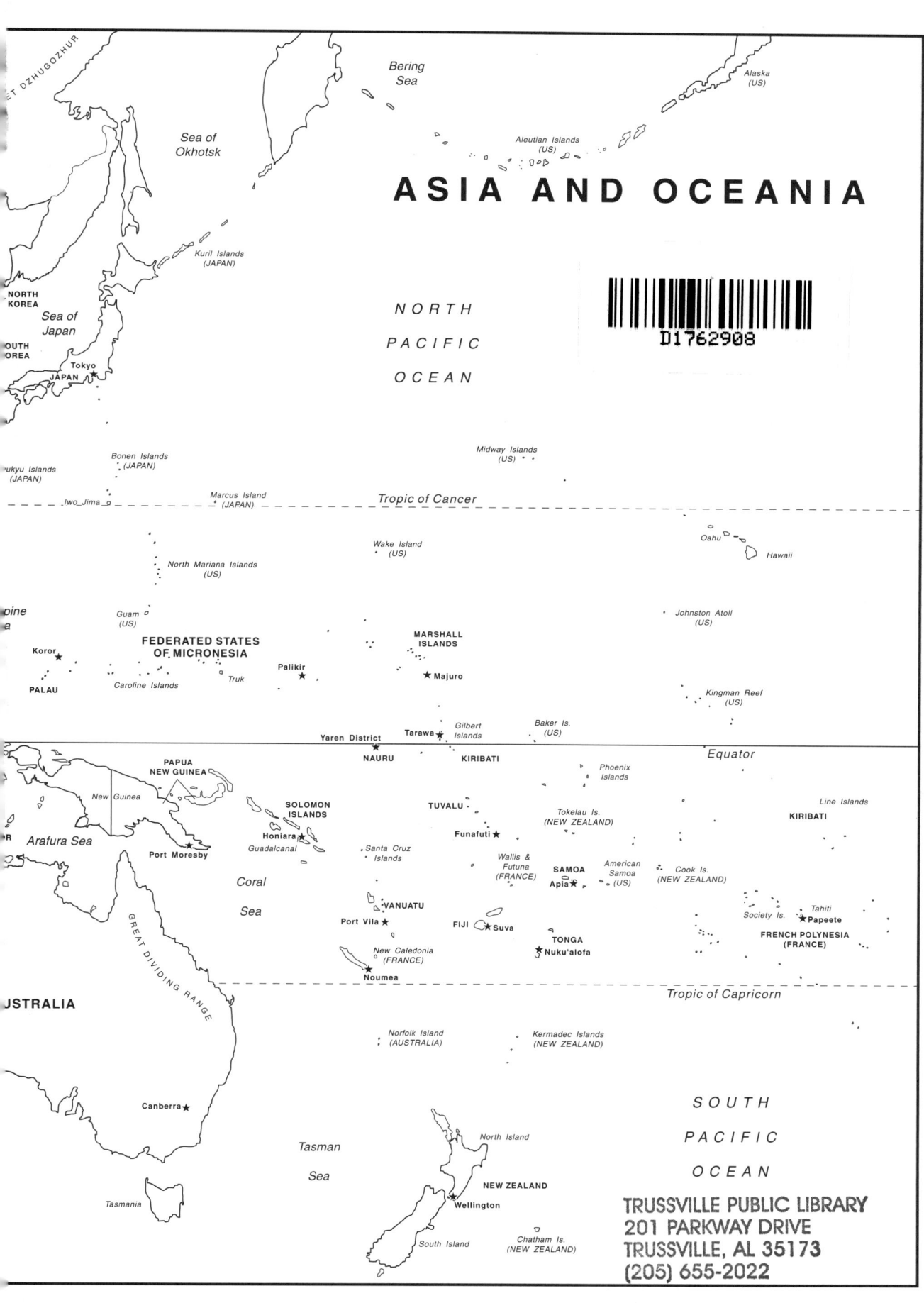

The Greenwood Encyclopedia of World Popular Culture

General Editor
GARY HOPPENSTAND

Volume Editors
MICHAEL K. SCHOENECKE, North America
JOHN F. BRATZEL, Latin America
GERD BAYER, Europe
LYNN BARTHOLOME, North Africa and the Middle East
DENNIS HICKEY, Sub-Saharan Africa
GARY XU and VINAY DHARWADKER, Asia and Pacific Oceania

THE GREENWOOD ENCYCLOPEDIA OF WORLD POPULAR CULTURE

ASIA AND PACIFIC OCEANIA

Gary Hoppenstand
General Editor

Gary Xu and Vinay Dharwadker
Volume Editors

GREENWOOD PRESS
Westport, Connecticut • London

Library of Congress Cataloging-in-Publication Data

The Greenwood encyclopedia of world popular culture / Gary Hoppenstand, general editor ; volume editors, John F. Bratzel ... [et al.].
   p. cm.
  Includes bibliographical references and index.
  ISBN-13: 978-0-313-33255-5 (set : alk. paper)
  ISBN-13: 978-0-313-33316-3 (North America : alk. paper)
  ISBN-13: 978-0-313-33256-2 (Latin America : alk. paper)
  ISBN-13: 978-0-313-33509-9 (Europe : alk. paper)
  ISBN-13: 978-0-313-33274-6 (North Africa and the Middle East : alk. paper)
  ISBN-13: 978-0-313-33505-1 (Sub-Saharan Africa : alk. paper)
  ISBN-13: 978-0-313-33956-1 (Asia and Pacific Oceania : alk. paper)
  1. Popular culture—Encyclopedias. 2. Civilization, Modern—Encyclopedias. 3. Culture—Encyclopedias. I. Hoppenstand, Gary. II. Bratzel, John F. III. Title: Encyclopedia of world popular culture. IV. Title: World popular culture.
  HM621.G74   2007
  306.03—dc22   2007010684

British Library Cataloguing in Publication Data is available.

Copyright © 2007 by Gary Xu and Vinay Dharwadker

All rights reserved. No portion of this book may be reproduced, by any process or technique, without the express written consent of the publisher.

Library of Congress Catalog Card Number: 2007010684
ISBN-13: 978-0-313-33255-5 (Set)
ISBN-10: 0-313-33255-X

ISBN-13: 978-0-313-33316-3 (North America)
ISBN-10: 0-313-33316-5

ISBN-13: 978-0-313-33256-2 (Latin America)
ISBN-10: 0-313-33256-8

ISBN-13: 978-0-313-33509-9 (Europe)
ISBN-10: 0-313-33509-5

ISBN-13: 978-0-313-33274-6 (North Africa and the Middle East)
ISBN-10: 0-313-33274-6

ISBN-13: 978-0-313-33505-1 (Sub-Saharan Africa)
ISBN-10: 0-313-33505-2

ISBN-13: 978-0-313-33956-1 (Asia and Pacific Oceania)
ISBN-10: 0-313-33956-2

First published in 2007

Greenwood Press, 88 Post Road West, Westport, CT 06881
An imprint of Greenwood Publishing Group, Inc.
www.greenwood.com

Printed in the United States of America

The paper used in this book complies with the Permanent Paper Standard issued by the National Information Standards Organization (Z39.48–1984).

10 9 8 7 6 5 4 3 2 1

To my graduate students.
G.X.

For Aparna, Aneesha, and Sachin.
V.D.

CONTENTS

FOREWORD: POPULAR CULTURE AND THE WORLD *Gary Hoppenstand*	xi
INTRODUCTION: POPULAR CULTURE IN EAST ASIA AND OCEANIA *Gary Xu*	xiii
INTRODUCTION: POPULAR CULTURE IN SOUTH AND SOUTHEAST ASIA *Vinay Dharwadker*	xxi
ARCHITECTURE	1
East Asia and Oceania *Yiju Huang*	
ART	
East Asia and Oceania *Jing Luo*	13
South and Southeast Asia *Vinay Dharwadker and Donna L. Halper*	22
DANCE	
East Asia and Oceania *Valerie H. Barske*	31
South and Southeast Asia *Beth Osnes and Vinay Dharwadker*	40
FASHION AND APPEARANCE	
East Asia and Oceania *Hui Xiao*	59
South and Southeast Asia *Vinay Dharwadker and Donna L. Halper*	69

Contents

Film
 East Asia and Oceania   91
 E. K. Tan

 South and Southeast Asia   105
 Wimal Dissanayake

Food and Foodways
 East Asia and Oceania   127
 Katarzyna J. Cwiertka

 South and Southeast Asia   137
 Vinay Dharwadker and Donna L. Halper

Games, Toys, and Pastimes   151
 East Asia and Oceania
 Erwei Dong

Literature
 East Asia and Oceania   161
 Eric Dalle

 South and Southeast Asia   172
 Jaina Sanga and Vinay Dharwadker

Love, Sex, and Marriage   189
 East Asia and Oceania
 Sheri Zhang

Music
 East Asia and Oceania   203
 LéJarie Battieste

 South and Southeast Asia   211
 Jeremy Wallach and Vinay Dharwadker

Periodicals
 East Asia and Oceania   227
 Shuyong Jiang

 South and Southeast Asia   239
 Aloke Thakore

Radio and Television
 East Asia and Oceania   259
 Donna L. Halper

 South and Southeast Asia   271
 Shelton A. Gunaratne and Amos Owen Thomas

Sports and Recreation   297
 East Asia and Oceania
 Jouyeon Yi-Kook and Monica Z. Li

Theater and Performance
 East Asia and Oceania   313
 Gary Xu

 South and Southeast Asia   320
 Beth Osnes

Contents

TRANSPORTATION AND TRAVEL
    East Asia and Oceania   337
    Bob Lee, Erwei Dong, and Aihua Zhang

    South and Southeast Asia   347
    David Atherton and Vinay Dharwadker

GENERAL BIBLIOGRAPHY   363

ABOUT THE EDITORS AND CONTRIBUTORS   367

INDEX   371

FOREWORD

POPULAR CULTURE AND THE WORLD

GARY HOPPENSTAND

Popular culture is easy to recognize, but often difficult to define. We can say with authority that the current hit television show *House* is popular culture, but can we say that how medical personnel work in hospitals is popular culture as well? We can readily admit that the recent blockbuster movie *Pirates of the Caribbean* is popular culture, but can we also admit that what the real-life historical Caribbean pirates ate and what clothes they wore are components of popular culture? We can easily recognize that a best-selling romance novel by Danielle Steel is popular culture, but can we also recognize that human love, as ritualistic behavior, is popular culture? Can popular culture include architecture, or furniture, or automobiles, or many of the other things that we make, as well as the behaviors that we engage in, and the general attitudes that we hold in our day-to-day lives? Does popular culture exist outside of our own immediate society? There can be so much to study about popular culture that it can seem overwhelming, and ultimately inaccessible.

Because popular culture is so pervasive—not only in the United States, but in all cultures around the world—it can be difficult to study. Basically, however, there are two main approaches to defining popular culture. The first advocates the notion that popular culture is tied to that period in Western societies known as the Industrial Revolution. It is subsequently linked to such concepts as "mass-produced culture" and "mass-consumed culture." In other words, there must be present a set of conditions related to industrial capitalism before popular culture can exist. Included among these conditions are the need for large urban centers, or cities, which can sustain financially the distribution and consumption of popular culture, and the related requirement that there be an educated working-class or middle-class population that has both the leisure time and the expendable income to support the production of popular culture. Certainly, this approach can encompass that which is most commonly regarded as popular culture: motion pictures, television, popular fiction, computers and video games, even contemporary fast foods and popular fashion. In addition, this approach can generate discussions about the relationship between popular culture and political ideology. Can popular culture be political in nature, or politically subversive? Can it intentionally or unintentionally support the status quo? Can it be oppressive or express harmful ideas? Needless to say, such definitions limit the critical examination of popular culture by both geography and time, insisting that popular culture existed (or only exists) historically in industrial and postindustrial societies (primarily in Western Europe and North America) over the past 200 years. However, many students and critics of popular culture insist that industrial production and Western cultural influences are not essential in either defining or understanding popular culture.

Indeed, a second approach sees popular culture as existing since the beginning of human civilization. It is not circumscribed by certain historic periods, or by national or regional boundaries. This approach sees popular culture as extending well beyond the realm of industrial production, in terms of both its creation and its existence. Popular culture, these critics claim, can be seen in ancient China, or in medieval Japan, or in precolonial Africa, as well as in modern-day Western Europe and North America (or in all contemporary global cultures and nations for that matter). It need not be limited to mass-produced objects or electronic media, though it certainly does include these, but it can include the many facets of people's lifestyles, the way people think and behave, and the way people define themselves as individuals and as societies.

This six-volume *Encyclopedia of World Popular Culture*, then, encompasses something of both approaches. In each of the global regions of the world covered—North America, South America, Europe, the Middle East, Sub-Saharan Africa, and Asia—the major industrial and postindustrial expressions of popular culture are covered, including, in most cases, film; games, toys, and pastimes; literature (popular fiction and nonfiction); music; periodicals; and radio/television. Also examined are the lifestyle dimensions of popular culture, including architecture; dance; fashion and appearance; food and foodways; love, sex, and marriage; sports; theater and performance; and transportation and travel. What is revealed in each chapter of each volume of *The Greenwood Encyclopedia of World Popular Culture* is the rich complexity and diversity of the human experience within the framework of a popular culture context.

Yet rooted within this framework of rich complexity and diversity is a central idea that holds the construct of world popular culture together, an idea that sees in popular culture both the means and the methods of widespread, everyday, human expression. Simply put, the commonality of national, transnational, and global popular cultures is the notion that, through their popular culture, people construct narratives, or stories, about themselves and their communities. The many and varied processes involved in creating popular culture (and subsequently living with it) are concerned, at the deepest and most fundamental levels, with the need for people to express their lifestyle in ways that significantly define their relationships to others.

The food we eat, the movies we see, the games we play, the way we construct our buildings, and the means of our travel all tell stories about what we think and what we like at a consciously intended level, as well as at an unintended subliminal level. These narratives tell others about our interests and desires, as well as our fundamental beliefs about life itself. Thus, though the types of popular dance might be quite different in the various regions of the world, the recognition that dance fulfills a basic and powerful need for human communication is amazingly similar. The fact that different forms of popular sports are played and watched in different countries does not deny the related fact that sports globally define the kindred beliefs in the benefits of hard work, determination, and the overarching desire for the achievement of success.

These are all life stories, and popular culture involves the relating of life's most common forms of expression. This *Encyclopedia of World Popular Culture* offers many narratives about many people and their popular culture, stories that not only inform us about others and how they live, but that also inform us, by comparison, about how we live.

INTRODUCTION

POPULAR CULTURE IN EAST ASIA AND OCEANIA

GARY XU

To compile an English-language volume on the popular culture in East Asia and Oceania is both exciting and challenging. It is exciting because this region has some of the richest cultural heritages in the world and is very dynamic in yoking the local with the global and the traditional with the modern. East Asia includes such geopolitical entities as China, Japan, North Korea, South Korea, Hong Kong, and Taiwan.[1] Oceania consists of Australia, New Zealand, Papua New Guinea, and other South Pacific islands such as Fiji and Tonga. Together with the American Pacific coast, this region forms the "Pacific Rim," whose economic development as a whole is so important to the world that the twenty-first century has been named the "Pacific century." Whether the Pacific Rim will replace the traditional power of the Euro-Atlantic remains to be seen; the cultural influences of this area have, however, undoubtedly become a major force that shapes every aspect of the human life around the globe. Wherever we are, we live in the midst of Chinese food, Japanese anime, Korean martial arts, Australian-style outdoor sports, or the mythical legends of the *Lord of the Rings*—made to come alive by New Zealand director Peter Jackson against New Zealand's mesmerizing landscape. These cultural traits and developments are as exciting as they are indispensable for understanding the world's popular culture.

The biggest challenge of this project lies in the diversity of this region, or, in fact, two regions. East Asia has a history that is drastically different from Oceania's. The ethnicities are different; so are the social customs or the ways of living. Even within each region, the popular culture of each geopolitical entity has distinctive characteristics. Generalization or overemphasis of intraregional similarities would risk exoticizing the "Oriental," a practice that reduces the rich and diverse cultures of the non–Euro-American into a singular fantasy.[2] A recent example is the Hollywood film *Memoirs of a Geisha* (2005). Starring the Chinese mega stars Zhang Ziyi and Gong Li, the film, albeit exquisitely made, neglects the ethnic and linguistic differences between China and Japan for the sake of telling a tale of the Oriental beauty. The potentially explosive and complex emotions of a Japanese geisha caught in historical vicissitudes are reduced to feminine jealousy and Confucian loyalty.

Introduction

Another challenge of this project stems from the dramatic—maybe even traumatic—ruptures that forever changed the popular cultures of East Asia and Oceania when outside forces pulled them into the modern age. Facing the extinction of nationhood when the Europeans sought to colonize East Asia in the nineteenth century, China, Japan, and Korea all had to "reform" in accordance with Western-style governance in order to survive. Japan's political, technological, economic, and cultural reform was earlier than the other two countries' and was the most successful. This resulted in Japan's determination to become a Europeanized colonizer of East Asia. Korea became its colony; China was soon invaded by Japan; and Taiwan was ceded to Japan as the result of China's defeat. Inner tensions grew, while Westernization penetrated every fiber of East Asian societies. Popular cultures changed accordingly. The popular in the West became equally popular in East Asia, and, inspired by the rationality of European Enlightenment, the voices of critiquing the traditional culture became louder in China, Japan, and Korea. In China, for instance, the early twentieth century saw enlightenment movements—widely known as the "May Fourth Movement"—calling for eradicating traditional Chinese culture and for complete Westernization. The result is that what appears "traditional" in contemporary Chinese culture can never be purely traditional—it must have been first destroyed and then rebuilt when the Chinese began to realize the importance of their own tradition. The rebuilt is no longer "pure," since it reflects the modern value system.

Ruptures happened in Oceania too. The European colonization beginning in the seventeenth century almost completely changed the Oceanian aboriginal cultures. What are the traces of the aboriginal culture that are still visible in contemporary Oceanian cultures? How did the clash of cultures figure in the cultural landscapes? How does one take these changes into consideration? How does one provide a balanced view between the premodern and the modern, or the local and the global? These questions are unavoidable for both the authors and readers of this volume.

In what follows, I adumbrate several aspects key to our understanding of the popular culture of East Asia and Oceania:

1. This area's popular cultures are ever shifting because of globalization and this area's tremendous economic growth at the turn of the millennium. What is popular in the world is most likely popular too in this area. Suffice it to mention the NBA, Hollywood films, McDonald's, Coca-Cola, and the FIFA World Cup.
2. Despite the fast-changing nature of this area's popular cultures, one may still grasp the trajectories of change through historicizing the ways in which culture is shaped by outside forces as well as intraregional tensions. China's fast rise as an economic superpower, for instance, helps boost the Korean film and television industry. Taiwan's history as a Japanese colony ironically makes Japanese popular culture most welcome when Taiwan looks for a non-Chinese past to establish its national identity in the shadow of China's military presence. Hong Kong, with its highly hybrid and Westernized popular culture, is reaffirming its Chinese roots after the handover from Great Britain to China in 1997. Australia and New Zealand, in the meantime, increasingly pay attention to their own aboriginal cultures and stress their ties with Asia in an effort to "de-Europeanize" or to "join Asia." To historicize helps us see the whole picture and avoid stereotyping and generalization.
3. The cultural trafficking between the Asian-Pacific and the Euro-Atlantic is multidirectional, not unidirectional. Although the modern period saw full-scale Westernization of the Asian-Pacific region, the popular culture in the West has been equally influenced by that of the East. Tea and Asian spices were crucial to not only European dietary changes but also Europe's overall organization of trade and commerce. Asian theater

INTRODUCTION

helped shape modern Western theater—that of Bertolt Brecht (1898–1956), Antonin Artaud (1895–1948), and others. Japanese aesthetics, which combines notions of impermanence with functional simplicity, was instrumental to Frank Lloyd Wright's (1867–1959) architectural designs. These are only a handful of examples. The instances of mutual influence are too numerous to be listed here. Western modernity, in fact, became possible only through contacts with and influences by the "Oriental."

4. In addressing the multidirectional cultural flows between the Asian-Pacific and the Euro-Atlantic, we must notice another instance of complexity: what is considered "traditional" in contemporary East Asia and Oceania is no longer purely traditional, due to the heavy cultural trafficking and to the modern condition. For example, the chapter on food and foodways in this volume makes it clear that the ultimate symbols of Japaneseness in present-day Japan—rice, soy sauce, and fresh seafood—were only recently turned into standard components of daily meals of all Japanese. Mass production of these food items and increasing nationalistic sentiments in the modern period made them the most important components in Japanese popular culture. In another interesting case, China's Great Wall was constantly rebuilt and made synonymous with China's national unity in the twentieth century. The fortune cookie, increasingly popular in China's Chinese restaurants, is an American invention. It is potentially misleading, therefore, to insist on finding the "authentic" elements in East Asian and Oceanian popular culture. In the modern period, the authentic is always already the result of interactions between the local and the global. Instead of searching for the authentic, we need to be open-minded about the hybridity of the local and understand the historical forces that shape hybridity.

To summarize: the popular culture of East Asia and Oceania is constantly changing; it is the result of both global influences and intra-regional tensions; it is mutually influential with the popular culture of the Euro-Atlantic; and it is highly hybrid even in its most localized and traditional forms.

The contributors to this volume have all done an outstanding job in taking these issues into consideration. They use the clearest language to introduce the various aspects of East Asian and Oceanian popular culture; they also strive to be original, to challenge common sense, and to correct stereotypes. This volume is thus a perfect combination of general knowledge and critical insights.

In **Architecture**, Yiju Huang is able to cover the incredible architectural diversities of the Asia-Pacific. Despite the wide range, she finds focus on the landmark structures that have witnessed the historical transformations of this region. In discussing Australia's architecture, she ties it to Australia's status as an immigrant nation and to Australia's colonial history. Providing the best evidence to the multidirectional nature of the cultural flows between East and West, she calls attention to the impact Frank Lloyd Wright had on Japanese architecture: Wright worked on reconstructing the Imperial Hotel in Tokyo in 1923 after he became fascinated with Japanese aesthetics. She also highlights the great architect I. M. Pei's contribution to world architecture in general and to Chinese architecture in particular. Three cities in this region have been the hosts of the Summer Olympics: Tokyo, Seoul, and Sydney. The fourth city, Beijing, will host the Summer Olympics in 2008. Huang is able to connect her material in this commonality and stresses the relationship between great urban architectural designs and the redrawing of the world geopolitical map.

One way to avoid generalization and stereotyping is to historicize—showing the remaining traces of earlier lives and putting these lives in their respective economic and geopolitical contexts. Jing Luo, in **Art**, is able to historicize by not only providing the historical context in

Introduction

terms of art's linear development but also linking art to people's ways of life. In discussing Chinese art, he details how it is reflective of China's topographical features, how its diversity stemmed from China's ethnic multiplicities, how ethics are central to Chinese society in general and to Chinese art in particular, and how modern Chinese art combines Western techniques with Chinese motifs. He has a vivid description of the ways in which the Japanese woodblock print was affected by Japan's urbanization since the Edo period. He also traces the Oceanian art to the Neolithic legacies on the Pacific islands. In his chapter, Luo restores the materiality of the art: the material conditions in which art is created.

Most of the contributors are experts in the field about which they write. They are thus able to combine their longtime research in specific areas with the overall picture of East Asian and Oceanian popular cultures. Nowhere is the combination of scholarly research with accessible general knowledge more evident than in the **Dance** chapter, written by Valerie H. Barske. An anthropologist, Barske has spent several years in Okinawa studying the area's folk dance. In her chapter, she is able to share her unique experience. She witnessed, for instance, the way Okinawan dances were highlighted as a means of marketing Okinawa to tourists in mainland Japan and around the globe during the 2000 Kyushu-Okinawa G8 Summit. She writes, "as world leaders including former president Bill Clinton entered the reception dinner at Shuri Castle, they were greeted by Okinawan dancers clad in traditional "*bingata*" court costumes. This official use of dance as cultural diplomacy contrasted with the actions of citizen groups in Okinawa who employ local dances in their political activism against the U.S. military bases." In this context, dance is not only a form of popular culture that we can all appreciate and live in, but also a political tool. The ability to add original arguments based on the ethnographic experience to the encyclopedic entry gives Barske's chapter an unusual depth.

In her chapter on **Fashion and Appearance**, Hui Xiao points out that "Asian fashion" seems an oxymoron in the fashion narrative dominated by the Euro-American. She then locates several important historical junctures when Asia was actually the center of world fashion. One juncture is China's Tang dynasty, during which Chinese fashion interacted with that of Persia along the famous Silk Road. As in the other aspects of popular culture, the advent of the modern shifted world's focus to the West instead of the East. As a result, Asian and Oceanian fashions in the modern period are highly mimetic of Euro-American fashions. One of Xiao's most important contributions to this volume is that she does not simply point out how Asia imitates the West. She complicates the picture by noting that most of the raw materials and labor the fashion industry relies on are from Asia while the West leads the trends in designs. This helps us understand that the global popular culture is based on unequal exchanges. Symbolic powers and labor exploitation are important in these exchanges.

Although the rupture separating the modern from the premodern has shaped most of the aspects of the popular culture, cinema is less affected by the rupture because it is exclusively the product of the modern. E. K. Tan, in **Film**, nevertheless finds continuity of the premodern in East Asian and Oceania cinemas. The premodern becomes either a thematic concern or the foundation on which a national cinema is built. To demonstrate how important the rupture is to cinema's representation of societies in transition, Tan cites Chinese films in the 1930s and 40s, Kurosawa's masterpiece *Rashomon*, Korean films made under the previous rule of the military government, and Australian auteur films focusing on the relationship between human emotions and the ancient landscape. To highlight the foundational role of the premodern in shaping national cinemas, Tan draws attention to the inevitable local film subsidy systems in Korea, Taiwan, Australia, and New Zealand. In these carefully fostered and government-endorsed national cinemas, Hollywood becomes the threatening other due to its modern appeal and industrialization. The premodern and the local are deemed essential for fending off the Hollywood invasion.

INTRODUCTION

Sometimes it is the popular culture that gives a region its identity, not the other way around. Writing about East Asian cultures, who would not immediately associate them with the use of chopsticks and the consumption of soybean-based food items such as tofu? Food defines cultural and national identity—this is an important point made by Katarzyna J. Cwiertka in her chapter on **Food and Foodways**. The incredibly rich culinary scene in East Asia and Oceania reveals the foundations of these different societies. Around the topic of food, we are shown festival celebrations, ritual performances, ethnic relationships, and political struggles related to hunger and poverty. The culinary transformation also forms a clear trajectory of these societies' modernization. Cwiertka cites the gradual invasion of East Asia by McDonald's to highlight the parallel between development and culinary changes: McDonald's entered Japan in 1971, Hong Kong in 1975, Taiwan in 1984, South Korea in 1988, and China in 1992. The timeline illustrates how culinary changes and economic liberalization go hand in hand. In many ways, Cwiertka serves as an ethnographer of food, paying attention not only to what people eat, but also to how they eat and why they eat certain things in certain historical periods.

Like the others, the chapter on **Games, Toys, and Pastimes** does not presume a stable set of traits associated with Asian and Oceanian popular cultures. Erwei Dong begins the essay with his solid research in recreational studies. He categorizes Chinese, and, by extension, East Asian games into five groups: strength, sports, intelligence, riddles, and gambling. Through these categories, we are shown a fascinating picture of the ways in which the ancient Chinese spent their leisure time: they played soccer, competed in archery, or kicked shuttlecock (*jianzi*) as daily exercise, or they gathered for a game of mahjong. The toys are similarly categorized so that readers can easily compare the traditional toys of East Asia and Oceania to the contemporary toys popular with kids worldwide. There is rich ethnographical information in Dong's chapter.

In **Literature**, Eric Dalle first poses the questions of definition: What is popular literature? What is literature? How can popular literature be divided by national boundaries? Dalle does not intend to answer these questions; his purpose is to call attention to the increasing blurring of boundaries between popular literature and serious literature, between traditional forms of literature and nontraditional forms such as manga and Internet blogging, as well as between national literatures. It is in the context of shifting boundaries that Dalle discusses the popular literature in each East Asian and Oceanian geopolitical entity: in China, works of popular literature, such as the novel *Journey to the West*, become national cultural treasures; in Japan, manga carries on the storytelling tradition and unique senses of aesthetics; in Korea, manhwa—the Korean term for animation—is less popular or ubiquitous than manga but is supplemented for popular cultural consumption by popular fiction and traditional Chinese and Korean stories; in Australia and New Zealand, the most popular form of literature is children's literature, which has produced an amazing number of outstanding writers and works that are considered as good as any other world literary masterpieces.

Among all the aspects of the popular culture, the most difficult to be accurately and thoroughly discussed is probably **Love, Sex, and Marriage**. This aspect contains a wide range of issues: clashes of values between traditional and modern, East and West; population regulation; abortion; homosexuality; family organization; generational gaps; and so on. All these issues are foundational to the ways in which a society is organized—this is why all of them are important campaign issues in American election politics. Sheri Zhang does an excellent job covering all these issues while paying attention to depth. We see in her chapter the transformation the Chinese family has gone through in the past century or so; we can find how the Japanese government copes with the aging of its population; we also get a clear picture of the influence of a laid-back postindustrial lifestyle on the love, sex, and marriage of peoples of Australia and New Zealand.

INTRODUCTION

Similar to film, the pop music in East Asia and Oceania is inherently modern and international. LéJarie Battieste gives an excellent account of the intraregional and international circulation of popular **Music**. On Chinese music, she details the generic differences and similarities among Cantopop, Taiwan pop, and mainland pop. Specifically highlighted is the way politics has shaped Chinese popular music and vice versa: how music could sometimes serve as voices of protest and how the June Fourth Tiananmen incident in 1989 cut short the promising careers of some young rock and roll stars. On Japanese music, she links the musical development to Japan's twentieth-century history. Each period—the early twentieth century, World War II, the postwar industrialization, the prosperous decades, and the post-bubble era—has its own corresponding popular music subgenre and style. She draws attention to Korea's megastar, Rain. She also details the ascendancy to international stardom of such Australian and New Zealand artists as Olivia Newton-John, Air Supply, and Crowded House.

In **Periodicals**, Shuyong Jiang shows another interesting aspect of the premodern/modern divide in Asian and Oceanian popular culture: the possibility that modernity happened around the same time in East and West. This possibility is particularly strong when it comes to mass printing in the form of the popular periodical, which has long been regarded synonymous with increasing literacy, notions of democracy, and modern technology. As Jiang's research shows, periodicals were first printed and circulated in China in 1815, and across East Asia and Oceania no later than the mid-nineteenth century. This was almost synchronous with Europe's development. Without assuming that all things modern traveled from West to East, Jiang draws a complete picture of the wide circulation of popular periodicals in Asia and Oceania. In China, the periodicals contributed to popularization of fiction, to women's liberation, and to the spread of modern ideologies. In Japan, the periodicals have always been closely linked to the formation of modern ways of life. In Korea, the fate of periodicals goes hand in hand with Korea's history as a Japanese colony and later a close U.S. ally. In Australia and New Zealand, the periodicals are instrumental to the development of national literatures and cultures. Jiang concludes her fascinating account by drawing attention to the two new phenomena in periodical publication: franchising of Western fashion magazines and the proliferation of Internet-based periodicals.

In **Radio and Television**, Donna L. Halper gives an excellent account of the history and current status of radio and television in East Asia and Oceania. This chapter is actually split into two parts, each introducing the distinctive histories and features of radio and television. For radio, we are told that China grew from three stations operated by the British or Americans in 1927 to countless stations run by the state at the turn of the millennium; Japan's radio history began at around the same time but grew at a much faster pace than China's or Korea's. Australia's and New Zealand's radio kept pace in development with other Western nations. For television, China did not broadcast any signal until the mid-1950s. These uneven developments, however, no longer matter during the current globalization of radio and television. Rupert Murdoch's Star TV has established strongholds from Australia to China while American entertainers can be seen, heard, and imitated all over Asia and Oceania. Halper hammers home an excellent point: radio and television, due to their inherent quality as the media that unify and facilitate global communication, are both creators and beneficiaries of globalization.

In **Sports and Recreation**, Jouyeon Yi-Kook and Monica Z. Li discuss both the historical development and the modernization of sports in East Asia and Oceania. They make an interesting observation: at any place in this area of discussion, sports can be categorized into the indigenous, the Europeanized, and the Americanized. Chinese wushu, Korean taekuanto, and Japanese judo are all sports locally developed in East Asia and globally dispersed at the turn of the millennium. Sports such as soccer and badminton show a more European influence, and basketball and baseball have distinctive American flavors. The two contributors further link sports to the nationalist discourse on national empowerment based on physical fitness.

In the chapter **Theater and Performance** I first call attention to what I call "referentiality," which is inherent in traditional East Asian and Oceanian theaters. Referentiality enables clear demarcation between performance and reality by referring to the performance's own fictitiousness and by ensuring that the audience understands the performance is fictitious. Because all theatrical performances are live actions, certain devices must be utilized so that the performance is not be confused with reality. These devices—such as the clearly marked yet minimally decorated stage, the high-pitched artificial singing voice, and the mask and, by extension, the face painting—are what make these traditional theaters expressionistic instead of mimetic. The expressionistic theater and the Western mimetic theater do, of course, interact. The former was instrumental to the development of the Western modernist theater, and the latter performed important roles in the changes of not only East Asian theaters but also East Asian societies in the modern era. Because of my training in East Asian literatures and popular cultures, I am able to provide in the chapter a concise yet rich description of the histories of Chinese, Japanese, and Korean theaters. The lack of information on Oceanian aboriginal theater and my lack of training in Oceanian studies contribute to the relatively short description of Oceanian theaters. This does not, however, imply that Oceanian theaters are any less important or creative than East Asian theaters. The resource guide will allow readers to further explore this important aspect of popular culture.

One of the most direct ways to understanding a nation's popular culture is through travel and transportation. When we think of China, we used to immediately conjure up the image of an ocean of bicyclists; for Japan, the immediate association is a bullet train zooming by Mount Fuji; for Hong Kong, it would be the motorized fishing boats in the Victorian Bay. The three experts on leisure studies—Bob Lee, Erwei Dong, and Aihua Zhang—give us a detailed description of **Transportation and Travel** in East Asia and Oceania. Their description provides a picture of change: China is no longer dominated by bicycles; the Japanese are joined by the Chinese, Korean, and other nationals as frequent international tourists; Fiji is more popular than ever as an exotic tourism destination thanks to its quickly expanding airports; and so on. Nor is this picture limited to leisure seeking; the three authors record faithfully the ways in which people get around for their everyday needs in East Asia and Oceania.

NOTES

1. The use of the term "geopolitical entity" instead of "country" is due to the fact that some of these areas are not widely recognized sovereignties despite their de-facto independence statues. Taiwan, for instance, has all the structures required of an independent country; it is nevertheless treated as a renegade province by the People's Republic of China and by most other countries in the world. We do not call these areas "countries" in order not to stir controversy and also not to subordinate culture to nation/state.
2. See Edward W. Said, *Orientalism* (New York: Vintage, 1979).

INTRODUCTION

POPULAR CULTURE IN SOUTH AND SOUTHEAST ASIA

VINAY DHARWADKER

GEOGRAPHY

South Asia and Southeast Asia are contiguous regions that stretch across the southern portion of Asia, from Afghanistan and Pakistan to the Philippines, and from Nepal to Indonesia and East Timor. Together, they are home to slightly more than 2 billion people, or just under one-third of the human race today. They contain an enormous diversity of geographical formations, natural environments, racial and ethnic groups, languages, religions, and cultures that are still little understood in the larger world. The popular cultures of these two regions are also remarkably diverse, with intricate connections among different art forms, classical models, folk traditions, national histories, and modern mass media.

From the viewpoint of the region itself, South Asia today consists of Pakistan, India, Nepal, Bhutan, Bangladesh, Sri Lanka, and the Maldives. These seven nations constitute the member states of the South Asian Association for Regional Cooperation (SAARC, founded in 1985), which continues to be the premier international network representing the region in Asian and global contexts. From the perspective of American and British foreign policy since the end of World War II, however, South Asia also contains an eighth nation: Afghanistan. This grouping reflects an older conception of the "Indian subcontinent" that was developed in the British-Indian empire in the eighteenth and nineteenth centuries. In the political turbulence following the attack on the World Trade Center in New York on September 11, 2001, the position of Afghanistan has become ambiguous: it seems equally connected to Pakistan and India in South Asia, and to Iran as well as the Islamic republics to its north and west, which constitute Central Asia. For our purposes here, the constellation of seven countries represented by SAARC provides the basic geopolitical definition of contemporary South Asia.

The conception of Southeast Asia is also a little blurry at the edges. The Association of South-East Asian Nations (ASEAN, founded in 1967 and expanded in the 1980s and 1990s), a regional network corresponding to SAARC in South Asia, currently identifies ten

INTRODUCTION

SOUTH ASIA: NATIONS, CITIES, LANGUAGES, AND RELIGIONS

Islamic Republic of Pakistan
Important Cities: Islamabad (capital); Lahore, Karachi, Rawalpindi
Major Languages: Urdu, Punjabi, Sindhi, Pashto, Balochi, English
Major Religion: Islam

Republic of India
Important Cities: New Delhi (capital); Delhi, Mumbai (Bombay), Kolkata (Calcutta); Chennai (Madras); Ahmedabad, Banaras (Varanasi), Bangalore, Chandigarh, Hyderabad, Jaipur, Nagpur, Patna, Srinagar, Trivandrum.
Major Languages: Hindi and English (official); constitutionally protected languages: Assamese, Bengali, Bodo, Dogri, Gujarati, Hindi, Kannada, Kashmiri, Konkani, Maithili, Malayalam, Manipuri, Marathi, Nepali, Oriya, Punjabi, Sanskrit, Santhali, Sindhi, Tamil, Telugu, Urdu.
Major Religions: Hinduism, Islam, Buddhism, Jainism, Sikhism, Christianity

Kingdom of Nepal
Important City: Kathmandu (capital)
Major Language: Nepali
Major Religions: Hinduism, Buddhism

Kingdom of Bhutan
Important City: Thimphu (capital)
Major Language: Dzongkha (official)
Major Religions: Buddhism (official); Hinduism

People's Republic of Bangladesh
Important Cities: Dhaka (capital); Chittagong, Narayanganj, Khulna
Major Language: Bengali
Major Religions: Islam, Hinduism

Democratic Socialist Republic of Sri Lanka
Important Cities: Sri Jayawandenepura (administrative capital); Colombo, Kandy, Galle, Jaffna
Major Languages: Sinhala, Tamil, English
Major Religions: Buddhism, Hinduism, Islam, Christianity

Republic of Maldives
Important City: Male (capital)
Major Language: Divehi
Major Religion: Islam

member states: Myanmar, Thailand, Laos, Cambodia, Vietnam, the Philippines, Malaysia, Singapore, Brunei, and Indonesia. Since 1999, however, East Timor has emerged as a separate national entity, after a long struggle against Indonesian occupation, which followed decolonization by the Portuguese in 1975. But despite its formal "independence" in 2002, East Timor's existence as a nation-state remains troubled and ambivalent, with the United Nations continuing to mediate its transition to autonomous nationhood. The coverage here is therefore limited to Southeast Asia as defined currently by ASEAN. Taken together, SAARC and ASEAN identify South and Southeast Asia as contiguous regions composed of seventeen countries in all, whereas alternative definitions add at least two other nations—Afghanistan and East Timor—to enlarge this portion of Asia at its westernmost and easternmost edges, respectively.

SOUTHEAST ASIA: NATIONS, CITIES, LANGUAGES, AND RELIGIONS

Union of Myanmar
- *Important Cities*: Pyinmana (Naypyidaw, capital); Yangon (Rangoon), Mandalay
- *Major Language*: Burmese
- *Major Religions*: Buddhism, Christianity, Islam

Kingdom of Thailand
- *Important Cities*: Bangkok (Krung Thep, capital); Chang Mai, Nakhon Ratchasima, Hat Yai
- *Major Language*: Thai
- *Major Religion*: Buddhism

Lao People's Democratic Republic
- *Important Cities*: Viangchan (Vientiane, capital), Louangphrabang
- *Major Languages*: Lao; French (for diplomatic communications)
- *Major Religion*: Buddhism

Kingdom of Cambodia
- *Important City*: Phnom Penh
- *Major Language*: Khmer
- *Major Religion*: Buddhism

Socialist Republic of Vietnam
- *Important Cities*: Hanoi (capital); Thanh Pho Ho Chi Minh (Ho Chi Minh City, formerly Saigon), Da Nang, Hai Phong
- *Major Language*: Vietnamese
- *Major Religion*: Buddhism

Republic of Philippines
- *Important Cities*: Manila (capital); Quezon City, Davao, Cebu
- *Major Languages*: Filipino and English (official); Tagalog
- *Major Religion*: Christianity

Federation of Malaysia
- *Important Cities*: Kuala Lumpur (capital); George Town (Penang), Melaka
- *Major Languages*: Bahasa Melayu or Malay (official); English, Chinese (various dialects), Tamil, Telugu, Malayalam
- *Major Religions*: Islam, Buddhism, Taoism, Hinduism, Christianity, Sikhism

Republic of Singapore
- *City*: Singapore (a city-state)
- *Major Languages*: English, Malay, Mandarin, Tamil
- *Major Religions*: Taoism, Buddhism, Islam, Christianity

Sultanate of Brunei
- *Important City*: Bandar Seri Begawan (capital)
- *Major Languages*: Malay, English, Chinese
- *Major Religions*: Islam, Buddhism, Christianity

Republic of Indonesia
- *Important Cities*: Jakarta (capital); Medan, Palembang, Bandung, Surabaya
- *Major Languages*: Bahasa Indonesia; more than 300 regional languages
- *Major Religion*: Islam

Introduction

Cultural Patterns

The societies of South and Southeast Asia have been in existence for a long time, and some of their cultural practices have more or less continuous histories going back to the beginning of the Common Era, if not to the preceding millennium. The consequence of such antiquity is that their popular cultures in modern times constantly draw on older precedents, complicating not only the materials, forms, ends, and means that are brought together in any given practice or product, but also the contexts in which artifacts are made, circulated, and received or in which activities are understood.

Part of the long social, political, and economic history of South and Southeast Asia is the fact that these two regions have been culturally interconnected for at least 2,000 years, and that many of the connections are still visible today. Vedic religion had appeared in the northern areas of South Asia by about 1000 BCE, encoded in voluminous texts (popularly known as "the Vedas" and "the Upanishads") composed in an early form of the Sanskrit language. Between about 600 and 300 BCE, poets in the Indo-Gangetic Plains composed the Ramayana and the Mahabharata in "epic Sanskrit." Around the middle of the first millennium BCE, Jainism (which has remained in India) and Buddhism (which migrated elsewhere at an early stage) appeared on the subcontinent as critical responses to the metaphysics and theology of Vedic religion. By the first centuries of the Common Era, the latter had evolved into what we now call Hinduism, and the epic poetry had given way to the more refined Sanskrit literature of the classical period, which lasted from about 200 CE to 1200.

Between about the first and fifteenth centuries, the classical Hindu-Sanskrit culture of India spread through trade and migration to Java and Bali (Indonesia), the Kingdoms of Funan (Vietnam, Cambodia, and Thailand, first to sixth centuries), Sukothai and Ayutthaya (Thailand), and the Khmers (Cambodia), exporting not only material goods and scripts, language, literature, arts, and aesthetics, but also philosophy and ethics, theology and ritual, and political theory and practice. Hinduism still survives in a transmuted form in Bali (Indonesia); the Ramayana and the Mahabharata continue to provide the staple stories and narrative contexts for classical and folk dances and dance-dramas across Southeast Asia, as well as for various forms of puppet and shadow puppet theater in the region; and postures, body movements, and gestures prescribed in Bharata's Natyashastra (Sanskrit treatise, probably second century) are part of the repertoire of today's classical dancers in Bali, Thailand, and Cambodia. Cotton migrated from India to Southeast Asia before the Common Era; the basic cotton wrap fastened at the waist remains the primary garment from South Asia to Myanmar, Thailand, Cambodia, Laos, Malaysia, and Indonesia; and the Indian dhoti is the historical model for the Khmer *yak rung* as well as the Thai *jong kraben*.

The presence of a shared classical Hindu-Sanskrit past in today's South and Southeast Asian cultures is complicated by other historical spheres of influence. In the centuries preceding the Common Era, Buddhism started to spread from north India, migrating a little later to Sri Lanka and Tibet, and dispersing from there to what are now Myanmar, Thailand, Laos, Cambodia, Vietnam, and Malaysia. In the first millennium CE, Chinese culture began to spread into Southeast Asia through trade, migration, and political domination, with a Chinese sphere of influence appearing especially in Vietnam, Laos, Cambodia, and Thailand. Starting in the eighth century, Islam entered South Asia (Pakistan, India, Bangladesh, Sri Lanka, the Maldives) and subsequently settled in what are now Indonesia, Malaysia, Singapore, and Brunei. Roman Catholicism arrived in the Philippines with the Spanish in the mid-sixteenth century, and became the dominant faith thereafter, making the Philippines the only Christian-majority nation in this part of Asia. In general, the influences of Buddhism, Chinese culture, Islam, and Christianity on particular societies in Southeast

Asia, and of Islam on South Asia as a whole, have been as far-reaching as the influence of classical Hindu-Sanskrit culture on South and Southeast Asia. Wherever they are the majority or official religions, Buddhism (in Bhutan, Sri Lanka, Myanmar, Thailand, Laos, Cambodia, and Vietnam) and Islam (Pakistan, Bangladesh, the Maldives, Malaysia, Brunei, and Indonesia) continue to shape people's ways of life comprehensively, and hence the popular cultures in which they participate.

All the societies of South and Southeast Asia are multiethnic. Each ethnic group tends to be racially, linguistically, and culturally distinct, and multiethnic societies therefore possess many different indigenous folk cultures. Because of its multiethnic composition, a nation in South or Southeast Asia today is unlikely to develop a single, unified popular culture; it usually has many coexisting popular cultures, each of which may be popular with a different social group, and some of which may become popular with several (but not all) such communities. In this zone of high ethnic differentiation, the indigenous folk cultures of particular groups often compete with each other and with dominant cultures for attention and recognition.

All the societies of South and Southeast Asia are also multilingual. The multilingualism of the countries in these regions not only increases their internal diversity by a factor of many, but also immensely complicates every aspect of everyday life and culture. India, to take probably the most complex example, has about 125 major languages belonging to four different language families they are written in a dozen different script systems and according to the 1961 Census of India (the last report to record such data), the country uses some 3,000 speech varieties on a daily basis. Hindi and English are the official languages of the republic, and federal government documents and records are maintained in both; the constitution protects twenty-two languages, which are associated with large communities of native users, many of them long-settled in specific regions of the country. In 2005, there were 60,413 registered newspapers in the country, and over 7,000 newspapers and 5,315 periodicals were published in 122 languages. The Indian school system requires every student to learn three languages (an ideal combination being a mother tongue, a lingua franca, and a classical language); street signs in cities are trilingual, with the name of the street provided in Hindi in the Devanagari script, English in the Roman script, and the local language in its own script.

The scale of India's multilingualism makes many forms of high and popular culture extremely complex, and questions of popularity are answerable only in relation to specific languages, but some of the complexity is reduced by the fact that each of about a dozen major languages also serves as a regional lingua franca, and is therefore comprehensible to the native speakers of several other languages in its region (most Indians are at least bilingual, if not trilingual). Television programming is currently broadcast in a dozen major languages, and in most cities standard cable service now includes channels in six to eight languages; contemporary artistic and commercial theater is most active in Bengali, English, Gujarati, Hindi, Kannada, Malayalam, Manipuri, Marathi, Punjabi, Tamil, Telugu, and Urdu, and a good or successful new play in one language is often translated into and staged in other languages within a few months of the original production. Songs are written, set to music, performed, recorded, and broadcast in at least two dozen languages: Kannada, Malayalam, Tamil, Telugu (the four main languages of south India), for instance, have their own large, thriving music industries. Documentaries and feature films are produced every year in eighteen to twenty languages, with the Hindi film industry being the largest, and with the film industries especially in Malayalam, Tamil, and Telugu also operating on a massive commercial scale. Contemporary Indian literature is most visible in about twenty-five languages, each of which has own its network of publishers, booksellers, and literary magazines. The Indian book industry in English is the second largest in the world in this language, next in size

Introduction

only to the book industry in the United States. As these quick examples suggest, multilingualism dramatically increases a nation's cultural diversity.

Given the patterns described above, most South and Southeast Asian cultures bring together four types of elements: (a) forms, styles, themes, or materials drawn from one or more "classical" sources, whether Hindu-Sanskrit, Buddhist-Pali, Islamic-Arabic, Taoist-Mandarin, or Christian-Latin in origin; (b) indigenous and even aboriginal folk traditions, often associated with specific ethnic and linguistic groups; (c) influences from the Euro-American West, chiefly from the early modern and modern periods; and (d) contemporary "mixed" or hybrid forms and practices that draw on a variety of local, regional, and international influences. Such elements converge, for example, in Indonesia's most popular and controversial contemporary music genre, *dangdut*. As Jeremy Wallach describes it in the chapter on music in this volume, dangdut is "a rhythmically propulsive cross between Indian film songs and Western hard rock," while also fusing "Latin American popular music, Jamaican reggae, Western disco, Egyptian pop, Malay folk music, and . . . Indonesian regional musics. These diverse influences have helped form a genre that fans claim is the true national music of Indonesia, neither an imitation of Western models nor representing a parochial ethnic tradition."

A similar convergence of the four elements identified above also occurs in very different cultural forms. In the case of apparel, for example, the convergence occurs in the various recent variations on the *Nyonya kebaya*, "a blouse made of sheer material, . . . traditionally worn with a Javanese batik sarong by women of old Chinese-immigrant descent in the Malay archipelago," but now also worn "as a top with jeans and Western-style skirts, as a blouse with pants, and even as a fashionable over-garment with Western-style sleeveless and spaghetti-strap dresses and casual tank-tops." Perhaps the most splendid fusion of classical, indigenous, Western, and hybrid forms is the *ao dai* ensemble—the extremely popular "national dress" for women in Vietnam—which consists of "a full-length, seamed and fitted, tuniclike dress with a high round collar, worn over loose pants," with the unusual feature that the upper garment has "four long slits, from hip to hem (two on the sides, and one each in the front and back), which produce 'four flaps.'" The fusion of multiple influences and the profusion of diverse languages, identities, artistic traditions, and aesthetic principles have provided the basis for enormous originality and creativity in South and Southeast Asian cultures in the past 2,000 years or more.

Political Conditions

Throughout the modern period, the formation, survival, and vitality of popular cultures in these two regions have depended heavily on their internal political conditions and economies. With the exception of Thailand, all of South and Southeast Asia was colonized and governed by various European powers and the United States at different times between the early sixteenth century and the mid-twentieth century. Decolonization began immediately after World War II, when Britain (on the Indian subcontinent), France (in Vietnam and Cambodia), the Netherlands (in Malaysia, Singapore, and Indonesia), Portugal (in various small colonies, from Goa to Macao and East Timor), and the Unites States (in the Philippines) started to transfer power to their subjects. The process of decolonization determined much of the political formation and subsequent history of the new nations that came into existence at this time.

The seventeen nations that make up the core of South and Southeast Asia at present fall into several groups with respect to their political organization. Five of the countries are monarchies, but with different features: Nepal is a Hindu kingdom with large Hindu and

Buddhist communities (population 26.3 million), whereas Brunei is a Muslim sultanate with Muslim, Buddhist, and Christian communities (population 374,000); Thailand (population 64.1 million) and Cambodia (population 14.8 million) are both Buddhist kingdoms with predominantly Buddhist populations, whereas Bhutan is a Buddhist kingdom with Buddhist and Hindu communities (population 2.4 million). Apart from the monarchies, several South and Southeast Asian countries have had long experiences with dictatorships. Pakistan (population 161.1 million) and Myanmar (population 50.7 million) both have military governments at present; Bangladesh (population 152.6 million) and Indonesia (population 225.3 million) have had extended military rule in the past; Thailand as well as Cambodia have suffered from intermittent military interventions; and the Philippines (population 82.8 million) has been subjected to an extended civilian dictatorship (under Ferdinand Marcos). In contrast, India, Malaysia (population 25.3 million), and Singapore (population 4.4 million) have functioned to different degrees as constitutional democracies, but have nevertheless endured short or long periods of civilian rule with authoritarian tendencies (under Prime Ministers Indira Gandhi, Mahathir Mohamad, and Lee Kuan Yew, respectively). The pattern in relation to culture across this array of authoritarian regimes has been quite consistent: they have all crushed political dissent, suspended civil liberties, curbed religious and artistic freedom, established state monopolies on key industries, and enforced censorship. Such conditions have throttled journalism and the press, literary writing and publication, painting and sculpture, dance and music, and theater and public performance, and they have even affected styles of food, clothing, furnishing, and decoration in the domestic sphere.

Several South and Southeast Asian nations have also been under socialist or communist regimes in the postcolonial period. Sri Lanka (population 19.4 million) officially continues to be a democratic socialist republic, though its recent governments have found their power base in ethnic, religious, and linguistic solidarities; Myanmar still identifies itself as a socialist "union"; Laos, a people's democratic republic (population 5.9 million), and Vietnam, a socialist republic (population 83.6 million), are among the last doctrinaire communist nations on earth; and Cambodia endured one of the harshest forms of communist totalitarianism under the Khmer Rouge (1975–79 and later). In the 1950s and 1960s, India and Indonesia, too, followed their distinct versions of socialist state policy under Prime Minister Jawaharlal Nehru and authoritarian President Sukarno, respectively. The predominance of socialism in Asia between the 1950s and 1980s meant that (a) many of these nations had more or less "closed," state-regulated, and planned economies, with elaborate import restrictions, limited export opportunities, and limited access to foreign goods and mass media; and (b) many of these governments actively canvassed against Euro-American capitalism and consumer products, while promoting the ideal of economic self-reliance. Most South and Southeast Asian nations emerged from Euro-American colonization in a state of deep impoverishment, and, in the long run, their broadly socialist policies in the early postcolonial decades failed to stimulate innovation or expansion in such technology-dependent cultural forms as newspapers, magazines, books, radio, television, and film, or in such industries as fashion and design, travel and tourism, and food and hospitality. "Popular culture," as we understand the category now, did not flourish in the shadow of socialism.

During the same period, a number of South and Southeast Asian countries were ravaged by international war or large-scale internal civil conflict. The partition of the Indian subcontinent in 1947 resulted in the death of an estimated 1.5 million people, and the forced migration of some 14 million individuals; Bangladesh's war of liberation in 1971 cost hundreds of thousands of lives and created 10 million refugees; Sri Lanka has been at war with the separatist Tamil Tigers since 1983, in continual violence that has already taken an estimated 65,000 lives; and

Introduction

the Maoist insurgency in Nepal, launched in 1996 on the model of the Shining Path movement in Peru, has resulted in about 12,000 deaths over a decade. Vietnam has only now begun to revive from the aftershocks of the war with the United States, which lasted from 1959 to 1975; and the Vietnam War also spread to Laos and Cambodia, further devastating those two nations. Between the communist regime of the Khmer Rouge and the overspill from the Vietnam War, an estimated 1.7 million people died in the "killing fields" of Cambodia alone. Each of these conflicts has exacted an enormous toll from human populations, natural environments, national economies, and local infrastructures, traumatizing entire societies and generations for years, if not decades. Under such circumstances, even the most basic forms and practices of everyday life have suffered, from nutrition, housing, sanitation, and health care to education, employment, entertainment, and the cultivation of the arts and crafts.

The Effects of Globalization

The globalization of capitalism and democracy since about 1990 has not yet solved any of these problems, but it seems to have begun an important transformation. At the political level, the most positive effect of globalization has been to exert pressure on many South and Southeast Asian countries to stabilize democratic institutions, to strive for greater transparency and accountability in government, and to be more responsive to their citizens' needs and concerns. In the 1990s, such pressures led to the restoration of elected governments in Bangladesh and Indonesia; and to an initial shift toward constitutional monarchies and shared decision making and governance in Brunei and Bhutan. In the first decade of this century, the pressure has also begun to create some (surprising) forms of political "openness" in Pakistan and Nepal, Malaysia and Singapore, and Cambodia and Vietnam. The direct effect of such changes in political conditions on the popular cultures of these nations has been to revitalize, to some extent, such arts as music, dance, painting, and theater and performance, and especially to give print, radio, television, film, and video media greater degrees of freedom than in the past. However, the salutary political effects of globalization have so far proved to be quite limited.

In contrast, the positive consequences of economic globalization are much more perceptible across South and Southeast Asia. Since about 1990, the nations in these regions have been under intense pressure on two fronts: on the one hand, to liberalize their trade policies and allow foreign capital and goods into their markets; and, on the other, to provide raw materials, labor, finished products, facilities, and services for corporations and consumers abroad. India, Thailand, the Philippines, Malaysia, Singapore, and Indonesia have been the best prepared to respond to this dual challenge, chiefly because of their earlier modernization, their large workforces (some of them highly skilled), their natural resources, and their enduring "cultural capital." As a result, their respective economies have "taken off" on an unprecedented scale in the past 15 years. In the first decade of the twenty-first century, the Indian economy, for example, has maintained an annual growth rate of 6 to 9 percent, comparable in scope to that of China. In practical terms, this has meant the creation of a larger, wealthier "middle class" in several of these nations over the last two decades. This class has greater purchasing power and more disposable income than in the past; it is now connected to much of the world through contemporary channels of communication (such as telephones and the Internet), as well as through travel, education, the mass media, and consumerism; and it now has the capacity to demand and pay for goods and services in its own immediate environment, for which there was little demand and virtually no supply earlier. The growth and spread of this consumer middle class, particularly in cities ranging from Lahore, Chandigarh, Delhi, Mumbai, Bangalore, Kolkata, Dhaka, and Colombo to

INTRODUCTION

Bangkok, Manila, Kuala Lumpur, Singapore, and Jakarta, implies that more people than ever before have access to commercial radio, cable and satellite television, film and video, and music on compact discs; can afford to buy fashionable clothes, accessories, and furnishings; want to eat out, go to dance clubs, take exotic vacations, watch professional sports, and cultivate expensive hobbies; wish to visit museums, attend live concerts, and go to the theater; and even to collect art and rare handicrafts. The empowerment of this middle class—consisting mainly of professionals, managers, bureaucrats, and entrepreneurs—has directly fed and fed off contemporary popular cultures throughout South and Southeast Asia.

At the same time, economic globalization has had a number of negative effects on these regions, some of them more than alarming in the long run. The growth of national economies and the statistical rise of incomes have been accompanied, in most cases, by an increased disparity between the rich and the poor, those who have the means and those who simply do not. In this context, globalization has largely benefited only a minority of the population in each country, consisting of the very wealthy and the educated, who already possessed the means to profit from this process. Moreover, economic globalization has driven a wider and deeper wedge between the urban and the rural, the trader and the farmer, the middleman and the craftsman, the professional and the rustic. There is very little "trickle down" from the city to the countryside at this stage, which has led to the migration of rural laborers in large numbers to metropolitan centers, where they live in sprawling slums or shantytowns. The establishment of enormous "world factories" and multinational manufacturing facilities—for goods ranging from shoes, apparel, and plastic wares to refrigerators and automobiles—in rural India and Indonesia, for example, has not only encroached on agricultural land, but has also begun to disturb the ecological balance, deplete natural resources without renewal, and increase greenhouse emissions and chemical pollutants to unacceptable levels. Most importantly, the advent of globalization has brought in exploitive wages, unhealthy and high-risk working conditions, and minimal job benefits for workers across Asia, whose degraded rights now deepen their poverty as well as their dependency on capital. These negative outcomes affect the majority of the population in many countries, so that South Asia, for instance, continues to be home to several hundred million of the poorest people on earth even in the midst of its current economic "boom," and it is not yet clear how globalization will alleviate this problem. In view of the larger picture, the whole category of popular culture—which assumes that its consumers are well integrated into a capitalist economy—becomes conceptually, politically, and ethically a very complicated one.

RELIGION AND CULTURE

The religious diversity of South and Southeast Asia, together with the long history of such diversity, also complicates the arena of popular culture. The religions with large or significant populations of followers in these regions include Hinduism, Islam, Buddhism, Jainism, Zoroastrianism, Sikhism, and Christianity, each of which is also internally quite diverse. Together with numerous indigenous varieties of faith and worship (which are often simply classified as "folk religions"), including forms of animism, *each* of the religions and its subvarieties has been an established factor in South and Southeast Asian societies for several centuries, if not for a millennium or more. Hinduism, Buddhism, Jainism, Taoism, and Zoroastrianism—all indigenous to Asia—have histories going back 2,500 to 3,000 years; Islam has a history in South and Southeast Asia going back nearly 1,300 years; and Sikhism and Christianity have been present in these regions continuously for almost 500 years. The

Introduction

key point for understanding the cultures of Asia, including its popular cultures in modern times, is that each of these religions and its subvarieties has established a whole way of life for its adherents for a very long time. Each of these faiths contains elaborate prescriptions and prohibitions for its followers on what (or what not) to eat and when to eat (or not eat) it, what to wear or not to wear, how to speak and behave, what to believe and think or not to believe or think, and so on; many of these faiths also dictate, regulate, or recommend what constitutes "literature," "music," "dance," "theater," and "art," or what does not, and whether or not these forms of presentation and representation are to be practiced. Orthodox Hinduism, for example, proscribes the consumption of beef, whereas orthodox Islam proscribes the consumption of pork; and much of what we know about "Hinduism" historically unfolds in literature, music, dance, theater, painting, sculpture, and architecture, with an emphasis on vivid representations of gods, humans, and other beings, whereas orthodox Islam prohibits such visual and plastic image making.

The detailed and comprehensive rules for specific ways of everyday life that religions have laid down for centuries in South and Southeast Asian societies have had a profound effect on what we today consider to be the defining forms and practices of "popular culture." Starting in the nineteenth century, if not much earlier, these societies have sought to adjust their older "religious" expressive and aesthetic traditions to the pressures of "secular" Western-style modernity and colonial-era modernization. In the process, they have often invented the "mixed" forms of literature, everyday prose writing, journalism, music, dance, performance, visual and plastic art, food, clothing, jewelry, handicrafts, housing, and architecture that we find everywhere in South and Southeast Asia today. The interaction, however, has *not* revolved around a mere polarization of secularism and religion, modernity and tradition, Western stimulus and Asian response, colonialism and nationalism. Rather, at its best, it has brought into play much deeper engagements with imagination and innovation, novelty and craft, discovery and exploration, aesthetics and expression, and change and self-transformation, especially on the part of Asian cultures. The chapters on various facets of popular culture in contemporary South and Southeast Asian countries demonstrate in detail how exactly this massive shift from an indigenous, local past to a globally accessible present has been accomplished in specific material forms and media.

Coverage in This Volume

The sections on South and Southeast Asia in this volume bring together an exciting group of distinguished specialists and emerging scholars in a spirited, multifaceted discussion of various forms of popular culture. **Literature**, by Jaina Sanga and Vinay Dharwadker, focuses on the complexity of the multilingual literary cultures of these regions; it describes the range of languages and traditions involved in the production, circulation, and reception of imaginative writing in print. It also analyzes some of the most widespread themes in literature and surveys some of the most significant developments in the novel, the short story, poetry, and drama. It highlights not only examples of popular writers and works in a dozen literary languages in ten Asian countries, but also some "popular classics," famous works that have become acclaimed films, and major authors who are prominent public figures. **Periodicals**, by Aloke Thakore, expands our understanding of print culture by succinctly summarizing the long history of journalism and publishing in South and Southeast Asia. It explains the political, economic, and social conditions of the popular press in each country, and it points to the multiple effects of globalization in a variety of languages. Thakore's account is particularly remarkable for its up-to-date overview of newspapers and magazines in these regions, and for its synthesis of a large amount of publication data in national as well as international contexts.

Theater and Performance, by Beth Osnes, showcases the extraordinary achievements of the long stage traditions of South and Southeast Asia, explicating both the influence of classical models and the interconnections among various national practices today. It describes the evolution of modern urban theater in countries such as India, Singapore, and Indonesia, even as it covers popular indigenous theater in detail, paying particularly close attention to folk and religious forms as well as the astonishing intricacies of puppet theater and shadow puppet theater. **Dance**, by Beth Osnes and Vinay Dharwadker, analyzes popular contemporary dance in South and Southeast Asia, relating it not only to the spread of film and television and the rise of a new urban middle class, but also to the growth of tourism and the mutual conflicts of religion, culture, and politics. It also discusses indigenous classical dance, classical dance-drama, and folk-dance in unusual depth, covering all the important national and regional varieties in these categories. Likewise, **Music**, by Jeremy Wallach and Vinay Dharwadker, examines the diverse indigenous musical traditions of South and Southeast Asia and their origins, and it links them to classical Indian and Chinese influences in earlier periods and to Euro-American and global influences in contemporary times. It provides unusual insights into the history of sound technology in Asia, the emergence of an unprecedented range of musical genres in Southeast Asia, and the popularity of classical, folk, and film music in South Asia.

The sections on cinema and broadcasting turn to the dominance and effects of mass media on different parts of Asian society. **Film**, by Wimal Dissanayake, is a circumspect account of the history of film making in South and Southeast Asia and the role of the medium in the public sphere. It explicates the preeminence of Indian commercial, art, and middle cinema in the global market, even as it encapsulates the histories of film making in other countries, from Pakistan and Sri Lanka to Thailand and the Philippines, charting the most popular genres and recent trends in each case. In contrast, the section on **Radio and Television**, by Shelton Gunaratne and Amos Owen Thomas, concentrates primarily on the infrastructure and contexts of broadcasting in South and Southeast Asia, mapping out the multilingual channels of mass communication in an age of digital and satellite technology. It reveals not only how radio and television programming reaches huge audiences, and what types of programs flood the airwaves, but also how complex the formation of networks and audiences is at the local, national, and transnational levels under globalization. **Transportation and Travel**, by David Atherton and Vinay Dharwadker, shows how deeply the transformation of roadways, railways, airlines, and other modes of transportation in the past two decades has affected local landscapes, national ways of life, and regional economies in South and Southeast Asia. Drawing on the geographical, historical, and technological contexts of transportation, it analyzes the boom in international tourism, the popularity of a range of tourist activities and destinations, and the volume and multifariousness of travel across Asia today.

The sections on **Art**, **Food and Foodways**, and **Fashion and Appearance** are all coauthored by Vinay Dharwadker and Donna Halper. "Art" offers a compact account of the interlinked developments in the traditional plastic arts of South and Southeast Asia, which bring together sculpture and architecture, engineering and craftsmanship, visual representation and religion. Against this historical background, it surveys the main trends in modern and contemporary art across the two regions, paying close attention to popular artists, forms, styles, and institutional networks and relating them to Euro-American modernist and postmodernist influences as well as to recent market conditions. "Food and Foodways" opens up a new perspective on its subject by looking at the emergent patterns of eating out in big

Introduction

cities in South and Southeast Asia, and by analyzing some of the most popular cuisines of these regions, with detailed discussions of ingredients, cooking methods, and famous dishes. It also examines the relations among food, ethnicity, and geography, as well as the unusual restrictions that some widespread Asian religions place on food and foodways. Finally, the section on "Fashion and Appearance" provides a comprehensive account of the history, social and economic contexts, and cultures of dress, textile production, garment design, and personal appearance that characterize South and Southeast Asia at present. It focuses on popular hybrid ideals of male and female appearance, fashions in various countries, the presence of Asian styles, textiles, and apparel in foreign markets, and a broad variety of indigenous garments, body treatments, and accessories. Taken together, the sections on South and Southeast Asia thus offer rich and varied accounts of the interdependence of contemporary popular culture and ancient cultural traditions, complex religious codes and shifting social conventions, economic factors and political institutions, indigenous identities, and global transformations.

ARCHITECTURE

EAST ASIA AND OCEANIA

YIJU HUANG

There have been profound changes in popular architecture over the course of the twentieth century. What was happening in East Asia and Oceania is reflective of dramatic changes in popular architecture worldwide. Several elements help explain the similarities. Some of the most prominent are technological innovation, population growth and urbanization, and the increased exchange and flow of ideas.

During this 100-year span, technological advances in building materials and methods spread rapidly. The use of reinforced concrete and steel frames, for example, allowed for the building of the first skyscrapers but also led to similarities in, or even the standardization of, practices in large-scale commercial and residential projects. In addition to those used directly in construction, other innovations—such as electric utilities, elevators, telephones, and plumbing—greatly impacted city planners and architects.

Another element contributing to similarities has been the need to respond to some of the same demands, particularly population growth and urbanization. Consider the change in China's urban population: in 1950 it was 69.5 million, and in 2000 it was at 455.8 million.[1] Those of other countries in these regions, while less dramatic, have more than doubled in the last 50 years. Successful projects dealing with high-density housing in one area, for example, are emulated in others. These patterns have also led to the development of similar urban entertainment and business districts; shopping malls are a more recent example of the same tendency.

While there is a long history of global exchange in these regions, particularly in East Asia, the scale and speed of exchange has increased exponentially in modern history. There were particularly volatile examples of colonialism, semicolonialism, and imperialism in East Asia and Oceania during the nineteenth century. Some of today's great urban centers were built during this time, where there had been few or no urban centers before. Examples of this type are Shanghai and Melbourne, both of which contain late nineteenth-century buildings modeled after trends then popular in Europe. In other instances, such as in Tokyo, new government and public buildings in a neoclassical style were incorporated into established

ARCHITECTURE

urban centers. Architectural ideals, philosophies, and techniques have continuously circulated in print media as well. Journals, magazines, and books have thoroughly explained, critiqued, and argued over each new trend and fashion, comparing what was happening globally with development and construction in the home country. Throughout the twentieth century, many university students of architecture spent time studying abroad. Professionals, likewise, have not been confined to one location. I. M. Pei, as example, is one of the most celebrated Chinese architects; he studied in the United States and eventually started his own firm there. His buildings can be found in numerous locations around the globe. International practice has been common among prominent architectural firms. Some of the most exciting examples come from the flurry of building that occurs when a country hosts the Olympic Games.

As striking as these similarities are, the architecture of the region has a great tendency toward variation. Some factors contributing to differences are internal to the various nation-states of East Asia and Oceania—economic and political forces behind development, for example—while others center on national and regional differences such as climate and topography. An example of building projects motivated by both of these factors is found in the adaptation of six regional models for apartment complexes in China during the 1950s that were patterned after Soviet building practices.

Additionally, many architects have been critical of building practices that ignore local culture and history. Conscious efforts have been made—with varying degrees of urgency across time and location—to resist the homogenization of cities. An early example is the reaction to the growing use of the International Style. The International Style was a functional design associated with aesthetic concerns of European modernism in the 1920s that could easily be employed in diverse climates. In Korea, Japan, and China, the desire to incorporate "traditional" elements into "modern" buildings has often resulted in elaborate rooftops. Other, less obvious elements of traditional design focused on the layout of buildings, such as to allow for courtyards and gardens.

CHINA

With an area of 9.6 million square kilometers (3.7 million square miles),[2] China experiences a wide range of weather patterns. The range in topography is just as striking, with mountainous regions, great deserts, and a long coastline. In south and central China, there are both tropical and subtropical climates that keep the winters mild, while northernmost regions experience extremely cold, harsh winters. Dry northwestern desert and semidesert regions contrast with the eastern and coastal regions with abundant rainfall. Three great rivers, Huang He, Chang Jiang, and Xi Jiang, cut through China. The valleys of these rivers and the coastal regions along the Pacific Ocean are the most populated areas of the country.[3] While China is known for having the largest national population, population density differs greatly, even between districts within the same urban area. In Beijing, for example, Xuanwu district has a population density of 99,281 per square mile, while nearby suburbs have a population density of 10,857 per square mile.[4]

Popular architecture, as it developed within China after the turn of the twentieth century, cannot be seen as a constant from city to city or from city to rural village. It is also not easily distinguished from traditional architecture. Shanghai, for example, with a semicolonial history, became a huge metropolis in a short period of time at the end of the nineteenth century. The city has long been famous for the Bund and its foreign quarters with French and English villas, coffeehouses, movie theaters, and racing tracks. This contrasts greatly with the history of new development in more established urban centers such as Xi'an, a city that still retains its city wall and moat, and Beijing, a city that tore down much of its city wall in an effort to modernize. The subway took the place of this wall beginning in 1965. Modernization has produced the construction of very diverse forms. Often, these were in opposition to traditional architecture, while at other times a balance was sought.

One predominant form in traditional architecture that was widely seen at the end of the Qing dynasty was the courtyard. The courtyard houses, *siheyuan*, still found in Beijing date, for the most part, to the Qing dynasty (1644–1911). The rectangular perimeter wall, built from grey brick, seals the home off from the outside. The entrance gate, located at the south or southeast section of the wall, is the only decorative part of the house visible from the outside. These gates can be decorated with ornate wooden eves, which mark the entrance leading from the narrow alleyway, *hutong*. Inside, one or more courtyards provide a secluded space for family. Along the perimeter walls are one- or two-room structures. The division of space—with the rear rooms reserved for parents, rooms for the sons and their families, and the front rooms for servants—reveals a hierarchical structuring. The courtyard design continues to be employed in China mostly in temples. Buddhist, Confucian, and Daoist temples and Muslim mosques[5] employ many of the same features. Temple of Chen in Guangzhou, built in the 1890s, is another example.

Attitudes toward modern city building in the Republic period led to more general discussions concerning whether or not to emulate the West in China's modernization efforts. This debate has resurfaced again and again with architects—both domestic and foreign—building in China. The Continental Bank Building in Beijing is an example of a modern classical building that makes no effort to incorporate traditional Chinese elements. Bei and Kuan designed this in 1924. Other buildings from this period incorporated traditional elements to varying degrees. The Peking Union Medical College, completed in 1918, was built by Henry H. Hussey; it incorporates various compounds and courtyards, complete with white concrete terraces and stairways, much like the architecture of the Forbidden City. The tiled roofs with upturned corners are obviously meant to give a strikingly Chinese feel. This same roof style is featured on entrance gates to the buildings. The limited height of three stories, in proportion to the width, compensates for the overall size of the buildings.

A major change in architecture followed the civil war period. The Soviet Union not only advised on construction and planning issues, but also initiated numerous joint projects and trained Chinese architectural students sent to the USSR. The Soviet Exhibition Hall, built in 1953, was designed entirely by Soviet architects. An example of Bauhaus architecture from the 1950s is the Beijing art district, Dashanzi. The brick buildings have serrated roofs and stark right angles. Originally used as a military electronics plant, and built with the help of East German engineers, many of the buildings are now used by artists, who enjoy the large workshop space and natural light. While functionalist aesthetics were often employed, the debate over incorporating traditional Chinese elements continued. One approach was to add tiled roofs, with upturned corners, to the tops of buildings. The Beijing Railway Station, 1958–59, has two clock towers, each with a double layer of such tiled roofs. The Western Railway Station, built in 1996, has a very similar effect. The large glass facade—just above the entrance and in between the towers—gives the appearance of a large gateway.

The Soviet model for standardized and industrialized housing was often used as well in the 1950s. These apartment complexes were constructed of concrete slabs that were relatively inexpensive and could be built quickly in response to housing shortages. In addition, the work unit was made responsible for housing its employees. Multiple buildings—four to six stories in height—were enclosed within the yard of a work unit. Buildings were very plain on the outside, forming rectangular blocks with uniform, square windows and simple entrances. These buildings would typically have multiple entrances on each side that led to a

ARCHITECTURE

TAIPEI 101

Taipei 101 is currently the record holder as the world's tallest building in three of four categories including highest structural top (at 509 meters), highest rooftop (449 meters), and highest occupied floor (439 meters). The fourth category, height measured to the highest antenna top, is held by the Sears Tower in Chicago.

High-rise structures serve as visual monuments to the economic importance and wealth of a city as well as to the region's ability to make use of new technologies and innovations in engineering. As such, laying claim to the title of the world's tallest building has been a source of competitiveness. The Chrysler Building became the world's tallest building in 1930, losing this title the following year with the completion of the Empire State Building. The Sears Tower held the title from 1973; however, when the Petrona Twin Towers were being built in Malaysia, heated debates occurred over how the world's tallest buildings should be measured. This centered on the planned use of "spires" on the Petrona Twin Towers, which made them technically taller than the Sears Tower, even though the rooftops were lower. In 1996, prior to the completion of the Petrona Twin Towers, the Council on Tall Buildings and Urban Habitat—an organization famous for listing the world's tallest buildings—specified the four categories to be included in its evaluation of tallest buildings, with measurements taken from the front sidewalk: the measurements to the highest structural top (including spires but not antennas); to the highest occupied floor; to the rooftop; and to the antenna top.

When considering the fifty tallest buildings in the world, it is noteworthy that the vast majority—thirty-five—are in the United States (18), China (17, including 6 in Hong Kong), and Taiwan (2).[6] What is even more remarkable is that, while the U.S. buildings listed in the tallest fifty were constructed between the 1930s and 1992, those in China and Taiwan were *all* completed during the 1990s or later, with nine of these in 2000 or later.

Taipei 101 may not hold the record for long. It had been rumored that the Shanghai World Financial Center—currently under construction and due to be completed in 2008—would hold the record; however, this was never to be the case.[7] The next most likely candidate is the Burj Tower in Dubai, United Arab Emirates. Under construction and due to be completed in 2008, this will have a structural height of 705 meters.[8] Furthermore, there are visionary plans for two superstructures in Shanghai, the M Tower and the Bionic Tower, which would, if ever realized, measure 900 meters and 1,128 meters, respectively.[9]

central staircase. Later, six new models were adapted to meet specific needs of the very different climate patterns across China.

Architecture of the 1980s took a new direction following the changes produced by the economic reforms of the Open Door Policy beginning in 1978. Modernization took on a new form. The Great Wall Hotel in Beijing is an example of the use of the all-glass shell that was popular around the world at the time. The hotel was designed by Beckett International, a firm from California. Wings of the hotel span out from the central shaft, on top of which is a large octagon that houses a restaurant. One renowned architect who has led the way in recent times is I. M. Pei. Originally from China, Pei studied at MIT and Harvard, teaching at the latter. He worked in the U.S. firm of Webb & Knapp in New York before starting his own

New York firm in 1960. Pei's buildings are located in many cities around the globe. His additions to the Louvre Museum in Paris are among his most well-known.

While projects such as the Bank of China tower over Hong Kong, leading the way for the building of an unprecedented number of modern skyscrapers, other projects have sought to blend in with traditional styles. The Fragrant Hill Hotel is a classic example of efforts to incorporate a stronger sense of Chinese aesthetics into a modern building. The hotel has 325 guest rooms, a large ballroom, conference rooms, restaurants, retail shops, an exercise room, swimming pools, and an atrium. Although it is a fully modern hotel, its courtyards, low-level building, and design are in harmony with the nearby Forbidden City. Another example comes from Taipei 101 in Taiwan, currently the world's tallest building. The exterior is shaped to form eight gold ingots, an ancient form of Chinese currency.

Conservation of traditional Chinese architecture and the blending of modern building with the structures of ancient areas has been an important issue. Wu Liangyong, Professor of Architecture at Qinghua University and frequent government building advisor, has argued for more efforts to be made to preserve a Chinese essence in modern building practices.[10] His project, Juer Hutong, reinvents the Qing Dynasty houses in Beijing. Today, because of the demands for housing in Beijing as well as efforts to modernize housing in China, many of the courtyard houses have been torn down and replaced with multistory apartment buildings. Those that remain typically house multiple families; makeshift structures fill the courtyards to accommodate more people. The Juer Hutong homes are multistory buildings that use a system of courtyards, roof styles, color schemes, and floor plans to continue a local style for Beijing housing. Xi'an is an example of efforts to conserve the ancient city feel while heeding the needs of modernization. The city walls still offer views of the city layout in all directions because of a limit on building height. Zones outside the city walls have been established for taller buildings. The Bell Tower and Drum Tower Plaza houses a two-story, below-ground shopping center.

Today, China is in the forefront of architectural design; with an unprecedented amount of new construction, China offers a rare opportunity for contemporary architects, both domestic and international. The 2008 Olympics, to be held in Beijing, has furthered current growth. In addition to structures to house Olympic events—the National Swim Center, the National Stadium, and the Olympic Green—construction of public buildings is being scheduled in time to awe visitors. The new CCTV headquarters and the National Grand Theater are sure to turn heads.

JAPAN

The archipelago of Japan has an area of 377,864 square kilometers and a population of 127.9 million.[11] Honshu is the largest island, south of Hokkaido and north of Shikoku and Kyushu. Many areas are mountainous, and there are some active volcanoes. The oceans have a great influence on Japan's climate throughout the year. Winter is dry in all but the northern latitudes; In the summer, typhoons are typical, and rainfall is relatively high.

While Japan is famous for its Tokyo skyline and highly developed urban architecture, traditional architectural practices are in many ways still alive. One example is the periodic rebuilding of wooden Shinto temples. The main temple on Ise has a tradition of being rebuilt every 20 years since 650 AD using specific techniques that have continued to be carefully passed down. The temple is built of white cedar beams held together with wooden pegs.

Traditional Japanese housing continues in many forms and has had a direct influence on modernism movements in the West. One- and two-story, single-family houses as well as row houses have been common in urban and rural areas throughout Japan. Wooden frames are set up in a rectangular formation. Inside the doorway is a small room called the *geikan*, an area to take off one's shoes before stepping up a level to enter the home. A notable feature is the ability to rearrange rooms using the sliding doors and walls. These lightweight panels are of wood with a paper or cloth covering. Tatami mats are used to measure room size and cover the floors. The spatial patterning; the shifting between inside and outside, between personal and private space; and the cubical modules of these traditional rooms have had a great influence on modernist movements in architecture around the world. Frank Lloyd Wright, for example, incorporated many of these elements in innovative ways.

Meiji-era architecture provided an extensive range of experimentation with European classical styles in conjunction with the goal of rapid modernization. At the same time aristocrats were dressing in Western attire, European mansions were being constructed. The Nara Imperial Museum, built 1894, is one such extant example. The facade is a combination of carved stone and stucco, with double columns on either side of an arched doorway. Western architects were invited to not only consult, oversee, and/or build government buildings, but also to teach Japanese architects. Josiah Conder, from Britain, was a prominent figure from this time. He taught at Tokyo's Imperial University. His buildings—of which there were over fifty built in Tokyo, including the Old Ueno Imperial Museum and the Kaitakushi bussan urisabakijo [marketplace]—ranged in style, or combination of styles, from Gothic to Renaissance to Tudor to Moorish.

The early decades of the twentieth century saw buildings that followed similar trends leading to modernism in the West, such as German expressionism. The Tokyo Department Store curves along the street corner where the main entrance is located. This expressionist building from 1931 is seven stories high with a rooftop plaza. Large-scale apartment complexes quickly became available in the 1930s. An early example is the Edogawa Apartments in Tokyo, built in 1934. These reinforced-concrete buildings form a perimeter around a courtyard park.

Also of great influence was Frank Lloyd Wright—who worked on reconstructing the Imperial Hotel in Tokyo in 1923—and the Swiss architect Le Corbusier. Le Corbusier's interest in urban living and city planning was particularly suitable to the rapid urbanization in Japan and influenced Japanese architects such as Isozaki Arata and Kenzo Tange.

Kenzo Tange emerged after World War II, in a time when Japan was hurriedly in the process of democratization. This opened the door to cutting-edge architecture more than before. Among his most celebrated works is the national Gymnasium, built in 1964 for the Tokyo Olympics. The sweeping roofs and the steel and concrete construction are unmistakably modern; however, the spatial design and proportions as well as the pillars in the walls hearken back to the cantilever principle of traditional Japanese wood buildings.

Special mention should be made on the construction of baseball stadiums throughout Japan. Baseball is among the top favorite sports in Japan, if not the favorite, and has a long history going back to the Meiji period. Simple parks, with wood-bench seating, can be found in schools and neighborhoods across the country. Mizuho Baseball Stadium in Nagoya city, built in 1947, is of a simple, yet elegant design, with a semicircle of stadium seating behind home plate; this same design is seen in more recent stadiums, such as the Toyama Civil Stadium built in 1992.

NORTH KOREA AND SOUTH KOREA

North Korea is a mountainous region that lies between the Korea Bay and the Sea of Japan. It shares its northern border, which follows the Yalu River, with China. It has a total area of

ARCHITECTURE

120,540 square kilometers and a population of 23.1 million.[12] Northern winds from Siberia produce cold winters, especially among the northernmost places. Both North Korea and South Korea experience a continental weather pattern, despite the fact that they are surrounded by water, and are atypically cold for their respective latitudes.[13] South Korea, between the Sea of Japan and the Yellow Sea, is not quite as mountainous and is further from the northern winds. Its total area is 98,480 square kilometers and the population is 48.8 million.[14]

Western architecture was introduced into Korea in the late nineteenth century. Myongdong Cathedral, built in Seoul in 1898, is primarily in a Gothic style. At the end of the Choson dynasty, a British architect was invited to build a royal residence in Toksugung Palace in 1900. This is very much in the Renaissance style. It is a two-story stone building. It was completed in 1909, after the Japanese occupation had begun, and was instead used as the National Museum. As with government buildings in Japan at the time, a variety of Western-style buildings were erected in Korea under the direction of the Japanese. Buildings such as the Seoul City Hall and the Seoul Railroad Station, both completed in 1925, remain today. Some South Koreans have voiced a desire to tear down the buildings since they are reminders of the occupation. The city hall building is in more of a neoclassical design, with an angular dome on top of the concrete structure. It has a white stone base that surrounds the entranceway. The railway station has more of a Byzantine dome. Its brick and stone facade and elaborate window ornamentation have a Renaissance feel. Little is known about Korean architects during the occupation. Two of the earliest known modern architects from Korea are Pak Kil-yong, who designed the Hwashin Department Store building, and Pak Tong-jin, who designed the main building of Korea University. The Korean War saw few resources for construction. After the war, rebuilding efforts in both North Korea and South Korea were extensive and the 1960s mark the beginnings of massive urban construction.

Pyongyang, the capital city of North Korea, was redesigned with widened streets, parks, and huge public buildings, often made of marble. The Grand Theater, Juche Tower, and the Palace of Culture are among these that show a strong Soviet influence in design. In the 1980s particularly, several massive building projects were begun as an attempt to outdo South Korea and to exemplify the benefits of communist state building. The Grand People's Study House opened in 1982 and currently houses over 30 million books. The Ryugyong Hotel was a massive building project begun in 1987 that has yet to be fully realized. It is built of reinforced concrete and takes the shape of a giant pyramid. At 105 stories high, it is the largest building in North Korea. Efforts to construct the hotel centered on gaining foreign investment, but construction eventually stopped in the early 1990s. Another grandiose project resulted in the world's largest stadium. The Kim Il-Sung Stadium seats 150,000 and was finished in time for the 13th World Festival of Youth and Students in 1989.

The city of Seoul, in South Korea, has become one of the largest urban centers in the world. Living standards have steadily improved, even after the 1997 financial crisis, which has only meant higher wages for the working class. The demand for housing led to the development of hundreds of quickly built apartment complexes. Many of these were modeled after U.S. building practices and designed by Korean architects trained in the United States. Bedroom communities, or suburban areas, also grew along commuter rail lines. Business centers helped define the emerging skyline of Seoul. The 63 Building was, upon completion in 1985, the tallest building in Asia at the time. Its simple, elegant form is covered in glass panels, which was very popular internationally in the 1980s.

With economic growth and a large urban population, theme parks provide a major source of entertainment. Dream Land is an amusement park equipped with sports facilities, a training field, campsites, and seasonal facilities as well as about forty entertainment facilities. Another example is Lotte World. Lotte World can almost be seen as a separate city. In addition to the giant shopping mall, there is a hotel, a swimming complex, a theme park, and a museum.

The 1988 Seoul Olympics saw the construction of an Olympic park and the opportunity for elaborate construction projects. Along with this new construction came new entertainment faculties, restaurants, and community centers. The number "88" is seen as auspicious and has been used in the names of nearby venues: 88 Gymnasium, 88 Golf Club, and 88 Swimming Pool are examples. The World Cup Stadium, which seats 64,000, offered another such opportunity for the development of an entertainment district, first in 2001 when it opened for the World Cup Soccer event, and again in 2003 when the area was renovated. Worldcupmall has been added; it houses a multiscreen cinema complex, a wedding hall, shopping malls, and a cultural center.

OCEANIA: AUSTRALIA AND NEW ZEALAND

The island continent of Australia has a relatively sparse population of 20.3 million in relation to its land area of 7.7 million square kilometers.[15] The north and northeast sections enjoy a tropical climate while the central desert regions, over half the total land area, experience warm to high temperatures and are dry most of the year. Australia's largest cities are along the coastal regions in the southwest—Perth has a population over 1 million—and the south and east, with Sydney and Melbourne being the two most populous, with populations over 3.5 and 3.1 million, respectively.[16] New Zealand has a mountainous topography on both major islands and receives a good amount of rainfall year round. The largest city is Auckland, with a population of 197,223.[17] The capital city, Wellington, has a population of 163,824 and a greater regional population, including the city's surrounding areas, of 423,765, making it New Zealand's third largest region.[18]

Australia's popular architecture, particularly as can be seen by its development during the nineteenth century, is closely tied to its status as an immigrant nation as well as to its colonial history. Early housing reflects the waves of Scottish, Irish, and English settlers who built them. An alternate example is Sydney's Chinatown, which moved to the Haymarket area in the early 1900s. As new standards and tastes developed in Europe, these were carried over and employed in the growing Australian cities and housing districts. Villas were the predominate favorite of the wealthy, who built Italianate and Romantic Gothic villas. British-appointed governors had been the ones to establish the guidelines by which Australia's cities were built. City planning extended beyond government building projects and included regulations that controlled, to varying degrees of effectiveness, how homes and other privately funded buildings were constructed. Such efforts, in turn, reflected adaptation to changing technologies such as electricity and plumbing, and new building materials such as reinforced concrete and steel. These ordinances also reflected lifestyle ideals, including the predominance of property zoned for single-family homes and regulations on room size.

As in Australia and the United States, many settlers emigrating out of Europe came to New Zealand and built their own houses. The styles employed from the mid-nineteenth through the early twentieth century reflected the new arrivals' places of origin, generally Ireland, Scotland, and England; however, the available building plans were also influential. Plans were sold locally with a variety to choose from; imported carpentry magazines also often included building plans. Common one- and two-story housing styles around the turn of the twentieth century included Queen Anne, Italianate, Gothic Revival, California Bungalow, art deco, Spanish mission, and many more. Elements were often blended in creative fashion.

In the cities, some of the earliest business districts have continued to be the heart of business in those cities. Collins Street in Melbourne, for example, was first laid out as a business district in 1839 and remains the center of the city's business today. Examples of Renaissance Revival architecture like the Old Treasury Building remain alongside newly constructed skyscrapers. As Australia's major cities, Sydney and Melbourne, were being developed and laid out, the gold rush added greatly to this growth as well as to the wealth of the city. Flinders Street Station in Melbourne is a good example of turn-of-the-century architecture in response to a rapidly growing urban center. Completed in 1899 in a grand Victorian style, this area also saw the use of the first steam engine in Australia.

In Australian rural areas, mining towns developed rapidly during the middle to late nineteenth century. While prefabricated homes were shipped, along with supplies, from England, many miners built their own homes with whatever material was on hand, just as farmers and urban dwellers had been doing. They selected from common forms that paralleled self-built homes throughout Europe: log homes, split-log slab homes, and various structures built of earth. Adobe was quite common, used on its own and also in combination with wooden frames.

Few examples of early wooden agricultural dwellings from this time remain. Wooden structures were rebuilt or replaced. An exception is Gulf Station in the Yura Valley. Built in the 1850s, this group of wood-frame houses was used until the 1950s. Today, it is a museum of Australia's agricultural past and showcases furniture, tools, and equipment from the past 150 years.

Turn-of-the-twentieth-century churches showcase an array of European styles that span the spectrum. Gothic wooden structures with steep roofs or towering steeples vie with castles in stone or brick. Melbourne's Cathedral of the Blessed Sacrament, built in 1904, is remarkable for its innovative construction methods as much as for its striking Italian and French classical design. Mass-produced elements, such as the arches and prefabricated panels on the doors and ceilings, allowed for relatively fast construction.

B. C. G. Burnett was an innovative architect not reliant on European trends. Burnett designed a number of homes in the early twentieth century that were specific to the tropical climate of Australia's Top End. Lightweight materials were employed in the construction: asbestos cement sheeting with windows of multiple glass slates allowed for adjustable shielding for various weather conditions; each corrugated roof formed a steep peak with a vent at the top. In addition many homes were built on stilts, similar to local building traditions throughout Micronesia.

Another architect, Harry Seidler, was a pioneer in modernist architecture. An early example is his famous Rose House, just outside of Sydney in Wahroonga, built in 1948. A white cube set in the hillside, this modest-sized home is built of stone, reinforced concrete, and wood; the rectangular framed windows span the entire front wall, allowing for views of the surrounding brush.

The 1960s was a time when cites once again experienced economic growth. New construction techniques allowed for larger buildings that fulfilled a range of needs. Australia Square, built in 1967, is a commercial building of this sort. The lower floors contain a large shopping center, a spacious restaurant is next to the shopping area, and offices occupy the upper floors. Several works of architecture from the 1960s and 1970s reveal an effort to establish unique symbols of Australia and to break away from generic styles. The Sydney Opera House and the Victorian Arts Center, Melbourne, are prime examples. By far, the Sydney Opera House has become Australia's most symbolic structure. Its location, seemingly afloat above Sydney Cove, has added to its worldwide visibility and status. Joern Utzon of Denmark designed the Opera House, with its unique white tile-clad roofs shaped like the sails of the ships in the cove. The project took 16 years from design to completion in 1973. Below the elaborate roofs, the main building is composed of reconstituted granite. Included within and atop the long rectangular outlay are a concert hall, an opera theater, a restaurant, and a large parking structure.

Two projects by Philip Cox Richardson Taylor & Partners reveal an effort to forge an architectural style unique to Australia and in tune more with specific needs and desires. The first is the Yulara Tourist Village. Set within viewing distance of Ayers Rock in the Northern Territory, this self-contained community fulfills its role as a tourist destination. The village contains a school, police station, and housing in conjunction with tourist accommodations such as a visitors' center, shopping center, community center, campgrounds, and two hotels. The spatial layout of the complex follows the natural valley path behind sand dunes. The coloring of the one- and two-story cube buildings—red sand walls and greenish blue rooftops—allows the village to blend into the surrounding landscape. Layout and construction also take special account of wind and sunlight because of the extreme heat and also to conserve energy. Solar panels and other environmental innovations help keep the village from being overly reliant on outside energy sources. A second design by Cox shows the building of a community in an already dense, urban setting. Golden Grove Street Housing in Newton, New South Wales, is a complex of low-cost housing units. Brick buildings of various heights are designed to house a range of family sizes as well as provide apartments for the elderly. The layout of the buildings forms several rows, which are diagonal in relation to the city block. This was a design feature meant to separate the community from surrounding buildings as well as to create community pathways and courtyards.

The 2000 Olympic Games in Sydney presented an opportunity for architects and city planners to showcase their efforts to the mass of spectators who came for the events. The Olympic Park now enjoys a variety of uses including concerts, festivals, children's camps and educational programs through the YMCA, and, of course, many sporting events. Sydney Olympic Park continues to be a site for development as new retail businesses, residential units, and restaurants are being built. Future planning includes "Vision 2025," a plan for a larger community built around the park as a showcase of sustainable urban development.[19]

Telstra Stadium, designed by Bligh Lobb Sports Architects as the centerpiece of the park, is an example of state-of-the-art building techniques. In addition to the many features enabling the stadium to accommodate a live audience of over 80,000—110,000 during the Olympics—there are separate rooms and facilities built in for media broadcasting. Even the great roof, an impressive saddle shape, is designed with television cameras in mind. The roof serves to reduce glare for the live audience as well, protecting the audience from rain while allowing in a maximum of natural light. Natural light filters into other areas of the building as well in an effort to conserve energy. Similarly, rainwater is recycled from the roof and used for the stadium toilets and other devices.

RESOURCE GUIDE

PRINT SOURCES

Australian Architects: Philip Cox Richardson Taylor & Partners. Manuka, ACT: Royal Australian Institute of Architects, Education Division, 1988.

Bognár, Botond. *The Japan Guide.* New York: Princeton Architectural Press, 1995.

Hill, Martin (Perry Martin). *Restoring with Style: Preserving the Character of New Zealand Houses.* Wellington, New Zealand: C. V. Ward, Government Printer, 1985.

Jackson, Davina. *Australian Architecture Now.* London: Thames & Hudson, 2000.

Knapp, Ronald G., ed. *Asia's Old Dwellings: Tradition, Resilience, and Change.* New York: Oxford University Press, 2003.

Lee, Leo Ou-fan. *Shanghai Modern: The Flowering of a New Urban Culture in China, 1930–1945.* Cambridge, MA: Harvard University Press, 1999.

Rowe, Peter G. *Architectural Encounters with Essence and Form in Modern China.* Cambridge, MA: MIT Press, 2002.

Troy, Patrick, ed. *History of European Housing in Australia.* Cambridge/New York: Cambridge University Press, 2000.

Wu, Liangyong. *Rehabilitating the Old City of Beijing: A Project in the Ju'Er Hutong Neighbourhood.* Vancouver: University of British Columbia Press, 1999

WEBSITES

Council on Tall Buildings and Urban Habitat. March 3, 2007. http://www.ctbuh.org/.

Emporis Buildings. March 3, 2007. A database on building and architectural data worldwide. Has a partnership with the Council on Tall Buildings and Urban Habitat. http://www.emporis.com.

New Zealand Institute of Architects. March 3, 2007. http://www.nzia.co.nz/.

Pei Cobb Freed & Partners Architects LLP. March 3, 2007. Architectural firm founded by I. M. Pei; includes descriptions of past projects by location. http://www.pcfandp.com/aN.html.

Sydney Olympic Park. March 3, 2007. http://www.sydneyolympicpark.com.au/.

NOTES

1. See *World Population Prospects*, United Nations Population Division 2004 Revision Population Database (accessed March 3, 2007), http://esa.un.org/unpp/.
2. See BBC News: Country Profiles (accessed March 3, 2007), http://news.bbc.co.uk/2/hi/country_profiles/default.stm.
3. Ibid.
4. See Demographia: Beijing (accessed March 3, 2007), http://www.demographia.com/db-beijing-ward.htm.
5. The Great Mosque in Xi'an is an excellent example of the courtyard layout.
6. See Emporis: World's Tallest Buildings (accessed March 3, 2007), http://www.emporis.com/en/bu/sk/st/tp/wo/.
7. See Emporis: World's Tallest Buildings (accessed March 3, 2007), http://www.emporis.com/en/wm/bu/?id=130957.
8. See Emporis: World's Tallest Buildings (accessed March 3, 2007), http://www.emporis.com/en/wm/bu/?id=182168.
9. See Emporis: World's Tallest Buildings (accessed March 3, 2007), http://www.emporis.com/en/wm/ci/bu/sk/li/?id=100213&bt=2&ht=2&sro=1.
10. See Wu 1999 (in Resource Guide).
11. See BBC News: Country Profiles.
12. See CIA, The World Fact Book (accessed March 3, 2007), https://www.cia.gov/cia/publications/factbook/index.html.
13. See BBC News: Country Profiles.
14. See CIA The World Fact Book.
15. See BBC News: Country Profiles.
16. See City Population (accessed March 3, 2007), http://www.citypopulation.de/Australia-UC.html.
17. See Statistics New Zealand (accessed March 3, 2007), http://www.stats.govt.nz/.
18. See Wellington, New Zealand, official tourism Website (accessed March 3, 2007), http://www.wellingtonnz.com/.
19. See Websites in the Resource Guide for additional information.

ART

EAST ASIA AND OCEANIA

JING LUO

The vast land mass described as East Asia is one of the earliest cradles of civilization. Its artistic creativity is one of the most diverse and productive. This chapter focuses on the modern artistic development of China, Japan, Korea, and Oceania. Within this limited scope, one has to pick and choose the events that only outline the traditions—and only in the areas of painting, sculpture, and crafts—leaving the rest for readers to discover on their own.

CHINA

With a territory of 3.7 million square miles, similar to that of the United States, China is the largest country in East Asia. China is primarily an inland country, with only a fourth of its borders facing the ocean. China's geography is basically mountainous. The topography features a "staircase" configuration, with the western territory the highest and the eastern territory the lowest. The Qinghai-Tibetan Plateau has an average elevation of 13,120 feet above sea level. The Himalaya Mountains rise up along the Sino-Nepalese border, forming the "roof of the world." Mount Everest, rising 29,140 feet above sea level, is the highest point in the world. Central China features low mountain ranges that rise 3,000 to 6,000 feet above sea level, and taper to plains in the east. Two of the world's longest rivers—the Yellow River and the Yangtze—flow from west to east across China. The Yellow River, a 3,395-mile long course, is credited as being the cradle of Chinese civilization. The 3,915-mile run of the Yangtze River divides the country into North and South, creating two worlds with different customs. The terms "Northerners" and "Southerners" represent a tremendous complexity of connotations that is often beyond expression in words.

For thousands of years, agriculture has been the foundation of China's economy. Today, given the rapid pace of urbanization since the 1990s, approximately 60 percent of the population is still dependent on farming. The mountainous terrain and agrarian way of life are the two main sources of classical Chinese art. The impact is clearly visible in Dong Qichang's landscape, in which mountains and rivers are mythically laid out. The conventional disproportion of objects in classical Chinese paintings is a unique style of artistic abstraction, and has become the fundamental feature of oriental art. Using this technique, the artist expresses his or her inner space, rather than the objective outside world.

Chinese art is a conglomerate of diversity. The Chinese population comprises 56 ethnic groups and today totals 1.3 billion. The Han Chinese represent more than 90 percent of the population and reside primarily in the eastern plain regions. The 55 minorities reside in three-fourths of the territory, mostly in small communities. The Tibetans, the Mongols, the Uygur Muslims, the Chinese Muslims, the Zhuang, and the Chinese Koreans are larger ethnic groups, each living in an autonomous region. Most ethnic communities, including Yunnan, Guangxi, and Guizhou, are located in the southern provinces. The Miao, Yao, Yi, Dai, and Jingpo are well-known for their embroidery craft. Their dress and hair decor are like living museums. Their artistically woven and died waxed fabric, which often features designs representing floral images, animals, and legendary heroes, is a unique tradition.

Chinese art is typically suggestive of the artist's moral pursuit. In ethics, the Confucian-Daoist system served for thousands of years as the guiding principle of human behavior. The principles of balance and neutrality and the worship of nature are transcendant in classical as well as modern artwork. Laozi's philosophy of nonaction and total submission to nature inspired most classical landscape art, and continues to underlie modern artwork. The Confucian emphasis on virtue, justice, and harmony forms the body of the spiritual pursuit of artists. In fact, the Chinese artist believes that all artistic creativity has to be part of an integrated cultivation. Few would like to be thought of as earning their living by the brush. The artist typically intends to use the brush to achieve the unification of three perfect things: calligraphy, poetry, and painting. Hence, what are viewed as conventional themes—bamboo, birds and flowers, landscapes showing scholars chatting in a garden pavilion while fishing—are vehicles of expression, the essence of which is harmony. As such, artistic transgression is unnecessary, and is in fact rare. In classical painting, variations of strokes seldom result in the expression of unfamiliar or disconcerting ideas. Harmony rises above all. This is particularly evident in the works of the Song (960–1279), Yuan (1279–1368), Ming (1368–1644), and Qing (1644–1911) dynasties. From the monumental landscapes of Fan Kuan and Guo Xi, to the works of Shi Tao and Badashanren, one can appreciate the harmony under the artists' brush, whether they have painted majestic mountains and streams or a leaf of lotus.

Toward the mid-nineteenth century, Chinese art encountered challenges from the West. After the Opium War (1840), China's door was open. As European art forms became increasingly popular, a great number of Chinese artists traveled to study in Europe and returned with new techniques and new ideas. This trend was further strengthened by the collapse, in the 1911 democratic revolution led by Dr. Sun Yat-sen, of the dynastic system that had lasted thousands of years. Democracy and science suddenly became the pursuit of intellectuals. Moreover, in the 1919 May Fourth Movement, intellectuals searched Chinese tradition for the roots of the nation's weaknesses. The New Cultural Movement launched by Chen Duxiu (1879–1942) and the Vernacular Speech Movement initiated by Hu Shih (1891–1962) condemned Confucian tradition for suppressing individual freedom. In literature, Ba Jin's *Storm* and his *Family, Spring, Autumn* trilogy denounced the traditional dominant-male family system. In art, enthusiastic study of Western styles and techniques was underway. For the first time, Chinese artists put aside the paintbrush and took up the charcoal to sketch the human body. Xu Beihong (1895–1953), a master classical painter, enjoyed great fame for successfully integrating Western techniques with traditional Chinese themes and framework.

Xu studied brush painting in his early years, and then studied art in France in 1919. He returned in 1927 to teach in the most prestigious school of art at the Central University. His painting, *The Old Foolish Man Removing Mountains*, is an example of Western technique melded with Chinese tradition. In this work, Xu depicted with paintbrush a traditional Chinese tale, but he apparently adopted the framework of Western perspective, which resulted in powerful characterization of the figures in the painting. Nudity and accurately outlined muscles and body cavities broadly explored in Xu Beihong's works are unseen in traditional Chinese painting.

Chinese art is based on a tradition of engagement. For some reason however, pure art has been a choice, although never a popular choice. Once equipped with Western artistic techniques, Chinese artists produced new art forms. Lu Xun (1881–1936), a great novelist, political commentator, and wood-cut artist, promoted the wood-cut movement in the 1930s. Although Chinese wood-block illustration of books traces to at least the Tang dynasty (618–960), the art of woodblock was mastered by Japanese artists and thrived in Japan in the nineteenth century. Thus, wood-block art was a "returnee" when it was adopted by the Chinese art world. In the 1930s, Lu Xun and other revolutionaries who rebelled against the Nationalist government and joined the Anti-Japanese invasion movements saw a unique means of expression in the powerful angular strokes of wood-block art.

Given its minimal material requirements and the convenience of duplication, wood-block art became one of the favorite art forms of Mao Zedong's (1898–1976) communist revolution. Mao envisioned his success as relying on the Chinese peasant masses, and found wood-block art to be an efficient tool of propaganda.

By tradition in China, art has been used by the government. Mao defined art as a tool to serve the Revolution, and denied the existence of pure art. In his theoretical framework, there was no middle ground in a class society. Mao understood everyone to belong to a socioeconomic class—to either the exploiting class or to the exploited class. As such, an artist who does not serve the Communist Revolution would be judged a servant to the bourgeoisie, and would therefore be labeled an enemy. Given the constraint of such ideology, a great abundance of wood-block artwork was produced in support of the Movement of Reduction of Rent and Taxes during the Anti-Japanese War (1937–45). This movement called on property owners nationwide to reduce rent and taxes on the poor to support the fight against the common enemy, the Japanese. Later, during the Civil War (1946–49) and in the early years of the New China period (b. 1949), wood-block art continued to be an effective means of communist propaganda. The anonymous work titled *Rent Reduction*, for example, shows peasants urging a landlord to reduce the rent on his land.

Art in the New China was bent to serve the government. For many years after the Liberation (1949), cultural authorities promoted a rural art movement. Although politically driven, the movement energized peasants and workers to apply their impressive creativity in praise of the New China's economic success and the Communist Party's leadership. Wu Shaoyun's 1958 painting, *We Sell Dry, Clean, Neat and Selected Cotton to the State*, is a good example. This propaganda poster not only depicts enthusiastic peasants harvesting cotton, but also celebrates the social equality to be enjoyed by women in the new society.

In addition to wood-block prints and traditional brush painting, other folk-art forms such as papercuts, mural painting, and posters were brought into play as well. The content of all artwork was sanctioned in order to guarantee political conformity, on the basis of which exaggeration was deemed a necessity to show loyalty to the Party. Workers, peasants, and soldiers—considered the most revolutionary members of the society—were typically featured in the focal section of paintings. Bringing in a bumper harvest was a typical theme. In answer to the Party's call, a number of villages sought to take the lead in art production. Huxian, a village in

ART

> ## MAO COLLECTIBLES
>
> Whereas Mao's statuettes and badges flooded homes and workplaces during the Great Cultural Revolution (1966–76), today they are highly sought collectibles. Apparently, Mao's iconographic value has gone from god-like to moneymaking. Owing to today's "commodification of Mao," a rare copy of "the little red book," *Quotations of Chairman Mao*, or a rare Mao pin, could bring more than $100 in street trading posts in China, and may be bid up higher on eBay. Some taxi drivers hang gadgets bearing Mao's image in their cabs as a totem for protection against road accidents.

Shaanxi Province, led the crowd. Today, decades after the height of the rural art movement, Huxian's artworks are still auctioned at respectably high prices. Huxian's peasants continue to supplement their income using the art production skills acquired in the 1950s.

On the heels of Deng Xiaoping's late-1970s political reform, modern Chinese art underwent tremendous change in becoming an outlet of individual expression. The rural political art campaigns died down as economic reform began in 1979. Mobilized by Deng Xiaoping's call to "get rich," rural artists converted the artistic skills they acquired in singing the praises of the Party into means of making money. As the latitude of political freedom widens, modern peasant art now often shows artists' sincere feelings and their introspection upon the relationship between humankind and the land. This work is sometimes labeled "naïve." A painting with qualities of naivete, *Vegetable Basket* by Zhu Yongin, won first prize in the 1996 National Contest of Peasant Painting and Calligraphy. Its simple colors and shapes express a sense of contentment with life.

If there is an art form considered to have prospered after the Liberation, it would be sculpture. Although sculpture is by no means a new form of art, its elevation to a position as dominant art form occurred following the Liberation. Obviously, from the 1950s through the 1960s, a great number of commemorative projects were in demand. Major projects included revolutionary landmarks, the Monument of the People's Heroes in Tiananmen Square, and particularly the statues of Chairman Mao that were erected in every public square. Additionally, abundant statues of local heroes; countless monuments to workers, peasants, and soldiers (the so-called leading class); and murals in relief commemorating historical events dotted the landscape across the country. From the artistic angle, sculpture for political propaganda has little artistic value. Every monument seemed to be a duplicate of another, except for differences in size. Moreover, after Mao died in 1976, the political and ideological principles championed by these artworks were challenged. The Great Cultural Revolution (1966–76) that led to the death and persecution of millions and the collapse of the economy had reduced Mao's image from god-like to deserving of oblivion. Toward the 1980s, the sculpture movement drew to an end. Most monuments, including Chairman Mao's statues, have been torn down; the few that remain standing today are maintained as historical relics.

Modern Chinese art is one of diversity. As China adopted an open-door policy in 1979, Western influence arrived. In the 1980s, the *Xin Chao* [New Wave] movement represented an avid acquisition of Western art. Writings of Nietzsche, Schopenhauer, Freud, Heidegger, and Sartre were translated into Chinese, and art salons sprang up. Young people were seeking new meanings of life, now that the authoritarian communist ideology had fallen apart. The avant-garde style was among the most popular trends. Geng Jianyi's *Barber Series* (1985), Zhang Qun and Meng Luding's *A New Era: Revelation from Adam and Eve* (1985), Miao Huixin's mixed media *Art's Enchantment* (1986), and Zeng Fanzhi's *Harmony Hospital* (1991) demonstrate an in-depth search for the soul in their abstract paintings. This is in contrast with the realist style of the pre-reform era.

Traditional Chinese paintings took a new direction in the 1980s. In this area, Gu Wenda's achievement is highly recognized. A student of Western oil painting, Gu Wenda returned to traditional brush painting. Traditional painting, as he puts it, allows him to break free from Western influence. Defying traditional designs and themes, however, Gu's paintings are abstract and filled with hidden messages. In *Sky and Ocean* (1986), for example, a white pillar of cloud rises from the sea, resembling a Greek statue. *Wisdom Comes from Tranquility* (1982–86) is a display of four panels of posters with Chinese characters in reversed structure. His recent work, *Feng Shui* (2003), presents an invented Chinese character that combines *feng* [wind] and *shui* [water] to imply an unconventional message.

Free of communism, Taiwan's art developed at a steady pace with more conformity to tradition than its mainland counterpart. Because Taiwan was occupied by the Japanese from 1895 to 1945, art was taught by Japanese instructors. *Nihonga* masters such as Takeuchi Seiho, Yokoyama Taikan, and Hishida Shunso left a strong impact. While the gentry continued to practice traditional painting, thousands of young artists traveled to Japan to study art. In addition, Japanese instructors such as Ishikawa Kin'ichiro (1871–1945) introduced Western art to Taiwan. Two events, however, precipitated changes in Taiwan's art world: one was Japan's surrender to the Allies in 1945; the other was the defeat of the Nationalist Kuomintang (KMT) Party in 1949. The influx of "provincials" (i.e., the nationalist service personnel from the mainland) brought fresh ideas. Meanwhile, an increasing American military presence exposed local artists to American art. Before the backdrop of Eastern and Western trends, the 1950s' *Fifth Moon* group revitalized traditional Chinese painting by integrating Western modernism. An impressive artwork was Liu Kuo-Sung's *The Earth Our Home* (1971), in which the traditional landscape is dominated by some cosmic force.

The Dongfang Huazhan (Eastern painting exhibition) was another group that experimented with abstract artistic expressions. Abstractionism was once labeled subversive by the same authorities who oddly contended that Picasso was simultaneously an abstractionist and a communist, and were thus suspicious of those who used cubist techniques.

The development of modern art in Taiwan was also facilitated by the end of the Cold War. Since the 1990s, the Taiwanese government has relaxed ideological monitoring and allowed artistic exchange across the Taiwan Strait. The opening up to mainland China and the prospect of reunification have brought new hope to the artistic mind. The sculpture titled *Expectation* (1991) reflects, in a way, the mentality of freedom in artistic pursuit.

JAPAN

Located east of China and comprising a long chain of volcanic islands, Japan's land mass consists of some 130,438 square miles of territory—slightly smaller than the U.S. state of California. The Japanese population totals approximately 127 million and is primarily uniform. After World War II, Japan emerged as a strong industrial power, and today ranks third in the world behind the United States and China.

Archeological discoveries suggest that Japan may have been populated earlier than China. For example, Japan's pottery production, known for its cord pattern, dates back some 10,000 years and spread throughout Japan during the Jomon period. China and Japan share a long history of cultural exchange. From the seventh through the ninth centuries, China grew to be the dominant nation in East Asia under the Tang dynasty (618–960). The Japanese court adopted the ranking system of the Chinese nobility, which was based on civil service examinations. Subsequently, hundreds of Japanese scholars and ambassadors studied in China and brought Chinese literature, painting, music, Buddhism, and the like back to

Japan. Japanese script, for example, was imported from China during the Heian period (794–1185). Japanese Buddhist art is characterized by the Chinese styles of the Tang dynasty. Much unlike the Chinese dynastic system, however, Japanese society was dominated by warriors and independent swordsmen, or *samurai*. The rise of the samurai occurred as the Japanese court weakened, toward the twelfth century. It is believed that the warrior's code of honor is an important part of the Japanese spiritual construct. In addition, the native Shinto religion, in conjunction with Buddhism and Confucianism, never stopped being venerated officially. In fact, during the Tokugawa period (the seventeenth through nineteenth centuries), many capable samurai wrote elegant Chinese and became highly knowledgeable of the Chinese classics.

The most prominent form of traditional Japanese art is wood-block art. Traditionally, wood-block art was a cheap and productive means employed by temples to duplicate religious tracts and images of deities. As it became a popular illustrative art, the art of the wood-block print was refined by integrating techniques of brush painting and calligraphy. The content was also widened to secular subjects, such as figures in literature. A masterpiece is Katsushika Hokusai's (1760–1849) *The Great Wave*. Apparently, Hokusai followed Western principles of perspective and shading to reflect Japanese landscapes.

Wood-block print has been inherited by such modern artists as Munakata Shiko (1903–75). Munakata was a practicing Buddhist. Many of his prints and paintings show religious subjects. The 1938 painting *Sutra of Kannon* is a well-known artwork. The thriving Buddhist worship of the postwar time also constituted an important focus of Kenzo Okada's (1902–82) wood-block work. Other subjects are taken from Japanese legends or from nature.

Japanese artists welcomed Western art with an open mind. During the Meiji era (1868–1912) Japan saw a great wave of Westernization. Rapid development of the military allowed Japan to win both the Sino-Japanese War (1894–95) and the Russo-Japanese War (1905). These military victories confirmed that the Meiji dream of achieving security and equality through acquisition of Western technology was more than realized. During the first half of the twentieth century, Japan rose to militarily dominate Asia, until falling at the end of World War II. In art, under the influence of the Meiji Restoration (1868), Western artistic concepts as well as new techniques were widely adopted. By the end of World War II, a marked rise in creativity was seen in all areas of art. In addition to Munakata Shiko's wood-block prints, the works of Kenzo Okada gained an equally great fame.

Kenzo Okada was born in Yokohoma, the son of a wealthy industrialist. He attended Tokyo Fine Arts University, where he painted in traditional realist style. He also studied Western painting in Paris and lived in New York City. By integrating the traditional and the Western techniques—particularly impressionist ones—Kenzo created works of world renown.

The works of the Japanese avant-garde reflected many aspects of postwar mentality. Like its European counterparts, Japanese avant-garde art represents rebelliousness in general. Antiorthodox and antipolitical conformity was a popular theme. One example is the artists' protest against the U.S.-Japan Security Treaty signed in 1951. To voice their concerns about the Japanese government's intention of rearming the country, members of the Neo Dada Organizers group participated in violent demonstrations. One well-known event was the artist Yoshimura posing masked and bandaged like a mummy in Neo-Dada poster paper in a street of Tokyo.[1] Other avant-garde shows included artists wrapped in strings of light bulbs. One artist was seen sticking his face into a bucket of water. He made bubbling sounds and then started shouting, "The War! The War! The Third World War!"[2]

In the 1990s, Japanese avant-gardism took a new direction to reflect Japan's quintessential contribution to modern technology. In general, the end of the Cold War and the rapid economic growth of the Japanese economy brought a sense of relief. Yet, the vision of Japan as the paradigmatic commodity culture became a source of concern. The works of Morimura Yasumasa's (b. 1951) in the early 1990s, for example, consisted of computer-scanned images. His immense, four-part *Playing with Gods* struck one man as an "irreverent decontextualization of the Crucifixion."[3] In this painting, Western religious figures are dressed in samurai and geisha clothing and wear what appear to be machined metal objects, all of which cast a rather mythologized cloud.

Meanwhile, a form of cartoon art known as *manga* (meaning "comics") has been popular since the end of World War II. Since the 1960s, manga has been sold mainly in the form of inexpensive weekly and monthly magazines. Each issue of these magazines contains ten to twenty separate series, all of which can be read in about an hour. Manga as an art medium carries an immense range of cultural themes through long-running stories. In adult manga, fanaticism, violence, politics, and sex are widely encountered. More than other art forms, the art of manga is particularly sensitive to changing political trends. Youth manga excels in magical stories of swords and battles. Transformed into TV series and video games, youth manga enjoys an international audience.

> **THE POPULARITY OF MANGA**
>
> To a great extent, the popularity of manga is the result of institutional promotion. The "manga industry" has been promoted by well-known organizations. In 1988 the University of California Press published an English edition of the manga series, *Japan Inc.: Introduction to Japanese Economics (the Comic Book)*. The Japan Foundation, two major manga publishers, and the U.S. Consulate General in Japan collaborated in presenting a large manga exhibition in 1992 at the San Francisco Cartoon Art Museum. In 1999 the Japan Foundation sponsored manga exhibitions at the Maison de la Culture du Japaon in Paris, and in the galleries of the Dutch Kunsthal in Rotterdam. In a sense, manga art has played the role of cultural ambassador more effectively than all the Japanese consulates stationed around the world.

THE TWO KOREAS

Sharing a land border with China, the Korean peninsula has maintained close ties with China for centuries. Historically, Korea was China's tributary state as well as China's protectorate. By the end of the nineteenth century, as the Chinese empire weakened, the Chinese court lost Korea. Korea was annexed by Japan in 1910. After World War II, a Republic of Korea (ROK) was established in the southern half of the Korean peninsula while a communist-style government, the Democratic Peoples' Republic of Korea (DPRK), was installed in the North. During the Korean War (1950–53), U.S. troops and UN forces fought alongside soldiers from the ROK to defend South Korea from DPRK attacks that were supported by China and the Soviet Union. An armistice was signed in 1953, splitting the peninsula along a demilitarized zone at about the thirty-eighth parallel. Thereafter, South Korea has gone on to achieve rapid economic development while North Korea has continued to struggle in poverty. Because of strict information control and deliberate political persecution, today little information manages to leave North Korea.

In its cultural tradition, the blighting influence of imperial Confucianism and its governing system made its mark on Korean history and remains strong today. Korean classical art faithfully follows the Chinese conventions. Variations, however, became prominent after the independence of the North and South. One landmark movement of art and culture in South Korea is the *Minjung* [masses].

ART

Modern South Korean art in the 1980s and 1990s was marked by the Minjung Cultural Movement. The movement gained momentum after what is known as the Kwangju Massacre of 1980, the violent suppression of peaceful demonstrators by the government of Chun Doo Huan. In condemning both classicism and art-for-art modernism, the Minjung artists defined their goal as speaking to the aesthetic needs of the middle class and lower-level working class. The word *minjung* means "masses." Hence the art stresses content rather than form, and intends to reflect the life of Minjung adherents as well as their political opinions. Minjung art gained prominence in actively creating works about student movements, and in supporting democratization, social justice, and reunification. In the 1990s, women's rights, consumerism, and sometimes nationalism also figured as popular Minjung themes. Given their political tendencies, Minjung artists were often accused of being communists trying to spread communist influence.

One renowned artwork is Chon Min-yong's flag painting. By integrating light bulbs on the striped banner to represent a number of different countries including South Korea, Chon intends to convey a strong message of dissent.[4]

While modern North Korean art is little known to the outside world, the few art and photo collections available on Websites, mostly posted by Chinese tourists, suggest that artistic freedom is nonexistent under the communist dictatorship of Kim Jung-Il and his Workers' Party. With a population of 23 million, North Korea is the last communist stronghold still on guard against the influence of the market economy, although its leadership allegedly has convenient access to Western art, similar to the situation in China in the 1960s and 1970s. The dominant ideological guidance—the "central spirit"—urges people to adhere to the central government's leadership. Individualism is inadmissible.

Another guiding principle, equivalent to China's Great Leap Forward (1958), is a radical economic ramp-up known as the spirit of the "thousand-mile horse." People are encouraged to deploy the spirit of selfless contribution and tireless enthusiasm to realize economic miracles. Monuments reflecting the spirit of the "thousand-mile horse" are popular across the landscape of North Korea. Information is tightly controlled. Even tourists from China, North Korea's top ally and a major source of its energy supplies, are treated as "foreigner guests" and are strictly monitored. Thus, the North Korean artistic scene is one of great familiarity: posters of workers, peasants, and soldiers working enthusiastically to construct the great fatherland; paintings depicting people grouped together in diligent study of what appear to be great leaders' works; and other artwork similar to what was popular in the communist bloc in the 1960s and 1970s. In North Korea, art is apparently geared to serve the government as a brainwashing tool.

AUSTRALIA AND OCEANIA

Oceanic art, whether in form or content, is distinct from the art of East Asia. Deeply embedded in the tradition of Oceanic art is a neolithic heritage, primarily in the form of tribal art crafts. The geographic scope of Oceania includes not only Melanesia, Micronesia, and Polynesia, but conventionally includes also Australia and New Zealand. Melanesia consists of a wide stretch of islands in the Pacific including Papua New Guinea, the Bismarck Archipelago, and the Solomon Islands. Off the coast of the Philippines and extending into the central Pacific are the Micronesian islands, which include the Carolines, the Marianas, the Marshalls, and the Gilbert Islands. Polynesian islands are located between the Hawaiian Islands and New Zealand. The aboriginals typically look Asian, but are much darker in complexion.

Australia, the world's smallest continent but sixth-largest country, has a population of approximately 20 million, concentrated along the eastern and southeastern coasts. Aboriginal settlers arrived from Southeast Asia about 40,000 to 50,000 years before the first Europeans began exploration in the seventeenth century. Since 1770 when Captain James Cook set foot on the continent, Australia was gradually occupied by the British. The six colonies created in the late eighteenth and nineteenth centuries federated and became the Commonwealth of Australia in 1901.

Southeast of Australia lies New Zealand, which has a territory the size of the U.S. state of Colorado. New Zealand's small population (of about 4 million) is 78 percent European and 14.6 percent Maori according to the 2006 census. Maori is the official language; English is popularly spoken. Discovered by Dutch sailors in the seventeenth century, the island was soon a British colony. New Zealand became an independent dominion in 1907.

Oceania shares a common aboriginal artistic tradition, as well as a common influence from European traditions in its modern arts. Oceanic arts are represented by wood sculptures of ancestors and deities. Decorations on sculpture and the human body (in the form of tattoo) are also popular. The Oceanic artistic tradition dates back thousands of years to the Paleolithic (approximately 10,000 years ago) and Neolithic (approximately 7,000 years ago) arts. From shape to content, modern oceanic arts preserve these traditions vividly and with great dedication. Researchers notice the prominent thematic motif of simple figuring used to represent ancestral spirit. Landscape art, on the other hand, is rare. In addition to the dominant spiritual and legendary themes, art for nonreligious purposes today is abundant. Tourists find fantastic art shows at festivals and farmers' markets. Farmers typically produce artwork to trade for cash. In Polynesia, pendants and hairpins carved from fish bone are exquisitely decorated; dining utensils are another preferred vehicle of carving and painting.

Although the wood carvings may appear simple, their real value is found within the tribal communities and religions. Colors, feathers, and leaf ornaments are perceived as the vehicles of hidden powers endowed by divine spirit. It is obvious that in every wooden carved object—whether it is a fish, a bird, or a human mask—there is a highly disciplined creative talent. Motifs and forms are brilliantly combined; nothing is left to chance. As shown in a dancer's mask, circles and lines are marvelously combined to stress facial features in ways that are both exotic and coherent.

A prominent theme of wood carvings, in particular, is the worship of male genitals. This tradition seems to be common to all Oceanic islands. The theme is also found in Taiwanese aboriginal arts. Recent genetic studies indicate that Polynesians may trace their genetic roots to Taiwanese aboriginal communities. Although most figurines are male, some are female. One aboriginal Taiwanese belief holds that worship of the male organ promises reproductive power to the family. While such beliefs may appear related to the traditional Chinese preference for larger families, the Oceanic message is different. In Oceania, the senses of protection and of divinity are more essential. Obviously, in terms of representation, Oceanic art shares little with Chinese artistic creation, which stresses landscape and shuns nudity. Seen in a live display, an Oceanic art object would be a reminder of timelessness and of the long distances that humans have traveled.

There is regional variation among the traditional arts of New Zealand and Australia. The Maori crafts of bone and stone carving are most characteristic of New Zealand. Most characteristic of Australia is the aboriginal art of "Dreamings," which depict the journeys and deeds of creators and ancestors, and express the artists' understanding of the natural world. Aboriginal Dreamtime stories demonstrate both good and bad behaviors in telling how the ancestors managed to hunt, marry, care for children, and provide defense against enemies.

It is the flourishing modern art of European origin, however, that makes New Zealand and Australia stand out in the scope of Oceania. Schools and groups with common aims have flourished from time to time, and produced works as similar to each other in style as those of the French Impressionists. In Australia, a most notable early group was the Heidelberg School, which flourished between 1885 and 1900. A more recent one, which may loosely be called "The Field," was popular from 1965 to 1970. The 1970s' Women's Art Movement in New Zealand generated paintings that typically reflected the themes of the feminist movement at the time. Jacqueline Fahey was one of New Zealand's first women artists to paint from a feminist perspective. Her domestic surroundings were the inspiration for her art, which centered on her interpretation of society. In Carole Shepard's painting *John* (1981), the artist created a modular work composed of individually boxed images. The multifaceted piece shows photographic images of the subject's face and parts of his body, and presents him in his different roles of father, musician, and lover. The work demonstrates an alternative to the convention of the erotic female nude. Obviously, although the brush strokes are of European styling, the content reflects the vision of these individual artists of Australia and New Zealand who are living in their own space and time.

SOUTH AND SOUTHEAST ASIA

VINAY DHARWADKER AND DONNA L. HALPER

The visual and plastic arts have exceptionally long and complex histories of indigenous origin and autonomous and interdependent development in South and Southeast Asia. South Asian sculpture and architecture were already sophisticated practices by the third century BCE, and began to spread with trade and migration (and without military conquest) from the subcontinental mainland to what are now Myanmar, Thailand, Indonesia, Cambodia, and Vietnam by about the first century CE. Between approximately 300 BCE and 1200 CE, a common Indian style of planning, design, construction, finishing, and representation emerged primarily in the dominant and interlinked domains of sculpture and architecture (and in the smaller domain of painting), which underwent some variation across the subcontinent and especially over time, creating distinct period and regional styles. This overall style was used in ancient and classical India chiefly to build monumental public buildings and complexes, such as places of worship and pilgrimage, monasteries, and royal palaces. In these cases, a building was usually conceived of as an enormous sculpture with abstract symbolic as well as concrete representational dimensions. Within this broad conception, actual sculpture—in relief and in the round—was integrated into the exterior, interior, and surroundings of buildings, using naturalistic but highly stylized representations of plants, animals, humans, demons, celestial beings, gods, and even landscapes and everyday objects. In the opening centuries of the Common Era, this approach to architecture and sculpture, including its choice and treatment of specific materials and its large repertoire of craft and technique, started to spread to various parts of Southeast Asia. Where it spread, the approach was adopted and adapted initially in relation to Hindu temples (as part of the Hindu-Sanskrit sphere of influence) and also subsequently in connection with Buddhist structures and monuments (as part of the later Buddhist-Pali sphere of influence).

Beginning in the eighth century, Muslim armies, traders, and Sufi practitioners moved incrementally into and across South Asia, bringing the active ancient and classical Indian tradition of building and sculpting (in their Hindu and Buddhist forms) to a close on the subcontinent with the ascendancy of Muslim political formations by the twelfth century. The Hindu model, however, continued to influence architectural and artistic practices in mainland Southeast Asia until about the sixteenth century, as in the monuments of the Khmer kingdom in Cambodia and the Sukhothai and Ayutthaya kingdoms in Thailand. Early in the twelfth century in north India and by the thirteenth century in Indonesia, much of the construction of state and public buildings and places of worship and pilgrimage started to follow Islamic principles, which in their orthodox form (but not in some of their Sufi and "secularized" forms) forbid the making of "idols" or the representation of any entity that is part of Allah's Creation, whether naturalistic or symbolic. Euro-Christian styles of architecture and art arrived in western and southern India with the Portuguese in the early sixteenth century, and in the Philippines with the Spanish a few decades later. Between the mid-eighteenth and mid-twentieth centuries, European colonial styles of building and visual and plastic representation spread throughout South and Southeast Asia, especially as the Portuguese, Spanish, Dutch, British, and French empires consolidated their control over specific parts of these two regions.

Over the course of the twentieth century, the broadly "modern," international genres of architecture, engineering, painting, sculpture, and decoration became pervasive in this portion of Asia. However, the Hindu, Buddhist, Islamic, and explicitly Christian traditions remain alive and productive, having adapted to modern circumstances in various ways and to varying degrees. In this context, the arts in South and Southeast Asia today continue to function in a very "mixed" cultural environment, in which the major traditions and influences of the past—sometimes the very ancient past—continue to exercise a vital force on the individual artist's imagination.

MODERN AND CONTEMPORARY ART

Modern drawing and painting in Western styles and media have flourished in most South and Southeast Asian countries quite extensively since the early or middle decades of the twentieth century, and in some cases since the nineteenth century. Realistic renderings of the human face and figure, of urban and rural scenes, of landscapes and natural objects and phenomena, and of everyday things and domestic interiors, together with abstract compositions in various modes, have been especially popular with artists, viewers, collectors, and institutions since the end of World War II. Drawings in charcoal, graphite, and pastel, and paintings in watercolor, acrylic, and oil colors on supports ranging from paper, wood, and metal to canvas and other fabrics are among the most commonplace genres of modern art in these parts of Asia.

Other forms of modern art are equally widespread across these regions but are less common, chiefly because they are less in demand in the contemporary market, or require more specialized skills or more expensive materials and facilities. Western-style printmaking—including relief printing with wood blocks and linoleum, intaglio printing using metal plates, lithography, and screen printing (including serigraphy, which uses silk screens)—has attracted a number of important artists in the past few decades. Similarly, modern sculpture in wood, stone, metal, and less durable media (such as terra-cotta and plaster) is practiced in most countries, but on a smaller scale than painting. South and Southeast Asian artists have also contributed significantly to the modern forms of the mural and the fresco, to stained glass and ceramic art, to mixed media and installation art, and to visual art forms using film, video, audio, and projection technologies.

A number of important art schools in Asia have been training artists in these and related media since World War I, if not earlier. Among the notable institutions in South Asia in this context are the Karachi School of Art, the National College of Arts in Lahore and Rawalpindi, and the Mayo School of Art in Lahore (Pakistan); the Sir J. J. School of Art in Mumbai, the Government College of Arts and Crafts in Kolkata, the Faculty of Fine Arts at the Maharaja Sayajirao University in Baroda, the Delhi College of Art, and the Triveni Kala Sangam in New Delhi (India); and the Institute of Fine Art, University of Dhaka (Bangladesh). Equally important institutions in Southeast Asia included the Art Institute of Teachers' Training and the State School of Fine Arts in Rangoon (Myanmar); the King Mongkut Institute of Art in Bangkok (Thailand); L'Ecole Superieure des Beaux Arts in Hanoi (founded in 1925), the Hanoi College of Fine Art, and the Gia Dinh National College of Fine Art in Ho Chi Minh City (Vietnam); the University of Santo Tomas in Manila, and the College of Fine Arts at the University of the Philippines-Diliman, which goes back to the Academia de Dibujo (Academy of Drawing) founded in 1823 (the Philippines); and the Department of Art at the University of Indonesia in Jakarta and the Faculty of Fine Arts and Design at the Bandung Institute of Technology (Indonesia). Besides their education at such institutions in their homelands, since the mid-twentieth century some artists from South and Southeast Asia have also been trained at major schools in Europe and the Americas.

Modern art in South and Southeast Asia is preserved and exhibited in an extensive network of national and local museums, which have been in existence since colonial times, and in private art galleries, which have mushroomed in recent decades with the growth of an international market for Asian art. Among the best-known museums are the National Art Gallery in Islamabad (Pakistan); the National Gallery of Modern Art in New Delhi (India); the Rangoon Museum (Myanmar); the National Art Gallery in Kuala Lumpur (Malaysia); and the Singapore Art Museum. Well-known private art galleries—some of which have played historic roles in the development of modern art in various parts of Asia—currently include the Chemould Gallery in New Delhi and the Jehangir Art Gallery in Mumbai (India), and the Valentine Willie Fine Art Gallery in Kuala Lumpur (Malaysia). State-run institutions that provide many types of support to contemporary artists in various media and genres, as well as to education and research in the arts, range from the Lalit Kala Akademi in New Delhi (India's national academy of the visual arts) to the famous Taman Ismail Marzuki Arts Centre in Jakarta (probably the largest such facility in Southeast Asia, with theaters, exhibition halls, an arts academy, and an archives department in a single complex).

Since about 1990, under globalization, the market for art from South and Southeast Asia has grown rapidly in size, value, and reach, with collectors and buyers appearing nationally and regionally as well as in the West, and including prosperous members of the Asian diaspora around the globe. This market now represents, promotes, and sells a wide range of artifacts from these regions, including antique art (such as miniature paintings, illustrated or illuminated manuscripts, sculpture, furniture, and decorative pieces, as allowed by laws regulating the export and import of antiques and art objects); high quality contemporary imitations and reproductions of traditional artifacts, genres, and styles (such as miniature paintings in specific regional styles from Pakistan and India; and metal, stone, and wood replicas of religious and artistic significance in the Hindu and Buddhist traditions from India and Sri Lanka); and originals and recent reproductions of more or less "exotic" colonial period genre paintings (such as Spanish, Dutch, British, and French landscape, still life, and figurative representations in oil and watercolor from the colonies). It also has successfully begun to show and sell works by contemporary painters, sculptors, installation artists, and multimedia artists (including artists in video and film) in various styles and genres, both domestically and abroad—a development that had remained elusive through much of the twentieth century, as modern forms and media of visual, plastic, and performance art entered and consolidated themselves in the cultural mix of South and Southeast Asia.

For much of the past 75 years, various kinds of modernist and postmodernist art that have emerged in Europe and America have migrated artistically to Asia, where they have tended to strongly influence indigenous practice, but have consistently undergone numerous local and regional modifications. In this sense, contemporary art in the so-called modern forms in South or Southeast Asian countries is not a mere imitation of Western schools or styles, but is strongly productive and innovative in its own right. Indian, Malaysian, Indonesian, Thai, Burmese, and Filipino trends over the past several decades, especially after World War II and decolonization, are therefore not always reflective of trends in France, Germany, England, or the United States, even though there are many points of coincidence and similarity. Precisely in order to escape from the power of colonial and Western influences, artists of the modern period in South and Southeast Asia have persistently pursued an ideal of originality and independence, and this shared but often unstated goal has resulted in a cumulative effect of great novelty around the turn of the millennium. Since about 1990 particularly, as artists from these regions have reached worldwide audiences under globalization to an unprecedented degree, the boldness and singularity of their vision, skill, and technique have become much more perceptible than ever before.

Some Individual Artists

The sheer variety and distinctiveness of figurative and representational art as well as abstract composition that marks contemporary South and Southeast Asian practices are perhaps best appreciated by looking at the works and careers of a selection of important painters and artists on an individual level. For the sake of brevity, a series of examples from Pakistan and India, followed by a brief description of two important collective shows in Southeast Asia early in this decade, may serve to represent the range of accomplishments across the two regions.

Shahzia Sikandar (b. 1969) is now the best-known woman painter from Pakistan. Trained as a traditional miniature painter at the National College of Arts, Lahore, she was subsequently educated in modern art at the Rhode Island School of Design in the United States, and has worked at the Glassell School of Art, Huston, and the Otis College of Art and Design, Los Angeles. Since the 1990s, her work has included miniatures, drawings, watercolors, large wall paintings, installation art in paper, photographs, video and digital media, computerized animation, and multimedia montages. She has exhibited at the Museum of Modern Art, New York; the National Gallery of Canada; the Musée d'Art moderne de la Ville de Paris; and the Venice Biennale 2005. In 2006 she gained further international attention when she became the first artist of South Asian origin to be awarded a five-year MacArthur Fellowship in the United States.

Among the major modern artists of India, the most famous and popular is M. F. Hussain (b. 1915). A self-taught painter with an enormous output in multiple media ranging from drawings and oils on canvas to large-scale murals as well as film, Hussain was associated with the Progressive Artists' Group in Mumbai in the 1940s and 1950s; he became famous worldwide when he was invited to exhibit with Pablo Picasso at the Sao Paolo Biennale in Brazil in 1971. His works are in the permanent collections of major art museums around the world, and also in numerous private collections. Since the 1980s, some of Hussain's paintings have sold for the highest prices for living artists in the international market.

Equally valued by connoisseurs around the world is Satish Gujral (b. 1925), who is known for his paintings, sculptures, and murals, as well as for his projects in architecture and interior design. Deaf since childhood, Gujral was trained at the Mayo School of Art, Lahore, and at the J. J. School of Art, Mumbai; in the early 1950s, he was an apprentice to Mexican artists Diego Riviera and David Alfaro Siqueiros. His works are in museums and private collections around the globe; his international awards include the Order of the Crown of Belgium (given for his design of the Belgian Embassy in New Delhi, chosen as one of the most distinguished buildings of the twentieth century), and the da Vinci Award, Mexico's international prize for lifetime achievement in the arts.

Of the other well-known and widely collected painters of the first postcolonial generation in India, six are especially popular. Jehangir Sabavala (b. 1922) was trained initially at the J. J. School of Art, Mumbai, and subsequently at the Heatherley School of Fine Art, London, and at private academies in Paris; he is famous for his tranquil but haunting abstract landscapes with occasional solitary, geometric human figures, painted in pastel tones in oil on canvas. S. H. Raza (b. 1922), a founding member of the left-wing Progressive Artists Group, trained at the J. J. School of Art and extensively in France, and has lived and worked for several decades in Paris and Gorbio, France. F. N. Souza (1924–2002) was a co-founder of the Progressive Group with Raza, and also trained at the J. J. School of Art, but left for Britain soon after India's independence and settled finally in New York. Raza and Souza are both painters who combine the realistic and abstract modes, and their works are represented in major museums in France, England, and the United States, and in numerous private and corporate collections around the world. Tyeb Mehta (b. 1925) has evolved over the past six decades an unmistakable style of figurative painting in abstract mode. One of the most prized contemporary Indian painters, he has exhibited at the Menton Biennale in France, the Museum of Modern Art at Oxford, the Singapore Art Museum, and the Tate Modern in London, among numerous international venues. Akbar Padamsee (b. 1928) mostly creates memorable abstract landscapes ("metascapes") and nonrealistic figures and portraits in oil, water color, and charcoal, and has also produced sculpture, films, and art criticism. Bhupen Khakhar (1934–2003), the first openly gay painter among Indian artists, has become popular for his large, complex compositions involving figures, cityscapes, and natural landscapes rendered in an abstract yet surreal style. His work is collected in the National Gallery of Modern Art (New Delhi), the British Museum and National Portrait Gallery in London, and the Museum of Modern Art (New York), among other collections worldwide.

Four younger male painters in India are especially notable for their distinctive drawings and paintings that have attracted numerous buyers, collectors, and viewers in the past three decades. Of these, Bikash Bhattacharya (b. 1940), who recently stopped painting as the result of a paralytic stroke, was trained in Kolkata and produced a large body of vivid, surreal figures, portraits, and cityscapes in the realistic mode. Rameshwar Broota (b. 1941) is best known for his large "monochrome" paintings with shadowy animal-like human figures, often grimly powerful in their psychological, cultural, and political resonance. Sudhir Patwardhan (b. 1949), a practicing radiologist, is a painter of unforgettable landscapes and cityscapes, often thickly populated with figures, machines, animals, and objects, and frequently concerned with the environment and problems of modernization and urbanization. The youngest of these prominent artists is Riyas Komu (b. 1971), whose work often focuses on the realistically rendered faces of ordinary people, painted in large scale and staring rivetingly straight out of the canvas.

Several important modern Indian painters are also distinguished writers in various indigenous languages or in English, very much in the small but worldwide tradition of poet-painters and writer-artists. Ram Kumar (b. 1924) is as well-known for his haunting abstract and fragmented landscapes as for his short stories in Hindi; G. R. Santosh (1929–97), a superb adapter of Tantric art and symbolism in modern media, was also an important poet in Kashmiri; Ghulam Mohammed Sheikh (b. 1939), a major innovator of complex compositions with human figures and built environments, is also a leading contemporary poet in Gujarati; and Gieve Patel (b. 1940), a practicing general physician, has been a popular thematic painter who works in a distinctive style of rendering stylized and realistic or semi-realistic figures in memorably portrayed urban and natural landscapes, and remains a significant Indian-English poet today. A number of women painters have distinguished themselves in the crowded contemporary Indian art scene. Among them are Anjolie Menon (b. 1940), who often focuses on female subjects, bodies, and issues; Arpana Caur (b. 1954), perhaps the most interesting figurative and compositional painter, who has memorialized such political and historical issues as war, violence, forced migration, and secularism; and Shruti Gupta Chandra (b. 1940), one of the most exciting and imaginative figurative painters to emerge in recent years.

> ## RECENT EXHIBITIONS OF MODERN ART FROM SOUTHEAST ASIA
>
> The vibrancy and popular appeal of contemporary art is best exemplified by some of the major exhibitions mounted in different parts of South and Southeast Asia in recent years.
>
> A representative instance is "Faith + the City: A Survey of Contemporary Filipino Art," curated by Valentine Willie and sponsored by the Magsaysay Maritime Corporation, Helu-Trans Art Movers, and the Singapore Tourism Board. Conceived as a regional exhibit, "Faith + the City" traveled to Singapore (October 2000), the National Art Gallery of Malaysia in Kuala Lumpur (January–February 2001), and Penang, Malaysia (March–April 2001). It displayed more than 100 works in various genres and media by forty-two artists from the Philippines, centering on the theme of religion and the urban experience today. Many of the remarkable artworks and artists featured in this exhibit can be viewed in the online catalogue uploaded by Valentine Willie Fine Art at http://www.artsasia.com.my/offsite/faithnthecity/.
>
> Another excellent example is "Telah Terbit [Out Now]: South East Asian Art Practices during the 1970s," a regional retrospective at the Singapore Art Museum (September–November 2006) on show at the time of the Singapore Biennale 2006 festival. Curated by Ahmad Mashadi, this exhibition displayed works by sixteen major artists from Indonesia, Malaysia, the Philippines, Singapore, and Thailand. The exhibition site as well as the works can be viewed at http://universe-in-universe.de/car/singapore/eng/2006, or via the respective Websites of the Singapore Biennale 2006 and the Singapore Art Museum.

TRADITIONAL ARTS

As indicated earlier, traditional arts remain enormously popular all over present-day South and Southeast Asia in two respects: artifacts produced in the past are popular among viewers, buyers, and collectors for a range of reasons; and forms, styles, and genres of traditional visual art remain part of the repertoire of artists in this region today, and hence continue to be popular among audiences. Artists are still trained in the traditional skills and techniques in many parts of Asia, and learn to work with the materials, media, themes, and motifs associated with them for centuries. The National College of Arts in Lahore (Pakistan), for instance, educates artists in the complex arts of Persian, Turkish, Central Asian, and Mughal-style miniature painting; the Government College of Arts and Crafts in Kolkata (India) trains Indian artists and craftsmen in many different genres of traditional art as well as handicrafts—in media ranging from paint to metal, wood, and textiles; and the school for traditional artists sponsored by the Maharajah of Jaipur at the City Palace in Jaipur (India) trains painters in several styles of premodern Rajasthani miniature painting (a school of art with nine main subdivisions that emerged independently of courtly Mughal-style miniature painting in north India in the sixteenth century).

The most important aspect of the popularity of traditional Asian arts is manifest in the vast annual flow of tourists and visitors, domestic and foreign, to historical sites around each country where works of art and architecture may be viewed in situ and in local museums that house artifacts preserved from important archeological recoveries. As noted above, for at least 1,500 years, much of the sculpture and architecture of South and Southeast Asia was fused into a single continuum of visual representation and building. This fusion, to some extent, also included within its ambit examples of painting and decorative art. An experience with ancient, classical, and premodern indigenous art forms has been a central focus in modern education in these regions. A large number of sites in countries ranging from Pakistan, India, Bangladesh, and Sri Lanka to Thailand, Cambodia, Vietnam, the Philippines, and Indonesia have been designated as World Heritage Sites by the United Nations Educational, Scientific and Cultural Organization (UNESCO) in recent decades, and they continue to attract tens or even hundreds of thousands of visitors each year.

Among the most popular and important World Heritage Sites where tourists, students, and researchers can view and study traditional artifacts—including relief and freestanding sculpture, monumental architecture, public engineering, fresco painting, and handicrafts, among other items—are Mohenjodaro (Pakistan) and Lothal (India), towns surviving from the prehistoric Harappan civilization around the Indus River and the west coast of the subcontinent. In contemporary India, premier sites include the Ajanta, Ellora, and Elephanta Caves in Maharashtra and near Mumbai, which contain exquisite Buddhist fresco paintings and colossal sculpture from the first millennium CE; the Buddhist monasteries and other monuments at Sanchi, Sarnath, and Bodh Gaya in north India; the major Hindu temple complexes at Konarak (Orissa), Khajuraho (Madhya Pradesh), and Mahabalipuram (Tamil Nadu), among other such locations; and the glorious Taj Mahal in Agra (Uttar Pradesh). In Sri Lanka, the most popular and important sites are Anuradhapura, Polonnaruva, Sigiriya, and Dambulla, with superb examples of Buddhist monumental sculpture, architecture, and painting dating to the beginning of the Common Era, many of which influenced Buddhist art in Southeast Asia over the next two millennia. In Southeast Asia, the ruins of the ancient cities of Sukhothai and Ayutthaya in Thailand contain some remarkable sculpture; in Cambodia, the Hindu temple complexes of Angkor Wat and Angkor Thom remain among the most astonishing achievements in world history in the visual and plastic arts; and in Indonesia, the enormous Hindu temple complexes at Borobudur and Prambanam continue to exemplify the originality and complexity of the Asian visual imagination. Each of these locations contains an entire history, sometimes more than a millennium long, and embodies a range of forms that represent the best of the traditional arts of South and Southeast Asia.

RESOURCE GUIDE

PRINT SOURCES

East Asia and Oceania

Luo, Jing. *Over a Cup of Tea—An Introduction to Chinese Life and Culture.* Lanham, MD: University Press of America, 2004.

Fairbank, John K., Edwin O. Reichauer, and Albert M. Craig. *East Asia—Tradition and Transformation.* Boston: Houghton Mifflin, 1989.

Hart, Frederick. *Art.* Upper Saddle Ridge, NJ: Prentice Hall, Inc., 3rd edition, 1989.

Hoffman, Franck. "Images of Dissent—Transformations in Korean Minjung Art." *Harvard Asia Pacific Review*, 1.2 (Summer 1997): 44–49.

Munroe, Alexandra. *Japanese Art after 1945—Scream against the Sky.* New York: Harry N. Abrams, 1994.

Schmitz, Carl A. *Oceanic Art—Myth, Man, and Image in the South Seas.* New York: Harry N. Abrams, 1971.

Sullivan, Michael. *Art and Artists of Twentieth-Century China.* Berkeley: University of California Press, 1996.

Thorp, Robert L., *Chinese Art & Culture.* Upper Saddle Ridge, NJ: Prentice Hall and Harry N. Abrams, 2001.

South and Southeast Asia

Coomaraswamy, A. K. *History of Indian and Indonesian Art.* New York: Dover, 1965.

Craven, Roy C. *Indian Art: A Concise History.* New York: Thames and Hudson, 1985, 1991.

Fischer, J., ed. *Modern Indonesian Art: Three Generations of Tradition and Change, 1945–1990.* Berkeley: University of California Press, 1990.

Islam, Syed Manzoorul, ed. *Contemporary Art in Bangladesh.* London: Arts and the Islamic World, 1999.

Rawson, Philip S. *The Art of Southeast Asia: Cambodia, Vietnam, Thailand, Laos, Burma, Java, Bali.* New York: Thames and Hudson, 1990.

Rowland, Benjamin. *The Art and Architecture of India: Buddhist, Hindu, Jain.* New York: Penguin, 1977.

Sivaramamurti, Calambur. *The Art of India.* New York: Abrams, 1977.

WEBSITES

East Asia and Oceania

Janes Oceanic Space. Accessed July 1, 2006. http://www.janeresture.com/index.htm.

North Korean Art. Accessed June 29, 2006. http://northkoreanart.com/index.html.

North Korean Art Outpost. Accessed June 29, 2006. http://www.orientaloutpost.com/proddetail.php?prod=1nks-5&cat=14.

South and Southeast Asia

Fabulous Ancient City of Anuradhapura. Accessed December 19, 2006. http://members.lycos.co.uk/withanage/Anuradha.htm?. Material, including pictures, on the ancient city of Anuradhapura, Sri Lanka.

Hernandez, Eloisa May P. "The American and Contemporary Traditions in Philippine Visual Arts." Accessed November 28, 2006. http://www.ncca.gov.ph/about_cultarts/. Informative short survey of key artists, genres, movements, etc., in twentieth century.

Hilario, Ronald. "Roots of Diversity in Philippine Contemporary Art." Accessed November 28, 2006. http://www.asianartnow.com/p_rh_main.html.

Historical Sites in Sri Lanka. Accessed December 19, 2006. http://www.galenfrysinger.com/polonnaruwa.htm. Excellent photographs of historical site at Polonnaruwa, Sri Lanka.

Indian Art World, Kolkata, India. Accessed November 24, 2006. http://indianartworld.com. A gallery that features the work of nearly fifty contemporary artists from the state of Bengal.

Information on Sri Lanka. Accessed December 19, 2006. http://www.infolanka.com/photo/vol12. Text and pictures of sculpture and architecture at various historical sites in Sri Lanka.

MacArthur Foundation. Accessed November 28, 2006. http://www.macfound.org. Listed among the 2006 MacArthur Fellows is information on Pakistani artist Shahzia Sikander.

Museum Nasional Indonesia, Jakarta. Accessed December 20, 2006. http://www.museumnasional.org/.

National College of Arts, Lahore, Pakistan. Accessed November 24, 2006. http://www.nca.edu.pk.

National Museum of Philippines, Manila. Accessed December 20, 2006. http://members.tripod.com/philmeseum/natartist.htm. Features works by the national artists displayed at the Philippine national museum in Manila, including Vicente Manansala, Ricarte Puruganan, Vistoria Edades, Simon Flores y dela Rosa, Cesar Legaspi, Jose Joya, Guillermo Tolentino, Fabian dela Rosa, Hernando R. Ocampo, Napoleon V. Abueva, Felix Resurrection Hidalgo, and Carlos V. Francisco.

National University of Singapore and Singapore Art Museum. Accessed November 24, 2006. http://www.scholars.nus.edu.sg/post/singapore4/arts/paintingov.html. This Website is developed jointly by the National University of Singapore and the Singapore Art Museum, and provides a very good overview of recent artists, works, and genres.

Palette Art Gallery, New Delhi, India. Accessed November 25, 2006. http://www.paletteartgallery.com. Features the works of more than 100 contemporary Indian artists in various media.

The Salmons Organization. Accessed December 19, 2006. http://www.thesalmons.org/lynn. Descriptions and photographs of the Ayutthaya and Sukhothai sites in Thailand. This Website also includes the UNESCO World Heritage List and provides links to material on all World Heritage sites in South and Southeast Asia.

Singapore Art Museum. Accessed January 8, 2007. http://www.nhb.gov.sg/SAM. This museum contains the world's largest collection of twentieth-century Southeast Asian art.

Thai Heritage Page. http://www.cs.ait.ac.th/ (accessed December 19, 2006). Includes text and pictures from Ayutthaya, Thailand.

Thavibu Gallery. Accessed November 24, 2006. http://www.thavibu.com. An excellent overview of contemporary artists, works, and trends in Burma, Thailand, and Vietnam, with features on many individual artists and the electronic text of articles from various sources.

Twenty-third Bienal Internacional, Sao Paolo, Brazil. Accessed December 20, 2006. http://www1.uol.com.br/bienal/23bienal/universa/iuashd.htm. Features the contemporary Indonesian artist Heri Dono.

University of Leiden, The Netherlands. Accessed December 19, 2006. http://www.leidenuniv.nl/pun/ubhtm/mjk/angkorwa.htm. Notes and pictures on the Angkor Wat temple complex in Cambodia.

Valentine Willie Fine Art Gallery, Malaysia. Accessed November 28, 2006. http://www.vwfa.net. Excellent showcase for works by dozens of contemporary Malaysian and Southeast Asian artists.

NOTES

East Asia and Oceania

1. Munroe, 1994 (in Resource Guide), 154.
2. Ibid., 151–152.
3. Ibid., 342.
4. Hoffman, 1997 (in Resource Guide), 44–49.

DANCE

EAST ASIA AND OCEANIA

VALERIE H. BARSKE

In the context of East Asia and Oceania, the category of dance encompasses a wide variety of movement forms. Dance traditions and acts of dancing remain intricately connected to religious practices, social structures, and cultural values. Individual dances may not be easily separated from other popular performance genres, including theater, drama, ritual, festival, music, and sport. For example, dance forms in East Asia include Korean farmers' dances with *kut* [shamanist ritual] elements, Chinese dance-dramas with various combinations of song, dance, spoken word, and acrobatics, and Japanese *matsuri* [festivals], which use dances to celebrate local *kami* [gods]. Similarly, movement forms designated as dances in Oceania include nightlong *sing-sing* rituals in Papua New Guinea, which blur the lines between performers and spectators, Micronesian dance mimes indexing sacred animals, and Maori *haka waiata* [action-songs or dance-chants].

As with other movement systems, dances intersect with complicated historical and cultural developments throughout East Asia and Oceania. From the end of the nineteenth century, dancing may be linked to specific dynamics of modernity in the region. With the spread of mass media culture, many established dance forms and court performance styles were popularized among various classes of people. New dances were often displayed and disseminated in public spaces, such as marketplaces and other sites of commerce. At the same time, dancing intertwined with modern struggles for power, including imperial expansion, national identity formation, and modernization as Westernization. Christian missionaries in the Pacific Islands banned certain indigenous dances as acts of sinfulness and sexual lasciviousness. Local dancers were forced to discover ways of altering "sexualized" movement elements and incorporating Christian hymns into their performance repertoires. The construction of a Japanese imperial nation and regional empire also involved strategies that targeted dancing as a vehicle of colonization and assimilation. Colonizing policies destroyed the position of *odori bugyō* [dance officials] in the Ryukyu Kingdom, prohibited Ainu dance rituals in Ezo (Hokkaido), enforced the study of Japanese *buyō* [traditional dance] in Taiwan, and forbade the practice of Yi court dances in Korea.

DANCE

During the 1920s, the concept of a modern, Westernized body, along with the flow of Western movement systems into East Asia, became filtered through the lens of Japan. Although Russian dancers were performing ballet and modern dances in China and Korea, performers in Japan have been credited with spreading the practice of Western dances in the region. For example, the introduction of modern dance to Korea has been attributed to Ishii Baku and his performance in Seoul in 1926. Trained in ballet and various dance genres, Ishii later founded a dance institute in Tokyo where future East Asian stars, including Choi Seung-hee of Korea and Li Ts'ai-e of Taiwan, studied ballet, eurhythmics, Japanese creative dance, and *neuer Tanz* [new dance]. Ishii's students worked to reinvent dances as expressions of Japanese national identity, but also to modernize Korean traditional dances and to create a genre of oriental dances as ethnic dance of East and Southeast Asia.

Following World War II, liberation, development, and nationalist movements revived many ethnic dance practices and folk-dances as hallmarks of cultural and political identities. As early as 1950 local schools in Papua New Guinea began hosting annual performances of dances from different provinces to foster a greater sense of group identity. In Taiwan the Kuomintang government initiated the "*Minzu Wudao* [national/ethnic dance] Propagation Movement" in 1952 to mobilize people against communism in mainland China. Beginning in the 1960s, revivals of festivals and religious ceremonies allowed Pacific Islanders to reclaim local practices, reaffirm group affiliations, and, in some cases, to endorse ethnic tourist ventures. The Aotearoa Traditional Maori Performing Arts Festival, started in 1972, became a national competition to support, develop, and protect Maori performance forms, including dancing.[1] Similarly, the Cape York Aboriginal Dance Festival, sponsored by the Queensland State Government in 1983, functioned as a dance competition to celebrate identities of aboriginal communities produced by Australian state development programs.[2] Many of these dance events continue to the present, offering opportunities for redefining communal identities through performance and providing venues for marketing local ethnobusinesses.

In addition to folk-dances and ethnic dance festivals, new forms of ballet and modern dance flourished in the postwar era. The Australian Ballet Company was founded in 1952, followed by the formation of the Royal New Zealand Ballet Company in 1953. Based on themes from Beijing Opera and incorporating Chinese percussive instruments, *The Treasured Lotus Lantern*, choreographed in 1957, became the first Chinese ballet.[3] Despite official attempts to discourage ballet as a performance form, the first Chinese ballet choreographed in Taiwan, entitled *The Grace of Love*, premiered in 1970. Contemporaneously, avant-garde *butō* dances and elaborate performance events proliferated in Japan. In 1968 Hijikata Tatsumi performed a dance-theater spectacle entitled *Hijikata and the Japanese: The Rebellion of the Body*, in which he challenged postwar concepts of gender, sexuality, religion, and Americanization.

During the 1980s world music and transnational dance trends, including hip-hop, breakdancing, swing, and jazz, became popular dance forms within East Asia and Pacific Oceania. By 1983 breakdancing and "bopping" (body popping) crews, such as Kinetic Energy and Juice Groove Breakers, were established in New Zealand. Maori producers created a chart-topping hit and a video with Maori bopping dancers in 1984.[4] New school-era Japanese hip-hop dance popularity expanded to television shows, including *Dance Kōshien* in 1989, a national street-dance competition of high school students. Beginning in 1998 the Japanese arcade game *Dance, Dance, Dance Revolution*, in which players perform movements on a flashing dance floor, became a huge sensation across Asia and the United States. Moving into the 2000s in China, street-dance groups have been producing a Beijing variant on hip-hop dancing, which combines *shaolin kungfu* elements with breakdance steps.

Although contemporary movement forms in the region may originate in Shanghai dance halls, rave parties in Hong Kong, and the club scene in Sydney, most recently dance crazes also spread via the World Wide Web. Streamlined audio/video clips and MP3 music files online allow performers in East Asia and Pacific Oceania to share new styles with global audiences and vice versa. For example, the popularity of Shanghai hip-hop music and dances spread when enthusiasts started downloading demos from groups such as Hi-Bomb. Blogs and chat rooms on the Internet provide a space for local groups to advertise performance events and for enthusiasts to discuss their favorite dance moves. Additionally, organizations promoting dance, such as the Ministry of Culture and Tourism in Korea and the National Library of Australia, publish dance-related Webpages or maintain full website on dance themes. In general, the Internet offers dance organizations and individual performers a chance to promote their work and expand the scope of dancing as a popular medium of expression both within the region and beyond.

CHINA

With at least fifty-six recognized ethnic groups, dances and dance traditions in China include a great variety of genres and styles. Although difficult to summarize, the dances may be organized into basic categories. For example, the category of *minjian wudao* represents folk-dances of ethnic Han Chinese, including dragon dances and liondances. *Gudian wudao* or classical dance refers mostly to Chinese court dances. In addition, performances by groups such as Miao, Tibetans, and Mongolians are often categorized as ethnic minority dances or *shaoshu minzu wudao*. During the late Qing period (1644–1911) popular dancing included various forms of folk-dances, performances of regional and ethnic groups, and several styles of dance-dramas staged by traveling theater troupes. Although formal performances were often commissioned by wealthy families and members of the Qing imperial court to celebrate events such as Empress Dowager Cixi's fiftieth birthday (1884), dances were also well integrated into the daily lives of peasants and common people.[5] Through dancing, people celebrated harvest rituals, prayed for good health and fortune, and commemorated rites of sacrifice to their ancestors. In addition, theater troupes, comprised mostly of male members, performed dance-dramas in permanent theaters, but also at teahouses, temple fairs, guild halls, or in the middle of marketplaces. These dance-drama styles included *kunqu*, a Southern movement system and musical genre originally created in the Kunshan area. Kunqu "emphasized the synthesis and synchronization of song and dance movements" and featured the "water-sleeve" action-sign, a popular component of drama techniques and dance vocabularies of the time.[6]

As mainland China struggled with the defeat of the Sino-Japanese War (1884–95), Taiwan became a colony of imperial Japan. During the Japanese occupation of Taiwan (1895–1945), dance education was implemented in elementary and intermediary schools. In order to modernize and assimilate the Taiwanese people, Japanese "educational dance" consisted of daily exercise sessions called *lazio taiso* or *rajio taisō* [radio calisthenics], creative dances accompanied by Western music, and courses on *nihon buyō* [Japanese dance].[7] The term "*wuyong*," which came to signify dance as an art form in Taiwan, also derived from the Japanese word and concept of buyō. Through the experiences of this complicated historical moment, Taiwanese dancers developed their skills as performers of ballet and modern dance. Particularly toward the end of the Japanese occupation, modern dance, as opposed to many art forms that were largely dominated by men, became a field in which women excelled in Taiwan and abroad.

Beginning in the 1920s and extending through the postwar era, the Chinese Communist Party (CCP) employed theater forms along with dances in their political rhetoric and cultural

DANCE

THE PEONY PAVILION

The popularity of *kunqu* has been on a decline because of the incompatibility of modern fast pace and the slow and elaborate movements of this dance-drama genre. In an effort to revitalize, modernize, and globalize *kunqu*, in 2000 New York's Lincoln Center for Performance showcased *The Peony Pavilion*, the most famous *kunqu* play. With multiple acts, *The Peony Pavilion* was performed only in short 2- or -3-hour segments, even during its heyday in China. However, Lincoln Center was audacious enough to stage the entire play—for a total of 19 hours! Directed by the Chinese-American artist Chen Shi-zheng, the production added numerous acrobatic and comical elements to the dance while preserving the original theatrical tension and the play's famous celebration of the power of love. Although the production received mixed reviews, it was an effective attempt to draw attention to China's national treasure in traditional dance theater.

policies. For instance, the communists appropriated northern *yangge* song-dances, originally performed during rice-planting seasons, to celebrate the village life of farmers. When the CCP assumed power in 1949, dancers performed yangge to announce the communists' victory in major Chinese cities.[8] Similarly, nationalists in Taiwan promoted the *minzu wudao* [national/ethnic dance] program, which promoted specific dances and other art forms in order to "extol national culture."[9] As political tensions increased in mainland China and Taiwan, dancing continued to serve as a site for moral and ideological battles of the time. Some dance forms, including the newly developed *wuju* dance-drama style, were banned during the Cultural Revolution (1966–76) and not revived until the late 1970s. Other forms were heralded for their political relevance and expression of proper political themes through cultural performance. For example, Chairman Mao Zedong celebrated two "revolutionary" ballets in 1964, *The Red Detachment of Women* and *The White-Haired Girl*. Both ballets combined classical ballet techniques with Beijing Opera themes and performance elements, but, more important, they focused on the theme of women and revolution.

In contemporary post-Socialist China, dancing continues to expand in popularity and to encompass a number of movement styles. At wedding receptions, both in China and in some Chinese diasporic communities abroad, liondances are often performed to bring good luck to the couple. Modern dance companies, such as the City Contemporary Dance Company (CCDC) of Hong Kong, sponsors dance development programs to "reflect on the multifaceted contemporary culture in China." CCDC also seeks to "facilitate exchanges between dance talents in China and Hong Kong, and with overseas artists" and "to bring the dance development in China to international attention."[10] On the Chinese island of Hainan, folk villages feature local Li ethnic dances such as the bamboo-beating dance to foster tourist ventures in the area.[11] By 1998 over 1,000 social dance halls in Shanghai had become popular sites for working-class entertainment.[12] As disc jockeys spin a mix of jitterbug tunes and modern Chinese songs, dance floors transform into sites for romantic interludes and sexually charged interactions. In general, the dance scene in China seems to support an ever growing leisure industry and remains a powerful medium for political and cultural commentaries.

JAPAN

Similar to dancing in China and other parts of East Asia, dance traditions in Japan interconnect with drama, festivals, and rituals. The theater genres of *kabuki* and *nō* may be categorized as *buyō-geki* dance-dramas, in which main characters perform dances to mark events in the storyline. The category of *nihon buyō* [Japanese dance] initially referred to *kabuki* dances transformed into individual pieces for separate stage performances. Folk-dances, such as *obon odori*, derive from popular religious ceremonies and *matsuri* festivals, in which people dance to celebrate local *kami* [gods]. During the Meiji period (1868–1912) female dancers and actresses returned to the stage after previously being banned from performing. Newly choreographed pieces featuring women became popular in professional theaters, but also in urban venues associated with geisha performances in the pleasure quarters of Tokyo and Kyoto. For example, a group of young female entertainers debuted in 1872 in a new spring dance program, *Miyako Odori*, in Kyoto's Gion district.[13]

At the same time that Japanese assimilation policies targeted dancing in Okinawa, Taiwan, and Korea, dancers in Japan struggled to define a new Japanese dance style. Through a movement called *shin buyō* [new dance], artists such as the famous playwright and dramatist Tsubouchi Shōyō sought to modernize traditional Japanese dance forms. Although Tsubouchi's experiments with new dance were not successful, the new dance movement continued by branching into various directions. Diverging from Tsubouchi's ideas, Ishii Baku combined modern Western dance elements from Isadora Duncan, Mary Wigman, and Emile-Jacques Dalcroze to produce his own version of modern dances. His school, the "Ishii Baku School of Dance and Physical Education," helped train famous modern dancers from Japan, Korea, and Taiwan. In addition to Ishii, a female dancer and choreographer known as Fujikage Shizuki (originally Fujima Shizue) became associated with the innovation of creative Japanese dances. Fujikage founded her own dance school in 1931, which trained several generations of female *buyō* dancers.

Following the Japanese defeat in World War II, artists in many fields, including literature and the performing arts, grappled with how to articulate experiences of intense loss and death. The Japanese avant-garde theater and *ankoku butō* [dance of darkness] movement began in this context. In the midst of the protests against the U.S.-Japan Security Treaty in the late 1950s, Hijikata Tatsumi performed *Kinjiki* [Forbidden Colors] (1959). Along with Hijikata, *butō* performers such as Ono Kazuo portrayed grotesque physical bodies to invert accepted notions of beauty as a means of political criticism and cultural production. At the same time, performers in Okinawa and mainland Japan sought to revive traditional Okinawan dances in order to redefine local identities. Immediately after the U.S. occupation ended and Okinawa reverted to Japanese sovereignty in 1972, Kodama Kiyoko presented a new dance-drama on the theme of 1,300 years of Okinawan history. The contrasting dance styles of artists such as Hijikata and Kodama highlight the complex struggles of redefining social values in postwar Japan.

In the 1980s popular dance trends included a "retro" movement, which revived 1950s American rock-and-roll, swing, and hop dances. This dance trend was extended to include a group of all-male "rock-a-billies" who began performing on weekends in public spaces in Tokyo. Still to this day, the group breaks out their leather outfits, Elvis-style hairdos, and rocker boots to perform free-style rock moves in Tokyo's Yoyogi Park. Overlapping with the retro rock phase, hip-hop and house music hit the dance scene in Japan. Modeled after American groups such as the Rock Steady Crew, Japanese hip-hop crews developed in places such as Fukuoka, Osaka, and Tokyo. In addition to the introduction of *Dance Koshien*, the national street-dance competition, another television show featured club dancers with a line dance resembling Soul Train and instructions on how to perform the latest dance steps.[14]

Beginning in the 1990s, in contrast with images of Japan as an ethnically homogenous country, dances of ethnic minorities also began to receive public attention. In 1997 the

Japanese government passed the Ainu Cultural Promotion Law to protect cultural practices of the Ainu population in Hokkaido. To promote transmission and preservation of Ainu rituals, the Japanese government provides funding for the performances of dance rituals such as *iyomante* [sending back the spirit of bears], *iwakte* [sending back the spirit of objects], and *shinnurappa* [ancestors' ceremony].[15] Additionally, during the Kyushu-Okinawa G8 Summit in 2000, Okinawan dances were highlighted as a means of marketing Okinawa to tourists in mainland Japan and around the globe. As world leaders, including former President Bill Clinton, entered the reception dinner at Shuri Castle, they were greeted by Okinawan dancers clad in traditional *bingata* court costumes. This official use of dance as cultural diplomacy contrasted with the actions of citizen groups in Okinawa who employ local dances in their political activism against the U.S. military bases.

Most recently dance crazes in Japan include reggae music and dance fests, university dance and sport events, and swing dances sponsored by the Tokyo Swing Dance Society. Also the Contemporary Dance Association of Japan represents 2,300 registered dance performance groups who present ballets, modern dances, and contemporary pieces across the country.[16] Plus an organization called Dance and Media in Japan is working on a collaboration between contemporary dance, theater, and media art forms entitled *Re-Mediation*. This program sponsors workshops and various performance events to generate networks of communication between different media and to "bring forth arts for the next generation."[17] Through the present, dancing in Japan continues to intersect with other forms of popular culture in the search for new media of expression.

KOREA

In Korea, dance traditions may be organized in three main categories: *kungjung muyong* [court dance], *minsok muyong* [folk-dance], and *cheui muyong* [religious or ritual dance]. Court dances are further distinguished between movement styles from China versus court practices from Korea. As performed today, the Chinese-derived court dances echo the water-sleeves movement, which is popular in Chinese dance forms and theater styles. Ritual dances include Confucian line dances performed at ancestor shrines, Buddhist dances performed by monks, and shamanistic ceremonies such as *kut*. Added to these traditional genres are Korean *shinmuyong* [new dances] and *ch'angjak muyong* [creative dances], plus Western modern dances and ballet.[18] Toward the end of the nineteenth century, even before Korea was officially colonized in 1910, classical dances and music of the Yi court were discouraged under Japanese political pressure. After 1910, colonial policies forbade the practice of traditional art forms, including dances, which were viewed as supporting Korean identity. Korean *kisaeng* [female entertainment dancers], analogous to Japanese geisha, were also forbidden to perform in public, although their dances continued at private parties.

Similar to its trajectory in Taiwan, modern dance in Korea developed from the colonial relationship with imperial Japan. After Ishii Baku's performance in 1926 in Seoul, the Korean dancer Choi Seung-hee returned with him to Japan and became one of his leading students of "new dance." Ishii's notions of *shin buyō* helped shape the concept of *shinmuyong* [new dance] in Korea more generally and specifically in the works of Choi. Many of Choi's dances were short solo performances, emphasizing the individualistic and expressive spirit of modern dance. She also created new Korean dances based on themes from traditional harvest songs, sword dances, and monks' dances. Choi proved a great success with Japanese audiences and even starred in a movie based on her life entitled *Hanto no Maihimei* [The Dancing Princess of the Peninsula] (1935).[19] Eventually Choi defected to North Korea, where she established a dance school until she was purged by the Communist Party sometime in the 1960s.

After World War II, the Chosun Dance Education Institute was founded in 1946 in order to develop dance education in Korea. But with the Korean War (1950–53), many of these early postwar dance developments ended abruptly. The Korean dance scene began to regain some momentum in 1959 with the creation of the Korean Dance Society. Unfortunately, the military coup d'état of 1961 in South Korea once again disrupted dance practices and the availability of public dance performances. Shortly after the coup, however, the National Theatre founded the National Dance Company in 1962, and Ewha Women's University established an official dance department in 1963. Beginning in the 1960s and expanding into the 1970s, Korean dances were also appropriated to support nationalist movements and articulations of national identity in both North and South Korea. For instance, the North Korean government provided funds to promote the *Chamo* [Alphabet] System of Dance Notation as the most comprehensive means for transcribing "traditional" Korean dances. In South Korea, mask dances were celebrated as symbolic expressions of "the people." The South Korean government established the Korean Culture and Arts Foundation in 1974, which provided financial support for the revival and perpetuation of dance traditions. Local farmers' *nongak* dances were also employed by student movements and political campaigns in the construction of a Korean ethnic national identity based on traditional cultural practices.

Since the 1970s dance performances, university dance departments, dance-related publications, and other dance activities have experienced a veritable boom in Korea. In 1979 the Korean Dance Festival (now the Seoul International Dance Festival) offered an opportunity for budding choreographers and dance companies to create new works for a national dance competition. According to statistics published by the Korean Culture and Arts Foundation in 1995, dance performances increased from 355 in 1989 to 778 in 1994, with nearly half of the total number of dance events held in Seoul.[20] In addition to Korean traditional dances, new Korean dances, ballets, and modern dances, avant-garde movement systems, including Japanese *butō* and the choreography of Meredith Monk, also became integrated into the works of Korean dancers such as Hong Sin-cha. One of Hong's more recent productions, *Labyrinth: In the Moon-Night* (2002), premiered in New York at the Asia Society and Museum. In this production, Hong employed Korean musical instruments, including a *kayageum* [twelve-string zither] and focused on the theme of "phases of the moon." Regarding this piece, Hong explains that, although she is an "avant-garde modern dancer" and her movements may not be considered traditional, still "the mood is very much Korean."[21] In some ways, dance forms in contemporary Korea continue to explore this very complex theme, the theme of how to express a sense of Korea and to redefine images of "Koreanness" through performance.

AUSTRALIA

In present-day Australia, popular dance styles often reflect the multicultural context of the country. People enjoy professional ballets, Irish folk dancing, lantern festivals for the Chinese New Year, Aboriginal performances, dances of the Torres Strait Islanders, plus contemporary choreographies that combine aspects of all of these styles. However, the current situation developed from a complex historical and cultural background. With the founding of the Commonwealth of Australia in 1901, artists, writers, and performers grappled with the question of how to represent Australian national identity. This discussion of identity was mediated by the race politics of the time and the promotion of policies such as the Immigration Restriction Act, which refused non-European immigrants. As a result, early twentieth-century white middle-class dance styles consisted mostly of movement forms from England, Ireland, and North America, to the general exclusion of indigenous dances and Asian influences. In 1929 the First Australian Ballet Company was established in Sydney by Louise Lightfoot and Mischa Burlakov.[22] However, in the 1920s and 1930s political representations of aboriginal cultures through indigenous performance also began appearing in Australian cities.[23] Eventually, indigenous music and dancing, formerly performed only in rural or outback areas, became staged in concert halls and other urban venues.

By the 1960s independent performance organizations and government agencies supported presentations of indigenous music and dancing. For example, in 1963 the Australian Elizabethan Theatre Trust and the Welfare Branch of the Northern Territory collaborated to promote an aboriginal concert, featuring songs, dancing, fire-making rituals, and reenactments of legends. Unfortunately, without the creative input of Aboriginal performers, these programs dismissed the specific cultural contexts and dance traditions of individual pieces. In general, the dancers seemed placed on display as embodiments of the "noble savage" and the exotic "other."[24] However, in the 1970s, Aboriginal artists gained greater access to portrayals of indigenous dances through the establishment of organizations such as the Aboriginal Islander Dance Theatre (AIDT). Founded in 1976, AIDT constituted an ongoing performance group with a repertoire based on traditional and contemporary dance and emphasized the goal of "promoting the modern Aboriginal/Islander identity."[25] Eventually AIDT developed into a performance school called the National Aboriginal and Islander Skills Development Association (NAISDA) College. In 1989 AIDT members created the Bangarra Dance Theatre and produced dances such as *Ochres* (1995), a piece described as developing a truly "Australian language of dance" by combining "indigenous traditions and international contemporary dance styles."[26] Bangarra performances continue to be popular with audiences and to win critical acclaim.

Reflecting late capitalist trends across the globe, dancing in Australia has also become a central component of ethnic tourism and the tourist industry more generally. For instance, the Tjapukai Aboriginal Cultural Park, created in 1996, features a dance theater as a main facet of portraying the Djabugay rain forest culture. The park is situated on land north of Cairns owned by the Tjapukai people and is one of the largest private employers of Aboriginal Australians. Dance performances at the Tjapukai Park include a night show where guests participate in an interactive recreation of a *corroboree* ritual and the ceremonial making of a fire. According to the official website, the park contributes to reconciliation efforts within Australia and represents an "incredible success story" for indigenous business, "the flagship for marketing Australian indigenous culture internationally."[27] Despite its economic successes, the park also has contributed to various problems for the Djabugay people, including the struggle of how, by whom, and for what purposes sacred dance rituals should be used to represent indigenous cultures.[28]

In addition to the increasing popularity of indigenous dance forms, dancing in Australia also has received international press and recognition through the release of films such as *Strictly Ballroom* (1992) and *Tap Dogs* (1996). These films depict a rather humorous side of the world of dance in Australia. Another key component in the promotion of all dance genres in Australia has been the development of a Website entitled *Australia Dancing*. The National Library of Australia designed this Website as a central location for dance information and research materials, past and present. Initially funded by the Australia Dance Council,

Australia Dancing features digitized pictures, original manuscripts, film clips, and so on, all easily accessible through online directories and search engines. The site also provides links to current dance industry information across the country. Through programs such as *Australia Dancing*, people may tap into the vitality and innovativeness of dance forms as they continue to expand throughout Australia.

NEW ZEALAND

Popular dances and dance traditions in New Zealand include settler folk-dances from England and Ireland, classical ballets, modern choreographed stage performances, but also numerous movement styles based on the cultural practices of the indigenous Aotearoa Maori. *Aotearoa* is the Maori word for the geographic area of present-day New Zealand, meaning "the land of the long white cloud." Although each Maori tribe presents a different performance repertoire, Maori dances are often categorized under the term *haka* [dance] or *haka waiata* [action-songs]. When European settlers arrived in the 1800s, Maori were performing various versions of *haka* as central to religious ceremonies and social rituals. In 1840 a group of Maori chiefs signed the Treaty of Waitangi with Lieutenant-Governor William Hobson, which established New Zealand as a British settler colony. With the increased popularity of European sports, especially rugby, Maori athletes began performing *haka* dances prior to rugby matches. Borrowing elements from *peruperu* war-dance *haka* and *Ka Mate* free-form *haka*, the players dance to announce their readiness for battle and to challenge the opposing team. When the New Zealand Native Team toured Britain in 1888, the players performed the first overseas prematch *haka*. During a subsequent sports tour in 1905, the New Zealand rugby team began to be called the "All Blacks," and, from this time on, the All Blacks have become famous for their powerful *haka* performances.[29]

In addition to rugby matches, popular entertainment during the 1920s and 1930s in cities such as Auckland and Wellington focused mainly on light operas, music in concert halls, and other European stage performances. Musical groups also performed in outdoor venues, especially to accompany Sunday promenades of the white upper and middle classes. Later, in the 1950s, people danced to big-band sounds in dance halls and cafés. Passenger boats carrying assisted immigrants traveling to New Zealand also featured social dances and talent competitions as part of on-ship recreation.[30] Around the same time, the Royal Ballet Company was founded in 1953 by Poul Gnatt, a Danish ballet principal dancer. When the company first started touring the country, the performers set up and took down the stage settings and relied on the hospitality of local community members for places to stay.[31]

Beginning in the 1970s the New Zealand government established festivals and dance events, such as the Aotearoa Traditional Maori Performing Arts Festival (ATMPAF), recently renamed the Te Matatini National Festival. Started in 1972, this national dance contest is staged in a different community every two years and features competitions in six dance categories, one of which is *haka*. Organized by a national committee and serving as the culmination of local dance contests, the Te Matatini in 2005 featured four days of incredible dance events, with over 1,200 performers and 35,000 attendees.[32] Contemporary Maori dance troupes, such as the Te Waka Huia, continue to compete in Te Matatini, placing overall second in the 2005 festival.[33] Groups such as Te Waka Huia and other competition finalists also officially represent New Zealand abroad at events such as the 1994 Commonwealth Games in Canada.

Through the present, dancing in New Zealand continues to increase in popularity, both domestically and internationally. Agencies, such as the National Arts, Education, and Service Agency for Dance in New Zealand or DANZ, support professional and recreational dances and dance education across the country. According to information reported by New Zealand's official statistics agency, an estimated 432,000 people, or roughly 16 percent of the population 15 years of age or over, attended Maori *haka* performances in 2005.[34] Along with live performances, Maori dances received widespread attention through the release of the popular film, *The Whale Rider* (2002). Featuring a young female Maori actress as the main character, the movie tells a touching story about the struggles of preserving cultural practices in the context of contemporary pressures. This film was followed by several media pieces that addressed Maori dancing, including a special on Pacific Islanders' dancing entitled *Dances of Life* (2005), which recently aired on PBS. In addition to traditional movement forms, Maori pop artists and dancers have gained attention for their contributions to hip-hop and other contemporary dance styles. Dalvanius Prime, a Maori producer and composer, released the song *Poi E* in 1984, which topped the charts for 4 weeks. The vocals are sung in Maori language, and the video features a Maori named Joe Moana performing "bopping" (body popping) dance moves. In 2001 the Aotearea Hip-Hop Summit was held in Auckland in 2001.[35] As events such as this summit and the ongoing Te Matatini Festival suggest, a great variety of New Zealand dance forms continue to develop and to branch into new directions across the country and abroad.

SOUTH AND SOUTHEAST ASIA

BETH OSNES AND VINAY DHARWADKER

Like music, dance in South and Southeast Asia is popular in many forms, contemporary and classical, indigenous and folk. The popularity of dance forms in these regions should be appraised in two ways: forms or styles that are widely practiced because large numbers of people have the skills necessary to do so and forms or styles that are widely appreciated by audiences who watch and listen to performers in these arts but do not themselves practice them in public spaces. Most contemporary dance forms and many indigenous and folk forms in various parts of Asia invite active participation, so large numbers of people not only watch performances in these forms, but also take part in them: the experiences and pleasures of dancing are qualitatively different from those of watching others dance, and many more individuals can dance in certain forms than can sing well or play musical instruments with sufficient skill. In contrast, all of the classical dance forms and some of the indigenous and folk forms of Asia require a great deal of training, discipline, and practice:

they can be performed only by dancers who have been educated in these arts, and the average person can experience them only as a member of an audience.

CONTEMPORARY DANCE

Contemporary dance as practiced in the West and internationally is popular in many South and Southeast Asian cities, which have their own local networks of dance clubs and discotheques, as well as underground establishments catering to specific clienteles. The popularity of contemporary dancing—which is often viewed as essentially foreign or imported even though it has been a part of Asian cultures for several decades if not longer—is related to social, economic, technological, and cultural factors. The spread of American and European rock and pop music across Asia since the 1960s through the music industry as well as through the broadcast media (radio and television) is closely connected to the interest in contemporary dance and to the establishment of discotheques and dance clubs in cities from New Delhi and Kolkata (Calcutta) to Manila and Singapore. The popularity of Hollywood films and Indian films, especially Bollywood's song-and-dance extravaganzas, has directly contributed not only to the popularity of various types of dance music, but also to that of particular styles of contemporary dance. The dissemination of audio cassette, video, and compact disc technologies over the past four decades—in which Asian markets have been extensively integrated into the international media industries from the start—has been vital to the popularization of contemporary dance in these regions. Key factors have included the rise of the music video industry (to which, in Asia, India contributed as much as the Americas) in the 1980s and the rapid, parallel growth of video and disc rental markets (which, in the 1980s and 1990s, flourished on the piracy of copyrighted material) in most parts of South and Southeast Asia.

Most important, however, the popularity of contemporary dance in many Asian cultures has been the result of several local or regional political and cultural factors. First, since decolonization in the 1940s, countries such as India, Thailand (the exception to colonization), the Philippines, Malaysia, Indonesia, and Singapore have witnessed the rise of a fairly extensive, modern, often Westernized middle class of urban professionals, people who are linguistically and culturally hybrid in a number of ways. Given the gradual internationalization of postcolonial economies in the 1970s and 1980s and their more rapid expansion under globalization and liberalization since about 1990, this middle class has had both the purchasing power and the leisure to pursue its eclectic cultural interests. Growing up in a technologically connected world, the second and third generations of this class have been avid fans, especially as teenagers and young adults, of contemporary music, dance, film, radio, television, as well as literature and print media, from around the globe.

Second, even in countries such as Pakistan, Bangladesh, Myanmar, Cambodia, the Philippines, and Indonesia—where dictatorships, totalitarian regimes, or fundamentalist religious groups have persecuted "dangerous" artists or tried to control arts, forms, and technologies of Western origin—contemporary international music and dance have persisted in underground networks. Since the 1950s and 1960s, Muslim Sharia law in Pakistan, Bangladesh, Malaysia, and Indonesia, for example, has repeatedly frowned on film, television, and video and disc media, as well as on musical and dance performances in contemporary forms in the public domain. Despite national controversies, legal prohibitions, police intimidation, government prosecution, and even public violence in many places—from Peshawar, Mumbai, and Dhaka to Rangoon, Kuala Lumpur, Jakarta, Phnom Phen, and Manila—alternative venues for contemporary music and dance have found ways to survive.

Dance

Third, the rise in domestic and international tourism across South and Southeast Asia since the 1960s, especially the dramatic escalation of tourist traffic since the early 1990s, has popularized contemporary international music and dance, both live and in the media, on a massive scale. Cities with Muslim majority populations, such as Lahore (Pakistan), Dhaka (Bangladesh), and Jakarta (Indonesia), as well as popular international tourist destinations, such as Kathmandu (Nepal), Mumbai and Goa (India), and Colombo (Sri Lanka), together with Bangkok and various resort towns and islands in Thailand and the city-state of Singapore, all have numerous bars, dance clubs, restaurants, and party places that cater primarily to international travelers but are also accessible to middle- and upper-class local residents. Around 2004, the metropolitan region of Mumbai (Bombay), for instance, was estimated to have about 2,000 establishments with public dancing, including dancing by professionals. The city of Bangalore (the emergent hub of the worldwide information technology industry, in southern India) has numerous dance clubs, music bars, and even establishments for rave parties for a transient and resident international workforce of several million people. Dance clubs in Kathmandu, Mumbai, Goa, Koh Samui (Thailand), and Bali (Indonesia) have been legendary party places for celebrities, international tourists, and wealthy local residents for about two decades now.

Dancers at Asian venues practice all forms of internationally popular contemporary dance, from retro styles of disco to the latest trends in American hip-hop. One important trend involves dance styles of Asian origin, the most widespread in the past 15 years being disco *Bhangra*, which involves continuous, vigorous, and simultaneous leg, arm, and shoulder movements and evolved out of the traditional north Indian folk-dance form. Disco *Bhangra* emerged as a musical and dance genre in London in the early 1990s, an innovation of the second generation of the Punjabi Sikh immigrant community in England (for whose ancestors *Bhangra* was the traditional folk-dance in the rural Punjab region of India and Pakistan). The most popular dance music for this form is that of Daler Mehndi, a folk singer from Punjab, India, and Apache Indian, an immigrant fusion musician based in London, both of whom have been international stars since the mid-1990s. As of 2006, the music and dance of disco *Bhangra* continue to be wildly popular in clubs as far apart as Bali and the islands of the Caribbean.

Another notable trend has been the emergence of Asian clubs that feature professional exotic dancers, with high-profile individual performers from abroad (e.g., from Iran, Eastern Europe, or Russia), as well as ensembles with elaborate dance routines backed up by multimedia, technologically advanced visual pyrotechnics. Such exotic dance items, which often feature erotic dancing by female as well as male performers, attract large crowds, justify substantial admission fees, set the mood for the evening, and invite audience participation.

A broader and longer trend across South Asia and parts of Southeast Asia (such as Indonesia) has been music and dance modeled on sequences in current Bollywood films, particularly from Hindi cinema. Most hit movies produced by the Mumbai film industry highlight major film stars in individual and ensemble dances performed to original songs that also, independently, become hits in India's internationally influential music industry; since the mid-1990s, many Hindi films have also explicitly incorporated item numbers, dances featuring international dance stars included in the story and the cast solely for the purpose of enhancing the movie's chances of box office success at home and abroad. Among recent Hindi megahits, *Hum Aapke Hain Koun?* (1994) featured dance numbers by Salman Khan, Madhuri Dixit, Mohnish Bahl, and others; *Dilwale Dulhaniya Le Jayenge* (1995), the longest running Hindi movie of all time, included popular dance sequences (some based on Indian folk forms) by Shahrukh Khan, Kajol, and others; *Dil to Pagal Hai* (1997) owed much of its popularity to the extraordinary dancing of Madhuri Dixit and Karisma Kapoor, as well as Shahrukh Khan; *Monsoon Wedding* (2001) highlighted festive north Indian and Punjabi popular folk music and ensemble dancing; and *Dil Chahata Hai* (2001) showcased remarkable fusion music, together with dances in a variety of forms and styles by Aamir Khan, Saif Ali Khan, Akshaye Khanna, Priety Zinta, Sonali Kulkarni, and others.

INDIGENOUS CLASSICAL FORMS

As in literature, theater, music, painting, and sculpture, the long cultural history of South and Southeast Asia has left the modern nations of these regions a rich legacy of classical dance. All classical dance forms require their practitioners to undergo arduous physical training and discipline over long periods, as well as rigorous education in the theory and aesthetics of performance. They also require apprenticeship under a legitimate master, formal initiation into training as well as performance, and continuous practice in the form throughout a career. Moreover, the classical dances of Asia involve training in makeup and costume, in stage preparation and (religious) performance rituals, and in live performance with musicians and, often, a small but complex orchestra. Each classical dance form comes with its particular style of music, and a trained dancer has to be completely at home in that style in order to perform the dance successfully.

These historical forms can be broadly divided into two categories: dances that are performed primarily by a solo artist (or by an ensemble troupe), with live or recorded vocal and instrumental accompaniment, and dance-dramas that usually involve an ensemble cast of dancers, singers, and musicians who enact a story on stage, sometimes with a narrator and often in a specific ritual or festive context.

Until the twentieth century, the classical dance forms of South and Southeast Asia flourished mainly under the patronage of royal courts or temples. In the past 100 years or so, most of these dance forms have entered the secular public sphere, with their practice supported by national ministries of culture, arts agencies, private foundations and associations, educational and research institutions, and private schools. Especially in the postcolonial period, classical dances have come to attract large local, national, and international audiences, both domestically and abroad, and are among the most visible objects of cultural pride in their home nations.

India

Several classical dance styles are popular in India today. The best-known dance form of north India (now also shared to some extent with Pakistan and Bangladesh) is *Kathak*, a centuries-long fusion of Hindu and Muslim dance conventions. *Kathak* is usually performed by a single artist, female or male, dancing to music provided by a vocalist, accompanied by a small orchestra (*tabla* for percussion, Indian harmonium or *sarangi*—a bowed lute—for melody, and *tanpura*—a plucked four-stringed instrument—for drone). The dancer wears anklet bells, and much of the focus of the performance is on the intricate footwork and the mathematical precision of the dance's complex percussive and physical rhythms. The footwork is coupled with slower arm movements and stylized hand and facial gestures. Since about the seventeenth century, *Kathak* has primarily represented the aesthetic play of love and erotic desire: in a Hindu context, it often uses lyrics in the Hindi language about the sacred love of Lord Krishna and his consort Radha, whereas in a Muslim context, it often uses lyrics in the Urdu language in the *thumri* and *ghazal* poetic-musical forms, all of which are set to Hindustani *ragas* in a classical or semiclassical style. Among the most famous exponents of *Kathak* in the later twentieth century were the male dancers Birju Maharaj and

> ## DANCE FESTIVALS IN INDIA, 1
>
> India showcases its rich and varied national heritage of dance, music, and related arts in a series of annual festivals held in different parts of the country. Each of these festivals lasts for several days or longer, involves recitals or performances by dozens or even hundreds of individual artists, and attracts domestic as well as international audiences of thousands (sometimes tens of thousands) of people.
>
> **Konark Music and Dance Festival.** This festival is held for several days, some time between December and February, at the marvelous Sun Temple on Chandrabhaga Beach, Konark, Orissa state. Built in black granite and known as the Black Pagoda, this temple is now a World Heritage site. The festival celebrates classical music and dance, including *Odissi*, *Bharata natyam*, *Manipuri*, and *Kathak*, as well as folk-dance forms such as *Chhau* (a narrative masked dance from Bihar state).
>
> **Modhera Dance Festival.** This three-day classical dance festival is held in January at the magnificent Sun Temple at Modhera (about 60 miles from Ahmedabad, Gujarat state). It features major dancers, in forms such as *Bharata natyam* and *Odissi*, in an outdoor historical setting.
>
> **The Taj Mahotsav.** This festival is held in Agra, near the Taj Mahal, for about 10 days in late February. It especially promotes many folk traditions of dance, music, and arts and crafts, as well as classical dance. It includes exhibitions of major north Indian handicrafts (marble inlay, wood carving, carpets, metal work, embroidery, etc.), plus a festival of north Indian cuisines.
>
> **Elephanta Music and Dance Festival.** This festival is held in February on the Elephanta Islands, six miles from Mumbai Harbour, Maharashtra state, on the Arabian Sea. The Islands are famous for their unique cave temples and sculptures (sixth century). In addition to classical music and dance, this festival features local fishermen's folk-dances, as well as local ethnic cuisines.
>
> **Khajuraho Dance Festival.** This week-long festival is held in February to March. It features *Kathak*, *Odissi*, and *Bharata natyam* dances and *Manipuri*, *Kuchipudi*, and *Kathakali* dance-dramas. It is located at the Khajuraho temple complex (eleventh century) in Madhya Pradesh state. Performances are given outdoors against the backdrop of the magnificent Chitragupta and Vishvanatha temples.

Gopi Krishan and the female dancer Sitara Devi. Among the actresses whose portrayals of historical and fictional *Kathak* dancers in Hindi films helped popularize this form immensely were Madhubala in *Mughal-e-Azam* (1960), Waheeda Rehman in *Guide* (1965), Meena Kumari in *Pakeezah* (1971), and Rekha in *Umrao Jaan* (1981).

A second important classical form, *Odissi*, comes from the state of Orissa, on India's eastern seacoast. Originally associated with young female dancers in Hindu temples, this form uses strong rhythms, beats, and pauses, during the last of which the dancer strikes sculpturesque poses, many of which are represented in the friezes and statues at the great Sun Temple at Konarak and at other notable temples in Bhubaneshwar and Puri in Orissa. Although *Odissi* strongly resembles the *Bharata natyam* style, in some ways it is the purest of the classical schools since it preserves the largest number of dance units described in Bharata's *Natyashastra*, the canonical Sanskrit treatise on drama, dance, music, and performance (second century CE). Two of the greatest modern *Odissi* dancers were Indrani Rehman and Sanjukta Panigrahi, who popularized this form in India as well as abroad in the 1960s and 1970s.

DANCE

In southern India, the most renowned classical dance form is *Bharata natyam*. Long associated with dancing girls in Hindu temples in what is now the state of Tamil Nadu (as well as in some parts of the states of Karnataka and Andhra Pradesh), this form emphasizes virtuoso footwork, total body movement, and expressive hand gestures and facial expressions. Accompanied by a classical Carnatic vocalist (who also plays a pair of small cymbals) and a percussionist (who plays the *mridangam*, a double-conical side drum), the female dancer usually performs a composition of about two hours, with a prologue invoking the gods and major portions devoted to dance phrases that mimic musical phrases, the evocative gestural interpretation of the emotions expressed verbally in a lyric and ecstatic, fast-paced expositions of pure dance. Among the most celebrated *Bharata natyam* dancers of the past 50 years are Rukmini Devi, Yamini Krishnamurthi, and Swapnasundari. The Hindi film actresses Vyjayantimala, Hema Malini, and Meenakshi Sheshadri were trained in this form and popularized it in their appearances on the silver screen.

Historically, India's Hindu culture and its canons, beliefs, and arts have strongly influenced the societies of Southeast Asia, from Myanmar, Thailand, and Cambodia, to Malaysia and Indonesia. One of the most important influences among them has been classical Indian dance. Many of the techniques and stylistic or aesthetic elements shared by *Bharata natyam* and *Odissi*, for example, also appear in Cambodian, Thai, Malaysian, and Javanese and Balinese classical dance forms, where they blend into new cultural contexts but nevertheless remain instantly recognizable.

Indonesia

Highly refined dance forms are abundant on the islands of Java and Bali in Indonesia. The Javanese dance form that most beautifully typifies the aesthetics of this island's culture is the *Bedoyo*, a court dance that commemorates the ritual marriage of the sultan's ancestor to the deity known as the Queen of the Southern Sea. Legend has it that, in the seventeenth century, a Muslim ruler of the state of Mataram ritually married this sea queen and she taught him this dance after the wedding, which symbolically links royal power to a divine source. The dance involves nine performers, who wear identical costumes and have indistinguishable faces so that they represent nine different aspects of one individual, theme, or idea.

The *Bedoyo* form emphasizes energetic and stylized walking during the performance, with arched insteps and toes curled upward. The dancers move slowly in highly controlled unison, personifying the qualities of balance and equilibrium; their legs are bent slightly at the knees, which are turned outward, revealing the enduring influence of classical Indian dance techniques. The costumes used in this form are very elaborate; it takes several hours for a dancer to dress for a performance. Each dancer wears a tightly fitted velvet bodice with a golden belt around the waist, a sarong, and a golden headpiece. In a courtly setting, the dance takes place in a pavilion built specially on the palace grounds for such performances, with a royal *gamelan* orchestra providing the accompaniment. The Javanese *Bedoyo* was performed to great critical acclaim at the Festival of Indonesia in Los Angeles in 1990 and at the 1990 Los Angeles Dance Festival.

A performance form that is exclusively Balinese and expresses the distinctive beliefs of this island's culture with great artistic exuberance is the *Barong*. This trance-dance enacts the struggle between good and evil, and it is performed ritually whenever evil seems to be outweighing good in a specific place. Good is represented on stage by a lion figure called *Barong* (most likely introduced from China at an early historical stage), and the dance uses multiple performers, one of whom manipulates the giant carved head with fierce eyes and pointed fangs, while the rest manipulate the long body that follows behind. The opposite is represented by a queen of evil spirits name Rangda, who is portrayed by a masked actor endowed with long, sagging breasts and long, sharp fingernails and whose movements are jerky and frighteningly erratic. Each performance starts with scenes, in dance and dialogue, from one of the ancient Indian epics, the *Ramayana* or the *Mahabharata*. At one point in the narrative, the male characters associated with the good lion figure try to kill Rangda, but her evil powers force them to turn their drawn weapons on their own bare chests: under her magic spell, the men wrestle their own daggers until a Brahmin priest appears and sprinkles holy water over them and they return to their normal state. Neither good nor evil is considered victorious in this battle; rather, a necessary balance between these two forces is restored in the world at the end.

CLASSICAL DANCE-DRAMA

India

The *Manipuri* dance style, which is recognized as one of the four main forms of Indian classical dance (along with *Kathak* and *Bharata natyam*, described previously, and *Kathakali*, discussed later) belongs to the state of Manipur in the easternmost part of the subcontinent. Manipuri female dancers wear stiff, cylindrical skirts, painted headpieces, and veils and highlight their femininity with undulating movements, slow rhythms, and elaborate hand gestures, whereas its male drummers emphasize their masculinity with frenzied beats and dancing. This form became popular with urban audiences during the renaissance of Indian classical dance in the 1920s and 1930s, when Rabindranath Tagore (Nobel Prize for Literature, 1913) included the *Manipuri* style in the curriculum of his school at Shantiniketan. In its modern version, the *Manipuri* style is most often used to perform dance-dramas based on Hindu themes, especially stories about Lord Krishna (as a young erotic god) and Lord Rama (as the hero of the ancient epic, the *Ramayana*).

Kuchipudi, in contrast, is a seventeenth-century village form of dance-drama from the state of Andhra Pradesh in south India. A traditional performance in the Telugu language enacts the mythological story of Satyabhama, the jealous wife of Lord Krishna, the universal divine lover: it involves a large cast of dancers directed onstage by a stage manager, with all of the roles played by men, all of the dancers singing their own parts, and a skillful use of dance, word, song, music, acting, and costume to communicate the nuances of emotion and narrative. In its modern version, a *Kuchipudi* recital by a single dancer or a pair of dancers offers one or more short episodes from the traditional story as a sample of the form. The best exponents of this style in recent decades have been Swapnasundari and the superb husband-wife team of Raja and Radha Reddy.

Kathakali, a major Indian style of classical performance, is one of the great forms of dance-drama in the world because of its unique bodily movements, hand gestures, facial expressions, costumes, makeup, narratives, and overall aesthetics. It comes from seventeen century Kerala in south India and uses the Sanskrit and Malayalam languages. A *Kathakali* performance takes place in a special theater in a temple complex and has strong religious and ritual dimensions; it enacts a story or theme from the *Ramayana*, the *Mahabharata*, or another Hindu canonical text. In this highly stylized and distinctive form, men play all of the roles. For an overall generic appearance that is completely unique in world dance and theater, the dancer-actors wear large and heavy headgear that is richly molded and painted; thick makeup, long fingernails, jewelry, and rings; and billowing skirts. The principal prop is

> ## DANCE FESTIVALS IN INDIA, 2
>
> **The Chennai Dance and Music Festival.** This festival is held in Chennai, in Tamil Nadu state, from late December to mid-January. It offers about 300 concerts and performances, with some 2,000 performers. It celebrates solo and ensemble south Indian dance (e.g., *Bharata natyam, Kuchipudi*) and Carnatic music (vocal and instrumental). The festival is a continuation of the Margazhi Festival of Dance and Music launched in Chennai in 1927.
>
> **Pattadackal Dance Festival.** This festival commemorates ten major temples at Pattadackal, a capital of the first Chalukya empire (mid-sixth to mid-eighth centuries), now a World Heritage Site near Badami, Karnataka state. It is unusual for temples at a single location to be in architectural styles from both north and south India. The festival is held in January and attracts major and popular classical dancers. It includes a handicrafts festival.
>
> **Mamallapuram Dance Festival.** This festival is four weeks long, from early January to early February. It is held in an ancient port city, Mamallapuram, about 40 miles south of Chennai, in Tamil Nadu state. It is the site of famous rock sculptures and stone and cave temples of the Pallava kingdom (seventh to eighth centuries). The festival showcases performances in all classical forms of dance and dance-drama (including *Kathak* and *Kathakali*) and select folk-dances in a spectacular outdoor seaside setting.
>
> **Natyanjali Festival, Chidambaram.** This festival is held for five days in February to March (beginning on the new-moon night of the Shivaratri festival). Chidambaram, in Tamil Nadu state, is about 150 miles from Chennai and is the site of the gold-roofed Nataraja Temple (twelfth to thirteenth centuries, dedicated to Lord Shiva in his dancing form). The festival attracts musicians and dancers in all classical forms to pay tribute to the god of dance.
>
> **The Other Festival.** India's only contemporary and avant-garde arts festival, featuring innovations in dance, music, drama, and visual art, includes Indian as well as foreign artists (recently, from the United States, Canada, France, Israel, and South Africa). It is held in early December, in Chennai, in Tamil Nadu state. The festival attracts many corporate sponsors and an audience of about 4,000 viewers.

a 12 × 6-foot curtain behind the performers; the accompanying vocalists and drummers stand on one side of the stage. A performance usually lasts from dusk to dawn, with the dancer-actors developing each scene in great detail, intent on bringing out expressively every shade of meaning in the story they have chosen to narrate.

Myanmar

Because of geographical proximity, dance in Myanmar has been heavily influenced by the traditions of India, China, and Thailand, but it has nevertheless developed its own style. The dance-drama *Zat Pwe* is the last remains of Burmese court dance-drama and can be found in central and southern Myanmar. Its movements combine classical Thai and Burmese elements, together with elements of the European ballet brought by the British when they colonized Burma in the eighteenth century. Both men and women sing, dance, and perform dialogue in this form, the stories of which are based on Burmese legends and usually highlight the comedic and humorous aspects of romance rather than conflict. A show lasts about nine hours, but the high point is after midnight, when the lead actors exhibit their virtuosity with short bursts of song and vigorous dance (which last less than a minute). Other performers follow suit, eventually joined by clowns (with up to ten highly skilled dancer-actors playing the latter roles). The performers wear ballet-style slippers, leaping and turning as in standard European balletic moves. But they also incorporate the turned-out elbows, bent legs, and low-torso postures that are characteristic of most Asian dance. Moreover, the articulation of their limbs often resembles the movements of the marionettes in *Yokthe Pwe* puppet theater (see the chapter on Theater and Performance). The musical accompaniment for a *Zat Pwe* dance-drama is provided by a *Saing* orchestra, which includes drums, gongs, bells, cymbals, a reed instrument, and a xylophone.

Thailand

Highly evolved forms of dance are a prominent part of Thailand's cultural heritage. Its indigenous traditions, however, have been heavily influenced by Cambodian dance and, through it, by classical Indian dance. They also belong to a common dance culture in Southeast Asia, so that the Thai *Manora*, for example, a folk-dance-drama performed in the south of the country, is the same as the *Manora* performed in the northern parts of Malaysia (see the following section).

One of the most recognizable expressions of Thai culture is the *Lakon Nai*, an all-female classical dance-drama adapted from a fourteenth-century Cambodian court dance and strongly resembling the Cambodian form *Lakon Kbach Boran*. The *Lakon Nai* form is noted for its small, elegant steps and graceful hand gestures, similar to those in classical Indian dance. These movements occur as the dancers shift from one stylized pose to another, all synchronized in choreographed patterns. The dancers wear tall, golden, tiered headpieces and wristbands of gold; their costumes consist of sleeveless fitted dresses with sarong-type skirts, and they dance with bare feet. The stories dramatized in the *Lakon Nai* are most often taken from the *Inao*, which is the Thai word for the *Panji* tales, the most famous written versions of which were composed by King Rama II (1809–24) especially for this dance form. A *Pin Peat* musical ensemble, made up of bamboo xylophones, bronze bowls, oboes, cymbals, and drums, accompanies the performance.

An all-male dance form is the *Khon*, a masked dance-drama performed for the royal court and believed to date to the sixteenth century. It may have evolved from *Nang Yai*, a form of shadow play in which dancers hold large figures over their heads and move behind a large screen on which their shadows are cast (see the chapter on Theater and Performance). The movements in *Khon* are broad and masculine, especially in scenes involving warrior characters; the fight scenes include choreographed acrobatics that conclude in a stylized pose. Two narrators, seated at the side of the stage, provide all of the dialogue and story. The dancers originally wore heavy makeup, which later evolved into masks with golden headpieces tiered to a high point. Among contemporary innovations in the *Khon* form are the conventions that only demons and monkey characters wear masks and that women perform the female as well as the more refined male roles. The stories are drawn from the *Ramakien*, the Thai version of the Indian epic, the *Ramayana*. Though the *Khon* dance-drama form remains popular among audiences, it can only be seen now at the Thai National Theatre.

Cambodia

Dance is considered to be the mother of Cambodian culture, and its teachers say that it takes 12 years to train a classical dancer: 6 years to learn body postures, hand gestures, and movement, and another 6 years to absorb the spiritual and emotional aspects of the art. A form of exquisite refinement and beauty is the *Lakon Kbach Boran*, a classical dance-drama performed mostly by women (and related to the Thai *Lakon Nai* form described previously). Two types of dance are contrasted in the *Lakon Kbach Boran*: narrative dancing, in which performers pantomime the meaning of the song lyrics, and non-narrative dancing, which focuses on pure movement. Female dancers portray heroes, princes and princesses, and demons; male dancers play the roles of old men, clowns, and monkeys. The women display slow, controlled movement with great, restrained energy that travels through their entire bodies, out to their flexed fingers and toes, their graceful composure contrasting sharply with the rowdy pranks of the male clowns. Although the form comes with an elaborate vocabulary of expressive hand gestures, it is the totality of movement and posture, music and costume, and song and language that conveys the meaning of a particular dance performance. The costumes include a snug silk bodice with a pleated skirt, headgear adorned with flowers, and elaborate jewelry at the neck and wrist. In recent times, the Thai influence has been visible in the tiered headpiece and the shoulder epaulettes. The *Ramayana*, *Panji* tales, and other such sources furnish stories for the *Lakon Kbach Boran*, whereas a *Pin Peat* orchestra provides the accompanying music. The National Khmer Classical Ballet Troupe, managed by the University of Fine Arts in Phnom Penh, is the only group able to perform this dance-drama now; its style is a Thai imitation of the original Khmer form now lost to history.

Indonesia

Many Indonesian dance forms originated in Java, where they are often still performed in courtly form, and then traveled to Bali, where they have evolved a more exuberant style than the Javanese original. The Javanese *Wayang Topeng* (or Balinese *Topeng*) is a masked dance-drama based on ancient masked dances performed to honor the spirits of the dead. Developed in the fourteenth century, this form is unique because it is performed both by dancers in a courtly tradition and by villagers in a folk tradition. Three or four performers play a number of roles from the *Panji* tales or local tales of kings and warriors. They change their masks and movement styles to change characters; they generally keep their legs bent slightly, and their knees and elbows pointed outward, leaving their hands free for sweeping expressive gestures. Only the clown characters speak, wearing half-masks to leave their mouths free, while all of the other characters communicate through pantomime.

Another form shared by Java and Bali is the *Ardja*, a romantic dance-opera performed by professional troupes at temple festivals and other events. Attractive young female performers play most of the roles and enact the stories through song and dance; the narratives are Javanese love legends from the twelfth to fourteenth centuries. Performances begin around midnight and continue until nearly dawn. In a convention adapted from classical India, the refined characters speak and sing in *Kawi*, the ancient Javanese language; the clown characters then translate the words into *Bahasa* or Balinese while engaged in physical comedy and witticisms. In Bali, *Ardja* is the only dance-drama that uses a front curtain.

The Balinese *Legong* is considered the ultimate expression of delicate femininity and grace. This dance-drama draws on the stories of Lasem and Semaradhana and is traditionally performed by three girls, all under the age of 12 or so. The dancers bring the chosen story to life through movement and gesture; a narrator, usually on the side, provides the dialogue and story. The *Legong* dance style, with its low body position and bent legs, which is maintained whether the dancers are moving or stationary, has probably been influenced by classical Indian dance. The dancers' sharp, precise movements require extreme discipline; their bare feet stamp strongly for emphasis or glide smoothly across the ground in small circular patterns. Their entire bodies highlight the contrast of hard, angular movements and fluid, graceful ones, alternating between the two. A distinctive element of this form is the flexed hand, positioned at shoulder height with the elbow out, with isolated fingers quivering back and forth like the wings of a small bird. A *Legong* performance begins with pure movement, in which one performer strikes a dramatic pose and, at a cue from the accompanying *gamelan* music, bursts into a brisk and lively dance; the other two dancers then join in, and they all flutter fans and execute intricate patterns.

In the last two decades, Bali has become a major international tourist attraction and also the site of terrorist incidents, but its arts continue to thrive and evolve despite the commercialization and politics. In the 1980s many Balinese dance masters collaborated with Eugenio Barba and his International School of Theatre Anthropology, a laboratory that actively compares performance techniques from around the world. In this setting, as with other collaborations, the Balinese have proved to be solidly based in their own traditions while remaining open to new artistic inspirations.

FOLK-DANCES

India

During the past two decades, one Indian folk-dance has become famous and popular around the world. *Bhangra* originates in the Punjab region in the northern part of the subcontinent, which is now divided between Pakistan and India. It is a dance form associated primarily with rural Punjabi farmers belonging to the Sikh religion, and it comes with a distinctive form of music (group singing to a fast-paced beat on the *dholak*, a large two-faced double-conical drum played with two asymmetrical sticks). The singing and dancing are usually done by a group of Sikh men, dressed in *kurtas* (loose north Indian shirts) and brightly-colored *tehbands* (ankle-length wraps fastened at the waist, often made of fabric with large check patterns), but women may join in from the audience as the performance heats up. Ensemble dancing is punctuated by short breakout performances by individual dancers who display their special skills and distinctive variations. The dance involves a vigorous movement of the entire body, usually emphasizing a continual pumping of the shoulders, the coordinated bending and unbending of arms and legs while in motion, hand gestures, twisting of the torso, and rapid footwork. Acrobatics include somersaults, leaps, dancing while crouching, hopping and shuffling on one leg, and other such feats of balance and endurance. Traditionally, the *Bhangra* is a festive harvest dance and a community dance performed in villages to celebrate folk-festivals, weddings, and other such occasions. Most of its songs are about love and desire, a woman's beauty, and the beauty of youth and passion; many of them are frankly erotic songs of invitation and seduction.

Since a significant portion of the Punjabi Sikh community has migrated out of India for economic and cultural reasons in recent decades, *Bhangra* music and dancing have spread with it to Europe and North America as well as other parts of the world. In the 1990s, *Bhangra* became popular among immigrant Sikh youth, especially in London's dance-clubs, and disco *Bhangra* music by Indian singers such as Daler Mehndi, as well as second-generation immigrant fusion artists such as Apache Indian, became globally available under Indian as well as Western music labels. In the present decade, disco *Bhangra* music and dance remain extremely popular from London to Jamaica, Bombay to Bali. *Bhangra* clubs are now widespread on American college campuses, and annual Bhangra competitions across the United States attract thousands of amateur dancers.

Because of its size, diversity, and long history, India has an immense variety of folk-dances. Among the nationally and internationally known forms are the following: *Chhau*, a narrative masked dance from Bihar state (with a variation without masks from Orissa state); *Garba*, a women's religious dance from Gujarat state, dedicated to Amba Mata (a benign form of Shakti, the Mother Goddess, or Parvati, the consort of Lord Shiva, known as Durga or Kali in her terrifying aspect); *Dindi* from Maharashtra state and *Dandiya Ras* from Gujarat state, in both of which male and female dancers whirl in circular formations, rhythmically striking pairs of short sticks held in their hands; and *Ghoomar*, a spirited and festive women's dance from Rajasthan state. Other folk forms practiced widely in specific social groups include *Karakam* from Tamil Nadu state and *Therayattam* from Kerala state, both ritual propitiations; *Kolyacha*, a fisherfolk's dance for men and women from the Konkan coastal region in Maharashtra state; and *Lambadi*, a women's dance (with men singing and drumming) from the Lambadi gypsy community of Andhra Pradesh state. Folk-dances that are associated with particular aboriginal, tribal, or minority ethnic groups in India include the yak dance, influenced by Tibetan dance, performed in Ladakh and in the Himalayan foothills near Assam state; bird and animal dances performed by the Juang tribe in Orissa state; the bison-horn dance, performed by men and women in the Muria tribe of Madhya Pradesh state; and various tribal dances performed by the Bhils, Gonds, Mundas, Santals, Nagas, and other peoples on the subcontinent. Each of these dances and forms is distinctive and is accompanied by its own form of music; many of them are performed in large groups, sometimes including up to 100 or more dancers; and some of them require complex bodily rhythms, difficult footwork, acrobatics, and great strength and agility.

Myanmar

Before Buddhism arrived in Myanmar, the Burmese people worshiped spirits known as *nat*s; remnants of this spirit worship are still evident in the country, from the shrines found in trees along roads to dance forms dedicated to them. *Nat Pwe* is a ritual spirit-medium dance, in which a female dancer assumes the role of a *Natkadaw*, a *nat* wife; during the performance, the spirit is believed to enter the performer's body and give her the vision to see the future. This form is very popular with local Burmese audiences for its predictions; they are usually more interested in hearing about the future than in appreciating the dance itself. Because of the spiritual nature of this dance, it is not performed for tourists.

Cambodia

One Cambodian folk-dance performed in the Siem Reap and Battambang region of the country is the *Trott*, or stag dance, which serves both a ritual and an entertainment function. Dancers impersonate deer and hunters and go from house to house seeking donations for ridding the area of drought and bringing good fortune in the coming year. The deer is conceived of as the golden deer in the *Ramayana*, which lures Rama and Lakshmana away from Sita. A second folk-form, still performed by the Royal Cambodian Ballet, is the coconut dance, a symbolic courtship performed by young male and female dancers who hold half of a desiccated coconut shell in each hand. In a series of quick turns and choreographed reaches, they hit each other's shells rhythmically in order to accent the rhythm of the music; the form is energetic, light hearted, and flirtatious. Another courtship dance includes the use of woven fishing baskets, which are most often set along the side of a river to catch fish but used here to fish for love among young male and female dancers. This folk-dance elaborates on the movements and gestures that are characteristic of the activity of fishing with these baskets and integrates them with the feigned flirtations, rejections, and seductions of love.

Vietnam

Dance in Vietnam combines indigenous elements with Chinese and Buddhist influences. The most indigenous in origin are folk-dances such as *Mua Chay Cay*, the dance of the plow. This form is popular in northern Vietnam and uses and develops the actions and gestures involved in the act of plowing. In Buddhist temples, mediums perform spirit-dances of folk origin in which they express ecstatically whatever spirit or god possesses them. The *Mau Phu Thuy* is a sorcerer's dance, which uses incense sticks, a small bell, or a small drum to keep away a disease or an evil spirit. The *Mua Luc Cung*, the dance of six offerings, is another form of folk origin, which is performed in the Buddhist temples by girls who are about 12 years old and who make ritual offerings of incense, flowers, candles, tea, fruit, and rice cakes.

Malaysia

The Malaysian *Manora*, a folk-dance-drama indistinguishable from the Thai form of the same name, dramatizes the *Jataka* stories, which narrate the previous births of Gautama Buddha. Performed in northern Malaysia with immigrant Thai dancers, it uses a southern Thai dialect and enacts the story of the princess of a mythical race of bird people, Manora, who is captured and falls in love with the prince of the land. While her beloved is away at war, she is sentenced to burn by those who fear her magical powers; she escapes death by ascending again to heaven, where her prince eventually finds her (at the highest point of the Himalayas). Traditional performances of the *Manora* last three days and nights: by day, a medium establishes contact with spirits on behalf of the person sponsoring the performance; by night, a number of dancers and a few clown characters dramatize episodes from the story. The male characters sometimes wear masks; the dancers' elaborate costumes include chest plates adorned with beads; and the princess's bird character wears wings.

Indonesia

The *Ludruk Bendang* is a Javanese traditional folk-dance of invulnerability, a demonstration of physical strength and magical powers. The dance is extremely rigorous, and male performers play all of the roles; the dance enacts the entire human life cycle and is followed by a ritual of offerings. The *Baris*, or war dance, of Java is also a completely masculine folk-form, performed at ritual feasts in villages. In this case, middle-aged men dance with long spears in a double line, making frightening noises and striking heroic poses; the music grows in intensity until extreme passion takes over their facial expressions and tension takes over their bodies; the dance concludes when one character symbolically slays another in a long, stylized battle. A *Baris* dancer should be able to squat low, with his body completely straight and his knees turned out; he wears tight pants with a short coat, layered scarves on his chest, and a white cloth headdress, with a high triangle in the back and fresh flowers along the front. A traditional Balinese *gamelan* orchestra accompanies the performance.

Some of the dance forms of Bali are relatively recent creations. One example is the male solo dance *Kebyar*, which was developed around the 1950s by a young man known as Mario, who had talent enough to combine the robust masculinity of the *Baris* war dance with the grace and refinement of the *Legong*, a feminine dance-drama (described previously). The *Kebyar* emphasizes the facial expressions and arm movements of the performer in a squatting *Baris* position; the goal is to respond in dance to a variety of musical moods and to interpret them visually.

Another folk-form, created in the 1930s, is the monkey dance or *Ketjak*, which is performed in several villages on the island. A group of 100 to 200 men sit tightly in a series of concentric circles, swaying back and forth in unison and rapidly chanting in varying rhythms the sounds made by a monkey. Drawn from traditional trance-dances, this monkey chorus is coordinated with vocal cues by one or more leaders. In the hypnotic mood induced by the chanting, a few young girls enter the clearing at the center of the circles and enact scenes from the *Ramayana* in pantomime and dance. In slow, controlled movement, they dance around the only light source, a many-branched candelabra, placed at the center. Often a masked dancer portraying Hanuman, the great monkey warrior of the Indian epic, also pounces into action. The men in the monkey chorus are bare chested but costumed in black-and-white checkered sarongs and a red sash around the waist. The girls are dressed in traditional Balinese dance costumes: golden headpieces adorned with flowers, sarongs, tight bodices made of long strips of golden cloth wrapped tightly around the torso, and ornamental golden wings at the elbows and wrists.

South and Southeast Asia offer an immense variety of indigenous dance forms, from supremely crafted and aesthetic classical dances for solo performers and ensembles, to extended dance-dramas based on epics and legends that require great training and discipline, to folk-dances of remarkable spiritual power, imagination, and originality.

RESOURCE GUIDE

PRINT SOURCES

East Asia and Oceania

Averbuch, Irit. *The Gods Come Dancing: A Study of the Japanese Ritual Dance of Yamabushi Kagura.* Vol. 79, *Cornell East Asia Series.* Ithaca, NY: East Asia Program, Cornell University, 1995.

Bowers, Faubion. *Theatre in the East. A Survey of Asian Dance and Drama.* New York: Thomas Nelson & Sons, 1956.

Brandon, James R., ed. *The Cambridge Guide to Asian Theatre.* Cambridge: Cambridge University Press, 1993.

Corona, Vicki. *China Folk Dance: Introductory Steps, Swirls & Choreography Suggestions for the Famous Long Silk Dance.* North Hollywood, CA: Dance Fantasy Productions, 1989.

———. *Maori Tribe of New Zealand: Choreographies.* Vol. 2, *Dance Fantasy Instruction Manuals.* North Hollywood, CA: Dance Fantasy Productions, 1989.

Craig, Barry, Bernie Kernot, and Christopher Anderson, eds. *Art and Performance in Oceania.* Honolulu: University of Hawaii Press, 1999.

Dao, Mailan, ed. *Chinese Dance: Old Traditions, Modern Visions.* 1st edition. Beijing: China Reconstructs, 1985.

Davis, Deborah, ed. *The Consumer Revolution in Urban China.* Vol. 22, *Studies on China.* Berkeley: University of California Press, 2000.

Denton, Meg Abbie, ed. *Dance in Australia: Influences and Presents [I.E. Present] Trends.* Netherlands: Harwood Academic Publishers, 2001.

DANCE

Dils, Ann, and Ann Cooper Albright, eds. *Moving History / Dancing Cultures. A Dance History Reader.* Middletown, CT: Wesleyan University Press, 2001.

Freund, Philip. *Oriental Theatre: Drama, Opera, Dance and Puppetry in the Far East, Stage by Stage, Variation.* London & Chester Springs: Peter Owen, 2005.

Goodman, David G. *The Return of the Gods: Japanese Drama and Culture in the 1960s.* Photo-reprint edition. Vol. 116, *Cornell East Asia Series.* Ithaca, NY: East Asia Program, Cornell University, 2003.

Gunji, Masakatsu. *Buyo. The Classical Dance.* Translated by Don Kenny. New York and Tokyo: Walker/Weatherwill, 1970.

Hoff, Frank. *Song, Dance, Storytelling: Aspects of the Performing Arts in Japan.* Vol. 15, *Cornell University East Asia Papers.* Ithaca, NY: China-Japan Program, Cornell University, 1978.

Jones, Mary. *The History of Sacred and Biblically-Inspired Dance in Australia.* Revised edition. Milsons Point, N.S.W.: Christian Dance Fellowship of Australia, 1981.

Klein, Susan Blakeley. *Ankoku Buto: The Premodern and Postmodern Influences on the Dance of Utter Darkness.* Vol. 49, *Cornell East Asia Series.* Ithaca, NY: East Asia Program, Cornell University, 1988.

Lawrence, Helen Reeves, ed. *Traditionalism and Modernity in the Music and Dance of Oceania: Essays in Honour of Barbara B. Smith.* Vol. 52, *Oceania Monograph.* Sydney: University of Sydney, 2001.

Luckman, Susan Heather. "Party People: Mapping Contemporary Dance Music Cultures in Australia." PhD dissertation, University of Queensland, 2002.

McLean, Mervyn. *Weavers of Song: Polynesian Music and Dance.* Honolulu: University of Hawaii Press, 1999.

Moore, Malcolm. *Dance Dialogue: A Strategy for the Development of Dance in Western Australia.* Perth: Department for the Arts, Government of Western Australia, 1989.

Pask, Edward H. *Enter the Colonies Dancing: A History of Dance in Australia 1835-1940.* Melbourne and New York: Oxford University Press, 1979.

Sanders, Dawn. *Dance New Zealand.* Auckland: Heinemann Reed, 1989.

Scott-Maxwell, Aline, and John Whiteoak. *Currency Companion to Music and Dance in Australia.* Sydney: Currency House, 2003.

The Korean National Commission for UNESCO, ed. *Korean Dance, Theater and Cinema.* Arch Cape, Oregon: Pace International Research, 1983.

Thomas, Allan. *New Song and Dance from the Central Pacific: Creating and Performing the Fatele of Tokelau in the Islands and in New Zealand.* Vol. 9, *Dance & Music Series.* Stuyvesant, NY: Pendragon Press, 1996.

Thrasher, Alan R. *La-Li-Luo Dance-Songs of the Chuxiong Yi, Yunnan Province, China.* Danbury, CT: World Music Press, 1990.

van Zile, Judy. *Perspectives on Korean Dance.* Middletown, CT: Wesleyan University Press, 2001.

Zi, Huayun, Sun Jingchen, and Luo Xiongyan. *Chinese Dance.* Translated by Jinhui Li, Jun Liu and Qizhi Zhang. Vol. 4, *Chinese Culture and Art Series.* Beijing: Culture and Art Pub. House, 1999.

South and Southeast Asia

Bandem, I Made. "Notes on the Development of the Arja Dance Drama." *Indonesia Circle* 3 (March 1983): 28–32.

Bowers, Faubion. *Dance in India.* New York: Columbia University Press, 1953.

Coomaraswamy, A. K. *The Dance of Shiva: Fourteen Indian Essays.* Rev. ed. New York: Noonday Press, 1962.

Covarrubias, Miguel. *Bali.* New York: Oxford Unversity Press, 1972.

Dhani Nivat, Prince. *The Khon.* Bangkok: Sivaporn, 1962.

Gere, David. *Looking Out: Perspectives on Dance and Criticism in a Multicultural World.* New York: Schirmer Books, 1995.

Jonas, Gerald. *Dancing: The Pleasure, Power, and Art of Movement.* New York: Harry N. Abrams, 1992.

Katrak, Ketu H. "'Cultural Translation' of Bharata Natyam into 'Contemporary Indian Dance': Second-Generation South Asian Americans and Cultural Politics in Diasporic Locations." *South Asian Popular Culture* 2 (October 2004): 79–102.

Massey, Reginald. *India's Dances: Their History, Technique, and Repertoire.* New Delhi: Abhinav Prakashan, 2004.

McKean, Philip. "From Purity to Pollution? The Balinese Ketjak (Monkey Dance) as Symbolic Form in Transition." Pp. 293–302 in A. L. Becker and Aram Yengoyan (eds.), *Imagination of Reality: Essays in Southeast Asian Coherence Systems,* Norwood, NJ: Ablex, 1979.
Meyer, Charles. "Cambodian Dances." *Nokor Khmer* 3 (1970): 2–27.
Sam, Sam-Aug, and Chan Moly Sam. *Khmer Folk Dance.* Newington, CT: Khmer Studies Institute, 1987.
Sariman, Chua. "Traditional Dance Drama in Thailand." Pp. 165–171 in Mohd. Taib Osman (ed.), *Traditional Drama and Music of Southeast Asia,* Kuala Lumpur: Dewan Bahasa Dan Pustaka Kementerian Pelajaran Malaysia, 1974.
Shapiro, Toni. "The Dancer in Angkor," *Asian Art and Culture* (Winter 1995): 9–23.
Singer, Noel. *Burmese Dance and Theatre.* New York: Oxford University Press, 1995.
Yousof, Ghulam-Sarwar. *The Kelantan "Mak Yong" Dance Theatre: A Study of Performance Structure.* Ann Arbor, MI: Proquest, 1976.

WEBSITES

East Asia and Oceania

Australia Dancing. National Library of Australia. March 28, 2006. http://www.australiadancing.org.
The Big Idea: An Online Community of New Zealand's Creative Industries. April 23, 2006. http://www.thebigidea.co.nz/.
Chinese Dance. 1995. National Endowment for the Arts. March 30, 2006. http://www.worldartswest.org/plm/guide/locator/chinese.shtml.
Chinese Liondance. June 11, 2001. The Chinese Historical and Cultural Project. March 29, 2006. http://www.chcp.org.
Collection Guide to Dance. 2003. State Library of New South Wales. April 23, 2006. http://www.sl.nsw.gov.au/collguides/dance/.
Gateway to Korea: Modern History of Korean Dance. 1999. Korean Overseas Information Services. April 23, 2006. http://www.korea.net/korea/kor_loca.asp?code=H0201.
Performing Arts: Chinese Dance. 1998. ThinkQuest Oracle Education Foundation. March 28, 2006. http://library.thinkquest.org/20443/dance.html.
Performing Arts in Korea. 2000. AsiaInfo.Org. April 23, 2006. http://www.asianinfo.org/asianinfo/korea/performing_arts.htm.
What Is Cultural Heritage? 2004. Indigenous Australia: Dreaming Online, Australian Museum. March 29, 2006. http://www.dreamtime.net.au/indigenous/culture.cfm.
What Is Nihon Buyo? 2003. Nihon Buyo Foundation. April 21, 2006. http://www.nihonbuyo.or.jp/eng/index.htm.
Wonder Okinawa. 2003. Okinawa Prefectural Government. April 23, 2006. http://www.wonder-okinawa.jp/index_en.jsp.

South and Southeast Asia

WebIndia. October 23, 2006. http://webindia123.com. A reliable source with basic information on Indian classical dance forms and contemporary dancers; useful information on current dance and music festivals in India, with good links to other Websites.]

VIDEOS/FILMS

East Asia and Oceania

The Art of Chinese Dance. ChinaSprout. 2002.
Dances of Life. Pacific Islanders in Communications and International Cultural Programming & KQED Public Television. 2005. Features Pacific Islanders dancing from Oceania, New Zealand, American Samoa, Guam, New Caledonia, and Palau.

DANCE

Japanese Dance: Succession of a Kyomai Master. Perf. Inoue Yachiyo IV. Films for the Humanities and Sciences. 2000. Kyoto-style Japanese dance, Yachiyo IV training her daughter to be her successor.

The JVC Video Anthology of World Music and Dance [30 VHS Tapes]. Dir. Katsumori Ichikawa, Kunihiko Nakagawa, Yuji Ichihashi, Tomoaki Fujii. Rounder Records [distributor], 1990. Note: v. 1–2, Korea; v.3–4, China; v. 5, China/Mongolia; v. 29, Micronesia/Melanesia/Australia; v. 30, Polynesia/New Zealand.

Kazuo Ohno & A Portrait of Mr. O. Dir. Daniel Schmid, Chiaki Nagano. Perf. Kazuo Ohno, Chie Ohno. Canta Ltd. 2004. About Japanese *butō* dancer Kazuo Ohno.

Mimi: An Evening with the Aboriginal Islander Dance Theatre. Dir. Andee Reese, Margaret Anne Smith. AFI Distribution. 1988. Performances by the AIDT dance company in Australia.

Shall We Dance? Dir. Masayuki Suo. Perf. Koji Yakusyo, Tamiyo Kusakari. Altamira Pictures Inc. 1996. Romantic comedy about a Japanese salaryman taking ballroom dance lessons.

Strictly Ballroom. Dir. Baz Luhrmann. Perf. Paul Mercurio, Tara Morice. M & A Film Corporation. 1992. A comedic portrayal of the world of ballroom dance in Australia.

The Survey of Korean Music. Multicultural Media. 1996. Video series demonstrating Korean dance, vocal music, and instrumental music.

Tamasaburo Bando – Kabuki Dance Series [6 DVDs]. Perf. Tamasaburo Bando. Marty Gross Film Productions, Inc. 2003. Six separate *kabuki* dance performances.

Tap Dogs. Dir. Dein Perry, Nigel Trifft. Warner Music Australia. 1996. Performances of a powerful tap dance group from Australia.

The Whale Rider. Dir. Niki Caro. South Pacific Pictures. 2002.

South and Southeast Asia

Cambodia: The People and the Performing Arts. Dir. Beth Osnes. Video, University of Colorado Theatre Department, 2003.

RECORDINGS

East Asia and Oceania

Cossey, Jenny. *New Zealand Music for Creative Dance.* UCA Recording, 2001.
Fanshawe, David. *South Pacific Island Music.* Nonesuch, 2003, 1981.
Laade, Wolfgang. *Australia.* Lyrichord, 1989.
Thrasher, Alan R. *La-Li-Luo Dance-Songs of the Chuxiong Yi, Yunnan Province, China.* World Music Press, 1990.

EVENTS

East Asia and Oceania

GuanDong Modern Dance Festival, Cultural Department of the Guangdong Province, Shuiyinhenglu, Shaheding, Guangzhou, China 51007. http://www.gdmdc.com/e_week_01.html. Held annually in Guangzhou May 1–7.

The Laura Dance and Cultural Festival (formerly the Cape York Aboriginal Dance Festival), Queensland State Government, Australia. Held biannually in different communities in Queensland.

Obon Festival, Tokushima Awa Odori Dance. Tokushima City, City Centre, Tokushima Prefecture, Japan. Annual festival, second week in August.

Okinawa Island-Wide Eisa Festival. Okinawa City Youth Council, Koza Sports Park Stadium in Okinawa City, Okinawa Prefecture, Japan. http://www.wonder-okinawa.jp/016/eng/kyot001.html. Dance competition and festival of Okinawan eisa drum dances.

Seoul International Dance Festival (formerly Korean Dance Festival). Room #401, Baum Bldg., 208-42 Buam-dong, Jongno-gu, Seoul, 110-817 Korea. http://www.sidance.org/. CID-UNESCO-sponsored annual dance event.

Te Matatini National Festival (formerly the Aotearoa Traditional Maori Performing Arts Festival). Level 12 Petherick Tower, 38–42 Waring Taylor Street, Wellington, New Zealand. http://www.tematatini.org.nz/editable/Home/home.shtml. Biannual dance contest held the last week in February.

ORGANIZATIONS

East Asia and Oceania

Ainu Museum. 2-3-4 Wakakusa-cho, Siraoi, Hokkaido 059-0902, Japan. http://www.ainu-museum.or.jp/english/english.html. Exhibits on Ainu culture, explanations about preserving dance rituals.

The Australian Ballet. The Australian Ballet Centre, Level 5, 2 Kavanagh Street, Southbank VIC 3006, Australia. http://www.australianballet.com.au/. National performance company.

Beijing Modern Dance Company. Phone (8610) 6757-3879. Fax (8610) 6758-0922. E-mail: bmdc@sina.com. City Contemporary Dance Company, Hong Kong, G/F, 110 Shatin Pass Road, Wong Tai Sin, Kowloon, Hong Kong. http://www.ccdc.com.hk/e_index.html. Professional stage performances, dance workshops, outreach programs.

Dance and Media in Japan, Head Office in Tokyo. 3-29-7-302 Chou Nakano-ku, Tokyo, Japan 164-0011. http://www.dance-media.com/e/index_e.htm. Collaborations between contemporary dance, theater, and media art in Japan.

DANZ: Dance Aotearoa New Zealand. Wellington Arts Centre, Ground Floor, 69 Abel Smith Street, Wellington, New Zealand. http://www.danz.org.nz/index.php.

Ministry of Culture & Tourism Republic Korea. 110-703, 82-1, Sejongno, Jongno-gu, Seoul, Korea. http://www.mct.go.kr/english/index.jsp. Provides resources on Korean culture, including the performing arts.

National Aboriginal and Islander Skills Development Association (NAISDA) Inc. PO Box 15, Millers Point NSW 2000 Studios, 3 Cumberland Street, The Rocks, Australia. http://www.naisda.com.au.

Kazuo Ohno Dance Studio. 1-20-15 Kamihoshikawa, Hodogaya, Yokohama, Japan. http://www.kazuoohnodancestudio.com.

Korean Culture and Arts Foundation, Republic of Korea. 1-130 Dongsoong-Dong, Chongro-Ku, Seoul 110-766 Korea. http://www.kcaf.or.kr/ehome3/emain.htm.

Tjapukai Aboriginal Cultural Park. Kamerunga Road (PO Box 816), Smithfield, Qld, 4878, Australia. http://www.tjapukai.com.au/. Cultural tourist attraction featuring Aboriginal dances.

NOTES

East Asia and Oceania

1. David Murray, "Haka Fracas? The Dialectics of Identity in Discussions of Contemporary Maori Dance" *Australian Journal of Anthropology* 11.2 (2000): 345–357.
2. This festival is now called the Laura Aboriginal Dance and Cultural Festival (see Resource Guide). See Rosita Henry, "Dancing into Being: The Tjapukai Aboriginal Cultural Park and the Laura Dance Festival" *Australian Journal of Anthropology* 11.3 (2000): 322–332.
3. De-Hai Cheng, "The Creation and Evolvement of Chinese Ballet: Ethnic and Esthetic Concerns in Establishing a Chinese Style Ballet in Taiwan and Mainland China," PhD dissertation, New York University (2000), p. 70.
4. HipHopNZ, March 29, 2006, http://www.hiphopnz.com/.

5. James R. Brandon, ed., *The Cambridge Guide to Asian Theatre* (in Resource Guide), 33.
6. Ibid., 34.
7. Ya-Ping Chen, "Dance History and Cultural Politics: A Study of Contemporary Dance in Taiwan, 1930s-1997" (Ph.D. dissertation, New York University, 2003), 18.
8. Brandon, ed., *The Cambridge Guide to Asian Theatre*, 40.
9. Chen, "Dance History and Cultural Politics: A Study of Contemporary Dance in Taiwan, 1930s-1997," 39.
10. City Contemporary Dance Company, Hong Kong, http://www.ccdc.com.hk/e_index.html (2005 [accessed March 29, 2006]).
11. Phillip Feifan Xie, "The Bamboo-Beating Dance in Hainan, China: Authenticity and Commodification," *Journal of Sustainable Tourism* 11.1 (2003): 5–16.
12. James Farrer, "'Opening Up': Sex and the Market in Shanghai" (PhD dissertation, University of Chicago, 1998), 222–223.
13. Masakatsu Gunji, *Buyo: The Classical Dance*. Translated by Don Kenny (New York: Walker/Weatherwill, 1970), 196.
14. Kozo Okumura, "Far East Coast Is in Da House: Examination of Hip Hop Culture in Japan," (MA thesis, Michigan State University, 1998), 9.
15. Ainu Museum, http://www.ainu-museum.or.jp/english/english.html (accessed March 29, 2006).
16. Contemporary Dance Association of Japan, http://www.alpha-net.ne.jp/users2/modance/en/index.html (2002 [accessed March 28, 2006]).
17. Dance and Media Japan, http://www.dance-media.com (2005 [accessed March 29, 2006]).
18. Judy van Zile, *Perspectives on Korean Dance* (in Resource Guide), 35.
19. Sang-Cheul Choe, "Seung-hee Choi, Pioneer of Korean Modern Dance: Her Life and Art under the Japanese Occupation 1910–1945" (PhD dissertation, New York University, 1996), 137.
20. Gateway to Korea, "Modern History of Korean Dance" http://www.korea.net/korea/kor_loca.asp?code=H0203 (2006 [accessed March 29, 2006]).
21. Alexis Menten, "An Interview with Sin Cha Hong, Korean Contemporary Dancer and Choreographer," http://www.asiasource.org/arts/sinchahong.cfm (June 24, 2002 [accessed March 27, 2006]).
22. National Library of Australia, http://www.australiadancing.org/subjects/29.html (2006 [accessed March 28, 2006]).
23. Fiona Magowan, "Dancing with a Difference: Reconfiguring the Poetic Politics of Aboriginal Ritual as National Spectacle" *Australian Journal of Anthropology* 11.3 (2000):308–321.
24. Ibid.
25. National Library of Australia, http://www.australiadancing.org/apps/ad (2006 [accessed March 28, 2006]).
26. Bangarra Dance Theatre Australia Limited, http://www.bangarra.com.au (accessed March 29, 2006).
27. Tjapukai Aboriginal Cultural Park, http://www.tjapukai.com.au (2006 [accessed March 28, 2006]).
28. Henry, "Dancing into Being."
29. Paul Waite, "Haka, the Silver Fern, and Rugby," http://www.haka.co.nz/haka.php (2000 [accessed April 20]).
30. New Zealand History Online, "The Voyage Out—Assisted Immigration to New Zealand," http://www.nzhistory.net.nz/culture/longjourney-voyageout (2006 [accessed March 27, 2006]).
31. Royal New Zealand Ballet, http://www.nzballet.org.nz/ (2005[accessed March 28, 2006]).
32. Te Matatini, http://www.tematatini.org.nz/editable/Home/home.shtml (April 20, 2006).
33. Te Waka Huia, "About Te Waka Huia," http://www.maoriperformingarts.co.nz/wawcs012419/tn-about-te-waka-huia.html (2005 [accessed March 29, 2006]).
34. New Zealand Official Statistics Agency, "Maori Performing Arts-Kapa Haka," http://www.stats.govt.nz/people/default.htm (April 2005 [Cited March 29, 2006]).
35. HipHopNZ, http://www.hiphopnz.com (2006 [accessed March 29, 2006]).

FASHION AND APPEARANCE

EAST ASIA AND OCEANIA

HUI XIAO

At the current intersection of economic integration and cultural flow, fashion can be regarded as a window through which the impact of globalization on people's everyday life can be clearly seen. An examination of fashion trends and dress styles in various Asian countries will provide not only case studies of transnational clothing politics but also a challenge to the orientalist rhetoric in Western fashion theory. When people around the world talk about fashion, they most likely would refer to the latest chic trends in Western metropolises such as Paris, Milan, London, and New York. In other words, "fashion has been defined a priori as a Western phenomenon."[1] On the other hand, Asian societies are considered static, unchanging, and thus representative of the traditional and the primitive. In short, in the dominant view of Western fashion theory, it seems an oxymoron to put together the two words Asian and fashion.

The recent rise of Asia's economic power is making people rethink the supremacy of Western fashion. In this rethinking process, contemporary Asian fashion and the historical development of multiple fashion centers in Asia have caught people's attention.

In the premodern period of Asian history during the Tang Dynasty (618–907 CE), Changan (present-day Xian city in the People's Republic of China) was the economic and cultural center of Asia. Students, ambassadors and merchants from Korea, Japan, Thailand, Persia, and many other Asian and European countries came to dwell in the city, dressing in Tang-style clothes, learning about the culture and local customs, and engaging in international trade of textiles and chinaware. With a sizable foreign population, the Changan city of Tang China was considered one of the most cosmopolitan cities in the eighth-century world. Modern scholars often compare it to today's New York City or Los Angeles. Changan was not only the regional fashion capital within Asia, but it also exerted its influences on people's clothing styles outside the geographic boundary of Asia. The Silk Road connected China proper with the Middle East, which served as a significant stop on the global trade route that allowed China to export textile products, particularly silk, to satisfy the need for the high-style clothing desired by European aristocrats and upper classes. However, these fashion influences were never unidirectional. Constant contacts with the Middle East made such a great impact on Chinese costumes during the Tang dynasty that many upper-class men complained their wives were dressing too exotically and becoming foreign. During the premodern period, the interplay of fashion trends on a global level was far more frequent and effective than could have been imagined.

When it came to the early modern era, this border-crossing flow of clothing styles and fashion trends took a different turn. Although Asian styles still appeared in European and U.S. dress designs, cosmetics, advertisements, and domestic decoration, the dominant model of fashion diffusion was moving from the West to the East. In the second half of the nineteenth century and the first half of the twentieth century, Japan, after its Meiji Restoration, became Asia's most industrialized country. As a new economic and cultural center in the Asian region, Japan also became the leader in producing and disseminating a new wave of Asian fashion. At the turn of the twentieth century, Western-style dress was considered modern and thus possessed a universal appeal. Japan adapted Western fashion trends and exported its own designs to other parts of Asia through its imperialist expansion and colonialist domination of Korea, Taiwan, Manchuria, and other parts of the Pacific-Asian region.

This picture of a single dominant fashion center in Asia has more recently been redrawn through the globalization of a regional economy and popular culture. Pluralism has become the key word of the global fashion arena. Although Tokyo still retains its leading position on the Asian fashion scene, many other metropolitan cities have begun to compete successfully with it in creating chic fads and "in" clothing styles. Seoul, Hong Kong, Taiwan, Singapore, Sydney, and most recently Shanghai have all emerged as new metropolises playing significant roles in the Asian fashion world. Although this multiple-center situation is not unique with Asia, Asian fashion has started to have universal impact. Asia has become the world's largest exporter of textile and clothing products. Asian fashion designers have challenged the monopoly of long-established Euro-American fashion tycoons. They have made important contributions to the Euro-American fashion scene and have chipped away a big chunk of high-style market share with their innovative designs. The accelerating ethnic diversity of internationally recognized top-ranking fashion designers has produced an increasing hybridization of clothing politics and dress codes in terms of variables such as materials, style, theme, texture, and patterns.

Furthermore, with the introduction of mass-produced clothing, the application of new textile-weaving technologies, and the radical changes in people's lifestyles and diets, Asian fashion has started to take on a new face, even though indigenous elements still play a significant role in providing inspiration for local and global designers. Numerous fashion programs and institutions have been established in Asian countries to produce an increasing number of professional designers equipped with a comprehensive knowledge of both local traditions and global trends. As the assumed supremacy of Western fashion has declined and the impact of Asian styles on Western fashion designs has grown, an unprecedented, large-scale global interconnectedness has manifested itself through people's experiences with fashion, renovating the fabric of our daily life.

CHINA

As the world's fastest-growing economy, China has gathered great export-oriented momentum thanks to its low-cost manufactured products. In 2004 the value of the exported textile and clothing products of China reached US$80.43 billion.[2] Although China is currently the world's largest clothing supplier and second largest textile producer, only recently has it started to emerge as one of the multiple high-style fashion centers in the Asian region. Currently, China not only provides low-end textiles and clothing products for Wal-Mart and K-Mart, but also for more upscale brands such as Burberry, Giorgio Armani, Hugo Boss, Nike, and Polo. In fact, various surveys show that China is the "supplier of choice" for major retail groups and brand-name marketers.[3]

China's appearance on the global fashion stage is in keeping with dramatic changes in the Chinese people's everyday lifestyle. Currently, a large percentage of urban women residents' disposable monthly income is spent to purchase trendy dresses and skincare products. More often than not, women will spend one's month's salary on an imported Prada handbag without a thought. With access to imported popular cultural products from Europe, America, Japan, and Korea, the Chinese people's sense of fashion has been reshaped by local, regional, and global fashion flows. As for the younger generation, although in most public schools it is mandatory for children to wear school uniforms, in their after-school time, children and teenagers prefer sportswear brands such as Puma, Nike, and Adidas. Recently, Li Ning, a national brand of sportswear, has also become popular among children and young people.

Immersed in this new fashion culture, Chinese people have started to spend more and more energy and money to take care of their physical appearance: a desirable image includes a well-groomed, tidy, sleek hairstyle; a fair-complexioned face free of wrinkles; and a well-shaped, slender body. Therefore, Japanese-made brightening and anti-aging skincare products targeting Asian consumers are considered most desirable by Chinese customers in spite of the prohibitive prices. In addition, beauty salons and body-shaping clubs have become fashionable resorts for both male and female urban inhabitants. Thanks to an increasingly sedentary lifestyle and the introduction of American fast food chains such as McDonald's and KFC, obesity is quickly becoming a social issue in contemporary China. A recent study into obesity rates in China has found that approximately 137 million Chinese people are overweight, and 18 million of those are obese. The study also discovered that people in cities are much more likely to be overweight, and that women are experiencing this problem more than men.[4]

The evolution of Chinese fashion has a very close link with the historical vicissitudes that affected the nation in the past century. In addition to the international interplay in Tang dynasty (618–907 CE) clothing politics, there were two more large-scale international communications in the history of Chinese fashion. Just as progressive, reformist intellectuals began embracing and advocating modern thoughts at the turn of the twentieth century, Western-style fashion was introduced to dress up the Chinese body. Breaking away from the confinement of traditional clothes and domestic restrictions, Chinese "Modern Girls" unbound their feet, bobbed their hair, and wore Western-style clothing, such as shorts and skirts, to demonstrate their feminine attractions in the public space. In the first half of the twentieth century, Shanghai became the most modernized city in China. With a large foreign population living in various foreign power concessions, Shanghai earned cosmopolitan fame as the "Paris in the Orient." During the 1930s' jazz age, *qipao* (also known as *cheung sam*) was the uniform outfit for Shanghai women of various classes, ranging from film stars to shop employees, while Western-style suits were the modern fashion for men. Since the tight-fitting and high-slit qipao flatters a woman's body, this time-honored Shanghai fashion continues to maintain its allure. Hong Kong filmmaker Wong Kar-wai's highly acclaimed film *In the Mood for Love*, released in 2000, can be used as the best guidebook for a tour of a glamorous *qipao* exhibition. In addition to its revival in China, Hong Kong, Taiwan, and other Asian countries, even a trendy Paris fashion show catwalk or a Hollywood blockbuster hit such as *Spider-Man* can employ the long-lasting beauty of this Chinese fashion. Even today, a hand-made *qipao* by a famous fashion designer can cost thousands of dollars.

The world of Chinese fashion changed completely during the Maoist era, which normally refers to the historical period from the foundation of the People's Republic of China in 1949 to the end of the Cultural Revolution in 1976. During this span of nearly three decades, except for a brief trend of borrowing Soviet Union clothing styles in the 1950s, anything related to Western fashion was frowned upon as bourgeois and decadent. Textile and clothing products were rationed and sold at regulated prices. China was cut off completely from the Western fashion world during this period. After the death of Mao Zedong in 1976, the post-Mao era was marked by a refashioning of China. With the market economy reform and the "Opening Up to the World," initially advanced by the CCP (Chinese Communist Party) under Deng Xiaoping's leadership beginning in the late 1970s, China rejoined the world of fashion and started to play a more important role.

In keeping with the shifting political and economic climate, Chinese lifestyles have also taken a new direction. The monotonous, dull blue and grey Mao-style suits worn by Chinese, whether male or female, were replaced by multi-toned, colorful dresses reflecting the latest trends introduced from the Western fashion world. In the early 1980s, Japan, Hong Kong, and Taiwan all exerted heavy influences in reshaping the Chinese sense of fashion. A large number of films and TV dramas imported from these parts of Asia provided Chinese with vivid visual images about how urbanites living in international metropolises dressed in fashionable ways. The sewing machine became one of the necessary betrothal gifts so that women could make their own clothes in order to catch up with the latest fashion trends. For the younger population, putting on a pair of imported jeans was fashionable in a rebellious way. Later on, more influences from America, France, and Italy started to further enrich the complexity of the Chinese fashion picture in the post-Mao era. Beginning in the 1990s, Korean popular culture created a stage to promote Korean hip-hop fashion, which continues to be crazily consumed by the Chinese younger generation.

Since Chinese people have paid greater attention to how they dress and how they look, both clothing and cosmetics industries have prospered. Compared to the dwindling production of skincare products during the Maoist era, in 1986 alone, more than 250 new cosmetic products were put on the market in Beijing. At that time, Huazi, a made-in-China cosmetic product, claimed that importing foreign advanced technology, particularly Japanese equipment and facilities, had enabled it to make an annul production of 4 million bottles, which sold well all over the country.[5] Two decades later, the number of cosmetic brands on Chinese market had increased dramatically. In 2005 the sales of cosmetic products was over 68 million *yuan* (roughly US$8.5 billion), which was 18 percent above total 2004 sales. Sales of men's skincare products are particularly on the rise.[6] Choosing skincare products and color cosmetics in large shopping malls or foreign-financed chain supermarkets, such as Carrefour (France) and Wal-Mart (United States), has become a new leisure pursuit for Chinese urban residents. The high-end cosmetic market has been dominated by L'Oréal, Procter & Gamble, Avon, and Shiseido products, while the national retailers are competing hard for the lower-priced market found mainly in small towns and the vast rural regions of China.

There is a similar situation with clothing purchases. The products of internationally recognized fashion designers such as Chanel, Prada, Versace, and Christian Dior appeal to the high-end Chinese market, while lower-priced brands such as Hang Ten, Baleno, and Giordano from Hong Kong and Taiwan are popular among college students and teenagers. International fashion shows have been held regularly in big cities such as Shanghai, Guangzhou, and Beijing. Numerous fashion magazines, such as *Vogue*, *Elle*, and *Cosmopolitan*, have released Chinese versions targeting various groups of Chinese consumers. Body-shaping clubs, fitness-training centers, and beauty salons have also flooded the streets of Chinese cities. Books written by celebrities about fashion, makeup, and weight loss have sold well. Chinese designers Coco Ma, Yvonne Ding Xue Lian, Chen Yifei, and Vivienne Tam come to the world fashion stage as top-ranking designers with acute fashion sense and the necessary artistic innovations to lead a new wave of global trends.

However, with the enlarging gap between the rich and the poor, the fashion market has also been stratified according to the purchasing capacities of different groups of consumers. The urban working class, including laid-off workers and migrant workers, and the vast number of peasants living in the countryside cannot afford the luxuries of international brands. Instead, people in these groups can only access locally made, less-expensive products that sometimes turn out to be counterfeit versions of the pricy brands. More often than not, those in the working classes count on tailors or on their own skills to make new clothes rather than purchase ready-made products. Correspondingly, their demand for cosmetics is much lower than that of more upper-class urban residents. This is also the case with national minorities living in the frontier areas of China, although they have kept more of their traditional clothing styles. Although the wave of global fashion has penetrated even to the remotest frontier area, the highly stylized clothing of those minorities frequently provides creative inspirations for fashion designers in Shanghai, Hong Kong, Taiwan, Tokyo, or Paris. For example, the avant-garde painter Chen Yifei has used indigenous Chinese elements in his cutting-edge fashion design and has made successful sales in the international market. Although the global economic and cultural exchanges have affected Chinese people's everyday experiences with the fashion world, details from the daily dress of Chinese people have also influenced the latest global trends in fashion.

> ### BEAUTY-PRODUCING INDUSTRIES IN CHINA
>
> In contemporary China, people have become so fashion conscious that the entire economy is said to be based on beauty-producing industries. Popularly termed *meinu jingji* (beauty economy) or *yanqiu jingji* (eyeball economy), these beauty-related activities include beauty pageants, TV advertisements, movies featuring beautiful actresses, cosmetics, weight-loss products, and fitness programs. In 2003 Wu Wei was selected the first Miss China. The same year saw the Miss World competition hosted by a Chinese city—Sanya—for the first time. A series of international beauty pageants mushroomed in China afterward. These have all been strongly endorsed by the Chinese government because of the belief that all these pageants help showcase China's modernization and boost the host cities' economies and the nation's GDP growth.

JAPAN

In the premodern period, Japan's clothing style was influenced by Chinese fashion, particularly that of the Tang dynasty. However, it does not do justice to traditional Japanese costume to imply that Japanese clothing has no unique aesthetic characteristics of its own. The kimono, the Japanese national costume, has long captured the elegance and exquisiteness of traditional Japanese aesthetics. In contemporary Japan, although people still wear pricy kimonos on special occasions like weddings or funerals, in their daily life, Western-style clothing such as suits, blouses, shirts, and skirts are preferred. Recently, China has become the principal supplier of clothing to Japan (77 percent market share).[7] Among young people, brands such as Nike and New Balance from the United States, as well as Puma and Adidas from Europe, are extremely popular. There is no longer much lag time between what is seen in Japanese and in Euro-American fashion. As the pioneering fashion producer and disseminator in the Asian region, Japan has also played a leading role in the global fashion scene. The annual global sales value of Japan's most visible pop icon, Sanrio's cartoon cat Hello Kitty, is US$1 billion. Teenagers and young people all over the world buy Hello Kitty accessories, including gloves, hairpins, and purses. For expensive, high-style clothing, Japan's most well-known fashion designer is Issey Miyake. Other currently successful Japanese designers with international fame include Hanae Mori, Kawakubo, Takeo Kikuchi, and Yohji Yamamoto.

Even when the economy slackens, Japanese consumers still buy imported luxury goods. Compared to other Asian districts and countries, Japan has the largest market for international high-end fashion products. The amount of money spent by the Japanese on dresses and cosmetics has ranked the highest in Asia. Louis Vuitton's boutiques make more money in Japan than anywhere else in the world. In 2005 Japan's total expenditures on consumption of clothing and cosmetics were lower than in 1997 by 13.4 billion yen. Still, the 2005 expenditures reached 15,000 billion yen (roughly US$13.27 billion), which was the highest total in the past eight years. This number was still growing in 2006. Maquillage (by Shiseido) and Revue (by Kanebo) cosmetic products, including foundation, mascara, eye shadow, and lipsticks, are the most welcome among women age twenty to thirty-nine. Other popular cosmetic brands include Kose, Shu Uemura, Clinique, and Lancôme.[8]

Thanks to the traditional diet consisting mainly of rice, seafood, tofu, and miso soup, the Japanese have the longest average life expectancy in the world. Although the recent expansion of American fast food chains in Japan has caused the number of overweight or obese teenagers to rise, most Japanese adults have maintained fit bodies. Compared to about 65 percent of adults in the United States, only 24 percent of Japanese age fifteen and older are overweight.[9] On the other hand, because of the strong obsession with having an extremely slim body, Japanese youth tend to be the ones making up all kinds of unconventional weight-loss programs, including using traditional Chinese acupuncture, drinking apple vinegar, and eating preserved soybeans.

In the last century, Japanese fashion went through a long evolution. In the first half of the twentieth century, almost simultaneously with other parts of the world including China, Korea, the United States, and South Africa, the image of "Modern Girl" came into fashion. This image became a symbolically subversive figure for Japanese women. To show their strong will and determination to break away from the domestic domain and gender subservience, Japanese "Modern Girls" invented a new fashion style by tailoring the traditional kimono. They deliberately violated the kimono aesthetics of restriction and elegance by cutting off some parts of the kimono to bare their shoulders and thighs. This modern feminist practice nudged out a space in the fashion world where Japanese women could utter their own voices in how to dress their bodies.

During the period of World War II, more innovations and reforms were made in Japanese women's fashion. During the war, Japanese women were mobilized to serve the government's agenda in expanding its imperialist regime. In order to produce healthier, stronger bodies, Japanese women gradually abandoned the kimono, since that style restricted their movements, and adopted Western-style clothing. Westernization of dress allowed Japanese women to become more athletic and active in outdoor sports and public activities. This fashion trend was further enhanced after Japan was defeated in the war and occupied by the U.S. military in the 1940s and 1950s. During this occupation, studying English and wearing American-style clothes both became national trends followed by all Japanese citizens, male and female.

This obsession with U.S. and, more generally, Western culture is embedded in contemporary Japanese society. Reflected in the Japanese fashion scene, this obsession has presented itself as the trend of dying dark Asian hair blond, or the trend of worshipping a fair complexion. The 2003 film *Lost in Translation* best showcases these trends in metropolitan Tokyo. In the highly internationalized fashion world portrayed in the movie, a Caucasian man is regarded as the ideal image of modernity in Japanese commercials. However, it would be an oversimplification to conclude that Japanese fashion is merely a product of the Westernization of Japanese culture. With the increase in regional and global economic and cultural exchanges, additional shifting patterns and nuances have been added to Japanese fashion. The Japanese younger generation not only dyes their hair gold but also red, green, purple, and many other colors to show their individuality rather than merely adopting the hair colors common to Caucasians. The current fashion-savvy generation uses all the minute details of accessories (e.g., cell phone cases) to express a sense of self.

As part of the current craze for a more athletic, outdoor lifestyle, younger-generation Japanese prefer more casual wear. Youthful and informal clothes with brand names such as Lee's, Levi's, Diesel, and Calvin Klein have come to dominate popular dress. This gives a boost to the retail sales of U.S. sportswear in the Japanese market. What is more, the growing preoccupation with a youthful appearance has stimulated the sales of anti-aging cosmetic products. At the same time, the long-standing worship of a fair complexion has also been replaced by a preference for suntanned skin. This has lead to a sharp decline in the sales of traditional brightening cosmetic products in the Japanese market. As a result, manufacturers of these kinds of cosmetic products are trying to expand their market in other parts of Asia, such as in China, Hong Kong, and Taiwan. However, with the increasing inter-Asian regional economic and cultural flows, fashion does not spread in one direction any more. Instead, the Korean Wave has left its mark on the Japanese sense of fashion. As in its past history, the Japanese fashion scene continues to be filled with examples of foreign inspirations and cultural fusions.

Before concluding this discussion of Japanese fashion, another important factor worth mentioning is the existence of subversive fashion trends invented by people at the margins. Marginalized people in Japan include ethnic minorities such as Koreans, Taiwanese, and the Ainu people living on Hokkaido. They have kept their own traditions and cultures by continuing to dress in traditional styles. In terms of gender, Japanese women are the subservient group. However, they are no longer satisfied with the famous Japanese *kawai* (youthful and cute) fashion culture. Rather, women have challenged traditional gender stereotypes by either dressing themselves in an androgynous way or by frequenting "Host Bars" to consume the sexual services and commodified types of romance provided by fashionable men. These emerging trends have also exerted their influences on the fashion scenes in other Asian countries and have caused dramatic changes in how people purchase and consume clothing and cosmetics. As a result, the more diversified and politicized fashion experiences in Asia have not reinforced traditional stereotypes; rather, they have undermined the assumption of a static world in Asian fashion.

SOUTH KOREA

Little information about fashion in North Korea, or the Democratic People's Republic of Korea, is available. Somewhat like China during the Maoist era, in North Korea, anything related to fashion is regarded as capitalist. People spend most of their money on food and other daily necessities and have little left for fashion or cosmetics. Therefore, this section will focus on fashion in South Korea.

Fashion and Appearance

Ever since the 1970s, the textiles and clothing sector has played a key role in South Korea's economic development. Although it experienced a slowdown during the 1997–99 economic crisis, the sector has recovered. South Korea's fashion market is divided primarily into domestically produced inexpensive apparel lines and a high-end market dominated by foreign designer brands imported mostly from Euro-America.[10] According to the Korea International Trade Association (KITA), the imports of low-priced Chinese garments are growing steadily. As of September 2005, South Korea's total apparel market was 7.25 trillion *won* (approximately US$7.68 billion).[11] The demand for cosmetic products continues to grow. Supermarkets, discount and specialty stores, and e-shops are the most popular distribution channels. World-class cosmetic brands such as Chanel and Lancôme have opened booths in Hyundai and Lotte department stores.

With a traditional diet consisting mainly of rice, Korean-style barbecue, and *kimchi* [salted Chinese cabbage], few South Korean adults are overweight or obese: 23.4 percent and 1.7 percent in men, and 24.9 percent and 3.2 percent in women, respectively.[12] Overall, Korean people possess fit bodies thanks to their enthusiasm for and money spent on fitness training, slimming products, and plastic surgeries.

Given its long history and the national trauma of the colonized past, contemporary South Korean society has a diverse fashion landscape that tends to separate along rural-urban lines, class stratifications, and generational divisions. Having followed fashion trends disseminated from Japan and Euro-America for the past decades, South Korea has started to emerge as one of the fashion centers and is propelling the popular culture of Korean Wave to other parts of the world.

The traditional South Korean outfit is called *hanbok*. The hanbok outfit worn by women normally consists of a short top and a long skirt, while hanbok for men includes a short blouse and a pair of pants with loose-fitting legs. The 2000 Korean film *Chunhyang*, directed by Im Kwon-taek, displayed a fabulous gallery of traditional hanbok costumes. At the turn of the twentieth century, there was a movement toward modernizing traditional Korean clothes. Korean "Modern Girls" announced that hanbok was restrictive. The top was so tightly bound around the chest and the back that women could not raise their arms, and the ground-sweeping skirt was so long that women could not walk freely. These "Modern Girls" modified the hanbok style by cutting the skirt shorter, and then putting on a pair of long stockings. In this way, they could move more easily without revealing their legs. At the same time, modernized Korean public schools adopted Japanese-style school uniforms for both boys and girls, while the upper classes preferred Western-style suits and dresses. Under the Japanese colonial regime, Korean clothing underwent Japanization and Westernization of its fashion almost simultaneously.

Strong influences from Japan and Euro-America on South Korean fashion remain. The latest trends from Tokyo are still enthusiastically embraced, although often with some modifications. For example, young women's fashion in South Korea is less funky and revealing. In addition, American hip-hop fashion from the United States has also been popular among the younger generations. For the urban residents, a "brand culture" has formed. South Korean consumers are both brand savvy and price conscious. They wear luxury brands to display social position and wealth. Younger people are so obsessed with internationally recognized designer brands such as Gucci, Chanel, Louis Vuitton, Dolce & Gabbana, and Abercrombie and Fitch that they would never hesitate to spend a large percentage of their income purchasing products with these labels. In addition to boutiques and department stores, mail order and e-market are also popular venues for fashion purchase among South Korean young people. Sometimes teenagers without much money will group purchase—they pool their money to buy a single name-brand item and then take turns wearing it.

Sometimes they will put a used item on the Internet for sale, and then buy another second-hand brand-name item with the money they have gained from the electronic transaction. Mixing and matching pricy items and cheaper ones is fashionable among South Korean youth. In contrast to younger people, the "baby boom" generation, those born between 1945 and 1960, constitute a powerful consumer group for luxury brands from Europe, Japan, and the United States.

This emphasis on imported fashion among South Korean urbanites is just part of the story. South Korea has also built up its own brands for export to the other parts of the world. Andre Kim, Chunghie Lee, and Lie Sang Bong are all internationally active fashion designers. In cosmetic production, the South Korean brands IOPE, LacVert, Innis, Taepyoung-yang, Isa Knox, and Mamonde are strong competitors with Japanese products and have gained a large market share. Shinwon, a big apparel retailer, recently opened a fashion-specialty building in Seoul that houses thirty different brand-apparel stores. What has been even more significant in boosting attention for South Korean fashion both regionally and globally has been the emergence of the Korean Wave in the first year of this century. Korean Wave refers to the fast, large-scale exporting of South Korean popular cultural products, including films, soap operas, popular songs, hip-hop dances, and fashion trends, to the other parts of the world. Under the impact of this powerful Korean Wave, current fashion trends have taken the reverse direction—spreading from Seoul to Tokyo as well as to other international fashion centers.

Compared to the high-style urban fashion, rural South Korea presents a different picture. Older generations still wear hanbok, although modified to suit the needs of manual labor. On special occasions such as the Korean Lunar New Year, the Korean Mid-Autumn Festival, weddings and funerals, rural residents and many urbanites as well still wear hanbok in different styles. For holidays and weddings, people wear colorful hanbok customized for the special occasion and costing an average of US$300. For funerals, family members wear white hanbok made of hemp, while guests coming to pay condolences normally wear black suits. For social gatherings, middle-aged women often wear hanbok to appear formal, while those of the younger generations normally prefer the more revealing Western-style evening dress. Recently, there has been a revival of hanbok. Greater numbers of younger urbanites have also started to wear hanbok for formal occasions. Because of the phenomenal popularity of the TV costume drama *Dae Jang Geum*, people all over Asia have become fans of traditional Korean food and clothing. As a result of all these trends, current South Korean fashion is highly hybridized in ways similar to the mixed approach of a modern South Korean wedding ceremony, which often consists of two parts: the Western-style part and the Korean-style part.

OCEANIA (INCLUDING AUSTRALIA AND NEW ZEALAND)

Compared to China, Japan, and Korea, both Australia and New Zealand have had a shorter history. New South Wales was formed in 1788. It was not until the early twentieth century that Australia and New Zealand achieved independence from Britain. Since Australia and New Zealand are both multiracial countries of immigration, it is hard to know what would be either country's traditional costume. As a result of past colonial history and current large immigrant communities, Australia and New Zealand both have diversified fashion scenes, with a mix-and-match amalgam of Scottish, Irish, English, Spanish, U.S., Asian, and local aboriginal styles.

Enjoying a mild climate, vast territories, rich natural resources, and a sparse population, people living in Oceania enjoy a more leisurely lifestyle compared to those in many other parts of the world. People in Australia and New Zealand generally dress well. They care about the tidiness of their physical appearance. Because of the tropical climate, people often wear comfortable T-shirts and shorts. Sun-block lotion is a must-have item because of the intense sunlight and extreme heat. In the workplace, people normally wear business suits and prefer a more conservative style. Clothes in the workplace are quite formal and gender specific. Men wear suits, and women often wear skirts or dresses and high heels. Among the younger generations, American hip-hop culture has caused a stir in the latest dress code and fashion trends. More casual sportswear is popular among children and teenagers.

The slower-paced life plus the high-fat and high-calorie European-style diet have caused a higher rate of obesity among Australian people. There have been large increases in the numbers of overweight and obese people living in Australia in the past 10 years. Results of the National Heart Foundation's National Risk Factor Prevalence Study showed that in Australia, 52 percent of adult males and 36 percent of adult females were either overweight or obese at the turn of the twenty-first century.[13] In New Zealand in 2002 to 2003, one in three adults was overweight and one in five adults were obese.[14] Perhaps, because of the fact that women in Oceania are often larger than Europeans, the beauty ideal of thinness has been less powerful. Recently, larger models such as Natalie Laughlan and Emme Aronson have made headlines as a deliberate counter to the image of the Barbie Doll. Currently, people in Oceania tend to appreciate the beauty of a natural shape and fuller body.[15]

Lately, the Australian clothing industry has become comprehensive and well developed. Just as Euro-American competitors in the industry, Australian retailers also outsource their production to China, Taiwan, and Hong Kong to make use of the cheap labor in these areas. The total retail sales value for the Australian textile and fashion industry was US$15 billion toward the end of the twentieth century, including US$4.8 billion for female outer clothing and US$2.8 billion for male outer clothing. The total annual output of the textile, clothing, and footwear (TCF) industries in Australia is estimated at US$4.75 billion, and the industries employ some 87,000 people. Since the beginning of the twenty-first century, sales numbers have been on the rise. Recently, China has out-performed Southeast Asia and other producers to become Australia's largest supplier of clothing (70 percent market share). In 2004 the import value of textiles and clothing products from China reached US$2.95 billion. Following China, New Zealand, the United States, India, Korea, Pakistan, Taiwan, and Hong Kong are also main suppliers of imported Australian textile and clothing products.[16]

Although a relatively late player in the fashion world, Australia has recently presented itself as a new power among fashion metropolises. Sydney and Melbourne along the coasts have become must-visit cities for fashion enthusiasts. During the Australian Fashion Week, discussions about beauty ideals, dress codes, and fashion tips fill TV screens and the pages of newspapers, popular magazines, and journals. Australian fashion designers always blend elements taken from a diverse range of national styles with the latest European and Asian trends to achieve artistic innovations. Celebrities have helped to shape people's sense of fashion. Australian actress Nicole Kidman, Naomi Watts, and internationally recognized supermodels have become fashion icons.

New Zealand includes two major islands and a number of smaller islands. Generally speaking, people in New Zealand prefer a natural and healthy physical appearance, which is in keeping with their beautiful natural scenery. People in New Zealand have access to a wide range of fashions and styles of different price ranges. The 1993 film *The Piano* gave global audiences a taste of Maori costume. The New Zealand director Peter Jackson's extremely successful trilogy *The Lord of Rings* (2001–03) has caused another influx of Euro-American tourists coming to visit the beautiful island country. The prosperous tourist industry brings in large groups of Euro-American travelers, who carry new examples of popular Western fashion with them. Teenagers and young people in New Zealand dress in current Western fashions and are more brand conscious. They like to keep up with latest European and American fashion trends. Leisurewear, sportswear, and college brands are very popular.

In the past decade, New Zealand has widened and extended its links with the global fashion world, substantially upgrading international textile and clothing products trade ties with Australia, Europe, and China among many other countries across the world. The total sales value for clothing was US$536.5 million in 2003 with local production of US$185 million. The country's main garment suppliers include China (71.3 percent), Australia (11.0 percent), Italy (2 percent), India (2 percent) and the United States (1.25 percent).[17] In big cities such as Wellington, people frequent department stores and smaller boutiques to get latest fashion items for their wardrobes.

Seeking a foothold in the global fashion world, New Zealand has rapidly expanded the influence of its fashion industry. Artist Deborah Crowe and fashion designer Kim Fraser co-established the brand Fraser Crowe in 1998. With its artistic elements and expressions of environmentalist concern, the brand has gained a reputation within New Zealand and overseas. With Crowe's Scottish background and Fraser's part-Maori ethnicity, their work is also informed with a strong consciousness of New Zealand's pluralistic cultural identity. They are managing to establish international fame in the global fashion scene.

SOUTH AND SOUTHEAST ASIA

VINAY DHARWADKER AND DONNA L. HALPER

The globalization of capitalism and democracy that began around 1990 forced many South and Southeast Asian countries to liberalize their national economies. This meant that new Asian markets were opened up to corporations in the developed world, even as markets in the developed world were opened up afresh to producers and suppliers in Asia. While the economic reality of this international order in the 1990s proved to be far more complicated and asymmetrical than such a statement suggests, the new arrangement did stimulate a general increase in capital flows, production, employment, wages, and consumer spending in many parts of Asia that had been relatively stagnant in the preceding decades. The prosperity brought by globalization has continued broadly, though unevenly, into the first decade of the twenty-first century, bolstering not only tourism and hospitality, mass media and communications, and entertainment and recreation, but also the textile, apparel, and fashion industries around the world. In contemporary South and Southeast Asia, "fashion and appearance" thus have as much to do with markets and consumers in these regions as with the outflow of goods and styles from these regions in other parts of the globe.

FASHION AND APPEARANCE

This section will focus on fashions in attire and trends in personal appearance through two different applications of these terms: the popularity of certain Western or international paradigms of appearance, categories of clothing and accessories, types of textiles and designs, and styles of self-presentation among consumers in South and Southeast Asia; and the impact of Asian ideas or ideals of beauty, garments and cosmetics, and fabrics and decorative techniques on Euro-American markets and consumers, as well as their use and popularity at home.

In both these contexts, terms such as "fashion" and "popularity" turn out to be slippery, especially because they are difficult to apply to many indigenous forms of dress and self-representation as well as to basic, everyday clothing and appearance. In most parts of South and Southeast Asia, what people wear on a daily basis, at home and at work, at social gatherings and in public places, depends greatly on their income and purchasing power as well as on their social rank and status. The same is true of their dress and adornment on festive occasions such as weddings and parties, on holidays and festivals, and at religious ceremonies or rituals. Their choice of clothing and personal appearance in any of these situations is also heavily determined by religion and caste, ethnic identity and cultural heritage, level of education and type of employment, provincial location and degree of urbanization, and various codes and conventions beyond their personal control. People's choices of dress and appearance in a given situation thus may not be "choices" at all. What is actually worn most widely or commonly in these parts of the world—including many indigenous forms of clothing and cosmetics—may, therefore, have little or nothing to do with what usually counts as "fashion" and, despite the large numbers involved, may not reflect anything resembling "popularity."

It is important to note that fashion that is driven by desire and popularity is a measure of choice: choices can be exercised and desires expressed or fulfilled only if one has the material means to do so. Under European colonization in earlier eras, and under globalization now, the majority of the population in most South and Southeast Asian countries has been too poor to pursue either free choice or desire in matters such as clothing or personal appearance. On one level, the enormous economic disparities among different social groups in these nations imply that Asian populations are not uniformly integrated into a Western-style consumer economy, or into a "global" market. On another level, the prevalence of poverty on such a scale means that "fashion" and "popularity" can be meaningfully associated only with the middle and upper classes in urban environments, those who have the leisure and the means—and hence the freedom—to pursue their desires and choices. Much of the discussion below, therefore, is limited to the interests, concerns, and tastes of a rather exclusive and privileged minority of people in the cities of South and Southeast Asia.

PERSONAL APPEARANCE

Societies in these parts of the world are characterized by an immense racial, ethnic, and cultural diversity, and hence by a great variety of body types, physiques, physiognomies, complexions, and other such attributes in their populations. Men, women, and children from these regions, therefore, do not fit into any one physical stereotype and also do not conform to a narrow Euro-American paradigm of what constitutes good looks or beauty, masculinity or femininity, a good bearing, or a graceful style of speech. Against this backdrop, Asia's urban and educated middle and upper classes—closely connected to the rest of the world through the information, communication, and entertainment media—seem to prize two kinds of "ideals" at once. On the one hand, they judge personal appearance according to indigenous aesthetic norms (often classical or traditional Asian in origin); on the other hand, they also judge themselves and others according to contemporary international norms (as projected by films, television, and advertising in the mass media). This "double standard" is actually a complex, hybrid standard of judgment rather than merely a self-contradictory stance: it simultaneously accommodates Asian physical features and cultural traits as well as Euro-American modes and fashions. Thus, a man may have characteristically "Thai" good looks but may nevertheless present himself in a highly Westernized form or style in his choice of clothes, shoes, and grooming, as well as his bearing, gestures, and speech, for example, without a conflict between the two aspects of his appearance. At the same time, he may present himself quite splendidly in traditional Thai apparel for a special occasion without having to relinquish his Westernization.

The best recent example of this hybridity is probably the Hindi film actress Madhuri Dixit, who became a national obsession in India and an international rage from Pakistan and Bangladesh to the Middle East and North America in the early1990s to the early years of this century. For millions of fans, Dixit seemed at once to fulfill the classical Indian criteria for female beauty (so that she looked "a picture of perfection" in a sari, with traditional makeup and jewelry, as in the 1994 film *Hum Apke Hain Koun?*), and also the modern Western or international criteria for a "brunette" (so that she looked equally stunning, for example, in a Lycra workout suit on a gym floor, practicing her dance moves in a contemporary pop style, as in the 1997 film *Dil to Pagal Hai*). India's leading twentieth-century painter, M. F. Hussain, paid an extraordinary public tribute to Dixit's hybrid beauty in the late 1990s by painting several portraits of her and directing *Gaja Gamini* (2000), a film that cast her as an archetypal artist's fantasy-muse, who combined both Indian and Western ideals of beauty down the ages.

The cultural logic of a combination of Asian and Western qualities in a hybrid personality of this type, especially as applicable to the appearance of women, has played out on a large scale for South and Southeast Asian contestants in recent international beauty competitions. The Miss World beauty pageant is a particularly instructive example. Before 1990, very few Asian competitors made it to the final stages of this contest; the only noteworthy exception was Reita Faria (India), who won the title in 1966. Between 1991 and 2006, however, a total of seventeen contestants from five nations in this region—India, Thailand, Vietnam, the Philippines, and Malaysia—either won the competition or received a high ranking in it. Over these 15 years, there were six semi-finalists, one fourth-place runner-up, three third-place runners-up, and two second-place runners-up, besides one ninth-place runner-up from either South or Southeast Asia. Among them were one woman each from Thailand and Vietnam, three women each from India and Malaysia, and five women from the Philippines. During this period, however, the four winners of the Miss World title who have been of either South or Southeast Asian origin have all come from India: Aishwarya Rai in 1994, Diana Hayden in 1997, Yukta Mookhey in 1999, and Priyanka Chopra in 2000. In all seventeen cases of success, the women have consistently represented characteristic "national" elements of beauty and appearance while also conforming to stringent Euro-American criteria that are not part of older, indigenous Asian paradigms: exceptional height and slenderness, athletic muscle tone without bulk, a formulaic distribution of body weight across torso and limbs, and a photogenic proportionality among facial features.

Together with the two Indian women who won the Miss Universe title during this period—Sushmita Sen in 1994 and Lara Dutta in 2000—the various winners and runners-up in the Miss World pageant mentioned above have collectively demonstrated the hybrid nature of their representations of female appearance, or of contemporary "womanhood," in South and Southeast Asia. At the same time, they have cumulatively exerted a strong reverse

Fashion and Appearance

> **MISS WORLD COMPETITION, 1991–2006: WINNERS AND RANKED CONTESTANTS FROM SOUTH AND SOUTHEAST ASIA**
>
> 1991 Semifinalist: Ritu Singh (India)
> 1993 Second runner-up: Sharmaine Gutierrez (Philippines)
> 1994 Winner Aishwarya Rai (India)
> Semifinalists: Caroline Subijano (Philippines), Rahima Yayah (Malaysia)
> 1996 Third runner-up: Joan Jeyraj (India)
> 1997 Winner: Diana Hayden (India)
> Third runner-up: Tanya Suesuntisook (Thailand)
> Semifinalist: Arianna Teoh (Malaysia)
> 1998 Second runner-up: Pick Lim Lina Teoh (Malaysia)
> 1999 Winner: Yukta Mookhey (India)
> 2000 Winner: Priyanka Chopra (India)
> 2002 Semifinalist: Katherine Manalo (Philippines)
> 2003 Third runner-up: Ami Vashi (India)
> 2004 Fourth runner-up: Ma Karla Bautista (Philippines)
> Ninth runner-up: Huyen Nguyen Thi (Vietnam)
> 2005 Semifinalist: Miss Philippines

pressure on international norms of feminine appearance: their presence on the world stage, displaying a great deal of the racial, ethnic, and cultural diversity of their homelands, has enabled South and Southeast Asian norms to significantly modify the Western or Euro-American models of beauty that had dominated the Miss World and Miss Universe competitions before about 1990.

There are no comparable pageants or contests for men, but the same may be broadly true of the standards by which male appearance currently is judged in South and Southeast Asia. If Bollywood films are any indication of such trends, then the immense popularity of male superstars such as Shahrukh Khan, Aamir Khan, Salman Khan, and Saif Ali Khan (all Indian Muslims) in the past two decades suggests that men also represent a hybrid norm. Whether playing a homely boy-next-door role, a historical character, an urban hunk, or a cosmopolitan living abroad, these actors constantly blend Indian (or South Asian, or even Asian) criteria with Western criteria for contemporary physical appeal. Aamir Khan, for example, has been as memorable in his appearance as a poor, barefoot farmer in indigenous clothes in nineteenth-century British India (*Lagaan*, 2002), as when he was cast as a hip college student in jeans and T-shirts in Mumbai and as a migrant entrepreneur in Armani business suits in Sydney, Australia (*Dil Chahata Hai*, 2001). The key point with regard to both men and women is that, especially since about 1990, mass audiences across Asia appear to have rejected any simple, one-sided imposition of only Euro-American ideals of physique, physiognomy, and personal presentation on their tastes. Audiences seem to celebrate a complex, shifting combination of the indigenous and the Western, the distinctive and the generic, the traditional and the modern.

Fashion Markets

Western Clothing and Westernization at Home

More generally, the cultures of Asian countries that were once colonized by European powers have largely emerged in the postcolonial period as "mixed" cultures, in which numerous indigenous institutions and practices of precolonial origin now coexist with various elements of Westernization and Euro-American modernity imported during the colonial period and after. Virtually none of these indigenous and foreign elements can be found in an unmixed form today: simply by surviving into the present, every local and national tradition has been contaminated by modernity, and every element of foreign origin has been domesticated, and hence altered by what is indigenous.

Such a cultural admixture is particularly visible in the garment and fashion industry, where a Westernized population in a South or Southeast Asian country constitutes a significant, preexisting market for goods from the developed world, and for goods in Western forms and styles manufactured domestically. This market was already well defined at the end of the colonial period in the 1940s (for most of South and Southeast Asia) and continued to consume Western-style clothes, cosmetics, and accessories on a moderate scale in several countries from the 1950s to the 1980s. Since the liberalization of several national economies in the 1990s, however, this Asian market has grown quite dramatically. Particularly in India, Thailand, the Philippines, Malaysia, Singapore, and Indonesia (and variably to a lesser extent in Pakistan, Nepal, Bangladesh, and Sri Lanka), it is now driven strongly by current local, national, and international fashions.

Against this backdrop, a broad range of Western-style clothing, accessories, and cosmetics has been used widely by Westernized middle- and upper-class consumers in South and Southeast Asian cities in the past half century. Among the most popular garments have been jeans and T-shirts for men, women, and children; trousers and shirts or blouses for men and women; shorts and T-shirts and shirts for boys; and dresses, skirts, and tops for girls. Suits and business clothing for men and women, including skirts, blouses, and dresses for women, have been less widely used because they are higher-priced, serve narrower needs, and cater to significantly smaller market segments. In the past two decades, sportswear of various kinds has become popular with a niche market on a comparable scale. An important factor in this popularity has been the use of synthetic fabric blends in Western-style garments, which are more durable, retain their finish longer, and are easier to care for than are the cotton and silk fabrics traditional to South and Southeast Asia.

The use of Western-style clothing, however, has been circumscribed in several ways. In many communities across Asia until the 1960s and 1970s, men wore Western clothes primarily in blue-collar and white-collar workplaces; at home, they often changed into traditional male attire (see below, under Indigenous Garments). Also, in many communities until the 1980s, men wore Western clothes more often than women did; if working women wore Western clothes, they frequently chose skirts or dresses in preference to trousers, and they hardly ever wore women's business suits at all. However, for most of the postcolonial period, the home/work and male/female divisions and restrictions of choice in Western clothing have applied only to adults: since the mid-twentieth century, urban Asian children have commonly worn Western garments in all situations, with shorts and shirts for boys and dresses or skirts and tops for girls being virtually ubiquitous.

The use of Western-style apparel has also been affected by religion and, unexpectedly, by government. In Islamic nations, where Qur'anic prescriptions and Sharia law apply (even if they are not enforced in everyday situations), men may be relatively free to wear Western clothes at work and in public places; women, however, whether young or old, are rarely permitted to be visible in skirts, dresses, or trousers in any public space (where they have to wear a burka, or "veil" that covers them from head to toe, as the outermost garment). In the Muslim majority populations in Pakistan, Bangladesh, and Indonesia, as well as in the Muslim minority populations in India, Thailand, the Philippines, Malaysia, and Singapore, for example, religious orthodoxy often restricts the use of Western apparel by women and girls and even by men and boys. The restrictions on Western clothing for religious reasons also extend more broadly to women's presence and appearance in public space, which is why many Muslim majority nations do not send national representatives to international beauty pageants (Turkey, which has long been committed to modernity, is a rare exception).

Fashion and Appearance

In Myanmar, Laos, Cambodia, and Vietnam, which are all Buddhist majority nations, totalitarian political regimes have officially prohibited or restricted the use of Western-style garments as part of their programs of postcolonial cultural "nationalism": the repression of such clothing is closely linked to these governments' persecution of Westernized artists and intellectuals in their midst, and their systematic censorship of Western or Westernized arts and cultural forms. This particular trend has not appeared so far in Sri Lanka, which is also a Buddhist majority nation, but one with a relatively durable tradition of parliamentary democracy, and hence much more open to Westernization and Western elements. Against such a background, the popularity of Western forms and styles of dress in South and Southeast Asia remains an outcome of Westernization that started in the colonial period and has continued and increased under globalization. But it has also been curtailed, sometimes severely, by the restrictions on the availability and public use of Western apparel imposed by some religions and repressive governments and political ideologies.

Outlets for Western Clothing in Local Markets

Until the 1980s, ready-made Western clothing (belonging to the *prêt-à-porter* category), manufactured in and imported from the developed world, was too rarely available (if at all) and too expensive for consumers in South and Southeast Asia. Individuals in these parts of the world usually acquired Euro-American jeans, T-shirts, skirts, blouses, and other articles of clothing while traveling abroad, through friends or associates who were able to travel abroad, or through underground black-market dealers in large Asian cities. Since about 1990, however, the general liberalization of Asian economies has relaxed import restrictions on apparel in many places, so that prêt-à-porter clothes designed and manufactured in the developed world are now widely available in mostly upscale garment stores, department stores, and shopping malls in countries such as India, Thailand, the Philippines, Malaysia, Singapore, and Indonesia (although government restrictions continue in Myanmar, Laos, Cambodia, and even Vietnam). Cities such as Mumbai, Delhi, Kolkata, Bangalore, Bangkok, Manila, Kuala Lumpur, Singapore, and Jakarta, in fact, are now among the "hottest" shopping places in Asia, offering local consumers as well as tourists a range of the latest prêt-a-porter garments (including a variety of fashionable Euro-American brand-name attire) imported from all over the world.

For much of the modern period in South and Southeast Asia, however, severe import restrictions on apparel and high prices for ready-made garments from abroad have resulted in a flourishing domestic custom-tailoring industry. Most of the demand for Western-style clothing among urban consumers in these regions has actually been met by local tailors, who operate out of small shops or workshops and produce moderately priced custom-made garments for men, women, and children using fabrics purchased separately by the customers at fabric stores. Until the present decade, most towns and cities in Pakistan, India, Nepal, Bangladesh, and Sri Lanka, as well as in Thailand, the Philippines, Malaysia, and Indonesia, had dozens if not hundreds of tailors and tailoring establishments in business, with the majority of urban dwellers using their services to acquire Western-style as well as indigenous clothing. Contemporary Bangkok, Manila, Kuala Lumpur, Delhi, and Mumbai, for example, still offer good-quality custom tailoring at reasonable prices—now a major attraction for international tourists in these cities. A competent tailor in Jaipur or Chandigarh, Bangalore or Chennai, can make you "look good" in clothes cut and stitched to the latest international design of your choice, and at a fraction of the price of an imported brand-name version of the same.

Since the mid-1990s, however, the long-standing custom tailoring industry and the fabric trade in countries such as India have been adversely affected by the advent of domestic prêt-a-porter garment manufacturing. Partly because of overstocks originally meant for export to the developed world, partly because of the recent "corporatization" of the apparel industry within South and Southeast Asia, and partly because of economies of scale in garment manufacturing in the face of labor problems and uncertain demand abroad, the merchandise from apparel producers in Pakistan, Indian, Nepal, Bangladesh, and Sri Lanka, as well as in Thailand, Vietnam, the Philippines, Malaysia, and Indonesia, has now crowded their local and national markets. Domestic consumers have adjusted to this development in complex ways, choosing relatively expensive ready-made options for some types of clothing but continuing with cheaper custom-tailoring options for other items.

Asian Presence in Foreign Markets

Moving in the opposite direction, South and Southeast Asian producers, sellers, and exporters have been supplying their goods to markets in the West for a long time (see below). Ever since decolonization in the 1940s, the textile and garment industries in these regions have been regular suppliers—although often on a limited scale—for clothing manufacturers, wholesalers, and retailers in Europe and North America. But until the 1990s, chiefly because of the trade agreements between Asian and Western countries, the labels on manufactured clothing in the West did not acknowledge the sources of their materials or assembly. Since the advent of globalization, however, and especially since the formation of the World Trade Organization and the signing of new international trade protocols, the extent of Asian participation in the apparel industry of the developed nations has become more visible. A high proportion of the South and Southeast Asian input—materials, techniques, skills, and labor—has been and continues to be for merchandise in the low-to-moderate price range. But in some exceptional sectors, clothing designed, manufactured, or assembled in factories in these regions has been featured at the high end of the Western fashion market, from Armani to Prada. The same has also been broadly true of accessories, such as moderate leather goods (e.g., belts, wallets, and bags) and fashion jewelry; the principal exception has been footwear, particularly sports shoes, such as those manufactured at Nike's "world factories" in Southeast Asia, which have remained high-priced items since the 1980s.

This new visibility of Asian materials and labor has had two significant effects. One is that, since the 1990s, Western designers and manufacturers have more explicitly incorporated, adapted, acknowledged, or drawn inspiration from South and Southeast Asian elements and motifs in their own products. At the beginning of the new millennium, for instance, Euro-American brand names such as Tom Ford and Prada showcased Indian elements, alongside Chinese and Japanese elements, in a series of products with "oriental" themes. This type of unprecedented move has helped open a new commercial portal for Indian fabrics, garments, designs, and trends, among others, which has had a wider—although perhaps transitory—impact on Western markets.

The other effect is that, for about 10 years now, Indian designer labels have found a place for themselves in the fashion market of the developed world. The first designers from Asia to have an impact at the international level appeared in the early 1980s, when Japanese names such as Hane Mori, Rei Kawakubo, Issey Miyake, and Yohji Yamamoto made inroads into the Paris establishment with their East-West fusion apparel. Ever since Ritu Beri received rave reviews at the Paris Fashion Week in the late 1990s, Indian designers generally have found favor with Paris and Milan, London and New York. Rohit Bal, J. J. Valaya, Tarun Tahiliani, Rina Dhaka, and David Abraham and Rakesh Thakore, for example, became "hot properties" in Europe as well as in America at the turn of the millennium. More recently, Suneet Varma, Manish Arora, Vivek Narang, Raghavendra Rathore, Rajesh Pratap Singh, Manish Malhotra, Anshu Arora Sen, and Puja Nayyar, among others, have also attracted widespread international attention. Designs by Dhaka, for instance, have been featured at Coin (Venice-based European conglomerate); by Arora at Maria Luisa (Paris and Europe); by Singh at Neiman Marcus (New York); by Abraham and Thakore at Bloomingdales (New York); by Varma at Moet and Chandon (subsidiary of the Louis Vuitton-Moet Hennessey Group); and by Sen at Selfridges (United Kingdom). Dhaka, Tahiliani, Arora, and Narang were highlighted in a group show at Lord and Taylor and at Saks Fifth Avenue (New York) in 2003; Varma has had important exhibitions in Singapore and Hong Kong; and several of these designers have figured prominently at such annual venues as the Milan Fashion Week, the Asia Fashion Week, and the Singapore Fashion Festival.

This success, however, has specific limitations. First, after World War II, Japan became a powerhouse in textile design and manufacturing, and by the 1960s its fabrics as well as manufactured garments were meeting the highest international standards of quality; this technological superiority provided the foundation for the success of Japanese designers in the Western fashion establishment in the 1980s, making Japan the "megacenter" of haute couture, fashion, and design in Asia. But no other Asian nation has been able to match or rival this accomplishment; despite their presence in the international market and the quality and distinctiveness of their products, many textile manufacturers in South and Southeast Asia are still unable to meet the highest contemporary technological or quality standards. As a result, designers from these regions who have made room for themselves in the international couture or prêt-a-porter markets are unable to deliver merchandise that can compete qualitatively with Japanese goods.

Second, the multisector success of the South and Southeast Asian garment industries is actually limited to the Indian design and manufacturing sectors. That is, while India has achieved competitive status in apparel design and in textile production, Pakistan, Nepal, Bangladesh, and Sri Lanka, as well as Thailand, the Philippines, Malaysia, and Singapore, have mainly provided labor for garment assembly. Third, Indian designers such as Bal, Valaya, Tahiliani, and Beri tried to replicate the strategies of their Japanese counterparts by focusing on haute couture in the 1990s. But, by the turn of the millennium, it became clear that Indian designers could not sustain such a presence in the international market, and so they have collectively shifted "downward" into prêt-a-porter garment markets. This, however, may not be a shortcoming or failure: while Japan has the capital, scientific, technical, manufacturing, and design capabilities to maintain "vertical" dominance, the South (and even the Southeast) Asian industries may be much better suited to a "horizontal" expansion and consolidation across borders.

In a parallel but independent development, Indian wholesalers and retailers have now opened outlets all over the world to cater to the demand of the Indian diaspora for fashionable clothing as well as everyday garments in Indian forms and styles. The "Little Indias" that have sprung up in England, Canada, the United States, Thailand, Malaysia, and Singapore, for example, feature ready-made clothing stores with the latest women's, men's, and children's fashions from urban India, reflecting trends in everyday wear in cities such as Delhi, Mumbai, Kolkata, Chennai, Ahmedabad, Chandigarh, and Bangalore as well as current tastes in high-priced items, such as ensembles for weddings and festivals. To a somewhat lesser extent, Pakistani, Bangladeshi, Sri Lankan, and some Nepali manufacturers and retailers have also joined in this expansion, serving their nations' immigrant communities in

Europe and North America as well as in Africa, Southeast Asia, and Australia. This diasporic retail market concentrates almost exclusively on indigenous apparel and fabrics that otherwise are impossible to obtain outside Asia. Given the size, spread, and purchasing power of South and Southeast Asian immigrant and migrant populations after about 1965, this market is also exceptionally large. Approximately 20 million people with origins in Pakistan, India, Nepal, Bangladesh, and Sri Lanka, for example, now live and work or are settled in some 125 countries around the globe, and the majority of them— belonging to an international middle class—continue to maintain strong ties with the cultures and lifestyles of their homelands. In the first decade of the twenty-first century, India's apparel industry alone has generated annual revenues in the range of US$12–14 billion, with nearly half of the amount coming each year from exports and sales outside the country.

TEXTILES AND TECHNIQUES

Silk is China's gift to the world. The culture of silkworms (sericulture) and the production and processing of silk yarn and silk cloth were established cottage industries in China by about 2500 BCE. The Chinese began to trade silk to South, Central, and West Asia around the middle of the first millennium BCE; sericulture and silk production probably spread from China to India via these overland trade routes in the mid-second century BCE. India was soon exporting its own raw silk and finished silk cloth to Persia, which became the Asian center for the silk trade to the Middle East and the Mediterranean region by the third century CE. Sericulture reached Byzantium only about 300 years later; it spread subsequently to Italy and France, where silk production flourished after the Renaissance. Within Asia, sericulture and silk production spread from China and India to Korea, Japan, and Thailand; these nations have remained primary producers of silk fabric and clothing down to modern times.

Cotton is India's gift to the world. The cotton plant was cultivated on the subcontinent in the third millennium BCE; by about 500 BCE, cotton spinning and weaving had become key cottage industries in the subcontinent's ancient economy. Primitive guilds and cooperatives of spinners and weavers in groups of villages supplied traders in the subcontinent's southern port cities, who were exporting cotton fabrics to much of the Indian Ocean region before the Common Era. Cotton production spread from India to China, Turkey, Egypt, and East Africa; in the early modern period, it became part of New World slave economies (especially in the United States, Mexico, and Brazil); and in the early twenty-first century, India and Pakistan remain among the world's leading cotton producers, along with Australia, Sudan, and the other countries mentioned previously.

The basic spinning wheels and handlooms for cotton and silk invented early in the ancient period remained in use in South and Southeast Asia until modern times. In cities such as Banaras (north India), Kanchipuram (south India), and Dhaka (Bangladesh), for example, which have been centers of silk and cotton fabric and garment production of world importance for at least 700 years, spinning and weaving technology changed very little until the British introduced the jacquard machine and the Hattersley domestic loom in the early twentieth century. Most cotton handloom and silk weaving work—for saris, for example—is still done in workshops located in weavers' homes, using techniques, patterns, and materials developed centuries ago. The cotton industry in eighteenth-century India was a key stimulus for the industrial revolution in England, which sought to replace handlooms with mechanized looms. Asia's first cotton mills were built under colonial rule in the later nineteenth century, which severely disrupted the indigenous cotton industry, changing product and supply, market and demand, price and economy. Synthetic fibers, yarns, and fabrics and synthetic blends (such as terecot, a blend of terelene and cotton) arrived in the third quarter of the twentieth century, further altering the landscape of textile production without fully replacing the old, indigenous crafts. Today, certain fabrics and garments, such as silk and cotton saris, continue to be woven on handlooms, but the weavers now use mill yarn. Moreover, in the past century or so, some of the traditional textiles of South (and also Southeast) Asia have been adapted for mechanized mass production.

For several millennia, Asian weavers have regularly used vegetable and mineral dyes (ranging from indigo to lead oxide) to produce brightly colored fabrics and garments. Most of these are not permanent and fade with repeated washings; nevertheless, many of the traditional dying methods and techniques, which also include the production of colored designs on finished cloth, continue to be used today. Among the most famous Indian products are the *lahariya* pattern (regular, wave-like curvilinear bands, produced on cotton by twisting the cloth while dyeing); Sanganer block-printed cotton (using small wooden blocks, carved in reverse relief, to reproduce design elements by repeated, high-precision imprinting by hand); *bandhani* work (Indian tie or knot dyeing, using waxed thread to protect patterned parts of cotton or silk while dying the rest); and *qalamkari* work ("brushwork"—originally in the seventeenth century, hand-painted cotton cloth with glowing colors that was used for coverlets and bedcovers; now, often machine printed).

Since the eighteenth century, the most popular textile from Southeast Asia in Western markets has been cotton dyed using the batik method, in which melted wax is applied to patterned areas to prevent them from absorbing color during immersion in dye. The wax is then boiled off, and successive applications of wax to other areas followed by immersions in vats with different colors produce richly colored and patterned fabric. Batik methods were refined mostly in Java (Indonesia), but important variations also evolved elsewhere in the region, as in Sulawesi. The Dutch began importing Indonesian and Southeast Asian batik cotton into Europe some 300 years ago. Other unique and superb fabrics from Indonesia include *ikat*, in which the yarn is dyed before being woven, and *geringsing* (or "double ikat" fabric), in which the yarn is dyed in patterns before weaving. Permanent petroleum-based dyes entered the Asian cotton and silk economies in the twentieth century; many of the traditional patterns and effects, such as lahariya, qalamkari, and batik can now be reproduced on cotton, synthetic fabrics, and blends using machine printing and permanent dyes.

Besides silk and cotton, the indigenous fibers and textiles of these regions include the remarkable fiber known as *pashmina*, or cashmere. True cashmere is not wool; rather, it is the very fine and soft hair from the downy undercoat of the goat native to Kashmir (now divided between India and Pakistan). The Kashmir goat is also bred for its hair in Iran, China, and Mongolia, but the finest fibers still come from Kashmir, India. This pashmina, or cashmere, is traditionally used in handmade shawls, which became famous worldwide in the early nineteenth century for their softness and beauty and as the models for the shawls of England, France, and Paisley (Scotland).

Among the most popular and distinctive indigenous techniques to adorn or enhance fabrics and garments are embroidery with silk thread on silk cloth (Thailand); *zari* work, embroidery with gold thread on silk to create elaborate borders for saris and various formal or festive garments (Pakistan, India, and Bangladesh); *chikan* work, fine embroidery with white cotton thread on plain muslin cloth (Bangladesh and north India); and mirror work, in which thin, penny-sized mirrors are appliquéd on richly embroidered cloth used for bed and divan covers, wall hangings, and indigenous forms of skirts, blouses, vests, and other garments (west India).

Indigenous Garments

The oldest, most basic, and most widely used form of clothing indigenous to South and Southeast Asia is the lower body wrap, a stretch of rectangular cloth that encircles the pelvis and legs one or more times and is tied at the waist. Using cloths of different lengths and widths, this wrap can be worn in many different ways or styles: one style yields the sarong of Southeast Asia, another the dhoti and the sari of India, and a third the *tehband*, *lungi*, and *longyi* of Pakistan, south India, Bangladesh, and Myanmar. Cotton wraps were probably in use in the towns of the Indus Valley and Harappan civilization of South Asia before 2000 BCE; silk wraps may have been in use in China even earlier; and cotton and silk wraps were probably quite widespread across many parts of Asia after about 500 BCE.

Cut, stitched, and fitted garments for the torso and the lower body were first made in Persia (Iran) by that date, probably with animal skins; in the centuries just before the Common Era, they appear to have spread along the Silk Road to China, where cloth pants and jackets were in use by the second century BCE. Fitted, seamed clothing entered South Asia with Muslim armies and Persian immigrants around the beginning of the second millennium CE and spread to Southeast Asia with Muslim and Hindu traders and settlers soon afterward. European-style clothes reached South Asia with the Portuguese at the end of the fifteenth century, and Southeast Asia in the next few decades.

South Asia

Numerous types of indigenous clothing continue to be common in these regions in the twenty-first century although their materials, methods of production, specific forms, and uses have changed over time. In India, the oldest male garment among Hindus is the dhoti, a lower body wrap tied at the waist, with one loose end pleated and passed between the legs, to be tucked in at the waist at the back. If the cloth is narrow and short, this wrap becomes a short dhoti, which covers only the pelvis and upper thighs, down to the knees; if it is shorter, it becomes a *langot*, or loincloth; if it is long and wide, it becomes a formal dhoti, reaching down to the ankles. From the seventeenth to the twentieth centuries, Hindus working for the East India Company and the British Raj wore formal cotton dhotis to work; in the first half of the twentieth century, Mahatma Gandhi made the short dhoti famous worldwide as his political "trademark" of protest against the British empire; in the late colonial and postcolonial periods, formal cotton dhotis have been used by village elders and officials, politicians, and orthodox urban Hindus; currently, formal, high-quality cotton and silk dhotis continue to be worn at Hindu weddings and festivals, among other occasions. Throughout the past millennium, short dhotis and loincloths have been the primary attire for most rural folk at work, whether on farms and in the fields, in forests and the hills, or on rivers and the sea.

Among rural Muslims since the thirteenth century and rural Sikhs since the sixteenth century in north India, the most common male version of the wrap has been a checkered or colored ankle-length cotton tehband, which is fastened at the waist and allowed to hang down like a sarong. Over the past 600 years or so, this has also been the most popular rural male attire in what are now Bangladesh and Sri Lanka, as well as in Myanmar, where it is called a longyi. The south Indian lungi is the same type of wrap, except that it is most often plain and white; it may be worn hanging down to the ankles, or with the bottom edge lifted up and tucked near the waist so that the garment is folded in half and reaches just above the knees.

For women, the principal variation on the lower body wrap over the past 1,500 years or so has been the sari (which, in parts of north India, is also called a women's dhoti). Across most of the northern half of the subcontinent, from Pakistan, through India and Nepal, to

FASHION AND APPEARANCE

Bangladesh, the common sari is rectangle 15 feet long and 3.5 feet wide, with a narrow ornamental border woven along one side of its length (which becomes the bottom edge of the wrap) and a much wider border along its width at one end (which becomes the *pallava*, *pallu*, or free top end). The sari is wrapped around and fastened at the waist from one end, usually with pleats hanging down the front to the ankles; the other end is then draped transversely across the torso and over the left shoulder so that it can hang freely at the back. In the states of Bengal and Gujarat and elsewhere, variations include draping the free end of the sari transversely across the back and over the right shoulder so that it hangs freely in front. In Maharashtra state, a distinctive variation on the garment itself is the 27-foot-long sari, which is worn much like the male formal dhoti, with one end passed between the legs and tucked with pleats at the back, and the free end draped over the left shoulder and around the other to the front again. Daily-wear saris are usually colored cotton; since the mid-twentieth century, nylon, georgette, and other synthetic fabrics have also become very popular. Silk saris, often with heavy gold-thread embroidery along the borders and other ornamentation and design work, are usually reserved for weddings, festivals, parties, and special occasions.

Until about 1200, saris were worn with the free top end serving as a loose wrap for the torso and shoulders; after the advent of Islam on the subcontinent and the arrival of Persian-style seamed and fitted garments, women in north India began to use a *choli*, or stitched blouse, for the upper torso, from which the modern sari-blouse (now universal in towns and cities) evolved in the mid-nineteenth century. Since just before World War I, the modern urban sari—whether cotton, silk, or synthetic—has also been worn over a narrow-skirted cotton petticoat with a drawstring at the waist, modeled after its European namesake. Except for the states of Bengal and Kerala, where white saris are the norm for everyday wear, white is reserved as the formal color for mourning; vermilion or red is reserved for brides at their weddings. In India, as in Pakistan, Nepal, Bangladesh, and Sri Lanka, saris are manufactured across an enormous range of fabrics (handloomed or machine-made, fine or heavy), colors (traditional or modern), patterns and borders (woven, printed, embroidered, dyed, appliquéd, ornamented, or hand painted), motifs (from geometrical to curvilinear, from symmetrical to irregular), and finishes, among other factors. Cotton and silk hand-loomed saris are especially prized because each piece is unique, as are some higher-priced machine-made ensembles. Although the sari was originally a Hindu garment for women in the northern Indian plains and on the peninsula, it also remains very popular among Muslims in Pakistan, India, and Bangladesh; Hindus in Nepal; Hindu Tamils in Sri Lanka; and women from all these communities in the South Asian diaspora around the globe.

Among cut, stitched or seamed, and fitted garments of indigenous or Asian origin in South Asia, the *paijama* [light-weight, comfortably fitted pants with a drawstring at the waist] and *kurta* [loose, flared shirt with long sleeves, worn without being tucked in] are the most common clothing worn by men. Europeans discovered the silk kimono in Japan and the cotton paijama-kurta combination in India, and then introduced both into Europe in the seventeenth century; the former became the basis for the modern Western bathrobe, housecoat, and dressing gown, whereas the latter was transformed into today's ubiquitous pajamas—another of India's gifts to the world. In Pakistan, India, Nepal, and Bangladesh, cotton and silk paijamas and kurtas, in appropriate varieties, constitute everyday wear at home and at work, as well as formal wear (for weddings, funerals, and festivals, for example). In all four countries, variations on this "indigenous pants-shirt" combination include the *churidar paijama* [cotton or silk pants, loose at the thighs but very closely fitted to the calves, made extra long and worn with multiple, layered "folds" between knees and ankles]

SHAMPOO, HAIRSTYLING, AND HEADDRESSES

The word "shampoo" is an English and European exoticism, derived from the north Indian Hindi word *champi*, which refers to a massage of the head and scalp with fragrant hair oil, followed by a lathering to cleanse the hair. The Indian style of champi was introduced into England by Din Muhammad (1759–1851, historically spelled Dean Mahomet), who ran a fashionable spa in Brighton for many years with his Anglo-Irish wife, Jane, and who in the 1820s served as a masseuse for King George IV and his royal household. Following the methods that Din Muhammad popularized, shampoo in its modern bottled form invites us to moisturize and massage the scalp with essential nutrients that are designed to cleanse and replenish the hair, give it body and volume, and restore its natural gloss.

In many parts of Asia, hairstyling and the grooming of head and facial hair is still influenced by premodern customs and religious practices. In many orthodox Muslim communities, for instance, from Pakistan, India, and Bangladesh to Malaysia, Indonesia, Thailand, and the Philippines, women are required to cover their heads in public, and men are required to cultivate beards. Among Hindus in India, Nepal, and Sri Lanka, men belonging to particular castes and ethnic communities customarily wear mustaches, and women maintain long, flowing tresses that are braided or wrapped in buns (with many orthodox Hindu communities still enjoining widows to completely shave their heads). Hindu men and women in particular have long used fragrant oils to add luster to their hair on a daily basis.

Among Sikhs, who are now scattered in many parts of South and Southeast Asia, men wear long, uncut hair, mustaches, and beards, with the hair dressed every day under styled turbans, and the mustaches and beards anointed close to the contours of the face; women wear their uncut hair in plaits or buns, often with elaborate coiffeurs. In the Malay archipelago and Indonesia, women of various ethnic groups have traditionally maintained long hair; women descended from old Chinese immigrants, for instance, wear their hair in chignons with precious ornaments. In contrast, in Thailand and Vietnam, for example, until the modern period, both men and women in various social classes wore their hair rather short, in what to outsiders often seemed a "unisex," masculine style.

On the Indian subcontinent, from Afghanistan to Bangladesh, Muslim, Hindu, and Sikh men have long worn different types of turbans, variously called *pagris* or *fetas*; men in Muslim communities throughout South and Southeast Asia also wear caps enjoined by their faith. Traditional turbans are often ceremonial and military, and tend to be adorned with ornaments crafted with precious metal and precious stones; everyday turbans are worn in styles specific to each community. In countries such as Thailand and Vietnam, common headwear for both men and women consists of handcrafted hats; the traditional Vietnamese gear for women, known as the *non bai tho*, is a conical hat made of dried young palm leaves, with poetry written on it.

and *achkan* or *sherwani* [knee-length, buttoned coat, with long sleeves and a round, snug collar at the throat, made of heavy fabric and often ornamented]. Especially among Muslims in Afghanistan, Pakistan, and Bangladesh, the male *shalwar* [very loose pants, tapered slightly toward the ankle] and *kameez* [an extra-long kurta-like shirt, with a closed, round collar], worn in colder weather with a short outer jacket (often of wool and shaped like a vest or waistcoat) are common.

Some of these indigenous items have influenced menswear around the world in modern times. Among the internationally famous and popular male garments derived from subcontinent models are these: jodhpurs, or long riding breeches, developed from the churidar paijama for equestrian sports and polo by the court tailors of the Maharaja of Jodhpur (Rajasthan state) in the late nineteenth century and subsequently adopted by the British; the Nehru jacket, developed from the traditional achkan or sherwani specially for Jawaharlal Nehru, the first prime minister of India (from 1947 to 1964), and adapted to a shorter length in Europe and the United States in the 1990s; and the "Chinese shirt," with its snug, round collar, also adapted from the fit of the achkan around the throat and torso.

For women, the major cut and stitched garments include the *ghaghra* (a wide-girth skirt, often of heavy cotton, with a drawstring at the waist and a length between knee and ankle) and choli (a "backless" blouse), traditional for much of the past millennium for Hindus in the states of Rajasthan and Gujarat and elsewhere in north and west India. This indigenous "skirt-blouse" combination is usually made of heavy dyed cotton and worn with a large upper-body wrap called a *chunari*, traditionally made of finer cotton. The ghaghra is the historical basis of the copious skirts of the Gypsies, who migrated out of these regions of India to the Mediterranean and Europe about 800 years ago; it is paralleled by the garara (wide-girth silk skirt) and its long-sleeved fitted blouse worn by Muslim women in Pakistan, India, and Bangladesh. Among other seamed garments are the salwar-kameez ensemble for women (the most popular dress in northern Pakistan and in the Indian Punjab, where it is most strongly associated with Sikh women) and the women's combination of churidar paijama and kameez (adapted from the garments described above for men). Both these ensembles are worn with a *dupatta*, a long, wide "scarf" that is pleated and draped across the torso in front and over both shoulders (adapted from the older chunari). The ghaghra-choli ensemble has been the apparel of rural Rajasthani and Gujarati women for centuries; in the postcolonial period, its upscale, urban version has become a high fashion item for middle- and upper-class consumers. In absolute numbers, the churidar-kameez combination is probably the most popular women's fitted-garment ensemble of the past four decades, cutting across religious, classes, and national boundaries as well as across the homeland-diaspora division, rivaling the sari in its frequency of use in public spaces.

Southeast Asia

Across Southeast Asia—and, further out, among some of the islands of Oceania—the most widespread and basic form of lower-body wrap is the sarong, which is used with variations and in different styles in Malaysia, Singapore, and Indonesia as well as in Thailand, Laos, and Cambodia. The traditional length of the sarong and some of the important styles in which it is worn relate it very closely to the male dhoti, tehband, and lungi; to the female sari on the Indian subcontinent; and to the longyi of Myanmar.

The military dictatorship in Myanmar requires its citizens to dress in traditional or indigenous clothes, and the most common attire for men and women is the Burmese longyi, worn in two distinct forms and styles. The male longyi is called *pa-so*; it is a long wrap worn by

JEWELRY, COSMETICS, AND BODY ART

For much of the past two millennia, South and Southeast Asian societies have been famous for their ornate and elaborate jewelry used by both women and men. The traditional crafts use gold as well as silver, a wide variety of precious and semi-precious stones, and also ocean pearls. The Indian subcontinent, Myanmar, Cambodia, Laos, and Vietnam are the historical centers for the production of artistic jewelry, with the traditions in Southeast Asia heavily influenced by Indian, Tibetan, and Chinese models.

Indian jewelry for women includes ornamental combs, hairpins, earrings, necklaces (often long and multistranded), armlets (worn above the elbow), bangles and bracelets (worn at the wrists and on the forearms), finger rings, waist belts (often with chain links and multiple strands), anklets, and toe rings. Burmese, Cambodian, Laotian, and Vietnamese jewelry contains many of these items as well as emphasizing brooches for the hair as well as for clothes. In the past 10 years or so, Indian-style bangles, anklets, and toe rings have become especially popular in Europe and North America.

Among indigenous cosmetics, most Hindu women still wear the *bindi* (a round mark made with vermilion powder in the middle of the forehead, designating married status), as well as *kumkum* (a streak of vermilion powder applied to the parting of the hair above the forehead, also designating married status). For Muslim as well as Hindu and Sikh women in South Asia, traditional eye makeup includes the application of *kajal* (a black ointment made with powdered antimony), an indigenous form of mascara.

Among South Asian Hindu as well as Muslim women, the most spectacular form of body art is *mehndi*, an herbal paste used to draw fine and intricate curvilinear, floral, and geometrical designs on the skin (especially on the palms, hands, forearms, soles, feet, ankles, and even on the throat, neck, and face), which dries several hours after application and, when rinsed off, leaves a deep saffron-hued imprint that can last for two to three weeks. For several hundred years now, mehndi has been a primary body-art form for bridal makeup in South Asia; as a result of globalization, it has become an internationally popular cosmetic style.

Tattoos and body piercing for both men and women have long histories in these regions. Thai men have traditionally worn black tattoos on their upper thighs, which are displayed prominently when wearing a short jong kraben. In Myanmar, men may tattoo their arms or chests with symbols for good luck and protection against harm. In rural west India (especially in the Rajasthan state), both men and women have long worn tattoos on their arms and have had their ears pierced for large and small earrings of gold or silver. Both Hindu and Muslim women across the subcontinent have also frequently practiced nose piercing, inserting a diamond stud or a precious metal nose ring (sometimes mounted with a pearl) above the left nostril.

folding it on both sides of the body and tucking it in at the waist (without tying or fastening it). The female version, called *hta-main*, is much shorter in length; it is worn with a single wide fold in front and tucked in on one side at the waist. Traditionally, both wraps have the same width (about 2.5 feet) and cover the legs down to near the ankles; men may fold the pa-so up to their knees for comfort, whereas women today may use a shorter width for a "higher hemline," although the length rarely rises above the knee. The fact that neither form of the longyi is tied at the waist (unlike the Pakistani, Indian, or Bangladeshi tehband and the south Indian lungi) means that, in order to keep them in place, both men and women frequently undo and retuck their wraps in public, with the necessary decorum. In their modern forms, both the pa-so and the hta-main now come in stitched, ready-to-wear versions, with the latter especially resembling a Western-style skirt. Most longyis for everyday use are made of cotton, with men's pa-sos often printed with checks or stripes, and women's hta-mains carrying multicolored floral or other patterns.

Thailand's most popular indigenous garment for men is the *jong kraben*, probably derived from the Khmer or Cambodian *yak rung* by the fifteenth century; both are versions of the Indian short dhoti described above. The Thai jong kraben may come down to the knees or the calves, or it may be short enough to be a loincloth, leaving much of the thighs exposed. In the sixteenth and seventeenth centuries, many ordinary Thai men covered only the lower body with a jong kraben, going bare-chested most of the time; since then, men have also worn this garment with a short- or long-sleeved shirt (in its formal version called *seur phra ratchathan*, which has a high collar), and with a sash or cummerbund at the waist. The most widespread dress for women is a sarong, specifically in the form called *pha-sin*: popularly known now as "the tube skirt," the wrap is fastened at the waist with pleated folds in front; it may be short or full length. The pha-sin is usually worn with a long-sleeved, high-collared blouse and a long, folded scarf known as a *sabai* draped transversely across the torso and over one shoulder. Until modern times, women of the poorer classes also wore the jong kraben like men, without a garment for the upper body—which led many early European visitors to assume that Thai apparel was "unisex." Late into the twentieth century, women of many classes also wore the jong kraben either with a *par tap* [a long cloth tied over the breasts] while at home, or with a *tabang marn* [a long cloth wrapped across the back and over the breasts and tied at the neck] outdoors. In the rural provinces of Thailand, the ubiquitous male garment is the *pa kao ma*, a basic lower-body wrap or male sarong like the tehband and lungi of the Indian subcontinent or the Burmese longyi; the universal women's garment is the pha-sin tube-skirt or female sarong. Currently, male and female jong krabens, men's ratchathans, and women's pha-sins and long-sleeved blouses come in many fabrics and patterns, with silk being the most common; they also appear in numerous provincial and rural variant forms. The Thai pha-sin and sabai are virtually identical to the pha-sin used in Laos and the sabai found in Cambodia, just as the Thai jong kraben is indistinguishable from the Cambodian yak rung.

Since the reunification of the country in 1975, Vietnam's national dress for women has been the *ao dai*, which was invented in the mid-eighteenth century and modernized in the mid-twentieth century, but then went out of production during the Vietnam War. Historically speaking, Malaysia, Indonesia, Thailand, and Cambodia, to a large extent, remained primarily in India's sphere of influence for centuries; in contrast, Vietnam has long remained in China's sphere of influence, much more so than Laos, Cambodia, or Thailand. The all-important consequence of this difference or division is that indigenous Vietnamese clothing is based on the model of Chinese stitched garments, rather than on the basic Indian-style wrap or its Southeast Asian derivatives. The splendid ao dai ensemble consists of a full-length, seamed and fitted, tunic-like dress with a high round collar, worn over loose pants: the unusual feature of the upper garment is that it has four long slits, from hip to hem (two on the sides, and one each in the front and back), which produce "four flaps." The dress and pants are traditionally made of fine silk (whether Chinese or Thai), but the current preference is for synthetic fabrics, which do not crush easily and drape well in this design. The whole ensemble is ideally custom made, so that the dress is contoured to fit the individual woman's body type perfectly; significantly, the open flaps flatter all shapes and proportions.

Since the 1990s, as Vietnam's economy has improved in some ways under globalization, the growing middle class in the country as well as the international tourist trade have sharply increased the popularity of the ao dai, which is now being mass produced in ready-made forms for export as well as for domestic consumption.

Among the indigenous garments of Malaysia and Indonesia, the "hottest" in the current decade has been the *kebaya*, a blouse made of sheer material, which is traditionally worn with a Javanese batik sarong by women of Chinese-immigrant descent in the Malay archipelago (who are known as the Nyonya). The kebaya is a formal and festive garment, and Nyonyas wear it at weddings, celebrations, and parties as part of a complex ensemble. The batik sarong (usually of high-quality silk) is pleated and fastened at the waist with a gold or silver chain-link belt; the top lapel of the blouse itself is secured with three brooches (*kerosang*). The hair is done up in a chignon (*sanggul*), using gold hairpins as well as flowers. The footwear is hand-crafted beaded shoes (*kasut manek*). The Nyonya kebaya as a type of blouse has attracted the attention of many designers recently: contemporary versions of it are now worn as a top with jeans and Western-style skirts, as a blouse with pants, and even as a fashionable overgarment with Western-style sleeveless or spaghetti-strap dresses and casual tank tops.

As the foregoing survey indicates, apparel is an exceptionally complex cultural domain in South and Southeast Asia. More than food, music, or dance, clothing reveals constant tensions between tradition and modernity, economics and class, religion and freedom, desire and practicality, politics and social convention, purchasing power and everyday life. For reasons that are not entirely "cultural," the majority populations in most societies in these regions—as in societies elsewhere—tend to be conservative in their choice of everyday clothes and appearance. For the great majority of Asians, what is most functional at home and at work, the least expensive to buy and maintain, and at the same time the most durable, familiar, and socially acceptable in their local contexts seems to predominate over what is fashionable or popular in the wider world. Nevertheless, even in the most provincial places, the contemporary mass media and market forces have made local residents acutely aware of trends that are popular at the national and international levels, and for those who have the material means and social freedom to do so, fashionable clothing, cosmetics, and accessories become essential elements in their self-definition in everyday life.

RESOURCE GUIDE

PRINT SOURCES

East Asia and Oceania

Bhachu, Parminder. *Dangerous Designs: Asian Women Fashion the Diaspora Economies.* New York: Routledge, 2004.

Brickell, Chris. "Through the (New) Looking Glass: Gendered Bodies, Fashion and Resistance in Postwar New Zealand." *Journal of Consumer Culture* 2.2 (2002): 241–269.

Bullis, Douglas. *Fashion Asia.* New York: Thames & Hudson, 2000.

Chua, Beng-Huat, ed. *Consumption in Asia: Lifestyles and Identities.* London/New York: Routledge, 2000.

Goodrum, Alison L. "Exhibition Review—The First New Zealand Fashion Week." *Fashion Theory* 8.1, (2004): 99.

Iwabuchi, Koichi, Stephen Muecke, and Mandy Thomas, eds. *Rogue Flows: Trans-Asian Cultural Traffic.* Hong Kong: Hong Kong University Press, 2004.

Kim, Youngjae. *Korean Costumes through the Ages.* Translated by Kiwon Lee, Janice Kim, and Jennifer Jung-Kim. Seoul: Korea National Folk Museum of Korea, 2003.

Kirby, Mark. "A Marriage of Art and Fashion in New Zealand." *Fiberarts* 25.4 (1999, January 1): 41.

Korea Fashion & Culture Association. *Fashion Art from Korea: Air of the East.* Seoul: Korea Fashion & Culture Association, 2000.

Lee, Leo Ou-fan. *Shanghai Modern: The Flowering of a New Urban Culture in China, 1930–1945.* Cambridge, MA: Harvard University Press, 1999.

Maynard, Margaret. *Fashioned from Penury: Dress as Cultural Practice in Colonial Australia.* Cambridge/New York: Cambridge University Press, 1994.

———. "Living Dolls: The Fashion Model in Australia." *Journal of Popular Culture* 33.1 (1999): 191–205.

Molloy, Maureen. "Cutting-edge Nostalgia: New Zealand Fashion Design at the New Millennium." *Fashion Theory* 8.4 (2004): 477–490.

Niessen, Sandra, Ann Marie Leshkowich, and Carla Jones, eds. *Re-orienting Fashion: The Globalization of Asian Dress.* Oxford/New York: Berg, 2003.

Steele, Valerie, and John S. Major, eds. *China Chic: East Meets West.* New Haven, CT/London: Yale University Press, 1999.

Roberts, Claire, ed. *Evolution & Revolution: Chinese Dress 1700s–1990s.* Sydney, AU: Powerhouse Publishing, 1997.

Tam, Pui-yim Jennifer. *Japanese Popular Culture in Hong Kong: Case Studies of Youth Consumption of Cute Products and Fashion Magazines.* Hong Kong: Hong Kong University Press, 2002.

Wood, Frances. *The Silk Road: Two Thousand Years in the Heart of Asia.* Berkeley/Los Angeles: University of California Press, 2002.

Wu, Ziyi. *Fashion @ Tokyo.* Taipei Shi: Huangguan, 2005.

South and Southeast Asia

Gahlaut, Kanika. "Designs on the World." *India Today* 2.38 (2003, September 16–22): 30–39.

Reddy, Vanita. "The Nationalization of the Global Indian Woman: Geographies of Beauty in *Femina*." *South Asian Popular Culture* 4.1 (April 2006): 61–85.

Runkle, Susan. "Making Miss India: Constructing Gender, Power and the Nation." *South Asian Popular Culture* 2.2 (October 2004): 145–159.

Taparia, Nidhi, and Eudore R. Chand. "All That Glitter." *India Today* 2.38 (2003, September 16–22): 41.

POPULAR FASHION MAGAZINES

China

Cosmopolitan China
Elle China
Ray China
Shanghai Fashion
Vogue China

Japan

An · An
Can Can
JJ
More

Say
With

Korea

An · An Korea
CeCi
Cosmopolitan Korea
Elle Korea
KiKi
Vogue Korea

Oceania

Elle Australia
Miss Australia Magazine
New Zealand Women's Weekly
Vogue Australia

WEBSITES

East Asia and Oceania

Air New Zealand Fashion Week. November 7, 2006. http://www.nzfashionweek.com. The official Website of New Zealand Fashion Week.
Apparel News. November 7, 2006. http://www.apparelnews.net. Regularly updated fashion and textile production news.
Asian Fashion & Apparel Accessories. November 7, 2006. http://www.fashion.ttnet.net. Regularly updated fashion and textile production news.
Australian Fashion Week. November 7, 2006. http://www.afw.com.au. The official website of *Australian Fashion Week*.
Economist Intelligence Unit. November 7, 2006. http://www.eiu.com. Regularly updated consumer statistics and forecasts.
Elle *Korea*. November 7, 2006. http://www.elle.co.kr. The official Website of the Korean version of *Elle*.
Fashion China. http://www.fashion.org.cn. Provides information about latest fashion trends in China.
Fashion in Australia. Australian Government Culture and Recreation Portal. November 7, 2006. http://www.cultureandrecreation.gov.au/articles/fashion. Government-sponsored Website promoting Australian fashion.
FashioNZ. November 7, 2006. http://www.fashionz.co.nz. A comprehensive introduction to the latest New Zealand fashion trends.
Infomat: Fashion Industry Search Engine. November 7, 2006. http://www.infomat.com. Fashion industry information services.
Japanese Streets. November 7, 2006. http://www.japanesestreets.com. This site explores Japanese street trends and includes interviews with Japanese designers and artists.
Japan Fashion Association. November 7, 2006. http://www.japanfashion.or.jp/english/index.html. The official Website of the Japanese Fashion Association.
Shanghai Tang. http://www.shanghaitang.com/shanghaitang/index.jsp. Chinese fashion lifestyle brand, with seasonal collections to view.
Thread. November 7, 2006. http://www.thread.co.nz/article/1110. New Zealand's fashion culture magazine and online store.
Tom.com. November 7, 2006. http://www.tom.com. China-related news on a wide range of topics including culture, leisure, fashion, and entertainment.

FASHION AND APPEARANCE

South and Southeast Asia

Ao Dai History. Anglo-Chinese Junior College, Singapore. Accessed November 12, 2006. http://www.acjc.edu.sg/Spectra/VibrantCulture/Vietnam/aodaihis.html.
Fashion Design Council of India. Accessed October 29, 2006. http://www.fdci.org.
IndiaMart. Accessed November 6, 2006. http://handicraft.indiamart.com/materials/textile.html.
Jackson, Peter. "Performative Genders, Perverse Desires: A Bio-History of Thailand's Same-sex and Transgender Cultures." *Intersections*, no. 9 (October 2003). Murdoch University, Australia, Internet journal. Accessed November 6, 2006. http://wwwsshe.murdoch.edu.au/intersections/issue9/jackson.html. Excellent discussion of the history of Thai clothing and appearance in relation to male and female gender roles and sexuality.
Miss World. Accessed October 28, 2006. http://www.missworld.com.
National Museum of Indonesia. Accessed November 6, 2006. http://www.museumnasional.org/textile.html.
Thailand Fashion Portal and Bangkok Shopping Guide. Accessed November 12, 2006. http://www.thailandfashion.net.

VIDEOS/FILMS

East Asia and Oceania

The Bold and the Beautiful (Australia, 1994). Depicts the world of the Australian fashion modeling industry and its commercial basis.
Chunhyang (Korea, 2000). Directed by Im Kwon-taek. A glamorous display of traditional Korean costumes.
Corset (Korea, 1996). Directed by Jung Byung-gak. Details the daily life of a Korean fashion designer, particularly her focus on losing weight.
Faces of Japan: The Fashion Model (Japan, 1988). "In Japan, models of mixed Japanese and Western heritage are prized for their exotic Western looks. Ironically, Chiharu's American/Japanese heritage has also made her an outsider in her own country."—Container.
Flowers of Shanghai (Taiwan/Japan, 1998). Directed by Hou Hsiao-hsien. Creates a picture of Shanghai fashion in the late nineteenth century.
In the Mood for Love (Hong Kong/France, 2000). Directed by Wong Kar-wai. Displays the beauty of Chinese cheongsam.
Korean Traditional Pattern (Korea, 1994). Opens with Korean-designed garments and fabric at a fashion show in Paris; also shows Korean fabric designers at work.
Lost in Translation (United States, 2003). Directed by Sofia Coppola.
Mao's New Suit (China, 1997). Directed by Sally Ingleton. Features two Chinese fashion designers who go to Shanghai to participate in a fashion show.
The Piano (New Zealand/Australia/France, 1993). Directed by Jane Campion. Shows New Zealand life in its colonial period.
Rock Kids (China, 1991). Directed by Tian Zhuangzhuang. Presents a picture of Chinese street trends and youth fashion in the 1990s.

NOTES

East Asia and Oceania

1. Niessen et al. (in Resource Guide), p. 245.
2. See Chinese Textile Industry Association Statistics, http://tongji.ctei.gov.cn/files (accessed March 1, 2007).

3. See Focus/Textile and Clothing, "Taking Stock in a Non-Quota World," http://www.aseansec.org/17306.htm (accessed March 1, 2007).
4. See "18 million Chinese adults now obese," *China Daily*, http://www.chinadaily.com.cn/english/doc/2005-04/15/content_434623.htm (accessed March 1, 2007).
5. See "Cosmetic Beautify and Benefit Beijing," *China Daily* (March 11, 1986), p. 8.
6. See "A Report of 2006 China's Cosmetics Market," http://www.ocn.com.cn/reports/2006075huazhuangpin.htm (accessed March 1, 2007).
7. See Focus/Textile and Clothing, "Taking Stock in a Non-Quota World," http://www.aseansec.org/17306.htm (accessed March 1, 2007).
8. See "Japan's cosmetics market," http://www.ruiyin.com/xwxt/list.asp?id=1609 (accessed March 1, 2007).
9. See "Japanese struggle with rising obesity rates," http://www.ctv.ca/servlet/ArticleNews/story/CTVNews/20060216/japan_obesity_060216?s_name=&no_ads (accessed March 1, 2007).
10. See *South Korea Textile Industry Statistics*, http://strategies.ic.gc.ca/epic/internet/inimr-ri3.nsf/en/gr-77931e.html (accessed March 1, 2007).
11. See "North Korean Apparel Occupies 3% of South Korea Domestic Market,"http://www.kita.net/tri/eng_tri/tri_research_viw.jsp?no=446 (accessed March 1, 2007).
12. See *Obesity Research* 12.3 (March 2004), pp. 445–453.
13. See "Trends and Challenges Relating to the Rising Incidence of Obesity," http://www.katelundy.com.au/obesity.htm (accessed March 1, 2007).
14. See "Obesity in New Zealand," http://www.moh.govt.nz/obesity (accessed March 1, 2007).
15. Margaret Maynard, "Living Dolls: The Fashion Model in Australia" (in Resource Guide).
16. See "The Australian TCF Industry—A Profile," Council of Textile and Fashion Industries of Australia, http://www.tfia.com.au (accessed March 1, 2007).
17. See Statistics New Zealand.

FILM

EAST ASIA AND OCEANIA

E. K. TAN

The motion picture is a product of modernity. After World War I, with modernization and the sudden change in social environments throughout the world, many people eagerly moved toward an industrialized, information-based, fast-moving modern life. The demands of modern life triggered the need to seek different forms of communication. The motion picture, with its characteristics that translate meanings through the universal language of the visual, naturally became the most convenient vehicle of communication in a rapidly transforming world. Hence, the motion picture offered an expedient way for the general public to adapt to the changing environment. By digesting images, people not only learned about the physical space they were in; they also learned to imagine outside the boundaries of everyday life.

The motion picture or film is more than entertainment; it is more than a mere art form. Film is an artifact of culture. The modern world has facilitated interaction between social and political communities with their diverse forms of communication; however, it also has separated communities with allegiances based on the concept of nation. Film, in some sense, functions as a mediator between the nation and the world. First, it helps a nation or an ethnic group define its identity and culture. With that as the basis, film uses its unique language of the visual to introduce that identity and culture to an outside audience.

Each of the countries in East Asia and the Oceania, with distinctive histories (often including colonialism or feudalism) and unique encounters with modernity, has constructed and is continuing to construct its own image in contrast to the others. Since the invention of film, Hollywood and Europe have been leading the industry, casting their influence over smaller regional film environments. China, one of the earliest East Asian countries to establish its film industry, was aided by U.S. experts in the profession. Japan, because of its eagerness to catch up with other developing Western nations, in particular the United States, saw filmmaking as one of the routes to that goal. Australia, following independence from the British colonial government, made films that depicted that struggle as a form of national identity construction. Historically and currently, the Hollywood filmmaking system seems to be the only standard for audiences worldwide. While working under the dominance of another culture, can cinema industries such as those in East Asian and Oceanic countries function as cultural standard-bearers to express uniqueness through visual images?

One common attempt to emerge from the dominant system has been to incorporate the film industry into the major project of nation building. Countries such as North and South Korea, China, and Taiwan all experienced stages when domestic films were made strictly for government propaganda. However, the specific manipulation of film as a political tool limited and hampered the creativity and development of the industry. An alternative was to subtly challenge Hollywood films by improvising and creating new genres and cinematic styles. Hong Kong, the Hollywood of the Far East, has been the most successful in doing so. Since the 1960s, Hong Kong has been extremely innovative with the films it has produced. From *huangmei diao* (Chinese opera genre), sword fighting, kung fu, martial arts, triad, and *mo lei tou* (nonsensical comedy) to Asian horror films, Hong Kong has not only successfully employed these genres as blockbuster formulae but also has attracted Hollywood production teams to adopt these refreshing genres and styles. Japan is another success story, with period films such as Akira Kurosawa's *Rashomon* (1950) and *The Seven Samurai* (1954). Kurosawa's unique psychological aura and visual aesthetics have inspired Hollywood remakes of the two films. Similarly, Australia has been able to entertain Hollywood and international audience with its *ocker* comedy that features a good-natured, naïve Australian male and his struggle to find the reality of life. South Korea, on the other hand, has successfully adopted the Hollywood melodrama and improvised that into its own genre.

Other countries and their directors have established international fame without having to impress Hollywood. Some directors accomplished this by participating in international film festivals. For example, Taiwanese cinema has grown tremendously over the past decades. Even though directors like Hou Hsiao-Hsien, Edward Yang, and Tsai Ming-liang are not as renowned in the United States as are Hong Kong and Mainland Chinese directors, European companies and organizations are keen financial supporters of their works. New Zealand director Jane Campion established her career in both Australia and France, first with her short film *Peel* (1982) and then with the feature *The Piano* (1993).

As the new millennium has settled in, global capital and transnational investment have taken over as the new order of the world system. This inevitably is reshaping the film industries in East Asia and Oceania. While the concept of national cinema continues to expand, with distinctive genres and styles that have originated in individual regions, filmmakers and investors are crossing national boundaries to produce high-profit and high-quality films as collaborative projects. Hong Kong/New Zealand director Peter Chan's *Perhaps Love* (2005) was jointly produced by Mainland China, Hong Kong, and Malaysia. Hong Kong director Lau Wai-keung's *Initial D.* (2005) is a film adaptation of the Japanese *manga* (comic book genre) of the same title. The film was made with a trans-East Asian cast, including Taiwanese singer-songwriter Jay Chou as well as Hong Kong and Japanese actors.

The global movement of and transactions among film industries in the regions of East Asia and Oceania offer a promising future for the industry in the next few decades. The concept of joint production has apparently pushed individual filmmakers to achieve new heights in filmmaking. Not only are they able to match up with Hollywood standards, but they also have often proven to be more innovative and courageous than their Hollywood counterparts.

The following sections separately describe the histories and characteristics of cinemas in the regions of East Asia and the Oceania.

CHINA

Shanghai, the cosmopolitan city occupied by different foreign settlements between the nineteenth and early twentieth centuries, was the starting point and center for Chinese cinema. Motion pictures were first introduced into Shanghai in 1896. However, it was not until 1905 that the first Chinese film, a Chinese opera performance, was produced. Since production studios at the turn of the century were all foreign owned, the Chinese film industry did not officially launch until 1916. With technical support and training from Western countries, particularly the United States, significant silent films such as Chen Bugao's *Spring Silkworm* (1933) were produced in the 1930s. These films not only marked the beginning of Chinese cinema, but they also functioned as vehicles to transport China to the modern era. The industry flourished almost immediately with heavy investments from two major companies, Lianhua and Mingxing. In addition to the emergence of talented directors, this golden period of Chinese cinema successfully groomed stars such as Ruan Lingyu in *The Goddess* (1934) and Zhou Xuan in *Street Angel* (1937). However, the vibrant filmmaking environment was wiped out when the Japanese invaded China in 1937. With the relocation of many actors and filmmakers to Hong Kong, the industry naturally migrated with the people.

Even though the film industry in Shanghai resumed after Japan surrendered in 1945, the city had lost its exuberance. Lianhua Film Company was reestablished along with a few other new companies, such as Wenhua and Minhua. One of the most acclaimed films in the 1940s was Fei Mu's *Springtime in a Small Town* (1948), produced by Minhua Production. Unfortunately, political intervention soon contaminated the freedom and creativity of film production. After the communists assumed power in 1949, cinema became a propaganda vehicle for the government. In addition, films from Hong Kong and Taiwan were banned or heavily censored by the communist government. Chinese cinema remained in a dormant state for several decades.

The Cultural Revolution in 1966 further hindered any potential revival of the industry. For the next decade, there was not much activity because of strict governmental regulations. However, the Cultural Revolution was not totally disruptive. A literary genre spawned by the revolution cast a strong influence on Chinese cinema beginning in the 1980s. To record the struggle of the people during the revolution, writers—one of the groups that suffered greatly during the event—started producing "scar-literature" to alleviate the pain they had experienced. Film adaptations of literary works were produced and were well received locally. Examples of such films are Xie Jin's *Tianyun Mountain* (1980) and *Hibiscus Town* (1986). The former was the winner of the Golden Rooster Award, while the latter was notably one of the most popular Chinese films at the time.

The mid-1980s saw the rise of fifth-generation Chinese directors. Like most of the U.S. "movie brats," such as George Lucas and Martin Scorsese, these Chinese directors had been formally trained at film school and had a collective identity as the avant-garde.[1]

These directors contributed greatly to Chinese cinema by introducing their films to international audiences through film festivals. Chen Kaige's *Yellow Earth* (1983) was one of the first films by the fifth-generation group that won international awards. Chen's fame extended with his subsequent films, *King of the Children* (1987) and *Farewell My Concubine* (1993). A story of forbidden love between two opera artists and their passion for art during the political upheavals in the late 1960s, *Farewell My Concubine* is the most internationally acclaimed film by Chen. Following in Chen's footsteps was his cameraman, Zhang Yimou. Zhang Yimou made his directorial debut with *Red Sorghum* in 1987. The film won the Golden Bear Award at the 1988 Berlin International Film Festival. In the United States, he is best known for his Venice Silver Lion award-winning film *Raise the Red Lantern* (1991). The film also marked the beginning of Gong Li's career as an international star. International audiences have often been fascinated by the rural settings and stereotypical culture icons in films by the fifth-generation directors, who attempted to evaluate culture and traditions through their aesthetics.

The transition to the twenty-first century was another big turning point for Chinese cinema. While the fifth-generation directors began seeking personal success on international and Hollywood platforms, the domestic scene became the experimental playground for amateur directors. Because of media censorship after the Tiananmen Square massacre in 1989, the so-called sixth-generation directors started an underground movement to produce low-budget avant-garde films that often deal with social issues in China. The raw documentary feel of these films resembles that of cinéma verité. Films such as Wang Xiaoshuai's *Beijing Bicycle* (2001), Jia Zhangke's *Platform* (2000), and Lou Ye's *Suzhou River* (2000) are products of this movement. Most of these films were not officially screened in China. Prints have sometimes been smuggled out to obtain foreign distribution rights. *Suzhou River* is one such example; a German distributor picked up rights to the film.

As the sixth-generation directors wriggled their way through to seek recognition at international film festivals, the fifth-generation directors' pursuit of the Hollywood dream did not necessarily prove fulfilling. For example, Chen Kaige's Hollywood thriller *Killing Me Softly* (2002) never played in a theater in the United States. To cater to the audience taste for blockbusters, Zhang Yimou produced two visually fascinating films with extremely weak plots: *Hero* (2002) and *House of Flying Daggers* (2004). Zhang's unique storytelling talent was reserved for Asian productions, such as *Riding Alone for Thousands of Miles* (2005).

HONG KONG

The film industry in Hong Kong began a little later in the 1930s than did the industry in Shanghai. Language was not an issue at the time since productions were still within the silent film era. With the outbreak of World War II, however, the industry was temporarily affected. Because Hong Kong was then a British colony, it did not suffer as much as Shanghai, which had to cope with the aftermath of World War II and civil wars.

By the early 1950s, the Hong Kong film industry resumed its productivity by collaborating with the Singapore-based production studio, Shaw Brothers. At that time, talent was in excess: many local filmmakers had returned to the industry after the war; in addition, there were also filmmakers who had fled to the colony from Shanghai during the war. The unique background provided Hong Kong cinema great diversity in form and content. As a result, several genres evolved over the years. The two most popular genres produced by Shaw Brothers were *wuxia pian* (sword-fighting genre) and *huangmei diao* (Chinese opera genre). Not only was filmmaking diverse in terms of genre at that time, but Chinese cinema was also not defined specifically by language. Films were made in both Mandarin and Cantonese, depending on genre. For example, most Cantonese films were melodramas.

As a keen competitor to Shaw Brothers, Golden Harvest Studio launched another popular genre in the 1970s. The kung fu genre, starring Bruce Lee, was not only a sensation in Asia; it traversed cultures and languages to mesmerize the international audience. Bruce Lee's career was short lived; although he died in 1973, his legendary role as a kung fu hero lingers on.

One of the most prominent directors during the period was Shaw Brothers' King Hu. His period piece *Kingdom and the Beauty* (1959) and his martial arts classic *Dragon Gate Inn* (1966), even though not officially released in the United States, were participating films at significant events such as the San Francisco Film Festival. The screening of *Dragon Gate Inn* was a major event not only for local Chinese but also for American moviegoers. The sacred status of the martial arts genre has been affirmed by the contemporary regeneration of the genre through pioneer Ang Lee's international blockbuster *Crouching Tiger, Hidden Dragon* (2000).

One unique trait of Hong Kong cinema is the studio system. In the 1980s, a group of new directors emerged from this system. Unlike Hollywood and European directors of the same period, these directors were not formally trained. They matured as directors through practical training in different areas of studio production, particularly as stuntmen. One such example is Yuen Wo-ping, the director of Jackie Chan's *Drunken Master* (1978). The success of the *Drunken Master* series prepared Jackie Chan for his Hollywood career and also groomed him as yet another director to benefit from the studio system. In 1983 Chan embarked on his first directorial project, the film *Project A*. The credit for the film's success goes to the hardcore action scenes Chan choreographed and performed on his own. The Asian hit also marked a new chapter in Chan's career as the modern action hero in Hong Kong cinema.

Emerging around the same period were directors who had been formally trained in foreign film institutes. The most acclaimed female director in Hong Kong, Ann Hui, spent two years at the London Film Institute before returning to Hong Kong. Hui's works were geared more toward melodrama and focused on the plight of ordinary Hong Kong people, especially women. Hui's best film, *Boat People* (1982), is a survey of the life of the boat people, which was an important aspect of Hong Kong history and identity.

Expounding on Chinese culture and history, director Tsui Hark examined identity by invoking legends and historical tales. A film graduate from the University of Texas–Austin, Tsui experimented with different genres in the industry until he came up with his own unique style: swordplay and martial arts fantasy. Tsui's popular works are *Zu: Warriors of the Magic Mountain* (1979), *A Chinese Ghost Story* (1987), and *Once Upon a Time* (1991). Jet Li's acting career took flight with the *Once Upon a Time* series.

In 1986 John Woo thrilled Asia with the triad movie, *A Better Tomorrow*. Woo's unique style soon caught the attention of Hollywood production companies. Companies such as 20th Century Fox and Touchstone Pictures had worked directly with Woo. Woo mesmerized the American audience with his trademark slow-motion sequences in *Broken Arrow* (1996) and *Face/Off* (1997), which latter became a popular trend incorporated into films such as *The Matrix* (1999). The success of *A Better Tomorrow* triggered excitement in the industry to produce more films under the triad-action genre. The genre soon became a trademark of Hong Kong cinema. Michelle Yeoh, one of the top Asian actresses in Hollywood, was groomed as an action star in such films.

As the industry became saturated with action and gore, Stephen Chow appeared with his mo lei tou (nonsensical) comedy. Chow's comedy came to the fore when Hollywood films were becoming more and more popular to the Hong Kong audience. After appearing in several comedies and creating his personal trademark performance, Chow began his directorial career with films such as *From Beijing with Love* (1994) and *The God of Cookery* (1997). Chow's popularity in the 1990s became apparent as his mo lei tou language and style greatly influenced different generations across East Asia.

Unfortunately, the Hong Kong film industry endured a huge crisis at the time of the handover of the island from the British government to Mainland China in 1997. An identity crisis haunted Hong Kong people to such an extent that even Stephen Chow's farcical performance and nonsensical jokes could not alleviate the anxiety of feeling rootless and disconnected. As a result, local productions mostly failed to sell; disillusioned directors left the industry, and some left the country. The only surviving group was the New Wave filmmakers, who received consistent support from international and art house audiences. The most internationally acclaimed among the group is Wong Kar-wai. With the aid of Quentin Tarantino's distribution company, Wong successfully invaded the U.S. market with *Chungking Express* (1994). The film was regarded as a classic postmodern film and is often taught in college film classes. Released in year 2000, his *In the Mood for Love* created another round of excitement when it premiered at the Cannes Film Festival. Wong's film captures the beauty of a chance encounter and the helpless displacement of feelings and identity.

As people in Hong Kong became accustomed to the new government, new studios, such as Milkyway Image Productions, were established to revitalize the once-vibrant industry. Different strategies were employed to help not only the domestic scene but also the general filmmaking environment in East Asia. Films such as the romantic comedy *The Truth about Jane and Sam* (1999) and the horror film *The Eye* (2002) were co-produced by Hong Kong and Singapore. Besides obtaining funding support from Southeast Asia, Hong Kong productions also began exploring the market and partnership possibilities in Mainland China. Peter Chan's *Perhaps Love* (2005), starring popular Hong Kong singer Jackie Cheung, mainland actress Zhou Xun, Korean soap opera star and Taiwanese/Japanese heartthrob Takeshi Kaneshiro, was a trans-East Asia project produced by Mainland China, Hong Kong, and Malaysia. This type of joint production creates an internal support system within Asia to counter Hollywood imports.

Between 2002 and 2003, the police thriller *Internal Affairs* trilogy became a huge commercial success in Asia. The success tempted Hollywood director Martin Scorsese to remake the film in 2006 under the title *The Departed,* which stars Leonardo DiCaprio and Matt Damon. The film won the Best Film Award at the 2007 Oscars.

The surprise return of Stephen Chow in 2001 with *Shaolin Soccer* proved that Chow's mo lei tou comedy was still widely loved by the general public. Miramax picked up the DVD for U.S. distribution. As a result, the film attracted a group of cult followers. *Kung Fu Hustle* (2004) even created a competition between Miramax and Columbia Pictures for the commercial screening rights of the film in the United States.

In general, Hong Kong cinema at present shows signs of merging with the mainland industry, emphasizing the trend of co-production.

TAIWAN

Taiwanese cinema can be dated as earlier as in 1920s during the Japanese colonial era. Two significant films of the period are *The Eyes of Buddha* (1922) and *Whose Fault Is It?* (1925). The industry was forced to a halt when the Sino-Japanese War broke out in 1937. It was not revived until the Kuomintang (KMT), the nationalist party led by Chiang Kai-shek, took over the island in 1945.

Under Republic of China administration, the movie industry in Taiwan produced mainly Mandarin films that were carefully sanctioned by the KMT Party. Production of Taiwanese- and Hakka-language films was not encouraged by the government, especially with Chiang Kai-shek's proclamation of Mandarin as the official language. As a result, dialect films were gradually phased out of the industry.

In the 1960s, the Taiwanese film industry supported the government's ideology of modernizing the country. In order to promote economic and industrial development, the Central Motion Picture Corporation (CMPC) adopted the melodrama genre in films to inject the belief in traditional values as the basis for the rapid development of the society and its economy. Two other important genres of the time were the conventional kung fu movies and the romantic melodramas adapted from the novels of the renowned author Qiong Yao.

In the 1980s, Taiwan underwent a huge political and social change. After approximately 30 years of martial law under the KMT government, the Taiwanese people were suddenly subjected to a new landscape of advanced technology, urban culture, and exploding informatics. The change inevitably brought about a revolution in the island's film industry. Transiting to a new era, Taiwanese cinema looked eagerly to the future as a way to break away from history. Taiwanese New Cinema evolved as the embodiment of creative aesthetic sensibility and nativist identity discourse. The termination of martial law in Taiwan triggered a sense of political and national anxiety in the society, arousing a collective desire to reshape the nation's history. A significant product of such change in political and social climate in the film industry was Hou Hsiao-hsien's *A City of Sadness*, a film released in 1989. *A City of Sadness* delineates the role of Taiwanese cinema as a cultural marker for a nation in the making by invoking history and reconstructing memories.

The haunting effect of historical instability encouraged filmmakers to engage in childhood-related themes. While lamenting the passing of time, such themes manipulate memories as content for nativist and realist representations. This cinematic style in Taiwanese cinema was transported from the 1980s to the 1990s. Some examples of nativist films produced in the 1990s are Edward Yang's *A Bright Summer Day* (1990), Wang Tung's *Hill of No Return* (1992), and Wu Nien-Jen's *A Borrowed Life* (1994). The unique style manifests visual representations of realism to map individual memories onto the greater history of the collective.

Even though realism was a dominant form of filmic representation in the 1990s, prominent filmmakers, including Hou Hsiao-hsien, often challenged it. The lack of creative flexibility in realist representation hindered Taiwanese cinema from advancing technically and aesthetically. Filmmakers began questioning the depiction of historical memory as a result of evolving discourses on historical truth and the pursuit of artistic sensibility in filmmaking. As a pioneer promoting Taiwanese cinema as historical genre, Hou Hsiao-hsien evolved in the 1990s to illuminate the discrepancies in the form. By dwelling on the dialectical representation of the tension between past and present, reality and fantasy, historical memory and history reconstruction, Hou succeeded in balancing historical realism and postmodern dialectics in films such as *The Puppetmaster* (1993) and *Flowers of Shanghai* (1998). This balance can often be identified as nostalgic sentiment.

A successor of Hou's film aesthetics is Stan Lai. Lai holds a doctorate from the University of California–Berkeley in dramatic art. His background as a stage director allows him to experiment with complicated and innovative spatial and temporal structures in order to compose a text of multiple meanings. In his debut film, *The Peach Blossom Land* (1993), he intermingled reality with history and mythology to address the contradictory yet complementary relationship between performing arts and real life, and the ambiguous relationship between Taiwan and Mainland China.

The aura of nativism in Taiwanese cinema waned as the country proceeded further into the decade. As politics and economics merged to form the country's absurd and chaotic social reality in the 1990s, popular culture generated a series of mesmerizing images that promoted a consumption culture. This environment further enhanced the sense of helplessness produced by the degeneration of ethical and moral beliefs toward the end of the millennium. Ubiquitous was an urban culture encroached upon by a suffocating atmosphere of decadence and hedonism. Isolation, anxiety, and everyday threats from the environment became daily concerns. This social backdrop inevitably became materials for Taiwanese filmmakers of the time. No longer using long shots and long takes just to capture visual unity and nostalgic imagination, Hou used these techniques to create images evoking the violence of helplessness and isolation.

FILM

> ### ACTRESS ZHANG ZIYI
>
> The face of China's twenty-first century transnational cinema is Zhang Ziyi. Beautiful, confident, multitalented, and fluent in English, Zhang is known for her roles in martial arts blockbusters such as *Crouching Tiger, Hidden Dragon*, *Hero*, and *House of Flying Daggers*. She also appeared in Wong Kar-wai's internationally acclaimed *2046*, and she starred in Rob Marshall's visually sumptuous *Memoirs of a Geisha*.

Goodbye South, Goodbye (1996) is an example of the haunting anxiety of helplessness at the end of a millennium. On the other hand, directors such as Chen Yu-hsun (*Tropical Fish*, 1995) and Wang Hsiao-di (*My Mental Illness*, 1997) preferred using montage as their approach to juxtapose experiences that were disjointed and absurd. The schizophrenic visual structure mirrored the experience of identifiable anxiety by the audience.

The films of Tsai Ming-liang, a Malaysian-Chinese director based in Taiwan, are evident representatives of the Taiwan New Cinema, which focuses on the themes of alienation and identity crisis. Tsai's films carry a worldview that embodies concerns about global issues and experience through minimalist form and claustrophobic themes. Even though Tsai's films have not been commercially successful in the local market, his international recognition has attracted foreign investment. After winning the Golden Lion at the Venice International Film Festival for *Vive l'amour* in 1994, Tsai's subsequent films, such as *The Hole* (1998), *What Time Is It There?* (2001), and *The Wayward Cloud* (2005), were funded by France. While investigating global themes and contemporary issues, these films pay tributes to film history in their own ways: *The Hole* uses music to display the desire to escape dystopia; *What Time Is It There?* celebrates *The 400 Blows,* the iconic work of François Truffaut; and *The Wayward Cloud* examines the relationship between avant-garde genre and pornography.

By focusing on the degeneration of social relationships in urban settings, Tsai foresees the inevitable human tragedy of ultimate isolation. Edward Yang, another internationally renowned Taiwanese director, sees the breaking down of social relationships, particularly within the family, as an effect of the traditions and values promoted by Confucianism. Yang's films are mostly satires that criticize the inflexible and suffocating teachings. *Yi Yi: A One and a Two* (2000), a film co-produced by Japan, questions the pretensions of traditions and the modern society built upon superficial relationships through the eyes of the naïve, untainted eight-year-old Yang Yang.

Trained in the United States at New York University in film studies, internationally acclaimed director Ang Lee did not establish his career with Hollywood productions. His debut film, *Pushing Hand* (1992), and the subsequent films *The Wedding Banquet* (1993) and *Eat, Drink, Man Woman* (1994) were winners of Government Information Office of the Republic of China (Taiwan) awards for screenplay. With the success of *The Wedding Banquet* in the United States and the applause for *Eat, Drink, Man and Woman* at numerous international film festivals, Ang Lee proceeded to the Hollywood scene with award-winning films such as *Sense and Sensibility* (1995), *The Ice Storm* (1997), and the controversial *Brokeback Mountain* (2005). Ang Lee's iconic film is the martial art film of the new millennium: *Crouching Tiger, Hidden Dragon* (2000). The film marked an important phase of contemporary Asian cinema, for it rejuvenated the martial arts genre, and in addition, it pioneered the trend of transnational production of Asian cinema with funds from Taiwan, Hong Kong, China, and the United States. The unique style of Ang Lee's film involves strong narratives, extravagant settings, mesmerizing scenery, and an Eastern philosophical aura. Not only is the combination refreshing for international audiences, but it also manages to strike a balance between popular culture and high art.

With the efforts of Hou Hsiao-hsien, Edward Yang, Tsai Ming-liang, and Ang Lee to introduce Taiwanese cinema to international audiences, newcomers such as Lin Cheng-sheng, Chang Tso-chi, and Chen Kuo-fu are working beyond the boundaries of the island in an attempt to further their potential in filmmaking.

JAPAN

Japanese cinema can be traced back to 1904 with the emergence of film studios. The development of Japanese cinema was curbed at two different times: first with the Tokyo earthquake in 1932, and second, after World War II when Japan surrendered to the United States. The American occupation of Japan further hampered the production potential of prominent Japanese directors.

Japanese cinema regained its energy and began to hit its peak after the end of the American occupation and the signing of the San Francisco Peace Treaty in 1951. Six production companies gradually emerged. Besides the production of films in two main genres, historical (*jidai-geki*) films and contemporary (*gendai-geki*) modern films, Japanese cinema at that time also consisted of films identified by popular American genres. Even though historical films required higher production costs and involved extravagant sets and costumes, Japanese companies preferred making films of this genre since they were commercial successes in local and in international spheres. The period piece that introduced Japanese cinema to the world was internationally acclaimed director Akira Kurosawa's classic *Rashomon* (1951). The film was the winner of Best Film at the Venice International Film Festival. Unlike what happens with most foreign films that are distributed by Hollywood currently, the Daiei Motion Picture Company was able to secure the rights to distribute its own films. This marked the unique structure of the Japanese film industry of the time as independent from Hollywood, despite a considerable degree of genre and pop-cultural influence. The year 1954 marked the first official introduction of Japanese cinema to the U.S. audience with the screening of Kurosawa's *Seven Samurai*, which was remade a few years later by John Sturges into *The Magnificent Seven* (1960).

Even though Japanese cinema was much influenced by Hollywood genres (for example, the western in the 1961 classic *The Bodyguard*), Japanese films were distinctively different from Hollywood films: they focused more on the psychological development of characters (an influence of European cinemas) instead of action. Mood and atmosphere were crucial as they supported the overall tone of such films. The mood and tone usually suffused from the unique mise-en-scène and cinematography put together by directors who were influenced by the sensibility of oriental art. In addition, especially in the case of the historical genre, conventional acting styles were often incorporated into Japanese films; for example, the use of Noh features and Kabuki characters in Kurosawa's period pieces combines a traditional popular style with the new media. A classic example is *Throne of Blood* (1957), an adaptation of Shakespeare's *Macbeth*; Kurosawa transformed Lady Macbeth into a Kabuki character. Each of her appearances involves a Noh performance. Kurosawa's contribution to film history was not limited to Japanese cinema; he influenced and inspired later filmmakers all over the world with his style and works.

Equally acclaimed is Kenji Mizoguchi, who invested most of his energy in making historical films. After making films for approximately two decades, Mizoguchi finally received international attention with *The Life of O'Haru* (1952), the winner of the grand prize at the Venice International Film Festival. Another prominent director under Daiei Motion Picture, Mizoguchi was a master of tracking shots. He used this cinematographic style to capture details of human behavior, specifically that of female characters. Unlike the masculine aura of Kurosawa's film, Mizoguchi's period pieces adopt sympathetic positions for the female gender through the depiction of their suppression by social and familial conventions.

Another master of Japanese cinema is Yasujiro Ozu, who chose to work solely on contemporary pieces. In terms of style and cinematography, Ozu deliberately challenged Hollywood conventions. Most of his films involved direct cuts, extra long shots, and narrative breaks. Often, the camera sits at eye level, assuming the role of an observer. The mood of Ozu's film is commonly described by Japanese cinema scholars with the term "mono no aware," which implies the impermanence of earthly things. Hence, the theme of change is easily recognized in the content of his films and even in their titles. One of the examples is *Late Spring* (1949). *Tokyo Story* (1953) is another one of Ozu's masterpieces.

In addition to the historical and modern genres, popular genres such as science fiction and gangster films also began to evolve in the 1950s and 1960s. In 1954 Ishiro Honda created an international frenzy over his monster hit *Godzilla*. The legend of *Godzilla* has been perpetuated over the years. Toho Film Company, the creator of *Godzilla*, has made over twenty *Godzilla* films since 1954, and the series has become an icon of Japanese popular culture for most U.S. audiences. Even as recently as 1998, the U.S. TriStar Pictures released a version of *Godzilla* set in contemporary New York, extending the popularity and influence of the Godzilla culture.

Between the 1960s and 1970s, a group of avant-garde directors emerged in Japan. Following in the footsteps of the French New Wave members, directors like Shohei Imamura began a movement to produce Japanese New Wave films that attempted to capture the modernist mode of visual sensation. Imamura's films are often invested in exploring human behavior and civilization as corresponding to other forms of life, such as that of insects and fish. Such modernist concerns are depicted in his classic film and Palme d'Or winner *The Eel* (1997). Another of his internationally recognized films, *Black Rain* (1988), surveys the consequences of modern world atrocities through the catastrophic event of the Hiroshima bombing.

Similar to the experience of other national cinemas, Japanese cinema underwent a period of crisis with the popularization of color television sets in the late 1970s and early 1980s. Many potential movie-goers chose to stay home instead of patronizing the theaters.

Japanese cinema took a rather interesting turn at the beginning of this century. Cinema as popular culture is represented by the innovative genre of animation. *Animé*, the Japanese term for animation, suddenly became the pop-culture icon for anyone who was interested in Japanese culture. Most animé films came from comic book materials known as manga. International sensations over animé began with the exportation of films like Manoru Oshii's *Ghost in the Shell* (1995) and Hayao Miyazaki's *Princess Monoke* (1997). Japanese animé is unique in the sense that the film is crafted with hand-drawn storyboards as the main material, while computer-generated effects are used as enhancing tools. In 2003, when the Oscar for Best Animation was given to Miyazaki's *Spirited Away* (2001), the film immediately became a household name in the United States. Because of Miyazaki's international fame, Buena Vista Pictures offered to produce his subsequent projects. The phenomenon of *Spirited Away* created another peak moment of Japanese animé films.

In addition to the stir created by Japanese animé in the United States, the sudden outburst of Japanese horror films in the late 1990s and early years of this century not only hit blockbuster charts in Asia but captured U.S. production companies' interest in the profitable genre. The biggest sensation, *Ringu* (1998), was remade with a Hollywood cast in 2002. Not only were American audiences excited by the remake, but the original Japanese version was also soon released on DVD for curious viewers.

Meanwhile, the Japanese gangster genre was revitalized internationally as an art house genre. Kitano Takeshi's *Zatoichi* (2003) won the Best Film award at the 2003 Venice Film Festival. The film is a remake of the popular TV series from the 1960s and 1970s.

KOREA

The sudden growth in Korean Cinema at the turn of the millennium has attracted great international attention. Not only were Korean films such as *Oldboy* (2003) and *Spring, Summer, Fall, Winter . . . and Spring* (2003) favorites at international film festivals, but films such as *My Sassy Girl* (2001) and *Oasis* (2002) were also blockbuster hits all over Asia. The breakthrough of Korean cinema after decades of slow development has Hollywood eyeing opportunities to profit from the growing global fever. With a history of remaking foreign films, Hollywood has chosen to remake Korean films to accommodate the U.S. audience rather than directly importing them. The remakes are, after all, not low-budget projects. For example, *The Lake House* (2006), a remake of Lee Hyun-seong's *Siworae* (2000) was directed by Argentinian director Alejandro Agresti and starred A-list U.S. actors Keanu Reeves and Sandra Bullock. The remake of the 2001 Asian movie sensation *My Sassy Girl*, originally directed by Kwak Jae-young, is scheduled for release in 2007 by Dreamworks.

The commercial success of Korean cinema is not at all incidental. Korean cinema underwent several stages of transformation. Between 1926 and 1935, the industry hit its peak with the production of high-quality silent films. This period is considered the golden age of Korean cinema. In 1935 the first sound film, *Chunhyang Jeon*, was produced by director Lee Myeong Woo, putting a halt to the era of silent film in Korea. At the same time, the ruling Japanese government imposed censorship on silent films and attempted to use film as propaganda. In 1942 the use of the Korean language was banned in Korean films, leading to the sudden decline of the industry.

The end of World War II liberated Korea from Japanese rule. The film industry was revived; however, films made at the time were only concerned with the end of colonial rule. Furthermore, the split of the country into North Korea and South Korea and the civil war in 1950 did not in anyway accelerate the revival of the film industry in the region. Even though production was never totally halted, not many films were made during this chaotic time.

Finally, between the late 1950s and early 1960s, Korean cinema enjoyed a second moment of glamour, which was known to many as "the second golden age" of Korean cinema. To revitalize the local film industry, South Korean president Lee Seung-man had given tax exemptions to the industry. In 1955 director Lee Kyu-hwan released his remake of *Chunhyang Jeon*, attracting a total of 200,000 over South Korea to theaters in a span of two months. In the same year, distinguished South Korean director Kim Ki-young launched his decades-long career with *Yang San Island* and *Box of Death*.

Without much financial constraint, Korean cinema began to mature in quality in the late 1950s and 1960s. Approximately 100 films were produced each year during the period. Two of the best Korean films made at the time were Kim Ki-young's *The Housemaid* (1960) and Yoo Hyun-mok's *The Aimless Bullet* (1960).

The Korean film industry experienced another transformation when Park Chung-hee became South Korea's president in 1962. Taking over Lee Seung-man's power after Lee was forced to leave his presidency, Park soon implemented the Motion Picture Law in 1963. The law consisted of a series of regulations that involved an inflexible quota system and stringent censorship that controlled the depiction of violence, obscenity, and communist themes.

FILM

Film production decreased from approximately seventy a year to fifteen after the law was passed. Fortunately, even though the production number dropped tremendously, the quality of the films was maintained.

The 1970s was one of the toughest times for Korean cinema. Beginning in 1973, Korean film was the equivalent of propaganda films under Park's government. Films produced then were known as "policy films"; they were not very popular with the general Korean audience, who were used to going to movie theaters to escape momentarily from reality. Similar to what happened in the United States in the 1960s, the introduction of home television also affected the local Korean film industry.

Korean cinema finally began to move away from the shadow of Park's government control toward the end of the 1970s with the assassination of Park Chung-hee and political events such as the coup d'état of December 12, 1979, which led to the Gwangju Massacre in 1980. Censorship and stern regulations were loosening as South Korea embarked on the route to democracy. It was almost at the same time that South Korean films became popular at international film festivals, mainly though the works of Im Kwon-taek. Even though Im's career had begun in 1962, it did not take flight until 1981 when his film *Mandala* received international acclaim. Im was often seen as a commercial director who made art house films. Im's films focus on issues relating to the modern Korean identity, a characteristic easily identified by the general population in South Korea. His biggest contribution to the industry has been his role in promoting the movement known as the New Korean Cinema. In 2000 he released another film version of the Korean legend *Chunhyang*, a significant work that explores the cultural identity of the Korean people. Like most of Im's films, the film was both a huge domestic and international success, and an art house favorite.

Even though South Korean cinema regained its vibrancy with the removal of government control, the opening of the local market to foreign films, particularly from the United States and Hong Kong, did not help the reception of local productions. This situation persisted through the 1980s and 1990s.

The year 1999 was a turning point for Korean cinema. The release of Kang Je-gyu's *Shiri* in 1999 was a box office success that exceeded records set by foreign imports such as *Titanic*. The film's success in local markets was a big encouragement to the Korean film industry. Focusing on similar themes relating to the ambiguous relationship between South Korea and North Korea and the suffering of the people caught up in the political and social chaos, Kang went on to direct another equally renowned film *The Brotherhood of the War* [*Taegukgi*] (2004). *Shiri* tells the story of a North Korean spy as she executes her mission in Seoul, while *The Brotherhood of the War* is a tale about two brothers during the Korean War.

In 2000 Park Chan-wook's *JSA* not only outsold Hollywood films screening at the same time but defeated the remarkable blockbuster record set a year earlier by *Shiri*. The following year, the comedy *My Sassy Girl* (2001), directed by Kwak Jae-young, topped the blockbuster chart, outshining films such as *The Lord of the Ring: The Fellowship of the Ring* and *Harry Potter and the Sorcerer's Stone*.

The blockbuster potential of Korean films produced at the turn of the millennium immediately caught the attention of Hollywood production companies such as Miramax, Warner Brothers, and Dreamworks. As a result, remakes of some of these Korean blockbusters have recently been released, and others are currently in production.

The international attention received by Korean film in the twenty-first century so far has not stopped the industry from pursuing the common themes of Korean cultural identity and the sentiments surrounding the split of the peninsula. While securing these unique traits, Korean cinema wants to further explore social issues using different genres and forms. Lee Chang-dong's *Oasis* (2002), winner of the second prize at the 2002 Venice Film Festival, is acknowledged as a representative work of Korean avant-garde film. The film focuses on the struggle of the handicapped everyman in negotiating between social and cultural expectations in life. Other examples are Park Chan-wook's Cannes Film Festival winner *Oldboy* (2003), a loose adaptation of Dumas's *The Count of Monte Cristo*, and 54th Berlin International Film Festival best director Kim Ki-duk's story of an adolescent prostitute titled *Samaritan Girl* (2004).

AUSTRALIA

The persistent domination of Hollywood films over the local industry triggered the Australian government to intervene in local film projects beginning in the 1970s. A government fund was created to support amateur filmmakers with their work; a media school focusing solely on film and television production was built to offer young artists with proper training in the field; and a national organization was formed to supply initial funds for film productions. These earlier stages of Australian cinema were part of the national culture-production process. Hence, most Australian filmmakers tended to focus on content relating to local history and cultural heritage, including both the settlement and the indigenous history and culture.

A common film genre that evolved at the time was the ocker comedy. Ocker refers to Australian English that came into being with the formation of the New South Wales in 1788, and its transformation through different stages of immigration history. Ocker comedy as a genre depicts the odyssey of a male character who experiences emotional and sexual tensions throughout the film. Such characters are usually down-to-earth, naïve, and good-natured Australians who play off ocker humor onscreen. Bruce Beresford's *The Adventures of Barry Mckenzie* (1972) is an example of early ocker comedy. Ocker comedy achieved its first international attention with Peter Faiman's *Crocodile Dundee* (1986), starring Paul Hogan. The film not only cast Paul Hogan as the naïve, down-to-earth Australian man but also depicted his challenges in adapting to the complicated city environment of New York for a week. This contrast illuminates the characteristics of the genre. Not only was the film the biggest box office success in Australia, beating Hollywood imports, but it also soared internationally, especially in the United States.

Emerging at the same period was the auteur-oriented art and period genre. Two representative pieces are Ken Hannam's *Sunday Too Far Away* (1975) and Peter Weir's *Picnic at Hanging Rock* (1975). A participant of the Cannes Film Festival, *Sunday Too Far Away* challenged conventional Hollywood themes and narratives. The story portrays the people who worked with cattle and sheep in the Australian outback, focusing on their struggles with their working conditions and their exploitative owner. Even though the film was officially released in the United Kingdom in the late 1970s, it was far from a success. Earning a different fate was Peter Weir's *Picnic at Hanging Rock*. Unlike the vulgar style of ocker comedy, *Picnic at Hanging Rock*, an adaptation of Joan Lindsay's eponymous novel, deals with subjects relating to upper-middle-class female characters in the late nineteenth century when Australia achieved independence from Britain. With support from the Australian Film Commission, Weir's task with *Picnic at Hanging Rock* was to define the cultural standards and endorse the Australian heritage through visual culture. The success of *Picnic at Hanging Rock* made Weir one of the core directors of the new Australian cinema. Before moving his career to Hollywood in 1980s, Weir produced other significant works that outlined different aspects of Australian history; these included *The Last Wave* (1977), a film on issues concerning the aboriginal people and native mythology, and *Gallipoli* (1981), a film depicting Australia's role in World War II. In Hollywood, Weir is best known for his films *Dead Poets' Society* (1989), *Green Card* (1990), and *The Truman Show* (1998). Even though content-wise Weir has departed from the genre of national cinema, his thematic trademark has always been consistent. Weir's films usually involve the struggle of an individual or a minority to cope with a changing or conflicting cultural and social environment.

A popular genre that evolved in Australia in the 1980s is the sci-fi/action thriller represented by George Miller's *Mad Max* series (1979, 1981, and 1985), starring Mel Gibson. The film is set in a dystopian future and involves the epic journey of Max, a police officer, to avenge his family. For decades the film was the holder of the Guinness record as the highest cost-to-profit-ratio film until the release of *The Blair Witch Project* in 2000. Unlike *Crocodile Dundee*, the series was dubbed and dialogues altered when the *Mad Max* movies were released in the United States. The success of the film established a long-lasting international career for the Australian star Gibson.

Like Peter Weir and others who left for Hollywood in the 1980s, Gillian Armstrong touched international audience with her *Little Women* in 1994. Armstrong, however, is one of the few who returned home to further her directorial dreams. Launching her career with *My Brilliant Career* in the 1970s, a film of the feminist genre, Armstrong returned to make films that integrate women's role in the construction of national and culture history. Two unique examples are *Oscar and Lucinda* (1997), the story of an Australian heiress played by Cate Blanchett (*Elizabeth*, 1998), and *Unfolding Florence* (2005), the story of Australian handprinted wallpaper artist Florence Broadhurst.

In 2001 *Moulin Rouge* earned Australian director Baz Luhrmann international fame for his flamboyant mise-en-scène, music video cinematography, and postmodern style. The film also relaunched Australian actress Nicole Kidman's career as an international star through the joint Australian/U.S. production. Luhrmann's success, however, can be traced back to his Australian debut with *Strictly Ballroom* (1992), an acclaimed film at the Cannes Film Festival. His Hollywood debut film *Romeo and Juliet*, like *Moulin Rouge*, has become a cultural icon since its release in 1996, attracting a large number of young cult fans.

NEW ZEALAND

New Zealand cinema came to the foreground in recent years with Peter Jackson's *The Lord of the Rings* trilogy (2001-03) and Niki Caro's short film *Whale Rider* (2002). The New Zealand government followed the example of the Australian government and formed the New Zealand Film Commission to finance local filmmakers with their projects. Directors who have benefited from the commission and produced internationally acclaimed films include Roger Donaldson (*Smash Palace*, 1982), Lee Tamahori (*Once Were Warriors*, 1994), and Niki Caro (*Whale Rider*).

New Zealand filmmaker Jane Campion won the 1993 Cannes Festival Palme D'Or for her film *The Piano*. Trained at the Australian Film Television and Radio School, Campion was the winner of the Palme D'Or in 1982 for her short film *Peel*. The initial success provided her with international support: *The Piano*, co-produced by Australia, France, and New Zealand, is one such example. Campion's film concerns issues relating to female sexuality and roles in a male-oriented society. Like Australian female director Gillian Armstrong, Campion's films often weave history, culture, and landscape together through the experience of women as seen in *An Angel at My Table* (1990). In 1996 Campion presented her audience with her first Hollywood project, *The Portrait of a Lady*. The success of the film was minimal. Her subsequent films were joint productions among the United States, the United Kingdom, France, Australia, and New Zealand.

The pinnacle of New Zealand Cinema is none other than Peter Jackson's *The Lord of the Rings* trilogy. Before the trilogy, Jackson was known for *Heavenly Creatures* (1994). The achievement of the trilogy affirms the status of New Zealand cinema. Not only were the films shot in New Zealand and produced by a New Zealand director, but the production team and the technical and technological support were also mostly from the region. Even though the trilogy was mainly funded by the United States, the international film series demonstrated the fact that New Zealand has the resources to make its own movies.

SOUTH AND SOUTHEAST ASIA

WIMAL DISSANAYAKE

INTRODUCTION

In the course of the twentieth century, films became a vital part of the lives of the people of South and Southeast Asia. National film industries appeared and grew quite rapidly in this region of the world, particularly after World War II and the withdrawal of European colonial powers. The evolution of indigenous cinema in various Asian languages meant that this medium began to reflect as well as shape (and reshape) local and national cultures extensively and in diverse and unpredictable ways. At the same time, as radio and television broadcasting, print and electronic communication, and satellite and cable transmission entered successive phases of development and became more widespread, South and Southeast Asian societies found themselves in close cultural contact with other parts of the globe to an unprecedented degree. By the beginning of this century, American, European, and Asian films had produced a fresh mix in cultural spaces stretching from Pakistan and India to Indonesia and the Philippines. One of the outcomes of this process is that cinema in many forms has become an essential ingredient in the popular culture of most Asian nations today.

Among the national film industries in South and Southeast Asia, the industry in India is the oldest and largest. Over the past several decades, Indian films have had a profound impact not only on the subcontinent, but also on countries such as Malaysia, Indonesia, and Thailand (which have been influenced by India—and also by China—for centuries). Any analysis of Asian cinema, and of cinema in Asia more broadly, must therefore begin with a discussion of the Indian film industry, which continues to play a transnational role in the region.

FILM

SOUTH ASIA

India

The Indian film industry is the largest in the world, producing an average of 800 films every year now in about twenty languages and reaching hundreds of millions of viewers in India and across the subcontinent, as well as in various parts of the world, from Asia and Africa to Europe and the Americas. Cinema, of course, is a form and a medium that was originally "imported" into India from the West. The Lumière brothers showed their epoch-making film, *Workers Leaving the Factory*, in Paris in March 1895, and thus inaugurated the art of cinema in its commercially viable form. The Lumière company organized the first film screening in India, which took place at Watson's Hotel in Bombay (now Mumbai) on July 7, 1896. European filmmakers, who saw the potential of India as an attractive location for film-making, shot several films there in the early years of the medium: among them, *Coconut Fair* (1897), *Our Indian Empire* (1897), *A Panorama of Indian Scenes and Processions* (1898), and *Poona Races '98* (1898, filmed at the famous colonial Poona Race Course, in what is now Pune). Since these exotic beginnings, India has adapted and absorbed film to the point where it has become a medium of art, communication, and entertainment all its own.

Around the turn of the twentieth century, a number of Indian artists and entrepreneurs were already keen to use the new art of cinematography to tell Indian stories. Dhundiraj Govind Phalke emerged as the pioneer among them, and he is generally regarded as the father of Indian cinema. He screened his first film, *Raja Harishcandra*, an entirely Indian production, on May 3, 1913. It was an immediate success, paving the way for the genre of "mythological films" that is central to popular Indian cinema. The first feature film made in south India was R. N. Mudaliar's *Kichaka Vadham* [The Killing of Kichaka] (1917). Both these inaugural films took their material from the two great Sanskrit epics of ancient India: *Raja Harishchandra* drew upon the *Ramayana*, while *Kichaka Vadham* drew upon the *Mahabharata*.

The first Indian sound film was *Alam Ara* (1931). It mixed realism and fantasy in interesting ways, and it was an instant hit. It also contained a number of melodious songs; song-and-dance sequences subsequently became a defining feature of Indian popular cinema. The year in which *Alam Ara* was made saw the release of as many as twenty-seven Indian films, which were made in four different languages (Hindi, Bengali, Tamil, and Telugu). By the early 1930s, a distinctive form of Indian popular cinema had begun emerging, in which realism and fantasy, singing and dancing, glamour and ordinariness were essential ingredients. Music started to assume great importance at this stage (the film *Indrasabha*, for example, is said to have contained some seventy songs). Contemporary Bollywood cinema (see below) is an outgrowth of this tradition.

Film was a popular form of entertainment in India from the beginning, but it also became a part of the public sphere and a vehicle of ideas at an early stage. Phalke was a filmmaker as well as an intellectual; his writings show that he wanted to use cinema as a vital educative force. In the 1930s Indian films started to explore social issues of contemporary significance, contributing thereby to lively public debate. V. Shantaram's film *Amritmantha* (1934) looked critically at theological absolutism. Two decades later, *Devadas* (1955), directed by Bimal Roy and starring Dilip Kumar, Vaijayantimala, and Suchitra Sen, proved to be a memorable critique of social conventionalism. Based on the popular early twentieth-century Bengali novella of the same name by Sharatchandra Chatterjee (a younger contemporary of Rabindranath Tagore), the Hindi version of the film had a screenplay by the writer Rajinder Singh Bedi (an important fiction writer in Urdu, with connections also to Hindi and

A SAMPLE OF INDIAN FILMS: SOME "CLASSICS," 1950–75

The lists of Indian films in this and the next sidebar include popular classics, commercial blockbusters, examples of middle cinema, and art films, as well as movies by women directors and by directors of the Indian diaspora. It includes several key genres; highlights films based on literary works, or those with screenplays by notable writers; and represents popular directors, actors and actresses, writers, cinematographers, and technicians of the past six decades.

Awaara (1951), directed by Raj Kapoor; featuring Raj Kapoor and Nargis; screenplay by Urdu writer Khwaja Ahmed Abbas.

Devdas (1955), directed by Bimal Roy; featuring Dilip Kumar, Vyjayanthimala, and Suchitra Sen; based on a Bengali novel by Sharatchandra Chatterjee; screenplay by Urdu writer Rajinder Singh Bedi.

"The Apu Trilogy": *Pather Panchali* (1955), *Aparajito* (1957), and *Apur Sansar* (1959), all directed by Satyajit Ray; featuring Kanu Bannerjee, Karuna Bannerjee, Uma Das Gupta, Soumitra Chatterjee, and Sharmila Tagore; based on Bengali fiction of Bibhutibhushan Bandopadhyay.

Tere Ghar ke Samane (1963), directed by Vijay Ananad; featuring Dev Anand and Nutan.

Sangam (1964), directed by Raj Kapoor; featuring Raj Kapoor, Rajendra Kumar, and Vyjayanthimala.

Charulata (1964), directed by Satyajit Ray; featuring Soumitra Chatterjee, Madhabi Mukherjee, and Shailen Mukherjee; based on a Bengali novella by Rabindranath Tagore.

An Evening in Paris (1967), directed by Shakti Samanta; featuring Shammi Kapoor and Sharmila Tagore.

Guide (1965), directed by Vijay Anand; featuring Dev Anand and Waheeda Rahman; U.S. version, *The Guide* (1965), directed by Vijay Anand and Tad Danielewski; based on an Indian-English novel by R. K. Narayan.

Jewel Thief (1967), directed by Vijay Anand; featuring Dev Anand, Ashok Kumar, Vyjayanthimala, and Tanuja.

Aradhana (1969), directed by Shakti Samanta; featuring Sharmila Tagore and Rajesh Khanna.

Anand (1970), directed by Hrishikesh Mukherjee; featuring Rajesh Khanna and Amitabh Bachchan.

Anubhav (1971), directed by Basu Bhattacharya; featuring Tanuja, Sanjeev Kumar, and Dinesh Thakur.

Pakeezah (1971), directed by Kamal Amrohi; featuring Meena Kumari, Ashok Kumar, and Raaj Kumar.

Garam Hawa (1973), directed by M. S. Sathyu; featuring Balraj Sahni, Farooq Shaikh, and Gita Siddharth; screenplay by popular Urdu poet Kaifi Azmi.

Rajanigandha (1974), directed by Basu Chatterjee; featuring Vidya Sinha, Amol Palekar, and Dinesh Thakur; based on a Hindi short story by writer Mannu Bhandari.

Chupke Chupke (1975), directed by Hrishikesh Mukherjee; featuring Dharmendra, Sharmila Tagore, Amitabh Bachchan, and Jaya Bhaduri.

Sholay (1975), directed by Ramesh Sippy; featuring Dharmendra, Sanjeev Kumar, Hema Malini, Amitabh Bachchan, Jaya Bhaduri, and Amjad Khan.

Aandhi (1975), directed by Gulzar; featuring Suchitra Sen, Sanjeev Kumar, and Om Prakash.

Nishaant (1975), directed by Shyam Benegal; featuring Girish Karnad, Shabana Azmi, Amrish Puri, and Smita Patil; original screenplay by Marathi playwright Vijay Tendulkar.

Punjabi), and it became a landmark in the evolution of Indian popular cinema. Other issues, such as untouchability and caste, individual freedom, equality, women's emancipation, and social injustice found extended cinematic expression at this time.

By the 1940s the Indian film industry had established a mass audience and a secure financial base for itself; it had also invented a distinctive mode of filmmaking, with a winning box office formula that consisted of song, dance, gesture, narrative, realism, spectacle, fantasy, and rhetoric. Like cinema in other Asian countries, film in India was an "imported" Western medium; but within a few decades of its arrival, it took on the strengths and confidence of an indigenous art form catering to the needs of indigenous audiences. The films and writings of Phalke and others clearly indicate how cinema has come to serve the continuity of Indian art and culture across millennia. By the mid-twentieth century, Indian film had developed a strong link with epic consciousness even at the popular level, and it had also emerged as a site for social criticism and for the negotiation of social meaning. In this context, the great Indian popular filmmakers of the period, such as Raj Kapoor, Mehboob Kahn, Bimal Roy, and V. Shantaram began to draw not only national but also international attention.

The 1950s are usually taken as constituting the "golden age" of Indian popular cinema. A number of highly talented directors, actors and actresses, musicians, writers, cinematographers, and technicians made their mark at this time, the first full decade in the experience of new nationhood (after independence and partition in 1947). India witnessed an urbanization and a modernization of consciousness as never before, and its cinema both led and reflected the process. Many of the most popular golden-age films, such as *Awaara* (1951), *Shree 420* (1955), *Pyaasaa* (1957), and *Kaagaz Ke Phool* (1959), explored various urban themes from diverse angles. *Awaara*, which was produced, directed, and starred in by Raj Kapoor, also starred Nargis and was a hit both nationally and internationally; based on a screenplay by notable Urdu and Indian English writer Khwaja Ahmed Abbas, it presents the city as both dream and nightmare.

Raj Kapoor—actor, director, and producer—was a seminal figure in the golden age of Hindi cinema. He came from a family associated with the theater (through his father Prithviraj Kapoor) and later involved extensively with cinema (along with his younger brothers, Shammi and Shashi Kapoor; his sons, Randhir and Rishi Kapoor; and Randhir's daughters, Karisma and Kareena Kapoor, all major actors). He became a cultural icon not only in India but also in most of the world outside Western Europe and North America, symbolizing the distinctiveness and international appeal of Indian popular cinema for audiences across cultures.

The 1950s also gave birth to India's art cinema. Satyajit Ray, the great Bengali filmmaker (who was honored by Hollywood in 1990 with an Oscar for his lifetime achievement), released his *Pather Panchali* in 1955. A neorealist slice of Indian rural life, it won eleven international awards (including one at Cannes) and is regarded as one of the finest films of all time. Ray followed *Pather Panchali* with *Aparajito* (1957) and *Apur Sansar* (1959), which together comprise the famous "Apu Trilogy." Among his other great films are *Devi* (1960), *Mahanagar* (1963), and *Charulata* (1964), as well as *Shatranj ke Khiladi* [The Chess Players] (1977, based on a short story by the major Hindi-Urdu writer Premchand) and *Ghare-Baire* [Home and the World] (1984, based on a novel by Rabindranath Tagore). Ray's cinema stood in sharp contrast to Indian popular cinema: his films were realistic, dealt with unglamorous aspects of life, preferred outdoor location shooting, eschewed song-and-dance sequences, stressed finely modulated method acting, and probed psychological depths and intellectual complexities from a broadly humanist point of view.

Another important Bengali filmmaker to emerge during the golden age was Ritwik Ghatak. His distinctive cinematic style drew substantially on the melodramatic traditions of Indian performance, combining a Marxist perspective with Jungian psychology and Indian

A SAMPLE OF INDIAN FILMS: SOME RECENT "GREATS," 1976–2006

Amar Akbar Anthony (1977), directed by Manmohan Desai; featuring Vinod Khanna, Rishi Kapoor, Amitabh Bachchan, Neetu Singh, Parveen Babi, and Shabana Azmi.

Bhumika (1977), directed by Shyam Benegal; featuring Smita Patil, Anant Nag, Naseeruddin Shah, Amrish Puri, Amol Palekar, and Kulbhushan Kharbanda; based on a popular Marathi book by Hansa Wadkar; original screenplay by Kannada playwright and actor Girish Karnad.

Shatranj ke Khiladi (1977), directed by Satyajit Ray; featuring Sanjeev Kumar, Saeed Jaffrey, Shabana Azmi, Victor Banerjee, and Tom Alter; based on a Hindi-Urdu short story by Munshi Premchand.

Junoon (1978), directed by Shyam Benegal; featuring Shashi Kapoor, Naseeruddin Shah, Deepti Naval, Shabana Azmi, and Tom Alter; based on an Indian-English short story by Ruskin Bond; screenplay in part by Urdu writer Ismat Chugtai.

Kalyug (1980), directed by Shyam Benegal; featuring Shashi Kapoor, Rekha, Raj Babbar, Kulbhushan Kharbanda, Anant Nag, and Amrish Puri; screenplay in part by Kannada playwright and actor Girish Karnad.

Akrosh (1980), directed by Govind Nihalani; featuring Om Puri, Smita Patil, Amrish Puri, Naseeruddin Shah, and Mohan Agashe; screenplay by Marathi dramatist Vijay Tendulkar.

36 Chowringhee Lane (1981), directed by Aparna Sen; featuring Jennifer Kendal and Karan Kapoor.

Ghare-Baire (1984), directed by Satyajit Ray; featuring Soumitra Chatterjee, Victor Banerjee, Swatilekha Chatterjee, and Jennifer Kendal: based on a Bengali novel by Rabindranath Tagore.

Bandit Queen (1994), directed by Shekhar Kapoor; featuring Seema Biswas and Aditya Srivastava.

Hum Aapke Hain Koun? (1994) directed by Sooraj Barjatya; featuring Madhuri Dixit, Salman Khan, and Mohnish Bahl.

Dilwale Dulhania Le Jayenge (1995), directed by Aditya Chopra; featuring Shah Rukh Khan, Kajol, and Amrish Puri.

Lagaan (2001), directed by Ashok Gowariker; featuring Aamir Khan.

Dil Chahata Hai (2001), directed by Farhan Akhtar; featuring Aamir Khan, Saif Ali Khan, Akshaye Khanna, Preity Zinta, Sonali Kulkarni, and Dimple Kapadia.

Monsoon Wedding (2001), directed by Mira Nair; featuring Naseeruddin Shah, Lilette Dubey, and Roshan Seth.

Mr. and Mrs. Iyer (2002), directed by Aparna Sen; featuring Rahul Bose, Konkona Sen Sharma, and Bhisham Sahni.

Bend It Like Beckham (2002), directed by Gurinder Chadha; featuring Parminder Nagra, Keira Knightley, Jonathan Rhys Meyers, and Anupam Kher.

Parineeta (2005), directed by Pradeep Sarkar; featuring Sanjay Dutt, Saif Ali Khan, and Vidya Balan; based on a Bengali novel by Sharatchandra Chatterjee.

Paheli (2005), directed by Amol Palekar; featuring Shah Rukh Khan and Rani Mukherjee; based on a folktale retold by Rajasthani writer Vijaydan Detha.

Apaharan (2005), directed by Prakash Jha; featuring Ajay Devgan, Bipasha Basu, Mohan Agashe, and Nana Patekar.

mythology. Among his films are *Nagarik* (1954), *Ajantrik* (1959), *Meghe Dhaka Tara* (1961), *Komal Gandhar* (1962), and *Subarnarekha* (1963). Relatively neglected for three decades, his films have re-awakened widespread interest since the1980s.

Satyajit Ray's pioneering art cinema inspired a new breed of filmmakers in the 1970s and later, who are often associated with the New Indian Cinema, Parallel Cinema, or Middle Cinema. Among them are Adoor Gopalakrishnan, Aravindan, Mani Kaul, Kumar Sahani, Shyam Benegal, Govind Nihalani, Buddhadeb Dasgupta, Gautam Ghose, and Ketan Mehta; equally significant are the important women directors Vijaya Mehta, Aparna Sen, Sai Paranjpye, Prema Karanth, and Parvati Ghosh. Over the past three decades, these filmmakers have collectively moved away from the popular tradition of song-and-dance fantasy as they have sought to present slices of Indian reality on the screen, often confronting the problems of modernization and contemporaneity. Adoor Gopalakrishnan's Malayalam film *Elippathayam* [Rat Trap] (1981), for example, portrays a pathetic, unmarried, middle-aged man who is unwilling to abandon his traditional ways and adjust to the imperatives of modernity, a tragic symbol of a dying class

By the 1970s, the two evolving traditions of Indian filmmaking—the popular and the artistic—were evidently in full flower. While Middle Cinema films were increasingly resonating with audiences at film festivals abroad, popular films at home were crossing new boundaries. Ramesh Sippy's *Sholay* (1975), for instance, created a new hybrid genre by fusing Indian social dramas and musicals with U.S. action, Western, and buddy films, tinged with shades of Akira Kurosawa's Japanese *Seven Samurai* (1954), John Sturges's American *The Magnificent Seven* (1960), and Sergio Leone's Italian spaghetti Western, *The Good, the Bad, and the Ugly* (1966). Carried by a stellar cast that included Dharmendra, Sanjeev Kumar, Hema Malini, Amitabh Bachchan, Jaya Bhaduri, and Amjad Khan, and written memorably by Javed Akhtar and Salim Khan, *Sholay* became one of the most popular Hindi films of all time.

The patterns sketched out partially and synoptically in the preceding paragraphs suggest that the evolution of Indian popular cinema is linked to several factors in Indian literature, theater and performance, and mass media (especially television), and to developments in film and mass media abroad (as discussed in the relevant chapters in this encyclopedia). First, there is the influence of the two ancient Sanskrit epics, the *Ramayana* and the *Mahabharata*, which provided the subject matter, plots, themes, and even narrative styles of some of the early films and of subsequent works in the genre of mythological films. Second, classical Sanskrit theater, especially through its theory of representation and performed emotion (*rasa*), has impacted Indian cinematic style. This impact has often been indirect, reaching modern times through the intermediate influence of post-classical folk performance genres, as the Yatra of Bengal, the Ram Lila of Uttar Pradesh, the Bhavai of Gujarat, the Bhagavata Mela of Tanjore, the Terukkuttu of Tamil Nadu, the Vithinatakam of Andhra Pradesh, and the Yakshagana of Karnataka (see the chapter on Theater and Performance).

Third, the popular, commercially successful Parsi theater of the late nineteenth and early twentieth centuries profoundly affected Indian popular cinema. The Parsi theater companies toured widely not only within India, but also in neighboring countries such as Sri Lanka; their plays combined melodious music, sensational plots, ingenious stagecraft, and raw humor to appeal to mass audiences. Fourth, the Hollywood musical served as a model for Indian popular cinema, but Indian song-and-dance sequences evolved quite differently over time, becoming "natural" extensions of the everyday life they represented. Fifth, in more recent times, the technical and stylistic innovations of MTV and the U.S. music video industry— riveting camera angles, quick cutting, superposed images, and narrative pace—have influenced Indian popular filmmaking, as evident from Mani Ratnam's films and box office successes such as *Satya* (1998) or *Kuch Kuch Hota Hai* (1998).

FAMILY DYNASTIES IN THE INDIAN FILM WORLD

In spite of the pressures of modernity and modernization, the family (both extended and nuclear) remains a strong unit in Indian society. The extended family is especially vital to the traditions of business, finance, and politics in India, and its fabric is unusually strong in the Indian film world. Since the 1940s the industry in Mumbai (Bombay) has witnessed the emergence of many family "dynasties" across generations, two of which are particularly noteworthy.

The Kapoor family has been legendary for decades. Prithviraj Kapoor entered the industry as an actor in the 1940s. His eldest son, Raj Kapoor, became a star actor, director, and producer in the 1950s. Prithviraj's other two sons, Shammi Kapoor and Shashi Kapoor, became star actors in the 1960s and 1970s, with Shammi dominating the popular market, and Shashi emerging as a principal figure (along with his wife, the English actress Jennifer Kendal) in the Middle Cinema movement. Raj Kapoor's two sons, Randhir Kapoor (who married the actress Babita) and Rishi Kapoor (who married the actress Neetu Singh), were prominent actors in the 1970s, with Rishi a major box office draw for some time; Randhir Kapoor's daughters, Kareena and Karisma, became star actresses in the 1990s. Shashi and Jennifer Kapoor's sons, Kunal and Karan, also have had significant acting careers in Hindi films.

The Jaywant-Samarth-Behl-Mukherjee-Devgan clan is larger and more complex. Rattan Bai Jaywant was a pioneering Hindi film actress in the 1930s and 1940s. Her daughter Shobhana Samarth (active mostly from the 1930s to the 1950s) and her niece Nalini Jaywant (mainly the 1940s and 1950s) also became famous actresses. Two of Shobana's daughters became stars in the next generation: Nutan, mainly in the 1950s and 1960s, and Tanuja, in the 1960s and 1970s. Nutan married Rajnish Behl outside the industry; their son, Mohnish Bahl, became a star actor in the 1990s. Tanuja married within the film industry: her husband, Shomu Mukherjee, a director and producer, is the brother of actors Joy Mukherjee and Deb Mukherjee (both active in the 1960s and 1970s) and of occasional director Ram Mukherjee. Tanuja and Shomu's elder daughter, Kajol, achieved superstar status in the 1990s; their younger daughter, Tanisha, became an actress in the first decade of this century. Kajol is married to the star actor Ajay Devgan, whose father, Veeru Devgan, was a prominent stunt director or action coordinator in the 1970s and 1980s. Ram Mukherjee's daughter, Rani Mukherjee—Tanuja and Shomu's niece and a cousin of Kajol and Tanisha—is currently the top-ranking female superstar in the Hindi film world.

Starting in the 1990s, the Hindi film industry based in Mumbai (Bombay) came increasingly to be referred to—sometimes humorously, sometimes derisively—as "Bollywood." This term refers to a style of cinema that has created a new structure of feeling in the popular entertainment in India and beyond, as evident in films such as *Hum Aap Ke Hain Koun*, *Dilwale Dulhania Le Jayenga*, *Dil To Pagal Hai*, and *Kuch Kuch Hota Hai*. This structure of feeling centers on light or frivolous entertainment, extravagant use of song and dance, celebration of life in a consumer society, and young love, as well as traditional family values, a cosmopolitan sensibility, and an erotic and spectacular display of the body. Clearly, these traits do not cohere easily, and the structure of feeling they construct is fragmented. Bollywood cinema, as distinct from older Indian popular cinema, seems to be an uneasy union of tradition and globality, as well as capitalism and modernity.

Pakistan

Most movie lovers outside Pakistan are unaware that this country, on average, produces about eighty films a year. This is so because Pakistani cinema is deeply overshadowed by the cinema of neighboring India, and because its films are largely intended for the domestic market. The film industry of Pakistan came into existence as an independent entity only after the partitioning of the subcontinent in 1947. Some directors, actors, and technicians moved at that time from Mumbai (Bombay) and Kolkata (Calcutta)—then the two principal sites of Hindi film production—to Lahore, which became the center of film production in Pakistan. As in India before and after independence, in Pakistan, too, a distinctive national film culture emerged quite rapidly. The singer and actress Noorjahan, who was popularly called "the melody queen," and the actor Sultan Rahi, who appeared in more than 500 movies, are perfect representatives of the distinctive qualities of Pakistani film culture.

Pakistan is a multilingual country, and languages such as Punjabi, Sindhi, Pashto, Balochi, and Seraiki are widely used in various provinces. But Urdu serves as the national language and lingua franca, and most Pakistani films are made in it. The first feature film in the new national tradition, *Teri Yaad*, was released on September 2, 1948; it featured Nasir Khan and Asha Posley in the lead roles. The first film by an "indigenous" Pakistani was Anwar Kamal Pasha's *Do Ansoo* (1949); Pasha went on to make a number of highly successful films thereafter, some of which attracted attention at international film festivals. During the 1950s, the industry as a whole grew in confidence and productivity; 1957, for example, saw the release of twenty-seven films, twenty-two of which were in Urdu and the rest in Punjabi. Despite political tensions between Pakistan and India throughout this period, film personnel in the two countries were able to continue their interactions with each other. But the size and resources of Indian cinema overwhelmed its neighboring industry. Many early Pakistani films were imitations of Indian films (*Badri* [1957], for example, was a copy of *Jagriti* [1954]), and the actor Kamal became a national star in Pakistan because he looked and acted like the Indian star Raj Kapoor.

In the early period, Pakistani films were mostly apolitical, focusing on family melodramas in the song-and-dance style of Mumbai movies. However, with the passage of time, movies began to deal with social corruption, injustice, and political issues. The Punjabi film *Katar Singh* (1959), for example, explored communal conflict (between Muslims, Sikhs, and Hindus) from a humanistic viewpoint, and it became a classic of Pakistani cinema. Similarly, Raza Mir's *Lakhon Mein Ek* (1967) dealt with Hindu-Muslim relations at a time of national crisis in Pakistan, and such a theme sparked strong responses from different sides. Subsequently, some films probed the nation's political problems more deeply. Sarwar Bhatti's *Maula Jat* (1979), for instance, alluded to the execution of former Prime Minister Zulfikar Ali Bhutto by the authoritarian military regime of President Zia-ul-Haq, then still in power. It stressed the view that no justice can be expected in a society where the rulers, the judicial system, and the government officials responsible for upholding the law are corrupt. Over the decades, Pakistani filmmakers have often complained that the state has not adequately recognized the importance of the film industry as an industry, or of film as a cultural artifact. Under Pakistan's various military regimes as well as its occasional democratically elected governments, most Pakistani films go unnoticed, except for films such as S. M. Yusuf's *Saheli* (1961).

In the 1970s, despite continuing and often severe obstacles, Pakistani films began to expand their repertoire of styles and themes. The new genres included outrageous comedies and satires, such as Rangeela's *Aurat Raj* (1979), and science fiction, such as Saeed Rizvi's *Shani* (1989). By the 1990s the impact of globalization was evident in all the Asian film industries, and Pakistani cinema kept pace with such developments. Film producers, for example, sought to promote co-productions between nations and on-location shooting in foreign locales; Shamin Ara's *Miss Hong Kong*, a forerunner of this trend, was shot on location in 1983, and she went on to make *Miss Colombo* (1984) and *Miss Singapore* (1985) in a similar fashion. Ghaffar Danawalla followed suit with his *Miss Bangkok* (1986), collaborating with Bangladesh and Nepal; the success of the series led Sri Lanka to launch similar projects of its own. Realizing the importance of international collaboration in a rapidly globalizing world, Pakistani filmmakers subsequently explored the possibilities of collaboration with the Philippines, Indonesia, Thailand, Singapore, Malaysia, and Hong Kong. Increasingly, actors and actresses from other nations—such as Babita, Nutun, Rozina, and Mustafa from Bangladesh; Sabita Perera from Sri Lanka; and Shiva, Minakshi, and Shushama from Nepal—began to appear on the Pakistani screen.

The evolution of Pakistani cinema over six decades points to a great deal of domestic talent in the directing, scripting, acting, and technical aspects of filmmaking. However, Pakistani cinema has yet to have an impact on the international stage in the way the Indian industry has made its mark. A number of factors seem to hold back Pakistani filmmakers. First, the country's general political climate, especially under military dictatorships and stringent censorship laws, is not conducive to bold, innovative, or independent filmmaking. Second, as many Pakistani film producers have pointed out, their successive governments have not adequately realized the importance of cinema in the cultural life of the nation, and they have therefore failed to support the industry. Third, the close presence of India's colossal film and media industries is a constant threat to the Pakistani market, with Indian films on video and compact disc and Indian television programs readily available across the border. Fourth, the growth of several new private-sector television channels that broadcast film reruns regularly has adversely affected the Pakistani film industry's share of the entertainment market. These and related factors make the expansion and consolidation of the Pakistani film industry in the early twenty-first century an uphill task.

Bangladesh

When the subcontinent was partitioned in 1947, the new nation of Pakistan consisted of West Pakistan (the territory now identified as Pakistan) and East Pakistan (the territory now identified as Bangladesh), with the two regions separated by a distance of nearly 1,500 miles. In 1971 East Pakistan broke away in a "war of liberation" and emerged as the independent nation of Bangladesh. This history of nationhood affects how we understand the cultural history of Bangladesh. The first film to be made in what was then East Pakistan appeared in 1956: Abdul Jabaar Khan's *Mukh O Mukhosh*. Bangladeshi cinema in the strict sense of the term began after independence in 1971. Very little is known about Bangladeshi films outside that country; during the last 35 years, the industry has had to face numerous difficulties, but it has created a vigorous and popular film culture. Dhaka, the capital, is the center of film production, and like the term "Bombay cinema," the term "Dhakai cinema" has gained currency.

Bangladeshi cinema caters largely to the Bengali-Muslim population of the country. The state, too, has sought to encourage this locally oriented cinema by adopting certain protective measures, such as discouraging the import and screening of Indian and Pakistani films. The tax system imposed by the government on film entertainment buttresses this protective posture. However, Indian and Pakistani films are widely available on video cassette and

DVD. Although on average over seventy-five films have been made annually in Bangladesh, the vast majority of these are sentimental melodramas that are artistically crude and leave much to be desired. The intelligentsia of the country have lamented the absence of a serious tradition of art cinema, pointing to the fact that the popular films have become increasingly vulgar and obscene. In the early years, Bangladeshi popular films were social dramas that dealt with family issues and questions of justice and injustice. In more recent times, under the twin influences of Hollywood and Bollywood, Bangladeshi film producers have increasingly turned toward action films with stunts and special effects.

Despite the fact that the preponderant majority of Bangladeshi films fail to qualify as serious works of art, a number of films have been shown at international film festivals and have received critical acclaim. Among such films are *Shurja Deeghal Bari* (1979), *Dahon* (1985), *Agami* (1985), *Chaka* (1993) and *Matir Moina* (2003). Moreover, a number of directors such as Sheikh Niamat Ali, Morshedul Islam, Tanvir Mokammel, Tareque Masud, Abu Sayeed, and Nasiruddin Yusuff have impressed the discerning movie-going public. Bangladeshi cinema, like most other Asian cinemas, is increasingly subject to the pressures and demands of globalization. This is reflected in the fact that Bangladeshi cinema has come increasingly under the influence of Bollywood. Bollywood actors such as Chunky Pandey have emerged as superstars in Bangladeshi films. The influence of globalization is also reflected in the desire of some directors, such as Suhanul Raman Suhan and Raju Chadhuri, to go to places like Nepal to shoot their films.

Sri Lanka

Sri Lanka is a small country, but over the 60 years since its inception, it has produced a number of distinguished films and filmmakers who have gone on to garner international recognition. The most important among them is Lester James Peries—the father of artistic filmmaking in Sri Lanka—who has won lifetime achievement awards at French and Indian film festivals, among others. There are three main languages in Sri Lanka—Sinhalese, Tamil, and English—but the number of films made in Tamil and English is negligible. The first Sinhalese film, *Kadavunu Poronduva*, was made in 1947, just one year before the country achieved independence. In the 60 years following the birth of Sri Lankan cinema, the indigenous film culture and industry have been growing steadily, if somewhat unevenly, punctuated by moments of upheaval, triumph, stagnation, and progress.

There appear to be two main streams in Sri Lankan cinema: the popular and the artistic. This is, of course, not an absolute distinction since the borders between the two are porous. Nevertheless, it is clear that filmmakers associated with art cinema have made an effort to define their work as the antithesis of popular cinema. But identity is relational, and the condition of its possibility is the recognition of difference, one aspect of which has centered round the concept of realism. Realism was seen as the hallmark of art cinema; many critics failed to recognize that realism is as convention-driven as any other modality of film representation.

The first Sri Lankan film, *Kadavunu Poronduva* (1927), was a sentimental, romantic melodrama as were most of the films that followed during the next 10 years. Among these, *Kapati Arakshakaya* (1948), *Varadunu Kurumanama* (1948), *Amma* (1949), *Peralena Iranama* (1949), *Sangavunu Pilithura* (1951), and *Umathu Vishvasaya* (1952) are particularly significant. While these films were melodramas designed for popular entertainment, they also raised issues connected to the public sphere. The dominant perception was that Sri Lankan cinema was unduly under the influence of south Indian cinema, and that it ought to

THE BIRTH OF AN INDUSTRY: THE INDIAN FILM MARKET

Movies reach an extremely diverse audience of about 1 billion people across Asia, who watch them in theaters and on video, disc, and television. Annual theater receipts for the Asia-Pacific region were conservatively estimated at about US$2.9 billion for 2005. A little over 70 percent of these (amounting to about US$2.1 billion in 2005) came from India alone.

The Indian cinema system has about 12,900 screens, which serve an estimated 13 to 14 million viewers every day, viewers who pay an average ticket price of less than 50 cents (prices in towns and cities may now range from about US$1 to $5 in most cases).

The Indian market is very different from the U.S. market, which has about 35,800 screens and sells between 1.5 and 1.7 billion tickets annually. With an average ticket price around $7, domestic U.S. theater receipts totaled about $12 billion in 2006.

The differences arise because Indian theaters are much larger (between 600 and 2,500 seats per screen) than American theaters (150 to 300 seats per screen), and the greater number of tickets sold annually in India is offset by prices that are much lower (by a factor of fourteen or so).

The Indian film industry employs approximately 6 million people, most of whom work on short-term contracts for specific tasks. On average, the industry currently produces more than 800 films a year in about twenty languages, and almost 90 percent of its revenues come from domestic audiences. Only Hindi films are released nationally; films in other languages are limited to appropriate regional and local markets. For a new Hindi film, the producer releases between 200 and 500 prints to distributors, depending on the film's anticipated audience appeal.

Film financing, production, distribution, and exhibition are separate sectors in India, and each is dominated by a different set of well-known family businesses. India's government did not classify filmmaking as an "industry" until recently, so the process of building a corporate structure for Bollywood has just begun. Since the death of the big Indian studios in the 1950s, a cumbersome mechanism has been in play: producers and directors rely on private financiers in the open market to fund their projects; producers release films to independent distributors for a share of net receipts; distributors pay rent and costs to (mostly) independent exhibitors to screen films in theaters. In such a system, financiers and distributors are particularly wary of risking their money on an untested product; historically, only one out of every six Hindi films has made a profit.

At the end of the twentieth century, the total media and entertainment market in India was estimated to be worth US$6 billion; projections suggest that this figure may double—or even triple—by the end of the first decade of this century.

strike out in a new direction that was true to local imperatives. Sirisena Wimalaweera's films were a response to this felt need.

Lester James Peries made *Rekhava* (1956) just nine years after the first Sri Lankan film was released. It was a landmark that signified the birth of an art cinema in Sri Lanka, just as the director Satyajit Ray had inaugurated the art cinema tradition in India one year earlier.

The entire film was shot on location; Peries had turned his back on the popular melodramatic tradition and had created a polished neorealistic work. In 1965 Peries was responsible for strengthening this art tradition with his film *The Changing Countryside*. Based on a critically acclaimed novel by the country's foremost novelist, it dealt sensitively with the collapse of feudal society and the rise of the middle class. This film won the Grand Prix at India's international film festival. Peries went on to make such internationally acclaimed films such as *Nidhanaya* (1960), *Baddegama* (1981), and *Age of Kali* (1983).

Thanks to the work of Lester James Peries, a reasonably large audience had been created for serious cinema in Sri Lanka. In the 1970s, a newer breed of film directors made its appearance. They are generally referred to as the second generation of art filmmakers, and they sought to build on the achievements of Peries while pursuing their own special interests. Among these filmmakers, Dharmasena Pathiraja, Vasantha Obeyesekera, Sumithra Peries, Tissa Abeysekera, and Dharmasiri Bandaranayake deserve special mention. Pathiraja's *Soldadu Unnahe* represents this generation's strengths; it is a socially committed film that deals with the nature of cultural hegemony and the social contours of subalternity. Among the films belonging to this group, Obeyesekera's *Dadayama* (1984), Sumithra Peries's *Ganga Addara* (1980), and Bandaranayake's *Suddilage Kathava* (1984) merit closer analysis.

The tradition of art cinema grew steadily, and a third generation of filmmakers emerged in the 1990s. Among the important directors of this generation are Prasanna Vithanage, Aasoka Handagama, Somaratne Dissanayake, Linton Semage, Sudath Mahadivulwewa, and Vimukthi Jayasundera. Many of their works have won prizes at international film festivals; Vimukthi Jayasundera's *Sulanga Enu Pinisa* (2005), for example, won a prestigious award at the Cannes Film Festival. The filmmakers of the third generation are innovative in terms of content as well as style. Asoka Handagama, in some of his films for example, has sought to incorporate the visualities characteristic of Buddhist temple paintings. They are also all deeply concerned with the civil war that has convulsed the island for the past quarter-century with deadly consequences, and their films reflect their anguish. Vithanage's *Pura Handa Kaluwara* (1999), for instance, explores the harmful impact of the ethnic conflict between the Tamils and the Sinhalese on everyday life in Sri Lanka. More broadly, Handagama's films, such as *Sanda Dadayama* (1999), *Me Mage Sandai* (2000), and *Tani Tatuven Piyambami* (2002), represent cinematic talent of a very high order, and the third generation of art filmmakers as a group inspires confidence in the future of Sri Lankan cinema.

Although art cinema has made an impact, the majority of films made in Sri Lanka belong to the popular tradition. Starting with the earliest film in this tradition, *Kadavunu Poronduva* (1947), Sri Lankan popular cinema modeled itself on Indian commercial films, a practice that continues with slight modifications to the present. The 1950 film, *Sujatha*, which became one of the most popular films ever made, extended this practice by basing itself on a Hindi film. Popular Sri Lankan films in this mold display all the features associated with Mumbai (Bombay) commercial cinema: their plots rarely develop in a linear fashion; digressions and detours are very common; and songs, dance, music, crude humor, fights, stunts, cabaret sequences, sentimentality, exaggeration, and excess dominate their content. Among the popular Sri Lankan films based on Hindi films are *Dinuma* (1986), *Jaya Apatai* (1986), *Ran Damvel* (1987), *Ahimsa* (1987), *Obatai Priye Adare* (1987), and *Raja* (1987). A shift away from the Indian commercial model has become evident only in the past 10 or 12 years, and films such as *Weediye Weeraya* (1996) and *Surayo Wedakarayo* (1997) evince an interest in Western action films.

The art films of Sri Lanka deal with serious issues, such as the moral ambiguities of modern living, the problems of patriarchy, the fault lines of nationhood, and the experience of subalternity. Although it is designed for mass entertainment, popular cinema in its own way has focused on issues related to cultural modernity and has tried to negotiate the complex and challenging pathways toward the "modern." What these films struggle with, in their own somewhat simplistic way, is the uneasy transition toward capitalist modernity and global consumerism.

SOUTHEAST ASIA

Thailand

In recent times, Thai cinema has generated great international interest partly because it has won awards at such prestigious film festivals as the Cannes Film Festival, and partly because it has begun to freely explore controversial themes of transgender and transsexual identity, for example, in films such as *Iron Ladies* (1999) and *Beautiful Boxer* (2003). When examining the growth of Thai cinema, it is useful to bear in mind that a triangulation of forces—the monarchy, the state (along with the military), and Buddhism—has had a decisive impact on it. Thailand is predominantly a Buddhist country, and Buddhism is closely intertwined with day-to-day life, which is evident at a number of levels in the generality of Thai films.

The first feature film in Thai, *Nang Sao Suwan*, was made in 1922, but it was directed by Henry A. Macrae of Universal Pictures. The first film in the Thai language to be made by a Thai director was Kun Anurakrathakarn's *Chok song Chan* (1927). Over the next two decades, the film industry in Thailand grew gradually, confronting numerous political, economic, and social issues along the way. In the 1950s about twenty-five films were made each year, and in the 1960s, the number rose to seventy. By the 1970s, the Thai film industry was displaying a certain degree of self-confidence, and there emerged a number of filmmakers, including Prince Chatri-Chalerm Yukala, Prempol Chuay-Arun, Euthana Mukdasnit, Channa Kraprayoon, Manop Udomdej, and Somboonsuk Niyomsiri, who were keen to strike out in new directions and make cinema an important adjunct of the public sphere. Examples of such efforts include Manop Udomdej's *Ya Pror Me Chu* (1985) and Euthana Mukdasnit's *Nampoo* (1984), which deal with the miserable sex life of an army major and his wife and with teenage heroin addicts, respectively. Another example is Mukdasnit's *Peesua Lae Dokmai* (1985), which won prestigious awards at international film festivals. It deals with the emotional relationship between two teenagers, depicted against the backdrop of poverty and social hardships, and it displays a lyrical surface that contrasts sharply with the social tensions in its narrative.

When the development of the Thai film industry during the last 15 years or so is examined, it becomes apparent that globalization has had a profound impact in terms of themes, styles, and techniques. Globalization seems to have set in motion three interesting trends. The first has been the attempt to make use of the vigor of commercial advertising and TV commercials, as evidenced in films such as *Sixty-nine* (1999) and *Ms. Nak* (1999). The second has been the desire of certain Thai filmmakers to base their stories outside Thailand and so to widen the territory of cinematic exploration. The third, which emphasizes history and cultural identity as countervailing forces to globalization, is visible in films such as Prince Chatri's *Suriyothai* (2000).

Vietnam

Broadly speaking, one can identify four stages in the growth of Vietnamese cinema: cinema under French colonization (until 1945), cinema during the liberation struggle (1945–54), cinema during the struggle for reunification (1954–75), and the cinema of reconstruction (1975 to present). Vietnamese cinema is distinguished from all other Asian cinemas by the fact that patriotism and war framed the entire filmic discourse until the

FILM

1990s. In March 1953 president Ho Chi Minh established the state enterprise for film and photography. Cinema was seen as an important tool of propaganda, national pride, and the battles against imperialism. It is not surprising that the first feature film, *Chung Mot Dong Song* (1959), directed by Nguyen and Pham ky Nam, sought to explore the violation of the Geneva Agreement by the United States. Films such as *Hai Nguoi Linh* (1962), *Nguoi Chien Sit Re* (1964), *Kim Dong* (1964), and *Em Be Ha Noi* (1974) had as their theme the dangers of war. After unification, many of the films dealt with the experiences of soldiers returning from the battlefront, and their adaptation to everyday life. The war remained the inescapable reference point, as evidenced in films such as *Chuyen Xe Bao Tap* (1977) and *Nhung Nguoi Da Gap* (1979). The much-needed healing process was the theme of some later films, such as *Huy Thanh Ve Noi Gio Cat* (1981) and *Xa Va Gan* (1983).

Since the 1980s the art of cinematography has made rapid strides. Dang Nhat Minh, for example, has emerged as one of the most important and innovative Vietnamese directors of the past two decades. His early films, *Thi Xa Trong Tam Tay* (1982) and *Bao Gio Cho Den Thang Muoi* (1984), as well as his subsequent works, such as *Co Gai Tren Song* (1987), *Tro Ve* (1994), *Thuong Nho Dong Que* (1995), and *Mua Oi* (2000), bear eloquent testimony to his desire to strike out in new directions.

A number of important changes are evident as the Vietnamese film industry enters the twenty-first century. Directors such as Le Hong, Phi Tien Son, and Vu Ngoc are changing the face of Vietnamese cinema, and a film such as *Gain Hay* (2003) illustrates their ambitions. These filmmakers are keen not only to adopt Western modes and styles of filmmaking but also to establish viable commercial cinema. Instead of the war and the people's heroic struggles, contemporary Vietnamese cinema deals with topics such as fashion, cabaret life, prostitution, and drug abuse. The younger generations of Vietnamese moviegoers, for whom the war is not even a memory, are attracted by this new direction.

The Philippines

The Philippines is also a large film-producing country in Southeast Asia, and its film culture is vitally connected to its popular culture. Filipino audiences were introduced to U.S. and European films at the very beginning of their association with cinema, and this had a determinate impact on their cinematic sensibility. Apart from the influence of Hollywood, Spanish cultural influence was considerable in the early years of Filipino filmmaking. Although the majority of films made in the Philippines are sentimental melodramas with a distinctly local flavor, a number of filmmakers, such as Lino Brocka, Ishmael Bernal, Maie-lous Abhaya, Kidlat Tahimik, in their different ways, have gone on to make films that have won high praise from discerning international audiences.

The first film made in the Philippines, *The Life of Rizal*, was a foreign production. The first local film, *Dalagang Bukid*, was made in 1919. The early films explored themes of patriotism, heroism, and sacrifice without overt criticism of the United States. The period around World War II witnessed the energetic growth of Filipino cinema. Directors such as Manuel Conde, Lamberto Avellana, Eddie Romero, Manuel Salos, and Gerardo de Leon made a deep impression on the cinema-going public. The 1970s saw the emergence of Lino Brocka, generally regarded as the best Filipino film director. He made a large number of films, most of which can be characterized as melodramas. At the same time, he made films such as *Tinimbang Ka ngunit Kulang* (1974), *Bayan Ko* (1984), *Macho Dancer* (1988), and *Orapronobis* (1989). In *Bayan Ko*, Lino Brocka boldly textualizes the formidable economic and social problems countenanced by the labor force in the unhappy context of an authoritarian concept of nationhood. Another filmmaker of this generation who has made a profound impression on local and foreign audiences is Ishmael Bernal. His film *Himala* (1982), which dramatizes the tragic story of a woman against the background of Filipino religious syncretism, displayed the strengths of local cinema.

The Filipino film industry has grown over of the last nine decades, with three main stages: the first was the early phase from 1897–1929; the second was from 1929 to 1970, when the Filipino film industry was established on a secure footing, and it began to grow with confidence; the third phase is the period from 1970 to the present, which marks the development of the New Cinema. Among the directors who have been closely associated with the progress of the New Cinema are Lino Brocka, Ishmael Bernal, Celso Castillo, Eddie Rumero, Marilou Diaz-Abaya, Mike de Leon, and Laurice Guillen. As the Filipino film industry began to embrace greater commercialism and consumerism, a number of filmmakers, such as Kidlat Tahimik, Raymond Red, Nick Deocampo, Lito Tiongson, Joey Agbayani, Roxlee, Louie Quirino, and Noel Lim, began to explore modes of alternative cinema.

Compared with most other Southeast Asian countries, the cinema of the Philippines is doing well in terms of the number of films produced annually. In the 1980s, about 140 films were produced each year; in 1997, 197 films were made. As the Filipino film industry entered the twenty-first century, there was a drop on film production. However, unlike other Southeast Asian countries, the Philippines still makes over 100 films annually.

Malaysia

Unlike the Philippines, Thailand, Vietnam, and Indonesia, Malaysia has not produced the type of outstanding artistic films that win international critical recognition. Malaysian cinema, beset with numerous economic, political and social problems, has yet to find its voice. Compared with other Southeast Asian countries, Malaysia's filmic output is not high either. The first Malaysian film, *Laila Majnun*, was made in 1933. This film propagated a style of filmmaking that was greatly indebted to Indian commercial cinema. By the late 1930s and early 1940s, the famous Shaw brothers had produced a number of films based on Chinese scripts; these do not seem to have generated a great measure of enthusiasm among local audiences. About 400 films were produced during the period from 1933 to 1975; among the films of this period, *Penggilan Pulau* (1954), *Anakku Sazali* (1956), *Sarjan Hassan* (1958), *Sri Mersing* (1961), and *Istana Berdarh* (1964) deserve attention.

The most important personality associated with Malaysian cinema is P. Ramlee. He was not only a talented and popular actor but also a singer, musician, comedian, composer, scriptwriter, and director. His film *Penarek Becak* (1955) became a great box office success. This film focused on the class divisions in society, which was a favorite theme of Ramlee and was to find articulation in some of his other films, such as *Antara Dua Darjat* (1960), *Ibu Mertuaku* (1962), and *Tiga Abdul* (1964). Ramlee was clearly influenced by the works of Japanese directors, most notably Akira Kurosawa. He was also successful in using humor to probe various social issues and problems. Ramlee's success as a director inspired others, including Jamil Sulong, M. Amin, S. Sudarmaji, Hussein Haniff, Salleh Ghani, S. Kadirisman, Mat Sentol, and Omar Rojik, to try their hand at directing.

By the 1980s most other Southeast Asian countries were making memorable films of a high artistic order. However, Malaysia still lagged behind, despite the attempts of new and talented directors such as Jins Shamsuddin, Rahim Razali, Hafsham, Sharom Mohm Dom, Nasir Jani, and Yasin Salleh to develop new approaches to filmmaking. A film such as *Mekanik*, which was shown at numerous international festivals and enjoyed wide popularity at home, underlined the fact that if Malaysia were to create a vibrant tradition of filmmaking, it needed to address all ethnic groups in the land. Hafsham later made a number of other films such as *Rahsia* (1987), *Ujang* (1988), *Driving School* (1990), and *Soal Hati* (2000); although these are not as artistically convincing as *Mekanik*, they displayed his gifts as a film director. The 1990s witnessed the rise of a fresh generation of filmmakers, including Aziz M. Osman, Arief Karmahani, Anwardi Jamil, and Yusof Haslam; of them, Aziz and Yusof have been the most successful commercially.

If the Malaysia film industry is to make greater progress, two things seem essential: First, film directors need to make films that attract all three ethnic groups—Malay, Chinese, and Indians—to theaters. Second, directors need to make films that attract international attention, such as Teck Tan's *Spinning Gasing* (2001), which will help expand the market for Malaysian films.

Indonesia

Indonesia is the fourth most populous country in the world, and the vast majority of its population is Muslim. It consists of thousands of islands, which are home to a large number of ethnic groups, languages, and cultures. The former Dutch colonial administration (until about 1945), and the Republic of Indonesia since then, have sought to forge a unity out of this diversity. This was no easy task. Cinema, and its dissemination of Bahasa Indonesia, as opposed to the various local languages, went a long way in contributing to this effort (see the section on Indonesia in the chapter on Periodicals for a discussion of the country's multilingualism). Except for a film such as Eros Djarot's *Tjoet Nja Dhien* (1988), in which characters speak in Acenese, most popular Indonesian films use dialog in Bahasa. Therefore, in an unusual way, Indonesian films may have, at one level, served to cement the idea of Indonesian nationhood; however, on closer examination, fissures in these filmic texts are evident.

The first Indonesian film was made in 1923, during the period of Dutch colonial rule. Over the past decades, Indonesia has produced over 2,020 feature films, no meager output. Indonesia is the largest film-producing country in Southeast Asia, although its films cater largely to its sizable local market. Film historians, for analytical convenience, tend to talk of the evolution of Indonesia cinema in three stages: the Old Order, the New Order, and the post-New Order. The Old Order and New Order coincide with the administrations of presidents Suharto and Sukarno, respectively. In terms of style and technique, the three periods do not display distinctive characteristics, but the political climate prevalent in each of them was different, and this had some impact on cinematic themes and content. During the first decade of film production in the country, Indonesian filmmakers drew heavily on traditional legends and myths, as well as on folk theatre. All the films at that time were made in Indonesia, but most were the works of European or Chinese directors and producers. The local immigrant Chinese community played a crucial role in the growth of the Indonesian film industry.

During the 1940s, when the Japanese occupied Indonesia, and the struggle for independence began to take shape, film production was at low ebb. However, with the dawn of the 1950s, film production bounced back. Films from America, India, China, and Hong Kong were shown. Usmar Ismail, who is generally regarded as the father of Indonesian cinema, made the first film by an Indonesia with an Indonesia theme, which was called *Long March Silwangi* (1950). Usmar Ismail subsequently went on to make a number of important films. Bachtiar Siagian was another early filmmaker who made a deep impression on Indonesia's cinema-going public. While Usmar Ismail was interested in making use of cinema for artistic and entertainment purposes, Bachtiar Siagian was more interested in the social meaning of films.

The first decade of Indonesia cinema saw the emergence of film directors such as Usmar Ismail, Bachtiar Siagian, Armijin Pane, D. Djayakusuma, Djamaludin Malik, and Asrul Sani. Their films were largely social melodramas. The Indonesian film industry moved forward, facing numerous ups and downs, largely as a result of local politics. Local film producers had to fight for their market share in the face of fierce competition from the film industries of India, China, and Hollywood. In the 1970s, a number of talented film directors made significant contributions to the growth of Indonesian cinema. Among them, Wim Umboh, Arifin C. Noer, Nya Abbas Akup, and Teguh Karya deserve special mention. Teguh Karya won national and international acclaim with films such as *Di Balik Kelambu* (1982), *Doea Tanda Mata* (1984), *Secangkir Kopi Pahit* (1984), *Ibunda* (1986), and *Pacar Ketinggalan Kereta* (1988). In all these films, Teguh Karya dealt with family conflicts, issues of ethnicity, and cultural identity with great sensitivity.

A film that won both national and international critical acclaim was Eros Djarot's *Tjoet Nja dhien* (1986), with the well-known actress Christine Hakim in the lead role. This film went on to win international awards. *Tjoet Nja Dhien* is significant for two reasons: First, this film, which deals with the story of a woman freedom fighter during Dutch colonial control, displays a strong female character. Second, the film is in Acenese with Indonesian subtitles. In the 1980s, the Indonesian film industry progressed well, with over 120 films made annually. By the 1990s, film production had dropped drastically, and the economic crisis of 1997 did not help. Despite hardships in the 1990s, a number of talented filmmakers sought to make serious films. Among them, Garin Nugroho has made a lasting impact.

At the beginning of the twenty-first century, the Indonesian film industry is facing severe difficulties. The new media and entertainment environment created by VCRs, DVDs, and cable and satellite television, as well as competition from the technologically superior Hollywood movies, pose serious challenges to Indonesian filmmakers. In addition, the younger generation of movie-goers has become more sophisticated and is demanding a newer and better type of cinema.

This section has presented thumbnail sketches of the status of film industries and film cultures in countries of South and Southeast Asia. Clearly, each country has its own distinctive trajectories of growth as well as its specific concerns and interests. However, there are certain commonalities as well. All the cinematic traditions discussed here relate to the issue of cultural modernity in interesting ways. Theorists such as Georg Simmel, Siegfried Kracauer, and Walter Benjamin have pointed out the complexities of modernity and their implications for cinema. Modernity is not one thing, as previously understood, but many things, and the cinemas discussed above focus on the sensory and experiential dimensions of cultural modernity in compelling ways. These cinemas also deal with the issue of nationhood: how films tend to strengthen as well as challenge and subvert the narratives of nationhood that are officially sanctified and propagated. Moreover, all cinemas in South and Southeast Asia address the issue of globalization and how globalization intersects with forces of locality. These films open interesting windows onto popular culture and general society across South and Southeast Asia.

RESOURCE GUIDE

PRINT SOURCES

East Asia and Oceania

Berry, Chris, and Feii Lu, eds. *Island on the Edge: Taiwan New Cinema and After*. Hong Kong: Hong Kong University Press, 2005.

Bordwell, David. *Planet Hong Kong: Popular Cinema and the Art of Entertainment*. Cambridge, MA: Harvard University Press, 2000.

———, and Kristin Thompson. *Film Art: An Introduction*, 7th edition. Madison, WI: McGraw-Hill Higher Education, 2004.
Bowyer, Justin. *24 Frames: The Cinema of Japan and Korea*. London: Wallflower Press, 2004.
Chow, Rey. *Primitive Passions: Visuality, Sexuality, Ethnography, and Contemporary Chinese Cinema*. New York: Columbia University Press, 1995.
———. *Sentimental Fabulations, Contemporary Chinese Films: Attachment in the Age of Global Visibility*. New York: Columbia University Press, 2007.
Fu, Poshek, and David Desser, eds. *The Cinema of Hong Kong: History, Arts, Identity*. Cambridge: Cambridge University Press, 2000.
McHugh, Kathleen, and Nancy Abelmann, eds. *South Korean Golden Age Melodrama: Gender, Genre, and National Cinema*. Detroit: Wayne State University Press, 2005.
Morgan, Albert, and Errol Vieth. *Historical Dictionary of Australian and New Zealand Cinema*. Lanham: Scarecrow Press, 2005.
Murray, Scott, ed. *Australian Film: 1978–1994*. Melbourne: Oxford University Press, 1995.
Nowell-Smith, Geoffrey, ed. *The Oxford History of World Cinema*. Oxford: Oxford University Press, 1999.
Shi, Chi-Yun, and Julian Stringer, eds. *New Korean Cinema*. New York: New York University Press, 2005.
Standish, Isolde. *A New History of Japanese Cinema*. New York: Continuum, 2005.
Stratton, David. *The Avocado Plantation: Boom and Bust in the Australian Film Industry*. Sydney: Pan Macmillan, 1990.
Teo, Stephen. *Hong Kong Cinema: The Extra Dimensions*. London: British Film Institute, 1997.
Wexman, Virginia Wright. *A History of Film*, 6th edition. Boston: Pearson Allyn and Bacon, 2005.
Xu, Gary G. *Sinascape: Contemporary Chinese Cinema*. Lanham, MD: Rowman & Littlefield, 2007.
Yau, Esther C. M., ed. *At Full Speed: Hong Kong Cinema in a Borderless World*. Minneapolis: University of Minnesota Press, 2001.
Zhang, Yingjing. *Chinese National Cinema*. New York: Routledge, 2004.
Zhen, Ni. *Memoirs from Beijing Film Academy: The Genesis of China's Fifth Generation*, trans. Chris Berry. Durham, NC: Duke University Press, 2002.

South and Southeast Asia

Ciecko, Anne Tereska. *Contemporary Asian Cinemas*. New York: Berg, 2006.
Dissanayake, Wimal. *Melodrama and Asian Cinema*. Cambridge: Cambridge University Press, 1993.
———. *Colonialism and Nationalism in Asian Cinema*. Bloomington: Indiana University Press, 1994.
——— and Ashey Ratnavibhushana. *Profiling Sri Lankan Cinema*. Colombo, LK: Asian Film Centre, 2000.
Ganti, Tejaswini. *Bollywood*. Routledge Film Guidebooks. New York: Routledge, 2004.
Gazdar, Mushtaq. *Pakistan Cinema (1947–1997)*. Oxford: Oxford University Press, 1997.
Gokulsing, Moti, and Wimal Dissanayake. *Indian Popular Cinema: A Narrative of Cultural Change*. Stoke-on-Trent, UK: Trentham Books, 2004.
Heider, Karl. *Indonesian Cinema*. Honolulu: University of Hawaii Press, 1991.
Lent, John A. *The Asian Film Industry*. Austin: University of Texas Press, 1990.
Mishra, Vijay. *Bollywood: Temples of Desire*. New York: Routledge, 2002.
Rajadhyaksha, Asish, ed. *Encyclopedia of Indian Cinema*, 2nd revised edition. London: British Film Institute, 1999.
Sen, Krishna. *Indonesian Cinema: Framing the New Order*. London: Zed Books, 1994.
Soto, Augustine. *Pelikula: An Essay on the Philippine Cinema, 1897–1960*. Manila: Cultural Center of the Philippines, 1992.
Van der Heide, William. *Malaysian Cinema, Asian Film: Border Crossings and National Cultures*. Amsterdam: Amsterdam University Press, 2002.
Vasudev, Aruna, et al., eds. *Being and Becoming: The Cinemas of Asia*. Delhi: Macmillan India, 2002.

FILM

WEBSITES

East Asia and Oceania

Asian Film Connections: China. May 12, 2006. http://www.asianfilms.org/china/.
Asian Film Connections: Hong Kong. May 12, 2006. http://www.asianfilms.org/hongkong/.
Asian Film Connections: Japan. May 12, 2006. http://www.asianfilms.org/japan/.
Asian Film Connections: Korea. May 12, 2006. http://www.asianfilms.org/korea/.
Asian Film Connections: Taiwan. May 12, 2006. http://www.asianfilms.org/taiwan/.
Australian Films@film.org.au: "The Best in Australian Film." May 11, 2006. http://www.film.org.au.
Bienvenue sur CinemAsie.com. May 12, 2006. http://www.cinemasie.com/en/.
Chinese Cinema Page. May 12, 2006. http://chinesecinemas.org.
Chinese Movie Database. May 12, 2006. http://www.dianying.com.
Chinese Taipei Film Archive. May 12, 2006. http://www.ctfa.org.tw.
Film in Australia—Stories from Australia's Culture and Recreation Portal. May 11, 2006. http://www.cultureandrecreation.gov.au/articles/film/.
HKcinema.net: Your Source of Asian Movies—Jet Li, Jackie Chan, Kung Fu, Martial Arts. May 12, 2006. http://hkcinema.net.
HK Film Archive. May 12, 2006. http://www.lcsd.gov.hk/CE/CulturalService/HKFA/.
Hong Kong Film Critics Society. May 12, 2006. http://www.filmcritics.org.hk/index.html.
The Internet Movie Database (IMDb). May 11, 2006. http://www.imdb.com.
Koreanfilm.org—Movie Reviews, News, Actor Info and More from Korea. May 11, 2006. http://www.koreanfilm.org.
Kraicer, Shelley. *A Chinese Cinema Site.* http://chinesecinemas.org.
The New Zealand Film Archive. May 11, 2006. http://www.filmarchive.org.nz.
Welcome to KOFIC (Korean Film Council). May 11, 2006. http://www.koreanfilm.or.kr.
Winter, Brendan. "The Best in Australian Film." *Australian Films@film.org.au.* http://www.film.org.au.

South and Southeast Asia

Asian Cinema Studies Society. http://astro.temple.edu/~jlent/ACSS/. Includes a link to the *Asian Cinema Journal.*
Asian Cinema Weekly. http://www.kinoasia.com.
Cinemaya. http://www.cinemaya.net/.
Internet Movie Data Base. http://www.imdb.com. A vast resource for information on individual South Asian and Southeast Asian films, actors and actresses, directors, writers, and other cinema personnel; has comprehensive and reliable listings, with excellent live links for cross-references, and a versatile search engine.

SELECTED VIDEOS/FILMS

East Asia and Oceania

The Adventures of Barry Mckenzie (Australia, 1972). Directed by Bruce Beresford.
The Aimless Bullet (Korea, 1960). Directed by Kim Ki-young.
An Angel at My Table (New Zealand/Australia, 1990). Directed by Jane Campion.
Beijing Bicycle (China/Taiwan, 2001). Directed by Wang Xiaoshuai.
A Better Tomorrow (Hong Kong, 1986). Directed by John Woo.
Black Rain (Japan, 1988). Directed by Shohei Imamura.
The Blair Witch Project (United States, 1999). Directed by Daniel Myrick and Eduardo Sánchez.
Boat People (Hong Kong, 1982). Directed by Ann Hui.
The Bodyguard (Japan, 1961). Directed by Akira Kurosawa.
A Borrowed Life (Taiwan, 1994). Directed by Wu Nien-jen.

Film

A Bright Summer Day (Taiwan, 1990). Directed by Edward Yang.
Brokeback Mountain (United States, 2005). Directed by Ang Lee.
Broken Arrow (United States, 1996). Directed by John Woo.
The Brotherhood of the War (Korea, 2004). Directed by Kang Je-gyu.
A Chinese Ghost Story (Hong Kong, 1987). Directed by Tsui Hark.
Chunhyang Jeon (Korea, 1955). Directed by Lee Kyu-hwan.
Chunhyang (Korea, 2000). Directed by Im Kwon-taek.
Chunhyang Jeon (Korea, 1935). Directed by Lee Myeong Woo.
Chungking Express (Hong Kong, 1994). Directed by Wong Kar-wai.
A City of Sadness (Taiwan, 1989). Directed by Hou Hsiao-hsien.
Crocodile Dundee (Australia, 1986). Directed by Peter Faiman.
Crouching Tiger, Hidden Dragon (Taiwan/China, 2000). Directed by Ang Lee.
Dead Poets' Society (United States, 1989). Directed by Peter Weir.
Dragon Gate Inn (Hong Kong, 1966). Directed by King Hu.
Drunken Master (Hong Kong, 1978). Directed by Yuen Wo-ping.
Eat, Drink, Man, Woman (Taiwan, 1994). Directed by Ang Lee.
The Eel (Japan, 1997). Directed by Shohei Imamura.
Face/Off (United States, 1997). Directed by John Woo.
Farewell my Concubine (China, 1993.) Directed by Chen Kaige.
Flowers of Shanghai (Taiwan/Japan, 1998). Directed by Hou Hsiao-hsien.
From Beijing with Love (Hong Kong, 1994). Directed by Stephen Chow.
Gallipoli (United States, 1981). Directed by Peter Weir.
Ghost in the Shell (Japan, 1995). Directed by Manoru Oshii.
The God of Cookery (Hong Kong, 1997). Directed by Stephen Chow.
The Goddess (China, 1934). Directed by Wu Yonggang.
Godzilla (Japan, 1954). Directed by Ishiro Honda.
Goodbye South, Goodbye (Taiwan, 1996). Directed by Hou Hsiao-Hsien.
Green Card (United States, 1990). Directed by Peter Weir.
Heavenly Creatures (New Zealand, 1994). Directed by Peter Jackson.
Hero (China, 2002). Directed by Zhang Yimou.
Hibiscus Town (China, 1986). Directed by Xie Jin.
Hill of No Return (Taiwan, 1992). Directed by Wang Tung.
The Hole (Taiwan/France, 1998). Directed by Tsai Ming-liang.
House of Flying Daggers (China, 2004). Directed by Zhang Yimou.
The Housemaid (Korea, 1960). Directed by Kim Ki-young.
The Ice Storm (United States, 1997). Directed by Ang Lee.
In the Mood for Love (Hong Kong/France, 2000). Directed by Wong Kar-wai.
Internal Affairs (Hong Kong, 2002). Directed by Lau Wai-Keung and Mak Sia-fai.
JSA (Korea, 2000). Directed by Park Chan-wook.
Killing Me Softly (United States, 2002). Directed by Chen Kaige.
King of the Children (China, 1987). Directed by Chen Kaige.
Kingdom and the Beauty (Hong Kong, 1959). Directed by King Hu.
Kung Fu Hustle (Hong Kong, 2004). Directed by Stephen Chow.
The Lake House (United States, 2006). Directed by Alejandro Agresti.
The Last Wave (Australia, 1977). Directed by Peter Weir.
Late Spring (Japan, 1949). Directed by Yasujiro Ozu.
The Life of O'Haru (Japan, 1952). Directed by Kenji Mizoguchi.
Little Women (Australia/United States, 1994). Directed by Gillian Armstrong.
The Lord of the Rings (United States/New Zealand, 2001, 2002, 2003). Directed by Peter Jackson.
Mad Max (Australia, 1979). Directed by George Miller.
The Magnificent Seven (United States, 1960). Directed by John Sturges.
Mandala (Korea, 1981). Directed by Im Kwon-taek.
The Matrix (United States, 1999). Directed by Andy and Larry Wachowski.
Moulin Rouge (United States, 2001). Directed by Baz Luhrmann.

My Brilliant Career (Australia, 1970). Directed by Gillian Armstrong.
My Mental Illness (Taiwan, 1997). Directed by Wang Hsiao-di.
My Sassy Girl (Korea, 2001). Directed by Kwak Jae-young.
Oasis (Korea, 2002). Directed by Lee Chang-dong.
Oldboy (Korea, 2003). Directed by Park Chan-wook.
Once Upon a Time (Hong Kong, 1991). Directed by Tsui Hark.
Once Were Warriors (New Zealand, 1994). Directed by Lee Tamahori.
Oscar and Lucinda (Australia, 1997). Directed by Gillian Armstrong.
The Peach Blossom Land (Taiwan, 1993). Directed by Stan Lai.
Peel (New Zealand/Australia, 1982). Directed by Jane Campion.
Perhaps Love (Hong Kong/China/Malaysia, 2005). Directed by Peter Chan.
The Piano (New Zealand/Australia/France, 1993). Directed by Jane Campion.
Picnic at Hanging Rock (Australia, 1975). Directed by Peter Weir.
Platform (China, 2000). Directed by Jia Zhangke.
The Portrait of a Lady (United States, 1996). Directed by Jane Campion.
Princess Monoke (Japan, 1997). Directed by Hayao Miyazaki.
The Puppetmaster (Taiwan, 1993). Directed by Hou Hsiao-hsien.
Pushing Hand (Taiwan, 1992). Directed by Ang Lee.
Raise the Red Lantern (China, 1991). Directed by Zhang Yimou.
Rashomon (Japan, 1951). Directed by Akira Kurosawa.
Red Sorghum (China, 1987). Directed by Zhang Yimou.
Ringu (Japan, 1998). Directed by Hideo Nakata.
Romeo and Juliet (Australia/United States, 1996). Directed by Baz Luhrmann.
Samaritan Girl (Korea, 2004). Directed by Kim Ki-duk.
Sense and Sensibility (United States, 1995). Directed by Ang Lee.
Seven Samurai (Japan, 1954). Directed by Akira Kurosawa.
Shaolin Soccer (Hong Kong, 2001). Directed by Stephen Chow.
Shiri (Korea, 1999). Directed by Kang Je-gyu.
Siworae (Korea, 2000). Directed by Lee Hyun-seong.
Smash Palace (New Zealand, 1982). Directed by Roger Donaldson.
Spirited Away (Japan, 2001). Directed by Hayao Miyazaki.
Spring Silkworm (China, 1933). Directed by Chen Bugao.
Spring, Summer, Fall, Winter . . . and Spring (Korea, 2003). Directed by Kim Ki-duk.
Springtime in a Small Town (China, 1948). Directed by Fei Mu.
Street Angel (China, 1937). Directed by Yuan Muzhi.
Strictly Ballroom (Australia, 1992). Directed by Baz Luhrmann.
Sunday Too Far Away (Australia, 1975). Directed by Ken Hannam.
Suzhou River (China, 2000). Directed by Lou Ye.
Throne of Blood (Japan, 1957). Directed by Akira Kurosawa.
Tianyun Mountain (China, 1980). Directed by Xie Jin.
Tokyo Story (Japan, 1953). Directed by Yasujiro Ozu.
Tropical Fish (Taiwan, 1995). Directed by Chen Yu-hsun.
The Truman Show (United States, 1998). Directed by Peter Weir.
The Truth about Jane and Sam (Hong Kong/Singapore, 1999). Directed by Yee Tung-Shing.
Unfolding Florence (Australia, 2005). Directed by Gillian Armstrong.
Vive l'amour (Taiwan, 1994). Directed by Tsai Ming-liang.
The Wayward Cloud (Taiwan/France, 2005). Directed by Tsai Ming-liang.
The Wedding Banquet (Taiwan, 1993). Directed by Ang Lee.
Whale Rider (New Zealand, 2002). Directed by Niki Caro.
What Time Is It There? (Taiwan/France, 2001). Directed by Tsai Ming-liang.
Yellow Earth (China, 1983). Directed by Chen Kaige.
Yi Yi: A One and a Two (Taiwan/Japan, 2000). Directed by Edward Yang.
Zatoichi (Japan, 2003). Directed by Kitano Takeshi.
Zu: Warriors of the Magic Mountain (Hong Kong, 1979). Directed by Tsui Hark.

FILM

South and Southeast Asia

The following list highlights popular classics, commercial blockbusters, examples of middle cinema, and art films, as well as movies by women directors and directors in the Indian diaspora.

Aandhi (India, 1975). Directed by Gulzar.
Akrosh (India, 1980). Directed by Govind Nihalani.
Amar Akbar Anthony (India, 1977). Directed by Manmohan Desai.
An Evening in Paris (India, 1967). Directed by Shakti Samanta.
Anand (India, 1970). Directed by Hrishikesh Mukherjee.
Anubhav (India, 1971). Dir. Basu Bhattacharya.
Apaharan (India, 2005). Directed by Prakash Jha.
"The Apu Trilogy": *Pather Panchali* (India, 1955), *Aparajito* (India, 1957), and *Apur Sansar* (India, 1959). Directed by Satyajit Ray.
Aradhana (India, 1969). Directed by Shakti Samanta.
Awaara (India, 1951). Directed by Raj Kapoor.
Bandit Queen (India, 1994). Directed by Shekhar Kapoor.
Bend It Like Beckham (India and UK, 2002). Directed by Gurinder Chadha.
Bhumika (India, 1977). Directed by Shyam Benegal.
Charulata (India, 1964). Directed by Satyajit Ray.
Chupke Chupke (India, 1975). Directed by Hrishikesh Mukherjee.
Devdas (India, 1955). Directed by Bimal Roy.
Dil Chahata Hai (India, 2001). Directed by Farhan Akhtar.
Dilwale Dulhania Le Jayenge (India, 1995). Directed by Aditya Chopra.
Garam Hawa (India, 1973). Directed by M. S. Sathyu.
Ghare-Baire (India, 1984). Directed by Satyajit Ray.
Guide (India, 1965). Directed by Vijay Anand. U.S. version, *The Guide* (1965). Directed by Vijay Anand and Tad Danielewski.
Hum Aapke Hain Koun (India, 1994). Directed by Sooraj Barjatya.
Jewel Thief (India, 1967). Directed by Vijay Anand.
Junoon (India, 1978). Directed by Shyam Benegal.
Kalyug (India, 1980). Directed by Shyam Benegal.
Lagaan (India, 2001). Directed by Ashok Gowariker.
Monsoon Wedding (India and USA, 2001). Directed by Mira Nair.
Mr. and Mrs. Iyer (India, 2002). Directed by Aparna Sen.
Nishaant (India, 1975). Directed by Shyam Benegal.
Paheli (India, 2005). Directed by Amol Palekar.
Pakeezah (India, 1971). Directed by Kamal Amrohi.
Parineeta (India, 2005). Directed by Pradeep Sarkar.
Rajanigandha (India, 1974). Directed by Basu Chatterjee.
Sangam (India, 1964). Directed by Raj Kapoor.
Shatranj ke Khiladi (India, 1977). Directed by Satyajit Ray.
Sholay (India, 1975). Directed by Ramesh Sippy.
Tere Ghar ke Samane (India, 1963). Directed by Vijay Ananad.
36 Chowringhee Lane (India, 1981). Directed by Aparna Sen.

NOTE

East Asia and Oceania

1. For the differences between the fifth and the previous four generations of Chinese directors, see Ni Zhen, *Memoirs from Beijing Film Academy* (in Resource Guide).

FOOD AND FOODWAYS

EAST ASIA AND OCEANIA

KATARZYNA J. CWIERTKA

INTRODUCTION

Cuisine is a very credible way of delineating Northeast Asia as a region. Food and foodways of China, Korea and Japan obviously differ, but they all rest on the foundations of the ancient Chinese civilization that once dominated this part of the world. The use of chopsticks and widespread consumption of processed soybeans (soy sauce, soybean paste, and soybean curd) rank among the most vivid indicators of the common heritage of the culinary cultures of China, Korea, and Japan.[1] However, this common ground by no means prevented those societies from developing quite distinctive foodways.

Along with the ancient imprint, an extensive spread of Chinese food in Japan and Korea took place during the first half of the twentieth century, propelled by the influx of Chinese traders and laborers. This movement of people was, in turn, inspired by the crumbling of ancient power structures in the region, with Japan gradually taking the lead as the most successfully modernizing nation of East Asia. As a consecutive adherent of culinary Westernization, Japan soon began to function as a vehicle and a filter in the process of popularization of Western food in Korea and Manchuria. Japan's imperialist expansion into other Asian countries also greatly contributed to the embrace of Chinese food by the Japanese population, and it was responsible for the introduction of Japanese food into Korea and of Korean food into Japan.[2]

After 1945, Japan's position on the frontier of Western culture in East Asia was further strengthened through its strategic alliance with the United States. The encroachment of American fast food made a start in the 1970s, and the penetration of East Asia by McDonald's—in Japan (1971), Hong Kong (1975), Taiwan (1984), South Korea (1988), and China (1992)—is emblematic of the trajectory by which global culinary influences spread throughout the region.

Foreign food notwithstanding, East Asian economic growth during the last decades of the twentieth century has, in the first place, brought about dietary affluence. The populations of

STARBUCKS AND THE RISE OF COFFEE-DRINKING CULTURE

Starbucks opened its first outlet outside of North America in Tokyo in 1996. A decade later, roughly 600 Starbucks coffee-shops were in operation throughout Japan; the country remains the company's most important overseas market. Japan was chosen as the first overseas investment by the Seattle-based coffee chain for a reason—by the mid-1990s Japan was already a coffee-drinking nation. Thus the impact of Starbucks on the consumption practices of the Japanese population was less significant than in South Korea and China, where it was responsible for the rise of a new coffee-drinking culture.

Before the late 1980s the South Korean coffee market was entirely dominated by instant coffee, which appeared first in the 1950s on the black market, traded illegally along with other components of U.S. military rations.[3] The opening of the first Starbucks in Seoul in 1999 marked a true watershed. Although the overwhelming majority of South Koreans today continue to drink instant coffee, it has acquired an aura of backwardness and is associated with a lower-class background. In contrast, a cup of freshly brewed Starbucks coffee has become a mark of distinction and sophistication. With its 125 outlets (as of 2006), Seoul has developed a true taste for the Starbucks experience, which is likely to have long-term implications for the place of coffee in the Korean foodways.

Starbucks has steadily expanded its operations in China as well. Over 100 stores (as of 2006) have opened since the first outlet in Beijing in 1999. Foreign tourists and expatriates and Chinese returnees who lived for an extended period abroad constitute a large proportion of Starbucks' customers. However, China's elite and the expanding urban middle class also successively embrace coffee drinking as a symbol of modern lifestyle and affluence, a world away from the ubiquitous tea.[4]

Japan, Hong Kong, Taiwan, Korea, and, of late, China have never before eaten as well as they do now. Ironically, culinary gentrification of recent years has inspired the nostalgic revival of (largely idealized) foods and consumption practices. Familiarity with global trends has, in turn, propelled a longing for lost or vanishing foodways that once reinforced an Asian sense of identity.

In other words, culinary cultures of contemporary East Asia (and many other localities) are continuously reshaped by the two contradicting forces: a growing interconnectedness sustained by global capitalism and a constant reinvention of the past as a means to reassert cultural distinctiveness and identity.

CHINA

Over the centuries, a variety of foodways developed throughout China, and these regional differences still prevail. The five cuisines, which emerged around the historically important cities, are nowadays recognized as the five major styles of Chinese cooking: (1) Beijing cuisine is celebrated for its noodles, dumplings (*paozi*, *jiaozi*), mutton hot-pot, and the renowned Beijing Duck; (2) Fujian cuisine is recognized by the prevalence of soups and sauces and for its congee (*chou*); foods are generally cooked more slowly in Fujian cuisine and seasoned more liberally than in other provinces; (3) Guangzhou cuisine is characterized by the use of a wide variety of vegetables and animals (including frogs and snails) and celebrated for its elaborate snacks (*tim sam*); (4) Sichuan cuisine has been largely influenced by Nepalese and Indian foodways, and it is distinguished by its piquant spicing and heavy reliance on pork; chili pepper now accounts for the pungent taste, but Sichuan pepper (*huajiao*) originally was the prevailing flavoring; (5) Zhejiang cuisine, developed in the surroundings of Shanghai, is considered the most sophisticated of all five; it is particularly celebrated for its seafood dishes, emphasis on freshness, and refined taste.[5]

A contrast between rural and urban foodways is perhaps the major unifying feature of the diverse culinary landscape of contemporary China. Rural areas lag significantly behind the rapidly changing urban lifestyle, and the restaurant boom is a prime example. Since the early 1990s large cities, such as Shanghai, Beijing, Tianjin, Shenyang, and Guangzhou, were swept by the enormous popularity of the transnational fast food industry. This foreign invasion, under the leadership of KFC and McDonald's, provided a strong stimulus for the emergence of native competitors, ultimately resulting in a true explosion of establishments for dining out.[6] Today urban areas boast of restaurants and food stalls of many kinds, offering a wide range of regional food from all over China for customers of every degree of affluence.

A significant motive behind the initial popularity of fast food restaurants among Chinese women is reported to have been the absence of alcohol. Despite regional differences in alcoholic beverages (*jiu*), the Chinese infatuation with alcohol is equally pronounced regardless the location. A family celebration without alcohol is unthinkable, and it is customary to serve it even at funerals. Drinking is not merely a form of entertainment, but also a way to shed inhibition and express social bondage. The social standing of the drinker determines how fancy the accompanying snack can be, but the cardinal rule is never to drink alcohol without nibbling on something in order to "make the wine go down" (*xiajiu*).[7]

In contrast to the gourmet lifestyle that the (affluent) citizens of urban China can experience, rural Chinese sustain themselves largely on a local diet and are able to sample the culinary culture of new China only via the media or occasional visits to the city. However, their nutrition has undoubtedly improved during the last decade, and their meals became far more varied.[8] In fact, a gradual improvement of food supply in China has been proceeding successively since it hit the rock bottom in the 1960s. The Great Leap Famine (1959–61), which resulted in 30 million deaths, became a powerful impetus for institutional innovation of Chinese agriculture; it was indirectly responsible for the reforms instituted during the 1970s and 1980s.[9] Still, until the late 1980s, even urban Chinese maintained a rather monotonous diet, usually taking meals at collective canteens in their work units. Tasteless food, unfriendly service, and uncomfortable environments were taken for granted and were indeed emblematic of this dining experience.[10]

The situation was different in the British colony of Hong Kong, whose sovereignty was transferred to China in 1997. Before the 1970s living conditions for the majority of the Hong Kong inhabitants remained poor because of the additional population pressure brought by the postwar influx of immigrants from mainland China and Southeast Asia. However, those same immigrants were responsible for the diversity that is so characteristic of the culinary landscape of contemporary Hong Kong. Restaurants specializing in local Chinese cuisines were opened by chefs who had fled from the mainland, and they, over time, became an important source of variety in Hong Kong's foodways. Western food had been strongly represented in the British colony since the nineteenth century, but the economic growth of the 1970s marked the beginning of Hong Kong as a global metropolis with a highly cosmopolitan palate.[11]

In the mid-1980s, when Hong Kong Chinese became familiar with fast food, supermarkets, and other emblems of globalized lifestyle, drinking herbal tea (*chìng lèuhng chàh*) began to emerge as a new fashion. It was part of a general trend toward natural foods that went hand in hand with the rise of health consciousness among consumers worldwide. However, in the case of Hong Kong, the revival of herbal tea shops, which peaked in the 1990s, was also a reaction to the identity crises that arose from the prospect of returning to China after 150 years of British rule. Nostalgic reconstruction of past foodways was part of reaffirming Chinese identity by the citizens of Hong Kong, an expression of yearning for a secure yesterday to counterbalance an uncertain tomorrow.[12]

MONOSODIUM GLUTAMATE (MSG) STIRS CONTROVERSY

The flavor enhancer commonly known as monosodium glutamate or MSG is intricately linked with Chinese cuisine. A set of adverse physiological symptoms (migraine headaches, nausea, heart palpitation, numbness, and dizziness) claimed to be caused by overconsumption of MSG are often referred to as the "Chinese Restaurant Syndrome."[13] This infamous association between MSG and Chinese food led, in turn, to a common assumption of its Chinese origin. In fact, MSG was invented by Ikeda Kikunae, a German-trained Japanese chemist and marketed by a Japanese manufacturer of iodine, Suzuki Chemical Company. Under the brand name of Ajinomoto, the product went on sale in Japan in 1909 and soon conquered the Taiwanese and Korean markets.

Despite initial successes, however, Ajinomoto encountered obstacles in China, where MSG became a symbol of Japanese imperialism and a favorite target of anti-Japanese protests. The nationalist response spurred the rise of myriad native imitators, who emphasized the fact that their product was domestically manufactured, not imported. The largest Chinese producer of MSG, the Tian Chu Company, called its brand "Buddha's Hand" (*foshou*) and marketed it not only as a cheap substitute for meat stock, but also as a vegetarian alternative.

By the late 1930s, MSG was widely used in urban China as well as among Chinese communities throughout Asia and the West Coast of the United States. American manufacturers of canned foods also recognized the capacity of MSG to make bland, inexpensive foods flavorful, and they were a chief importer of Ajinomoto at the time.

Chinese Restaurant Syndrome was discovered in 1968, in the midst of the rise of environmentalist consumer consciousness in the United States. MSG was labeled a chemical additive and began to be perceived increasingly as harmful to health. Despite the extensive use of MSG by the food industry as a whole, it is the Chinese restaurants that had the misfortune to acquire the negative association with this Japanese invention.

A similar process of reaffirmation of national identity through food has been taking place recently in Taiwan. In face of China's emergence as a global economic power, the concept of Taiwanese cuisine has been used increasingly by the government and the media as a symbol of Taiwanese culture. As in Hong Kong, Taiwanese foodways are a patchwork of the foods and practices of the people who arrived on the island throughout the twentieth century and those who had settled there earlier. Taiwanese cuisine rests on the foundations of the Fujian cuisine since the majority of Chinese who reside in Taiwan hailed from this province. Moreover, as a consequence of half a century (1895–1945) of colonial rule, Taiwanese cuisine is saturated with Japanese influences.

The proliferation of Taiwanese cuisine as a melting pot among the Taiwanese population, as well as among the tourists, is, in itself, not unique. However, the timing of the governmental support for the publications, exhibitions, and other activities that popularize the concept of Taiwanese cuisine implies that it is one of Taiwan's various efforts to elude the shadow of the motherland.[14]

Japan

Multiculturalism is the defining feature of the culinary scene in contemporary Japan and is clearly reflected in the food choices made daily by every Japanese. An average day may begin with a Western-style breakfast of toast, coffee, and fried eggs or a Japanese-style breakfast of rice, *miso* soup, pickles, and grilled fish. Lunch may be either a Japanese-style *obentō* (a boxed meal of rice and several small side dishes) or a quick bite at one of the ubiquitous fast food restaurants, noodle shops, or an array of other lunch establishments. Many factories and schools operate their own canteens, in which indigenous fare prevails, but with strongly pronounced Chinese and Western influences. This also holds true for Japanese home meals. Although they are often centered on white boiled rice, side dish mainstays that are served with the rice may range from Chinese-inspired stir fries such as *mabōdōfu* and *yasai itame*, Western-inspired breaded and deep-fried *tonkatsu* and *korokke*, and Korean-inspired *kimuchi nabe*. The Japanese character of the entire meal is secured by its structure of rice, soup, and side dishes. Moreover, the side dishes are often "Japanized" by the addition of soy sauce (*shōyu*), the most important flavoring in contemporary Japanese cooking.

For present-day Japanese, rice, soy sauce, and fresh seafood are the ultimate symbols of Japaneseness. Yet these three ingredients have only recently turned into standard components of daily meals for all Japanese. The symbolic importance of rice in the Japanese history is indisputable—it was, to be sure, a preferred staple. However, until the 1960s, there was not enough of it to feed everybody. Similarly, soybean paste (*miso*) rather than soy sauce was the prevailing flavoring in most rural areas. The latter was much more costly and labor-intensive to manufacture. The consumption of seafood had also been relatively limited and confined to the areas with easy access to the sea, and the standard of freshness maintained today was impossible to attain before contemporary transport and preservation technologies. During the twentieth century, formerly expensive and exclusive types of food became universally affordable, and the daily meals of people of different social and economic status who reside in different parts of Japan have grown increasingly similar.

Dining at restaurants—a genuine luxury for most Japanese before the 1970s—was transformed into a routine component of daily life in the urban as well as rural areas. The number of eating and drinking establishments operating throughout the country more than doubled between the 1960s and 1990s. As of 2004 an average household spent 19.6 percent of its food budget on dining out, as opposed to 7.9 percent in 1970.[15]

The variety of dining establishments throughout Japan today is dazzling. First, there is wide range of native restaurants, from upmarket ones serving exclusive *kaiseki* cuisine (see sidebar) to inexpensive noodle and sushi bars. Cheap eateries specializing in Chinese food and in Korean-style barbeque (*yakiniku*) rank among the most ubiquitous eating establishments, alongside American fast food chains such as McDonald's and KFC. Larger urban centers offer an even wider selection of dining choices, including fancy French and Italian bistros and eateries that claim to serve food from such exotic places as India, Vietnam, Malaysia, and Ethiopia.[16]

In addition to restaurants and fast food outlets, 24-hour convenience stores (*konbini*) supply basic ingredients, a variety of snack foods, and ready-to-eat meals 7 days a week. Moreover, Japan's ubiquitous vending machines dispense not only soft drinks, alcoholic beverages, candy, and ice cream, but also steaming noodles and grilled rice balls.

These are only the most obvious places where one encounters food in Japan. Long-distance train travelers can dine in buffet cars or purchase food to eat in their seats from catering carts. Catering carts and rail station kiosks also stock a large variety of food souvenirs, usually specialties of the region, such as locally grown fruit and vegetables, pickles,

> ## THE KAISEKI IDEAL
>
> Nutritiously balanced simplicity, deep artistic sensibility, and spiritual connection with nature constitute the key components of the idealized image of Japanese cuisine inside as well as outside Japan. In fact, this specific attitude toward food and cooking was characteristic of the *kaiseki* cuisine (*kaiseki ryōri*) that emerged in the sixteenth century as a style of dining designed especially for the purpose of being served before a tea ceremony (*chanoyu* or *sadō*)—a highly ritualized procedure during which powdered green tea is prepared by a skilled practitioner and served to a small group of guests.
>
> Over the centuries, this particular style of cooking and serving food—with the adjoining philosophy that guides it—gradually shifted from the periphery to the center of the culinary scene in Japan. It was born in the elite circles of the practitioners of the tea ceremony, largely influenced by the spirituality of Zen Buddhism. Gradually, however, it was also embraced by upmarket restaurateurs who successively transformed the character of the kaiseki meal from that of ritualized tranquility to epicurean enjoyment of excellent food. The kaiseki ideal as it is known today was crystallized during the twentieth century. The economic affluence of the 1960s and 1970s endorsed the nationwide spread of the kaiseki ideal beyond the exclusive circle of tea practitioners, chefs, and gourmets. Endorsed by home economics education and perpetuated by mass publications and televised media, the attributes of kaiseki were disseminated among the entire population and became synonymous with the concept of culinary Japaneseness. The kaiseki aesthetics functioned as a vital homogenizing component in the creation of a Japanese national cuisine.

and confections. These treats are distributed among colleagues, friends, and family to mark the end of a journey and to offer a vicarious sharing of the experience. For centuries food has been a typical and welcome gift in Japan: it is relatively inexpensive and easy to choose, share, and dispose of. Edible souvenirs and gifts are only one example of how food remains an important means of communication in Japan.

The prominence of food in Japanese society is best reflected by its continual appearance in the media. Food is a regular feature, if not the centerpiece, of visual entertainment in Japan.[17] Culinary fashions are constantly invented and reinvented in print and televised media. The recreational and entertainment value of food is trumpeted in books and brochures dealing with food history, in recipes, in restaurant reviews in magazines, and in food-related quiz shows, contests, and documentaries. Even serious daily newspapers regularly include information related to the native and foreign culinary heritage. Serialized soap operas and home dramas are often staged at restaurants or in traditional food workshops, and popular animated characters bear food-related names, such as the celebrated Anpanman (Mr. Beanpaste Bun) and Sazae-san (Mrs. Top-Shell). Travel programs invariably focus on cuisine. No journey is considered complete without tasting local food, regardless of whether it is a refined meal at one of Japan's celebrated spas or a baguette in a Paris bistro. Moreover, each channel has several cooking shows targeted at specific audiences—housewives, children, and men, for whom cooking is a hobby. One of the reasons why cuisine rates so highly on Japanese television is the premium placed on the appearance or presentation of food in contemporary Japan. The emphasis on the aesthetic harmony between the food, the vessel, the setting, and the season in which it is served has turned into the defining feature of contemporary Japanese cuisine (see sidebar).

Despite being caught in a complex web of commercial interests, food still retains strong spiritual and religious connotations in Japan, largely because of its prominent role in Shinto and Buddhist rituals. As elsewhere, the connection between food and religion is particularly pronounced on festive occasions, such as the New Year's celebration, when a pyramid of pounded rice cakes (*kagamimochi*) is displayed in almost every household, or during the *obon* (autumn equinox) festival, when ancestors are worshipped with offers of fruit, vegetables, and *sake* in addition to the food they favored when they were alive. Gravestones covered with tangerines and small *sake* containers are familiar scenes in cemeteries throughout Japan.[18]

In real life, however, beer has long surpassed *sake* as the most popular alcoholic drink, despite the recent revival of local *sake* varieties (*jizake*) produced by small, independent brewers.[19] Although the consumption of coffee in Japan ranks among the highest in the world and various carbonated beverages are available, green tea remains Japan's national drink. In 1995 the sales of tea drinks (including green as well as black teas) surpassed sales of all carbonated beverages combined, reversing the steady decline in green tea consumption since the 1950s. The launch of canned green tea has undoubtedly contributed to this success. Its popularity was generated chiefly by the rising demand for healthy, sugarless drinks.[20] However, a nostalgic return to Japanese foodways, after decades of infatuation with foreign culinary fashions, has an equal share in this trend.[21]

(SOUTH) KOREA

Owing to the current popularity of barbequed meat, Korean cooking tends to be mistakenly perceived as a meat-centered cuisine. However, before economic growth took off in the 1970s, meat was by no means a component of daily meals for the common people in Korea, but rather was intended to strengthen physical resistance against extreme weather conditions.[22] In fact, the consumption of animal products (beef, pork, chicken, eggs, and milk and dairy products) in South Korea increased more than twenty times during the last three decades. A more appropriate label for Korean cooking would be a vegetable-centered cuisine—extensive consumption of vegetables has always been the distinguishing feature of Korean foodways.

Pickled vegetables, generally referred to by the name of *kimch'i*, remain an indispensable element of every Korean meal. There are hundreds of varieties of kimch'i—every region, village, and even every individual family used to cherish its own special recipe, applying slightly different preparation methods and using slightly different ingredients. Napa cabbage is the most common type, followed by radishes. Basically, vegetables are first placed for several hours in brine, washed with fresh water, and drained. Then condiments such as ginger, chili pepper, spring onions, garlic, and raw or fermented seafood are added, and the mixture is packed into pickling crocks and allowed to mature.

Since the 1960s, when factory-made kimch'i appeared on the market for the first time, the number of urban families that continue to make their own kimch'i has gradually diminished. With the rising consumption of meat and seafood and the popularization of Western-style food, the quantity of kimch'i consumed by Koreans has successively declined in recent years. A growing number of Korean children are reported to express aversion toward this traditional food. However, it is still an indispensable component of practically every meal and continues to be considered Korea's national symbol.[23]

Chili pepper, sesame oil, garlic, and spring onions, along with soy sauce (*kanjang*), soybean paste (*toenjang*), and red bean paste (*koch'ujang*), constitute what might be called the Korean flavoring principle. The combination of all or a selection of some of these ingredients gives Korean dishes their characteristic taste. Ginger, semisweet rice wine (*ch'ongju*) and honey or sugar are other crucial components of Korean flavor.

Food and Foodways

KOREAN ROYAL CUISINE

September 15, 2003, marked a turning point in the attitude of ordinary citizens of South Korea toward Korean Royal Cuisine (*kungjung ŭmsik*)—the most refined art of the Korean cooking. This was the first day of the broadcast of the popular TV drama "Taejanggŭm," which followed the life history of the legendary female who combined the career of a royal chef with that of King's private physician in early sixteenth-century Korea. "Taejanggŭm" made history as the most popular historical drama ever aired on Korean television, but its implications have been much greater.

Since 1971 Royal Cuisine has been recognized as a part of the Korean cultural heritage and designated the Intangible Cultural Asset No. 38. The Intangible Cultural Asset system was founded by the South Korean government in 1962 with the aim of fostering national pride through the promotion and careful portrayal of specific aspects of Korea's unique history and culture. However, before autumn 2003, kungjung ŭmsik was scarcely known among young Koreans and admired only by people with specific culinary interests. Thanks to the "Taejanggŭm" series, however, the exclusiveness of Royal Cuisine has been turned into a nation-wide trend.

Royal Cuisine for the Home (Ch'ŏngnim, 2004) is one of several cookbooks published in response to the "Taejanggŭm" craze. The back cover declares:

> Royal Cuisine—each time you watched "Taejanggŭm" you regretted so much that it was a feast for the eyes only! Yet, anybody can prepare it with no effort if only easily accessible ingredients and easy to follow cooking techniques are used.
>
> Set the "King's table" at home now, as a daily meal or as a banquet for your guests. Honest, home-made cooking prepared devotedly with health in mind. Once a week eat like a King.

Chinese, Japanese, and American influences are becoming increasingly pronounced in the Korean foodways, especially outside the home. Yogurt and Western-style snack food have become the staple of Korean children, and American fast food chains (McDonald's, KFC, and Pizza Hut), particularly popular among the youth, have successively enlarged their share of the Korean restaurant market. Koreans of older generations prefer Chinese restaurants, which have been popular for decades, to the more recent Japanese and Italian establishments. However, foreign food remains largely within the categories of both snacks and dining out. With the exception of convenience foods, such as pizza and noodle soup (*ramyŏn*), and occasionally cooked pasta or Japanese-style curry, foreign dishes rarely find their way into Korean kitchens.

The differences in the food that Koreans consume at different times of day are little pronounced. Supper is usually more elaborate than breakfast and lunch, but, generally speaking, every meal is centered on plain boiled rice (*pap*), soup (bouillon–like *kuk* or a more hearty *t'ang*) and pickled vegetables (*kimch'i*). Side dishes (*panch'an*) extend this core menu, and their number depends on the occasion, three to five side dishes being the norm in most contemporary households. A variety of wheat and buckwheat noodles (*kuksu*) also frequently appears on the Korean table. Noodles are usually served in soupy liquids; stuffed dumplings (*mandu*) can be steamed, pan-fried, or simmered in soups (*manduguk*). Noodles and dumplings are popular lunch dishes. They have also been traditionally served at birthdays because of their symbolic association with long life. However, two holiday foods that managed to retain their important position within the Korean society are pine needle-scented rice cakes (*songp'yon*), which are intricately connected with the Harvest Moon Festival (*Ch'usok*), and the rice cake soup (*ttokkuk*) served during the lunar New Year's Day celebrations (*Sollal*). For example, asking "How many bowls of rice cake soup have you eaten?" is a polite way of asking about someone's age, as if failing to eat a bowl of rice cake soup would deprive a person from a complete New Year's experience.

Korea is a culinary exception in East Asia in the sense that it did not develop a tea-drinking culture. Water and *porich'a*, scorched-rice tea—made by boiling water over the rice that sticks to the bottom of the rice pot—remain the two most important drinks to accompany meals. Green tea is more popular than black tea; it has been popularized during the last decade or two under the Japanese influence.

For celebrations, most Koreans drink either beer (popular for several decades) or traditional *soju*. *Soju* is made of grain or sweet potatoes, with the alcohol content of up to 45 percent. Another popular alcoholic beverage is *makkŏlli*, a milky liquid with the alcohol content of 6 to 8 percent. It used to be a lower-class drink—hence its alternative name, *nongju* (farmers' wine)—but it experienced a true revival in recent years. Alcohol is never drunk in Korea without elaborate snacking. Practically all side dishes can be served for this purpose; they are called *anju* (not *panch'an*) on such occasions. Anju can be small snacks, similar to French hors d'oeuvres or Spanish tapas, but not necessarily. Stews and large savory pancakes (*chŏn*), including vegetables, meat, and seafood, are also typical drinking snacks.

South Korea's GNP allows the majority of its population today to enjoy a diet that was only affordable to the very rich in the past. Koreans are also able to follow worldwide culinary trends if they so desire. Consumer expansiveness intensified to such an extent in the early 1990s that the government Public Information Office began a campaign against *kwasobi*, the term applied to the phenomenon of consuming beyond what was considered appropriate.[24] The major Korean dilemma concerning consumption in the 1990s was the desire to be nationalistic and global simultaneously. Following the Seoul Olympics of 1988, a remarkable increase in the supply of imported consumer goods was observed, linking South Koreans to the rest of the world and expanding their knowledge of the lifestyles of other people. At the same time, however, people feared that, through the consumption of foreign products, Korean culture would fall victim to Japanese or Western infiltration. Although crowds of customers at McDonald's, Baskin Robbins, and Starbucks, along with the rising sales of imported food items, seem to undermine this precept, there is a general ambivalence toward achieving a globalized lifestyle and losing Korean identity in the process.[25]

The Korean resistance to dietary globalization is most concisely expressed in the slogan *shint'o puri*, which, in its popular usage, means that food from Korean soil is best for Korean bodies. The ideology is widely covered by the media, where consumers are taught to distinguish foreign foods from Korean-grown foods. Foods produced in Korea are often promoted to be and are commonly believed to be better tasting than their foreign counterparts. Among the foods of concern are beef and Chinese-grown vegetables such as chili peppers and garlic. The irony of shint'o puri with regard to Korean beef is that cattle and all other Korean farm animals are not fed with plants produced in Korean soil but with imported feedstuffs. Yet activists argue that these animals are raised in Korea by Korean farmers.[26]

AUSTRALIA AND NEW ZEALAND

The proximity of Australia and New Zealand to Asia has, until recently, hardly been manifested in their foodways. The culinary cultures of both societies rests on a strong British heritage, the food and drink carried by the Irish, Scottish, and English settlers who, since the nineteenth century, began to dominate over the indigenous population of the islands. Because the port of Sydney served as the base from which New Zealand's resources were exploited, Australian influences on New Zealand were strong and remained so for decades. Moreover, the immigrants to both islands were from similar socioeconomic backgrounds, which accounted for the similarities between the two culinary cultures.[27]

WAGAMAMA: FROM SELF-INDULGENCE TO HEALTHY LIVING

Regular Japanese-English dictionaries translate *wagamama* as selfishness, self-indulgence, or waywardness. However, many Australians associate the word with the phrase "positive eating + positive living"—registered trademark of the restaurant chain named Wagamama, representing the establishment's emphasis on the healthy appeal of the food it serves: from freshly squeezed fruit juices and a wide choice of vegetarian alternatives to the ability to cater for customers with food allergies. The core of the Wagamama menu is formed by a variety of (modified) Japanese noodle and rice dishes, including the Japanese version of British curry, which was brought in the mid-nineteenth century to the Land of the Rising Sun by the British residents of the treaty ports. Wagamama calls itself a noodle canteen, and it certainly looks like one—an open space filled with communal wooden tables and benches (not chairs), with the capacity to seat 100 to 150 customers. It is an original creation of Alan Yau, the son of Cantonese immigrants who had run a Chinese takeaway in Norfolk on the eastern coast of England. The first Wagamama venue opened for business in London in April, 1992, and, 14 years later, the enterprise was operating 42 restaurants throughout the United Kingdom. Wagamama has also opened establishments in Dublin, Cork, Amsterdam, Copenhagen, Istanbul, and Dubai, but the second most successful market is Australia.[28]

Wagamama operates in twelve locations in Australia: six in Sydney, two in Melbourne, two in Brisbane, one in Perth, and one in Erina (near Newcastle).[29] The popularity of the restaurant formula highlights recent transformations within the Australian food culture: the steady decline of meat consumption, the growing concern about the connection between health and nutrition, and a passionate embrace of Asian cuisines. On the other hand, the Wagamama case reveals that the time-honored ties with Great Britain, although not strong as in the past, still play a role in the shaping of the culinary culture of its former colony.

In the beginning, the settlers' diet was basically that of Britain's urban underclass—potatoes, bread, tea with a little sugar and milk, and occasionally bacon—mixed with the diet of the immigrants of rural background, which was centered on potatoes, bread, cheese, peas, turnips, and small quantities of meat. Rations provided for the convicts in the penal colonies of Australia resembled seamen's fare of biscuits, salt pork, dried peas, oatmeal, cheese, butter, sugar, coffee, and tea. The food habits of the middle-class immigrants were represented by roasted meat, accompanied by cabbages, carrots, and spinach, and followed by flour-and-suet puddings. The colonial elite dined according to the latest European fashion and, similar to other Western enclaves in different parts of the world, subsided on imported provisions, including champagne, *fois gras*, and tinned plum pudding.[30]

As elsewhere, the settlers retained food practices and preferences of their place of origin for many decades. As was the case in the United States, for example, the fundamental difference that developed over the years between the diet of Australians and New Zealanders and their counterparts in Great Britain was abundance.[31] Because of the successful development of pastoral economies, in particular that of sheep grazing, even working-class families could afford large amounts of meat on a daily basis: mutton chops for breakfast, cold beef at luncheon, and roast or boiled mutton at dinner were by no means unusual. Five-course dinners and enormous portions were standard practice in middle-class households. Until about the mid-twentieth century, afternoon tea remained a fixed accompaniment to the three main meals; it was the accepted way for entertaining guests and used to be particularly lavish on Sundays. Many of the dishes that Australians and New Zealanders claim as their own, such as pumpkin scones, hokey-pokey biscuits, and the Pavlova—a crisp-shelled soft meringue cake spread with whipped cream and decorated with fresh fruit—belong to the world of the afternoon tea.[32]

By the early twentieth century, industrially processed food manufactured by American and European firms (i.e., Heinz, Kellogg, Kraft, Nestle, Cadbury) acquired a firm position in Australian and New Zealand kitchens. The American influence intensified even more because of the presence of American troops during and after World War II. Coca Cola, supermarkets, and American fast food outlets (McDonald's, KFC, Pizza Hut) had established themselves by the 1960s as the new options for dining out for most Australians and New Zealanders, forming stiff competition for traditional fish-and-chips shops, meat-pie carts, and, at the top end, dining rooms of hotels that served a standard menu of roast meats, mashed potatoes, and boiled vegetables. However, a true revolution in the foodways of both islands, as was the case with the Great Britain itself, was brought about by Asian cuisines. This is particularly true for Australia, where Asian cuisines constitute the center of its culinary culture. This shift took place during the last two or three decades, in concert with the relaxation and, during the 1970s, abolishment of the discriminatory immigration policies generally known as "white Australia policy." The Immigration Restriction Act of 1901, which drew on similar legislation in South Africa, restricted nonwhite immigration to Australia, while promoting white, European immigration.[33]

Today, Chinese-Australians and Vietnamese-Australians rank among the largest ethnic groups of Asian origin residing in Australia.[34] The Chinatowns of Sydney, Brisbane, and Melbourne, which date back to the early Chinese immigration to the island propelled by the 1850s' gold rush, are thriving. Along with Chinese and Vietnamese restaurants, Thai, Japanese, and Korean cuisines are also very popular. After two centuries of British culinary domination, Australia has finally embraced the food of its Asian neighbors.

SOUTH AND SOUTHEAST ASIA

VINAY DHARWADKER AND DONNA L. HALPER

The foods of South and Southeast Asia are immensely varied and can be grouped into national cuisines, the cuisines of particular religious or ethnic communities, and regional and local cuisines. Classified by country, the cuisines of Thailand and Vietnam, for example, are among the most distinctive and popular, not only within their national borders, but also outside. Indian cuisine, in contrast, is actually a composite category, in which many prepared dishes, ingredients, cooking methods, and styles of dining are shared by communities across Afghanistan, Pakistan, India, Nepal, Bangladesh, and Sri Lanka. Likewise, the cuisines of Malaysia, Singapore, and Indonesia constitute a regional constellation, which has important historical, cultural, and culinary connections with Chinese cooking. The foods of Muslim communities in different parts of Asia have certain commonalities that set them apart from the foods of Hindus; similarly, the cuisines of the Parsis, the Jains, and various Christian communities in South and Southeast Asia tend to be very different from the cuisines of their neighbors. Within any given Asian nation, cuisine also varies by region, locality, ethnicity, and socioeconomic class. The everyday food and eating habits of poor peasants, for example, are different from those of urban factory workers, which in turn are different from those of middle-class professionals.

EATING OUT IN BIG CITIES

The metropolitan areas in South and Southeast Asia, from Karachi and Lahore to Manila and Jakarta, now offer an international array of popular cuisines in established restaurants, as well as at stalls and vendors' vans and carts in markets, at bazaars, and on roadsides. In each of the large Asian cities, consumers can thus choose from a wide variety of prepared foods and dishes, a spectrum of kinds of ambience and types of service, and a range of prices. Since urban centers in these regions now attract large numbers of international tourists and serve a significant migrant workforce (including foreign executives and diplomats), they usually offer European, American, fast food, and international fusion cuisines in eateries ranging from McDonald's and Pizza Hut to fine dining in upscale hotels. Depending on their clientele and location, they also provide an assortment of Asian cuisines, especially Chinese and Thai, with Korean, Vietnamese, and Indonesian food sometimes added to the mix. Moreover, each of these cities serves large numbers of domestic tourists, together with hundreds of thousands (or millions) of middle- and upper-class residents, so their outlets include a broad selection of national, subnational, and local cuisines. Any Asian metropolis today has a rich, cosmopolitan culture of food and foodways.[1]

In Pakistan, for example, Karachi (on the southern coast) offers quality Thai food at Ban Thai; good Japanese cuisine at Fujiyama; French, Italian, American, Chinese, as well as Pakistani dishes at Lasania; and excellent Afghan cooking at Bar-B-Q Tonight, Pakistan's largest restaurant. Other popular offerings in Karachi include a sumptuous Pakistani buffet (with Mughlai dishes) at Lal Qila, which has a fort-like setting resembling the Red Fort in Delhi; and different types of *biryani* (rice cooked with spices and meat, poultry, or vegetables) at Biryani Center. Lahore (in the north) is a diner's paradise for delicacies in the centuries-long Indo-Muslim culinary tradition. Famous Lahori specialties include *gosht karahi* (goat meat or chicken cooked relatively dry with ground spices) at restaurants such as Pakasia, Butt, and Nirala Butt; *murgh chhanni* (chicken) at the Manna, Tooba, Shaihi, and Ghulam Rasool restaurants; roasted goat meat and *murgh-emussallam* (chicken stuffed with rice and dry fruits) at Tabbaq and the Paradise Canteen; and *seekh kababs* (minced goat meat rolls on skewers) at stalls in the Mochi Gate area and at the Bhayya Kabab Shop. Among the most popular spots for delicious Lahori food are the food street in Gawal Mandi; and distinctive settings, such as Coocoo's Den, which occupies a five-story, 300-year-old *kothi* or manor. International cuisines are available in Lahore at the Copper Kettle and the Gun Smoke Restaurant, as well as at Freddy's Café, which serves Mexican, Italian, Continental, and Afghan dishes.

New Delhi's numerous eateries are best known for their Indian, Asian, and Euro-American food. The range is well represented, for example, in the set of upscale restaurants at the Le Meridien Hotel (at Windsor Place, near Connaught Circus): Golden Phoenix serves Szechwan and Cantonese dishes; Pakwan features Indian, Pakistani, and Afghan cuisine, with live *ghazal* music; Le Belvedere specializes in fine French food; Monsoon caters to Mediterranean tastes; the Aloha Bar is popular for its Polynesian ambience; and La Plaza, a café, offers sandwiches, pastries, patties, and tarts. Among Delhi's most unique and popular restaurants are Karim (Nizamuddin area), which features fabulous Indo-Muslim cooking not found anywhere else; and Naivedyam (Hauz Khas Village), known for its south Indian and vegetarian dishes. The best establishment, and one of the world's great restaurants (which American President Bill Clinton ranked as his favorite in the mid-1990s), may be Bukhara, located in the Maurya Sheraton and Towers, near the city's diplomatic enclave: it specializes in Northwest Frontier cuisine (the cuisine of the Peshawar region in Pakistan and of Afghanistan) and is famous for its *rotis* and *nans* (unleavened breads), *kababs* and *tikkas* (grilled chicken, fish, and meat), roasts and curries (goat meat and chicken), and *biryanis*. Among New Delhi's numerous Chinese restaurants, Daichee (South Extension area), for example, offers excellent Cantonese and Szechwan dishes at moderate prices; among its popular, moderate restaurant clusters, the eateries at the Pandara Road Market offer spicy Sikh-Punjabi cooking; and, of its many snack houses and sweet-shops, those at Bengali Market, South Extension, and Green Park, for example, continue to be among the most popular for north Indian *samosas*, *kachoris*, *tikkis*, *gol gappas*, *paapri*, and *chaat*, as well as a great variety of milk-based Bengali sweets.

In Sri Lanka, the capital of Colombo likewise offers an international array of foods and flavors. Chesa Swiss, for example, specializes in Swiss cuisine, with fondue, *raclette* (melted cheese over boiled potatoes, with ground black pepper, accompanied by pickled pearl onions and gherkins), and *rosti* (grated potato mixed with oil, shaped into patties and pan fried or baked); Il Ponte provides quality Italian food; and La Rambla is popular for its Mediterranean fare. The Gallery Café is housed in the former workshop of Sri Lanka's most famous architect, Geoffrey Bawa, and is best known for its fusion menu and desserts. Navratna, located in the Taj Samudra Hotel, offers north Indian cuisine; The Mango Tree is widely known for its innovative South Asian dishes; and Shanti Vihar, a moderately priced restaurant, specializes in vegetarian south Indian food.

Bangkok, widely regarded as the city with the best range of restaurants in Southeast Asia, is one of the world's great havens for food lovers. Some of its best restaurants for European, American, and international fusion cuisines are concentrated in the Silom Street, Banglampoo, and Sukhumivit areas, which house most international tourists; a variety of Chinese eateries are located in Chinatown; and a number of Indian restaurants are clustered in the Pahurat and Bangrak areas. Among the city's best known Thai and Chinese restaurants are Baan Chiang, located in an old Thai house, and Golden Dragon Chinese Restaurant, noted for its deep-fried aromatic duck, served with pancakes and Beijing sauce. European cuisines can be sampled in various forms and at various prices at Le Banyan, a moderate French eatery; Le Bouchon, a popular French restaurant in the red-light district; Gianni's, well-known for its creative menu and excellent service; Heidelberg, prominent for its Swiss and German dishes, including three types of Swiss fondue; and Euro de Café, famous for its fast food, which includes sausages, French fries, and unusual salads.

Of Bangkok's Middle Eastern and African foodways, Shoshana is an inexpensive Israeli hangout, popular with students and backpackers for its *schnitzel*, *falafel*, and *hummus*; Roots serves African and Caribbean food and features reggae music; and Sarah specializes in Arabic, Yemeni, Lebanese, and Thai cuisines. Among the city's many Indian restaurants are Rang

Mahal, a lavish fine dining establishment in the Rembrandt Hotel; Mrs Balbir's, which offers excellent home-style north Indian dishes; and Delhi's Delights and Akbar, which serve a range of north Indian and Indo-Muslim dishes. American-style eateries include the classic Fireplace Grill, recently refurbished at the Intercontinental Hotel, which displays and custom-cooks beef steaks on a charcoal grill; Hamilton's Steak House, which offers a conservative ambience with dark wood paneling; and the Rib Room, which specializes in prime rib and offers a grand view of Bangkok's skyline.

Kuala Lumpur's eateries cover spicy Malay food, numerous varieties of Chinese cooking, Nyonya cuisine (a 400-year long hybrid of immigrant Chinese and Malay styles), and north as well as south Indian cuisines, in addition to Thai, Japanese, Korean, and Portuguese food. Popular restaurants include Koon Kee Wantan Noodle, probably the best place for its type of Chinese food; Highway Café, where the menu ranges from charbroiled steaks and Continental dishes to seafood and Malaysian delicacies; La Bodega, a Spanish *tapas* bar; Bombay Palace and Bangles, both Indian restaurants; and Seri Melayu, considered the city's best Malay restaurant.

In Singapore, the Just Steak restaurant features exceptional Wagyu beef (from the select Wagyu breed of cattle); Margarita's serves moderately priced Mexican dishes and memorable deserts; and Coriander Leaf offers a unique menu of Indian fusion cuisine, which includes notable preparations of chicken *tandoori* (roasted in an open clay oven) and cod with *miso* (soybean paste). Whole Earth specializes in home-style Peranakan and Thai vegetarian food, and its menu includes Buddhist vegetarian preparations (which exclude onion and garlic); whereas African Heartbeat and Mama Africa specialize in African cuisines, with ingredients ranging from yams to ostrich meat.

In Jakarta, diners' choices include Oasis, a boutique restaurant with an international menu, housed in the former home of a famous Indonesian painter, Raden Saleh. Oasis is noted for its *Rijstaffel*, a Dutch colonial rice table, a large buffet-style meal that is now served only in select upscale Indonesian and Malaysian restaurants: it offers up to thirty varied dishes, all eaten with steamed white rice; the main dishes include several kinds of *satay*, Indonesian egg, bean, and prawn *sambals* (*sambal celek* is a red chili paste, of Indonesian origin, but also used widely in Malay and Thai cooking), braised chicken, beef *rendang*, grilled fish, and coconut and vegetable curry, and Balinese-style pork; and the accompaniments range from fresh pineapple and grated coconut to frittered plantain and peanuts, crisp, fried *krupuk* (starch crackers flavored with dried shrimp), and pressed and dried *melinjo* nuts. Other distinctive choices in Jakarta include Natrabu and Sari Bundo, both Padang restaurants, the former representing the best of this western Sumatran style of food presentation in the city.

The range of foods and cuisines available in some of the major metropolitan areas of South and Southeast Asia is immense, diverse, and distinctive: unprecedented internationalization and cosmopolitanism now mark the foodways of this part of the world. The picture becomes even more multifarious by including Kathmandu in Nepal, Dhaka in Bangladesh, Ho Chi Minh City in Vietnam, and Manila in the Philippines, not to mention the great cities of Mumbai (Bombay), Kolkata (Calcutta), Chennai (Madras), Bangalore, and others in India. The foregoing survey, of course, limits itself to established restaurants and hotels in large cities, which represent only a small portion of the food and hospitality industries in Asian countries. If street vendors, roadside food stalls, and food shops in markets and bazaars in both urban and rural areas are included, the sheer variety of available foods increases exponentially. From Pakistan to Bangladesh, Sri Lanka to Myanmar, and Laos to the Philippines, vendors, food stalls, and local shops are the outlets where most people eat on the go or where they order takeout on a routine basis. In a sprawling metropolis such as Mumbai, which has some 2,000 established bars and restaurants, the number of smaller, unregulated food outlets runs into the tens of thousands, as it also does in a poorer country such as Vietnam, where street food is the norm for most consumers.

POPULAR CUISINES

The two cuisines from South and Southeast Asia that have achieved global popularity since about 1975 are north Indian cuisine (which shares many features with the cuisines of Afghanistan, Pakistan, Nepal, Bangladesh, and Sri Lanka) and Thai cuisine. The foods of Vietnam and Indonesia, as well as of south India and Malaysia, are also well known internationally, but not to the same extent as the foods of north India and Thailand. Within any given Asian nation, its own cuisine, along with many of its regional and local varieties, is the most widely consumed, foods from other parts of Asia and the world are also quite popular. North Indian and Thai are two popular cuisines that exemplify patterns found in a larger spectrum of national and transregional culinary and gastronomic traditions.

North Indian Cuisine

This is a composite culinary tradition common to most of the Indo-Gangetic Plains region and its surrounding areas, so that its terrain stretches from northern Pakistan to north India proper. Its repertoire is related to many elements in Nepali and Bangladeshi cooking, and has more indirect links to Afghan and Sri Lankan food. Among its characteristics are fresh flatbreads made of wheat flour, usually unleavened, and cooked on a hot griddle, in an open clay oven, or directly over a flame; vegetables, meats, poultry, or fish cooked with particular combinations of spices, for dishes that range from dry and semidry preparations to those that have a high proportion of gravy (usually called *curry*); and a range of spices, from turmeric, chili pepper, and cumin, coriander, and mustards seeds to cardamom, clove, cinnamon, and asafetida. North Indian cuisine also makes fairly extensive use of ginger, garlic, fresh coriander, lime, tamarind extract, and saffron, as well as onion and tomato, to create the basic flavor, texture, and consistency of a variety of dishes; it traditionally employs ghee (clarified butter) as its cooking medium, now often replaced with vegetable oil or unsalted butter; and it uses distinctive methods of preparation and cooking to achieve its tasteful effects.

Among the characteristic techniques of this cuisine are the cracking of cumin and mustard seeds in very hot oil before the addition of other ingredients to the pot; the slow frying of sliced or chopped onion to a golden brown in a little ghee or oil, often along with ginger or garlic (finely chopped or ground to a thick paste) in a *karahi* (the heavier Indian counterpart of the Chinese wok), as part of the base of a curry or gravy; and often the slow and long cooking of all of the ingredients together in the liquid, to bring out a multiplicity of aromas and flavors. The variety of wheat breads in this cuisine ranges from *chapatis* (thin flat rounds, cooked on a griddle) and *rotis* (often thicker rounds, cooked on a griddle or on a flame) to *paranthas* (thick flatbreads, with internal layers glazed with oil and basted on the outside with oil while cooking on a griddle), and *naans* (flatbreads, occasionally leavened and sometimes stuffed with chopped vegetables or minced meats, cooked in a *tandoor*), as well as to several types of deep-fried breads (such as *puris* and *bhaturas*). North Indian cuisine also supplements its staple wheat breads with different kinds of rice preparations, which include white steamed rice, *pulao* (rice cooked with spices, vegetables, or meat), and *biryani* (rice cooked with spices and meat in a particular Indo-Muslim style).

Among the most popular nonvegetarian dishes in this cuisine are chicken curry, the simplest and most generic preparation of this type, with chicken pieces browned and cooked slowly in a spicy gravy; and meat curry, with goat meat instead of chicken in a more heavily spiced gravy—both of which may be eaten with *rotis*, *naans*, or steamed rice. More complex or sophisticated preparations include Punjabi-style butter chicken, in a tomato-based curry; and numerous Indo-Muslim preparations, such as karahi chicken (or meat, a drier, heavily spiced dish), *korma* (with chicken or meat, cooked with whole spices and ginger and garlic paste, but without onions or water), and *murgh-e-mussallam* and *raanmussallam* (whole chicken and leg of goat, respectively, marinated, stuffed with a mixture of fried onions and dry fruits and other ingredients, and slow-cooked in a covered pan). Some of the most popular dishes and breads in this cuisine, such as *tandoori* chicken and *naan*, are cooked in a *tandoor*, a waist-high cylindrical clay oven that narrows to a circular opening at the top, which is fired with coals at the bottom. Meat, poultry, and fish, placed on long skewers (inserted vertically through the oven's opening), are roasted; *rotis* and *naans* are stuck to the clay sides on the interior and also cooked rapidly at high temperatures. Other popular dishes, such as *seekh kababs*, are usually cooked more slowly on skewers placed horizontally over an open coal grill.

North Indian vegetarian dishes commonly use potatoes, green peas and beans, cabbages, cauliflowers, capsicums (sweet green peppers), brinjals (purple eggplants), spinach and mustard greens, and a range of indigenous squashes and gourds (*ghiya*, *tori*, and *karela*, the last being a remarkably bitter gourd). Some of these vegetables are cooked in combination with onions and tomatoes or used with other distinctive ingredients, such as *paneer* (a tofu-like cake made with milk curds). The simplest *sabji* (vegetable preparation) with any one or more of these ingredients is spiced with turmeric, chili pepper, and either cracked mustard seeds or cracked cumin seeds in tandem with powdered coriander seeds. More elaborate recipes require the preparation of a complex gravy with additional or other sets of spices and other flavoring ingredients, such as garlic, ginger, or tamarind paste, and even full cream and yogurt. In addition, north Indian food draws on ingredients such as chick peas (*kabuli chana*); as well as a large assortment of legumes, known as *dals* (such as *tur*, *chana*, *urad*, *maa*, *moong*, and *masur*—the penultimate being dried Chinese mung beans and the last being lentils in American parlance). Popular vegetarian dishes include *matar paneer* and *palak paneer* (green peas and spinach, respectively, with cubed paneer); *navratan korma* (a preparation with nine assorted vegetables in a rich, creamy curry); *dum aloo* (whole potatoes cooked with whole spices and yogurt); *tandoori gobhi* (a whole cauliflower, marinated in yogurt and spices, roasted in a *tandoor*); stuffed capsicum (with mashed potato and spices); *chana masala* (chick peas cooked in a spicy gravy); and *dal makhani* (a cooked *dal* topped with butter). Vegetarian accompaniments to most north Indian meals include *raita* (chopped or shredded vegetables, among other possible ingredients, blended into mildly spiced yogurt) and pickles (mango, lime, garlic, and other such ingredients pickled in a heavily spiced oil).

Thai Cuisine

Like north Indian cuisine, Thai food is immensely varied, bringing together numerous ingredients in memorable combinations and highlighting unusual tastes, textures, and flavors. The staples of Thai cuisine, like much other food in Southeast Asia, are white rice and alimentary paste made of rice flour (or an equivalent starchy medium), dried into noodles or sticks of various lengths that are either round or flat in cross-section. Nonvegetarian ingredients include beef, pork, chicken, duck, and a wide variety of fish and seafood; vegetarian ingredients range from onions and shallots, cabbages (several varieties, including *bok choy*), peas, mung bean sprouts, eggplants (several varieties, including small, round, green and white ones), and mushrooms (many varieties), to lettuce, bamboo shoots, seaweed, radish, and squashes (a few varieties), as well as to tofu (processed soybean cake) and tapioca pearls (processed cassava starch).

Among the numerous spices and flavoring ingredients are cardamom, cloves, white and black pepper, star anise, turmeric, peanuts, and coriander, cumin, sesame, and fennel seeds, as well as basil, fermented soy and other beans, chili peppers (several varieties, fresh and dried), garlic, ginger, chives, coriander leaf, limes, mint, tamarind seeds and paste, vinegar, sesame oil, and fish, oyster, and soy sauces. Many of the distinctive and unusual flavors of Thai food come from its use of secret flavoring agents such as coriander root, *kaffir* lime leaves and lime rind, *kah* or *galangal* root, lemongrass, salted plums, and dried shrimp, together with prepared bean, chili, and shrimp pastes. One of the key elements in this cuisine (probably derived from the foods of Goa and Kerala on the Indian west coast and shared with Malaysian and Indonesian cooking) is coconut, used in its fresh and dried (grated) form and especially in the form of coconut milk, which provides the base and medium for many Thai dishes.

The preparation and cooking methods of Thai food are quite elaborate. Thai curries, such Panang, green, red, and peanut, involve prior preparation of complex pastes with multiple spices and flavoring agents, which are soaked, chopped, and pounded or ground until blended smooth. Some of the dipping and cooking sauces (such as ground chili sauce, vinegar sauce, and garlic sauce) can be made in advance, but others (such as spicy fish sauce and lime sauce) have to be prepared shortly before serving. Much of the actual cooking is done in a large wok or a large frying pan; prepared ingredients are often cooked quickly at high heat, being added serially during the cooking process; many dishes are assembled additively in the end. Some dishes, however, require a limited amount of slow cooking under a lid, at low heat; some ingredients, prepared in advance or in bulk, require extended cooking times. In most of its steps and techniques, Thai cooking can seem utterly different from north Indian cooking.

Among the most popular Thai dishes are *gai dom kha*, a creamy soup of chicken in mildly spiced coconut milk; *pad thai*, a rice noodle dish with an absorbed sweet-and-sour sauce and eggs, green onions, bean sprouts, and some shrimp, chicken, or pork, topped with roasted chili pepper, peanuts, and lime juice; *gang kiew wan gai*, chicken with green curry, a hot preparation of chopped chicken cooked in coconut milk spiced with green curry paste; *bla nuang*, ginger-steamed fish, in which a whole fish, such as trout or a small red or yellow

THE POPULARITY OF *PHO*

Although Chinese cuisine has enjoyed years of popularity all over the world, the number of Vietnamese restaurants is now growing in countries from Australia to America, and not just Vietnamese immigrants eat at these restaurants. Because Vietnamese cuisine tends to be hearty but inexpensive, both students and people on a budget have become big fans.

Vietnamese cuisine made its debut in the United States around 1961, when one of the first Vietnamese restaurants opened in New York City. The Viet Nam Restaurant introduced Americans to a uniquely Vietnamese dish called *pho*, which was an instant success. To this day, people go to Vietnamese restaurants worldwide to enjoy a bowl of this unique noodle soup, which can be eaten for lunch or dinner.

Actually, calling pho noodle soup is an oversimplification. Pho is a meal in itself. A bowl of pho is aromatic, thanks to spices such as anise and ginger, and usually consists of a tasty broth with rice noodles and thin slices of beef. It often has bean sprouts, slices of lime, and chili peppers as garnishes. There is also a version made with thin slices of chicken rather than beef. Vietnamese restaurants have their own unique way of making pho, with variations in the kinds of spices or the cuts of meat. Most Westerners do not realize that while pho looks as though it rhymes with "doe," it is actually pronounced to rhyme with "duh." In any case, the many fans of this Vietnamese soup say there is nothing as good as pho!

snapper, is steamed with a mixture of ginger, mushrooms, green onions, salted plums, and a little ground pork; and *nue nam tok*, grilled beef with seasoning, thin slices of grilled flank steak topped with a hot and sour dressing and served on a bed of lettuce, garnished with coriander and basil leaves. Other popular dishes include noodles with coconut milk (*mee gati*), ground pork salad (*nam sod*), stir-fried beef with mint or basil (*nue gra pao*), dried beef (*nue swan*), pork with green beans (*moo pad prig king*), and sweet-and-sour pork (*pad priew wan*). Some of the best vegetarian dishes in this cuisine are stir-fried eggplant (*pad ma kua yaow*), stir-fried tofu with bean sprouts (*pad tohoo gob tua ngog*), stir-fried bamboo shoots with chilies (*pad prig nomai*), and spicy green beans (*pad ped tou kag*).

Malay, Singaporean, and Indonesian cuisines share many preparation and cooking methods with Thai food, especially the general handling of rice and various alimentary pastes (the staples). All four cuisines share some techniques with mainland Chinese cooking. Vietnamese, Cambodian, and Laotian cooking also fall into this broad circle of interrelated cuisines, even though they differ from Thai cuisine, often for economic and environmental reasons, in their choice of ingredients, cooking methods, highlighted flavors, and especially the preparation of bases for some kinds of dishes.

FOOD, GEOGRAPHY, AND ETHNICITY

Food in South and Southeast Asia differs broadly by race, ethnicity, and geographical setting. The wide swath of land stretching from Pakistan, through north India, to Bangladesh, and down to the Indian state of Maharashtra, is still inhabited predominantly by ethnic groups of Indo-European origin. Wheat is the staple cereal, accompanied by several legumes and an array of fresh vegetables and fresh and dry fruits, for this population (along with the population of Nepal, which is culturally influenced by it, despite ethnic differences). Cow's and buffalo's milk provide a range of dairy products, and, for select communities, eggs, chicken, and goat meat provide the common nonvegetarian fare. Beef and pork are relatively rare because of religious proscriptions (see the following); rice supplements wheat in specific contexts, or replaces wheat as the staple grain in particular regions (such as the Indian state of West Bengal, and Nepal and Bangladesh); and fresh-water and salt-water fish become primary in some areas for geographical and environmental reasons.

Much of the region in peninsular India, south and east of the state of Maharashtra, and the northern portion of Sri Lanka are occupied by ethnic groups of mostly Dravidian origin. The food of Dravidian peoples centers around rice, selected legumes, a range of fresh fruits and vegetables (some of which are different from those widespread in the north), and a variety of dairy products derived from cow's and buffalo's milk. Relatively few communities in the Dravidian region consume chicken, goat meat, or even eggs; fish is restricted mostly to coastal communities, for whom it becomes a primary food for geographical and environmental reasons; and wheat is almost completely excluded from the food economy.

In contrast, Southeast Asia is occupied by numerous ethnic groups in different geographical environments, but its food broadly centers around rice as the staple grain (to the exclusion of wheat), with the soybean as its principal legume (which is different from the variety of legumes used all over the subcontinent), and almost completely without any dairy products based on cow's or buffalo's milk (the only real exception being the milk of the Philippine buffalo or *carabao*). This economy uses a variety of rice and soybean products, especially in the form of noodles and paste, together with a wider range of meat, poultry, and fish than in South Asia; a broad selection of fresh and preserved vegetables and fruits, some of which are different from those in South Asia; as well as an array of fresh-water foods and seafoods, ranging from nuts and weeds to marine life unknown in South Asia. Geography and environment (as well as economic and cultural history) thus vitally determine many of the qualitative differences among South and Southeast Asian cuisines.

RELIGION AND FOOD

From Pakistan to the Philippines, food habits also differ from community to community by religion and related factors. Among Muslim populations throughout the region, from majority communities in Pakistan, Bangladesh, Indonesia, and Brunei to minority communities in India, Sri Lanka, Thailand, the Philippines, Malaysia, and Singapore, pork and its products are proscribed. Among Hindu populations, the majorities in India and Nepal and often small or tiny minorities in Bangladesh, Sri Lanka, Thailand, Malaysia, and Singapore, religious beliefs prohibit the consumption of beef and its products. In contrast, Asian Christians, from India and Sri Lanka to the Philippines, regularly consume both beef and pork but have to do so under conditions that do not offend neighboring Hindu or Muslim communities. The followers of the Jain religion, concentrated mostly in India, forego all forms of nonvegetarian food under all circumstances and therefore often limit their consumption only to food prepared under familiar and controlled conditions. The same is true of many castes in the extensive Hindu social system, which now extends well beyond the borders of India and especially into Nepal, Sri Lanka, Malaysia, and Singapore.

Complex sets of further restrictions and proscriptions come also into play in most of these communities during particular religious festivals and observances: Muslims, for example, substantially modify their diets during the holy month of Ramadan (September to October); nonvegetarian Hindus limit themselves to specific types of vegetarian foods during festivals such as Diwali (the Hindu new year, in October or November), temporarily joining more orthodox vegetarian Hindus in their dietary restrictions. Religious proscriptions and prescriptions, both in general and for specific occasions, have a profound effect on the sales of food items, prepared foods, and the market cycles of foodways, as well as on the locations and conditions in which food may be prepared, sold, and consumed outside the home in both South Asia and Southeast Asia.

Within the world of Hinduism, which has almost 850 million followers in India alone, the caste system imposes a series of strict restrictions on its members with regard to the choice, preparation, consumption, and exchange of food and foodstuffs. As a result, the majority of orthodox Hindus in rural and semiurban India do not consume food prepared outside of their family kitchens or the kitchens of other members of their caste. Even in large cities, many Westernized and modernized Hindus still resist eating out often or regularly and may systematically avoid restaurants that are owned, operated, serviced, or patronized by foreigners, people of other ethnicities and religions, or people of lower caste status. Hindus who practice any version of their caste's code of dietary purity also travel with homemade food and beverages, even on extended journeys.

In the course of the twentieth century, India's hospitality industry has developed large nationwide networks of niche hotels and restaurants that cater specifically to orthodox Hindu clientele (300 million people or more); the names and signs of such establishments clearly announce which particular cuisine they offer and what types of patrons they serve. In many ways, the widespread Hindu practice of dietary purity undercuts the very notion of popular food in public foodways and broadly resembles the practice of kosher diets among orthodox Jews. Given the kinds of restrictions that various branches of Hinduism place on their caste members, the attempts under globalization by American food corporations, such as McDonald's, KFC, and Pizza Hut, to exploit the size of India's consumer market have frequently run into unforeseen obstacles.

RESOURCE GUIDE

PRINT SOURCES

East Asia and Oceania

Bailey, Ray, with Mary Earle. *Home Cooking to Takeaways: Changes in Food Consumption in New Zealand during 1880–1990.* Palmerston North: Massey University, 1999.
Bestor, Theodore. *Tsukiji: The Fish Market in the Center of the World.* Berkeley: University of California Press, 2005.
Chu, Young-ha. "Origin and Change in *Kimch'i* Culture." *Korea Journal* 2 (Summer 1995): 18–29.
Cwiertka, Katarzyna. *Modern Japanese Cuisine: Food, Power and National Identity.* London: Reaktion Books, 2006.
———. "Soy Sauce Industry in Korea: Scrutinising the Legacy of Japanese Colonialism." *Asian Studies Review* 30 (December 2006): 389–410.
———, with Boudewijn C. A. Walraven, eds. *Asian Food: The Global and the Local.* Honolulu: University of Hawaii Press, 2002.
Du Bois, Christine M., Chee-Beng Tan, and Sidney W. Mintz, eds. *The World of Soy.* Urbana: University of Illinois Press, 2007.
Farquhar, Judith. *Appetites: Food and Sex in Postsocialist China.* Durham: Duke University Press, 2002.
Ishige, Naomichi. *The History and Culture of Japanese Food.* London: Kegan Paul, 2001.
Jing, Jun, ed. *Feeding China's Little Emperors: Food, Children, and Social Change.* Stanford: Stanford University Press, 2000.
Lee, Chun Ja, Hye Won Park, and Kwi Young Kim. *The Book of Kimchi.* Seoul: Korean Overseas Culture and Information Service, Ministry of Culture and Tourism, 1998.
Ohnuki-Tierney, Emiko. *Rice as Self.* Princeton: Princeton University Press, 1993.
Reinschmidt, Michael. "Rice in South Korean Life: The Transformation of Agricultural Icons." Pp. 509–25 in Roy W. Hamilton (ed.), *The Art of Rice: Spirit and Sustenance in Asia.* Los Angeles: UCLA Fowler Museum of Cultural History, 2003.
Roberts, J. A. G. *China to Chinatown: Chinese Food in the West.* London: Reaktion Books, 2002.
Sand, Jordan. "A Short History of MSG: Good Science, Bad Science, and Taste Cultures." *Gastronomica* (Fall 2005): 38–49.
Symons, Michael. *One Continuous Picnic: A History of Eating in Australia.* Adelaide: Duck Press, 1982.
Watson, James L., ed. *Golden Arches East: McDonald's in East Asia.* Stanford: Stanford University Press, 1997.
Wu, David Y. H., and Tan Chee-beng, eds. *Changing Chinese Foodways in Asia.* Hong Kong: The Chinese University Press, 2001.
Yan, Yunxiang. "Of Hamburger and Social Space: Consuming McDonald's in Beijing." Pp. 201–25 in Deborah S. Davis (ed.), *The Consumer Revolution in Urban China.* Berkeley: University of California Press, 1999.

South and Southeast Asia

Acharya, K. T. *A Historical Dictionary of Indian Food.* New Delhi: Oxford University Press, 1998. A detailed yet compact guide to much South Asian food.
Collingham, Lizzie. *Curry: A Tale of Cooks & Conquerors.* Oxford University Press, 2006.
Crawford, William, and Kamolmal Pootaraksa. *Thai Home-Cooking from Kamolmal's Kitchen.* New York: New American Library, 1985. An excellent exposition of Thai cuisine, with recipes.

Katz, Solomon H., and William Woys Weaver, eds. *Encyclopedia of Food and Culture.* New York: Scribner's, 2002.
Ramanujan, A. K. "Food for Thought: Towards an Anthology of Hindu Food-images." Pp. 73–95 in Vinay Dharwadker (ed.), *The Collected Essays of A. K. Ramanujan.* New Delhi: Oxford University Press, 1995. Informative and stimulating essay on the "system" of Hindu food.
Tyabji, Surayya. *Mirch Masala: One Hundred Indian Recipes.* Bombay: Sangam Books, Orient Longman, c. 1975. A small gem of a book, with many remarkable Indo-Muslim and north Indian recipes.

WEBSITES

East Asia and Oceania

EatingChina.com. http://www.eatingchina.com (accessed March 7, 2007).
Introduction to Korean Food. http://english.tour2korea.com/05food/Introduction/lifestyle_food. asp?konum=1&kosm=m5_1 (accessed March 7, 2007).
Research Centre for the History of Food and Drink. http://www.arts.adelaide.edu.au/centrefooddrink (accessed 7 March 2007).
Soyfoods Center. http://www.thesoydailyclub.com/Shurtleff.cfm (accessed March 7, 2007).
Tokyo Food Page. http://www.bento.com/tf-recp.html (accessed March 7, 2007).

South and Southeast Asia

AsiaRecipe.Com. http://asiarecipe.com (accessed October 9, 2006). Contains notes on and recipes from various national cuisines.
Sally's Place. http://www.sallys-place.com/food/ethnic_cusine (accessed October 9, 2006). Contains useful short essays on specific Southeast Asian cuisines by Nancy Freeman.
Starwood Hotels. http://www.starwoodhotels.com (accessed October 9, 2006). Links to Sheraton and Le Meridien hotels in Asia, with descriptions of their restaurants.
World66. http://www.world66.com (accessed October 9, 2006). Contains listings, with consumers' notes and ratings, on restaurants in Asian cities.
World Executive: Hotels and Resorts Direct. http://www.worldexecutive.com/cityguides (accessed October 9, 2006).Lists restaurants in Asian cities, sometimes with comments.

VIDEOS/FILMS

East Asia and Oceania

Eat, Drink, Man, Woman. Directed by Ang Lee. MGM, 1993.
Tampopo. Directed by Junzo Itami. Fox Lorber, 1987.
Peking Restaurant (aka: *The Great Chef*). Directed by Kim Ui-Seok. Dawoori Entertainment, 1999.

NOTES

East Asia and Oceania

1. Du Bois et al. (in Resource Guide).
2. Young-Kyun Yang, "Jajangmyeon and Junggukjip," *Korea Journal* 2 (Summer 2005): 60–88; Cwiertka, *Modern Japanese Cuisine* (in Resource Guide), chapter 6.
3. Sangmee Bak, "From Strange Bitter Concoction to Romantic Necessity: The Social History of Coffee Drinking in South Korea," *Korea Journal* 2 (Summer 2005): 37–59.

4. See http://www.starbucks.cn/.
5. See E. N. Anderson, *The Food of China* (New Haven: Yale University Press, 1988), pp. 194–228, or Solomon H. Katz, ed., *Encyclopedia of Food and Culture* (New York: Charles Scribner's Sons, 2003), vol. I, pp. 384–398.
6. Yunxiang Yan, "Of Hamburger and Social Space: Consuming McDonald's in Beijing" (in Resource Guide).
7. François Sabban, "China," in *The Cambridge World History of Food*, ed. K. F. Kiple and K. C. Ornelas (Cambridge: Cambridge University Press, 2000), vol. II, p. 1172.
8. Jun Jing, "Food, Nutrition, and Cultural Authority in a Gansu Village," pp. 135–159 in Jing, ed., *Feeding China's Little Emperors: Food, Children, and Social Change* (in Resource Guide).
9. Dali L. Yang, *Calamity and Reform in China: State, Rural Society, and Institutional Chang since the Great Peal Famine* (Stanford: Stanford University Press, 1996), pp. 240–242.
10. Yan, "Of Hamburger and Social Space," pp. 86–87.
11. Sea-ling Cheng, "Eating Hong Kong's Way Out," In *Asian Food: The Global and the Local*. (in Resource Guide), pp. 16–33.
12. Sea-ling Cheng, "Back to the Future: Herbal Tea Shops in Hong Kong," pp. 51–73 in *Hong Kong: The Anthropology of Chinese Metropolis*, ed. Grant Evans and Maria Tam (Richmond: Curzon Press, 1997).
13. Jordan Sand, "A Short History of MSG: Good Science, Bad Science, and Taste Cultures," *Gastronomica* 4 (Fall 2005): 38–49. See also Keun-Sik Jung, "Colonial Modernity and the Social History of Chemical Seasoning in Korea," *Korea Journal* 2 (Summer 2005): 9–36.
14. See http://www.gio.gov.tw/taiwan-website/5-gp/culture/food/; http://202.39.225.132/jsp/Eng/html/about_taiwan/gourmet.jsp, and http://202.39.225.132/jsp/Eng/html/travel_tour/subject_introduce.jsp?subject_id=11+11&update=2002-09-17 (accessed 1/7/2006). I would like to thank Chen Yujen for providing information on Taiwanese cuisine.
15. *The Asahi Shimbun Japan Almanac 2006*, Tokyo: Asahi Shinbunsha, 2005, pp. 195, 200.
16. Michael Ashkenazi and Jeanne Jacob, *The Essence of Japanese Cuisine: An Essay on Food and Culture* (Richmond: Curzon Press, 2000), pp. 119–134.
17. See T. J. M. Holden, "'And Now for the Main (Dis)course . . .,' or Food as Entrée in Contemporary Japanese Television," *M/C: A Journal of Media and Culture*, 7 (1999), http://www.uq.edu.au/mc/9910/entree.php (accessed 10/01/2006); Bestor *Tsukiji* (in Resource Guide), pp. 133–140; T. J. M. Holden, "The Overcooked and Underdone: Masculinities in Japanese Food Programming," *Food and Foodways* 1–2 (2005): 39–65.
18. Jane Cobbi, "*Sonaemono*: Ritual Gifts to the Deities," Pp. 201–209 in *Ceremony and Ritual in Japan*, J. van Bremen and D. P. Martinez, eds. (Richmond: Curzon Press, 1995); Robert J. Smith, *Ancestor Worship in Contemporary Japan* (Stanford: University of California Press, 1974), pp. 90–91, 105, 133–134.
19. Noriya Sumihara, "Changing Sake in Global Challenge: Crisis Paves Ways for Tradition," paper presented at the 14th EAJS meeting, Warsaw, 2003.
20. Sarah Hanson, "Hip Drinks Bring Cool Profits in Japan." FAS Online, http://ffas.usda.gov/info/agexporter/2000/September/hip.htm (accessed 1/07/2006).
21. Cwiertka, *Modern Japanese Cuisine*, chapter 7.
22. Boudewijn C. A. Walraven, "Bardot Soup and Confucians' Meat: Food and Korean Identity in Global Context," pp. 101–106 in *Asian Food: The Global and the Local*, ed. Cwiertka with Walraven (in Resource Guide).
23. Walraven, "Bardot Soup and Confucians' Meat," pp. 97–101.
24. Laura C. Nelson, *Measured Excess: Status, Gender, and Consumer Nationalism in South Korea* (New York: Columbia University Press, 2000), pp. 126–130.
25. Sangmee Bak, "McDonald's in Seoul: Food Choices, Identity, and Nationalism," pp. 150, 154, in *Golden Arches East: McDonald's in East Asia*, James L. Watson, ed. (in Reousrce Guide); Nelson, 2000, p. 25.
26. Robert W. Pemberton, "Wild-Gathered Foods as Countercurrents to Dietary Globalisation in South Korea," Pp. 79–80 in Cwiertka with Walraven (in Resource Guide).

27. Brian Murton, "Australia and New Zealand," in *The Cambridge World History of Food*, vol. II, pp. 1345–1346.
28. Cwiertka, *Modern Japanese Cuisine* (in Resource Guide), pp. 197–198.
29. See www.wagamama.com.au (accessed September 7, 2006).
30. See, for example, Michael Symons, *One Continuous Picnic: A History of Eating in Australia* (Adelaide: Duck Press, 1982); David Burton, *Two Hundred Years of New Zealand Food and Cookery* (Wellington: Reed, 1981). See also J. A. G. Roberts, *China to Chinatown* (in Resource Guide), pp. 66–70.
31. Harvey Levenstein, *Revolution at the Table: The Transformation of the American Diet* (New York and Oxford: Oxford University Press, 1988), p. 7.
32. Barbara Santich, "Australia and New Zealand," in *Encyclopedia of Food and Culture*, vol. I, pp. 140–143.
33. See Laksiri Jayasuriya, David Walker, and Jan Gothard, eds., *Legacies of White Australia* (Claremont: UWA Press, 2003).
34. For detailed statistics see www.immi.gov.au/media/index.htm (accessed September 7, 2006).

South and Southeast Asia

1. The information on specific Asian cities, restaurants, cuisines, menus, and dishes summarized in this section of the chapter is current as of late 2006. The information was gathered from World66, online at www.world66.com; Starwood Hotels, online at www.starwoodhotels.com; and World Executive Hotels and Resorts Direct, online at www.worldexecutive.com, accessed as noted in the Resource Guide at the end of this chapter.

GAMES, TOYS, AND PASTIMES

EAST ASIA AND OCEANIA

ERWEI DONG

Mainland China, Taiwan, Korea, and Japan are geographically located in East Asia. Heavily influenced by Chinese language, religions, and political systems from ancient times, East Asian countries have many similarities in art, music, leisure, and the like. As a form of leisure, games and toys have been developed since ancient times in East Asia. Many games and toys played by the Chinese, Koreans, and Japanese are similar despite slightly different names and variations.

The aboriginal and Maori people were among the first settlers in the continent of Australia and in New Zealand. The European immigrants arrived in Oceania only several hundred years ago. In addition to indigenous people and European settlers, people from other continents have also been immigrating to Oceania for the last 60 years, leading to great social diversity in Australia and Newland. Multicultural games are played, including indigenous games, traditional European games, and the diverse games played by Australians and New Zealanders.

The rapid growth of modern toys in East Asia has influenced the sort of toys that children in East Asia enjoy, but traditional folk toys continue to be popular in contemporary East Asian culture.

CHINA

Games in modern Chinese society are strongly linked to ancient Chinese games, and some traditional games are still influential and popular in modern China. Chinese ancient games can be categorized as games of strength, sport, and intelligence; as riddling games; and as gambling games.[1]

Games of strength include human strength games (e.g., wrestling and tug-of-war) and animal strength games (e.g., cockfighting, bullfighting, bird fighting, and cricket fighting). In human strength games, tug-of-war is still very popular in schools and at company socials as both a kind of game and a sport. The animal strength game of cricket fighting spread widely throughout China and has become popular among adults and children today. In major Chinese cities, cricket-fighting clubs and societies host competitions in residential areas and in the streets and parks, although it is banned in some regions of China because it invites illegal gambling.

In ancient China, there was no significant difference between sports and games, and sports today are also thought of as games. Sports and games include arrow-shooting games (e.g., archery), ball games (e.g., *cuju*, polo), and jumping games (e.g., shuttlecock and skipping rope). In the language of ancient China, *cu* meant "kick" and *ju* meant "ball." The game of cuju can be dated to the Song dynasty (960–1279) and is the predecessor of modern soccer. Although cuju was a very popular and widespread game in ancient China, it has been replaced by modern soccer today. Chinese shuttlecock is now referred to as *jianzi*, which is a favorite game in China today. The game of jianzi is like badminton played without rackets.[2] Players primarily use the feet but also other parts of the body except the hands to keep the jianzi shuttlecock from touching the ground. Skipping rope has a 1,500-year history in China. This game was originally played by children during the Spring Festival in ancient times, and has gradually become a fun game for both children and adults.

The ancient Chinese played a variety of games to improve their intelligence. Among the intelligence games, both *weiqi* [Go] and *xiangqi* [Chinese chess] were developed as tools to develop intelligence, make friends, enhance mental health, and improve morality.[3] It is widely held that Emperor Shun (2255–06 BCE) originally invented Weiqi to help his son develop intelligence and enhance learning ability. Moreover, Chinese archaeologists found written evidence of Weiqi in the pottery of ancient times, and discovered a Weiqi board in a Tang dynasty tomb. It is confirmed that Xiangqi was played as early as the fourth century BCE in China. A Weiqi set has 361 stones—181 black stones and 180 white stones. The Weiqi board can be either flat or (by tradition) mounted on legs as a floor board. Two players use either black or white stones to compete and capture territory on the surface of the board. Like Weiqi, Xiangqi is played by two opponents on a board that is nine lines wide and ten lines long with each player commanding. At first Weiqi and Xiangqi were played only by the aristocracy, but both games gradually became favorite leisure activities for all classes and age groups in China. In modern times, both games have professional and amateur associations in China, and some Chinese devote their entire lives to the game and its ranking system. In leisure time, both games are played in the home and in parks, the streets, and other public places.

In ancient times, riddle games were initially created by emperors and aristocrats for amusement while they hosted drinking parties, and to show their wisdom. In the Song dynasty (960–1279), riddling emerged during the Lantern Festival, which occurs on the fifteenth day of the first month of the Chinese lunar calendar. Riddles—called Lantern Riddles—are written on pieces of paper and posted on lanterns or walls. Anyone who solves the riddle can be awarded a prize. Riddle games have become popular among all social classes in China now.

Surprisingly, gambling games had a variety of forms in ancient China. Gambling games include dice, dominoes, and card games. Both Mahjong and poker have become extremely popular in China. The Chinese philosopher Confucius developed Mahjong about 500 BCE. Mahjong is a domino game for four players whereas Western-style poker is played by players who vary in number from two to ten. As important leisure activities for Chinese people's daily life, people meet friends and get relaxed through playing the games during their leisure time. In most areas of China, Mahjong and poker are invariably associated with gambling. Although most Mahjong and poker lovers make very small bets "to make the game more interesting," high-stakes gambling has led many individuals to loose their entire earnings or become addicted.[4]

Chinese children are believed to have been playing with folk toys for 6,000 to 10,000 years. Based on their function, Chinese folk toys can be classified as festival toys (e.g., lanterns, fireworks), decorative toys (e.g., clay masks, rice flour–made human figures, and centimeter-long wooden sculptures), toys with sounds (e.g., drums, rattles, and bird-shaped whistles), intelligence toys (e.g., the *tangram*), and practical toys used in both child's play and daily life (e.g., a tiger-shaped pillow, human-shaped candy).[5] Moreover, some toys can be considered instrumental in playing games and sports such as kite flying, jianzi, and cuju.

At the same time, because of the rapid spread of high-speed Internet, play with electronic games is increasing dramatically. In 2004 there were 20 million Internet gamers between the ages of 15 and 30 years in China. The value of the Chinese Internet game market reached US$220 million in 2003.[6] It is interesting that Chinese Internet gamers quickly adapt to Korean games. This is true because Korean games were created mostly on the basis of historical adventure, fantasy, and martial arts.[7]

JAPAN

Historically since 300 BCE, Chinese culture influenced Japanese culture. During the Tang dynasty, Japan sent envoys to China to learn Chinese culture and technology. Because of the cultural exchange between China and Japan, Japanese lifestyles and culture were deeply influenced by the culture of the Tang dynasty. As a result, some traditional Chinese games spread to Japan and became popular in modern Japan. The Japanese word for the Chinese game of *Weiqi* (which spread to Japan from China around 600 CE) is *Igo*, and the Japanese word for *Xiangqi* (also originally from China) is *Shogi*. However, with the influence of Western culture since the middle of the nineteenth century, Japanese culture has evolved greatly over the centuries to form a distinct culture in the arts, crafts, cuisine, and traditions, which is deeply influenced by Asia, Europe, and the Americas.[8]

The Japanese maintained their own games created in Japanese society. At the same time, they developed many games originally created in non-Japanese society that became well-known in the rest of world. The origin of the term *origami* refers to the Japanese art of paper folding. *Ori* means "folding" and *kami* means "paper" in Japanese. However, origami was not created by the Japanese. It began in China in the first or second century and then spread to Japan during the sixth century. The Chinese developed early paper-folding techniques, which later spread to Japan after the technique of papermaking was introduced to Japan by China during the early seventh century. The most well-known origami creation is the paper crane, which has developed into a worldwide symbol of children's desire for peace. Origami is used as a teaching tool for its educational worth and to inspire creativity in kindergarten and elementary schools in Japan. Origami is not only a form of children's amusement, but is also widespread as a hobby among adults. There are now many origami associations formed around the world by origami lovers.

In addition to traditional pastimes such as Igo, chess, and origami, the Japanese developed computer and video games, first invented by Americans in the 1940s. Now Japan is a major exporter of games that have gained popularity around the world. The Japan-based game companies Nintendo, Sega, Namco, Konami, and SONY dominate the Japanese domestic market as well as the international market. The top Japanese content providers in the electronic game market are always looking for cutting-edge game development software. The value of the Japanese game market in 2001 was approximately US$5.2 billion.[9]

In the past decade, the rapid development of Internet and broadband connections has resulted in bringing new life to the game industry. In Japan, even traditional games like Mahjong and Igo can be played on Mahjong arcade machines and on computers that are connected to others over the Internet.

GAMES, TOYS, AND PASTIMES

> ### PACHINKO: THE JAPANESE ADAPTATION OF PINBALL
>
> Pachinko parlors can be found in every big train station in Japan. Pachinko is a gambling game similar to pinball. Customers in pachinko parlors play quite passively. Pachinko parlors can be recognized easily because they are bright and colorful. Inside a parlor, women and men of different ages play in the loud and smoky environment. According to Web Japan in 2006,[10] nearly 27 million Japanese are playing pachinko. The game of pachinko has developed into and been maintained as a leisure activity for pleasure-seekers in Japan.[11]

Whereas computer and video games can be played at home by children and adults, Japanese game arcades have become increasingly popular as testing grounds for all sorts of new and innovative games, such as dancing and drumming games, railroad train simulation games, and other games that cannot be played at home.

Gambling games are favorites among adults, and are legal activities in Japan. Gambling games in Japan can be categorized into animal gambling (e.g., horse racing), vehicle gambling (e.g., boat racing, Keirin [cycle] racing, and car racing) and machine gambling (e.g., pachinko). Gambling advertisements can be easily found on TV and in newspapers and magazines every day. Among Japanese gambling games, pachinko can be thought of as the most famous game to have widely spread to the rest of the world.

In ancient times, Japan's unique geographic location influenced the creation of several hundred folk toys. The characteristics of the isolated agricultural island-nation and its diverse four seasons have profoundly influenced how and why the Japanese made folk toys. However, because of the deep influence of Western culture since the nineteenth century, folk toys are gradually disappearing. The result is that few folk toys are popular nowadays. Dolls such as the Daruma doll, Hina doll, and Kokeshi doll are still popular among Japanese children. Toys that symbolize good fortune and success in life can also be thought of in the same sense as games and sports. Hagoita, for example, is a Japanese style of badminton played with a wooden paddle. On one or both sides of the paddle, good luck symbols or the image of a woman are portrayed. Koinobori are wind-sock-style flags styled as carp, which represent success in life. These are flown outside of houses for the Boys' Day Festival.[12]

KOREA

Korea has a 5,000-year history. In the fourth century, the adoption of art, language, religion, architecture, and other aspects of culture from China had a profound effect on Korean culture. Because of Korea's unique geographic location between China and Japan, some Chinese traditional games spread to Japan through the Korean peninsula. Except for about 20,000 Chinese who live in Korea, the rest of the population is Korean.[13] Therefore, Korean games were created by and are played in a homogeneous society, although Korean people maintain some Chinese traditional games.

While Korean culture was influenced by Chinese and Japanese culture as well as by Western culture, a variety of games were created by Koreans based on their own social gatherings, social strata, gender classification, and celebrations of the harvest, resulting in the unique Korean *Nori* [play or game] culture. Korean games can be generally grouped as strength games (e.g., *Neolttwigi, Gu-nae, Chajon-nori*), sports games (e.g., Korean wrestling, taekwondo), board games (e.g., *Jjanggi*, similar to Chinese chess; *Baduk*, similar to *Weiqi* and *Yut-nori*), and card games (e.g., *Hwatu*).[14]

Neolttwigi [seesaw] and Gu-nae [swing] are traditional girl's games. Neolttwigi involves a long board that is put on a rolled-up straw mat. Two girls, who usually wear *Hanbok* (traditional Korean women's costumes), play the game by jumping at each end of the board. Because women were not allowed to go outside the home in ancient Korea, women used the Neolttwigi to jump up to see outside over the walls of their homes. Whereas Neolttwigi could only be played inside the home in ancient times, nowadays it is an outdoor game. Girls also enjoy Gu-nae (Korean swing) during traditional Korean holidays. Unlike swing in other countries, Gu-nae became a girls' competition game that one or two players can play, with one swing to bounce their bodies as high as possible.

Chajon Nori is one of the traditional strength games played by Korean men. The creation of the game dates to the latter of the Three Kingdoms period, about 1,000 years ago. The purpose of the game is to celebrate the harvest. After players divide into two teams, teammates push their opponents to pull them down to the ground.

Jjanggi and Baduk are two typical board games played by all age groups. After the games spread to Korea from China, their rules slightly changed. Baduk is a game played in China, Korea, and Japan, and also became popular as a sport for which regular competitions are annually hosted in China, Korea, and Japan.

Yut-nori is a traditional board game unique to Korea. The group-based game usually involves more than four players and is usually played during the Lunar New Year in Korea. Yut is played with four wooden sticks, each with one flat face and one round face. The sticks are tossed in the air and the score is calculated based on the position of the sticks when they land.

Invented in Japan, *Hwatu* [flower card game] is one kind of card game popularized in Korea. Hwatu is strongly associated with gambling because most people play it for money. However, Hwatu lovers can be easily found in parks, at restaurants, on trains, and in any other public place.

Aside from traditional Korean games, the Korean electronic games market is rapidly growing, making South Korea one of the world's biggest game-user counties. The nation's 17 million gamers (who account for 35 percent of the population) are obsessed with playing electronic games.[15] Furthermore, next to the broadcasting industry, electronic games have become the second-largest entertainment industry in Korea. The value of the Korean electronic games market was expected to reach approximately US$1.76 billion in 2002.[16]

Like the people of China and Japan, Korean people have created toys since ancient times. However, folk toys are gradually replaced by modern toys. While some toys still maintain popularity, they are also used for game and sports' purpose. Top, kite, and shuttlecock are three kinds of toy for Korean children, but they became popular games and sports among the children.

AUSTRALIA

While Australia is an English-speaking country, the first immigrants from Southeast Asia arrived on the continent about 40,000 years before Europeans began coming to the island in the seventeenth century.[17] Because the 43 percent of the Australian population who were born overseas embrace the heritage of the indigenous Australians, of the early European settlers, and of the new immigrants from more than 200 countries, Australia can be considered a highly multicultural society.[18]

It is difficult to generalize about the games of every cultural group on the basis of just several games, but Australians do enjoy a variety of games in their multicultural society. The value of the toys and games market (including video games) in Australia is estimated at

Games, Toys, and Pastimes

US$660 million, with an annual growth rate of 4 percent.[19] Australian people enjoy playing traditional European games (e.g., table games), multicultural games (e.g., dominoes), indigenous games, and electronic games. However, with the rapid growth of technology in the world, computer and other electronic games have become games commonly shared within Australian society regardless of cultural identity.

According to the Australian Bureau of Statistics, Australian children under age 14 were daily involved in 2004 in organized cultural activities, organized sports, and leisure activities. Among all activities, 70.7 percent of the children (81.8 percent boys and 58.9 percent girls) participated in playing electronic and computer games.[20] A contrary view was reported in the Exercise, Recreation, and Sport Survey (ERASS) conducted by the Australian Sports Commission in 2004, which listed 164 different activities. Lawn bowling was one of the top-ten organized activities cited by a number of participants in the 2004 survey of Australian adults age 15 and over.[21] Historians believe lawn bowling originated in Egypt and spread to European countries, and that European settlers introduced the game to Australia in the 1800s. Lawn bowling became one of Australia's favorite games, with more than 4,000 clubs active around Australia.[22] In the ERASS activity list, European traditional lawn games such as croquet, carpet bowls, and bocce; table games such as snooker, pool, billiards; and American-style pinball were also considered favorites among Australian people.

While indigenous Australians account for only 1 percent of the population, the indigenous culture has made a unique contribution to Australia. Indigenous Australians form their diverse games commensurate with Australia's unique geography and weather; they use games for social gatherings and appreciation of nature.

However, because indigenous people have been acculturated by the majority, very few traditional games continue to be played in Australia. According to the Australian Sports Commission in 2006, a total of 18 games are still popular among the indigenous people. Among the 18 games, 14 games are ball games played by large groups outdoors.

Since the indigenous people moved to the continent, the population inevitably had to interact with nature in making their living, which resulted in the creation of games associated with the natural environment.[23] The game of *Kolap* is named for the beans of the Kolap tree, which are used as throwing objects. In North Queensland, a game of throwing skill called *kee'an* is played by throwing a large animal bone over a net into a hole. On Bathurst Island, children play the game of *Tarnambai*, in which they collect the seed heads of spring rolling grass. The players chase the seed heads and try to pick them up while running at full speed. In Arnhem Land in Australia's Northern Territory, *munhanganingin* is the word for a small nocturnal gecko lizard, and is the name given to a children's running game. Some games of Munhanganing are restricted by gender because of cultural constraints. The game of *Gori* is played only by boys or young men, whereas the game of *Wana* is played only by girls; girls and boys are not allowed to play together after a certain age.

Indigenous Australian children often make their own toys. Because the children's lifestyle is influenced by the environment, some toys—boomerangs, spears, baskets, boats—are models of traditional tools and weapons, whereas some toys, such as special throwing objects, are created specifically for indigenous games.[24]

New Zealand

The Polynesian Maori were the first settlers in New Zealand in about 800 CE, followed in the nineteenth century by large numbers of migrants from the United Kingdom. Four million people from more than 145 countries chose to make New Zealand their new home.[25]

Like Australia, New Zealand is a multicultural society in which a variety of games are played. New Zealanders generally consider toys and games to be an integral part of children's play. Although New Zealand is geographically isolated from the rest of the world, children are able to easily access such mass media as TV, radio, and the Internet. Because European immigrants account for nearly 70 percent of the population, some traditional European games are still popular in New Zealand. Traditionally, New Zealanders are raised playing board games such as Monopoly, Scrabble, and Snakes and Ladders.[26] Furthermore, surveys of New Zealand Sport and Physical Activity conducted by the Association of Sport and Recreation New Zealand (SPARC) in 2006 found lawn bowling to be one of the top-fifteen sport and active leisure pastimes of New Zealand adults.[27] Without exception, computer games remain popular, resulting in the fact that 29 percent of adults of all cultural groups play computer games at home. Japanese game companies such as Sony Nintendo dominate the market. Males are the major users of Nintendo and Playstation. However, these days it is also common for girls to play with Barbie dolls and for boys to play with train sets, for example.

Because of the country's cultural diversity, the government in 1995 initiated the New Zealand Framework for Cultural Statistics, which conducts a Measure of Culture for the purpose of developing statistics on cultural activities in New Zealand. Although the survey asked questions regarding *Tanoga tuku iho* [Maori cultural activities], heritage, library services, literature, the performing and visual arts, film and video, broadcasting and the Internet, and community and government activities, games and hobbies are not listed in the questionnaire.[28] Therefore, game playing as a form of culture is not easily measured in this multicultural society.

However, in discussing the traditional games of New Zealand, only the Maori people's games can be considered traditional, for the Maori have lived in New Zealand longer than any other cultural group. Although Maori people account for only 7.9 percent of the population, the games they created are diverse. Toys are used in playing games and for sports purposes among Maori people. Games are played not just by Maori children, but are also a form of relaxation for adults. Maori games can be categorized into physical games, games played with toys, games of dexterity and mental agility, string games, stick games, and hand games.[29] Physical games include running, wrestling, and other forms of sports. Flying kites and spinning tops are popular games played with toys. Although kite flying is generally regarded as a sport or hobby in other East Asian countries, kites are viewed as a form of toy, and kite flying is considered a game by the Maori people.[30] The games of jumping jack and knucklebones are introduced in Alan Armstrong's book as games of dexterity and mental agility. A jumping jack can be considered a Maori-style puppet—a Maori toy as well as a kind of game. The games of knucklebones and string figure are very popular with East Asian children of all cultural groups. However, the stick game and hand game are games played uniquely by the Maori people. Nowadays, the stick game has become a musical game that requires players to follow the rhythm of the music to catch sticks thrown by other players. Hand games are usually played by two people with fast movement of the hands.

Because of the acculturation of the Maori people, they are enjoying modern games just as other cultural groups do. The SPARC survey in 2006 found that 35 percent of the Maori people play computer games at home, compared to only 28 percent of European New Zealanders.

RESOURCE GUIDE

PRINT SOURCES

Armstrong, Alan. *Games and Dances of the Maori People.* Wellington, New Zealand: Viking Sevenseas, 1992.
Barbarash, Lorraine. *Multicultural Games.* Champaign, IL: Human Kinetics Press, 1999.
Bell, Robert. *Board and Table Games from Many Civilizations.* New York: Dover, 1979.
Braman, Arlette N. *Kids Around the World Play! The Best Fun and Games from Many Lands.* New York: Wiley, 2002.
Corbett, Doris, John Cheffers, and Eileen Crowley Sullivan. *Unique Games and Sports Around the World: A Reference Guide.* Westport, CT: Greenwood Press, 2001.
Devoogt, Alexander, and Larry Russ. *The Complete Mancala Games Book: How to Play the World's Oldest Board Games.* New York: Marlowe, 1999.
Hamilton, Leslie. *Child's Play Around the World: 170 Crafts, Games, and Projects for Two-to-Six-Year-Olds.* New York: Perigee, 1996.
Kirchner, Glenn. *Children's Games from Around the World*, 2nd edition. Boston: Allyn and Bacon, 2000.
Masuda, Yasuhiro, ed., *Asobi no daijiten.* Tokyo: Tokyo Shoseki, 1989.
Nelson, Wayne E., and Henry Glass. *International Playtime: Classroom Games and Dances from Around the World.* Carthage, IL: Fearon Teacher Aids, 1992.
Orlando, Louise. *The Multicultural Game Book (Grades 1–6).* New York: Scholastic, 1999.
Pu, Lu. *China's Folk Toys.* Beijing: New World Press, 1990.
Sierra, Judy. *Children's Traditional Games: Games from 137 Countries and Cultures.* Phoenix, AZ: Oryx Press, 1995.
Sutton-Smith, Brian. *The Games of New Zealand Children.* Berkeley, CA: University of California Press, 1959.
Wang, Lianhai. *Zhongguo min jian wan ju zao xing tu ji.* Beijing: Beijing gong yi mei shu chu ban she, 1984.
Wang, Lianhai. *Zhongguo min jian wan ju jian shi.* Beijing: Beijing gong yi mei shu chu ban she, 1992.
Zaslavsky, Claudia. *Math Games and Activities from Around the World.* Chicago: Chicago Review Press, 1998.

WEBSITES

Chinese Chess Web. http://www.cchess.com/huangye/lishi4.html (accessed March 10, 2007). This is a Chinese chess information Website.
China Weiqi Web. http://weiqi.cycnet.com/index.php (accessed March 10, 2007). This is a Weiqi information Website.
The Online Guide to Traditional Games. http://www.tradgames.org.uk/ (accessed March 10, 2007).

ORGANIZATIONS AND MUSEUMS

Auckland Museum, Auckland, New Zealand. +64(9)3090443. http://www.aucklandmuseum.com. The museum has a collection of Maori and Pacific treasures reflecting the natural, cultural, and social history of New Zealand.
Australian Museum, Sydney, Australia. +612(9)320 6000. http://www.amonline.net.au/index.cfm. The museum has an international reputation for its natural history exhibitions and indigenous studies research.
Beijing Toys Association, Beijing, China. +86(10) 64247064. http://www.bjwj.org.cn/index.asp This is a professional organization concerned with toy manufacture and research.
China Weiqi Academy, Beijing, China. +86(10)51029122. http://www.weiqi.cc/weiqi. This is the headquarters of the largest Weiqi association in China.
Yong-in-si [Korean Folk Village], Gyeonggi-do, Korea. +82(31)2880000. http://www.koreanfolk.co.kr/folk/english. This is an open-air folk museum that displays Korean folk culture.

Japan Mahjong Museum, Izumi City, Chiba. http://museum.takeshobo.co.jp. The collection includes 3,000 Mahjong sets and 10,000 Mahjong documents.

Japan Toy Museum, Hi meji City, Hyogo, Japan. +81(79)2324388. http://www.japan-toy-museum.org/english/eindex.htm This museum has a collection of more than 80,000 items, including Japanese folk toys and toys and dolls from 140 countries.

NOTES

1. See Renshan Zhang, *Zhongguo gu dai min jian yu le* (Beijing: Shang wu yin shu guan guo ji you xian gong si, 1996).
2. Ibid.
3. See China Weiqi Academy, "Di yi zhang: zhong shuo fen yun de we qi qi yuan," http://www.weiqi.cc/weiqi/news_detail.php?id=44 (accessed May 1, 2006).
4. See Mahjong Museum, "A Brief History," http://www.mahjongmuseum.com/brief.htm (accessed May 1, 2006).
5. Wang 1992 (in Resource Guide), pp. 7–8.
6. See Xiaoming Liu, Lou qin jian: si da cuo shi fa zhan min zu te se de ruan jian you xi chan ye, http://www.ceic.gov.cn/detail?record=1&channelid=94&presearchword=ID=136738 (accessed September 1, 2006).
7. See Strategis, 2005, Online game market in China, http://commercecan.ic.gc.ca/scdt/bizmap/interface2.nsf/vDownload/ISA_4033/$file/X_4944443.DOC (accessed September 1, 2006).
8. See Masuda 1989 (in Resource Guide).
9. See Strategis, 2003, Japanese entertainment content provider SEGA is looking for cutting-edge game development software, http://strategis.ic.gc.ca/epic/internet/inimr-ri.nsf/en/gr114986e.html (accessed September 1, 2006).
10. See Japan Fact Sheet, "Leisure, A trend toward increased free time," March 10, 2007; http://web-japan.org/factsheet/pdf/LEISURE.PDF.
11. See *The Culture of Japan as Seen through Its Leisure*, edited by Sepp Linhart and Sabine Fruhstuck (Albany: State University of New York Press, 1998), p. 359.
12. See Masuda 1989 (in Resource Guide), p. 946.
13. See Central Intelligence Agency, "The World Factbook: South Korea," http://www.cia.gov/cia/publications/factbook/geos/ks.html (accessed May 1, 2006).
14. See Korean Folk Village, http://www.koreanfolk.co.kr/folk/english (accessed May 1, 2006).
15. See MSNBC, "South Korea frets over video game addicts," http://www.msnbc.msn.com/id/9608614/from/RL.1 (accessed May 1, 2006).
16. See Vectis International, *The Korean Electronic Games Market: Selling Game Content and Applications to the World's Most Avid Electronic Games Players* (Kirkland, QC, Canada: Author, 2002).
17. See Central Intelligence Agency, "The World Factbook: Australia," http://www.cia.gov/cia/publications/factbook/geos/as.html (accessed May 1, 2006).
18. See Department of Immigration and Multicultural Affairs, Australian Government, "Australian Multicultural Policy," http://www.immi.gov.au/multicultural/australian/index.htm (accessed May 1, 2006).
19. See Strategis, 2006, Toy industry in Australia, http://commercecan.ic.gc.ca/scdt/bizmap/interface2.nsf/vDownload/ISA_3198/$file/X_3080250.DOC (accessed May 1, 2006).
20. See Australian Bureau of Statistics, 2003, "Children's Participation in Cultural and Leisure Activities, Australia," http://www.abs.gov.au/AUSSTATS/abs@.nsf/DetailsPage/4901.0Apr%202003?OpenDocument (accessed May 1, 2006).
21. See Australian Government, "Exercise, Recreation and Sport Survey (ERASS) 2004," http://www.ausport.gov.au/scorsresearch/erass2004.asp (accessed May 1, 2006).
22. See Bowls Australia, "Membership Statistics," http://www.bowls-aust.com.au/Default.asp?pg=about&spg=statistics (accessed May 1, 2006).

GAMES, TOYS, AND PASTIMES

23. See Australian Government, "Australian Sports Commission—Indigenous Sport Program—Services," http://www.ausport.gov.au/isp/traditional.asp#14 (accessed May 1, 2006).
24. See Australian Museum Online, "Family," http://www.dreamtime.net.au/indigenous/family.cfm (accessed May 1, 2006).
25. See Central Intelligence Agency, "The World Factbook: New Zealand," http://www.cia.gov/cia/publications/factbook/geos/nz.html (accessed May 1, 2006).
26. See Strategis, 2003, Toys, http://strategis.ic.gc.ca/epic/internet/inimr-ri.nsf/en/gr111511e.html (accessed September 1, 2006).
27. See Sport and Recreation New Zealand, "SPARC Facts '97–'01," http://www.sparc.org.nz/research-policy/research-/sparc-facts-97-01 (accessed May 1, 2006).
28. See Statistics New Zealand, "New Zealand framework for cultural statistics," http://www.stats.govt.nz/analytical-reports/new-zealand-framework-for-cultural-statistics.htm (accessed May 1, 2006).
29. Armstrong 1992 (in Resource Guide), p. 5.
30. See New Zealand in history, "Traditional Maori sport and games," http://history-nz.org/kite.html (accessed May 1, 2006).

ARCHITECTURE

ARCHITECTURE: Taipei 101 (officially named the Taipei Financial Center) in Taiwan, the tallest building in the world. Courtesy of Shutterstock.

ARCHITECTURE: Flinders Street Station, Melbourne Australia. This station, completed in 1899 in fine Victorian style, saw the first steam engine in Australia. Courtesy of Shutterstock.

ART: Porcelain worker dolls in a Chinese market include Chairman Mao, who is very popular as an image. Courtesy of Shutterstock.

ART: *The Great Wave of Kanogawa* by the Japanese artist Katsushika Hokusai (1760–1849), a woodblock print, is considered a masterpiece. This work and other woodblock prints created by other Japanese artists continue to be popular reproduction items worldwide. © The Art Archive / Claude Debussy Centre St Germain en Laye / Dagli Orti.

ART: Part of an outdoor fence painted with traditional Maori warriors. © Wendy Kaveney/Dreamstime.

DANCE

DANCE: A dancer from the famous Beijing Opera, China. Courtesy of Shutterstock.

DANCE: The traditional South Korean fan dance. As in other Asian countries, dance is a vibrant artistic expression and very popular. Courtesy of Shutterstock.

DANCE: A colorful character from the exciting traditional Barong dance in Bali, Indonesia. Courtesy of Shutterstock.

FASHION AND APPEARANCE

FASHION AND APPEARANCE: Japanese designer Issey Miyake is applauded by his models at the end of the 1997/98 fall-winter ready-to-wear collection he presented in Paris. © AP Photo/Remy de la Mauviniere.

FILM

FILM: Zhang Ziyi (as Mei) in Zhang Yimou's *Shi mian mai fu* [House of Flying Daggers] (2004). © Sony / Elite Group / Photofest.

FILM: Keisha Castle-Hughes (as Pai) in Niki Caro's *Whale Rider* (2003). © Newmarket Films / Photofest.

FOOD AND FOODWAYS

FOOD AND FOODWAYS: A Starbucks outlet in the Forbidden City, Beijing. Courtesy of John Horne.

FOOD AND FOODWAYS: Korean women preparing *kimch'i*. Courtesy of Katarzyna Cwiertka.

FOOD AND FOODWAYS: The colorful street food of India. Courtesy of Shutterstock.

GAMES, TOYS, AND PASTIMES

GAMES, TOYS, AND PASTIMES: With onlookers advising, a group of people make themselves comfortable on a sidewalk in China, playing a game of mahjong. Courtesy of Erwei Dong.

GAMES, TOYS, AND PASTIMES: Origami cranes, created from the Japanese art of paper folding, are made to pray for the return to health of sick or injured people. Courtesy of Shutterstock.

LITERATURE

EAST ASIA AND OCEANIA

ERIC DALLE

Several factors contribute to the complications involved in understanding the notion of popular literature of East Asia and Oceania. Geographically, this area contains individual nations that are culturally distinctive and possess indigenous literary traditions. Similarly, literary traditions throughout the areas known as East Asia and Oceania have influenced and created each other. In this increasingly globalized world, in which national literary traditions and representative works migrate across boundaries, it becomes increasingly difficult to locate popular genres specific to each national literature.

Within East Asia, the long history of Chinese poems, histories, and oral tales has provided the base for the literary traditions of Korea and Japan. Large canonical narratives such as *The Romance of the Three Kingdoms* and *Journey to the West* constitute a base for the traditions of East Asia. Both of these narratives were transmitted orally in earlier centuries, eventually appearing in written novel form attributed to Luo Guanzhong and Wu Chengen respectively. These stories have proven popular not only within the auspices of literature, but they also have contributed to the popular consciousness of the countries. The classics of East Asian literature are often disseminated to consumers via graphic novels (comic books such as *manga* in Japan or *manhwa* in Korea) as well as through television programs and storytelling. Particular characters (such as Guan Yu of *The Romance of the Three Kingdoms*) have also become deified over time, adding another dimension to the relationship between popular story, religion and spirituality, literature, and popular cultural consciousness.

The notion of literature is an ideologically specific concept implying for Western audiences a high art that comes in print form and is consumed accordingly. The contemporary world of the Internet and other developing methods of transferring text have challenged our notions regarding print literature. The Internet provides access to classical works via Websites as well as through Web logs (blogs), both of which offer to the contemporary reader unprecedented literary corridors.

LITERATURE

> ### BLOG: *THE SEXUAL DIARY OF A YOUNG CHINESE WOMAN ON THE INTERNET*
>
> One example of new textual innovations and popular literature can be seen with the works of the writer Muzi Mei in Mainland China. Muzi Mei entered into the spotlight with her blog; it recounts her sexual exploits and showcases her personal search for meaning in the contemporary world through a confessional display. Her online diary has been read by half of the Mainland Chinese population with Internet access. Her Web log was eventually published in book form. Although initially banned by the Chinese government, the book achieved international fame with its translation into French as *The Sexual Diary of a Young Chinese Woman on the Internet*.[1]

The literatures of Australia and New Zealand pose other difficulties. These national literatures are, by default, inheritors of an Anglophone tradition based primarily on the literature of England. The literature of Australia and New Zealand attempts to create a national identity outside of, yet bound to, the literary heritage from which it sprung. National literatures are often complicated in this manner. How does one define an Australian literature? How does one separate this from a New Zealand literature? In many ways these national literatures must also address the existence of the prior traditions of indigenous peoples.

Global marketing of publications provides the most difficult challenge in understanding how to define the popular literature of East Asia and Oceania. Taking the extraordinary and unmatched popularity of J. K Rowling's *Harry Potter* series as an example, the consumption of these books far outweighs the purchase of home-grown works in specified countries. In fact, Rowling's popularity has affected every single country listed in this encyclopedic section. The sales of *Harry Potter* books far outweigh those of regional popular pieces, complicating the manner with which we equate consumption, readership, and popular literature of the individual nations. In a sense then, the focus is not necessarily on what the country or region reads; rather, the focus is on what popular pieces have been produced and what works can be used to position a nation and its particular form of popular production.

The popular literature of East Asia and Oceania as a whole reveals a hybrid of literary traditions that interact as well as conflict. What is the inherent literary trend within each country? What is being exported outside, and what is being consumed within? All forms of narrative must be considered, including Websites, blogs, printed materials, and video games. This section will avoid the discussion of "what is literature" and, by extension, "what is popular literature?" Rather, it will examine what has been produced and provide an overview, however brief, of the world of popularized narratives indicative of East Asian and Oceania.

EAST ASIA

China

The history of Chinese literature spans many centuries and has influenced the traditions of East Asia as well as many parts of Southeast Asia. The history of the Chinese literary past has favored certain genres over others. Because of the influence of Confucian philosophy, history was considered one of highest forms of literature. Poetry was also considered more literary than novels or fiction in general. In the present, favoring one genre over another does no justice to the ways in which the literary tradition of China has entered into the contemporary popular consciousness. Large canonical novels such as *Romance of the Three Kingdoms*, attributed to Luo Guanzhong; *Journey to the West*, by Wu Chengen; or *Dream of the Red Chamber*, by Cao Xueqin, are known by almost every person raised in the Chinese cultural tradition. Furthermore, many of the novels were popular as oral stories, dramatic performances, and short fiction before being written in novel form.

These large works of traditional literature form the basis of many children's books and comic books. *Journey to the West* is a prime example of how a work can span the literary and popular arenas. The work tells the story of a monkey, Sun Wukong or simply Monkey, who searches for enlightenment. The monkey is eventually forced to take a pilgrimage to India to find sutras and bring them back to China. The narrative is loosely based on a historical pilgrimage by a Tang dynasty monk named Xuan Zang. The story of *Journey to the West* appeals to children who find the antics of Monkey and his ragtag bunch of cohorts, including Pigsy and Sandy, very amusing. On another level, the work has an extremely powerful spiritual aspect, examining the transformation of the soul from mortality to immortality. Just as many other popular works of literature, *Journey to the West* has also been serialized on television. The story is the basis of many children's books, comic books, and dramatic performances. In the modern world, the character of Monkey has been attributed in influencing the creation of other popular characters, such as King Kong, Son Goku of the Japanese manga titled *Dragon Ball*, and the antagonist in the popular 1980s video game Donkey Kong. *Journey to the West* exemplifies how it is difficult to assume a "popular literature" that is distinct from other areas of the national and cultural literary tradition.

Traditional dramas have also played a major role in the contemporary literary consciousness of China as well as provided the basis for narratives in film, television, dramatic performances, and published works. The best example is the Ming dynasty drama *Peony Pavilion*, written by Tang Xianzu and published in 1599. The work is written as a southern Chinese style of drama known as *chuanqi*. This particular form of drama is defined by extensive works: the play *Peony Pavilion* contains fifty-five acts. It is the story of a young maiden who begins her lessons of poetry at an early age. She pines away and dies for the image of her young lover, whom she finds in a dream. Her soul returns to the mortal world, where she must finally find her real lover and consummate their marriage. The work is enjoyed by many young readers, particularly females. *Peony Pavilion* is perhaps the most famous love story in Chinese literature.

Chuanqi is the textual representation of the work, and it has often been represented in popular performance through the operatic style of *kunqu*. *Peony Pavilion* has recently experienced a contemporary revival among Chinese and international audiences. The director Chen Shi-zheng toured international stages with a bold project, performing all fifty-five acts of *Peony Pavilion* in kunqu style. This was perhaps the first time in history that this feat had been accomplished; traditional kunqu often picked only several highlighted scenes to perform. Chen Shi-zheng's performance took three days to complete. Similarly, the writer Bai Xianyong has worked on performing a kunqu performance of *Peony Pavilion* on Taiwanese and Mainland Chinese stages. His project of revitalizing kunqu, now considered an endangered performance art, is slowly gaining popularity.

Kunqu is just one form of dramatic performance associated with China. Perhaps the most famous form of modern Chinese operatic performance is Peking Opera. This style of performance involves particularly stylized singing, somewhat similar to kunqu; however, Peking Opera also uses elements of acrobatic performance. Peking Opera grew extremely famous at the turn of the century and eventually become considered the national Chinese art form—similar to opera in Italy. One of the most famous Peking Opera pieces is *White Snake*, which tells the story of love and heartbreak between a snake spirit and her mortal lover.

Literature

> ### REVOLUTIONARY OPERAS
>
> With the creation of the People's Republic of China in 1949, Peking Opera grew and transformed in many different ways. During the Cultural Revolution (1966–76), only a handful of operas were deemed acceptable for performance. These revolutionary operatic performances were politically motivated but took the form of traditional Peking Opera. Popular revolutionary operas included *Taking Tiger Mountain by Strategy* and *The Red Detachment of Women*. Another piece, *The White Haired Girl*, became a popular ballet that also featured the political propaganda of the time.

At the beginning of the twentieth century in China, there arose a school of romance novels that were originally referred to derogatorily as the School of Mandarin Ducks and Butterflies—so called because of heavy references to mandarin ducks and butterflies as traditional symbols of lovers. These traditional love type stories proved quite popular, especially in Shanghai, the first modern metropolis of China. In that city, the existence of a publishing industry as well as the wide availability of newspapers and serializations promoted these types of stories. One of the first and most widely read was the work by Xu Zhenya, *Jade Pear Spirit* (1912). The work not only proved highly popular, but it also sparked interest among middle-class urbanites in the popular fiction of the day. The term Mandarin Ducks and Butterflies was also used as a blanket term to refer to a spectrum of popular fiction of the early twentieth century, including detective fiction, knight errant stories, and traditional love stories. Popular literature, although highly popular among urban circles, drew the critical wrath of literary innovators of the May Fourth Movement, who advocated a modern social consciousness in the literary works of authors. Nevertheless, the works that sprang from the Mandarin Ducks and Butterflies school represent a modern popular literary production of Chinese stories in urban areas of the early twentieth century.

During the middle part of the twentieth century in Hong Kong, Taiwan, and overseas Chinese communities, the martial arts genre, particularly the novels written by Jinyong, exploded upon the scene. Jinyong, the pen name of Zha Liangyong, who was also known by his English name Louis Cha (b. 1924), was the foremost writer of the martial arts genre in the twentieth century. His most popular works available in English include *The Deer and the Cauldron*, a several-volume work, and *Fox Volant of the Snowy Mountain*.

Japan

Japan's most popular and culturally pervasive literary form is manga—or comic books. This specific Japanese form of comics has played a major role in the twentieth century as a vehicle for propaganda, entertainment, pornography, instruction, and industrial communications. Manga (as opposed to *animé*, which is the film version of the manga style of illustration) has a long history within Japan. The word manga can be located as far back as the 1700s. In the nineteenth century, the term referred to woodcuts that featured comic themes. The word found popular usage in the Showa period (1926–89). Today manga remains the most well-known form of popular narrative from Japan, and its influence can be observed worldwide.

Manga is a visually rich form of narrative featuring particularly stylized blocks. These blocks present dialogue, commentary, and codified sounds indicating particular background noises. Manga has its own particular form of visual representation that has evolved over the years.

The word manga represents a particular type of visual representation and storytelling form. Manga is the product of a variety of events occurring in twentieth-century Japanese history. Strip comics began to become popular in the 1920s. 10 years later they were available in cheaply produced pulp book style. As World War II progressed, a government reform movement reduced the number of artist associations and refocused the purpose of the comics to support the war movement. Comics were then used to educate young audiences about the war effort as well as to promote anti-Western rhetoric. The Japanese government wielded control over comic representation, banning newspaper publication of comics from 1944 until the end of the war. Another factor, the shortage of paper, also influenced representation. Picture card shows, known as *kamishibai*, used a narrator to tell a story depicted on illustrated plates. Kamishibai become quite popular as a form of storytelling and public entertainment. As late as 1953, it is estimated that as many as 5 million people a day attended kamishibai.[2]

Economic factors also affected the popularity and circulation of comics in Japan. Comic books were rented out, similar to the way videos and DVDs are rented at video stores and other locations today. This practice allowed migrant workers, who had been moving to the large cities, an affordable entertainment venue. Manga and television developed their popularity simultaneously. As opposed to what happened in many parts of the world, where film challenged the consumption of printed materials, in Japan it was the reverse: the popularity of manga challenged the development of film in Japan, always remaining a more popular industrialized form of entertainment.

Manga originally appealed to younger audiences, but the readers of manga matured along with the genre. In the 1970s manga began to specialize into a variety of themes and subjects not necessarily for children. An official attempt to denounce manga as a frivolous and childish pastime did little to sway its popularity within Japan. Linguistic attempts to camouflage and relegate manga to a youth-only demographic failed. Any Japanese person on a train, any businessperson, or any high school student can be seen reading comic books.

Manga can be classified by target audience as well as theme. *Kodomo* is manga geared toward children. *Josei manga* refers to comics for young adult females. This type of manga is often written by women artists. The opposite is *seinen*, which caters to younger male audiences, although it is often enjoyed by older readers as well. Certain themes also define the specific genre of manga. Robots are central to the Japanese comic imagination and hold a place equivalent or comparable to the role of the superhero in American comics.

In the 1980s the thematic specialization of manga reached into the areas of pornography and eroticism—referred to by the term *hentai*. Depictions within hentai manga can include heterosexual relationships as well as gay (*yaoi*) and lesbian (*yuri*) sex. Various comics also cover a variety of fetishes including *ecchi* (derived from the English letter *H* to refer to hentai), which refers to partially clad characters insinuating a thinly veiled sensual representation. *Lolicon* (an abbreviation of "Lolita Complex") shows younger females in suggestive poses and situations. The opposite, *shotocon*, shows younger boys, usually as a sexual object of an older male's desire. *Futanari* shows hermaphrodites or women displaying exaggerated male genitalia.

Manga has become an international phenomenon. Its influence has spread across Asia, where it has transformed Chinese and Korean comics. In Europe, Japanese comics have fused with and influenced the Franco-Belgian style of the visual graphic novel. In the United States and Canada, manga remains popular among certain sections of the comic book–reading population. Despite various efforts over the past decades to decry manga as a low and juvenile art form, it has remained the most popular type of entertainment in Japan. It is such a

Literature

part of the contemporary world that certain industries have created manga-style manuals for their employees. In 1986 *Japan Inc.*, a manga about Japanese economics, was published. *Japan Inc.* has been used to make a potentially difficult and complex subject accessible to larger number of people. It was published in English and eventually French. *Japan Inc.* represents a trend of using manga for purposes outside of mere entertainment. Other subgenres of manga immediately followed, including political manga, education manga, and documentary manga.

There have been so many different manga series over the years that it is difficult to offer any representation of its popularity with just a few examples. Some of the more popular in Japan and among international audiences include *Dragon Ball*, *Ghost in the Shell*, and *Sailor Moon*. These works have also been popularized through animé film and television series, video games, role-playing games, and theater. Although the main characters and plots remain fairly consistent, there are noticeable differences among the many representations of the narratives.

Dragon Ball was originally a manga by Akira Toriyama about the lifelong adventures of Son Goku, who becomes the world's best martial artist. His life holds many similarities to the character Monkey (Sun Wukong) of the legendary Chinese tale *Journey to the West*. The manga was serialized between 1985 and 1995 and eventually made into an animé. It appeared as an American comic book under two titles and versions: *Dragon Ball* and *Dragon Ball Z*.

Ghost in the Shell, by Masamune Shirow, tells of the adventures of a National Public Safety Commission agent named Motoko Kusangi. The futuristic tale explores the realm of cyberpunk as characters fight and hide within an electronically circuited world. Limits of human existence and reality are examined in this work, which proves to be highly philosophical as well as entertaining. The manga was produced as animé films and as an animé television series. A sequel, *Ghost in the Shell 2: Man/Machine Interface*, has also been published in English.

Naoko Takeuchi created the *Sailor Moon* serialization surrounding the fantastical outer space adventures of a team of young girls with magical powers known as Sailor Senshi (or Sailor Soldiers). The character of Sailor Moon is one of the Sailor Senshi; other characters include Sailor Mercury, Sailor Neptune, and Sailor Venus. All characters have their own adventures and are opposed mostly by a band of evil sailors, which includes Sailor Galaxia, the most pernicious enemy of Sailor Moon.

The rapid development of manga in the twentieth century in Japan shows how a particular genre can enter the national and cultural consciousness, influencing local as well as international audiences. The future of manga remains uncertain as the popularity of personal computers and video game entertainment units has affected the overall sales of manga. Many of the current video games, such as *Dragon Ball*, are based specifically on manga. The competition between manga and video games can perhaps be seen more as a genre transformation than as a complete replacement. Regardless of the future direction of these two forms, it remains indisputable that manga, along with the permutations of animé and various video games, are true indicators of the popular literary tradition of late twentieth and early twenty-first century Japan.

Korea

Popular literature and the publishing industry in Korea have reacted directly to the social and political changes of the past centuries. The history of Korean literature usually assumes two periods: a classical age and a modern age. The classics of traditional Korea date back to many centuries and were heavily influenced by the Chinese literary and linguistic tradition. With contact with the West and its literatures, Korean literature began the struggle for national identity. The importation of Christianity and the arrival of new styles of written works also influenced how writers composed their works. Later, the Japanese occupation of the Korean peninsula (1910–45) greatly affected literary output since speech and publications were generally censored by the ruling Japanese.

The separation of the peninsula into North Korean and South Korea isolated each part of the country from its other half. The establishment of the Republic of Korea in 1948 and the gradual economic development of the country brought with it the founding of many publishing houses. Today the publishing industry of South Korea is one of the largest in the world, actively participating in international fairs and importing and exporting popular works internationally.

The fluctuation of the economic climate in Asia directly affected the publishing industries and, by extension, trends in readership. An initial economic boom of the mid-1990s ushered in an influx of blockbuster best sellers from the international market, including such authors as Daniel Steele and John Grisham. The high-tech boom at the turn of the twenty-first century created a huge interest in more technical works about business and computer science. The booms and shifts in the publishing industry did not occur without particular adversities. The Asian economic crisis of 1997 saw the demise of several large and reputable publishing companies. Market trends of the early twenty-first century also presented the industry with new challenges and competition from global competition, the Internet, and the push toward consumer-based marketing. In 2002 Chongno Book Center, one of Seoul's oldest and best known publishing houses, closed its doors after 95 years in the business.

A look at the 2003 publishing year as an example shows that the publishing industry is a several-billion-dollar industry in Korea. Best seller lists, particularly those from the large chains such as Kyobo and Youngpoong, often affect popular readership, displaying the power of the publishing industry and of market forces in South Korea. The current lack of South Korean writers with international recognition has resulted in a literature that emphasizes special interests within the country. South Korean books that are popular in the market fall into the genres of self-help or business. Bookshops have begun to list self-help and business in the same category, so these two genres are increasingly being merged into one. Two-thirds of the national best sellers can be considered business/self-help books. Translated works also make up a good percentage of book sales (roughly 20 percent). Recent international mega blockbusters have affected the national market for books. Examples of extraordinarily popular blockbusters include J. K. Rowling's *Harry Potter* and J. R. R. Tolkien's *Fellowship of the Ring*.[3]

The popular genre of comics (known in Korea as manhwa) has recently become relegated to the area of children's literature. Manhwa is similar to Japanese manga but has several notable linguistic differences—Korean is typically read left to right, as in English. Although there are some notable visual differences between the two national cartoon styles, manga has influenced manhwa. Within South Korea, however, the popularity of manhwa is in no way comparable to that of its comic counterpart in Japan. Comic books in South Korea have never reached readership among adults and other audiences. The advancement of the video game industry has also presented the sale of comic books with challenges. Further impacting a difficult market, sales of comic books have dropped recently because of pressure from parents for greater availability of books that interest young children in serious literature and other academic subjects in order to prepare them for school. Certain restrictions have allowed the publishing industry some protection against the influence of online book sellers.

LITERATURE

The future of the Korean book industry remains uncertain and is dependant upon changes in market trends.

OCEANIA

Australia

There has always been a relationship between the literary production of Australia and the Anglophone and European traditions. Although Australian writers had taken steps to create a national literary identity, international acclaim for major writers did not occur until Patrick White (1912–90)—author of *Voss* (1957), *Riders in the Chariot* (1961), *The Twyborn Affair* (1979), and *Memoirs of Many in One* (1986), among others—became the first and only Australian to win the Nobel Prize for literature in 1973.

Another author who has gained international fame with popular novels is historical fiction writer James Clavell (1924–94). His most popular works include *King Rat* (1962), *Tai-Pan* (1966), *Shogun* (1975), *Noble House* (1981), and *Gai-Jin* (1993). All of his novels take place in Asia, except for *Whirlwind* (1986), which is set in Iran. His first work was inspired by his experience abroad as a POW in a Japanese camp during World War II. His set of Asian works, known collectively as *The Asian Saga,* narrates the encounter of the East and West immediately following the age of discovery.

Born in 1937, Colleen McCullough was originally trained as a neuroscientist but has published prolifically over the past 30 years. Her novel *The Thorn Birds* (1977) is perhaps her most famous work; it follows 40 years in the lives of the Cleary family in the Australian outback. The novel was serialized for television and proved quite popular among American audiences. Her larger historical project to date, the *Masters of Rome*, details the fall of the Roman empire with rigorous historical accuracy. The series contains six works altogether: *The First Man in Rome* (1990), *The Grass Crown* (1991), *Fortune's Favorites* (1993), *Caesar's Women* (1995), *The October Horse* (2002), and *Caesar* (2003). Her current work continues to explore various genres, and she recently published a murder mystery, *On, Off* (2006).

Peter Carey (b. 1943) began his literary career with the publication of two sets of short stories, *War Crimes* (1979) and *The Fat Man in History* (1980), both included in *Collected Stories* (1995). He is also the author of several novels and the recipient of numerous awards. His novels include *Bliss* (1981), *Illywacker* (1985), *Oscar and Lucinda* (1988), for which he received the Booker Prize, *True Story of Kelly Gang* (2000), and *Theft* (2006). Carey's works represent a trend in modern Australian fiction to move away from realistic representation and search among the global and international for subject matter. He has been heavily influenced by writers such as James Joyce, William Faulkner, and Gabriel García Márquez, just to mention a few.

Australia's best-selling female novelist, Di Morrissey, has made a career by crafting stories of intensely Australian themes. Her works explore love, loss, and the many challenge of modern life from a uniquely and intrinsically Australian perspective. Her novels, which have sold well, include *Heart of the Dreaming* (1991), *Follow the Morning Star* (1993), *Last Mile Home* (1994), *Tears of the Moon* (1996), *When the Singing Stops* (1997), *The Bay* (2002), *Kimberley Sun* (2003), and *Barra Creek* (2004).

Australia has had a long tradition of children's literature that has developed since the mid-nineteenth century. Children's literature has been employed throughout history for a variety of purposes, including instruction in proper moral behavior, escapism, or simply providing an outlet for didacticism. Although children's literature has been prevalent among many literary traditions, serious scholarly research and appreciation of the genre did not occur until the twentieth century. Australia has a multitude of children's book writers and has enjoyed a large number of national and regional awards celebrating those authors.

The first work for children in Australia was *A Mother's Offering to Her Children: By a Lady Long Resident in New South Wales* (1841), published by the *Sydney Gazette*. The identity of the "Lady Long Resident" is unknown, although speculation suggests that she was Lady Gordon Bremer, whose husband was in the Royal Navy and had been ordered to the north of Australia in 1823. *A Mother's Offering to Her Children* consists of conversations between a Mrs. Saville and her children, Clara, Emma, Julius, and Lucy. The purpose of the work is to instruct children in the ways of proper moral and polite behavior. This type of didactic novel was not indigenous to Australia: in the English and French traditions, stories written for children often included discussions on acceptable conventions.

Other types of children's books appeared in the latter half of the nineteenth century, including adventure stories targeted at boys. Books in this category include *The Kangaroo Hunters; or, Adventures in the Bush* (1859) by Anne Bowman, *The Boy in the Bush* (1869) by Richard Rowe, and *Twice Lost: A Story of Shipwreck and Adventure in the Wilds of Australia* (1881) by W. H. G. Kingston. Other themes for Australian children's books include fairy tales, aboriginal folk tales, and family stories that tell of family togetherness as well as adventure.

One of the most popular literary writers of the early twentieth century was Ethel Turner (1872–1958). Born in England, Ethel Turner moved to Australia with her parents when she was only eight years old. During her lifetime, she published thirty-eight works. She can be considered a writer of children's literature as well as adolescent books because of the thematic elements she addressed. Many of her works are still read today, such as *Seven Little Australians*, *The Little Larrikin*, and *Miss Bobbie*. Her third work, *The Story of a Baby* (1895), is geared more toward adults because of the novel's complex emotional situations.

As the twentieth century progressed, a national interest in the country's children's literature increased. The year 1946 saw the establishment of the Children's Book Council awards, aimed at promoting and applauding quality publications. Currently, the different Australian states and territories also feature regional awards, in which local children can cast their votes for their favorite book of the year. Some of these regional awards include Books I Love Best, an annual award in Queensland; Young Australians Best Book award in Victoria; and the Children's Yearly Best Ever Reads in Tasmania.

Creating a list of popular and widely read Australian children's writers is problematic since popular literature for children is vast and has a long history within the country. The following writers are popular among a wide range of readers but only constitute a slice of this large and influential genre. Nan Chauncey (1900–70) won the Children's Book Council book of the year award for older readers (twelve to mid-teens) several times. Her winning novels were *Tiger in the Bush* (1958), *Devil's Hill* (1959), and *Tangera* (1961). She was also awarded a Hans Christian Anderson diploma of merit. She produced fourteen novels in all and enjoyed a wide readership for many years.

Mem Fox (b. 1946) is currently considered the most popular Australian children's writer. She was born in Melbourne but spent her childhood in Zimbabwe, where her parents worked as missionaries. She attended drama school in England and moved back to Zimbabwe for a brief period of time. She then worked in Australia as a teacher and storyteller.

Mem Fox has had quite a prolific career; some of her more recent and popular works include *Possum Magic* (1991), *Koala Lou* (1994), *Wombat Devine* (1999), and *Where Is the Green Sheep* (2002). Her books attempt to avoid stereotypic gender roles. Her works also try to counteract the racial profiling of Aborigine and African characters that she finds inherent in many other children's books.

New Zealand

Like Australia, the literature of New Zealand has been influenced by the anglophone tradition. As New Zealand writers produced works intended for their home audience, they also sought international appreciation, particularly from British and American audiences. Recognition proved difficult; however, influence was definitely present. An early example was Edith Littleton (1873–1945), who published a novel titled *Jim of the Ranges* (1910), written particularly to appeal to American readers with themes of the frontier and the Australian outback. One character, the Cisco Kid, would become the subject of an American western film years later.

One of the earliest New Zealand writers to gain worldwide popularity was Ngaio Marsh (1895–1982). With the publication of the millionth copy of her novels, she joined Agatha Christie and two others as one of the four grandes dames of detective fiction. She published thirty-two novels during her lifetime, but only four of them take place in New Zealand. The majority of her novels take place in England, although New Zealand plays a role in many of her works. Ngaio Marsh's novels have proven quite popular among international audiences that crave crime fiction. She did not consider the genre of detective fiction as an outlet for escapism; rather, her works explore deep psychological and thematic questions. A brief list of her novels includes her first novel, *A Man Lay Dead* (1934), as well as *Vintage Murder* (1937), *Dead Water* (1963), *Photo Finish* (1980), and her last work, *Light Thickness* (1982).

In the 1950s New Zealand experienced a boom in the production of light romance novels. This resulted in part from the influence of extremely powerful publishing firms, most notably Mills and Boon, although the Robert Hale firm also played a part. Romance novels would become one of the most popular and most influential genres from New Zealand in the twentieth century. One of the earliest and most famous writers to be promoted by Mills and Boon was Essie Summers. She was an extremely prolific writer. Some of her most noteworthy works include *New Zealand and Inheritance* (1957), *Bachelors Galore* (1958), and *No Orchids by Request* (1965). Some of the other earlier writers who would make their career with Mills and Boon were Gloria Bevan, Rilla Berg, Mary Moore, and Karin Mutch. Mills and Boon continued to influence the publication of books and advance the careers of many romance writers from New Zealand throughout the twentieth century. Later writers who became popular in the 1990s included Robyn Donald, Daphne Clair, and Susan Napier. All three writers have proven to be particularly prolific, and sales of their books have steadily remained in the millions. These writers have also become internationally known as translations of their works have received worldwide distribution, including in China.

Many other popular genres emerged toward the end of the twentieth century, including science fiction novels and thrillers. One of the first to write thriller novels that reached a worldwide readership was Colin Peel. He remained popular among international circles even though his works were not necessarily known within New Zealand. Colin Peel had published twelve novels before the 1990s; he reached greater success in the last decade of the century with such works as *Atoll* (1992), *Covenant of Poppies* (1992), *Armada* (1995), and *Blood of Your Sisters* (1996). Other writers of thriller novels remained known and read within the country although they are not well known internationally. Gaelyn Gordon writes for a variety of audiences, mostly young adults. Some of her works include *Above Suspicion* (1990), *Strained Relations* (1991), and *Deadlines* (1996). One of the most recent writers to appear on the New Zealand scene is Paul Thomas. His works include *Old School Tie* (1994), *Inside Dope* (1995), and *Gorilla Season* (1996). Science fiction has never been the most popular fiction genre in New Zealand; however, Philip Mann, who writes of empire and aliens, is one writer who has proven to be quite successful in this genre. His novels include *The Eye of the Queen* (1981), *Master of Paxwax* (1986), *Pioneers* (1988), and a four-part epic titled *A Land Fit for Heroes* (1993–96).

Children's literature has had a long history in New Zealand and reflects the various elements that have developed the island into a modern nation: exploration, the idea of the frontier, nationalism, and the culture of the Maori (aboriginal people often referred to as "New Zealanders"). The first two books that began the history of New Zealand literature were *Stories about Many Things, Founded on Facts* (1833) and *Emily Bathurst* (1847). These two works were published anonymously in London. Both books deal with experiences within the newly founded territory, including encounters with the Maori. W. H. G. Kingston's works *Holmwood; or, The New Zealand Settler* (1869) and *Waihoura; or, The New Zealand Girl* (1872) also recount initial Western experiences with the Maori. Kingston's novels, however, take the position that the Maori were savages before their encounter with the British, and having been Christianized, they were now model individuals. This racist sentiment toward the Maori changed as children's works and writers of the twentieth and twenty-first centuries began giving literary credit to the aboriginal tradition. Children's literature has also sought a New Zealand identity. The previous books mentioned as well as the majority of works written in the nineteenth century were all published abroad and were never considered to be children's literature specifically indigenous to New Zealand.

The twentieth century produced worldwide interest in children's picture books, particularly with the fame of Beatrix Potter at the turn of the century. No picture books were published in New Zealand until the 1940s. By the end of the twentieth century they would become one of the trademarks of New Zealand's children's literature. One of the first quality picture books published in the country was Joan Smith's *The Adventures of Nimble, Rumble, and Tumble* (1950). Advances in printing technology allowed an integration of color, picture, and text in the 1960s and encouraged the publication of a large number of picture books. Many of the works of this period stressed strong relations with the Maori and expressed New Zealand nationalism. Examples include Jane Hill's *Hey Boy* (1961), Pat Lawson's *Kuma Is a Maori Girl* (1961), and Ans Westra's *Washday at the Pa* (1964).

With a new understanding of the need for indigenous New Zealand literature for children, a boom in such works occurred in the 1970s and 1980s. This increase in publications of children's literature was coupled with scholarly attention to the genre. Four authors, each of whom published their first book in 1969, have received international acclaim: Rugh Dallas, Anne de Roo, Joy Cowley, and Margaret Mahy. Of these, Mahy was the most prominent in advancing publication of and interest in picture books in the 1980s. Her works addressed a variety of themes, including Maori legends. Children's books have been an expanding field of popular literature in New Zealand since the 1950s. They contribute to an understanding of New Zealand nationalism and a respect for the traditions of Maori culture. They are an intricate and vital aspect for readers of popular books from New Zealand.

LITERATURE

SOUTH AND SOUTHEAST ASIA

JAINA SANGA AND VINAY DHARWADKER

INTRODUCTION

The countries of South and Southeast Asia are mostly multilingual, and their literatures are often composed, preserved, circulated, and read in a number of languages. In each of these nations, populations belonging historically to different races, ethnicities, religions, and socioeconomic classes (among other groupings) often use different languages. But many of these linguistic groups are also multilingual in themselves: they use a shared "mother tongue" at home and in their community, and a different "market" language for practical transactions in their local environment. At the same time, they also use one or more "official" languages (including a national language) in the spheres of education, bureaucracy, government, and professional life. In such a setting, popular literatures reach large or mass audiences in complex ways, while "popularity" itself becomes a complicated term. In the absence of reliable information about publication, sales, circulation, and readership, the popularity of much Asian literature today can be measured best by broad public visibility.

The long-standing and widespread multilingualism of South and Southeast Asian societies varies in degree and kind by nation, and it affects the institutions of literature accordingly. Pakistan's literature, for example, is dominated by writing in Urdu, which is the most widely spoken language in the country and also the national language. But it also includes important though smaller literatures, such as those in Punjabi, Sindhi, and English. Each of these other literatures reaches a majority of the readers in a specific community and, therefore, may be "very popular" within that market segment.

In India today, newspapers and periodicals are published in nearly 125 languages and cater to a broad range of readerships. In this range, small audiences may vary from several hundred to a few thousand readers, whereas large audiences may run into tens of millions of readers. About 60 of India's languages are used for literary composition today. Literatures in some 25 of these languages (including English) are large and vibrant, comparable in size, scope, historical longevity, aesthetic quality, and cultural complexity to some of the literatures of Europe. In contrast to India, Sri Lanka has long literary traditions in just two contemporary languages, Sinhala and Tamil. It also has an older, mostly religious literature in Pali (the language of Theravada or Hinayana Buddhism) as well as a younger colonial and postcolonial literature in English.

In further contrast, literature in the Philippines has been dominated historically not by one but by two colonial languages: Spanish and English. Since the mid-twentieth century, however, literary cultures have flourished in a number of indigenous languages, such as Filipino, Tagalog, and Pangasinan, which also have large audiences now for newspapers, magazines, radio, television, and other mass media. Malaysia and Indonesia essentially share a major language in Bahasa. But Malaysia has literary traditions in Bahasa Melayu (earlier called Malay) as well as Chinese (a legacy of the Chinese diaspora), Tamil (a legacy of the south Indian diaspora), and English (a colonial legacy). Indonesia, on the other hand, has literary traditions in Bahasa Indonesia (a form of Malay), in indigenous languages such as Javanese and Balinese, and in the diasporic and colonial languages of Chinese, Dutch, and English. Popular writers and literary works, stories and poems, and forms and styles thus find different kinds of homes for themselves in different parts of South and Southeast Asia.

The following survey is organized by theme and form, not by language or nation. The principal focus is on the contemporary varieties of the novel, the short story, poetry, and drama. For each form under discussion, select examples—mostly of individual writers and works—suggest wider patterns and processes in Asian literatures. For writers and works in indigenous Asian languages, representative examples that are accessible in English translation have been included.

THEMES

Over the past 50 years or so, a number of themes have become particularly popular in South and Southeast Asian writing. These themes—which range from home to war, from women at the center of the family to outcasts at the bottom of society—represent relatively serious concerns shared by popular authors and their large audiences. They stand beside the "perennial favorites" of love, romance, and sex, which are treated at the popular level in formulaic ways, whether in periodical or book form (or in the mass media, such as in film and on television), and appear in inexpensive, mass-produced "genre" publications, as in much of the rest of the world.

Many authors from Asia turn to home and family as their primary concerns, so that stories, poems, and plays with a domestic or familial setting are especially common. Since many communities in Asia conceive of the family as an extended structure rather than as a nuclear one, familial narratives frequently cover larger kinship networks. The heroes and heroines or protagonists of many modern novels, plays, and short stories—in Indonesia, Malaysia, the Philippines, Sri Lanka, Nepal, or Pakistan, for example—thus tend to be figures set in the midst of family, kinship, and community networks. Even when they struggle against such traditional ties, and seek personal freedom and independence, they resist becoming isolated, merely self-serving individuals. We see this pattern, for example, in many well-known short stories, such as Shahnon Ahmad's "Woman" (Malay; Malaysia), Asoka Colombage's "The Smell of a Baby" (Sinhala; Sri Lanka), and Zamiruddin Ahmad's "Purvai—The Easterly Wind" (Urdu; Pakistan-England). The same is true even of English works in the Indian-American diaspora, such as Bharati Mukherjee's famous story, "The Management of Grief," and A. K. Ramanujan's well-known poem, "Small-Scale Reflections of a Great House." In these examples, different types of modern Asian families become microcosms of the larger societies within which they exist. "Family" and "home," in fact, are more than themes: they often serve as elaborate metaphors for a variety of structures, experiences, and phenomena in modern life.

Other themes are equally popular. For writers from former European colonies, stories of empire, colonial subjugation, and nationalist struggles for freedom are of great historical and political significance. Many of them devote their best creative energies to the quest for a new national identity, and to the search for a viable form of self-governance in postcolonial times. The best-known example of this kind of writing is Pramoedya Ananta Toer's *Buru Quartet*, a sequence of four long novels that reconstructs much of the Dutch colonial history of Indonesia, as well as the history of its nationalist movement and its larger struggle for nationhood.

For writers in Pakistan, India, and Bangladesh, a major theme is the decolonization of the subcontinent that occurred in 1947–48, and the related stories of national liberation and the birth of new nations. This includes the horrific saga of the partition of India and Pakistan in mid-1947 and later, which took the lives of at least 1 million Hindus, Muslims, and Sikhs—and displaced an estimated 14 million people in a matter of months, in what is the largest known mass migration in human history. The narratives of the partition have been recounted

THREE PERENNIAL FAVORITES

Mirza Asadullah Khan, known universally by his poetic pseudonym, Ghalib, was the first major modern poet in any of the Indian languages. Ghalib (1797–1869), a Muslim aristocrat of Turkish origin, spent most of his life in Old Delhi (near New Delhi, India's capital), struggling for financial survival. An exact contemporary of Shelley, Keats, and Heine, he is the most popular—if not the greatest—poet in Urdu, which is used across India and is the national language of Pakistan. He was a master of Urdu and Persian poetry in the *ghazal* form, and also of Urdu prose (in his letters) and Persian prose (in his diary of the Indian rebellion of 1857 against British rule, with its accounts of the horrifying aftermath). Millions of people know some of his poetry by heart. His poetry, letters, and diary circulate widely in Urdu and Persian, and in several English selections and translations.

In 1913, Rabindranath Tagore (1861–1941) won the Nobel Prize in literature, the first Asian to do so. A poet, short story writer, novelist, and dramatist in Bengali, he was also a major musical composer and lyricist (with about 2000 songs in the Rabindra *sangeet* style he created) as well as an innovative visual artist (with several thousand drawings and paintings in various media). In the second half of his career, he traveled all over the world as a public intellectual and cultural ambassador, lecturing in English to audiences in Europe, the Americas, and Asia. Large selections of his work are available in his own English translations. Excellent new versions include *Selected Poems* (1985, rev.1987) and *Selected Short Stories* (1991), translated by William Radice; *Quartet* (1993), translated by Kaiser Haq; *Gora* (1997), translated by Sujit Mukherjee; *The Oxford Tagore Translations* series (2000–), edited by Sukanta Chaudhuri and others; and *Three Plays* (2001), translated by Ananda Lal.

Premchand was the pen name of Dhanpat Rai Shrivastava (1880–1936), considered the "father" of the modern novel and short story in both Hindi and Urdu. Despite persistently poor health, he wrote ten novels and novellas and some 300 short stories over three decades, besides dozens of essays, lectures, reviews, and sketches, and hundreds of letters. A self-styled practitioner of "idealistic realism" that contrasted sharply with Tagore's explicitly spiritual "universal humanism," Premchand's literary output remains comparable in quality and impact to that of his more famous Bengali contemporary. Works, selections, and commentary available in English include novels *The Gift of a Cow* (1968), translated by Gordon Roadarmel, and *Nirmala* (1999), translated by Alok Rai. Books written about Premchand include David Rubin's *The World of Premchand* (1969), featuring selected stories, and Amrit Rai's *Premchand: His Life and Times* (1991), a biography.

in numerous short stories, novellas, novels, sequences of novels, biographies, autobiographies, and other works (including films), in languages ranging from Urdu, Punjabi, and Hindi to Bengali and English.

The related stories of 1971 and after, when East Pakistan broke away from West Pakistan to become Bangladesh, have figured prominently in the literary imaginations of writers in Bangladesh as well as in India, especially those written in Bengali and English. The Bangladeshi war of independence and the civil war that erupted around it also took the lives of about 1 million people, and drove 8 to 10 million refugees into India. In Sri Lanka the parallel theme has been the civil war that started in 1983 and continues into the present. This conflict has pitted an insurgent Hindu Tamil community in the north (descended from immigrants from south India, who mostly arrived between the thirteenth and nineteenth centuries), and the Sinhala-Buddhist majority, especially in the south, represented by Sri Lanka's national government. A poignant view of this lengthy conflict, which has claimed more than 60,000 lives and driven some 1.5 million people from their homes and livelihoods, appears in *Anil's Ghost* (2000), the best-selling novel in English by Michael Ondaatje, who was born and raised in the Dutch-colonial "burgher" community of Sri Lanka but subsequently migrated to Canada.

Other common themes of popular interest are the status and treatment of women in society, the position of marginalized and disenfranchised ethnic or religious minorities as well as that of larger disempowered social groups, and the clash between orthodox views and emerging values of modernity. The need to change the condition of women, to educate female children, and to protect women in vulnerable situations (such as single mothers, abused or abandoned wives, and widows) has been a long-standing concern of "reformist" writing across Asia. Early examples include the famous novels, novellas, and short stories of Rabindranath Tagore and Saratchandra Chatterjee, which were written in Bengali between the 1890s and the 1940s but remain immensely popular today. Contemporary classics of such "feminist" writing include stories like Pramoedya Ananta Toer's "Inem" (Bahasa Indonesia), Shahnon Ahmad's "Woman" (Bahasa Melayu), and Marianne Villanueva's "Siko" (English, the Philippines). Among the most popular works on themes related to women are the short stories of Ismat Chugtai (Urdu) and Mahasweta Devi (Bengali), both considered to be among the finest women writers of the twentieth century from a global perspective.

In the case of India, one of the most widespread themes in this cluster is the condition and experience of former "untouchables" in the caste system, most of whom are now known as Dalits (*dalit* in Marathi means "crushed, ground, or milled to a powder," and hence "downtrodden"). Mulk Raj Anand's English novels, *Untouchable* (1935) and *Coolie* (1936), were early treatments of this and related themes. Since the 1950s the large body of nonliterary writings in English by the activist and popular leader B. R. Ambedkar has become a "classic" at the center of the history of the Dalit movement. The works of Dalit writers, such as Namdeo Dhasal and Vasant Moon, have reached large audiences in India and abroad.

Finally, one of the popular themes that run through South and Southeast Asian literature is the celebration of indigenous, traditional, or aboriginal ways of life. Works on this theme usually focus on particular communities outside the modern, urban world; use folk tales or other folk material to create "authentic" narrative structures; and emphasize the vitality of a premodern or precolonial way of life, including its underlying spiritual or religious dimension. A large number of modern Asian novels, novellas, short stories, poems, and plays adopt this broad strategy to valorize the local, the indigenous, and the national over and against Westernization, modernity, and European colonization.

FORMS

The Novel

In South Asia, Munshi Premchand (1887–1936) is the most important and perennially popular figure from the beginning of modern prose fiction in two major languages: Hindi (one of two official languages of India) and Urdu (the official language of Pakistan). Premchand is famous for bringing an unusual brand of realism to the Urdu and Hindi novel, which he called "idealistic realism." He painted a large and detailed portrait of modern India, focusing especially well on peasant and village life in the north Indian countryside (which he knew intimately), and drawing out the conflicts and contradictions that marked modernity in urban India under colonial rule. He published ten novels in his relatively short lifetime, preparing versions of most of them in both Hindi (in the Devnagari script) and Urdu (in the Persian-Arabic script). They include *Sevasadan*, *Rangamanch*, *Ghaban*, *Nirmala*, and *Godan*, many of which have been translated into several languages, including English.

Major Hindi novelists of the post-independence period, whose works have remained popular over the years, include Yashpal, Upendranath Ashk, Hazari Prasad Dwivedi, and S. H. Vatsyayan (pseudonym: Agyeya). Since the 1970s, Amritlal Nagar, Giriraj Kishore, Rajendra Yadav, and Nirmal Verma have been among the most well-known and widely read novelists, together with a number of women writers, such as Krishna Sobti, Mannu Bhandari, Usha Priyamvada, Mridula Garg, Raji Seth, and Alka Saraogi. The novels and other prose writings of Nirmal Verma (1929–2005), currently available selectively in English translation, are widely considered to be classics of contemporary Hindi fiction. Amritlal Nagar's *Bhookh* [Hunger], originally published in 1946, has proven to be a modern classic in a wider context and was translated into English in 1990. The story focuses on the wartime famine of 1942 in pre-partition Bengal, which then included what are now the Indian state of West Bengal and the country of Bangladesh. The protagonist, Panchu Gopal Mukherjee, is the headmaster of a village school, and the horrors of the great famine are rendered through his eyes and thoughts. Although hunger ravishes the land, the local *zamindar* (land owner) and the rich traders are least affected; in fact, they thrive on profiteering from the war. Mukherjee is reduced to penury and wonders whether to sell off the few things left in his house or the furniture of his much-beloved school. Around him he witnesses the carpenter's widow selling her body, food riots erupting in the streets, and the scavenging dogs and birds eating the corpses left by the roadside. Despite this, the novel ends on a hopeful note: Mukherjee picks up a newborn child whose mother has just died; he takes the child home, and his wife, Mangala, although starving, is nonetheless happy with the new arrival.

In India, the woman novelist Qurratulain Hyder (b. 1927) remains the preeminent fiction writer of the postcolonial period in the Urdu language, chiefly for her novel *Aag ka Darya* (1959), translated into English as *River of Fire*. The novel, and Hyder more generally, is celebrated for the innovative use of stream-of-consciousness techniques to represent modern Indian consciousness as well as South Asian and Muslim history and culture, both past and present. In Bengali, popular classics include the novels of Rabindranath Tagore and Saratchandra Chatterjee, written in the first half of the twentieth century. Among the major figures of the post-independence period in this language are Bibhutibhushan Bandyopadhyay, Manisankar Mukherjee, and Sunil Gangopdhyay, whose fiction was popularized particularly by Satyajit Ray, who made several films based on their works. In other Indian languages, widely acknowledged and admired novelists since independence in 1947 include Gopinath Mohanty (Oriya), Ashokamitran (Tamil), O. V. Vijayan (Malayalam), U. R. Anantha Murthy (Kannada), and Vyankatesh Madgulkar (Marathi). Among women novelists, the best-known figures include Ashapurna Devi (Bengali); Amrita Pritam (Punjabi); and Ruth Prawer Jhabvala, Kamala Markandeya, Anita Desai, and Arundhati Roy (English), together with the others mentioned above and below.

South Asian literature in English—mainly from Pakistan, India, and Sri Lanka—occupies a special place in this context. Although Indian-English literature had its beginnings between about 1794 and 1834, it was not until the 1930s that the Indian novel in English really took hold. Three major novelists—Mulk Raj Anand, R. K. Narayan, and Raja Rao—began their

POPULAR WRITERS AND FILMS BASED ON THEIR WORK

The popularity of many Asian writers in recent decades has been enhanced by films based on their work. The Malaysian fiction writer Shahnon Ahmad's novel set in Malay, *Ranjau sepanjang jalan* [No Harvest but a Thorn] (1965), was made into a film of the same name in 1966, directed by Jamil Sulong. The Bengali woman writer Mahasweta Devi's short story "Hajar chaurashir ma" [The Mother of Prisoner Number 1084], which she turned into a stage play, was also turned into a film in Hindi, *Hazar Chaurasi ki Ma*, by Indian Middle Cinema director Govind Nihalani. W. S. Rendra, Indonesia's leading poet, dramatist, and theater personality, has acted in several films, including *Yang Muda Yang Bercinta* [The Young Who Love].

In the Indian film industry, cinema based on literary works has been commonplace since the early twentieth century. The fiction of Bengali writer Saratchandra Chatterjee (1876–1938), a younger contemporary of Rabindranath Tagore whose works have been translated in print into most of India's major modern languages, has been a favorite of moviemakers as well as audiences. Between 1922 and 2005, some twenty of his novels and stories were adapted for the silver screen, some repeatedly and in different languages. Among the Saratchandra "classics" of Indian film are various versions of *Devdas* (1928, 1935, 1936, 1953, 1955, 1974, 1979, 2002), *Parineeta* (1942, 1953, 1969, 2005), *Badi Didi* (1939, 1961), *Majhli Didi* (1950, 1967), *Biraj Bahu* (1954), and *Swami* (1977).

The two leading stage dramatists in India, Vijay Tendulkar (b. 1928) and Girish Karnad (b. 1938), have also had remarkably prolific careers in the film industry. Tendulkar has written original stories, scripts, dialogue, lyrics, or screenplays for thirteen films in Hindi and Marathi, including the Indian Middle Cinema classics *Samna* (1974), *Nishaant* (1975), *Manthan* (1976), *Arvind Desai ki Ajeeb Dastaan* (1978), *Aakrosh* (1980), *Umbartha* (1982), and *Ardh Satya* (1983).

As a leading and supporting actor, writer, and director, the dramatist Girish Karnad has contributed to the making of more than fifty films in Hindi, Kannada, and other languages, with equal facility in commercial and art cinema. Among his numerous credits as an actor are memorable roles in *Samskara* (1970), *Nishaant* (1975), *Manthan* (1976), and *Swami* (1977); as a screen writer, he has had a hand in *Bhumika* (1977), *Kalyug* (1980), *Utsav* (1984), and *Agni Varsha* (2002); and as a director, he has made *Kaadu* (1973), *Godhuli* (1977), *Ondanondu Kaladalli* (1978), *Kanaka Purandara* (1988), and *Cheluvi* (1992).

Among other important contemporaries associated with film is the Urdu writer Khwaja Ahmad Abbas (1914–87), who was the director of thirty-three films in Hindi, Urdu, and English; a screen writer for twenty-six films; and a producer for six films. His credits included the notable commercial movies *Awaara* (1951), *Shree 420* (1955), *Sapno ka Saudagar* (1968), *Bombai Raat ki Bahon Mein* (1968), *Saat Hindustani* (1969), *Mera Naam Joker* (1970), and *Bobby* (1973). Rajinder Singh Bedi (1915–84), a writer in Urdu, Hindi, and Punjabi, directed four films, including Dastak (1970); he was also a screen writer for twenty-two films, including *Daag* (1952), *Devdas* (1955), *Madhumati* (1958), *Dooj ka Chand* (1964), *Anupama* (1966), *Satyakam* (1969), *Abhiman* (1973), and *Ek Chadar Maili Si* (1986). Among other important figures are the Hindi woman writer Mannu Bhandari (*Rajnigandha* [1974] and *Swami* [1977]) and the Urdu poets Kaifi Azmi (1914–2002), who served as a song writer for over forty films, and Akhtar-ul-Iman (b. 1915), who also was a screen writer for over forty films. (See the Film chapter on South and Southeast Asia for more information on films.)

careers at this time. Known as the "grand masters" of the Indian novel, they are noted for their contributions to the literary aesthetics of the genre. For instance, Anand, like James Joyce, experimented with the technique of compressing a single day's events into a narrative (as in *Untouchable* [1935]). Narayan, who is widely beloved for creating the imaginary locale of Malgudi as a typical small town in south India, focuses on rendering minute details and posits his characters within local rather than heroic predicaments; for examples, see *The Financial Expert* (1952) and *The Man-eater of Malgudi* (1962). Rao, in contrast, celebrates Indian village life as in the superb, experimental *Kanthapura* (1938); he also attempts to promote a philosophical and spiritual "classical" Indian worldview in his later fiction and prose.

In tracing the rise of the contemporary South Asian novel in English, the seminal influence of Salman Rushdie's *Midnight's Children* (1981) perhaps created the tremendous international "boom" in South Asian writing, inspiring novelists in English to write in a brave new way. The novel tells the dramatic story of Saleem Sinai, the first-person narrator, who was born at midnight on August 15, 1947, at the exact moment of India's independence. Saleem is linked telepathically to one thousand other "midnight's children," also born during the hour of independence. Saleem's life mirrors that of the nation, and the novel becomes a rendition of the trials and tribulations of modern India as told through the narrator's fractured perceptions. Rushdie's innovative narrative strategies in this novel—and in his other fiction—were brilliantly adapted from numerous sources in world literature, ranging from Sterne's *Tristram Shandy* and Joyce's *Ulysses* and *Finnegans Wake* to García Márquez's *One Hundred Years of Solitude*. His importing of Indian words and idioms into the English text; his evocation of Indian attitudes, experiences, and history; and his engagement with current political themes not only anchored a place for him within the canon of contemporary literature, but also paved the way for other South Asian writers of the postcolonial generation. Among the most notable and popular South Asian novelists in English who emerged after Rushdie, mostly in the South Asian diaspora in Europe and North America, are Vikram Seth, Hanif Kureishi, Rohinton Mistry, Bapsi Sidhwa, Amitav Ghosh, Shashi Tharoor, Arundhati Roy, and Hari Kunzru (all with connections to India or Pakistan); and Michael Ondaatje and Shyam Selvadurai (with connections to Sri Lanka).

The development of the novel in Southeast Asia, both in the indigenous languages of the region and in European colonial languages (such as English) is similarly complex, and even less well known outside the region. Pramoedya Ananta Toer (1925–2006) was the leading novelist in postcolonial Indonesia, the quality and impact of whose large, sustained output in Bahasa Indonesia (under extremely difficult personal circumstances) placed him in the front ranks of modern world literature. The same is true of a writer such as Nick Joaquin (1917–2004), whose novels, poetry, plays, essays, and journalistic writings in English made him a national figure in the Philippines, during the Marcos regime as well as after, and placed him among the most distinctive figures in contemporary world literature.

The Short Story

More than the novel, it is probably the modern short story form that has emerged as the central driving force and achievement in the modern literatures of South and Southeast Asia. In most of the literary languages of the region, the short story has proved to be particularly adaptable to new experiments and techniques, often improvising upon and even extending Euro-American modernist, avant-garde, and postmodernist models. Equally significantly, however, the Asian varieties of the modern short story have been able to echo,

FOUR CONTEMPORARY ASIAN AUTHORS

Pramoedya Ananta Toer (1925–2006), known internationally by his first name, was one of Indonesia's most famous literary figures in the post-independence period, and the leading fiction writer in Bahasa Indonesia. He was imprisoned by the Dutch colonial government in the late 1940s for his "anticolonial" activities. The authoritarian Suharto regime imprisoned him without trial as a political dissident in the notorious Buru Island facilities between 1965 and 1979, and kept him under virtual house arrest thereafter until 1992. The severe beatings and forced hard labor of the Buru period permanently damaged Pramoedya's hearing and his hands, but he composed four novels orally and narrated them to his fellow prisoners; given access to a typewriter after 1973, he recorded the narratives on paper, which were published upon his release as "the Buru quartet"—translated as *This Earth of Mankind* (1980), *Child of All Nations* (1980), *Footsteps* (1985), and *House of Glass* (1988). For biographical and bibliographical details on Pramoedya's astonishing life and prolific career, see his biography page at http://www.kirjasto.sci.fi/pram.htm.

Shahnon Ahmad (b. 1933) is generally regarded as Malaysia's most important prose writer in modern times, with a large output in Bahasa Melayu in the novel, novella, short story, and essay forms, and with one film based on his work. His fiction explores a broad range of vital social, economic, historical, and religious issues in contemporary rural as well as urban life. A verbal and stylistic innovator of the first order, Ahmad practices both social realism and idealistic satire. His most famous novel, with the title *Shit* (1999) in English but the text in Malay, is one of the most brilliant political satires of recent times. It caused a national furor in Malaysia, resulting in retaliation by the authoritarian government of Prime Minister Mahathir against Ahmad. For an overview of Ahmad's life and achievements, see http://www.kirjasto.sci.fi/shahnon.htm.

Mahasweta Devi (b. 1926), known by her given name, is one of the most important living women writers in Asia. She was born in Dhaka (now in Bangladesh) but has lived in West Bengal (India) since adolescence. A fierce activist, who works tirelessly for the rights of women, children, the rural as well as urban poor, and India's aboriginal peoples, Mahasweta has published more than 100 books in the past five decades, including novels, short stories, plays, historical fiction, contemporary documentary studies and reports, and essays, many of which have become "classics" of contemporary Bengali prose. In addition to a film and dramatic productions based on her work, translations into English and interviews and commentaries in English have enabled her work to have an international impact in recent years. For a basic guide to Mahasweta's life and writings, see http://www.english.emory.edu/Bahri/Devi.html.

Nick Joaquin (1917–2004) was the leading Filipino writer and journalist in English of his age. Famous for his nuanced prose style, his historical probing of the Philippines' Spanish colonial past, as well as his psychological and metaphysical understanding of human characters, Joaquin produced a large body of poetry, novels, short stories, essays, sketches, and historical and cultural studies over 50 years, in addition to his prolific reportage and journalism. The authoritarian regime of Ferdinand Marcos in the Philippines first courted, then actively marginalized, him; he survived this retaliatory technique on the strength of his national popularity as a writer with "militant artistry," driven by a "cultural mission" to create "the true portrait of the Filipino soul."[1]

translate, incorporate, or innovate upon long-standing indigenous traditions of folk and literary storytelling.

In Bengali, a literary language of the first importance both for India and for Bangladesh, Rabindranath Tagore single-handedly invented the modern short story in the 1880s. Available widely in excellent new selections and English translations since the 1980s and 1990s, his short stories remain among the most popular Indian examples of the form internationally. As with the novel in Hindi and Urdu, Premchand is the progenitor of the modern short story in these two languages, cutting across the post-independence divide between India and Pakistan.

In Hindi subsequently, Mohan Rakesh (1925–72), Nirmal Verma (1929–2005), and Bhisham Sahni (1915–2003) were among the pioneers of the *Nai Kahani* (new short story) movement of the 1950s. They responded creatively to the influence of Premchand's "idealistic realism," his Marxist vision of Indian society and history as well as British colonialism, and his relatively linear narratives and minimally embellished prose. Their achievement was to revolutionize the Hindi short story with new representations of the individual, of consciousness and desire, and of social relations—and with new narrative structures and techniques, as well as new voices and styles. In recent decades, popular short story writers have included Phanishewarnath Renu, Amritlal Nagar, Rajendra Yadav, Kamleshwar, and Giriraj Kishore. Also among this group of writers are Raghuvir Sahay and Kunwar Narain (both well-known poets), as well as Ram Kumar (also a popular painter) and the women writers Krishna Sobti, Mannu Bhandari, Usha Priyamvada, and Mamta Kalia (also a poet in English).

Ruskin Bond (b. 1934) is perhaps India's most prolific and widely recognized short story writer in English. His stories capture the sights and sounds of his youth in Dehra Dun, and his current home in Mussoorie, both in the Gharwal region of north India. Some of these stories depict people who, often unconsciously, need each other—they are people in love or in need of love. Some of his stories are quiet, satirical studies of village life, with their small-town braggarts and petty officials. His most memorable collections are *The Night Train at Deoli and Other Stories* and *When Darkness Falls and Other Stories*. Among Indian-English writers with earlier reputations, the short stories of Mulk Raj Anand, R. K. Narayan, Raja Rao, Khwaja Ahmed Abbas, Khushwant Singh, Ruth Prawer Jhabvala, Anita Desai, Bhabhani Bhattacharya, and Manohar Malgaonkar remain the most popular today. Of the post-1980 generations, Salman Rushdie, Rohinton Mistry, and Shashi Tharoor have published some of the best-known short stories in English. Among the women writers, Bharati Mukherjee, Chitra Divakaruni Banerjee, Padma Perera, Githa Hariharan, and especially Anjana Appachana (also author of a terrific but neglected novel *Listening Now*) and Jhumpa Lahiri have produced a number of remarkable short stories. Lahiri's *The Interpreter of Maladies* (1999), a collection of short stories about Indian immigrants in the West, won the Pulitzer Prize for fiction in 2000.

The short story has been a vital form since the early twentieth century in Nepali writing as well as in what is now the Bengali literature of Bangladesh. An important new development in the case of Nepal was the publication of Samrat Upadhyay's *Arresting God in Kathmandu* (2001). Upadhyay is an immigrant Nepalese writer who lives in the United States and writes in English. His stories focus on the clash between the spiritual and the material by exploring the nature of desire and transcendence in both the public and the private realms. In Bangladesh, writers such as Sayeed Ahmad, Abu Rashd, Abu Jafar Shamsuddin, Shaheed Akand, and Nuzhat Amin are among the most prominent in relation to the short story form. Among collections that have become available and noticed in recent years are Niaz Zaman's *The Dance and Other Stories* (1996), written in a fantasy folktale style; Shamim Hamid's *Zuleikha's Dream and Other Stories* (2002), which invokes feminist issues and depicts the struggles of Bangladeshi women; and Ahsan Senan's *The Tenth Victim* (2003), an unusual collection of detective stories emulating the popular international genre.

In Pakistan, the short story has served as an important vehicle for documenting the atrocities that occurred during the partition of the subcontinent. Saadat Hassan Manto (1912–55) maintained a sufficiently objective yet passionate view of the genocide on both sides of the border to achieve the status of a "classic." Manto's collection, written originally in Urdu and titled *Mottled Dawn: Fifty Sketches and Stories of Pakistan* (1997), is a powerful rendition of the tragedies of partition. More broadly, many readers believe that the short story in Urdu, as cultivated in Pakistan as well as in India, has steadily emerged as the best example of the genre in South Asia. Its major practitioners include Intizar Hussain, Abdullah Hussein, Enver Sajjad, Hasan Manzar, Muhammad Salim-ur-Rahman, and Zamiruddin Ahmad in Pakistan (or the Pakistani diaspora abroad); and Rajinder Singh Bedi, Khwaja Ahmed Abbas, Balraj Manra, Surendra Parkash, and Naiyer Masud in India (or its diaspora). Among the important women writers of short stories in this language are Khalida Asghar (Pakistan), Qurratulain Hyder and Ismat Chugtai (India), and younger writers such as Mumtaz Mufti and Rukhsana Ahmed. The fiction and nonfiction of Chughtai (1911–91) has been posthumously collected in English translation in *Lifting the Veil* (2001). Perceived most often as a feminist writer, she is best known for stories exploring female sexuality in its social, psychological, and existential contexts.

As in South Asia, the short story has been a principal site of innovation and representation in modern Southeast Asian literatures, from Indonesia and Malaysia to Thailand and the Philippines. Shahnon Ahmad (b. 1933) is the most important prose writer in modern Malay or Bahasa Melayu. His large output includes novels and satires, but he is most famous for his short stories. His language is particularly innovative: he creates a rich, resonant verbal texture by combining words, phrases, echoes, and allusions from Kedah, Prak, Johore, Negri Sebilan, and Minangkabau with Sanskrit, Javanese, and Arabic. His fiction deals with a variety of historical and contemporary themes and issues, whether social economic, political, or religious. One of his most popular stories in translation, "Woman" (1980), is about Siti, a girl in a poor Muslim community along Malaysia's rural coastline. Siti's parents decide to find her a husband, but she wants to resist that arrangement with all her being. The unflinching representation of Siti and her well-intentioned parents reveals a painful conflict between adult dutifulness and youthful rebellion, conservative caution and obstinate desire, and natural disposition and social convention. From narratives such as these, Ahmad emerges as a masterful observer and critic of economic and social realities, and especially of the moral, ethical, and spiritual tensions of everyday life.

The short story has also played a central role in the development of modern Philippine literature. Among the best-known figures associated with this form in the postcolonial period are Manuel Arguilla, Amador Daguio, Nick Joaquin, and Marianne Villaneuva. Some of the best stories by these writers center on the great common themes of Asian writing. Arguilla's "How My Brother Leon Bought Home a Wife" and Daguio's "Wedding Dance," for example, are multifaceted and unusual explorations of home and family. Daguio's story and Villaneuva's "Siko" are both set in villages far from the modern city and urban life; they celebrate indigenous cultures that connect independently and powerfully with nature, the earth, and a world of spirits. Joaquin's remarkable story "The Summer Solstice" also explores the interconnections of spirit world and mundane world, ancient and new, male and female, and reason and instinct, but it dramatically reasserts the primacy of the female in human culture, in a style strikingly reminiscent of Latin American magical realism.

The short story remained much more dormant in Vietnamese writing until the beginning of the twenty-first century. The partition of the country under the French in 1954, the subsequent occupation of the south by the United States, and the outbreak of the long war between the north and the south severely disrupted Vietnamese literary culture for several decades. Since the end of the Vietnam War in the mid-1970s, lyric poetry has become the most widely practiced form, used both by writers in the unified homeland under reconstruction and by writers of the Vietnamese diaspora in the West. But such fiction writers as Nguyen Huy Thiep, who began to publish his work in Vietnamese in the 1980s, have gradually developed specific thematic concerns in their short stories. Thiep often explores history and myth even as he writes realistically about contemporary society, but a well-known story such as "Salt of the Jungle" engages with the interaction between the human world and nature on a much wider imaginative canvas.

Poetry

Poetry, in some respects, is the most popular form in many parts of the South Asian mainland and elsewhere in Asia. In many modern Asian cultures, poetry circulates widely in both oral and printed forms; it is quoted in conversation, sung to music, recited on social occasions, and read for both cultural knowledge and personal pleasure. In South and Southeast Asia, the great bulk of the poetry in circulation in modern times has been composed in indigenous languages. Many communities across the region believe that the poetry in their "mother tongues" best expresses and communicates their most intimate and profound feelings, emotions, and experiences, and hence also best represents their individual and collective identities.

In languages such as Hindi and Urdu, older poets such as Kabir (fifteenth century), Mirabai (sixteenth century), Tulsidas (seventeenth century), and Mirza Ghalib (1797–1869) continue to be the most popular: the majority of educated people in north India know at least a few verses by each of them by heart. In Bengali, both in India and in Bangladesh, the most widely-known and quoted poet is Rabindranath Tagore (1861–1941); other popular older poets in the language are Michael Madhusudan Dutt (nineteenth century) and Kazi Nazrul Islam (mid-twentieth century), the national poet of Bangladesh. All three of them were born in or were long associated with the land that is now Bangladesh, and public monuments to them are the most popular tourist destinations in that country today.

Modern South Asian poets in the indigenous languages have explored most varieties of poetry: major epics on national-cultural and historical themes; short and long narrative poems; dramatic poems in dialogue form, verse-plays, and dramatic monologues; songs; lyric poetry in Romantic, modernist, and postmodernist styles; poems that experiment radically with language, form, conventions, and subject matter; protest poetry and anti-poetry; poems in meter and rhyme as well as in free verse and prose; poetic sequences; and meditative and reflective poetry. Examples of many of these varieties (except for some long forms) can be found in anthologies such as Vinay Dharwadker and A. K. Ramanujan's *The Oxford Anthology of Modern Indian Poetry* (1994), and in Vinay Dharwadker's comprehensive *The Columbia Book of South Asian Poetry*.

In Bengali, some of the more popular poets after Tagore have been Jibanananda Das and Buddhdev Bose, on whom there are important books in English; Amiya Charavarty, Bishnu De, Shakti Chattopdahyay, and Sunil Gangopadhyay (also a major novelist); and the women poets Nabaneeta Deb Sen, Kabita Sinha, Vijaya Mukhopadhyay, and Anuradha Mahapatra. In Kannada, another major language of poetry, Gopalkrishna Adiga is the dominant modern figure, regarded by many as the best twentieth-century poet in India; other significant innovators include K. S. Narasimhaswami, Chandrashekhar Kambar (also a major dramatist and theater practitioner), P. Lankesh (also a fiction writer), and the bilingual poet and multilingual translator A. K. Ramanujan.

Marathi poetry, which has been influential as well as popular, has been widely represented by the early innovators B. S. Mardhekar and P. S. Rege; by the proponents of *nava kavya*, or "new poetry," especially Indira Sant (a remarkable woman poet), Vinda Karandikar, Vasant Bapat, and Mangesh Padgaonkar; by trend-setting Dalit and subaltern poets, such as Narayan Surve, Namdeo Dhasal, and Hira Bansode (a boldly experimental "downtrodden" woman poet); and, not least, by the internally renowned bilingual poet Arun Kolatkar (both Marathi and English). Telugu has a broad range of well-known modern poets, from the multifaceted Sri Sri to the astonishing N. Revathi Devi (a woman poet who committed suicide early). So, too, does Malayalam, from G. Shankara Kurup and the versatile K. Ayappa Paniker to postmodernist experimenters such as K. Satchidanandan and women poets such as Savithri Rajeevan. The most widely known but controversial poet in modern Punjabi is Amrita Pritam, a prolific woman writer with seminal achievements in the novel, short story, and autobiographical genres as well.

Hindi has also produced a number of poets with national and international reputations. Among the early twentieth-century pioneers are Mahadevi Verma and Suryakant Tripathi (pseudonym: Nirala). In the middle of the twentieth century, prominent experimentalists and progressives included S. H. Vatsyayan and G. M. Muktibodh; in the postcolonial period, *nai kavita*, or "new poetry," and important later "schools" came to be represented by figures such as Kunwar Narain, Raghuvir Sahay, Shrikant Verma, Kedarnath Singh, and Dhoomil, some of whom have been among the most widely circulated poets until the present decade. Urdu poetry flourished during this period in India as well as Pakistan. After Mohammad Iqbal (considered the national poet of Pakistan), the single dominant poet has been Faiz Ahmed Faiz, now translated quite extensively into English. Other well-known Urdu poets of the post-1947 period include N. M. Rashid and Kishwar Naheed (Pakistan) and Akhtar-ul-Iman, Firaq Gorakhpuri, Ali Sardar Jafri, Kaifi Azmi, and Nida Fazli (India). Unlike most other South Asian languages, Urdu has persisted with metrical poetry in fixed forms, derived from the long Persian or Farsi poetic tradition, a feature that has proven to be a source of weakness and strength at once.

English is a common medium of poetry in India, Pakistan, Bangladesh, and Sri Lanka. In post-independence Indian-English poetry, the most popular figures have been the bilingual poets A. K. Ramanujan (English and Kannada) and Arun Kolatkar (English and Marathi). Other poets with international reputations in the first postcolonial generation are Nissim Ezekiel (of Bene–Israeli Jewish descent), Dom Moraes (of Goan Christian descent), Jayanta Mahapatra (also a translator of Oriya poetry), Keki Daruwalla and Adil Jussawalla (both from the Parsi community), and R. Parthasarathy (also a translator of Tamil poetry). The most celebrated women poets are Kamala Das, Eunice de Souza, Imtiaz Dharker, and Sujata Bhatt. Among the younger English poets of the Indian diaspora are Saleem Peeradina (also a translator of Gujarati poetry), Meena Alexander, Agha Shahid Ali (also a translator of Urdu poetry), Vinay Dharwadker (also a multilingual translator), and Jeet Thayil in the United States, roughly contemporaneous with figures such as Melanie Silgardo and Tabish Khair in Europe, Leela Gandhi in Australia, and Manohar Shetty in India.

The counterparts of the Indian-English poets include these: in Pakistan, Alamgir Hashmi; in Bangladesh, Kaiser Haq; and in Sri Lanka, Patrick Furtado, as well as the remarkable woman poet Jean Arasanayagam (a "burgher" by descent, but married to a Tamil), whose social origins and background have given her a unique perspective on the Sri Lankan civil war of the past three decades. The patterns and cycles found in South Asian poetry in English are also present, with important variations, in the experiences and work of English-language poets in Southeast Asia and its diasporic cultures. Among the major figures to be explored in such a context are Shirley Geok-lin Lim, born in Malacca (Malaysia) and now based in the United States and Hong Kong, who writes poetry as well as autobiographical prose and fiction in English, besides scholarly criticism; Li-Young Lee, born in Jakarta, Indonesia, into an immigrant Chinese family and relocated via Hong Kong, Macau, and Japan to the United States, where he is now a celebrated immigrant poet in English; and Edwin Thumboo, immigrant of Indian descent who is perhaps Singapore's most distinguished poet and literary scholar in English today, with a professional career that has significantly changed understandings of the contemporary world.

Drama

Among the Asian nations, India, Sri Lanka, and Indonesia have the liveliest cultures of original dramatic writing, with complex links to contemporary urban theater as well as to older folk and rural performance traditions. Since India's independence in 1947, a large number of playwrights have appeared in a number of Indian languages. The major and most popular playwrights in Hindi are Mohan Rakesh (1925–72), who was also a short story writer, and Dharamvir Bharati (1926–97). Habib Tanvir, whose plays are often developed in workshops with folk and urban performers, has created nine important plays in Hindi, Urdu, and the Chattisgarhi dialect, the most popular being *Charan Das the Thief* (1974). The premier playwrights in Bengali are Badal Sircar (b. 1925), with sixteen plays to his credit, among them the classic *Evam Indrajit* [And Indrajit] (1962); and Utpal Dutt (1929–93), also a noted stage and film actor, with eleven plays, most of them unflinchingly political in theme.

The most visible post-independence drama has appeared in Marathi, which has a remarkably modern urban theater in cities such as Bombay (Mumbai), Poona (Pune), and Nagpur. The best-known playwrights in Marathi are Vijay Tendulkar (b. 1928), also a writer of fiction and essays as well as for film and television, who has published over thirty plays; G. P. Deshpande (b. 1938), with six plays to his credit to date; Mahesh Elkunchwar (b. 1939), also an actor, who has authored fifteen plays so far; and Satish Alekar (b. 1949), also a director and an actor, with ten plays in print. The contemporary classics of Marathi drama include Tendulkar's *Silence! The Court Is in Session* (1967), *Sakharam the Book Binder* (1972), *Ghashiram Kotwal* [Constable Ghashiram] (1972), and *Gift of a Daughter* (1983); Deshpande's *The Ruined Sanctuary* (1974); Elkunchwar's *Old Stone Mansion* (1985); and Alekar's *The Great Departure* (1974) and *Begum Barve* (1979).

Kannada, the language of Karnataka, has also been a principal medium of dramatic and theatrical production in recent decades. The major playwrights, whose work has been widely appreciated, are Chandrashekhar Kambar (b. 1938), also a director and producer, with ten important plays to his credit; and Girish Karnad (b. 1938), also a noted film actor as well as a writer and translator in English, with a dozen plays in print. For many readers and theater audiences in India and around the world, Vijay Tendulkar in Marathi and Girish Karnad in Kannada (and some English) are the best Indian playwrights of modern times.

Other important Indian dramatists include K. N. Panikkar (b. 1928), with some eight plays in Malayalam; Ratan Thiyam (b. 1946), with ten unusual plays and performance texts in Manipuri (the language of the state of Manipur in northeastern India, near the border with Myanmar); and Mahesh Dattani (b. 1958), who has published nearly a dozen plays in English. Among Indian women playwrights and theater figures, the most prominent are Mahasweta Devi and Usha Ganguli (both Bengali), Vijaya Mehta (Marathi), Neelam Mansingh Chowdhry (Punjabi, Hindi, English), and Manjula Padmanabhan (English).

Sri Lanka's modern theater has also supported a number of original dramatists. In English, the most prolific and successful playwright has been Ernst McIntyre (b. 1935), who formed a theater group in the 1960s and has staged international plays in English as well as his own plays. McIntyre migrated to Australia in the 1970s, but even his later works, such as *Let's Give Them a Curry: An Australian-Asian Comedy in Three Acts* (1981) and *Rasanayagam's Last Riot* (1990), created a cross-cultural dynamic between Sri Lankan and Anglophone theater. In the Sinhala language, an important contemporary playwright was Simon Navagattegama (1940–2005), also an actor, who was influenced by Chekhov and Kafka and published five plays, among which *Suba Saha Yasa* is considered a masterpiece. Sugathapala De Silva (1928–2002), often called the "architect" of modern Sinhala drama and theater, launched a theater company and translated and adapted plays by Tennessee Williams and Luigi Pirandello for Sri Lankan audiences. He also wrote several original plays that captured the mood of the new middle class in Sri Lanka after independence. Among them are *Thattu Geval* and *Boarding Karayo*, as well as his best piece, *Dunna Dunu Gamuwe*, a serious political play written just after the insurrection of 1971. Over the past two decades, Sri Lanka has also witnessed the growth of a new commercial theater, which offers popular entertainment with political satire, stage gimmicks, and risqué humor. Nihal Siva's *Sergeant Nallathamby* was probably the first Sinhala play to achieve large-scale commercial success, playing even to expatriate audiences in the Middle East.

Over the past five decades, Indonesian drama and theater have been dominated by the enormous creative presence of W. S. Rendra (b. 1935), the country's most celebrated poet, playwright, stage director, and performer. Born in Java and trained in theater arts in New York, he is the author in Bahasa Indonesia of several major collections of poetry, including *Potret Pembangunan dalam Puisi* [Portrait of Development in Poetry], *Bersatulah Pelacur-pelacur Kota Jakarta* [Jakarta's Prostitutes, Unite!], and *Blues untuk Bonnie* [Blues for Bonnie]. Besides performing his poetry to music and acting in films, he is an internationally recognized human rights and social justice activist. He launched his Bengkel Teater Group (Theater Workshop) in 1967, and he was associated with the anti-state Taman Ismail Marzuki, the arts center in Jakarta, in the 1970s. Imprisoned by both the Sukarno and Suharto regimes in the 1960s and 1970s, he was banned from performing during much of the 1980s. His landmark plays include *A Flower Red as Blood* and *The First Jolt* (both 1953); free Bahasa adaptations of Western works, such as Ibsen's *The Wild Duck* and Ionesco's *The Chairs;* as well as *Bip-Bop* (1968), the first example of *teater mini kata* or the theater of the minimal text. Subsequently, his works included the protest plays *Mastodon* and *Condor* (both 1973), *The Struggle of the Naga Tribe* (1974), *Regional Secretary* (1976), and *Panembahan Reso* [Baron Reso] (1986), and such late and sometimes controversial works as *Selamatan Anak Cucu Suleiman* [A Ritual for Suleiman's Descendants] (1988), a mini-*kata*, and *Kantata Taqwa* [A Cantata to Piety] (1990), a multimedia extravaganza performed in a sports stadium.

RESOURCE GUIDE

PRINT SOURCES

East Asia and Oceania

Craig, Timothy J., ed. *Japan Pop! Inside the World of Japanese Popular Culture.* Armonk, NY: M. E. Sharpe, 2000.
Guanzhong, Luo. *Three Kingdoms.* Translated by Moss Roberts. Berkeley: University of California Press, 1999.

LITERATURE

Gelder, Ken. *Popular Fiction: The Logistics and Practices of a Literary Field.* New York: Routledge, 2004.
Gravett, Paul. *Manga: 60 Years of Japanese Comics.* New York: Collins Design, 2004.
Hamm, John Christopher. *Paper Swordsmen: Jin Yong and the Modern Chinese Martial Arts Novel.* Honolulu: University of Hawaii Press, 2005.
Kinsella, Sharon. *Adult Manga.* Honolulu: University of Hawaii Press, 2000.
Link, E. Perry, Jr. *Mandarin Ducks and Butterflies: Popular Fiction in Early Twentieth-Century Chinese Cities.* Berkeley: University of California Press, 1981.
McDougall, Bonnie. *Popular Literature and Performing Arts in the People's Republic of China 1949–1979.* Berkeley: University of California Press, 1984.
Pratt, Keith, and Richard Rutt, eds. *Korea: A Historical and Cultural Dictionary.* Surrey, UK: Curzon Press, 1999.
Powers, Richard G., and Kato Hidetoshi, eds., *Handbook of Japanese Popular Culture.* Westport, CT: Greenwood Press, 1989.
Saxby, H. M. *A History of Australian Children's Literature 1841–1941.* Sydney: Wentworth Books, 1969.
Schodt, Frederik L. *Dreamland Japan: Writings on Modern Manga.* Berkeley: Stone Bridge Press, 1996.
———. *Manga! Manga!: The World of Japanese Comics.* New York: Kodansha International, 1983.
Scott, Dorothea Hayward. *Chinese Popular Literature and the Child.* Chicago: American Library Association, 1980.
Sturm, Terry, ed. *The Oxford History of New Zealand Literature in English*, 2nd edition. New York: Oxford University Press, 1998.
Tang, Xianzu. *The Peony Pavilion.* Translated by Cyril Birch. Bloomington: Indiana University Press, 2002.
Turner, Graeme. *National Fictions: Literature, Film, and the Construction of Australian Narrative.* Boston: Allen & Unwin, 1986.
Wu, Cheng-en. *Journey to the West.* Vols. 1–4. Translated by Anthony Yu. Chicago: University of Chicago Press, 1984.

South and Southeast Asia

Biddle, Arthur W., ed. *Contemporary Literature of Asia.* Upper Saddle River, NJ: Prentice Hall, 1996. Contains introductions to and selections of contemporary short stories and poems from Pakistan, India, Nepal, Sri Lanka, Vietnam, the Philippines, Malaysia, and Indonesia; notes on authors and texts; and bibliographies. Includes English translations of many of the stories and poems mentioned or discussed in this chapter.
Chaudhuri, Amit, ed. *The Picador Book of Modern Indian Literature.* London: Picador, 2001.
De Souza, Eunice, ed. *Nine Indian Women Poets: An Anthology.* New Delhi: Oxford University Press, 1998.
Dharwadker, Aparna Bhargava. *Theatres of Independence: Drama, Theory, and Urban Performance in India since 1947.* Iowa City: University of Iowa Press, 2005; New Delhi: Oxford University Press, 2006.
Dharwadker, Vinay, ed. *The Collected Essays of A. K. Ramanujan.* New Delhi: Oxford University Press, 1999. Excellent essays on Indian and South Asian literatures and folklore.
———, ed. *The Columbia Book of South Asian Poetry.* New York: Columbia University Press, forthcoming.
———, and A. K. Ramanujan, eds. *The Oxford Anthology of Modern Indian Poetry.* Delhi: Oxford University Press, 1994. Broad selection of twentieth-century Indian poets in fourteen languages; includes excellent English translations.
Gentleman, Amelia. "In India, a Maid Becomes an Unlikely Literary Star." *New York Times* national edition (2006, August 2): B3.
Khwaja, Waqas Ahmad, ed. *Mornings in the Wilderness: Readings in Pakistani Literature.* Lahore: Sang-e-Meel, 1988.
Natarajan, Nalini, ed. *Handbook of Twentieth Century Literatures of India.* Westport, CT: Greenwood, 1996.
Rahman, Tariq. *A History of Pakistani Literature in English.* Lahore: Vanguard, 1991.

Rushdie, Salman, and Elizabeth West, eds. *The Vintage Book of Indian Writing: 1947–1997* (also titled *Mirrorwork: Fifty Years of Indian Writing: 1947–1997*). New York: Henry Holt; London: Vintage: 1997.

Sanga, Jaina, ed. *South Asian Literature in English: An Encyclopedia.* Westport, CT: Greenwood, 2004.

Wijesinha, Rajiva, ed. *An Anthology of Contemporary Sri Lankan Poetry in English.* Colombo, Sri Lanka: English Association of Sri Lanka, 2000.

WEBSITES

East Asia and Oceania

Angles, Jeffrey. *Japanese Literature-Related Resources on the Web.* September 28, 2006. http://homepages.wmich.edu/~jangles/jlit.htm. A guide to related Internet sources.

Literature in Australia and New Zealand. Postcolonial Web. University Scholars Programme, National University of Singapore. October 7, 2005. http://www.postcolonialweb.org/australia/auslitov.html.

Modern Chinese Literature and Culture (MCLC). http://mclc.osu.edu/jou/mclc.htm.

Saito, Satoru. *Japanese Popular Literature Overview.* 2000. http://www.columbia.edu/~hds2/BIB95/00poplit_sato.htm.

Yuldo.net: A Korean Studies Site. http://www.yuldo.net/literature.htm. A guide to related literature sources, including cyberliterature, journals, and contemporary literature.

South and Southeast Asia

Baldauf, Scott. "Indian Housemaid Pens Dickensian Memoir of Poverty." August 7, 2006. *Christian Science Monitor* online edition. Accessed October 3, 2006. http://www.csmonitor.com/2006/0807/p01s04-wosc.html. Article on Baby Halder, popular Indian writer.

International Movie Database. http://imdb.com/. Accessed October 3, 2006. Superb search engine; contains entries on numerous films and all those involved in their production; provides information on several authors mentioned in this section, and on movies based on literary works.

"Mahasweta Devi." Postcolonial Studies at Emory. Accessed October 3, 2006. http://www.english.emory.edu/Bahri/Devi.html.

Pegasos. http://www.kirjasto.sci.fi. Accessed October 3, 2006. Very good biographical and bibliographical articles on Pramoedya Ananta Toer (/pram.htm), Shahnon Ahmad (/shahnon.htm), and Nick Joaquin (/joaquin.htm).

Pisharoty, Sangeeta Barooah, "A Life Less Ordinary." May 15, 2006. *Hindu* online edition. Accessed October 3, 2006. http://www.thehindu.com/. Article on Baby Halder in this Indian daily newspaper.

Ragan, David Paul. "Pramoedya Ananta Toer: Meeting a Dissident Writer." http://www.neh.gov/news/humanities/1998-03/dissident.html.

NOTES

East Asia and Oceania

1. The French translation is *Journal sexuel d'une jeune chinoise sur le net* published by Albin Michel. An online blogger's description of her online journal with links can be found on http://www.bloggersblog.com.
2. Schodt, *Manga! Manga!* (in Resource Guide), 62.
3. For more up-to-date information about the Korean publishing industry, consult the Website http://www.booksfromkorea.org, which gives lists of the top publishing houses as well as best-seller

LITERATURE

lists. The Website also includes several links to Korean and English sites of interest. Another report, found at http://www.accu.or.jp/appreb/report/abd/abd3014.html, gives recent statistics about the number of bookstores and the effect of the International Monetary Fund (IMF) on the publishing industry in the late 1990s.

South and Southeast Asia

1. See Pegasos, http://www.kirjasto.sci.fi/joaquin.htm.

LOVE, SEX, AND MARRIAGE

EAST ASIA AND OCEANIA

SHERI ZHANG

Family values in East Asia, including the moral rules governing love, sex, and marriage, had developed under the traditional Confucian view for more than two millennia when Japan became the first country to open up to the West during the latter half of the nineteenth century; China and Korea followed during the first half of the twentieth century. Australia and New Zealand, the two major countries in Oceania, consolidated their societies around the same time, basing them on their European cultural heritage and overriding the indigenous cultures. East Asia and Oceania both have been influenced by European and more recently U.S. ideas on free love and sex, which resulted in radical changes in the traditional concept of marriage.

In Australia and New Zealand, where societies are dominated by more recent European influences and lack traditional restrictions from past cultures, men and women are free to choose in respect to love, sex, and marriage. In view of the high divorce rate in these two countries, many choose to remain single or live in common-law unions instead of getting married. This attitude is fundamentally different from that in the countries of East Asia, where the traditional rules governing love, sex, and marriage are deeply rooted in society. However, views of personal freedom and independence are rapidly being accepted by an increasing number of people in East Asia; their attitudes are shifting from Confucianism toward Western-style freedom, and from collectivism toward individualism. At the same time, teenagers in East Asian countries are under huge pressure to pass the university entrance exams. They cannot afford the relatively free life of their peers in Oceania, where higher education is well developed and more easily accessible than in the more restrictive environment of East Asia, including in China, Japan, and Korea.

Similar to the sexual revolution of the 1970s in Western countries, which was accelerated by medical progress and the availability of contraceptives, China is currently experiencing a sexual revolution after many years of treating the topic as taboo. Other East Asian countries or regions such as Japan, South Korea, Taiwan, and Hong Kong had already popularized the Western style of free dating and courtship, which is now gradually replacing Asia's traditional arranged dating and marriage rituals. Commercialization of romantic relations, such as observing Valentine's Day, is further promoting freer relationships among the young generation.

In East Asian countries, a woman is expected to be a virgin when she gets married. However, because of Western influences beginning in the last century, premarital sex is becoming more common among teenagers and becoming a part of dating and courting, leading to an increased number of teenage abortions. Although the tradition of the arranged marriage is fading away, most people in Asia are still family oriented as a result of their heritage based on Confucian ethics and family values. Confucianism originated as an ethical system of rules defining the relations between sovereign and subject, father and son, and among other family members; it is based on principles formulated 2,500 years ago by the Chinese educator, Confucius. In the China of the 1970s, this philosophy was criticized as being chauvinistic and suppressive of women. At present, Confucius is being rehabilitated as China's first teacher and carrier of Chinese culture. An example of this rehabilitation is the current practice of naming each of the approximately 100 Chinese language and culture institutes, to be established overseas under the sponsorship of the Chinese government, as a "Confucius Institute."

CHINA

After 30 years of government-imposed birth control and one-child policy, China's population in 2005 was an estimated 1.3 billion. Without the restrictions started in the 1970s, population growth would have reached catastrophic levels. By the 1960s, it was common for all Chinese families, whether in urban or rural areas, to have several children; many families had seven or eight, and some even ten. For the peasants in the countryside, having many children meant guaranteed support in their old age, and over 90 percent of Chinese were peasant farmers at that time. China's population problem was not addressed in the government agenda until the late 1970s, after the Cultural Revolution of 1966–76 had ended. Since then, there has been a trend away from the multiple-birth family to the one-child family of modern times. Under China's one-child policy, implemented since 1979, almost all families in China's urban areas have only one child. The policy mandates fines for additional children born without pre-authorization from the parents' working units. To further control the population growth, the government promotes late marriage and late pregnancy.

China's educational system has been improved significantly since 1949. Currently, every child goes through nine years of mandatory basic education. Students must pass high school admission exams, and, to attend a university, they must pass a national university entrance examination. The university admission rate of high school graduates is estimated to have doubled over the past two decades. From the late 1970s on, birth control education was offered everywhere from working units to educational institutions, but sex education has always been an underdeveloped program.

As guides for the behavior and conduct of individuals and officials in traditional Chinese society, the philosophy of Taoism and the ethics of Confucianism were as influential as Christianity was in the west. Therefore, many Chinese, following the influence of traditional thinking, found it hard to accept the one-child policy, especially those families with only female children. Under the old value system, it was important to have a son to continue the father's family line. Accordingly, the one-child policy enhanced the traditional Chinese preference for male descendants. Often a woman would keep getting pregnant until she had a son, afraid that with "only" daughters, her husband would leave her and remarry someone else in hopes of having a son.

Chinese attitudes toward love, sex, and marriage changed dramatically after the socioeconomic reforms of the late 1970s. The Chinese open-door policy transformed the socioeconomic system and raised the standard of living. After years of suppression during the austere, hard-line socialist period of 1949–76, China experienced the fall of sexual taboos and a sharp increase in the divorce rate, which continues to grow. Currently, divorced women are not considered persons without virtue as much as they were in the past. As society is becoming more Westernized, people's minds are also changing: in present-day China, most divorce cases are initiated by women.

With China's divorce rate on the rise, the traditional principle of "living together till the hair turns grey" no longer applies. While most Chinese still regard marriage as a lifetime commitment, others regard the recent divorce trend as a sign of social progress since many women are able to break free from unhappy marriages. However, it is not a trend encouraged by Chinese officials and older people; members of these two groups have launched various campaigns admonishing the young generation to take a serious attitude toward marriage. Ever since the founding of the People's Republic of China, divorce has been discouraged by government policies and by the courts. Couples who were determined to divorce were often reconciled through "persuasion" by officials and Party cadres. But in modern China, divorces have lost the stigma of failure and are becoming more common, especially among young people and the well educated.

Homosexuality still does not officially exist in China, and there is hardly anyone who dares to be openly gay or lesbian. Most gays in China are likely to be married men who use marriage as a disguise for their homosexual orientation. Various Western media report that there are gay groups in China whose members engage in sexual activities, for which they face public criticism. It has also been reported that Chinese gays gather in clubs or parks to arrange sexual assignations.[1]

Today in China, sex is not a taboo as it was two decades ago. Starting from the 1980s, the Chinese have become gradually more tolerant toward premarital and extramarital relations. The traditional Chinese view does not allow for premarital sex. However, since the country opened its door to the West more than three decades ago, Western influences have been transforming the Chinese people's attitudes toward sex, and now greater numbers of Chinese have started to taste the forbidden fruit at an earlier age than was true of their elders. In a 2005 survey, 70 percent of Beijing residents said they had sexual relations before marriage, compared with 15.5 percent in the 1980s.[2] People's attitudes toward sexual behavior, both inside and outside of marriage, have shifted from the traditional Chinese discipline toward greater individual freedom. But in general, under the leadership of the Chinese Communist government, with its stress on discipline, the system continues to frown upon premarital and extramarital sex. In 1949 the new Communist government banned prostitution and keeping concubines as relics of the old, semifeudal society.

In present-day urban areas, young people have easy access to Western culture and fashion. They celebrate Valentine's Day and often ignore traditional Chinese holidays. They expend effort to make themselves look attractive, quite in contrast to the years before 1976 when pretty looks and graceful clothing were not accepted, and when looking "sexy" was considered shameful. In those days, men and women alike dressed in shapeless, blue cloth "Mao-style" outfits—a proletarian style that was considered revolutionary and was glorified as antibourgeois. Today, many Chinese admire Western fashion and Western lifestyle, adapting both to their lives. Dating is commonplace, and people prefer to choose their spouses themselves rather than accepting the use of a go-between. The quest for true love is not limited only to new couples, and even those who have children are reclaiming their delayed and lost loves through divorce and remarriage.

On the other hand, the Chinese tradition of the arranged marriage is still very much alive in urban and rural areas of China. A friend in the work unit, a parent, or a relative might act as a go-between for single young people. Once young people are in their twenties, social pressure mounts on them and on the entire family to find a spouse. While some young people find marriage partners on their own, it is difficult for others. At the universities, students are discouraged from dating, and they are too busy worrying about their jobs and careers. For those continuing on to graduate studies, the chance of finding a marriage partner diminishes further, especially for females since they are expected to marry before the age of thirty. As a result of spending time doing university and graduate work, there are many well-educated young single women without suitors. This phenomenon worries many parents. In the larger cities, an informal version of matchmaking has evolved: parents take photos of their sons/daughters and go to parks to try to arrange dates for their adult children.

Since China implemented its family-planning policy a few decades ago, abortion has become quite common. After a couple has had a child, they normally do not plan to have a second child. In case of failed birth control, abortion would be the default. While urban couples usually settle for one child, most rural parents want to have two. When a family was free to have several children, there was a natural mix of boys and girls. Now, with the limit of one, every couple wants a boy. Ultrasound equipment is available throughout China and is often used for prenatal sex determination, although the practice is illegal. The abortion that apparently often follows is devoid of taboo in China and easy to arrange. The government has tried to put an end to this widespread practice of sex-selective abortion.

After China's opening up to the West in the 1980s, the criteria for choosing a marriage partner also changed. Before, the main parameter for selecting a spouse was his/her family background—whether it was the family of an official, a revolutionary family, a family of academics, and so on. Currently, the money culture of modern consumer society is reshaping family values in China. The condition for marriage eligibility can be the ownership of a car or a house. Usually, the family of the groom fulfills the material demands of the bride. The economic pressure on husbands to have a big income often puts great strain on marriages.

Many modern Chinese are critical of the new money culture. They believe that the obsession with money has led people to ignore the traditional emphasis on good personal character and behavior. They are troubled by studies showing rising levels of early teen sex, and they advocate stronger moral education.

HONG KONG AND TAIWAN

Hong Kong was a British colony from 1842 to 1997, when it again came under the control of China. During colonial times, Hong Kong was a place of Chinese tradition mixed with Western culture. In Hong Kong, the social concepts of love, sex, and marriage did not undergo the stern sociopolitical reforms common to the People's Republic of China, and even in the 1970s, it was common for wealthy Hong Kong men to have concubines. The number of concubines supposedly reflected the size of a man's fortune. This form of polygamy was part of the Chinese feudal tradition; it had been kept alive by the rich families of China, but it was abolished under the marriage law of 1950, which notably was the first law to be adopted after the founding of the People's Republic of China. When Mainland China started its economic reforms in the late 1970s, many Chinese businessmen with concubines came in from Hong Kong and Taiwan.

Like Hong Kong, Taiwan never went through the radical changes that transformed Mainland China during the second half of the twentieth century. After the government of the Republic of China, which had been established in 1911, withdrew to Taiwan in 1949, Taiwan became the protector of Chinese tradition; at the same time, it was included in the American sphere of influence. In the absence of government restrictions, during the past half century the island has become thoroughly Westernized in a general way and has experienced the specific development of a sex industry.

Hong Kong and Taiwan were influenced by Western culture earlier than Mainland China. When Hong Kong was under British rule, porno magazines and sex toys were openly available for sale in evening markets. When Mainland China opened up to the world after the Cultural Revolution, pop music and love songs that entered from Taiwan and Hong Kong were considered decadent and "unhealthy." Communist China would not accept music and songs from capitalist Taiwan. For example, the songs of Teresa Teng, among them "When Will You Come Again?", "How Would You Explain It Today?", "The Moon Represents My Heart," and "Do You Know Whom I Love?" were banned in the 1970s because of their love themes. Nevertheless, the strong traditional component makes Hong Kong and Taiwan societies appear more "Chinese" than the society in the People's Republic of China. Tradition in Hong Kong and Taiwan is visible everywhere, especially in the forms of palm readers, geomancers, temples, religious organizations, and other historical and cultural phenomena.

> **CONTEMPORARY MARRIAGE LAWS**
>
> In 2001 China thoroughly revised its 1950 marriage law. To reflect changes over time, new elements were added to address adultery, marriage nullity and revocation, property division, and domestic violence. Most notable is the section—pointed directly at those members of the newly rich who take de facto secondary wives—that deems bigamy to be criminal and punishable by up to two years imprisonment. A second major change dealt with marriage dissolution. A recent *Los Angeles Times* report indicated that 6 million married couples in China divorced in 2004, which was a 21 percent jump from 2003.[3] China's divorce rate has jumped to about 20 percent from 4 percent since the passage of the newly revised marriage law. Many link the jump to changes in the law, which made divorce much easier than before.

JAPAN

Japan today is characterized by having fewer children and more senior citizens than ever, and the trend is proceeding at a faster pace than anywhere else in the world. Although Japan never had a one-child policy, its population growth for 2005 was estimated at 0.05 percent, one-tenth the rate of China. Since the baby boom of the 1950s, the birth rate in Japan has plummeted. In 1980 the average number of children born to one woman was 1.75. In 2002 it was 1.32, and by 2005 it had further decreased to 1.29.[4] The reason for Japan's birthrate decline has been an increase in the number of late marriages, and an increase in the number of men and women remaining single. A further reason is the Japanese working woman's reluctance to have her career interrupted by having children, especially because the inadequacy of publicly provided child care would negatively impact her ability to hold a job and raise children at the same time. The trend toward fewer children is accelerated by the growing number of young women attending university and getting a job. In Japan the percentage of women who continue their formal education after high school is unusually high. In 2003, for example, half of all women graduating from high school entered universities or junior colleges.

Over the past decades, the Japanese government has paid close attention to the declining birthrate, passing laws and amendments to protect women's rights and encourage childbirth.

Love, Sex, and Marriage

An example is a law passed in 2005 that increases the maximum childcare-leave period from one year to one-and-a-half years.

Before the Westernization of Japan after World War II, love, sex, and marriage had been governed by the traditional principles of the major religious and ethical belief systems of Shinto, Buddhism, and Confucianism, accompanied by some ideas from religious Taoism, which was the antitraditional philosophy of ancient China.

Shinto ("the divine way") is the indigenous nature religion of Japan; it has been part of people's lives from the beginning of an organized Japanese state up to modern times. It is not a religion of moral commandments or ethical rules, and it does not have any official sacred scriptures; rather, Shinto emphasizes ritual purification and cleanliness in one's dealings with the gods and with nature. According to Shinto beliefs, gods reside in sacred stones, trees, mountains, and other natural phenomena—similar to beliefs in the nature religions of native populations in North America.

The philosophy and ethics of Buddhism, with its concept of suffering and salvation, is more oriented toward human life than is the nature religion of Shinto. Buddhism originated in India around the fifth century BCE and came to Japan via China and Korea. After Buddhism arrived in Japan in the sixth century CE, Shinto and Buddhist beliefs began to interact. The present peaceful coexistence between Buddhist temples (*tera*) and Shinto shrines (*jinja*) is the defining characteristic of Japanese religion, with the latter frequently serving as the background of traditional Japanese wedding ceremonies. Both Shinto and Buddhism are very popular as religions in modern Japan, although lately their marriage rituals have had to compete with the Christian wedding ceremony, which is becoming increasingly common.

Confucianism in Japan is not a religion; rather, it is a set of ethical principles and social rules for proper behavior and human interaction, especially within the family. The Confucian concepts of family ethics originated in ancient China around the fifth century BCE and were introduced into Japan in the formative period of the Japanese state, beginning in the sixth century CE. They have been adapted and integrated into Japanese society in the course of the past centuries. The original Confucian *Analects* are still included in the curriculum of Japanese High Schools, with Japanese annotations.

Although the Confucian canon does not make detailed statements about marriage or the relationship between the sexes, its rules of proper behavior such as filial piety, loyalty, and other virtues still form the backbone of the Japanese family. But many young people in modern Japan are living lives different from those of their parents, and the Confucian tradition of the eldest son caring for his elderly parents is slowly disappearing. Young people in Japan like what they see as the U.S. lifestyle, without a lot of family worries or burdens. In addition to the Chinese heritage of Confucianism, the influence of religious Taoism in Japan can be seen in the use of the Chinese calendar and in popular beliefs and superstitions such as fortune-telling and believing in auspicious phenomena.

Since Japan opened up to the world during the Meiji period (1868–1912), Western ideas have entered and have contributed to the country's modernization in many areas, including the area of women's rights. As of the beginning of this century, more Japanese women were obtaining a university or college education and wanting to work on an equal basis with men. As a consequence, fewer women feel pressure to get married before age twenty-five. Many young men and women do not follow their parents' example of settling down and getting married: they fear that getting married would disturb their careers and independent lifestyle. Thus, an increasing number of young people in Japan either get married late or remain single.

Japan traditionally has had a lower divorce rate than has been the case in many Western nations, apparently related to its Confucian cultural tradition and rigid social structure. The crime rate in Japan is also significantly lower than elsewhere, and modern Japan presents itself as a safe country of harmony and social stability. Recently, however, Japan has seen a sharp increase in divorces, affecting young and elderly couples alike. Despite the rising divorce rate, Japanese women are rooted in the Asian cultural tradition regarding their role in society. A 1996 survey found that 37 percent of Japanese women strongly believed that a home and children is what they really want, compared to only 7 percent of American women.[5] Nevertheless, by 2005 the Japanese divorce rate had caught up with the average divorce rate of the European Union, although it is still behind that of the United States.

The Japanese hold a different attitude toward divorce than do people in the West, especially regarding child custody. In Japan, the divorced parent without child custody is not allowed to meet the child (or children), and the child normally does not know who or where the other parent is. Visitation rights are unknown in Japan, and a divorce means the child loses a parent just as if that parent had died. A recent high-profile divorce case involves the former Prime Minister Koizumi. He was granted custody of two of his children, while one child stayed with his ex-wife, and the children have not met with the other parent in the years since their divorce. As an example of the way Japanese implement child custody, the son who grew up with his mother could support Koizumi's political campaign only from a distance, and would not be allowed to be in contact with his father. The closest he has ever gotten to his father was in the crowd during a political campaign.[7]

Homosexuality is now more accepted in Japan than it was 40 years ago. Japan is a conservative country, and because gays were not accepted until recently, they did not usually reveal their sexual orientation since to do so would have been scandalous. The movement to end discrimination against homosexuals and lesbians came into full force during the 1990s, but many conservative Japanese still resent same-sex relations.

A unique type of "comic" called manga, which contains sexual material, developed in Japan after World War II and has become the most popular literary genre. About half of all books and periodicals sold in Japan are manga-style comics. The ubiquitous Japanese manga typically contain sexually explicit cartoons with sadistic pornography that would appear morbid, if not obscene, to the average Western viewer. Recently, a manga comic book depicting genitalia and sexual acts in two-thirds of its content was ruled obscene in a landmark court case that sparked a debate over freedom of expression in Japan.[8]

Although greater numbers of young women currently attend universities and get white-collar jobs, most of them do not plan to be life-long office workers since they want their own homes and family lives. The young professional women in Japan—often called an *oyaji* girl,

ADOLESCENT STANDARDS OF BEAUTY

Japanese teenagers devote great efforts to pursuing the image of a beauty icon, not just in their looks but also in their behavior. Speaking in a childlike voice, or with a voice an octave higher than normal, combined with deep bowing and a naïve smile that does not show the teeth are considered good manners. Young girls with tiny red mouths and big eyes, complete with mascara, are ubiquitous on posters, in commercials, and in real life in Japan. In recent years, almost all teens in Japan undergo eyelid surgery and have their Asian eyelids cut open to achieve the Western double-eyelid look.[6] This simple operation changes their "Asian" slit eyes to big round "Western" eyes. Pictures of Asian girls on posters, whether advertising cosmetics or announcing a movie, show they have had this kind of cosmetic eye surgery. For those who do not want to go through the surgery, special eyelid glue that temporarily produces the fashionable Western round-eye look is being sold everywhere.

with oyaji used as a stereotype that originally described a busy "salary man"—does not want to remain an oyaji girl who works hard and plays hard; rather, she wants to get married when she meets "Mr. Right" at the right time. Japanese women, particularly women with children, are happy to stay out of the corporate rat race. Married women prefer a lifestyle described as *onna tengoku* [women's heaven], which means having a part-time job while taking care of small children, enjoying hobbies, and participating in community work.

A common stereotype for men in Japan is the *sarariman* [salary man]: the employee who spends all day at work and often stays in the office after hours. He uses the workplace as his home, works long hours in the evening, and spends his late evening with colleagues in restaurants and bars. Since his family hardly sees him at home, there is usually little communication between husbands and wives. When the husband retires, the elderly couple often realizes they have nothing in common—a situation that is contributing to the growing number of divorces among retired employees in Japan.

A large number of Japanese men seek prostitutes, fueling the vast sex industry of Japan. It is a well-known fact that human traffickers bring in young foreign women as sex workers. These women hold "entertainment" visas, but in fact, they have little talent as song-and-dance entertainers. The Japanese government has long turned a blind eye to the influx of sex workers, who come mainly from the Philippines and some South American and Eastern European countries. In 2004 the United States put Japan on its human-trafficking watch list, and then issued a warning that Japan was not far from being lumped in with North Korea and Myanmar. As a result of outside pressure, Japan has recently begun to restrict the issuance of entertainment visas.

Teenagers in Japan face a strict education system and strong social pressure to succeed in exams, similar to their peers in China. In contrast to party-going North American teens, Japanese high school students spend all their time studying to gain entrance into a good university, preferably a state university. It is common to see students studying from their textbooks on commuter trains.

Regarding birth control and abortion, in 1998 Japan had an abortion rate of 50.2 per 1,000 women of childbearing age (between 15 and 49). In 1952 the Japanese government advocated a family planning program for married couples similar to the approach taken in China. Subsequently, for about a decade after 1955, the annual abortion rate decreased dramatically. Since the mid-1960s, abortions have continuously declined but at a slower rate than in the previous decade.[9] It seems that the introduction of birth control in Japan has had similar effects to those in China.

Although abortions occur, the Japanese hold a different attitude toward abortion than do the Chinese. In China the topic is discussed openly; in Japan, however, people are usually silent about it, with feelings of remorse and guilt when an abortion is actually performed. After paying the medical fees for an abortion, which in Japan are not covered by medical insurance, many women—especially the religious ones—buy a small stone figure of *Mizuko Jizō*, the guardian deity of children in modern Japanese Buddhism. When walking through a city in Japan, one passes these stone figures of children wearing cloth bibs and woven hats standing beside one another in the shade of the big old trees, usually close to a Buddhist temple. Each of these statues was ordered by parents as a way to grieve for their miscarried or aborted children. The deity's role as the guardian of unborn, aborted, miscarried, and stillborn babies was not assigned to the god Jizō in earlier Buddhist traditions from mainland Asia; rather, it is a modern adaptation unique to Japan. This understanding and use of Mizuko Jizō began in Japan in the 1960s in response to a human need: to relieve the suffering of the large number of women who had undergone abortions after World War II.

KOREA

After World War II, Korea was divided into North Korea (Democratic People's Republic of Korea) and South Korea (Republic of Korea). Since information is not available from North Korea, information in this section refers only to South Korea.

In 2006 North Korea had an estimated population of 23 million, while South Korea had an estimated population of 50 million. While North Korea is a closed communist country, South Korea is a capitalist country with Confucian traditions in the background, similar to Japan. Fast population growth in South Korea used to be a serious social problem, but it is now under control through family planning campaigns and attitude changes. In the 1960s South Korean families with six or more children were common; now most families have two children.

Just as modern Chinese and Japanese, modern South Koreans keep the Confucian tradition alive by taking family relations and education seriously. Children in South Korea attend six years of elementary school, three years of middle school, and three years of high school, followed by four years of higher education. Graduate courses leading to the degree of PhD are offered at certain universities and colleges. There are also junior colleges and vocational colleges where two- or three-year programs lead to graduation. Among the two types of South Korean high schools, the vocational high schools teach skills needed for careers in such fields as agriculture, engineering, and business, while the general high schools prepare students for entering university. Numerous different religions coexist in South Korea, including Shamanism, Catholicism, Protestantism, *Cheondogyo* [an indigenous Korean nationalist movement] and Islam, but the religion of Buddhism and the ethics system of Confucianism remain the most influential spiritual forces in South Korea.

Following the Confucian family-oriented tradition, most Koreans officially oppose divorce. Even early in this century, match-making services did not have any customers who had been divorced. When a wedding candidate was introduced as "single," everyone thought he/she had never been married before. No South Korean would think "single" could also refer to a divorced person. Although still firmly anchored in the Confucian patriarchal family values, South Korea is also an open, Westernized society with advanced technology, a pop culture, and a Western, individualist lifestyle. Recently, a social transformation has begun, including a change in attitudes toward family values such as marriage, childbearing, cohabitation and divorce. Although more couples are getting divorced, the number of people getting remarried has doubled over the past decade.[10] This massive shift in traditional family values has resulted in soaring divorce rates that are now second only to those of the United States. As South Korean society becomes more Westernized, fewer couples are willing to put up with unhappy marriages. Amid this social transformation, as the divorce rate soars, people are becoming more apprehensive about marriage, and cohabitation is gradually gaining wider acceptance in Korean society. Although the formula for calculating the divorce rate has been disputed, the Korean divorce rate is now one of the highest in the world and probably the highest in Asia.

With Confucian family ethics so deeply rooted, it is hard to understand this sudden change in South Korean society. If not for the strong Western influence, the South Korean people would probably have continued to follow the traditional social rules of Confucianism, which placed severe restrictions on women. According to tradition, a woman had to be obedient in three ways: she had to show obeisance to the father before marriage, to the husband upon marriage, and to the son after the husband's death. Female submission in the Confucian social model was not based on innate female weakness or inadequacy, but rather on the strict organization of society: a woman's domain was home and family, while the man's role was outside. As in most traditional societies, the South Korean woman's duty is to raise children, take care of her husband, cook, and sew—and thus create the environment for her husband to concentrate on the larger issues of society. The South Korean government officially promotes the Confucian "Five Relationships" of (1) father and son, (2) husband and wife, (3) elder and younger brothers, (4) ruler and subject, and (5) friend and friend. The traditional concept that genders have different roles in society has affected not just the roles of husband and wife, but virtually all relations between the genders. From early childhood, children in South Korea grow up segregated by gender, because "boys and girls at the age of seven should not be allowed to sit in the same room."[11]

The situation regarding homosexuality in South Korea is similar to that in China: people neither admit nor acknowledge the existence of homosexuals in the country. Because of people's strong prejudice against homosexuality, gays in South Korea do not publicly admit their sexual orientation.

Abortion was legalized in South Korea in 1973 by the Maternal and Child Health Law. In 1983, in the course of controlling population growth, the government began suspending maternal care insurance benefits for pregnant women with three or more children. It also revoked education expense tax deductions for parents with two or more children.

OCEANIA: AUSTRALIA AND NEW ZEALAND

Situated in the South Pacific region, the once very much isolated British colonies of Australia and New Zealand have developed into prosperous Western democratic countries. The estimated population of New Zealand was 4.1 million in 2005. Before the arrival of the European immigrants, New Zealand had been the home of the Maori people. The population in Australia reached 20 million in 2005, with its indigenous peoples making up only a tiny fraction of the whole population. In the middle of the twentieth century, Australia's immigration policy attracted large numbers of white settlers, mainly from Northern Europe and the Baltic, followed by those from Southern Europe. Recently, most of the immigrants have been from the Middle East, Asia, and South America. In contrast to present-day China, where families are limited to one child, the Australian government encourages population growth through more children. In 2005, a quarter of all babies born in Australia were born to unmarried women.

The first university established in Australia was the University of Sydney in 1850, followed by the University of Melbourne in 1853, with several others opening soon after. Australia's higher education experienced a boom after World War II, especially between the 1950s and the 1970s.[12]

The New Zealand school system makes it possible for children to enter school at age five, and schooling is compulsory for children between 6 and 16 years of age. Students graduate at age 17 from secondary education. Most of these graduates attend government-funded schools, which are known variously as secondary schools, high schools, colleges, or area schools. Most schools use English as the common language, but some schools teach in the Maori language since New Zealand is officially English/Maori bilingual. At present the universities in Australia and New Zealand attract large numbers of international students, especially from China. Students from many other Asian countries are enrolled at all levels in Australian and New Zealand institutions of higher education.

Australia remains a democratic country with a predominantly Christian society, largely as a result of its early history of immigration from Europe. Similarly, more than half the population of New Zealand is affiliated with a Christian religion, with Anglicans, Catholics, and Presbyterians as the largest groups; the non-Christian religions with the most followers are Buddhism, Hinduism, Islam, Spiritualism, and the New Age religions.

Three decades ago, more than half of Australian families typically had two or more children. By the end of the twentieth century, this number had decreased significantly because of the larger numbers of single parents and childless couples. Almost half of all first-time marriages in Australia end in divorce. Although still behind the high divorce rates in countries such as the United States, Britain, and South Korea, Australia ranks high on the current divorce-rate list.

With an increasing proportion of New Zealanders remaining unmarried through their thirties, it is likely that fewer will ultimately marry. A growing proportion of New Zealanders cohabit, just as their counterparts in Australia, North America, and Europe. New Zealand's marked trend toward later marriages started in the early 1970s; at that time, one-third of all brides were in their teens, compared with just 3 percent at the turn of the current century. The shift away from early marriage has resulted in fewer men and women marrying in their teens, following a trend toward later marriage common in most developed countries. Another shift occurred in remarrying: 30 years ago, 67 percent of remarriages were between divorced men and women, whereas in recent years 90 percent of remarriages are between divorcees.[13]

As a result of legislative changes introduced in New Zealand in 1981, there was a sharp rise in the number of divorces in the early 1980s. The new law enabled many couples to satisfy a two-year separation requirement (for Australia, it was 12 months) as a single ground of irreconcilable marriage breakdown and seek dissolution of their marriages in a family court. Consequently, a temporary spike in divorces was recorded in 1982. After this peak, the divorce rate dropped, but the trend has turned upward again since the late 1980s.

As far as homosexuality is concerned, Australia has banned same-sex marriages, stating that only a man and a woman can be married in that country, while New Zealand recognizes same-sex unions. The controversial legislation recognizing civil unions of gay couples was passed in 2004 by New Zealand's parliament.

In 2003 Australia ranked toward the top of the list of the world's advanced countries in terms of teenage pregnancy and abortion: it was sixth in teen pregnancy and third in teenage abortion. The rate of teenage childbearing in New Zealand is high by Organization for Economic Cooperation and Development (OECD) standards, which has generated considerable interest and discussion among social researchers and policy makers. As more teenage pregnancies are now ending in abortion, however, there are fewer teenage mothers; the number of abortions now is 44 percent higher than it was 10 years ago.[14] Abortion data for New Zealand were not available before 1980, which shows that family planning was not an important issue there as it was in many other countries.

In view of an estimated 1 million divorcees in their country, modern Australians seem to show little interest in getting married, or perhaps make decision about getting married later. More than half of all married couples became married after cohabiting. Besides being married or living as a single, cohabitation has become the third choice for Australians, often not just as a transition to getting married but as a permanent state. Cohabitation is also becoming very common among Chinese Australians. In New Zealand, the trend toward late marriage means an increase in unpartnered people through their twenties and thirties, and a growing number of people living in de facto unions.

Australian demography is characterized by a strong pattern of intermarriage or interpartnering. The most rapidly growing group in Australian society includes couples that bring both Anglo-Celtic and non-Anglo-Celtic ancestry to their marriages or unions. About one-quarter of Australians have no Anglo-Celtic background. Thus, Australia is becoming increasingly multicultural, with marriages or partners coming from extraordinarily diverse origins.

In New Zealand, the composition of families is changing, and there are growing numbers of single-parent and de facto–couple families. Although just over three-quarters of New Zealand children live in two-parent families, changing patterns of family formation, dissolution, and reformation have promoted a growing diversity of family types. In particular, the number of single-parent families has grown rapidly over recent years. Over the past 20 years, the proportion of children under 15 living in single-parent families has risen and fallen. After first increasing from 16 percent to 24 percent, the growth slowed between 1991 and 1996, when the proportion of children living in single-parent families increased by only two percentage points. The fastest-growing group of children in single-parent families includes those whose parents were never married. Maori children, and to a lesser extent Pacific Island children, are more likely than children from other ethnic groups to live with only one parent. Some 41 percent of Maori children lived in single-parent families in 1996 as compared with 29 percent of Pacific Island children, 17 percent of European children, and 12 percent of Asian children.

Differing from today's China, Japan of the 1960s, and South Korea of the 1970s, the Australian government encourages women to have more children by offering incentives. A pregnant woman can collect government subsidies for her unborn child. In New Zealand, in contrast, the number of induced abortions has increased by 171 percent in the last two decades, from fewer than 6,000 in 1980 to over 16,000 in 2000. While the general trend has been upward, there have been small drops in the annual number of abortions on three occasions: 1985, 1992, and 1998.

In summary, a consolidation of people's attitudes toward love, sex, and marriage is taking place in the countries of East Asia and Oceania, mainly through the increasing influence of Western pop culture accompanied by a lifestyle of greater freedom and individualism. In contrast to the Asian countries, where the common heritage of Chinese Confucian ethics is still prevalent and arranged marriage is still practiced, Australians and New Zealanders face less social pressure and prejudice; in addition to conventional marriage, they have the choice to remain single, get divorced, or simply cohabit. The East Asian principle of collectivism still encourages people there to work and live in larger groups, rather than in pairs or couples. In the traditional environment of East Asia that is being transformed through Western influences, the realm of love, sex, and marriage remains controversial, polarized between the sexual revolution and deeply rooted Confucian moral attitudes.

RESOURCE GUIDE

PRINT SOURCES

Adams, B. N., and J. Trost, eds. *Handbook of World Families*. Thousand Oaks, CA: Sage Publications, 2005.
"AIDS in China: Anatomy of an Epidemic." *Economist* (2005, July 30–August 5): 36–38.
Bornoff, N. *Pink Samurai: Love, Marriage, and Sex in Contemporary Japan*. New York: Pocket Books, 1991.
Keneally, T. *The Commonwealth of Thieves: The Story of the Founding of Australia*. New York: Nan A. Talese/Doubleday, 2006.
Leeder, E. J. *The Family in Global Perspective: A Gendered Journey*. Thousand Oaks, CA: Sage, 2004.
Patterson, B., ed. *Ulster-New Zealand Migration and Cultural Transfers*. Dublin: Four Courts Press, 2006.
Yan, Y. *Private Life under Socialism: Love, Intimacy, and Family Change in a Chinese Village, 1949–1999*. Palo Alto, CA: Stanford University Press, 2003.

WEBSITES

Australian. Accessed March 2006. http://www.theaustralian.news.com.au/. Australian newspaper.
BBC News. http://news.bbc.co.uk/.
China Daily. Accessed March 2006. http://www.chinadaily.com.cn/home/index.html. Official newspaper of mainland China.
Economist. http://www.economist.com. British magazine with an Asian section.
"Induced Abortions." *Statistics New Zealand.* 2001. http://www.stats.govt.nz/analytical-reports/dem-trends-01/part-7-induced-abortions.htm.
Japan Times. Accessed March 2006. http://www.japantimes.co.jp/. The most popular English-language newspaper in Japan.
Seoul Times. Accessed March 2006. http://theseoultimes.com/ST/. South Korean newspaper.
Women of China. Accessed March 2006. http://www.womenofchina.com.cn/. Official Chinese newspapers focusing on women's issues.
"Women's Issues: Roles in a Changing Society." *Japan Fact Sheet.* http://web-japan.org/factsheet/woman/aging.html.

NOTES

1. See "AIDS in China: Anatomy of an Epidemic" (in Resource Guide).
2. See "Sex, Please—We're Young and Chinese," *Time Magazine* Canadian edition (December 12, 2005), p. 4.
3. See Don Lee, "'Second Wives' Are Back," *Los Angeles Times* (November 22, 2005).
4. See "An Aging Society," *Japan Fact Sheet* (in Resource Guide).
5. See "The New Women in Japan—Free at Last?" *Economist* (1997), http://www.economist.com/displaystory.cfm?story_id=145042.
6. See L. T. Cullen, "Changing Faces," *Time Asia* (2002), http://www.time.com/time/asia/covers/1101020805/story.html.
7. See M. Sheridan, "Japanese PM Keeps Lost Son at Bay," *The Times* (2005), http://www.crnjapan.com/articles/2005/en/20050904-koizumijunichiroyoshinaga.html.
8. See *China Daily,* "Japanese Sex Comic Book Ruled Obscene," January 2004, http://www.chinadaily.com.cn/en/doc/2004-01/14/content_298736.htm.
9. See Goto et al., "Abortion Trends in Japan, 1975–95" (2000), http://www.hsph.harvard.edu/faculty/reich/japan.pdf#search='abortion%20in%20Japan'.
10. See C. Gluck, Koreans Learn to Live with Divorce," *BBC News,* 2003, http://news.bbc.co.uk/2/hi/asia-pacific/3011119.stm.
11. See *Korea.net,* "Gateway to Korea: Social Life," http://www.korea.net/korea/kor_loca.asp?code=G0501.
12. See "Universities in Australia," http://www.unixl.com/dir/university_and_college/australia/.
13. See *Statistics New Zealand,* http://www.stats.govt.nz/default.htm.
14. See *Statistics New Zealand,* http://www.stats.govt.nz/analytical-reports/dem-trends-01/part-7-induced-abortions.htm.

MUSIC

EAST ASIA AND OCEANIA

LÉJARIE BATTIESTE

INTRODUCTION

Music doesn't develop in isolation. A combination of indigenous and Western musical styles characterizes modern popular music in the countries of East Asia and Oceania. Imitation has evolved into adaptation and resulted in distinctive and innovative musical genres. A growing multilingual population and transnational flow of popular culture in East Asia have resulted in one of the largest populations of music consumers in the world. Modern popular music in the Oceanic islands of Australia and New Zealand is as diverse as their renowned spectacular landscapes. The fusion of indigenous musical traditions with urban musical styles has given rise to a new movement of Pacific music that is garnering global attention.

MODERN POPULAR MUSIC IN CHINA

Mixing the Old with the New: Gangtai and Liuxing in China

The introduction of popular music to mainland China occurred in 1976 after the death of China's leader, chairman Mao Zedong. The ensuing rise to power of Deng Xiaoping and the adoption of the open door policy allowed an influx of popular music from the West, Japan, and Hong Kong. The *liuxing* style of music, once popular in China during the 1940s, was reintroduced in the ensuing decades with a more contemporary style. Nevertheless, *gangtai* music, which had been popularized in Taiwan and Hong Kong, became the primary choice of popular music on the mainland. Cassette tapes of gangtai songs by Taiwanese singer Teresa Teng were some of the first popular music on the mainland. The romantic lyrics of gangtai and the use of soft Western harmonies with traditional Chinese pentatonism were in sharp contrast to the revolutionary opera music of the Mao era and provided a more appealing soundtrack to the modernization and social changes that would sweep mainland China. During the 1980s, realizing music's potential for influence and profit with a population of millions, the Chinese government began to use television to broadcast official pop music, which initially mixed government ideology with the smooth gangtai style of music.

Chinese Rock

The birth of *yaogun*, or rock and roll, on mainland China is linked to the musician and songwriter Cui Jian. Born in Beijing, he started his musical career as a member of the prestigious Beijing Philharmonic but would eventually leave in order to form a small rock band. In 1986 Cui Jian performed the song "Nothing to My Name" ("Yi Wu Suo You") from his debut album at a World Peace Concert in Beijing. His honest lyrics and rough vocal style were in sharp contrast to the soft and sentimental styles of gangtai songs. His popularity triggered a new movement in music called *xibeifeng* (northwest wind), which often featured political lyrics, fast Western beats, and an aggressive bass, combined with a style of folk singing from the northwest regions of China. The songs "My Beloved Homeland" and "Young Sister Go Boldly Forward," from the movie *Red Sorghum*, would become some of the most famous rock songs in the xibeifeng style. Some of China's most famous rock bands Breathing, Tang Dynasty, the Females Rock, and Black Panther were established. Eventually, Cui Jian's first album, *Rock N Roll on the New Long March*, would become China's biggest selling album in history.

The decline in the popularity of rock and roll is often associated with the Chinese government's reaction to several bands performing in support of the demonstrating students in Tiananmen Square before the violent crackdown on June 4, 1989. In the following decade the Chinese government attempted to divert the public's attention away from politics by implementing restrictions on rock performance and broadcast. However, rock music reemerged in the late 1990s. In 2006, in order to celebrate the Twentieth Anniversary of the Birth of Rock 'N' Roll in China, Cui Jian performed with the Rolling Stones at their first concert performance in China.

Pop Music in Mainland China

Chinese people on the mainland were listening to smuggled cassette tapes of *Cantopop* and *Mandopop*, from Hong Kong and Taiwan, respectively, since the 1970s. The free market economies and close ties with Western countries produced a style of pop music common to both *Cantopop* and *Mandopop* that was an appealing mixture of Western pop and indigenous music. Both *Cantopop* and *Mandopop* produced a bevy of popular songs and singers, such as Andy Lau, Jacky Cheung, Leon Lai, and Aaron Kwok—the Four Heavenly Kings of Cantopop. The *Cantopop* music industry reached its peak in the 1990s, as the Chinese government began to loosen control over the media, and *Cantopop* stars achieved immense popularity in the neighboring Southeast Asian countries. By the late 1990s pop musicians began to release albums in both Cantonese and Mandarin.

The light vocals and guitar-based music of *Mandopop* has helped it remain a staple in mainland China and Taiwan, producing such Taiwanese stars as Jay Chou and the boy band named F4. Easy production and lack of originality caused the *Cantopop* market to slow down in the middle and late 1990s, as illegal music downloads and music piracy became rampant. In the early 2000s approximately 90 percent of the recorded music sold in China was from pirated sources.[1] In the 2000s girl and boy singing duos became popular. The girl duo, Twins, became huge pop stars, and Easan Chan and Joey Chung are the current top of *Cantopop*.

POPULAR MUSIC OF JAPAN

Early Japanese Popular Music: Kayokyoku

At the turn of the twentieth century, hit theatrical plays were a ready source of many early popular songs in Japan. The first hit ballad was from a theatrical production of *Tolstoy's Resurrection*, called "Kachusha no uta," ["Katherine's Song"], which combined Western and European harmonies with traditional Japanese music styles. The new record and radio broadcasting companies emerging in the 1920s and 1930s were eager to provide the growing Japanese public with the latest *kayokyoku* [popular songs]. One of the first hit *kayokyoku* songs from the period, "Sake wa Namida ka Tameiki ka" ["Is Sake My Tears or My Sighs?"], used a traditional Japanese music singing style called *yuri*, voice ornamentation, and a *yonauki* scale with instruments such as the ukulele, the violin, and the guitar.

In the postwar years (1945–51), with the occupation of Japan by the Allied Forces, Western styles of music—jazz, blues, boogie-woogie, country, pop, and even French chansons—flooded into the country. Japanese popular songs relied on Western pop melodies and harmonies, but the lyrics reflected the desire to lift the spirits of Japanese citizens after the devastating war. The song "Ringo no uta" ["Apple Song"], released in 1945, and the upbeat boogie rhythm of "Tokyo Boogie Woogie," released in 1947, succeeded in boosting morale in the postwar years. As Japan rapidly began to industrialize in the late 1940s and 1950s, more Japanese moved from rural areas to large cities, creating nostalgia. Although many Japanese singers were imitating Western music, the melancholy *enka* tunes of singer Misora Hibari (1937–89) captured the hearts of the postwar Japanese with the popular tunes "Ringo Oiwake" and "Kanashii Sake" ["Sad Sake"], which displayed her renowned vocal ornamentation and her superb natural singing voice.

Rock, Folk, and Pop Music in Japan

In the roughly two decades following the end of World War II, Japan experienced tremendous prosperity, and Western pop and rock and roll music streamed from radios and televisions all over Japan. A combination of American rock and roll and country music called *Rokabiri* (rockabilly) found a niche in Japan, resulting in the tune "Hoshi was Nan demo Shiteru" ["The Stars Know All"] becoming the first hit rock song. Popular music in Japan in the 1960s relied heavily on imitation and adaptation of Western and Japanese music styles. An outstanding example is Kyu Sakamoto's rendition of "Ue o Muite, Aruko," which charmingly blended traditional Japanese vocals on top of a Western pop beat and became the only Japanese song ("Sukiyaki" in America) to date to go to number one on the

---

LEGENDS OF CANTOPOP

Two legends of Hong Kong pop are Anita Mui and Leslie Cheung, who both began their careers as winners of local singing contests. Female *Cantopop* singer Anita Mui's deep and melancholy voice won her a legion of fans and she was deemed the "Madonna of Hong Kong" because of her ever-changing style. Legendary Hong Kong singer Leslie Cheung achieved critical acclaim for his self-titled album *Leslie* and, although he also starred in several popular TV dramas and movies throughout his career, he shot to stardom with his acting role in the John Woo movie *A Better Tomorrow*. His role in the Oscar-nominated movie *Farewell My Concubine* gained him international recognition. The shock of the untimely deaths, of Leslie in April 2003, of an apparent suicide, and Anita, a few months later in December 2003, from complications of ovarian cancer, reverberated throughout Asia and with their legions of fans in America and Europe.

American music chart. Throughout the 1960s Japanese musicians continued to draw inspiration from pop musical trends in America and Europe. Instrumental rock music, made popular in America by such groups as The Ventures, inspired many Japanese musicians to take up electric guitars. The colossal success of the Beatles and The Rolling Stones were the inspiration for such Japanese bands as The Tigers and The Fingers, who were some of the most prominent of the *gurupu saunzu* [group sounds] trend.

By the 1970s Japanese musicians began to find their own voice. Spurred on by such folk musicians as Yosui Inoue and the huge success of his single, "Kori no Sekai" [World of Ice], which sold an unprecedented 1 million copies, a new music genre developed, based on the folk music style but with a new added personal perspective. In 1975 singer and songwriter Yumi Matsutoya's album *Cobalt Hour* became a hit with the prosperous baby boomers, who appreciated her new blend of folk music with contemporary American and European pop. In the latter half of the 1970s, Japanese musicians pushed rock to new and innovative boundaries. The Yellow Magic Orchestra, a techno-pop group comprised of three young men, became one of the first Japanese groups to have a worldwide impact on the music scene by pioneering the use of synthesizers and drum machines, creating music full of electric beeps. They would eventually release a U.S. album and become one of the first Japanese music groups to tour worldwide.

The sugary pure pop tunes and irresistibly cute pop idols in the 1970s provided a consistent source of hit songs. The pop song "Young Man" had Japanese youngsters all over Japan on their feet and made pop idol Hideki Saijo a hit sensation. New sex appeal was brought to the pop industry by the female duo Pink Lady, with their disco-inspired, booty-shaking routines and the success of their single "U.F.O" (also the name of an instant noodle), which launched them to the status of super idols. Rock music would also enjoy immense popularity during the 1980s and 1990s, most notably because of the male singer-songwriter duo Chage & Aska, who would have twelve number one albums in their career and perform to sellout crowds in Japan and Asia.

The Japanese "Aidoru" Takes Control

The manufacturing of pop idols became a million-dollar industry in the late 1980s and 1990s, owing to the increasing buying power of teenagers in Japan. Johnny's Jimusho (Johnny and Associates) was one of the first talent agencies at the time to focus on not only live performance, but also on mass media appeal. The roller-skating boy band, Hikaru Genji, was one of Johnny's most novel and popular idol groups during the early 1980s. Boy bands, such as Johnny's Juniors, V6, Tokio, and the megapopular group SMAP, dominated the pop music charts. The foremost idol group to exemplify successful mass media appeal is the megapop group SMAP. The current five members each stars in his own extremely popular TV variety show, *SMAP X SMAP*, and each individual member has starred in several popular TV dramas, movies, and TV commercials while consistently performing top-selling hit songs.

By the late 1990s Japan's music industry had become the world's second largest market and included music groups from genres such as hip-hop, rap, rock, and dance. The dance-music singer Namie Amuro and the groups SPEED and T.R.F. released several chart-topping hits. Illegal music downloads and the availability of downloadable music caused a decline in music sales, but, as Japan entered the twenty-first century, its music industry continued to thrive, as the American-born Japanese pop and rhythm and blues singer Hikaru Utada, pop singer Ayumi Hamasaki, and South Korean-born star and super idol BoA dominated the music charts.

MODERN MUSIC OF KOREA

Early Popular Music

Popular music in Korea can be traced to the 1920s, when a *yuhaengga* (popular) song called "Sa-ui chanmi" [Adoration of Death] became an unprecedented hit in Korea. The song's tale of a miserable life resonated with Koreans suffering under oppressive Japanese colonial rule. Many early *yuhaengga* were indigenized cover versions of Japanese songs, but they stylistically characterized early popular music by using a lighter vocal production than that of traditional Korean music. *Gisaeng*, female entertainers, briefly came into Korea's burgeoning music industry in the mid-1930s as singers of *sinminyo* or new folk music.

Because of the restriction placed on the performance and expression of Korean music by the Japanese colonial government, Japanese music dominated in Korea, and, eventually, a local variant style of Japanese *enka* emerged as one of the most resilient Korean musical genres. "Trot music" or *teuroteu* is a combination the pentatonic scales and the duple-meter structure of *enka*, with lyrics typically depicting tales of the lovelorn. But it was the lyrics that portrayed the daily struggles of life that deeply resonated. *Teuroteu* remained a popular musical genre throughout World War II, but its popularity waned in the 1950s and 1960s, as easy listening music became the preferred musical choice of the younger generation in South Korea. Nevertheless, teuroteu can still be heard blaring from taxis and coffee shops, and renewed interest was sparked in 2004 by a young female singer, Jang Yoon Jeong, with her hit *trot* song entitled "Oh My Goodness."

The Korean War (1950–53) devastated the country and resulted in the division of Korea into two nations with opposing musical landscapes: traditional and nationalist music in communist North Korea and heavily Western-influenced popular music in democratic South Korea. Big band, rock and roll, and jazz music flooded into South Korea via the military bases maintained by the United States and its allies. Many popular songs during this period were cover versions and imitations of Western styles of music. In the 1960s and 1970s, the *tong*, (box or acoustic) guitar-based music, and *norae undong*, a politically aware style of music, struck a cord with the growing youth population, who were increasingly influenced by American musicians such as Bob Dylan and Joan Baez.

The Korean Wave

In the 1980s and 1990s South Koreans were listening to American, Japanese, and Korean homegrown pop, rock, rhythm and blues, and hip-hop. The South Korean music group Seotaiji and Boys was one of the first homegrown bands to blend pop, hip-hop, and rhythm and blues successfully. In response to a growing and affluent teen population and a considerable number of teenagers listening to Japanese pop music,[2] music management companies began to focus efforts on cultivating homegrown talent. The answer was H.O.T.: a five-member boy band trained by SM Entertainment, one of Korea's top music management companies, to sing pop,

---

KARAOKE: A BRIEF HISTORY

The word *karaoke* is the combination of the Japanese words *kara* (empty) and *oke* from the Japanese word *okesutora* (orchestra). The first karaoke machine was invented haphazardly in 1971 by a part-time bar musician who, at the request of a friend, prepared a cassette tape of music without vocals and only instrumentation. Karaoke was first performed at small Japanese clubs or bars called "snacks," but now it is most often performed in karaoke boxes in Asia, which are private rooms. Most Japanese music singles released today contain a karaoke version so that fans can sing along.

MUSIC

HALLYU

Terms such as "Korean Wave" or *hallyu* or even "Kim Chic" have come to be used to describe the popularity of Korean TV soap operas, music, fashion, food, and even eyebrow shaping in China, Taiwan, Hong Kong, Singapore, and Japan. In 2004 the export value of Korea's cultural content was at $800 million, and the Korea Culture and Contents Agency expected the upcoming figure to exceed $1 billion as a result of the *hallyu*.[3]

rhythm and blues, and hip hop music, and to do the latest dance moves. H.O.T. became the seminal K-pop group, as their fashion, music, and cute looks gained them a legion of fans not only in South Korea, but also in Southeast Asian countries. The terms "Korean Wave" or *Hallyu* were initially coined to describe the continued fascination with the band H.O.T in China even after the group disbanded.

By the 1990s Korean pop music, or K-pop, had become a million-dollar industry. With the increase in profitability of K-pop, music management companies regularly held auditions several times a year to find the next big star. Music management companies claim to spend anywhere from $40,000 to $400,000 to groom the young stars in music and dance.[4] Their highly stylized performances combined with large marketing campaigns have led to the crossover success of many K-pop groups in Southeast Asia. As a consequence of the pop music industry's hunger for the next big pop idol, the music industry came under heavy criticism for its lack of ingenuity and suspicions that they were monopolizing music charts. In the early 2000s several of the top K-pop groups sued their music management companies, claiming unfair contracts, resulting in a Korean Fair Trade Commission investigation.

A second Korean Wave was spurred by the phenomenal success of the South Korean female pop and rhythm and blues artist BoA in Japan. As an SM Entertainment protégé, BoA was groomed for five years in dance and taught to sing in Japanese and English before her debut in 2000. BoA's first album, *ID: Please B*, sold 1.21 million copies in South Korea, but her single from the second album, *Listen to My Heart*, took her to the status of a mega idol by consistently topping the Japanese Oricon music charts.

The South Korean pop music industry also suffered greatly due to the increase in illegal and legal music download, with sales reaching 410-billion won in 2000 and then sharply down turining to 180-billion won in 2003 according to the Music Industry Association of Korea (MIAK). However despite declining music sales, K-pop music continued to be immensely popular both domestically and throughout East Asia. The South Korean pop music industry was entering a new phase by 2005 in which attempts were made, this time with the eager support of the South Korean government, to push the Korean Wave beyond its Asian neighbors to the West and Europe.

POPULAR MODERN MUSIC OF OCEANIA: AUSTRALIA

The Early Days: Rock 'n' Roll and "Beat Music"

The sometimes raucous and rebellious nature of rock 'n' roll music coming from America in the 1950s found a very receptive youth audience in Australia with bands Johnny Rebels and the Rebels, The Planets, and aboriginal singer Jimmy Little representing some of the early successes. By the early 1960s, Australia had its first rock 'n' roll star, Johnny "The Wild One" O'Keefe. Greatly influenced by his idols, Elvis Presley and Little Richard, O'Keefe's debut single "You Hit the Wrong Note (Billy Goat)" was the first of several hits on the Australian music charts, and eventually his popularity also made him a pioneer on television: he became the first Australian rock star to have his own music television show, *Sing, Sing, Sing*, on which a young Olivia Newton-John won the top prize of a trip to the United Kingdom in 1967. Imitation prevailed during the 1960s, with surf and instrumental music, influenced by the California surf music craze, dominating the music charts (1961–63). The band called The Atlantics strived to establish their own instrumental guitar music sound; it is considered one of the most successful Australian groups in the genre. The 1960s also saw the quirky

> **MUSIC FORECAST: RAIN**
>
> In 2005 the male K-pop singer and actor RAIN became the first K-pop star to perform in New York's Madison Square Garden for two nights to sell-out crowds. In 2006 *Time* magazine named the South Korean pop sensation RAIN (whose Korean name is Bi; in Japan, his name is pronounced as Pi) the second most influential World Artist in Asia (after two-time Oscar winner, Chinese director Ang Lee).

Australian tune "Tie Me Kangaroo Down, Sport" become a number one hit and its singer, musician and artist Rolf Harris, eventually achieve cult status in the United States.

Inspired by the immense popularity of The Beatles, "beat music" topped the Australian music charts also in the 1960s with The Easybeats' hit song, "Friday On My Mind," topping both the Australian and U.S. charts. Early beat music singers, The Brothers Gibb, later modified to The Bee Gees, resided in Australia for eight years (1958–66), releasing several singles. Despite their popularity as TV performers, a hit song eluded them until 1966, when "Spicks and Specks" went to number one in Australia, but they returned to the United Kingdom in 1967 because of lack of recognition. Popular 1960s bands The Missing Links and The Pinks Finks drew inspiration from the British Invasion, and pop solo singer Johnny Farnham had the biggest Australian single in the 1960s; he remains a popular performer.

New Music and International Recognition

Music in the 1970s began to evolve from an imitation of popular American and European bands to a more distinctly Australian sound. The progressive or hard rock group Billy Thorpe & the Aztecs was one of the most successful and influential bands from that period, and their single "Most People I Know (Think I Am Crazy)" is still regarded as a classic of Australian rock. Another progressive rock band, the Skyhooks, became famous for their flamboyant performances and outrageous song lyrics and for being one of the most successful rock groups at making Australian Music. Their debut album, *Living in the Seventies*, was the best-selling album of that time. The media became more significant in promoting local talent as the TV pop show, *Countdown*, and the radio station, Double Jay, played important roles in launching the careers of numerous Australian artists in the 1970s. Aboriginal Australian musicians also began merging traditional music instruments and sounds with contemporary music, most significantly, with reggae, as spearheaded by bands such as No Fixed Address, US Mob, and Warumpi Band.

In the late 1970s and throughout the 1980s, the Australian music industry saw many of its local groups make inroads into the overseas market. British-born pop and country singer Olivia Newton-John achieved international fame with the huge success of the tunes "Hopelessly Devoted" and "You're the One That I Want" from the hit movie musical *Grease*. From the opposite musical spectrum, hard rock band AC/DC became one of the most influential bands worldwide, achieving the majority of their fame after Bon Scott replaced the original leader singer. Scott's larynx-shredding vocals and the energetic guitarist clad in a

> ## MIDNIGHT OIL
>
> By voicing the plight of Australia's aboriginal settlers and impoverished miners, the rock band Midnight Oil established itself as one of Australia's most compelling politicized bands. Their 1983 album, *10,9,8,7,6,5,4,3,2,1*, spent two years on the top of the Australian music charts. The single "Beds Are Burning," from the breakthrough album *Diesel and Dust*, topped both the American and the Australian charts. The band's most notable protest occurred 1990, when it performed in front of Exxon Corporation's New York City headquarters in order to bring attention to the company's handling of the Alaskan oil spill.

school uniform solidified them as the global leaders of hard rock. Their album *Back in Black* became a monster hit, selling over 10 million copies in the United States alone.

The punk music phenomenon manifested in late 1970s Australia with bands such as The Scientists and Young Charlatans. By the mid 1980s alternative pop band Pseudo Echo was making a name for itself locally while Men at Work, Air Supply, and Icehouse also found success abroad. The most popular of the alternative pop bands to emerge from the Australian pub scene was INXS, with their first single, "Underneath the Colours," in 1981. Their stylish music and their lead singer Michael Hutchence's famous strut made them stick out from the bunch. Later hits, such as "What You Need," laid the groundwork for their 1987 album *Kick* and their second album *Original Sin*, with its fusing of rock and dance, which turned them into international superstars. Although their popularity began to wane in the late 1990s, INXS maintained a dedicated following until the death of Michael Hutchence in 1997. The grunge band Silverchair and the electronic pop duo Savage Garden are prominent Australian bands to debut in the 1990s.

The 1990s saw a wide variety of diverse music groups gain mainstream success in Australia. The first Aboriginal rock band to garner mainstream success was Yothu Yindi, when the single "Treaty" hit number 11 on the Australian music charts. The band's fusion of high-tech music with traditional aboriginal instruments extended the genre of rock music, and their elaborate dancing and stage lighting left an indelible mark on the Australian music scene. In the new millennium, roots music and singer-songwriters came to prominence. The Australian dance music scene also came into the limelight with the phenomenal success of acts by Kylie Minogue and Slinkee Minx in the United Kingdom, Europe, and the United States. Australian hip-hop music also achieved success with Hilltop Hoods and MC Trey. In the early twenty-first century, Australia's long tradition and affection for country music, evident from the unofficial national anthem "Waltzing Matilda" and the tremendous popularity of country music legend Slim Dusty, continued with the crossover popularity of contemporary country music stars such as Lee Kernaghan, Tania Kernaghan, Kasey Chambers, and New Zealand-born (but raised in Australia) Keith Urban.

Popular Music of New Zealand: A Brief History

Throughout the 1950s and 1960s, New Zealand produced a number of successful rock 'n' roll bands and pop and country singers, some reflecting strong American influences and indigenous musical traditions. However, New Zealand didn't have a recognizable music scene until the 1970s and 1980s; with the support of an increasing number of record labels, rock bands such as the Chills, the Headless Chickens, and the Cleans achieved prominence. During this time the soul music also emerged, spearheaded by indigenous Maori groups Ardijah and Dalvanius Prime, who innovatively combined traditional Maori vocal chants and Polynesian drumming with funk beats and breakdancing performances. Bands such as Dread Beat and Herbs became renowned for their politically aware Maori and Polynesian style of reggae music. The urban hip-hop group Upper Hutt Posse released the first hip-hop album in New Zealand, and their single "E Tu" ["Stand Proud"] was a breakthrough for its unique blend of politicized rap in Maori and English, reflecting the issues of increased urbanization and multicultural society.

The pop-rock group Crowded House became one of the most internationally popular groups from New Zealand in the late 1980s and 1990s with their massive international hit "Don't Dream Its Over" and other notable songs such as "Something So Strong" and "Weather with You." The 1990s saw acts by urban hip-hop group Supergroove rise to prominence and the hip-hop and pop group OMC top international charts with the single "How Bizarre."

In the twenty-first century, with the increasing collaborations of musicians from Polynesia, a new form of hip-hop laced with Pacific pride emerged called Urban Pasifika, in which the group Nesian Mystick and rapper Scribe are prominent. A reggae and soul style called Pacific Dub gained international awareness because of the success of the groups Fat Freddy's Drop and Salmonella Dub. New Zealand's rock music scene continued to flourish, as pop rockers Elemenop and the Datsuns consistently top the music charts, and the immense popularity of the album *Beautiful Collision* by singer-songwriter Bic Runga reflect the diverse nature of New Zealand's thriving music industry.

SOUTH AND SOUTHEAST ASIA

JEREMY WALLACH AND VINAY DHARWADKER

Many types of music, disseminated through various mass media, reach large audiences in South and Southeast Asia today. Recorded and live music are broadcast on radio, performers and performances are featured on television, music is published on audiocassettes and compact discs (also in the Video Compact Disc [VCD] and Digital Compact Disc [DVD] formats), musical numbers and performances are sold and rented on videotapes, and film music is prominent on the silver screen and its associated technologies. As computer technology has spread through these regions since the 1980s, Asians have also begun to access music on the Internet and the World Wide Web. Moreover, music lovers in these parts of the world encounter musicians and music in a variety of live settings: performances in private homes; small performances in villages, urban neighborhoods, or community centers; commercial performances in modern theaters and auditoriums; and megaconcerts in stadiums and other large public spaces. The kinds of music encountered in these forms is immensely varied: it ranges from international pop and rock to local folk, from classical and exotic to religious and secular, from film song and dance number to elevator music and karaoke performance. Music is everywhere—in streets and temples, shops and homes—and it makes its presence felt in many forms and styles.

ORIGINS AND INFLUENCES

The popular music of Southeast Asia today is the product of centuries of influence from other Asian civilizations—particularly China and India—as well as imported elements from European colonizers and, in more recent decades, a globally dominant American popular culture. The indigenous musical traditions of the region are tremendously varied and include varieties of both ornate and rarefied court music and diverse and lively forms of folk performance. Many ensemble traditions, such as the Javanese *gamelan* in Indonesia, the Thai *pi phat*, the Burmese *pat waing*, and the Vietnamese *vong co*, have been celebrated internationally for their musical subtlety and stately refinement. These characteristics stand in marked contrast to the loud, coarse, unruly sounds of Western rock and heavy metal that have become so popular in the region in recent decades. Moreover, the civilizations that brought Buddhism, Hinduism, and Islam to Southeast Asia in the first and second millennia of the Common Era have had a tremendous impact on the region's mass media industries down to the present. Recorded popular music is no exception, and Indian film music, Chinese pop, and Middle Eastern secular and religious music have all been, and remain, important sources of instrumentation, rhythmic patterns, melodic contours, vocal techniques, and visual styles of contemporary Southeast Asian popular music.

Beginning in the sixteenth century, European colonialism brought Western instruments, tunings, and ideas about music to this part of the world. In some cases, the new imports were absorbed into pre-existing musical traditions. A dramatic example is the incorporation of the Western piano (introduced by British colonizers) into Burmese classical music, where, played seemingly without any semblance of Western chordal harmony or playing technique, the piano's sound blends in seamlessly with other more traditional Burmese instruments. Also notable in this regard is the retuning and re-functioning of Western stringed instruments in *langgam Jawa*, a Javanese popular genre that resembles *gamelan* music but is performed on ukuleles and cellos instead of tuned gongs and xylophones. In other cases, Western and Western-influenced genres and repertoires have crowded out and replaced indigenous musical forms. European military marching bands and various European folk music traditions (especially from Spain and Portugal) have played an important role in local forms of popular music in Southeast Asia, including the Spanish-derived *zarazuela* dance of the Philippines, the brass band *tanjidor* ensembles of Indonesia, and the Portuguese-influenced, guitar-and-accordion-based folk music performed by ethnic Malays in peninsular Malaysia and on the coast of Sumatra.

The global political and economic dominance of the United States and the planetwide spread of American popular culture in the later half of the twentieth century have further contributed to the process of musical Westernization in Southeast Asia, such that many cultural commentators in nations across this region have remarked that their national popular music is virtually identical to American pop in every respect, save the language in which it is sung. In Singapore, where English is an official language, even this final mark of difference is often absent from locally produced popular music. In the 1990s the entrance of MTV, the global music television channel, into the region's largest national markets—Indonesia, Thailand, Malaysia, Singapore, and the Philippines—had a dramatic impact on popular music and led to the rise of new youth-oriented styles such as pop punk, hip hop, and alternative rock.

In South Asia, questions of origin and originality, influence, and hybridity take a more complex turn. Music had originated on the Indian subcontinent by 1000 BCE, and a remnant of that antiquity survives today in the ritual Vedic chant—a specialized style of intoning and reciting the mantras of the Vedas, the earliest Hindu scriptures. The classical period of India's indigenous literature and art, roughly from 200 to 1200 CE, developed an elaborate system of theatrical music, with songs sung by actors on stage and accompaniment as well as background music provided by singers and an orchestra off stage. In the middle period, beginning roughly around 1200 and continuing until about 1800, influences from Persia and Afghanistan (brought in by the subcontinent's Muslim conquerors and immigrants), especially Sufi schools of music, combined with Hindu principles, forms, and styles of music to redefine the region's classical, folk, and religious musical traditions. As they emerged in the first half of the past millennium, these branches of Indian music not only laid the groundwork for the subcontinent's modern practices, but also—carried abroad by merchants, migrants, and Muslim, Hindu, and Buddhist missionaries—deeply influenced music in different parts of Southeast Asia.

Between the thirteenth and seventeenth centuries, Indian musicians and musical theorists had developed two major types of classical music: Hindustani classical, a hybrid Indo-Muslim system that is now common to the northern traditions of India and Pakistan, and Carnatic classical, a southern system common to the states of Karnataka, Andhra Pradesh, Tamil Nadu, and Kerala in peninsular India. Both systems use two key elements in musical performance: a melody based on a *raga*, a tonal structure with a set of progressions and melodic and rhythmic patterns on which the performer improvises variations in order to express the mood and meaning of a chosen theme, and a rhythm based on a *tala*, a measure of beats patterned according to duration, tempo, and stress. On the one hand, the *ragas* and *talas* of the two classical systems emerged from and systematized numerous premodern rural, folk, religious, and ritual musical forms and practices. On the other hand, they became resources for all subsequent musical styles and forms so that even Indian folk music today offers rich glimpses of classical melodies and rhythms. In this sense, Hindustani classical music especially serves as a great reservoir for the melodic contours and rhythmic patterns found in most forms of rural, urban, folk, religious, ritual, and popular song and instrumental music in Pakistan, India, Nepal, and Bangladesh.

The traditions of South Asia thus blur any sharp distinction between the classical and the nonclassical and lie along a continuous spectrum that includes the folk and the popular. These traditions have also been syncretistic or assimilative for a long time: north Indian or Hindustani classical music is itself a centuries-long fusion of Hindu and Muslim schools of discipline and performance. Since the late eighteenth century, both the Hindustani and the Carnatic classical systems, as well as most other types of music in South Asia, have interacted closely with and absorbed the influences of many musical traditions from around the world. The violin has been the most common secondary melody instrument in Carnatic classical music for about 200 years; the Indian harmonium, adapted from the European instrument of the mid-nineteenth century, has been a common secondary melody instrument in both Hindustani and Carnatic classical music as well as the subcontinent's musical theater and popular music for at least 125 years. In the twentieth century, Indian film music has absorbed elements from American jazz, rhythm and blues, and hip hop; international rock and pop; German and Irish folk music; Caribbean calypso and reggae; east and west African percussion; and even Hawaiian, Australian Aborigine, and Maori vocal and instrumental music.

MUSIC

SOUND TECHNOLOGY: THE BEGINNINGS

Thomas Alva Edison invented the first successful phonograph in 1877, which recorded sound on tinfoil wrapped around a rotating cylinder. But it was the German-born Emil Berliner who invented the process of recording sound on a flat disc in 1887, of reproducing the master disc in the form of records, and of reproducing the sound from a record on a machine called the gramophone.

Berliner launched The Gramophone Company in the United States in 1893–94, and in England in 1898. The following year the Company bought the Liverpool painter Francis Barraud's picture of his brother's dog Nipper listening intently to a Berliner gramophone. It patented and started using that image, along with the title of Barraud's painting, "His Master's Voice" (HMV), as its trademarks in 1910.

Over the next few decades, HMV became the biggest and most famous label in the music business. In 1931 The Gramophone Company and the Columbia Gramophone Company, both in England, merged to form Electric and Musical Industries Limited, the precursor of today's media conglomerate commonly known as EMI. Toward the end of the twentieth century, when compact audio discs essentially replaced vinyl records, EMI created EMI Classics as a replacement for its HMV trademark.

Emil Berliner also invented the microphone in 1876, which was initially used as a voice transmitter for the telephone. In the 1890s, The Gramophone Company began to record and sell the work of some of the popular musicians of the day, Enrico Caruso and Dame Nellie Melba being among the earliest.

The Gramophone Company of England established its first overseas branch in Bombay, India, in 1901 (with another Asian branch appearing in Japan three years later). It launched its long future collaboration with Indian artists in 1902, when it ceremonially recorded Gauhar Jan, a famous dancer and singer of Calcutta; it began its association with cinema when it recorded the first song in an Indian film for *Alam Ara* in 1931.

The branch was incorporated as an independent Indian company in 1946 and became a publicly traded corporation in 1968, but it remained a member of the EMI conglomerate until 1985. By 1998, the Gramophone Company of India, still popularly known as HMV throughout the subcontinent, had metamorphosed into Saregama India Limited, a member of the RPG Group. Saregama now owns nearly 50 percent of all of the music ever recorded in India and hence controls the largest music archive in the country and one of the largest in the world.

Parts of Asia and some of its music have been at the forefront of the international music industry since its very inception and continue to make up a large proportion of its global market.

SOUTHEAST ASIA

Music lovers in Southeast Asia, like their counterparts anywhere else, do not listen to music produced only in their own countries. Throughout this region, imported music from North America, Europe, and other parts of Asia (particularly China, Japan, and India) maintains a strong presence in local music markets. In addition, the popular music of Southeast

Asian countries often finds an audience in neighboring nations with similar languages. Examples include the ubiquity of Thai pop ballads in Laos and the popularity of Indonesian pop and *dangdut* music in Brunei Darussalam, Malaysia, and Singapore.

Myanmar

"To come to Burma, one of the few places where despotism still dominates, is to take both a physical and emotional journey, a critical ascent into fear and to become caught up, like most Burmese, in the daily management of fear," writes anthropologist Monique Skidmore.[1] Like most dictatorships, Myanmar's military regime—in power since 1962—has attempted to limit the influence of foreign cultural imports, including popular music, on its captive populace. This attempt, as elsewhere, has not been entirely successful. One of the world's most isolated and poorest countries, Myanmar is nonetheless home to its own underground rock scene—featuring groups such as The Playboy and The LPJ (Love, Peace, and Joy)—that operates furtively in the shadow of state-controlled and state-promoted pop music.

Although sanitized, colorful displays of Burmese traditional music and dance dominate television broadcasts of state-sponsored national floric performances, Myanmar's embattled ethnic minorities, many of whom have for decades fought bitterly for independence, have created their own popular music, sung in local dialects, in the shadow of the central government. Among the most successful of these musicians is Shan rock star Sai Mao (known as "the Mick Jagger of Shan State"), who has won committed fans in Burma, Laos, Thailand, and Southwest China.[2]

Cambodia, Laos, and Vietnam

The populations of these Buddhist mainland nations, especially the people of Cambodia, have been deeply scarred by war and dislocation over the last half-century. Among the victims of the Khmer Rouge's four-year reign of horror in Cambodia (1975–79), for example, were an estimated 90 percent of the country's musicians and entertainers. Musicians have fared somewhat better in Laos and Vietnam, but many popular musicians went into exile following the communist takeovers of both these countries. Vietnam's popular music scene is particularly well known for its vitality and cultural distinctiveness. Rather than consisting of imitations of Western pop, Vietnamese popular music is often derived from a highly popular, mass-mediated operetta form called *cai luong*, which incorporates both Western-style music (*tan nhac*) and indigenous Vietnamese music (*vong co*).

Like nearly every other form of cultural production, popular music in Cambodia, Laos, and Vietnam is controlled and promoted by national governments, which attempt to use it as a propaganda tool. The 1980s Laotian disco star Bouangeune Saphouvong, for example, began his career by singing motivational revolutionary songs for the Communist Pathet Lao regime. More recently, Laos's newest teen pop sensation, the half-Lao, half-Bulgarian singer Alexandra Bounxouei, has performed under the auspices of the Laotian government in both international and national venues.

A large portion of contemporary popular music sung in the Khmer, Lao, and Vietnamese languages is actually recorded in the United States by performers in the diasporas of those respective countries. In Asian grocery stores in the United States, it is possible to purchase karaoke DVDs of Lao pop music featuring lyrics written in two different alphabets scrolling across the bottom of the screen: the ancient Lao script and, for those Laotian Americans who speak the language but do not read it, the Latin alphabet. Much of the music produced in the diaspora suggests a widely felt nostalgia for the pre-Communist era in the homeland. Tango music, a holdover from the period of French colonial rule in Vietnam (then part of French Indochina), was incorporated into *cai luong* musical theater in the 1920s, and it remains a vital pop and karaoke genre in Vietnamese-American communities, where it evokes memories of Old Saigon. (One translation of the phrase *vong co* is "longing for the past.")

Thailand

Thai popular music is generally divided into two categories: *sakon* and *luktoong*. *Sakon* consists of Western-style pop songs sung in Thai, usually containing themes of romance and sentimental love. *Luktoong* (also called *phleng luktoong*, literally, "child of the fields") is a modernized folk music from Northeast Thailand, in which the songs often deal with the hardships of life in the countryside. Northeast Thailand, home to many ethnic Lao (Isan) and the poorest region of the country, has a similar status in the Thai national imagination as the American South in the United States. Important non-Western instruments in *luktoong* include the *pin* (three-stringed lute) and the *khaen* mouth organ, a Lao instrument that has long been part of Thai musical culture. The "Queen of Luktoong" was vocalist Pompuang Duangjan, who died in 1992 at the age of thirty-one after a life of both celebrity and hardship. Reportedly over 200,000 people attended her funeral, a testament to her popularity as well as the popularity of this genre.

Since the early 1970s, popular musicians have played a role in the student-led movement to democratize Thailand, a turbulent constitutional monarchy where social change has been hard-won and gradual and military governments have been common. Caravan, a rock group founded by Bangkok university students, played a politicized form of folk rock music (called "songs of life") that was more challenging musically and thematically than previous *sakon* styles. In the 1980s the group Carabao carried on the songs of life tradition and became one of the most successful musical groups in Thai history. Contemporary Thai music is diverse and keeps up with the international styles popularized by MTV: its performers range from the heavy metal band Thrash Project to a variety of hip-hop artists.

Brunei Darussalam, Malaysia, and Singapore

Authoritarian governments, aided by general economic prosperity, maintain order in the divided multiethnic societies of Brunei, Malaysia, and Singapore. The diverse populations of these former British colonial possessions are the result of waves of immigration from China, Europe, and the Indian subcontinent to areas originally inhabited by ethnic Malay peoples. Today, Malaysia is roughly 50 percent Malay, 39 percent Chinese, and 11 percent Indian, whereas, in Singapore, the Chinese-majority population is only 14 percent Malay. Consequently, imported popular music sung in Indian languages (particularly Hindi and Tamil film songs) and Chinese (Mandarin or Cantonese) plays a significant role in the musical life of the three countries, although the appeal of such songs is generally limited to the South Asian and Chinese communities, respectively. Domestically produced Malay-language music tends to attract the largest multiethnic audience. One reason for this crossover in Malaysia is that schoolchildren are required to learn Malay regardless of their ethnic background.

Malay popular music, both religious (Muslim) and secular, is admired for its polish and professionalism but is also sometimes criticized for its lack of distinctively Malay musical elements. Veteran pop divas, such as talented and wholesome Siti Nurhaliza (known to her fans as "the Malaysian Idol"), the urbane, jazz-influenced Sheila Majid, and rock singer Ella can claim thousands of fiercely loyal fans, as do a strikingly large number of Malaysian heavy metal groups, including Cromok, FTG, Suffercation, XPDC, and the all-female band Candy. Malaysian "slowrock" is a unique national genre that combines the ballads and romantic themes of pop with the volume and blistering guitar solos of metal; this style has also caught on in Indonesia. Additionally, commercial recordings of regional music genres, such as the Islamic *dikir barat* from Kelantan state, provide an indigenous alternative to the Westernized sounds of Malay pop for local markets. Indonesian dangdut music also has a large, non-elite Malay audience, and a number of Malaysian artists have made successful careers performing this genre.

Raihan is one of Malaysia's most successful pop groups, and their devout Islamic-themed pop music has inspired many other Muslim groups to adopt a similar message and style. This music, sometimes called *nasyid*, has won a regionwide audience with its sophisticated production techniques, polished vocal harmonies, and the appealing, boy-band images of many of its stars. Song texts, which are in Malay, Arabic, and English, range from the didactic to the militant. Most songs, however, emphasize the importance of following the religious teachings and practices of Islam, while promoting tolerance and social harmony rather than the fundamentalist jihadism that has taken root among a minority of Southeast Asian Muslims.

Not all of the inhabitants of the three countries are Malay, Chinese, or Indian. *Orang asli* ("original people") is the name given by the Malaysian government to non-Muslim indigenous groups who live in Borneo and in relatively isolated rainforest areas on the peninsula. Although they make up a tiny percentage of the country's overall population, the music of *orang asli* groups, featuring characteristic bamboo stampers, zithers, and mouth organs (*sompoton*), has recently entered Malay popular music, often accompanying songs that convey patriotic messages of social justice and ecological consciousness.

Indonesia

Indonesia is by far Southeast Asia's largest music market. The world's fourth most populous nation, Indonesia's national motto is "Unity in Diversity." This phrase is apt, as this vast archipelagic nation—home to hundreds of different cultural and linguistic groups—is united by a single national language, Bahasa Indonesia, and a robust national culture. Popular music sung in Bahasa is one of the most important components of this national culture, which is centered in Jakarta, the nation's massive, sprawling capital.

Indonesian popular music genres can be placed along a continuum from the least acculturated traditional forms to the most Westernized. At one end are regional (*daerah*) types of music—folk and classical traditions of Indonesia's various ethnic groups—and at the other is the national genre, pop Indonesia, which refers to Western genres (rock, heavy metal, pop, hip-hop, etc.) sung in Bahasa. Successful pop Indonesian artists of the past two decades include solo artists Krisdayanti, Melly Goeslaw, and Titi DJ, and the alternative pop groups Cokelat, Gigi, Potret, Sheila on 7, and the wildly successful Padi. Between the two poles (often described as representing the opposites of tradition and modernity) lies dangdut, Indonesia's most popular music genre and also its most controversial. Most published accounts describe dangdut music as a rhythmically propulsive cross between Indian film songs and Western hard rock. Although this description is largely accurate, other important ingredients in the dangdut sound include Latin American popular music, Jamaican reggae, Western disco, Egyptian pop, Malay folk music, and the occasional borrowing from other Indonesian regional music styles. These diverse influences have helped form a genre which fans claim is the true national music of Indonesia, neither an imitation of Western models nor representing a parochial ethnic tradition. Since the 1970s dangdut superstars, including male singers such as Rhoma Irama, Meggi Z, and Mansyur S and female vocalists such as Rita Sugiarto, Elvy Sukaesih, and Titiek Nur, have performed songs about the hardships and heartbreaks of everyday life, especially in the lives of Indonesia's poor. These veteran artists have been joined by more recent stars such as Iis Dahlia, Evie Tamala, Lilis Karlina, and the dangdut girl group Manis Manja.

By far the most famous musical artist of the current decade in Indonesia is Inul Daratista, a former village-level dangdut singer whose onstage undulating dance (*goyang*) first brought her fame and fortune and then condemnation by conservative Muslim clerics. Remarkably, a broad coalition of moderate Muslims, politicians, feminists, and ordinary fans rose to Inul's defense and defied not only the clerics, but also the moralistic "King of Dangdut" himself, Rhoma Irama, who had decried Inul's dancing as pornographic. Besides dangdut, genres of note in Indonesian popular music include *keroncong*—a languid, Portuguese-derived hybrid entertainment music associated with the 1940s anticolonial struggle against The Netherlands—and *jaipong*, a nationally popular dance genre that draws on West Javanese musical traditions and, unusually, does not incorporate any Western instruments or tunings.

The Philippines

The Philippines was first colonized by Spain in the mid-sixteenth century; between 1898 and 1946, however, the United States ruled this island nation. Not surprisingly, Filipino popular music has been heavily influenced by imported American sounds, but at times its most celebrated performers adopt a position of resistance toward America's economic, political, and cultural dominance. This trend is prominent in *pinoy*, the national pop rock music sung in Tagalog, which deals with the concerns and aspirations of ordinary Filipinos. The most celebrated *pinoy* artists are Freddie Aguilar and Joey Ayala, whose music combines trenchant social criticism with calls for progressive social change.

As in the rest of the islands of Southeast Asia, hard rock is popular among youth; successful Filipino hard rock bands include Slapshock, Wolfgang, and Razorback. The country is also important regionwise as an exporter of highly skilled cover bands, which perform at diverse venues throughout Southeast Asia—from the Hard Rock Café in Kuala Lumpur and Planet Hollywood in Singapore, to small cafés in remote outposts in the Borneo rainforest that cater to expatriate oil workers. These Filipino bands not only perform the latest Anglo-American pop and rock hits, but also popular favorites in Cantonese, Malay, Mandarin, and other Asian languages.

SOUTH ASIA

The popular music of South Asia is perhaps better surveyed by genre rather than by nation, since many of its forms and styles slice across boundaries on the mainland. As in Southeast Asia, Western musical genres are popular with large audiences, especially youth, in South Asia, but their popularity is far outweighed by that of the indigenous traditions, largely because the richness and originality of the music styles of South Asia (however hybrid they may be in actuality) undercut any simple equation of tradition with the indigenous and of modernity with merely the Western. Moreover, the Indian subcontinent's long experience of colonial subjugation left it with a deeper appreciation of its own cultural heritage and a greater suspicion of and resistance to the superficialities of Westernization.

SOUTHEAST ASIAN WORLD-BEAT FUSION GROUPS

Inspired by the international success of world-beat music, many Southeast Asian musicians have elected to forge their own ethnic pop hybrids without the benefit of high profile Western collaborators or producers. West Java and Bali, both well known for the richness of their traditional music cultures as well as their savvy cosmopolitanism, are the home bases of some of Indonesia's most creative world beat artists.

Hailing from Bandung, West Java, Krakatau's rhythmically propulsive music represents the most sustained and serious attempt to combine the traditional gong-, drum-, and xylophone-based traditional music of Island Southeast Asia with the technologies, instruments, and techniques of Western popular styles—specifically jazz and rock, with a touch of new age. Balawan is a Balinese guitar virtuoso whose album *GloBALIsm* is a compelling blend of Balinese gong *kebyar* (the flashiest, most aggressive style of Balinese *gamelan*), jazz, and pop. Other important world-beat or ethnic fusion artists from Indonesia include Samba Sunda, Djaduk Ferianto's Kua Etnika ensemble, and the Batak artist Viky Sianipar.

Sabah Habas Mustapha (a.k.a. Colin Bass), a member of the Balkan pop world-beat group 3 Mustaphas 3, is the most internationally known artist who dabbles in Indonesian ethnic fusion music. Mustapha's musical collaborations with local studio musicians in Bandung and Jakarta have resulted in three albums that received critical acclaim in the Western world music press. In Indonesia itself, a relatively straightforward pop song he composed, "Denpasar Moon," became a huge surprise hit in the mid-1990s—both in its original English-language version and with several inventive cover versions sung in Indonesian (or Sundanese) that ranged in style from *dangdut* disco to *jaipong* to *keroncong*.

The Filipino group KONTRA-GAPI (Kontemporaryong Gamelan Pilipino), founded in 1989 by Professor Pedro R. Abraham Jr. of the University of the Philippines, combines musical traditions from the Philippines and from all over the Malay archipelago to create a unique contemporary *gamelan* music that conveys a message of Asian cultural pride and resistance to colonized attitudes.

For instance, over six decades of independence, intellectuals, activists, and artists in India have invested a great deal of creative energy in defining their own alternative modernity, which is particularly manifest in the subcontinent's contemporary styles of music.

Classical Music

The category of popular music on the subcontinent spans a spectrum of forms and genres. Hindustani classical music, as practiced today, attracts hundreds of thousands of listeners to national classical music festivals and hundreds of local concerts annually across India and supports a large industry for publishing classical music. The same is true of Carnatic classical music, although on a smaller scale in most respects. Since the 1960s numerous Hindustani and somewhat fewer Carnatic classical concerts and festivals have also been held outside India, with instrumental music in the two streams proving to be especially popular among European and North American audiences. Since the 1980s communities in the South Asian diaspora have also sponsored concert tours by Hindustani and Carnatic vocal and instrumental artists and ensembles to most parts of the world, from Sydney and Singapore to Nairobi, Paris, and Chicago. These two forms of exposure abroad have contributed significantly not only to the international sales of South Asian classical music in recorded form, but also to the spread of education in this art at various types of institutions around the globe.

In the past four decades, the major classical stars among Hindustani instrumentalists have been Ravi Shankar, Vilayat Khan, and Nikhil Banerjee on the *sitar* (a plucked, long-necked fretted lute) and Akbar Ali Khan on the *sarod* (also a plucked lute, but with a shorter neck and without frets); Alla Rakha, Vasant Achrekar, and Zakir Hussain on the *tabla* (a pair of small drums); and Bismillah Khan on the *sheh'nai* (a double-reed wind instrument resembling the oboe). Musicians of comparable mastery on other important classical instruments include Hariprasad Chaurasia (*bansuri*, side-long bamboo flute); Shivkumar Sharma (Indian *santoor*, a hammered dulcimer often made of walnut wood, with 70 to 100 strings; derived from the 72-string Persian *santur*; with a sound like the harp or harpsichord); Ram Narayan (*sarangi*, a short-necked, bowed lute); and Appa Jalgaonkar on the Indian harmonium. Among Carnatic classical instrumentalists, the most noted performers have been Lalgudi Jayaraman on the violin and Palghat Mani Iyer on the *mridangam* (double-conical, two-headed drum). The major stars of this period among Hindustani classical vocalists have been Bhimsen Joshi, Kumar Gandharva, and Pandit Jasraj (all male) and Kishori Amonkar (female); the best-known Carnatic vocalist has been the woman singer, M. S. Subbalakshmi. Among the younger masters of Hindustani classical singing are the women artists Parween Sultana, Ashwini Bhide Deshpande, and Veena Sahasrabuddhe. All of these artists are from India, and, as the details of their busy careers indicate, many of them have averaged fifty to sixty concerts per year (if not more), drawing several hundred to a few thousand listeners on each occasion.

Ghazal and Folk Music

The *ghazal* is a high literary form, mostly of love poetry (both mundane and mystical), that emerged in Arabic (eighth century), achieved canonical status in Persian (eleventh to twelfth centuries), and then spread to Turkish (fourteenth to fifteenth centuries) and Urdu (seventeenth to eighteenth centuries), among other languages. On the subcontinent, the Urdu *ghazal* came to be set to music and performed under courtly patronage and in aristocratic circles in the late eighteenth century and came to be used more widely in poetry, music, and dance by the end of the nineteenth century. Since the decolonization and partition of the subcontinent in 1947, the Urdu *ghazal* has become the single most popular literary form in musical performance in the region. Urdu, the national language of Pakistan, is virtually indistinguishable in its common spoken form from Hindi, the official language of India, and Hindi–Urdu, as a linguistic continuum, is understood by some 600 million people on the subcontinent's mainland, from Pakistan to India, and even to Nepal and Bangladesh. In the age of mass media, and especially because of its use as a common lyric form in Hindi film music since the 1940s, the *ghazal* sung in Urdu reaches at least a few hundred million listeners in South Asia and the South Asian diaspora.

Over the past 30 years or so, *ghazal* singing has broken away from its initial media linkage with Hindi film music and become a performance genre in its own right. The pioneering stars in this transformation have been the light classical Pakistani *ghazal* vocalists Ghulam Ali and Mehdi Hasan and the Indian singers Jagjit Singh and Chitra Singh (a husband and wife duo), who began to appeal to urban subcontinental audiences with live concerts and recordings (then on vinyl records and audio cassette tapes) in the 1970s. By the 1990s these four *ghazal* singers had achieved international fame and fortune, with performances for South Asian diasporic communities around the globe and global sales in the compact disc format. Among other popular *ghazal* performers today are Pankaj Uddhas, Anup Jalota, and Bhupinder and Mitalee Singh (India) and Abida Parveen (Pakistan).

Since about 1990, several folk traditions belonging to specific parts of South Asia have also achieved national and international popularity. In the 1980s subcontinental Sufi music became very popular with singer Runa Laila (born and raised in Pakistan, she migrated to Bangladesh as an adult), whose rendering of "Dama dam masta qalandar," a Sufi folk song, was an enormous hit in India. In the 1980s and 1990s, the more complex Sufi tradition of Hindustani classical singing reached spectacular heights of international popularity in the career of the Pakistani singer Nusrat Fateh Ali Khan, trained traditionally in the genre of *qawwali* (a devotional Sufi group song, with a lead singer and a chorus and multi-instrument accompaniment, but characterized especially by rhythmic hand clapping). Nusrat recorded 125 *qawwali* albums in his lifetime (the world record for the genre in *The Guinness Book of Records*); collaborated on fusion compositions with Canadian guitarist Michael Brook; contributed to the soundtracks of the Hollywood films *The Last Temptation of Christ*, *Dead Man Walking*, and *Natural Born Killers*, among others; and developed a close friendship with Peter Gabriel, whose Real World label released five of Nusrat's albums worldwide.

Bhangra music and dance, originally a rural tradition of the Punjab (a region divided between India and Pakistan) and associated with group dancing at harvest festivals and other celebrations, achieved a different kind of popularity under the conditions of globalization. In the 1990s this music and dance combination emerged as disco *bhangra* in England and North America, a hybrid urban form, popularized by the Sikh and Punjabi diaspora, with Daler Mehndi as its star performer from India. At the turn of the millennium, an astonishing new folk form from South Asia reached the international stage. Siddi Goma, a large performance troupe, consists of members of a community of Muslim African immigrants who have lived in India for several centuries, but who still practice their African Sufi devotional music and African ritual dancing, using several languages (from different continents) and several African folk instruments. Their success and popularity in India, Europe, America, and elsewhere have not only altered understanding of the long-term fusion of different musical traditions, but also of the history and anthropology of South Asian cultures in general.

Hindi Film Music

In the great carnival of popular music in South Asia, Hindi film music occupies a special place. Hindi film songs are embedded inside stories; thus they are always associated with particular characters, situations, and episodes, and often with particular dance sequences. Hence they are inevitably linked, in their audience's minds, with specific actors, actresses, and dancers. This narrative embedding, which has antecedents in classical Indian drama and theater, makes a Hindi film song more than just a song—it gives it a resonance that exceeds its melody, rhythm, and words. The immense popularity of Hindi film music over the past seven or eight decades has evolved around this suggestive or associational power of its performance setting.

In the evolution of Indian cinema, Hindi film music has produced a number of superstar playback singers, who have lent their musical voices to several generations of actors and actresses who have only mimed their songs before the camera. The major male voices in the industry from the 1950s to the 1980s were Mohammad Rafi, Mukesh, and Kishore Kumar, whereas the major female voices were the sisters Lata Mangeshkar and Asha Bhosle (Lata holds the world record in *The Guinness Book of Records* for the largest number of songs ever recorded over a lifetime by a single artist—more than 25,000). Each of these five singers had several dozen, if not a few hundred, hits in the course of 30 or 40 years, preserved in the memory of tens of millions of followers. Somewhat less prominent yet popular other singers in the Hindi film world before the 1990s include K. L. Saigal, Talat Mehmood, Manna Dey, Hemant Kumar, S. D. Burman, R. D. Burman, and Suman Kalyanpur. Among important popular artists of the past ten years or so are Udit Narayan, Shankar Mahadevan, Kumar Sanu, and Kunal Ganjawala among the men, and Sonu Nigam, Alka Yagnik, Sunidhi Chauhan, Shreya Ghoshal, Vasundhara Das, and Hema Sardesai among the women.

The most popular music composers for Hindi films from 1950s to the 1980s included Shankar and Jaikishan, S. D. Burman, Salil Choudhury, Lakshmikant and Pyarelal, Madan Mohan, and R. D. Burman, as well Naushad, Khayyam, and Vanraj Bhatia. In the past two decades, A. R. Rahman has probably been the most innovative and sought-after music composer in the industry. Among the most popular lyricists or songwriters since the 1950s have been Kaifi Azmi, Firaq Gorakhpuri, Sahir Ludhianvi, Majrooh Sultanpuri, Hasrat Jaipuri, Shailendra, Anand Bakshi, Gulzar, and Javed Akhtar. As the complex structure of Hindi cinema production suggests, a film's story and direction, lyrics and musical composition, actors and singers, cinematography and dancing, all have to come together before a hit song emerges in the public imagination. The best Hindi film songs—which are often the most popular with a surprisingly discerning South Asian audience—balance the counterweights of word and emotion, mood and melody, scene and rhythm, experience and imagination, to fix themselves in the hearts and minds of their countless listeners.

RESOURCE GUIDE

PRINT SOURCES

East Asia and Oceania

Baker, Glenn A., ed. *Australian Made: Gonna Have a Good Time Tonight.* Sydney: Fontana Collins, 1997.

Baranovitch, Nimrod. *China's New Voices: Popular music, ethnicity, gender, and politics, 1978–1997.* Berkeley, CA: University of California Press, 2003.

Brace, Timothy. "Popular Music in Contemporary Beijing: Modernism and Cultural Identity." *Asian Music* 22.2 (1991): 43–66.

Chung, Kyung-Wha. *The New Groove Dictionary of Music and Musicians.* New York/Hong Kong: Macmillan, 1980.

Cockington, James. *Long Way to the Top: Stories of Australian Rock & Roll.* New York: ABC Books, 2001.

Craig, Timothy. *Japan Pop! Inside the World of Japanese Popular Culture.* New York: M. E Sharpe, 2000.

de Kloet, Jeroen. "'Let Him Fucking See the Green Smoke beneath My Groin': The Mythology of Chinese Rock." Pp. 239–74 in Arif Dirlik and Xudong Zhang (eds.), *Postmodernism and China.* Durham, NC: Duke University Press, 2000.

Dix, John. *Stranded in Paradise: New Zealand Rock and Roll, 1955 to the Modern Era.* Wellington: Penguin New Zealand, 2005.

Dunbar-Hall, Peter, and Chris Gibson. *Deadly Sounds, Deadly Places: Contemporary Aboriginal Music in Australia.* Sydney: UNSW Press, 2004.

Eggleton, David. *Ready to Fly: The Story of New Zealand Rock Music.* Nelson, NZ: Craig Potton, 2003.
Howard, Keith. *Riding the Wave: Korean Pop Music.* Honolulu: University of Hawaii Press, 2006.
Huang, Hao. "Voices from Chinese Rock, Past and Present Tense: Social Commentary and Construction of Identity-Yaogun Yingue from Tiananmen to the Present." *Popular Music and Society* 26 (2003): 183–202.
Japanese Encyclopedia of Popular Culture (Taishu bunka jiten). Tokyo: Kobundo, 1991.
Jones, Mason. *Japan's Edge: The Insiders Guide to Japanese Pop Subculture.* San Francisco: Viz Media LLC, 1999.
Kang, Man-gi. *A History of Contemporary Korea.* Translated by John B. Duncan. Los Angeles: Center for Korean Studies UCLA, 2005.
The Korean National Commission for UNESCO. *Traditional Korean Music.* Seoul: Pace International Research, 1983.
Lee, Byong Won. *Styles and Esthetics in Korean Traditional Music.* Seoul: National Center for Korean Traditional Performing Arts, 1997.
MacIntyre, Donald. "Flying Too High?" *Time Asia Magazine*, July 29, 2002.
McClure, Steve. *Nippon Pop.* Tokyo/Boston: Tuttle Publishing, 1998.
McFarlane, Ian. *The Encyclopedia of Australian ROCK and POP.* St. Leonards, NSW: Allen & Unwin, 1999.
Richie, Donald. *Image Factory: Fad and Fashion in Japan.* London: Reaktim Bookmax, 2000.

South and Southeast Asia

Barendregt, Bart, and Wim van Zanten. "Popular Music in Indonesia since 1998" in "Particular Fusion, Indie and Islamic Music on Video Compact Discs and the Internet." *Yearbook for Traditional Music* 34 (2002): 67–113.
Davis, Sara. *Song and Silence: Ethnic Revival on China's Southwest Borders.* New York: Columbia University Press, 2005.
Lockard, Craig. *Dance of Life: Popular Music and Politics in Southeast Asia.* Honolulu: University of Hawaii Press, 1998.
Manuel, Peter. *Cassette Culture: Popular Music and Technology in North India.* Chicago: University of Chicago Press, 1993.
Neuman, Daniel M. *The Life of Music in North India: The Organization of an Artistic Tradition.* Chicago: University of Chicago Press, 1990.
Skidmore, Monique. *Karaoke Fascism: Burma and the Politics of Fear.* Philadelphia: University of Pennsylvania Press, 2004.
Tan, Sooi Beng. "The Performing Arts in Malaysia: State and Society." *Asian Music* 21.1 (1989/1990): 137–171.
Ubonrat, Siriyuvasak "Commercialising the Sound of the People: Pleng Luktoong and the Thai Pop Music Industry." *Popular Music* 9.1 (1990): 61–78.
Wong, Deborah. "Thai Cassettes and Their Covers: Two Case Histories." *Asian Music* 21.1 (1989/1990): 78–104.

WEBSITES

East Asia and Oceania

Australian Music Online. Australia Council for the Arts. http://www.amo.org.au. Australian music and artists' information.
Australian Recording Industry Association. http://www.aria.com.au. Australian Record Industry Association.
BoAjjang. http://www.boajjang.com (English). All about South Korean pop sensation BoA.
C4TV. http://www.c4tv.co.nz. All the latest information on New Zealand music industry.

Chosun. http://www.chosun.com (Korean, English and Japanese). The electronic version of the Korean Newspaper *Chosun.*

Cui Jian's Website. Beijing Eastwest Productions. http://www.cuijian.com. Latest information of the father of Chinese rock and roll.

jpop.com. http://www.jpop.com (English). All about what's popular in Japan.

KoreaPop.com. http://www.koreapop.com (English). Korean music shop and webzine.

Mai FM 88.6. Mai Media Ltd. http://www.maifm.co.nz. Auckland's No. 1 youth radio station with the news and information on urban music.

Melon. http://www.melon.co.kr (Korean). A Korean pop music and culture site with the latest rankings and music news.

MTVCHINESE.COM. MTV Networks. http://www.mtvchinese.com (Chinese). Music, reviews, and interviews.

MusicAustralia. http://www.musicaustralia.org. Detailed resources on Australian Music.

nippop. http://nippop.com (English). Japanese music artist information and music industry news features.

NZMUSIC.COM. http://www.nzmusic.com. Latest on New Zealand music charts and industry information.

Oricon Style. http://www.oricon.co.jp (Japanese). Japanese music chart rankings and information.

Recording Industry Association of New Zealand (RIANZ). http://www.rianz.org.nz. The Recording Industry Association of New Zealand Website, with album and single chart information.

rip it up online. http://www.ripituponline.com. New Zealand's oldest music magazine online.

Seoul Selection. http://www.seoulselection.com (English). Website with the latest trends and links about South Korea.

9SKY.COM. http://www.9sky.com (Chinese). Chinese music and entertainment site.

S.M. Town. S.M. Entertainment Co., Ltd. http://www.smtown.com (English, Korean, Japanese, Chinese). Features the latest information on all of Korea's top SM Entertainment idols.

Vibe Australia. http://www.vibe.com.au. Website showcasing Australian Aboriginal and Torres Strait Island's music and culture.

South and Southeast Asia

BollywoodWorld. http://www.BollywoodWorld.com *and* http://www.desimusic.com. Accessed October 21, 2006. These two Websites, among many, offer informative and interesting glimpses into the commercial world of popular music in South Asia.

Emile Berliner—The History of the Gramophone. http://inventors.about.com. Accessed October 21, 2006. See various entries on Emile Berliner, inventor of the microphone and the gramophone.

Saregama India Limited. http://www.saregama.com. Accessed October 21, 2006. Official Website of Saregama India Limited, the successor to The Gramophone Company of India (which carried the HMV label).

WebIndia123.com. http://www.webindia123.com. Accessed October 21, 2006. Useful source on Indian music, music festivals in India, etc.

RECORDINGS

East Asia and Oceania

AC/DC. *Back in Black.* Albert/EMI, 1980.
Ardijah. *Take a Chance.* WEA, 1987.
BoA. *Vol. 2–No. 1.* SM Entertainment, 2002.
Cheung, Leslie. *Leslie.* Capital Artists, 1998.
Chills, The. *Soft Bomb.* Slash/ Liberations. 1992.
Cui, Jian. *The Best of Cui Jian 1986–1996.* EMI, 2006.

Headless Chickens. *Donde Esta la Pollo.* Flying Nun Records, 1997.
Hibari, Misora. *Golden Best Vol. 1.* Sony Japan, 2004.
Hikaru, Utada. *Single Collection V.1.* EMI, 2004.
H.O.T: *The Best/HOT.* Avex, 2002.
INXS. *Kick.* WEA, 1987.
Matsutoya, Yumi. *Cobalt Hour.* Toshiba-EMI, 1975.
Midnight Oil: *Diesel and Dust.* CBC, 1986.
Mui, Anita. *Bad Girl.* Capital Artists, 1985.
Once We Were Warriors. (movie soundtrack). Milan Records, 1995.
Rain: *Vol. 3—It's Raining.* Seoul Records, 2004.
Seotaiji. *Seotaiji Live Tour Zero 04.* Yedang Entertainment) 2004.
SMAP. *SMAP VEST.* JVC, 2004.
Upper Hut Posse. *E Tu.* Jayrem Records, 1988.
Yellow Magic Orchestra. *The Best of Yellow Magic Orchestra.* Restless Records, 1993.

South And Southeast Asia

Aguilar, Freddy. *The Best of Freddy Aguilar.* Selected tracks at http://moriki.hp.infoseek.co.jp/Freddie_htm/Aguilar.htm.
Ali, Ghulam. *The Best of Ghulam Ali: Ghazals.* Calcutta: The Gramophone Company of India Limited, 1984; Saregama India Limited, 1998. CD.
Amonkar, Kishori. *Live Concert: Swar Utsav 2000. Kishori Amonkar.* Vols. 1–2. New Delhi: Living Media India Limited, 2001. CD.
Bhosle, Asha. *Golden Collection: Sizzling Hits.* Calcutta: Saregama India Limited; London: Saregama plc, 2003. CD.
Bounxouei, Alexandra. http://www.alexandrabounxouei.com. Official Website; offers sample tracks from recent releases.
Chaurasia, Hari Prasad. *Sangeet Sartaj: Hari Prasad Chaurasia.* Vols. 1–2. New Delhi: Living Media India Limited, 1990 and 1992. CD.
Duangjan, Pompuang. Various compilations of songs listed at http://www.thaimegamart.com. The Thai MegaMart Website also lists recordings of contemporary music by a large number of other singers and musicians from the country, including the popular Thai groups Caravan and Carabao.
Gandharva, Pandit Kumar. *Sangeet Sartaj: Kumar Gandharva.* Vols. 1–2. New Delhi: Living Media India Limited, 1993 and 2002. CD A 02057-58 DDD; 2-CD set.
———. *Pandit Kumar Gandharva in Concert.* Calcutta: Saregama India Limited; London: Saregama plc, 1996. CD
Hasan, Mehdi. *Life Story.* Vols. 1–2. Mumbai: Universal Music India Private Limited, 2002.2-CD set.
Jasraj, Pandit. *Maestro's Choice, Series One: Pandit Jasraj.* Living Media India Limited, 1991. CD.
Joshi, Pandit Bhimsen. *Live at the Town Hall in Calcutta.* Calcutta: Hindusthan Musical Products Limited, 2000. CD.
———. *Maestro's Choice: Bhimsen Joshi.* Living Media India Limited, 1991. CD.
Khan, Bismillah. *Maestro's Choice, Series One: Bismillah Khan.* New Delhi: Living Media India Limited, 1991. CD.
Khan, Nusrat Fateh Ali, and Party. *Akhian.* North Bergen, NJ: M.I.L. Multimedia LIC, 1997; licensed from Interra Records.
Krakatau. *As.* Musea, 2006. CD. Listed at http://www.starpulse.com/Music/.
Kumar, Kishore. *Legends: Kishore Kumar, The Versatile Genius.* Vols. 1–5. Calcutta: The Gramophone Company of India Limited, 2000.
Kurnia, Detty. *Dari Sunda: Woman of the World, Vol. 6.* Riverboat, 1996. CD. See biography and discography listed at http://www.starpulse.com/Music/.
Majid, Sheila. http://www.sheilamajid.com. Website of major Malaysian pop singer and performer.
Mangeshkar, Lata. *Lata . . . Forever.* Vols. 1–5. Calcutta: Saregama India Limited, 2001. 5-CD collection.

Mao, Sai Sine. *Ta Yawar Thar*. Music video at http://www.innwa.com. The Innwa Website also lists a large number of other currently popular musicians from Myanmar and the Burmese diaspora.

Mehndi, Daler. *Ho Jayegi Balle Balle*. Mumbai: Magna Sound India Limited, 1997.

Mukesh. *Anmol Ratan*. Vols. 1–2, 4–5, 7. Calcutta: Saregama India Limited; London: Saregama plc, 2002. 5-CD set.

Nurhaliza, Siti. http://www.sitizone.com. Malaysian pop diva's Website.

Rakha, Alla, and Zakir Hussain. *Maestro's Choice, Series One: Alla Rakha and Zakir Hussain, Tabla*. New Delhi: Living Media India Limited, 1991. CD.

Sethi, Satnam Singh. *Japji Sahib Raehraas Sahib*. Noida, India: Super Cassettes Industries Limited, 1996. CD.

Shankar, Pandit Ravi. *Shankar: Sitar Concertos and Other Works*. Economic Times Editor's Choice. EMI Records Limited, 1998; Mumbai: Times Music, 1998.

———, with Ustad Alla Rakha. *Ragas Hameer and Gara*. Music India 1988; Mumbai: PolyGram India Limited, 1999. CD.

Sharma, Pandit Shivkumar, Rahul Sharma, and Ustad Zakir Hussain. *Santoor Virasat: Raga Hansadhwani*. Mumbai: Ninaad Music and Marketing Private Limited, 1998. CD.

Singh, Jagjit and Chitra. *The Unforgettable Hits of Jagjit and Chitra Singh*. Calcutta: The Gramophone Company of India Limited; London: Saregama plc, 1999. CD.

Slapshock. *Project 11–14*. EMI Philippines, 2002. CD. Biography and discography at http://www.starpulse.com/Music/.

Sultana, Parween. *Bhavani Dayani: Vocal*. Calcutta: The Gramophone Company of India Limited, 1997. CD.

3 Mustaphas 3. *Play Musty for Me*. Omnium, 2001. CD. See biography and discography at http://www.starpulse.com/Music/.

NOTES

East Asia and Oceania

1. Johnny Kennedy, CEO of IFPI (International Federation of Phonographic Industry), Speech in Shanghai May 25, 2006, titled "Unlocking the Music Market in China."
2. In 1998, the South Korean government announced that it would gradually lift the more than 50-year ban on Japanese cultural items, which includes movies, television, animation, and music. The ban was stalled in 2000 and 2001 over issues related to Japanese history textbooks' description of the Korean War. Prior to the lifting of the ban, South Korean teenagers purchased illegal copies of Japanese music cassettes and CDs on the black market.
3. *The Korean Times* newspaper, December 22, 2005, *Culture Contents Exports to Top $1Billion*.
4. See "Korean Pop: Flying Too High?" *Time Asia Magazine*, July 29, 2002 (cover story).

South And Southeast Asia

1. Skidmore (in Resource Guide), p. xi.
2. Davis (in Resource Guide), p. 75.

PERIODICALS

EAST ASIA AND OCEANIA

SHUYONG JIANG

East Asia and Oceania began publishing periodicals during the early mid-nineteenth century, at the same time that this form of print appeared in Europe and North America. The first periodical was published in China in 1815. In Oceania, the first robust growth of periodical publishing began during the founding days of the colonies. Australia issued its first magazine, *Australia Magazine*, in 1821; New Zealand's first newspaper was published in 1839. Although each of these countries was experiencing similar industrial development, the development of the popular press was far from synchronous. Each country had its own time, and in some cases the gap between initial periodical publication from one country to another could be decades apart. The nature of these periodicals constituted the unparalleled development of the popular press. The spontaneity, dynamics, and temporality of popular periodicals, and their reciprocal relations with other subcultures, make this medium very sensitive to economic, social, and political changes. Therefore, this section on the overall development of the periodical press of East Asia and Oceania concentrates on the evolving stages of the periodical publication without necessarily linking it to a uniform timetable.

The term "popular periodicals" is not "popularly" employed in many Asian countries; this phrase is generally used in the West. In China, the term "popular" may be used to describe literary periodicals that are not designed for a high-society reading audience. When it comes to periodicals, the division is based on the subjects—such as literature, science, or sports—and the type of audience—such as women, youth, or frequent as opposed to infrequent readers. Many of these categories include both academic and nonacademic periodicals. In Japan, "popular magazines" have some historic and political connections that represent particular stages in the development of periodical publication.[1] Therefore, the popular periodicals discussed in this chapter are rather loosely defined to include all nonscholarly serial publications, regardless of their forms, styles, or subjects.

The newspapers, or news sheets, appeared long before the nineteenth century in some countries. The indigenous news press appeared as early as the eighth century in China.[2] Nevertheless, the development of popular periodicals in the region can only be considered outgrowths of the modern mechanical era, and the development was greatly influenced by Western journalism. During the early years of the nineteenth century, stimulated by the prosperous economy, industrialization, and advanced printing technology, magazines boomed as a source of leisure reading in Europe. Shortly thereafter, they expanded into markets in the rest of the world. At the beginning, the periodical press in East Asia and Oceania was either colonial or foreign in nature. In China, from 1807 to 1842, there were periodicals published in both Chinese and English by Western missionaries. From 1815, when the first *Cashisu meiyue tongjizhuan* [Chinese Monthly Magazine] (1815–21) was founded by Robert Morrison (1782–1834) and William Milne, to the end of the nineteenth century, there were about 200 foreign periodicals in China, which amounted to 80 percent of total periodicals published during that period.[3] Many of these periodicals were issued for the purpose of missionary propaganda. In order to reach the Chinese readers, these foreign publishers had hired Chinese editors and managers. Thus, foreign influence helped train Chinese journalists and foster the modern press in China.

In Australia the first newspaper was issued by a British printer, George Howe (1769–1821), a son of the first government printer in the West Indies, who had served on the *London Times* for a period of time. Howe published Australia's very first *Sydney Gazette and New South Wales* in 1803.[4] During the founding days of the colony, to satisfy the reading appetite of the immigrants from Great Britain, who brought with them the culture of magazine reading, many periodicals were inaugurated. Most of these early magazines were imitations of European originals and were customized for "colonial readers."[5] For example, the first illustrated popular magazine in Australia, *Melbourne Punch* (1855–1925), was initially a satirical publication; its editorial ideas were clearly influenced by its British predecessor, *Punch*.

Japan's first magazine appeared in 1867; it was called *Seiyo-Zasshi* [Western Magazine]. The first all-around magazine, *Meiroku-Zasshi*, was founded in 1874 by a group of Meiji scholars who had studied Western culture. The translation of the word "magazine" is *zasshi* in Japanese, similarly *zazhi* in Chinese, which means "miscellaneous records," echoing its French origin of *magasin* to suggest variety in entertainment, information, and taste. In Korea, development came later. The word "newspaper" was first mentioned in 1874 by a scholar official, Kang Wi, who heard about it during his trip to Peking. It was not until 1881 that Korea published its first newspaper. Even then the *Choson Shinbo* was only published after a group of Japanese businessmen imported printing equipment from Japan.

Following the initial period of imitating and learning, local publishers and editors began to produce their own periodicals. This trend introduced the notion of the press as a venue for politically motivated or otherwise opinionated voices. The local and national news gazettes and weekly magazines increased rapidly in most of those countries during the last decades of the nineteenth and the first decades of the twentieth centuries. These periodicals focused on national and international events that were interesting to the reading public of the time. The most successful magazines were geared to national political, social, and cultural concerns and problems. They served as sources for immediate news, and for both local and nationwide information. Among these different types of publications, the weeklies experienced the most success since they were timely enough to cover current events and to devote pages to entertainment as well. In Australia the weekly periodicals were established with both journalistic and commercial success between 1880 and 1900. In 1870 Australia had only one monthly magazine but a lot of weeklies. Australia's most celebrated weekly periodical, the *Bulletin*, was founded in 1880. In Japan, after the inaugurations of *Shukan-Asahi* and *Sunday Mainich* in 1921, weekly periodicals dominated the periodical market through the 1920s and 1930s. In New Zealand the weeklies are still going strong in the periodical market.

The combined circulation of the top three women's weekly magazines sell 352,000 copies each week, more than one-third of total periodical readership.

During its early development, the popular periodicals also played an important role in popularizing literature and promoting national writers. There were reciprocal benefits for having renowned authors writing for magazines: it could result in mass circulation on the one hand, and provide writers with effective means for presenting their stories on the other. The famous Australian literary magazine, *Australian Journal* (1865–1962), was essentially a magazine for popular stories written by Australian authors, some of whom later became well known in Australian literature. During its 97 years, the *Australia Journal* formed a close bond with many Australian writers and employed "the ablest of colonial pens of the day,"[6] including Marcus Clarke, whose best-known novel, *For the Term of His Natural Life*, first appeared in the *Australian Journal*.

In Japan literary magazines created an innovative genre, "intermediate novels," which aimed at a level that was not purely literary, nor purely entertainment, and therefore able to appeal widely to the reading public. In China, the popularization of literary periodicals was associated with revolutionary reforms of Chinese literature and society. In the first two decades of the twentieth century, the "New Fiction" movement, proclaimed by Liang Qichao (1873–1929), China's leading reformer at the end of the nineteenth century, created a sensational boom for fiction magazines. The influence of the movement and success of the four flagship fiction magazines of the time— *Xin xiaoshuo* [New Fictions] (1902–06), *Xiuxiang Xiaoshuo* [Embroidered Fictions] (1903–06), *Yueyue Xiaoshuo* [Monthly Fictions], 1906–09), and *Xiaoshuo lin* [Fiction Forest] (1907–08)—changed the traditional notion of fiction and promoted the idea of fictional writing as a means to benefit society.

The wartime and postwar periodical press in the region became increasingly distinct among the countries. After the 1920s the popular press in China declined, especially during the Sino-Japanese War (1935–45). Many magazines and newspapers were forced to close; only a small number of them remained in the foreign settlements of Shanghai, and some moved to Hong Kong. In Taiwan, under the Japanese occupation, Chinese language periodicals were prohibited. In Australia, many periodicals reduced their shape and size because of the shortage of paper and labor. However, relative to the harsh wartime conditions, the Australian popular press learned that the entertainment feature of the popular periodicals was as important as filling the pages with wartime news. Some new magazines were published to address the problems created by the war. Once the war was over, publishers of many of these were enthusiastic to modernize their formats and to revitalize themselves for postwar presentations.

Throughout the twentieth century, and especially after World War II, countries in the region underwent many social changes. One of the major changes was in the status and role of women in society. This change was mirrored in the proliferation of women's magazines that were published in East Asian and Oceania. In many of these countries, women's magazines enjoyed wide circulation. In many categories, women readers surpassed any other groups in periodical readership.

As a continuing publication, the newspaper or the magazine builds up a relationship with its audience by catering to the tastes of its readership. Since the 1950s, the prospering economy, modern technology, and the ever-expanding tastes of the public have created opportunities, as well as challenges, for the popular press. While radio, television, and computers may take the public away from their reading habits, each of these also stimulates new ideas for periodical publishing: sports, games, comics, fashion, home improvement, hobby, music—wherever there is an interest, there is a magazine for it. The public's interests have become increasingly diverse, and hence popular periodicals have become more specialized and selective. Even as some well-established, large-circulation magazines vanished without a trace, new ones always arose. Some periodicals build circulation in the millions by appealing to an audience of highly diversified tastes and interests, and some build it by seeking out smaller publics within the population at large. Many periodicals reinvented themselves to become integral parts of the popular culture. A good example is the Japanese *Weekly Sankei*, a long-troubled traditional newspaper-magazine. It successfully revived itself by changing to a subculture magazine as *Weekly SPA!* in 1988.

In the later twentieth century, popular periodicals also became a major venue for advertising. Although the profits of many popular periodicals still rely on their sales, advertising expenditure has been increasing across the countries. Magazine advertising even helped the public accept many rising subcultures and trends. For example, in 1988 in Japan, *Hanako*, a new gourmet-oriented information magazine, drove many young ladies to the restaurants that were introduced in the magazine, and influenced the development of a reader group of highly consumer-oriented women, the *Hanako-zoku* ["Hanako-tribe"]. Moreover, studies also have shown that, in Australia, magazine advertisements help promote brand-name products.[7]

The twenty-first century brings two new phenomena to periodical publication: a global market and a new electronic genre of periodicals. Leading international periodicals found their way into the East Asian market. One can find *ELLE*, *Reader's Digest*, and *Vogue* on street stands and in bookstores in China, Japan, and Korea. Many of them are as successful in these countries as they are in Europe and America. Publications produced in the region are likewise distributed across countries. *Ray*, a Japan-based fashion magazine, is a favorite fashion and style magazine in China. It is even more popular than the world-leading fashion magazines.

In the current periodical market, and more than ever, the popular press faces serious challenges and also opportunities for reaching and maintaining readership and audience share. According to an ACNielsen study, people now spend more time on the Internet than with newspapers or magazines.[8] The impact of the Internet on popular periodical publishing is revolutionary. Electronic access and distribution have brought popular periodical publishing to a new level. Not only do print magazines often offer online subscriptions, but e-journals are also emerging. The popular publications now have a new medium for publishing and for global dissemination. The Internet and digital publishing have also changed the way magazines interact with readers. If it is being done correctly, electronic publishing can also boost the sales of print copies. There are many successful examples of turning an online popular publication into a print version, or using Internet to promote print publications. It is a matter of either seizing the moment or losing it. In the past, popular magazine publishing has confronted the challenges of other emerging media, such as radio and television broadcasting. However, this time, the moment is unfolding against a background of globalization and an integrated international market in an electronic era.

CHINA

With a population of more than 1.3 billion, the market for popular periodicals in China is full of potential. The first boom in popular periodicals occurred at the beginning of the twentieth century but was almost demolished during wartime. By 1949 there were only 257 periodicals left. Because of political conditions and other factors, the popular press experienced even harsher conditions in the 1960s and the 1970s, during which there were only 20 or so titles in existence. It was not until after 1977 that popular periodical publishing in China really took off. In 1979 the total number of magazines increased to 1,470. In 2004 a total of 1,922 newspapers were published, and the total number of published magazines reached 9,490 titles, with an average of 4.3 million printings per issue and a total printing of 47.27 million copies. Among the more than 9,000 titles, less than 4 percent (about 353 titles) were all-around magazines; about 2,000 titles were popular magazines.[9] There were 140 publications that exceeded 2.5 million in circulation, but almost two-thirds of these titles were either government and Communist Party publications or tutorial materials.

In 2001 China launched a government-sponsored "China Magazine Square" project. It selected 1,518 titles from the more than 9,000 periodicals and listed them in a hierarchy of four groups. The top group included 24 of the best and most widely circulated magazines. Next to the *Banyue tan* [China Comment], a political publication by the Communist Party, four popular magazines dominated the top five: *Gushihui* [Storytelling Club], *Duzhe* [Readers], *Zhiyin* [Bosom Friend], and *Jiating* [Family Magazine].

The *Storytelling Club* was inaugurated in 1963; *Revolutionary* was added to its title between 1974 and 1978, but it returned to its original name in 1979. There were more than fifty storytelling periodicals with total of 8.63 million copies in circulation in 2002; *Storytelling Club* alone had 4 million copies in circulation, almost 50 percent of the total.[10] The secret of *Storytelling Club* is its editorial policy: collect raw materials from real stories of real people and make them suitable for storytelling. Its success proved that good stories are more powerful than the literary skills of telling them.

The *Readers* magazine is the most circulated magazine in China and in 2006 was fourth worldwide.[11] Its circulation of 10 million and 30 thousand copies in April 2006 was a record high yet to be surpassed. It has been estimated that since the inauguration of its first issue in 1980, approximately 200 million people have read the magazine and total of 1.1 billion copies have sold.[12] Without relying on fancy design, beautiful cover girls, or star powers, the magazine retains its standard of good quality and provides careful editorial review for each article it publishes. In so doing, *Readers* has won itself a reputation as a digest magazine with a wide range of interests, a combination of domestic and international matters, and frequent reflections on a variety of cultural and social issues. These methods have kept it in touch with a large reading audience.

Both *Bosom Friend* and *Family* magazines specialize in presentation of the contemporary Chinese scene. The *Bosom Friend* is known for its news reporting. Its columns keep a balance between serious muckraking stories and gossip about celebrities. Its cover stories are provoking and shocking, often causing a sensational chain reaction. The *Family* magazine, on the other hand, addresses marriage, love, parenting, and issues modern families are facing every day.

Led by these general and family magazines, the popular periodical market has recently been expanding. Diverse and specialized periodicals emerge every day. The number of specialized magazines increased from 5,000 to 8,000 from 1988 through 1999, and continues to grow.[13] Using magazines targeted for a parental audience, the division of age group can be very specific. For example, *Mammy's Baby* is designed for parents with children age birth to three years old; *For the Children* is for those with children age three to seven; *For Today's Parents* is for parents with children age eleven to eighteen. Similarly, for car lovers, there are targeted automobile magazines such as *Utility Cars*, *Sports Cars*, *Old Cars*, *Car Repairs*, and more.

The government played an important role in the development of periodical publications. The General Administration of Press and Publication of the People's Republic of China (GAPP) is the government agency for policy and management of periodical publishing. It manages the publishing industry through its regular working conferences and documents. It issued the "Periodical Registration Ephemeral Procedures" in 1952. Since 1978 GAPP has issued more than forty regulations for the management and the regulation of the periodical publishing industry and the popular periodical market. Between 1997 and 2003, GAPP issued several documents and policies. The "Periodical Market Regulation," issued in 2003, encourages the fair competition of periodical publishing; it is a policy for industrial operations and market competition in periodical publishing.

Since 2001 GAPP has sponsored periodical exhibitions and core periodical projects to encourage periodical publishing. The government's policies on periodicals with foreign investment and Chinese editions of internationally acclaimed periodicals have been developed and enhanced. Commercial periodical publishing is growing. However, the popular periodical industry in China is still at an early stage. Government censorship still has the most control over what can or cannot be published. Every year thousands of periodicals are ordered to close for various reasons, political and nonpolitical alike. Compared to other countries, the number of the periodicals per person is relatively low, with only 2.98 per person. Minority publications comprised less than 30 percent of the total number of periodicals published in 2005, and periodicals in minority languages other than Han language numbered fewer still.

In 2007 the Federation of International Periodical Press Congress will hold its 36th World Magazine Congress in Beijing. This event will certainly stimulate the popular press in China in a positive way.

HONG KONG

Hong Kong holds a special place in the Chinese popular press because of its status as a free port and world market. The earliest modern Chinese daily newspaper, *Chung Ngoi San Po (Zhong Wai xinwen* [Sino-Foreign News]), began in Hong Kong around 1860. For a time, Hong Kong's news press served as a model for Shanghai's news press before Shanghai became the base of modern Chinese journalism at the beginning of the twentieth century. During the Sino-Japanese War, when most of the land in China was under Japanese occupation and the Chinese periodical press was prohibited, many newspapers in Shanghai and other cities moved to Hong Kong. Two famous newspapers of the time, *Min Li Bao* [People Independent] and *Da Gong Bao* [Great Public], became influential news gazettes in Hong Kong after they moved from Shanghai in 1937. *Tiantian Ribao* [Every Day Newspaper] was the first newspaper that took advantage of color printing technology. On November 1, 1960, it published its first color issue and became the first color daily newspaper in the world.

Today, Hong Kong produces a variety of newspapers. The daily circulation of Hong Kong newspapers is as much as 16 million, within a population of 72 million, which means that one newspaper could be allotted to about every three people over the age of ten. There are independent newspapers and newspapers published by parties from both sides of the Taiwan Strait. The majority of magazines published in Hong Kong are consumer periodicals. TV weeklies and entertainment weeklies are the most circulated magazines, among which the *Ming Bao Weekly* and *Hong Kong TV* are the two most circulated ones.

Several print media companies have emerged recently, with products that cross national and geographic boundaries. Noteworthy examples include Next Media and its *Apple Daily* and *Next Magazine*, which are leading newspapers and weekly magazines in both Hong Kong and Taiwan. The leading women's magazine in Hong Kong, *Jessica Hong Kong*, is the brand magazine of Jessica Publications Group. The magazine's average circulation was 76,647 copies per issue in 2004.[14] Jessica Publications Group was established in 2000 as a magazine publisher. Its targeted audience is career or urban women. This is also the aim of its other publications, including *Jessica Code*, a monthly fashion and beauty magazine that provides the most up-to-date trends in fashion and beauty; *Lisa Tastes*, a biweekly family magazine; and *Jessica's Complete Women's Handbook*, a four-in-one weekly magazine with topics from women's life styles through money management. All of these magazines are designed for an audience of affluent women.

TAIWAN

Compared to the mainland China, the number of periodicals per 10,000 persons in Taiwan is much higher, with 6,500 periodicals published for a population of 23 million. Popular periodicals account for 600 to 1,000 of these publications, with gross profits of HK$6 billion a year.[15] About one-third of the revenue of the periodical industry comes from advertising. In 2004 the registered Taiwanese newspapers had increased from 31 in 1988 to more than 700, and the regularly published newspapers numbered more than 50.[16] Among them, *Freedom Times*, *China Times*, and the *United Daily News* are the three major newspaper groups. In addition to these aggregated newspapers, there are also specialized newspapers on business, theater, technology and sports. The rising star of the news press is *Apple Daily*, a Hong Kong–based newspaper. Its Taiwanese edition was inaugurated on May 2, 2003. In order to attract readers, the paper is geared to social problems and scandals. Its marketing strategies include a promotional selling price of NT$5 per copy, all-year-round publishing, and a reader hot line for muckraking that is open 24 hours a day, seven days a week. The age group 12 to 39 forms the main body of its readership.[17] Between July and December 2005, its daily sales reached an average of 527,609 copies, and it has become the most circulated newspaper in Taiwan.[18] In spite of the success of the *Apple Daily*, Taiwan's newspaper market is declining in competition with other media, such as TV and the Internet. In recent years, the readership of newspapers has decreased from 76 percent to 48 percent.[19]

In 2004 monthly Taiwan magazines had the largest circulations. Among the top twenty monthlies, women's fashion magazines swept the top six. These six titles are a combination of indigenous Taiwan titles, such as *Sugar* and *Meirenzhi* [Beauty], and imported titles such as *ELLEgirl*. According to the *Yearbook*, Taiwan's magazines cover a wide rage of interests, but categories of business and economic, fashion, as well as recreation and entertainment, are still the most popular. Many publishers also avidly publish digital versions of newspapers and magazines to increase their readership and circulation.

Taiwan's open policy for periodical publishing encourages fair competition and creates a diverse market. Many famous international periodicals have established their Chinese editions in Taiwan: *Vogue*, *Bazaar*, *ELLE*, and *Marie Claire*, as along with *Non No* from Japan, are just a few of the numerous fashion magazines that are imported regularly. Taiwan's periodical publishing is also dynamic. Every year there are new periodicals created and old periodicals ceasing publication in response to trends in the periodical press and public interest.

The government's media press policy was not always so favorable to the free press in Taiwan. During the Japanese occupation (1895–1945), no Chinese newspapers were allowed to publish, and only Japanese publications were permitted. After 1945 Taiwan was free from Japanese rule, so the periodical press began to grow. But although free from one type of censorship, the periodical press was still restricted under another: from 1950 to1988, the periodical press in Taiwan suffered a long period of censorship.

After the Republic of China government moved to Taiwan, it issued many regulations to secure control over the periodical press. In 1949 it issued the "News and Periodical Capital Restriction Act" and several other regulations in the following two or three years to restrict the use of newspapers. The government restricted the development of new papers; it also regulated the number of pages an existing paper could have. In 1950 the government issued a "Press Administrative Act during the Martial Law Enforcement," which started its 36-year control over the periodical press. This act eliminated any freedom to publish antigovernment opinions and news. Newspapers and magazines were obligated to send three copies to the Security Headquarters for scrutiny. In 1951 Taiwan's government issued an order to restrict the registration procedure for new periodicals. Under these restrictions and government control, the periodical press in Taiwan ceased to grow, and for a very long time, there were only thirty one newspapers published in the country.

In 1988 Taiwan lifted the ban on new periodical registration; the periodical press began to grow rapidly, along with rapid economic development. In 2004 the number of newspapers had increased to 2,524. The yearly circulation was 45 million, and advertising expenditure reached NT$150 billion.[20] The periodical press in Taiwan also established several highly functional organizations to self-regulate and coordinate among their members. Currently, the Taipei Magazine Association has 300 members, and a total of 400 magazine titles. It accounts for 80 percent of the consumer periodical market. Taiwan now has the second largest popular periodical market in Asia, its numbers surpassed only by Japan.

JAPAN

The Japanese popular press has enjoyed much more freedom and a steadier development over time than have those of some other Asian countries/regions. Despite temporary interruptions during wartime and occupation, the Japanese press has grown into a remarkably large enterprise. Japan has been one of most productive countries for periodical publishing. In 2004 there were 4,529 magazine titles, with sales as high as ¥1,965,183,040,000 and annual sales of 4.4 billion copies. That equals an average of twenty to thirty copies per person, ten times the average of two copies per person in China.[21]

Periodical publishing in Japan had enjoyed steady development until very recently. Many popular magazines have had a long life span. Some of the top magazines have been running since the end of the nineteenth century. In 2006 *Shincho*, a leading literary monthly, celebrated its 100-year anniversary. There are several popular women's magazines that have also enjoyed a long life span. For example, *Shufu no Tomo* [Companion of Housewives] was created in 1903 as *Katei no Tomo* [Companion of Family] and changed to its current name in 1917. It is still running strongly, with 291,519 copies sold in 2004.[22] *Shukan Josei* [Weekly Women], which started in 1956, and *Josei Jishin* [Women Themselves], launched in the following year, are two leading women's magazines today. Most of the frontrunner weeklies of the nineteenth century, such as *Shukan Asahi* (1922), *Sundy Mainishi* (1922), *Shukan Shincho* (1956), *Shukan Bunshun* (1959), and *Shukan Geidai* (1959) are still going strong, although overall weekly magazine sales decreased slightly in 2004. *Shukan Bunshun* topped the list with sales totaling 581,433 copies between January and June in 2005.[23]

The stability and productivity of the periodical press in Japan benefited from a prospering economy, high technology, and free market infrastructure. More importantly, this stability has come from a sophisticated industrial structure and mature reading public. Originally, magazines were published by major national papers. With a large, established newspaper-reading audience, it was an effective way to guarantee sales circulation. Before 1956 the periodicals, mostly weeklies that focused on news, were generally created by newspaper companies. For example *Weekly Asahi* is published by Asahi Newspaper as its Sunday edition. *Sunday Mainichi* is published by Mainichi Newspaper Company, with a similar idea of expanding daily newspapers to meet public demand for news and socially relevant information. Their main focus is national and international news reporting, rather than opinion. The publishing houses that issue weekly magazines, on the contrary, intend to be subjective and cynical. The first publishing-house-issued weekly magazine was *Shukan Shincho*, published by Shincho Publishing in 1956. Japanese publishing houses produce both monographic and periodical publications, and form their specialties and strength in periodical publications. For example, Shogakukan, as a leading company for comic periodicals, has several leading comic periodicals for youth and adults. Its comic periodical for young women, *Chao*, had a circulation of 1.0 million copies in 2004.[24] Not only popular in the domestic market, it also has opened overseas markets in the United States and other countries.

> ## COMIC, OR MANGA, MAGAZINES
>
> Comic magazines are customized to meet the tastes of different reader groups, usually organized by age or gender. Children's comics, such as *Monthly Shonen Gangan* and *Kokokmikku* by Shogakusha, and *Shukan Shonen Jampu* by Shuinsha, were well accepted in 2004. Two of the most popular adult comic magazines were *Biggu Komiku* [Big Comic] and *Big Comic Original*, by Shogakukan. Comic magazines are usually several hundred pages long. These magazines may have several concurrent running stories, with installments of twenty to forty pages for each series.

Publishing weekly magazines became a part of brand-making for publishing houses. Before the *Weekly Shincho*'s inauguration, Shincho publishing company had already been publishing two literary magazines. The earliest one, *Shincho*, had been established in 1906; it is the oldest, and still one of the leading literary magazines in Japan. *Shosatsu Shincho*, a literary magazine of "intermediate novels," was added in 1945. These were combined with the company's other periodicals to form the brand known as *Shincho* periodicals. The other large publishing houses, such as Shogakukan, Heibansha, and Bungei Shunju, all have their brand series of magazines. These brand products cover a range of different audiences, cater to the various interests of the reading public, and also bring the benefit of promoting the company's various products.

Publishing houses have played an important role in promoting the idea of proletarian media in Japan. Heibansha was a leading publishing company that claimed periodical publishing for the proletariat, including women and young readers. It inaugurated a proletarian magazine, *King* (1925–57), as the flagship product that would promote the idea of popular magazines for the general public. *King* created a sensational phenomenon when it was issued and quickly gained in popularity. Its first issue sold 740,000 copies. This was the largest first issue sale, making it the most popular magazine of the time. The editorial policy of publishing for the public regardless of age, gender, or class was the reason *King* was such a popular magazine. *King* ceased only when entertainment became more individualized, with the introduction of radio and TV as alternative leisure activities, and when public interests became more diverse. These changes called for more specialized periodical publication.

Another special type of magazine in Japan that has enjoyed wide popularity is the comic book, or *manga*, as it is known in Japan. All three major publishing houses, Kodansha, Shogakukan, and Shueisha, publish comic periodicals. Manga magazines made up 39 percent of sales value for magazines in 2004, with a total sale value of ¥504.7 billion.[25] The core manga periodicals include thirteen weekly magazines and ten biweekly magazines, plus approximately twenty influential monthly magazines. At least ten of these magazines can easily boast sales over 1 million copies per issue.[26]

PERIODICALS

When manga stories prove to be popular, they are bound into books or made into animé or TV series. The mixed-media strategy becomes an effective way to stimulate sales and increase popularity. A recent successful example is *Nana*. It expanded its readership by publishing an accompanying CD movie, *Hagane no Renkin-jutsu-shi* [Full Metal Alchemist]; later, it was made into a TV cartoon series.

Manga is not only the most popular genre in Japan, but it has also become "a focus of international interest."[27] It first gained popularity among East Asian countries and regions, such as South Korea, Hong Kong, Taiwan, and China in the early 1970s, and then in Indonesia, Thailand, and other East and Southeast Asian countries. It became very popular in Europe, especially in Italy and France. As early as the mid-1990s, some U.S. comics had already begun to show manga influences, both in drawings of the characters and in the layout on panels. The first English manga magazine, *Shonen Jump* [Boy Jump], was published in the United States by VIZ, a California-based company, in 2002. The initial issue sold 250,000 copies.[28] The manga effect is phenomenal and beyond the genre itself. The reasons for the popularity of manga are many. One may say manga is "something for everyone," or "a window on Japan";[29] most of all, though, it is because of "its unknown potential to evolve into a conglomerate for TV programs, videos, and films, game software and characters for toys and other merchandise for the children's and young adult segments."[30]

KOREA

The growth of the popular periodical press in Korea has been bumpy since the first modern newspaper, *Hansong Sunbo*, was published by the Government Printing Office (Pangmun-guk) in October 1883. From 1904 to 1945, when Korea was under the control of Japan, the Japanese governor general in Korea employed various measures to eliminate Korea's news press and shut down all the nationalist newspapers. After South Korea gained independence in 1948, the periodical press was governed by the registration system. Newspapers and other periodicals mushroomed. But this temporary boom only resulted in more censorship. In 1972 the Park Chung-hee government exercised prepublication censorship. The South Korean periodical press experienced a so-called dark age, which lasted until 1979. In 1987 Roh Tae-woo, a presidential candidate, issued a declaration for democratization of Korea, including the guarantee of press freedom. In 1988 the Seoul Olympics drew thousands of journalists to South Korea. With the relaxation of government censorship, the South Korean press began a new era of free publication. While mass communication in North Korea is still under rigid authoritarian control, the South Korean media, including the periodical press, began to benefit from a greater freedom of expression.

In the last five years, the total of periodicals published in South Korea numbered more than 6,000. In 2004 the total number of periodicals reached 6,938 titles.[31] According to ACNielsen research, 55.93 percent of South Koreans read newspapers. There are twenty-four central newspapers and twenty-two local newspapers. The central newspapers are further classified as general dailies, economic newspapers, sports dailies, and foreign language newspapers.[32] Periodicals are divided by frequency of publication: weekly, every ten days, every 15 days, quarterly, biannually, and annually. In recent years, riding with the "Korean Wave," popular periodical publishing has roared.

However, the shadow of the past still affects the periodical press today. The press may no longer be censored, but periodicals are still considered something to regulate, rather than to encourage, by the South Korean authorities.[33] In this respect, government policy has not been favorable in supporting the periodical industry as it faces the challenges and difficulties in the decline of advertising revenue. The readership of South Korean magazines decreased from 28 percent in 1990 to 20 percent in 1998, and the situation worsened in 2005. Currently, almost one-third of the magazines registered with the Ministry of Culture and Tourism, about 1,034 titles, among them some long-standing magazines, are closed or suspended.

One of the reasons for the decrease in magazine readership may lie in the convention of the usefulness of the magazines. Magazines are viewed as "socially intellectual and well-cultivated products," and the idea of magazines as "commercial and fun" is not well received.[34] This is also reflected in the development of the digital press. Thus, professional or academic journals have grown faster than popular periodicals that are purely for leisure and entertainment.

Another factor that may contribute to the limitation of the periodical market in South Korea is the distribution system. About 40 percent of sales are by subscription through the mail, 15 percent at bookstores, 3.3 percent at street stands, and 3.6 percent by home visits. The rising postal cost has been a big contributor to the decline in readership. Online bookstores and magazine subscriptions may help to stimulate more readerships, but the key will still be a government policy to support periodical publishing in general. The South Korean periodical industry needs to expand commercially generated revenue from advertising in both digital and print periodical publications.

OCEANIA: AUSTRALIA AND NEW ZEALAND

Australia

Compared to a circulation of 6.86 million for *Readers* in China, the 615,139 copies of the most circulated magazine in Australia, the *Australian Women's Weekly*, would not count for much if the success of popular magazines were measured only by the total number of copies in circulation. In spite of the limited population of 19 million, Australians are among the top spenders on periodical reading, with an estimated $1,356 billion spent on magazines in 2000. In 2005, more than 226 million copies of magazines were sold, which means that, per capita, Australians 14 years and over buy an average of 13.6 magazines per year.[35]

Among the types of magazines, women's magazines dominate the market with a 56.5 percent share of gross annual copies sold in 2004–05. There are a total of twelve ABC (Audit Bureau of Circulations)-audited women magazines, nine fashion and lifestyle titles and four health/parenting titles, amounting to one-fourth of the total audited titles, but only 62.2 percent of the market share. The second largest categories are men's interests and life style, current affairs and business, home and garden, food, entertaining, and fashion.[36]

Although a majority of popularly acclaimed magazines in Australia are imported ones, including international titles such as *Reader's Digest*, *Better Homes & Gardens*, and *Cosmopolitan*, some of Australia's own, long-standing publications are also top sellers. The *Australia Women's Weekly* and the *Bulletin* are two noteworthy examples. The *Australia Women's Weekly*, commonly known as the *Weekly*, is a monthly magazine, which started as a weekly in 1933 and retained *Weekly* in its title when it changed to monthly publication in 1983. The magazine was designed for middle-class women, with a laid-back style in dealing with social changes. Its emphasis on leisure interests and domesticity and its well-known recipes have "influenced almost every Australian family at some stage of their lives."[37] It is no surprise that the *Weekly* topped the list of top 100 magazines in circulation in Australia in 2005.

The *Bulletin* is certainly among the most celebrated and famous Australian publications, and it is the longest-running magazine in the history of Australian periodical publishing. Established in 1880, its policy was to foster and encourage Australian writers and artists. The 1890s were the golden years of the *Bulletin*. Because of its success in promoting national writers, "the influence of *The Bulletin* was such that this era of the legendary nineties [1890s] is regarded as the source of our national culture."[38] The present status of the magazine has changed; it is no longer as influential as it was 100 years ago, but its policy of focusing on the Australian scene and current affairs has remained unchanged.

In 1998, the Magazine Publishers of Australia launched the Magazine of the Year Awards to celebrate achievement and excellence in the editorial and publishing professions. The awards include "General Excellence" in categories of General Interest and News, Home & Food, Lifestyle, and Special Interests. It also recognizes the Magazine of the Year, Editor of the Year, Story of the Year, Columnist of the Year, and Feature Writer of the Year. The event is held in August each year and continually generates the reading public's interests and passions.

New Zealand

The periodical press of New Zealand shares a great number of similarities with that of Australia. First of all, New Zealanders are as avid as Australians in consuming periodicals. It has been estimated that they annually spend an excess of $270 million on magazines. New Zealanders consume well in excess of 2 million magazines a week; of those, 1.3 million copies are weekly magazines and business weekly newspapers.[39] Similar to Australia, the New Zealand popular press also has an annual awards event. The annual awards have similar categories for editorial and journalistic achievements.

New Zealand shares its periodical market with Australia publications, as well. The periodical market is a mix of internationally acclaimed titles, popular Australian titles, and New Zealand's own publications. The women's magazines in the top-ten list in 2005 demonstrate the composition of the shared magazine market: the *NZ Woman's Weekly* (first place) is published by New Zealand Magazines, but *Woman's Day* (the fourth), *Australia Women's Weekly* (the sixth), and *New Idea* (the ninth) are Australia's top three magazines. The influence of Australia's periodical press on the New Zealand market is well illustrated here.

Overshadowed by overseas publications, especially by Australia's periodical publishing, many of New Zealand's periodicals have lacked originality since the early days. This was one of the reasons their pioneer newspapers and magazines often have had very short life spans. Many of the early newspapers were local and are now hard to find. In recent years, with the internationalization of periodical publishing, there are some new and successful general interest magazines, such as *Metro* and *North and South*. The *New Zealand Herald* has been New Zealand's number one daily newspaper for many years. Its average circulation amounts to more than half a million a day.

Some action has been taken to preserve the older newspapers. The National Library of New Zealand has launched its "Papers Past" project. Including New Zealand's earliest newspaper, *The New Zealand Spectator*, there are a total of forty-one nineteenth-century New Zealand newspapers and periodicals, and an estimated 250,000 digitized pages. The project Website provides public access to this collection of important cultural and historical value. As the project continues, the number of titles and the size of the database will increase.

SOUTH AND SOUTHEAST ASIA

ALOKE THAKORE

INTRODUCTION

Southeast and South Asia are home to slightly more than 2 billion people, who use more than 1,500 different languages on a daily basis. The political regimes in the countries of these two regions range from military dictatorships and theocratic states to monarchies and multiparty democracies. No generalizations can be made, therefore, with fairness or ease about the variety of periodicals and the conditions under which they are published. What unifies this part of the world, however, is a shared history of printing and print culture, and the development of the modern press. Printing technology and journalism (in the modern sense of the term) arrived in Asia with European missionaries and colonizers. The first presses were set up by the Portuguese in India (who were in Goa as early as 1510), the Spanish in the Philippines, the Dutch in Indonesia, the French in Vietnam, and the British in Malaysia. Even in Thailand, the one country that did not fall to European colonizers, it was an American missionary who started a press.

For Christian missionaries, the press was primarily an instrument for spreading their religion. The printing press that landed in Goa (west India) on September 6, 1556, was used by Portuguese Jesuits to print the *Conclusões e outras coisas* and the *Doutrina Christā*. In the Philippines, Spanish friars printed the *Doctrina Cristiana* in 1592. Between the seventeenth and nineteenth centuries, Christian scriptures and tracts were translated and published extensively in local Asian languages, and churches also started periodicals for their communities. For European colonial administrations, the press was also a potential instrument of control and power. What they did not anticipate, however, was how quickly their fellow Europeans (followed by their Asian subjects) would start using the press in the colonies as it was used back home—to challenge authority.

The credit for starting the first newspaper in the Indian subcontinent goes to the Irishman James Augustus Hicky. He launched the *Bengal Gazette* in Calcutta (now Kolkata) on January 29, 1780, as a "weekly political and commercial paper open to all parties, but influenced by none," designed to expose the corruption of officials and practices in the British East India Company, which subsequently led to a major investigation by English parliament. In the Philippines the Spanish governor general started the *Del Superior Gobierno* in 1811, but the authorities in Spain may have shut it down shortly afterward because it was inadequately vetted. In the course of the nineteenth century, printing technology become widely available across Asia, and once Asian entrepreneurs began to invest in it, print culture became unstoppable in the colonies. Newspapers (largely weekly, occasionally daily) and magazines (monthly and bimonthly) became widespread by the turn of the twentieth century.

The second phase in the development of the press in South and Southeast Asia coincided with the protracted struggle for independence in the European colonies, during which nationalists used the press to garner political support for their anticolonial causes. Nationalist movements appeared at different times in different countries and took different forms, but they adopted a common strategy: they sought to mobilize large groups of colonized people, to help them reclaim their identities and cultures, and to reach them in their own languages (rather than the languages of their colonizers). Numerous nineteenth- and twentieth-century nationalist periodicals with political, social, and cultural themes were published in indigenous languages; some used existing Asian scripts, cast in metal type in European and Indian foundries, while others adopted the Roman script.

The emergence of nationalist discourse in various parts of South and Southeast Asia had two significant consequences. One was that European colonial administrations responded by creating harsh laws to control the vernacular press, and by implementing a variety of obstructive and repressive measures: for example, licensing for publication, prohibitions against or restrictions on the ownership of printing technology, heavy duties and tariffs on printing paper, restrictions on imports, and aggressive censorship of books and periodicals. (An extreme instance of the effects of censorship was the unusual decision by the *Amrita Bazaar Patrika*, the most popular Calcutta daily, to change its language of publication overnight from Bengali to English, in order to circumvent draconian British-colonial legislation designed to smother nationalist Indian-language publications.) The other consequence was that, in the long run, the growth of the periodical press and journalism in various Asian languages led their users (often belonging to distinct ethnic groups) to demand separate nationhood for their communities, or greater constitutional protections and rights for themselves. Such linguistic nationalism was vital in the cases of Urdu in Pakistan, Bengali in Bangladesh, tribal languages such as Karen and Kachen in Myanmar, Chinese in Singapore, and Tamil in Sri Lanka. The pivotal role of such languages in mass political movements in colonial as well as postcolonial times has also resulted in the growth of newspapers and magazines published for specific communities, and in the greater diversity of languages and media in any given nation-state.

Decolonization in South and Southeast Asia began in the late 1940s and continued into the 1980s. For most of the nations formed in this period and later, political independence brought the promise of a great new freedom to publish and print any type of material in any form. Most of the emergent nation-states, however, retained versions of their colonial press and censorship laws and institutions, and significant differences began to appear among them soon enough. Some countries opted to become multiparty democracies, which engendered a free and vigorous post-independence press; despite some abuse of constitutional provisions, India remains a good example of this type. Pakistan began as a democracy but came under successive military dictatorships after the mid-1950s, all of which prosecuted certain kinds of oppositional publications aggressively. Nepal, a monarchy with a parliamentary system, has largely had a government-controlled press. Sri Lanka had an early experience of large-scale ethnic and political discord that was compounded by several governments willing to restrain the press, which has resulted in the state taking over the largest publishing house in the long term.

Myanmar (Burma), which had a brief period of democracy followed by military rule, has had a deeply repressive state-controlled press until recently. Indonesia started with complete freedom for the press, but military coups resulted in the press being controlled rather strongly under two successive regimes that lasted from the mid-1950s to the early 1990s. Malaysia and Singapore emerged as democracies but were dominated by single political parties, which either ideologically compromised the press or subjected it to government ownership and control. The situations of Vietnam, Laos, and Cambodia proved to be very different: the extended Vietnam War, with its cascading impact across the region, made the very presence of the press a largely precarious one. Thailand became a constitutional monarchy, but it suffered numerous coup attempts in the twentieth century, and whether the press has been free or restrained at any given time has depended on the politics of the moment.

It needs to be noted that newspapers and periodicals can only flourish under conditions that make it economically viable to print them. In the case of an advertising-supported model, there should be enough economic activity in the country to provide for advertisements, or the government has to support the media with advertisements. In the case of a subscription-supported model, the presence of either a paying public or an organization or institution that underwrites the cost is imperative. In South and Southeast Asian countries with functioning democracies and basic economic freedoms (such as India), an advertising-supported model came into existence after independence. Even in these countries, however, the governments often emerged as the largest advertisers and thus came to exercise considerable influence on the press. In countries with limited freedoms or single-party rule, the government has been the primary or only publisher of newspapers and magazines, and thus uses them to promote its views (as in Vietnam). In some democratic nations dominated by a single political party (such as Singapore), a distinction has emerged between political news and nonpolitical news, and the former has come to be controlled while the latter was left free.

Control of the supply of printing paper has also proven to be a key factor in the freedom of the press. For much of the second half of the twentieth century, most Asian countries have had to import newsprint from the West, and their governments have often placed complex restrictions on the purchase and use of newsprint. This has been an effective means of checking political dissent and criticism even in the most open countries. Moreover, at the national policy level as well as in common political discourse, most former colonies in South and Southeast Asia have retained a general suspicion of and resistance to the European and Western press. As a result, since independence, many of them have not allowed the reprinting of foreign publications on their shores, some have curbed the distribution of Western periodicals, and others have simply forbidden the entry of European and American periodicals into their territories.

Under globalization, the last decade of the twentieth century and the beginning of the twenty-first century witnessed economic liberalization and the removal of import restrictions in many parts of Asia, bringing in foreign media, regime changes from single-party rule to multiparty democracy, and free market enterprise even under authoritarian systems. Three broad patterns, largely in keeping with their earlier trajectory, are still visible in the environments in which periodicals are published, and they determine the content, printing quality, distribution, and reception of newspapers and magazines. The patterns in question may be called "periodical friendly," "periodical neutral," and "periodical hostile." These are not watertight boxes into which different countries may be placed; rather, they are different points on a continuum on which various Asian countries find themselves placed today. Particular countries may move from one point of the spectrum to another because of a change of regime or new legislation, for example, thus transforming a periodical-hostile environment into a periodical-friendly one in a matter of months.

India stands at one end of this spectrum, with an enduringly periodical-friendly environment. There is constitutional protection for the press; newspapers and magazines are free to publish almost anything, within reason. The constitution does contain provisions for checking free speech under special circumstances, but they have been invoked rarely. Source privilege and strong defense of individuals' views as political speech prevails. Neighboring Myanmar stands at the opposite end of the spectrum, where the military junta controls the press rigorously, and nothing can be published that sits even marginally ill with the rulers. Possession of printed material deemed to be against the government is treason. Vietnam occupies a similar position: it has opened its economy to international companies under its *doi moi* policy, which has resulted in a plethora of new publications in the country, but the Communist Party's control of the press is complete. Brunei, Bhutan, and the Maldives also fall in the same category, although each of these countries publishes only a handful of periodicals.

Indonesia, the Philippines, and Thailand are closer to the Indian end of the spectrum. There has been a media explosion in Indonesia since the fall of the Suharto regime; the post-Marcos Philippine media have also experienced new freedom and expansion; and Thailand continues to have a largely open press, even though its *lèse-majesté* provisions to protect the monarchy cause problems. In each of these three Southeast Asian countries, however, the press is in the hands of a few big companies that are directly or obliquely aligned with particular political parties. Pakistan, Bangladesh, and Sri Lanka can be grouped together as countries that come next in the degree of freedom enjoyed by the press. In Bangladesh and Sri Lanka, the government or important political groups have a stake in the running of some newspapers. In Pakistan the freedom of the press is at the whim of the rulers, but sometimes a military regime may be more tolerant than a democratic government. In these three South Asian countries, however, the violence used by political groups outside the government can have as chilling an effect on press freedom as that of state institutions.

In another variation along the spectrum, both Singapore and Malaysia have a free press, but they have to operate within the limits of what the state construes to be good for the nation. In Singapore the press is state controlled, while in Malaysia the ruling coalition has a financial stake in the largest newspapers. But in both these countries, while news remains under the watchful eye of the government, non-news publications are largely free, which has encouraged a flourishing magazine industry with popular titles pertaining to topics such as sports and entertainment. Nepal, caught between violent insurgents and an authoritarian monarchy, shifts between a relatively free press working in a hostile environment and a stifled press, in which journalists are subject to summary arrest at the king's will. The experience of the press in Laos, Cambodia, and East Timor has been quite uneven in the short time since the return of peace to their respective lands; it is too early to say how the press will develop there, but all three nations have seen an increase in the number of publications since the end of the violence and strife.

Anyone making a voyage from Pakistan to the Philippines will discover a wide array of periodicals. The staid broadsheet and the shocking tabloid (in content, but not in size), the compacted broadsheet and the afternoon tabloid (in shape, but not in content), scholarly journals with low circulation and news magazines with high circulation, the de rigueur fashion and life style magazines, sensational crime magazines and conservative educational periodicals, sports magazines and literary magazines, community publications and local adaptations of international publications, and even widely circulated comics and party propaganda publications—all jostle for space on the news stands, fight for the attention of the readers, root for the patronage of the advertisers, and sometimes cringe for the approval of the political masters. From the latest technology to primitive methods of printing, from newspapers that sell upward of 10 million to those that have a three-digit circulation, from presses that use satellite technology to print multiple editions to those that rely on antiquated methods, from periodicals delivered to a wide subscriber base to those exclusively meant for a select clientele, from readers vigorously reading and discussing in underground metros and parks to families reading with an eye on the door, Southeast and South Asia has all possible variations in periodical content, publishing, advertising, distribution, and reception.

South Asia

Pakistan

Pakistan has a population of about 161 million and a literacy rate of approximately 49 percent. The chief languages are Punjabi, Sindhi, Siraki, Pashto, Balochi, Hindko, Brahui, Burushaski, Urdu, and English. When the Indian subcontinent was partitioned in 1947, the part that then became West Pakistan (and is now Pakistan) had four regional newspapers: *Pakistan Times*, *Zamindar*, *Nawa-e-waqt*, and *Civil & Military Gazette*. During partition, *Dawn*, *Morning News*, *Jang*, and *Anjam* also moved to Pakistan from locations now in India, rapidly expanding the periodical press in the new nation. Pakistan has seen several military dictatorships, interspersed with several short-lived, democratically elected governments; as a result, its press has oscillated between considerable freedom and severe restraints. Under globalization various Pakistani governments have relaxed a number of restrictions on the press since about 1990, but the environment for periodicals remains volatile. Besides continuous pressure from the military (whether in power or not), journalists and publishers have to negotiate constantly with violent political groups outside government, including fundamentalist religious organizations, terrorist groups, and regional separatist and opposition parties. Despite its difficult environment, however, the Pakistani press has consistently been at the forefront of criticizing the government.

Today, the press in Pakistan is largely an Urdu press with *Jang* (850,000) and *Nawa-e-waqt* (500,000) as the dailies with the largest circulations. *Dawn* (109,000), *Nation*, and *News International* (120,000) are the three leading English dailies. The state has controlled the press through the National Press Trust in the past; now three publishing groups dominate periodical publication. The Jang Group publishes *Jang*, *Akhbar-e-Jahan* (Urdu weekly), *News* (English morning paper), *Daily News* (English eveninger), and *Awam*; the Herald group publishes *Dawn*, *Star* (eveninger), and *Herald* (monthly magazine); and the Nawa-e-waqt organization publishes *Nawa-e-waqt*, *Nation*, and *Family* (Urdu weekly). The Jamaat-e-Islami, a political party, publishes its own Urdu newspaper, *Jasarat*. On the whole, Pakistan currently publishes a total of 303 dailies and 247 nondailies, which include a wealth of magazines and periodicals devoted to religion, sports, music, and the arts, as well as to various social, cultural, and historical issues—a range that is far greater and more open than in many other Islamic nations.

India

Statistically speaking, India is home to almost half the population of South and Southeast Asia combined, and more than one-third the total land area of the two regions. It has 22 major languages protected by its constitution, and nearly 3,000 distinct speech varieties used on a daily basis by a population of approximately 1.1 billion (with a literacy rate of almost 60 percent). Of the 60,413 registered newspapers and more than 7,000 registered periodicals, over 7,000 newspapers and 5,315 periodicals are published in 122 languages. The most important and widespread languages in which periodicals are published include Assamese, Bengali, English, Gujarati, Hindi, Kannada, Konkani, Malayalam, Manipuri, Marathi, Nepali, Oriya, Punjabi, Sanskrit, Sindhi, Tamil, Telugu, and Urdu. Hindi (67.04 million), English (27.29 million), Gujarati (8.35 million), Urdu (8.11 million), Malayalam (7.69 million), Marathi (7.08 million), Bengali (6.52 million), Tamil (5.17 million), Telugu (4.64 million), Oriya (4.60 million), Kannada (2.75 million) and Punjabi (2.66 million) have total periodical circulations in excess of 1 million each.

The story of this staggering array of periodicals in the country goes back to the colonial era when James Augustus Hicky's *Bengal Gazette* made its appearance in 1780. This four-page, 11.5 inch × 14 inch paper did not survive more than two years, but it inaugurated an industry that turned from cottage to organized over the decades, and learned to survive, grow, and flourish in the colonial era and after independence in 1947. It also survived a brief but sordid interregnum, in some cases gloriously and in others cravenly, when Prime Minister Indira

PERIODICALS IN INDIA: SOMETHING FOR EVERYONE

The size, diversity, and multilingual and cultural complexity of India's periodical press in the post-1990 period are best appreciated by looking at a sample of newspapers and magazines across genres, themes, periodicities, and readerships. Such a list would include the largest-circulating English daily in the world, the multi-edition *Times of India*; the largest single-edition English daily in the world, the *Hindustan Times*; the highest-circulating newspaper in India in any language, *Dainik Jagran*; the highest-circulating periodical, *Saras Salil*; the astrological monthly *Astrological Magazine*; the sports magazine *Sports Star*; the trust-owned and operated *Tribune*; the children's magazine, with multiple-language editions, *Chandamama*; the historically important *Kesari*; the satirical periodical *Tughlak*; the Communist Party newspaper, *Deshabhimani*; the nationalist organization Rashtriya Swayam Sevak Sangh's *Panchjanya*; the government-owned *Employment News*; the women's magazine *Griha Shobha*; the religious monthly *Kalyan*; the education-oriented monthly *Competition Refresher*; and the children's monthly *Wisdom*.

Gandhi imposed a state of emergency on the country from June 1975 to January 1977, in an effort to retain power illegitimately, and press freedom and civil liberties were smothered.

The Gujarati daily *Bombay Samachar*, which was first published in 1822, is the oldest newspaper in India, while *Divya Bhaskar*, another Gujarati newspaper that was started in 2003 with a first-day print run of over 350,000, may well claim to have had the biggest newspaper launch in the country. Straddling both *Bombay Samachar* and *Divya Bhaskar* is a story of newspaper and periodical growth that is varied and astonishing. The three features that are most noticeable about the contemporary Indian press are the explosion in circulation and the wide-ranging content of newspapers and periodicals in the era of globalization; the growth of large corporate houses that control more of the circulation pie, and have decided to reap the benefits that a liberalized economy has presented them; and the freedom with which the media operate.

While many of today's major newspapers were launched in the nineteenth century, their growth was largely subdued till the last decade of the twentieth century. While there were some attempts at starting multi-edition newspapers, with the Indian Express Group and the Times of India going to second-tier cities, the ability to increase circulation was hampered by a smaller reading public. The principal constraints until the 1980s were lower literacy levels, restricted advertising budgets in a socialist-style economy that was driven by a greater reliance on essential commodities that needed little or no advertising, and the generally low growth rate of the economy. The economic liberalization of the 1990s changed this scenario. Growth rates picked up, multinational companies were welcomed even in non-core sectors, and literacy levels had risen enough for a large reading public to come into being. Companies also had to seek more consumers away from the large metropolises of Mumbai (Bombay), Kolkata (Calcutta), Delhi, and Chennai (Madras). Newsprint, which had been strictly regulated since independence, could now be freely imported. In the short span of about 15 years since liberalization, fresh newspapers have been launched, and papers that had only one or two editions earlier have expanded into large chains of multicity newspapers. Remarkable examples of the latter phenomenon in a dozen or more languages include *Andhra Jyoti, Deccan Chronicle, Dainik Jagran, Dinamalar, Eenadu, New Indian Express, Times of India, Dainik Bhaskar, Rajasthan Patrika, Amar Ujala, Malayala Manorama, Mathrubhumi, Lok Mat, Sakal, Hindustan Times*, and *Vijaya Karnataka*. For magazines, the new environment has meant improving their distribution (especially so as to penetrate semi-urban areas), and even expanding their publication to other Indian languages (as in the cases of *India Today* and *Outlook*, both originally English, which added Hindi national editions).

What stands out in this enormous expansion since about 1990 is that the old media houses, which already had access to capital and infrastructure, were strongly positioned to seize the initiative. Some were only regional players, but in a market of India's size, a regional player can be much bigger than the entire press of several other countries combined. Virtually no new major companies emerged in the print business, while the existing companies used the capital market to gather weight and clout. In the race for more advertising revenue, there was a fresh democratization of newspaper content, which inevitably meant that serious, literary material was (distressingly to some) sidelined. Those who were interested in such material would have to seek it in specialized sources, and such fare would no longer be served on the daily platter that large-circulation or truly mass-market publications would offer.

The legal environment within which this newspaper and periodical outburst took place was as free as any that could be imagined. The Indian Constitution provides for reasonable restrictions on freedom of speech, but in only two cases are restrictions enforced: speech that may incite religious violence and pornography. Anything else is fair game, and no topic is really taboo. As a consequence, smaller periodicals often publish extreme views that may appeal only to a minority of readers. There is an active political press in India, in which political or quasi-political parties, which represent all positions on the political spectrum, publish periodicals with significant circulations. Journalists are free to express their views, but the Liebling dictum, that the freedom of the press belongs to those who own it, is as true in India as anywhere else.

Nepal

Nepal is a landlocked country of over 28 million people, with a literacy rate of approximately 45 percent. The main languages are Nepali, Maithili, Bhojpuri, Tharu, Tamang, Newari, Magar, Awadhi, and English. The history of the press goes back to the end of the nineteenth century: *Sudhasagar* was published in 1898, and the hereditary prime ministers who then ruled the kingdom established *Gorkhapatra* in 1901, which continues to be printed under state control today. The political uncertainties of the country in the late twentieth century have deeply affected the press. Nepal, a monarchy, reinvented itself as a multiparty democracy in 1990, but its record, at best, has been uneven. The royal family has repeatedly reasserted its traditional authority, and since 1996 a violent Maoist insurgency (modeled on the Shining Path in Peru from some years earlier) has disrupted civilian life all over the country.

Despite conditions of peril and uncertainty, the press has witnessed perceptible growth in Nepal in the 1990s, with the appearance of new newspapers and periodicals. *Gorkhapatra*, the state-owned paper, continues to have the highest circulation. A private company launched *Kantipur* in 1993; it now also publishes the *Kathmandu Post*. Other newspapers include the *Kathmandu Times* (English) and *Awaz* (Nepali). Among magazines, *Himal* appears in English; *Asmita* is a monthly devoted to women's issues; and *Saptahik Bimarsha* is a weekly devoted to news and analysis. The larger trend can be glimpsed in the fact that Nepal has 298 registered dailies, of which 89 are still being published; 1,442 registered biweeklies, of which 381 continue to be published; and 273 registered fortnightlies, of which 40 are still in circulation.

Bangladesh

Bangladesh has a population of just over 147 million and a literacy rate of about 43 percent. The majority language is Bengali; the other major language is English, but it is used only by a miniscule minority. Bangladesh appeared as an independent nation in 1971; between 1947 and 1971, it constituted East Pakistan; before partition in1947, it constituted East Bengal (see the General Introduction to South and Southeast Asia).

Kabita Kusumabati and *Dhaka Prakash* (both Bengali) were started in this region in 1860s. During partition, two newspapers, *Azad* and *News*, relocated their operations from Calcutta to Dhaka, and two important dailies, *Sangbad* (1950) and *Ittefaq* (1955), were launched soon after. The period from 1947 to 1971 was one of linguistic nationalism, with many newspapers supporting greater autonomy for Bengali-speaking East Pakistan and subsequently demanding independence from West Pakistan.

The periodical press grew rapidly after independence in 1971, but the state of emergency imposed in 1974 brought draconian laws and severe restrictions, many of which remained in effect until 1991. During this period, journalists could be arrested without bail; they could be handed five-year prison sentences for printing, publishing or distributing prejudicial reports; they were required to identify all sources of information; and the government could seize documents, ban publications, and search premises without warrants. Until recently, the state managed the dailies *Dainik Bangla* and *Bangladesh Times*, the weekly *Bichitra*, and the fortnightly *Anand Bichitra* through a trust.

Since 1991 conditions have broadly improved, with more than 200 dailies and 180 weeklies printed in Bengali, English, and other languages, and many Indian periodicals widely available in the country (especially from the neighboring Indian state of West Bengal). Two houses, the Ittefaq group and the Inquilab group, currently dominate the media scene, but the government is still able to influence the newspapers: it is the largest advertiser, and it also controls the distribution of newsprint. The principal Bengali dailies currently are *Ittefaq* (215,900), *Dainik Inquilab* (180,140), *Janakantha* (150,000), *Daily Manarzamil* (100,000), *Sangbad* (73,000), *Bhorer Kagoz* (70,000), *Daily Sangram* (50,980), *Jugantor*, and *Prothom Alo*. The main English newspapers are *Bangladesh Observer* (42,830), *Daily Star* (30,010), *Morning Sun* (18,125), *Daily Independence* (15,000), and *New Nation* (10,920). The most popular magazines are *Jay Jay Din*, *Mashik Madina*, *Purnima*, *Binodon Bichitra*, and *Anandadhara*.

Sri Lanka

Sri Lanka is an island nation with a population of more than 20 million, and a literacy rate of over 93 percent. Its main languages are Sinhala, Tamil, and English. The earliest newspaper published in Sri Lanka was the *Government Gazette* (1802), with the *Colombo Journal* (1832) as well as the *Observer and Commercial Advertiser* and *Ceylon Observer* (1834) appearing soon after. A number of Sinhala newspapers were launched in the 1860s, with *Lankaloka* (1860) and *Lakminapahana* (1862) among the more prominent. *Dinamina* (1909) continues to be in circulation.

Three media houses, all of which are based in Colombo and one of which belongs to the government, control the press in Sri Lanka. The Associated Newspapers of Ceylon Limited (also known as Lake House) was nationalized in 1973; it is aligned with whichever party is in power. Its stable includes *Dinamina* (Sinhala), *Sunday Silumina* (Sinhala), the *Daily News* (English), *Evening Observer* (English), *Sunday Observer* (English), and *Thinakaran* (Tamil). The Lake House newspapers enjoy the benefit of state advertising and have the biggest reach. Upali Newspapers Limited has *Divaina* (Sinhala), *Sunday Divaina* (Sinhala), *Island* (English), and *Sunday Island* (Sinhala) in its stable. Wijeya Newspapers Limited has *Lankadipa*, *Sunday Lankadipa*, *Daily Mirror*, and *Sunday Times*.

The civil war between the national government (which represents the Buddhist Sinhala majority of the population) and the rebel Tamil Tigers (who represent the Tamil-speaking immigrant Hindu minority), which has raged continually since 1983, has created a difficult situation for the press. The displayed and perceived partisanship of the Sri Lankan press poses a persistent problem. The Colombo-based periodicals, seen as representing Sinhala interests, are hardly read in the northern and eastern parts of the island, where the Tamils are largely located and where the local Tamil paper, *Uthayan* (20,000) has the highest circulation. The freedom of the press is precariously poised, since a host of legislation provides for multiple forms and levels of control. The Official Secrets Act, the Prevention of Terrorism Act, and various emergency provisions can be used to stifle or discourage accurate reporting. Moreover, the presence of the Sri Lankan army and the armed Tamil group has created a range of security problems for journalists covering the ethnic strife. The state's position vis-à-vis the press can be inferred from the fact that it seized 75 percent of Lake House shares in 1973, and then vested them in a trust charged with selling them to the public (to spread media ownership), but the government has taken no steps to make the sale so far. Every successive government has thus violated a provision of the law, thereby retained control of the largest newspaper house in the country.

SOUTHEAST ASIA

Myanmar

Myanmar (formerly Burma) has a population of over 42 million, with a literacy rate of approximately 85 percent. The great majority of the population is ethically Burmese, but there are significant pockets of other ethnic groups, including Karen, Karenni, Rakhine, Shan, Tavoyan, and Mon. While Burmese is the country's principal medium of communication, various minorities also use English and a range of ethnic languages. The earliest newspapers—*Morning Star* in Karen and *Moulmein Chronicle* in English—were published in 1836 in the town of Moulmein in the Tenasserim region. The Burmese paper *Moulmein Times* appeared soon after. *Myanmar Alin*, published simultaneously in four languages, was started in 1914.

Myanmar achieved independence from Great Britain in 1948. The period of freedom lasted till 1962, when a military junta came to power and abrogated all fundamental rights. This situation has continued into the present, except for a few months in 1988, when protests broke out against the regime, and briefly in 1990, when an election brought a pro-democracy government to power.

The state-controlled paper is *The New Light of Myanmar* (Burmese and English). Since 2003 the military dictatorship has permitted an Australian entrepreneur to publish the *Myanmar Times*, which has circulations of 200,000 in Burmese and 35,000 in English. The allowances made to this new daily are especially surprising, given that the Myanmar regime is among the most repressive in the world, prohibiting its citizens from even possessing material that it considers incendiary. This is an unfortunate chapter in the history of a country where, in 1874, King Mindon Min blessed a newspaper, *Ranabon Naypyidan*, by giving its editorial staff free access to the royal palace and permission to publish articles critical of him, his queens, and his officials whenever they were at fault.

Thailand

Thailand, which has a population of almost 65 million and a literacy rate of nearly 93 percent, is the only country in South or Southeast Asia that did not experience European colonization. Thai and English are the primary languages. A U.S. Protestant missionary started the first newspaper, *Bangkok Recorder*, in 1844; the first magazine, *Vajiravana*, was launched in 1884. The absolute power of the monarch was curtailed by a constitutional coup in 1932, and since then, the freedom of the press has been largely dependent on the prime minister, or the military dictator, who has held power. The constitution of 1997 promises protection of freedom of expression and of the media, but its provisions have yet to be implemented.

During the economic and financial crisis of 1997 in East Asia, the press in Thailand suffered a severe setback. Since several newspaper owners also had other business interests, the sharp drop in the economy meant either closing down newspapers or heavily slashing staffs, print runs, and budgets. The economy has rebounded subsequently, but the media industry is now stuck with proprietors that have distracting interests in politics or in other businesses, rather than with families whose primary commitments are to journalism. The ascendancy of politicians who have media connections especially means that they exercise greater control over journalists and publishers under the guise of promoting governance and economic development. The editors and publishers of periodicals have offset such patterns by forming a self-regulatory body called the Press Council of Thailand, and so far the major newspapers have accepted its decisions.

Thailand has over 1,200 periodicals, ranging from newspapers to magazines and tabloids. The English dailies with the largest circulations are *The Bangkok Post* (55,000) and the *Nation* (50,000), the latter founded by staffers of the former who wanted a Thai-owned English daily. The most prominent Thai dailies are *Thai Rath*, a crime and politics paper known for its aggressive tabloid-like journalism, with a weekday circulation of 850,000 and a weekend circulation of 1 million; the *Daily News*, with a weekday circulation of 750,000 and a weekend circulation of 900,000; the *Post Today* (100,000); and *Kom Chat Luek* and *Khao Sod*. Thailand's oldest Chinese daily is *Sing Sian Yit Pao*, and its 10,000 circulation caters to the Chinese minority. The country also has community newspapers in the provinces close to the borders in Songkhla, Chianngmaim, and Nakorn Ratchasima. Among the major magazines are *Siam Rath Subda Vijarn, Matichon Sud Subda, Phiyatkarna Rai Subda*, and *Nation Sud Subda*. A popular crime magazine named after Thailand's emergency telephone number is *191*, and its stories are even gorier than those of the *Thai Rath*.

Laos

Laos is a landlocked country of almost 6.5 million people, with a literacy rate of about 66 percent. The country, which has had an uninterrupted rule by the Communist Lao People's Revolutionary Party since 1975, uses three main languages: Lao, French, and English. For much of this period, the government has not allowed a nonofficial press to exist. The economy was opened in 1986, but the news and periodical media were not; privately owned media were allowed to enter the economy only in 2002. Even today, most of the fifty-six newspapers in the country are owned by the state. *Pasason* (3,000), *Vientiane Mai* (3,600), and *Pathet Lao* (3,000) are published in Lao; *Vientiane Times* (3,000) appears in English, and *KPL News* is half in English and half in French. The weekly tabloids, *Pasason Van Athit* (Lao), *Vientiane Social and Business* (Lao), and *Le Renovateur* (French), are associated with these newspapers. *Pasason* (1950), the oldest newspaper, was established during the anticolonial freedom movement and was known then as *Lao Haksat*. Four magazines owned by private companies currently are in circulation: *Update, Sao, Lao Culture*, and *Lao Trader*. A sports magazine that has a circulation of 1,500 was started in 1994. Most of these magazines are sustained by advertising.

Cambodia

Cambodia has a population of nearly 15 million and a literacy rate of almost 74 percent. The principal languages are Khmer (over 90 percent), Vietnamese, and Chinese. The press in the country has seen momentous changes recently: more than 183 newspapers and 38 magazines are currently in circulation, although most of them have very small readerships. Only in the first few years of the twenty-first century has Cambodia managed to recover from the aftermath of the Pol Pot regime, which took over in 1975 by overthrowing the monarchy that had gained independence from the French in 1953. The brutal Pol Pot regime rendered civil life nonexistent. After the regime capitulated, a 13-year civil war broke out among the Vietnamese, who had invaded Cambodia; surviving factions of the Khmer Rouge; and groups aligned with the old monarchy that the Khmer Rouge had replaced.

The growth of modern media began in the mid-1990s, after some normalcy had been restored. At present, the main Khmer newspapers are the *Rasmei Kampuchea* (20,000), *Koh Santepheap* (47,000), *Kampuchea Thmey* (20,000–30,000), *Chakraval* (8,000), and the opposition-owned *Voice of Khmer Youth* (3,000). The main English newspaper is *Phnom Penh Post* (3,000–5,000). The two bilingual papers, published in English and Khmer, are *Cambodia News* (7,000–10,000) and *Cambodia Daily* (3,600). *Cambodia Soir* (3,000) is published in French. *Bayon Pearnik*, *Indradevi*, and *The Popular Magazine* are three important magazines currently.

Vietnam

Vietnam has a population of nearly 84.5 million people, with a literacy rate of approximately 90 percent. The major languages in common use are Vietnamese, English, French, Chinese, and Khmer. Vietnam's first periodical was the *Bulletin de l'Expedition de la Cochinchina* (1861), in French; its first newspaper in Vietnamese was *Gia-Dinh bao* (1865). The changing political landscape of Vietnam in the twentieth century—first a French colony, then an independent nation, then a country divided between a communist north and a French- and American-backed south, and finally a unified Vietnam under the communists—has meant that diverse kinds of publications devoted to different political causes have dominated its history. Since the country was unified under communism between 1973 and 1975, it has only had a state-owned and state-sanctioned press.

In 1986 Vietnam adopted the doi moi policy, which has brought about a vast change in the media landscape. Removal of subsidies, greater reliance on advertising, and openness has resulted in tabloids with overtly sexual content; magazines focusing on lifestyle, fashion, and romance; and even periodicals devoted to satirical cartoons and sports. But the control rests with the Vietnam Communist Party's Ideology Department, which oversees all the media in conjunction with the Ministry of Culture and Information.

Nine national dailies, 108 weeklies, 45 local dailies, 144 local weeklies, and 333 magazines dot the periodical landscape. The major newspapers in Vietnamese are *Nhan Dhan* (180,000), *Quan Doi Nhan dan* (70,000), *Tin tuc* (50,000), *Hanoimoi* (50,000), *Sai Gin Giai phong* (100,000), *Lao dong* (100,000), *Tien Phong* (90,000), *Thanh nien* (150,000), and *Tuoi te* (280,000). The principal English dailies are *Viet Nam News* (10,000) and *Saigon Times* (14,000). The chief weeklies are *Thoi bao Kinh te Viet Nam* (30,000), *Tap chi cong san* (53,000), and *An ninh the gioi* (500,000). Other current weeklies include *Vietnam Economic News*, *Vietnam Investment Review*, *Vietnam Pictorial*, and *Heritage*. The only French daily is *Le Courier du Vietnam*, with a circulation of 4,000.

PERIODICALS

The Philippines

The Philippines is an archipelago; its population of nearly 89.5 million people, with a literacy rate of some 93 percent, uses more than eighty languages on a daily basis. The most important of these are English, Filipino, Tagalog, Cebuano, Ilocano, Hiligaynon, Bicol, Waray, Pampango, and Pangasinan. The press, however, is restricted to English and Filipino. The history of the press dates back to 1637, when the first newsletter, *Succesos Felices*, appeared in Spanish. The first Philippine paper, *Del Superior Gobierno* (1811), appeared almost two centuries later. But the press never came into its own under Spanish rule; rather, it developed only after the United States became the colonial power. The first Tagalog publication, *Ang Patnubay ng Catolico*, appeared in 1890; the two English dailies, *The Manila Times* (1898) and the *Manila Daily Bulletin* (1900), started publication at the turn of the century and continue into the present. The 1920s also witnessed a surge in women's magazines, which were products of women's clubs; among them were *Women's Outlook*, *Woman's World*, and *Woman's Home Journal*. When the country gained independence in 1946, the press became relatively free; however, when it came under military rule in 1972, the press was smothered. It was some 20 years before democracy and the freedom of the press were restored.

The country's principal English newspapers are *Manila Bulletin* (280,000), *Manila Times* (180,446), *Newspaper Malaya* (150,000), and *Philippine Daily Inquirer* (257,416). The Philippines also has more than 400 community newspapers, with an average circulation of 2,000; of these provincial publications, 30 are dailies, 292 are weeklies, and the rest have different periodicities.

Magazines have a vigorous presence in the country, with more than forty in circulation. Summit Media has sixteen titles, with a total print run of 700,000 copies; ABS-CBN has thirteen titles; and Mega has eight. Movie magazines such as *Gossip*, *Glitter*, *Kislap*, *Hot Copy*, *Rumors*, and *Moviestars* are popular. What sets the Philippines apart, however, is the huge readership for comic books that are published either weekly or twice a week. They are called *komics* and have an aggregate readership of about 16 million. With names like *Aliwan*, *Lovelife*, *Beloved*, *True Horror*, *True Ghost*, *Shocker*, and *Halimaw*, these komics mostly focus on stories of love, heroism, adventure, magic, and horror.

Since the resumption of democracy in the Philippines, the media environment has been free, and the unusual safeguards for the freedom of the press included in the country's constitution now seem to be a reality. The country has an active press association. However, the concentration of press ownership among families that own other big businesses can impact journalistic freedom and responsibility. Some pressure also comes from violence directed at journalists.

Malaysia

Malaysia is home to over 24 million people, with a literacy rate of almost 89 percent. Bahasa Melayu is the official language, while English, Chinese, and Tamil are the other major languages. The *Prince of Wales Island Gazette* (1805) was the first newspaper published in Malaysia; *The Straits Times* (1845) was launched later in Kuala Lumpur. In the nationalist period, two early twentieth-century Islamic reform journals, *Al-Iman* and *Neracha*, were particularly prominent. The earliest newspapers in Malay were *Utusan Melayu* (1907–21), *Lembaga Melaya* (1914–31), and *Warta Melaya* (1931–41). The independence movement in the country was led by the United Malays National Organization, which was able to align itself with the Malaysian Chinese Association and the Malaysian Indian Congress. These parties forged a long-standing pact among themselves, and their coalition, known as Barisan Nasional, has been in power since independence. Over the decades, the ruling coalition has restricted the freedom of the press, especially where political reportage and criticism are concerned.

At present, three major groups—The New Straits Times Press (Malaysia), Star Publications (Malaysia), and Utusan Melayu—own all the major English and Malay newspapers. The principal English papers are *Star* (307,019), *New Strait Times* (135,040), *Malay Mail* (35,251), and *Sun* (142,645); the main Bahasa Melayu papers are *Utusan Malaysia* (246,006), which doubles its circulation on Sunday, *Berita Harian* (228,462), and *Harian Metro* (149,675). The Chinese press is dominated by *Sin Chew Daily* (342,425), *China Press* (204,901), *Nanyang Siang Pau* (326,000), and *Guang Ming* (131,581); the chief Tamil newspapers are *Tamil Nesan* (35,000) and *Malaysia Nanban* (54,000). An important recent change has been the unprecedented popularity of an opposition newspaper, the *Harakah* (300,000), owned by the Parti Islam SeMalaysia (PAS).

Among the more than 240 magazines in circulation, the important ones are *Aliram Monthly* (a reformist monthly), *Kuntum* (a magazine for children), *Shanh Hai* (an authoritative Chinese magazine), *Galaxie* (an English light-reading magazine), *Keluarga*, and *Kemaja*. An interesting feature is the cartoon magazine genre, aimed at the Malay reading public and highlighting the aspirations of this ethnic majority.

Singapore

Singapore is an island city-state with a population of over 4.5 million and a literacy rate of about 93 percent. The principal languages are Mandarin Chinese, English, Malay, Hokkien, Cantonese, Teochew, and Tamil. Singapore is a democracy, but it has been ruled by the same party since independence in 1965. The press is controlled through a unique management system, in which two kinds of shares in companies are mandated: ordinary shares, with one vote each, making up 99 percent of the company's stock; and management shares, with 200 votes each, making up 1 percent of the stock. The government holds all the management shares in companies in Singapore, and no entity is allowed to hold more than 3 percent of a company, while any company has to have a minimum of fifty shareholders. In effect, the state controls the business sector as well as the press.

Singapore Press Holdings owns all the main newspapers in the city, including the two papers that go back to colonial times, the *Straits Times* (English) and *Tamil Murasu* (Tamil). The other papers are the *New Paper* and the *Business Times* (both English); *Lianhe Zaobao*, *Lianhe Wanbao*, and *Shin Min Daily News* (all Chinese); and *Berita Harian* (Malay). Recently, a private company rolled out *Singapore Gazette*, which has editions for housing estates and is an example of a zoned community–based newspaper. The press in Singapore is clearly at the service of the government, and journalists would prefer to avoid conflicts with the ruling party. Non-news publications are not rigorously controlled, and most international publications are available in Singapore, but anything that goes against the "public interest" is stopped at the borders. Over 120 magazines focusing on lifestyle, trade, sports, and special interests are also in circulation, among which *Her World* is very popular.

Indonesia

Indonesia is a vast archipelago of 17,508 islands, of which about 6,000 are inhabited by a total population of over 245 million, with a literacy rate exceeding 87 percent. The principal languages are Bahasa Indonesia (a form of Malay), Javanese, English, Chinese, and Dutch. The historic trajectory of Indonesian periodicals follows a well-recognized pattern: Dutch colonial publications, followed by nationalist periodicals, followed by an assortment of periodicals with checkered careers in the post-independence period.

The earliest publication was a bulletin of the Dutch East India Company, the *Memorie des Nouvelles* (1615). The first Indonesian-language publication was *Bromartani* (1855), published in Javanese. Two important publications in Malay, *Soerat Kabar Bahasa Melajoe* (1856) and *Slompret Melajoe* (1860), followed soon after, but they were brought out by Dutch publishers. The first completely Indonesian paper was *Medan Prijaji* (1907). The Chinese, an important ethnic minority, had *Sin Po* (1907), *Ik Po* (1904), *Tjhoen Tjhiou* (1914), and the leading periodical of the nationalist movement, *Sin Tit Po*. The importance of the press in the nationalist period can be gauged by the fact that Indonesia's great modern novel, *This Earth of Mankind* by Pramoedya Ananta Toer, is based on the life of a nationalist journalist, Tirto Adi Suryo.

The development of the press after independence in 1945 was interrupted within a few years, when President Sukarno established a "Guided Democracy" and took away most press freedoms. This continued when President Suharto, also a military dictator, assumed power in 1966 and imposed a "New Order" on the nation. Suharto used numerous methods of repression, including mandatory licensing, the jailing of journalists, and the revocation of permits. Only with the advent of democracy in 1994 did the press become relatively free. In 1997 the number of publications was around 300; by 1998–99 the number had gone up to 1,200.

At present, Indonesia has about 500 periodicals, including over 170 dailies, but their ownership is concentrated largely in the hands of five big media groups. The Kompas Gramedia Group owns fourteen newspapers and thirty-five periodicals, besides broadcasting and publishing companies; it owns *Kompas* (1965), the Indonesia daily with the highest circulation (500,000). The Jawa Pos Group owns eighty-one newspapers and twenty-three weeklies; it runs the *Jawa Pos* (1949), which has a circulation of over 430,000, as well as the *Pos Kota* (1970), a newspaper for blue-collar readers, which has a circulation of 500,000. The Femina Group is primarily a magazine group that targets "niche" audiences, especially women; it publishes *Femina* magazine, which has been in circulation for over 30 years. The latest entrant to this league is the MRA group, which owns the Indonesian franchises of *Cosmopolitan*, *Harper's Bazaar*, *MTV Trax*, and *FHM* magazines. There are three English newspapers, *Indonesian Observer* (1955), *Indonesia Times* (1974), and *Jakarta Post* (1983), the last of which has the largest circulation in this category with 100,000 copies. Other important publications are *Suara Merdeka* (176,000), *Rakyat Merdeka* (200,000), *Media Merdeka* (200,000), *Koran Tempo* (200,000), *Republika* (200,000), *Kendaulakan Rakyat, Pikiran Rakyat* (183,000), and *Suara Pembaruan* (200,000), the last a Protestant Christian publication. Indonesian political parties also run their own newspapers—*Demokrat* is published by Partai Demokrasi Indonesia-Perjuangan, *Amanat* by Partai Amaner Nasional, *Dute Masyarekat* by Paratai Kebonghitan Bangsa, and *Abadi* by Partai Bulan Bintang.

RESOURCE GUIDE

PRINT SOURCES

East Asia and Oceania

Blackwell, Janet. *NZ Woman's Weekly: The First 60 Years, 1932–1992*. Auckland: Moa Beckett Publishers, 1992.

Britton, Roswell S. *The Chinese Periodical Press, 1800–1912.* Shanghai: Kelly & Walsh, 1933.
Gravett, Paul. *Manga, Sixty Years of Japanese Comics.* London: Laurence King, 2004.
Greenop, Frank S. *History of Magazine Publishing in Australia.* Sydney: K. G. Murray, 1947.
Hamilton, Stephen. "New Zealand English Language Periodicals of Literary Interest Active 1920s–1960s." PhD dissertation, University of Auckland, 1996.
Kim, Chie-woon, and Lee Jae-won, eds. *Elite Media amidst Mass Culture: A Critical Look at Mass Communication in Korea.* Seoul: NANAM, 1994.
Lewis, Dana. "Unlikely Ambassadors: The Surprising Appeal of *Manga* Overseas." *Japan Foundation Newsletter* 27.3–4 (March 2000): 7–9, 11.
Li, Yansheng. *Zhongguo bao kan tu shi* [A Pictorial History of Chinese Newspaper and Magazine Publishing]. Wuhan: Hubei People's Publishing, 2005.
Lindesay, Vane. *The Way We Were: Australian Popular Magazines 1856–1969.* Melbourne, Oxford University Press, 1983.
Misaka, Kaoru. "The First Japanese *Manga* Magazine in the United States." *Publishing Research Quarterly* 19.4 (Winter 2004): 23–30.
Natsume, Fusanosuke. "Japan's *Manga* Culture." *Japan Foundation Newsletter* 27.3–4 (March 2000): 1–6.
Oka, Mitsuo. *Fujin zasshi janarizumu, josei kaiho no rekishi to tomoni.* Tokyo: Gendai Janarizumu Shuppankai, 1981.
Ozaki, Hotsuki, and Asako Munetake. *Zasshi no Jidai, sono kobo no dorama.* Tokyo: Shufu no Tomosha, 1979.
Ross, Penny Griffith, and Harvey Keith Maslen, eds. *Book & Print in New Zealand: A Guide To Print Culture in Aotearoa.* Wellington: Victoria University Press, 1997.
Schodt, Frederik L. *Dreamland Japan: Writing on Modern Manga.* Berkeley, CA: Stone Bridge Press, 1996.
———. *Manga! Manga! The World of Japanese Comics.* Tokyo: Kodansha International, 1983.
Scholefield, G. H. *Newspapers in New Zealand.* Wellington: Reed, 1958.
Shen, Guofan. *Jiedu Gushihui: yiben Zhongguo qikan de shenhua* [Decoding the *Storytelling Club:* The Myth of Chinese Periodical Publishing]. Shanghai: Shanghai Social Science Publishing House, 2003.
Sun, Yanjun, et al. *Qikan Zhongguo* [Periodical China]. Beijing: Chinese Social Science Publishing House, 2003.
Tregenza, John. *Australian Little Magazines, 1923–1954: Their Role in Forming and Reflecting Literary Trends.* Adelaide: Libraries Board of South Australia, 1964.

South and Southeast Asia

Coronel, Sheila S., ed. *Access to Information in Southeast Asia and Beyond.* Uppsala: Dag Hammarskjold Centre, 2003. Useful essays on India, Thailand, the Philippines, and Singapore.
Dharwadker, Vinay. "Print Culture and Literary Markets in Colonial India." Pp. 108–133 in Jeffrey Masten, Peter Stallybrass, and Nancy J. Vickers (eds.), *Language Machines: Technologies of Literary and Cultural Production.* New York: Routledge, 1997. Informative overview of the early history of printing and print culture in India and South Asia.
Parker, Elliott S., and Emelia M. Parker, eds. *Asian Journalism: A Selected Bibliography of Sources on Journalism in China and Southeast Asia.* Metuchen, NJ: Scarecrow Press, 1979. A useful guide to older literature on journalism in Southeast Asia.
Peiris, G. H., ed. *Studies on the Press in Sri Lanka and South Asia.* Kandy, LK: International Centre for Ethnic Studies, 1997. Essays on the history of Sri Lankan journalism and political aspects of journalism and mass media in Sri Lanka and South Asia.
Romano, Angela Rose, and Michael Bromley, eds. *Journalism and Democracy in Asia.* London: RoutledgeCurzon, 2005. Includes essays on print and broadcast journalism in India, Cambodia, Singapore, and Indonesia, as well as in other Asian countries.
Williams, Louise, and Ronald Rich, eds. *Losing Control: Freedom of the Press in Asia.* Canberra: Asia Pacific Press, Asia Pacific School of Economics and Management, Australian National University,

PERIODICALS

2000. Conference papers on aspects of government and the press, press freedoms, and journalism and politics in Asian countries.

WEBSITES

East Asia and Oceania

AllYouCanRead.com. May, 23, 2006. http://www.allyoucanread.com. A portal to 22,800 magazines and newspapers from around the world. Features include lists of top magazines and newspaper by countries.
Bulletin. Accessed May 20, 2006. http://bulletin.ninemsn.com.au.
China Journalists Network. http://press.gapp.gov.cn/index.php.
Chuban nianjian [Publication Annual]. Government Information Office, Republic of China. 2005. http://www.gio.gov.tw/info/publish/yearbook/10-03.htm.
Dragonsource Magazine Online Store. May 20, 2006. http://www.qikan.com/gbqikan/jcategoryjournallist.asp. Includes over 800 electronic Chinese magazines, with a brief introduction to each magazine as well as its table of contents.
Go, Tchiei. "A History of *Manga*." *Dai Nippon Printing.* May 10, 2006. http://www.dnp.co.jp/museum/nmp/nmp_i/articles/manga/manga1.html.
Jessica Publications Group. 2006. http://www.corp.jessicahk.com/index.htm.
Kanzaki, Masahide. "History of Magazines in Japan: 1867–1988." July 7, 1996. *Web Kanaki.* Accessed April, 28, 2006. http://www.kanzaki.com/jpress/mag-history.html.
Lee, Sim. "Present Status and Prospect of Korean Magazine Market." Presented at the FIPP-Seoul Conference on April 17, 2002. Accessed May 10, 2006. http://www.magazine.org.tw/events/fippseoul/presentation/S-I%20lee-sim.pdf.
Media in China. 2005. http://www.mediainchina.com/.
Natsume, Fusanosuke. "Japan's *Manga* Culture." *Japan Foundation Newsletter* 27.3–4 (March 2000): 1-24. Accessed August 31, 2006. https://www.jpf.go.jp/j/publish_j/jfn/pdf/jfn27_3.pdf.
Nielsen Media Research, Australia. Accessed May 10, 2006. http://www.nielsenmedia.com.au/industry&issues.asp.
News and Magazine Publishing Network. http://www.mediainchina.com.cn/.
Papers Past Project. National University of New Zealand. April 28, 2006. http://paperspast.natlib.govt.nz/about.html.
Shogokukan Manga 2005. http://www.shogakukan.co.jp/english/htm/m_manga.html#.

South and Southeast Asia

British Broadcasting Corporation. August 30, 2006. http://www.bbc.co.uk. Easy access to country profiles from the BBC home page, with reliable and informative overviews of South and Southeast Asian countries; excellent links to various media Websites in each country.
Daily News. August 29, 2006. http://www.dailynews.lk. Nationally circulated Sri Lankan English newspaper published since 1916, with weekend English and Sinhala editions.
Dawn Group of Newspapers. August 28, 2006. http://www.dawn.com. A leading English news group in Pakistan, with daily, evening, weekly, and monthly print and electronic publications and a news wire service; publishes multi-edition *Dawn*, paper launched by Mohammad Ali Jinnah, Pakistan's founding father.
Hindu. August 28, 2006. http://www.thehindu.com. English daily in India with national circulation, offering meticulous and balanced news coverage.
India Today Group. August 28, 2006. http://www.india-today.com. Major Indian media group, with operations in periodical and book publication, music, printing, education, and entertainment.
Jakarta Post. August 28, 2006. http://www.thejakartapost.com. Leading Indonesian English daily, with very useful online resources.
Manila Times. August 30, 2006. http://www.manilatimes.net. Filipino daily in English with high circulation; a newspaper with a rich history, first published in 1900.

PERIODICALS

SELECTED POPULAR MAGAZINES AND NEWSPAPERS

East Asia and Oceania

Apple Daily Online. Hong Kong: Next Media, 1990. http://appledaily.atnext.com.
Apple Daily Taiwan. Hong Kong: Next Media, 2003. http://www.appledaily.com.tw/AppleNews/index.cfm.
Australian Women's Weekly. Melbourne, Australia: 1980.
Bulletin. 1880. http://bulletin.ninemsn.com.au/.
Duzhe [Readers]. Lanzhou: Gansu People's Press, 1993.
Gushi hui [Storytelling Club]. Shanghai: Shanghai Literature and Art Publishing, 1963. http://www.shwenyi.com/news/news_default.asp?cataid=54.
Jessica. Hong Kong: Nanhuang Media, 2000. http://www.jessicahk.com/index.htm.
Jiating [Family]. Guangzhou: Jiating Magazine Publishing, 1982.
Meirenzhi [Beauty]. Teibei: Beauty Magazine Publishing, 1994.
NZ Woman's Weekly. 1932.
Yi zhoukan [Next Magazine]. Hong Kong: Yeung Wai Hong, 1900.
Zhiyin [Bosom Friend]. Wuhan: Bosom Friend Magazine Publishing, 1984.
Ziyou shibao [Liberty Times]. http://www.libertytimes.com.tw/.

RADIO TALK

East Asia and Oceania

"Manga, Animé and Japanese Culture in America." January 31, 2005. National Public Radio *Talk of the Nation.* Accessed August 31, 2006. http://www.npr.org/templates/story/story.php?storyId=4472410. Neal Conan with guests Peter Carey, author of *Wrong about Japan: A Father's Journey with His Son* (Knopf, 2005); Calvin Reid, comics editor for *Publisher's Weekly*; and Elizabeth Kawasaki, managing editor at VIZ, a publisher of Japanese manga.

EVENTS

East Asia and Oceania

Golden Tripod Awards [*Jinding jiang*]. http://info.gio.gov.tw/mp.asp?mp=24. Taiwan government-sponsored awards. Founded in 1976 and presented annually since 1981 to individuals and publishers for outstanding achievements in magazines and books.
Magazine of the Year Awards (Australia). http://www.magazines.org.au/default.asp?page=/events/mpa+awards. Established in 1998 by the Magazine Publishers of Australia (MPA) and held annually in August.
Magazine of the Year Awards (New Zealand). http://www.mpa.org.nz/index.html?mode=display&section_id=&parent_id=0&content_id=29&id=29. Held annually since 2001.

ORGANIZATIONS AND MUSEUMS

East Asia and Oceania

Association of Taiwan Journalists, 5F, 88 Shinyi Rd.Sec.2, Taipei, Taiwan, ROC. Phone_886-2-23419944; Fax: 886-2-23216121; E-mail: journaly@ms10.hinet.net. http://www.atj.org.tw/atj.
General Administration of Press and Publication of the People's Republic of China (GAPP), 85 S. Dongsi dajie, Dongchengqu, Beijing 100703, China. E-mail: webmaster@gapp.gov.cn. http://www.gapp.gov.cn.
Government Information Office, Republic of China (Taiwan), 2 Tianjin St. Taipei, 100, Taiwan, R.O.C. http://www.gio.gov.tw/.

Periodicals

Japanese Magazine Publishers Association (Nihon Zasshi Kyokai), Tokyo-to Chiyoda-ku Kanda Surugadai 1-7, Japan 〒101-0062. Phone: 03-3291-0775; FAX: 03-3293-6239. www.j-magazine.or.jp.

Korea Magazine Association. Phone: 02-780-2112; Fax: 02-785-9494. http://www.kmpa.or.kr and http://www.kmpa.or.kr/english/index.html.

Korea Magazine Museum. Phone: 02-7359464; Fax: 82-7372485; E-mail: webmaster@kmpa.or.kr. http://www.kmpa.or.kr/museum/.

Magazine Association of the Republic of China, 2F, No. 42, Sec. 1, Luosifu Road, Taipei 100, Taiwan, ROC. Phone: 02-2393-4684; Fax: 02-2396-4638.

Magazine Business Association of Taipei, 8F, No. 81, Sec.2, NanChang Rd., Taipei 100, Taiwan, R.O.C. Phone: 886-2-23569484; Fax: 886-2-23569485; E-mail: mbat@magazine.org.tw. http://www.magazine.org.tw/web-eng/home.asp.

Magazine Publishers Association, New Zealand (MPA), 409 New North Road, Kingsland, Auckland. Mail: PO Box 2778, Shortland Street, Auckland, New Zealand; Phone: 64-9-846-4653; Fax: 64-9-815-7143; E-mail: info@mpa.org.nz. www.mpa.org.nz.

Magazine Publishers of Australia (MPA), Level 11, 53 Walker Street, North Sydney NSW 2060 Mail: PO Box 513, North Sydney NSW 2059; Phone: + 61-2-9923-1568; Fax: + 61-2-9460-1450. http://www.magazines.org.au.

NOTES

East Asia and Oceania

1. According to the author of *Kingu no Jidai*, the development of popular press in Japan experienced three stages: "general magazines," "popular magazines," and "national magazines." See Sato Takumi, "*Kingu*" *no jidai, kokumin taishu zasshi no kokyosei* (Tokyo: Iwanami shoten, 2002).
2. The earliest indigenous newspaper of the world was the "*Jin zhou yuan zhuang*" from 887, which is now held at the British Museum.
3. See Tan Shulin, "Zaoqi Lai Hua Jidujiao chuan jiaoshi yu jindai zhong wai wen qi kan [Early English and Chinese Magazines and Foreign Missionaries in China]," *Shijie zongjiao yan jiu* [World Religious Studies] 2 (2002), pp. 81–82.
4. See *Australian Dictionary of Biography*, online edition, accessed Sep. 7, 2006, http://www.adb.online.anu.edu.au/biogs/A010519b.htm.
5. See Joni Johnson-Woods, "The History of the Popular Press in Australia," accessed March 30, 2006, http://www.thecore.nus.edu.sg/post/australia/press.html.
6. See Johnson-Woods, "Popular Periodicals: *The Australian Journal*," accessed March 30, 2006, http://www.thecore.nus.edu.sg/post/australia/press.html.
7. See "Magazines Boost Brand Performance," Magazine Publishers of Australia, accessed May 17, 2006 (in Resource Guide), http://www.magazines.org.au/driver.asp?page=mpa/news/latest+news/magazines+boost+brand+performance&flashver=7.
8. Steve Warshaw and Phil Cara, "Online Advertising Really Moves Offline Product," accessed March 27, 2007, http://www2.acnielsen.com/pubs/documents/2004_q3_ci_cover.pdf.
9. See "2004 Basic Information of Press and Publishing in China," General Administration of Press and Publication of the People's Republic of China, "accessed April 28, 2006, (in Resource Guide).
10. See "Preface to *Jiedu Gushihui*," in Shen 2003 (in Resource Guide), p. 1.
11. Sun et al. 2003 (in Resource Guide), p. 3.
12. Ibid.
13. Ibid., p. 425.
14. Jessica Publications Group, accessed May 11, 2006 (in Resource Guide).
15. Data from *Chuban nianjian* 2005 (in Resource Guide), p. 95. See also Yu Ren and Li Jun, "Taiwan qikan fazhan dui dalu tongye de qishi" [Inspiration from the Development of Taiwan Periodical Publishing], accessed March 6, 2006, http://press.gapp.gov.cn/news/wen.php?val=news&aid=10097.

16. Data from *Chuban nianjian* 2005 (in Resource Guide), p. 11.
17. See Chen Zongyi, "Tabloid Journalism Trumps Politics in Taiwan" (original article in Chinese), *New Taiwan* 489 (August 8, 2005) accessed September 6, 2006, http://www.newtaiwan.com.tw/bulletinview.jsp?period=489&bulletinid=22438.
18. See "Next Media Limited Annual Report 05-06," Accessed September 6, 2006, http://www.nextmedia.com/v4/investor.html.
19. See Zhou Zhaoliang and Yang Zhikai, "Zhuazhu zhuazhu baozhi duzhe de xin, Taiwan baozhi meiti duzhe zhuanhuan yinsu tantao" [Discussion on Newspaper Readership in Taiwan]. *Chuban nianjian* (in Resource Guide), p. 34.
20. Ibid., p. 35.
21. Sun et al. 2003 (in Resource Guide), p. 429.
22. See *Shuppan nenkan 2006* [Publishing Yearbook] (Tokyo: Japan shuppan nyususha, 2006), p. 275.
23. Ibid., p. 274.
24. See Data from "Japan Magazine Publishers Association Japanese Magazine Data," JMPA (in Resource Guide), accessed May 12, 2006, http://www.j-magazine.or.jp/data_001/index.html.
25. See "Japanese Publishing Industry," JETRO Japanese Economy Division, *Japanese Economic Monthly* (July 2005), p. 1–10.
26. Go, "A History of Manga'" (in Resource Guide).
27. Natsume, "Japan's *Manga* Culture" (in Resource Guide), p. 1.
28. Misaka, "The First Japanese *Manga* Magazine in the United States" (in Resource Guide), p. 23.
29. Lewis, "Unlikely Ambassadors: The Surprising Appeal of *Manga* Overseas" (in Resource Guide), pp. 7–9, 11.
30. Misaka (in Resource Guide), p. 23.
31. See Korea Ministry of Culture & Tourism Website, accessed May 10, 2006, http:// www.mct.go.kr/english/index.jsp.
32. Based on material from Nielsen Media Research, accessed May 10, 2006, http://www.acnielsen.co.kr.
33. See Kim Ki-tae, "Korea: Falling Readership Hits Magazine Industry," June 15, 2005, *Korea Times*, accessed May 15, 2006, http://asianmedia.ucla.edu.
34. Lee 2002 (in Resource Guide).
35. See Nielsen Media Research, http://www.nielsenmedia.com.au, Magazine Publishers of Australia, accessed May 10, 2006 (both in Resource Guide).
36. Ibid.
37. Lindesay 1983 (in Resource Guide), p. 131.
38. Ibid., p. 7.
39. See "A Decade of Exceptional Growth," Magazine Publishers Association, New Zealand, accessed May 10, 2006 (in Resource Guide).

RADIO AND TELEVISION

EAST ASIA AND OCEANIA

DONNA L. HALPER

On the surface, the countries of northeast Asia (China, Japan, and North and South Korea) could not be more different from those of Oceania (Australia and New Zealand). And yet, while their languages are different, there are historic colonial ties that have bound these countries together. Today, colonialism has been superseded by globalism. And in an increasingly global economy, these countries have more ties than ever. One good example of this can be found in broadcasting.

From its earliest years, radio has made the world a little bit smaller. Because AM radio signals were capable of traveling long distances, on a night when atmospheric conditions were right, a listener in Australia might hear a station in New York. Some magazines of the 1920s introduced a new game called "Radio Golf," in which the object was to receive signals from far-away cities; the miles were tallied up, and a monthly prize was awarded to the person who pulled in the most distant stations. And when shortwave broadcasts came along a few years later, it became even easier to receive stations from all over the world. Educators capitalized on this by using radio to teach geography, while radio equipment manufacturers such as Philco put out publications including *The Radio Atlas of the World*, with full-color maps and descriptions of the stations in each country.

But the idea of a station in Australia playing music from China or a station in Taiwan using American slogans (or hiring American announcers) is a product of our modern age. And it is no longer unusual for stations in the East to pattern themselves after the style of broadcasting in the West. So a station in Shanghai began to call itself JoyFM, and FM100 in Taiwan says on its Website—in English—that it features "music and fun." Stations from Australia and New Zealand began using U.S.-style station names in the recent past (for example, 2DayFM, and Triple M), and some of these stations have even hired U.S. radio consultants. This blending of styles and images is not just a radio phenomenon. The U.S. cable channel MTV, which features popular music videos aimed at young adults, has branched out to include a version that broadcasts in Japanese, another in Chinese, and a third in Korean. Today's radio and television in Asia offer "canto-pop," which is popular music in Cantonese;

Radio and Television

"Mando-pop," or popular music sung in Mandarin; and "J-pop," Japanese pop music. A recent addition is the Korean Wave, as Korean artists and pop culture also spread throughout Asia.[1] One Hong Kong broadcasting company (TVB) now provides everything from music videos to soap operas to Chinese-speaking communities in over twenty countries. And South Korea is exporting TV dramas throughout Asia—one business publication estimated that in 2002 South Korea's TV exports were at only US$29 million, but by 2005 that figure had leaped to $100 million.[2] It is also not unusual for Asian stations to play some American and British hit songs, as well as Asian cover versions of those songs. Meanwhile, Asian young adults can also see American popular movies (with subtitles) and learn about the fads and catchphrases that are popular in the West. It's not exactly Radio Golf, but the exporting of popular culture by multinational media conglomerates has certainly brought Asia, Oceania, and North America closer together.

However, although there are an increasing number of common ties, there are also areas of difference. Countries such as North Korea maintain a rigidly controlled state-run system of broadcasting. The government of Mainland China, on the other hand, has moved away from the severe restrictions on Western popular culture that were the norm during the time of Chairman Mao Zedong; today, there are few complaints about the prevalence of Mando-pop, and both Taiwanese and Hong Kong performers are heard. But the government also makes sure that these performers do not take stands on politics, and that local broadcasters are not too critical of government policies. Importing MTV, with its message of commercialism and consumerism, is accepted, but censorship of news and current events persists. This is a far cry from what goes on in Oceania, where news broadcasters hold a variety of political views, and the government can be criticized on talk shows. Hong Kong is trying to maintain its free press; as a former British colony, it was returned to Mainland China in 1997, and Hong Kong media professionals fear that China will exert more influence over what can and cannot be broadcast. Already, there are critics who see evidence of a new conservatism and self-censorship. But for the most part, countries such as Taiwan, Japan, and South Korea have media that express a variety of opinions, whereas North Korea and mainland China still lack such a system.

Radio History: The Early Years in China and Hong Kong

According to the *New York Times*, there were only twenty-two radio stations in all of Asia at the end of 1927. These included three in China and three in Japan. By comparison, in Oceania, Australia already had twenty-four radio stations. This was not accidental. Almost from the beginning, Asia has had a love-hate relationship with new forms of media, starting with the telegraph and extending to print journalism and broadcasting. This may be partially because the first companies to bring modern technology to the region were either British or American. Which group would control communication, especially in large and important countries such as China, became an ongoing power struggle as well as a source of controversy.

In China the Imperial Telegraph Company was founded in October 1880, and it was able to construct telegraph facilities between several major cities, greatly improving communications as a result. But British and Danish companies established telephone service, and French, British, and American concerns set up the first wireless telegraph stations. And it was a British entrepreneur who introduced Western-style print journalism. In late April 1872, a new daily newspaper, *Shen Bao* (in some sources, *Shun Pao*) made its first appearance in Shanghai. Published by Ernest Major and a Chinese staff, it tried to imitate Western newspapers by focusing on mass appeal rather than on scholarly work. *Shen Bao* featured editorials, giving opinions on current events and maintaining considerable independence from the official Chinese government viewpoint. *Shen Bao* was quick to embrace technology: by late January 1874, it had begun carrying dispatches sent by telegraph, becoming one of the first Chinese newspapers to do so. Getting news by telegraph meant that readers received breaking news in a timely fashion. Even after Major left China, his newspaper continued its positive relationship with new technology. When radio came along, *Shen Bao* put its own station on the air in mid-1924, sending out programs of music and education four times a day.

But before the *Shen Bao* station succeeded, there were several other attempts. The first radio stations in China were set up by individual entrepreneurs with ties to American or British manufacturing concerns, and who wanted to appeal to Westerners doing business in China. The first station was started by an American journalist named E. G. Osborn, who began to broadcast in Shanghai in late 1922 (some sources say January 1923). The Osborn station did not last very long, nor did another set up by an American engineer, Robert F. Gowen, in 1923. Gowen remarked to a radio magazine that his biggest challenge in teaching the Chinese how to broadcast was the fact that their language contained no words for any of the terminology of radio technology. Gowen and his translator had to create a new vocabulary so that the subject could be taught.[3] Another American entrepreneur, Charles H. Robertson, who came from a missionary background, taught radio courses in China during the early 1920s under the auspices of the YMCA. There was a small but active amateur radio society in Shanghai, and Robertson was a frequent speaker during its formative years. Soon, a local university began offering college-level courses in radio engineering. Even though the fledgling stations and radio courses were popular, the Chinese government, which had never been comfortable with the new technology, asserted itself into broadcasting almost immediately. To the chagrin of Chinese radio fans, the government decided that radio equipment was illegal, a decision that one radio magazine called "absurd."[4] With the parts necessary to build receivers now declared contraband, only a select few could listen to radio, thereby giving the government a measure of control.

Ultimately, the government relented somewhat and began setting up its own stations in major cities such as Beijing and Harbin by the late 1920s; a few local warlords did the same. The instability and factionalism in the country during the 1930s contributed to the slow pace of radio's growth. That was ironic, given radio's proven ability to unite a nation and give the public a shared popular culture as demonstrated in other countries. But the Chinese government still had great ambivalence about radio, and that attitude was slow to change. The one place where radio flourished was the city of Shanghai, which remained a center for music, theater, and literature. Several radio stations operated successfully there in the late 1920s and early 1930s, exposing listeners to cultural events they might never have been able to access, and even giving news bulletins, thanks to relationships the stations had established with local newspapers. A national radio service, supervised by the Chinese Communist Party, did not begin broadcasting until 1940 when the government finally became convinced that radio would be a valuable tool for dissemination of the Party's official message. The Communist Party began to commemorate December 1945 as the official anniversary of the "people's radio broadcasting," and on the twentieth anniversary, Chairman Mao Zedong even spoke about the importance of radio. Other government officials, too, praised radio's ability to spread the message of socialism and educate the Chinese people, even those who lived in the most distant rural areas.[5]

In Hong Kong, which was a British colony until 1997, the government displayed the same conservative attitude about radio that was slowing down forward progress in China. So the

DEFINING RADIO'S ROLE IN THE 1920s

Radio broadcasting in Asia was at first considered a hobby, an educational pastime for young men; in the 1920s, it was rare for an Asian woman to be encouraged to study electronics, although a few seemed to have done so, mentored perhaps by a brother or a husband. Early radio was dominated by engineers and amateurs (or "hams"), and at first everyone was content to join radio clubs and perfect their Morse code skills. But once having built receivers, the amateurs began "listening in" to stations in other parts of the world, and they quickly realized that radio was not just educational—it could also be entertaining. As early as December 1922, the *North China Herald* (an English-language newspaper popular with Western businessmen and their families who were living in Shanghai) editorialized on the importance of radio. The newspaper spoke enthusiastically of the new medium's potential, and the editor expressed the hope that Shanghai would soon be at the forefront of broadcasting in Asia.

But that was not to be. The Chinese government was wary of radio and put a number of roadblocks in the way of its development. As a result Japan was ahead of China in creating a national broadcasting service (known as NHK). Like many other government-run services, NHK saw its mission as informing and educating as well as entertaining. Even though in other parts of the world, including Australia and New Zealand, stations were successfully offering a combination of the popular and the educational, in most of Asia, what was heard on the radio reflected the tastes of the ruling elites. Thus, when China finally did begin regular broadcasts in several major cities, playing American jazz or pop music was considered improper. Most Asian governments believed that the role of radio was to expose the public to "good music"-opera, classical and folk—as well as to provide educational talks by famous scholars. News broadcasts were frequently censored, especially in China and Korea. The idea of a mass-appeal radio station aimed at the general public was virtually unknown.

Hong Kong Telegraph decided to try to bring about some change. Having heard from readers who were interested in the new medium of broadcasting, the newspaper helped to start an amateur radio club in early 1923. The Hong Kong Radio Society hoped that the government would soon give permission for a commercial station. One hundred amateurs convened for the first meeting on May 4, 1923, to plan their strategy. When they met a second time, they sent a formal letter requesting such permission, but the government was concerned that a commercial station would interfere with its naval and military stations, and setting up a station for entertainment was not yet a priority. It would not be until June 1928 that a station was finally permitted to operate. GOW, Radio Hong Kong, which changed its call letters to ZBW in early 1929, was the only station in Hong Kong till the mid-1930s; a Chinese-language service called ZEK did not make its debut until 1934.

The programming on ZBW was heavily influenced by the BBC style of radio; a majority of it was in English, making it especially popular with the educated middle- and upper-class residents of Hong Kong. Even when there was only one station, radio broadcasting acquired a loyal group of fans. In December 1929 Hong Kong hosted a radio exhibition, which was held at City Hall. Large crowds came to see the newest in radio equipment, and fourteen companies (including some from the United States and Great Britain) displayed their receivers. But since receivers were still too expensive for the average person, and licensing fees had to be paid, only about 5 percent of households owned a radio in the late 1920s through the early 1930s.[6] It was not until after the World War II that more mass appeal (and more ethnically Chinese) programming would be heard on Radio Hong Kong.

EARLY RADIO BROADCASTING IN JAPAN AND ITS TERRITORIES

Similar to the reaction by the Chinese government, the government of Japan was equally reticent to let the new radio craze proceed. Although Japan had numerous amateur radio fans in the early 1920s, and a successful radio exhibition was held in Tokyo (or Tokio, as it was then spelled) in April of 1923, the first station did not receive permission to go on the air until late March 1925. But this was not entirely the result of government hesitation; there had been a natural disaster that had slowed the process considerably. In early September 1923, a major earthquake had struck Japan. A courageous wireless telegrapher, Kaichiro "T. K." Yonemura, had stayed at his post to transmit messages that kept Western newspapers informed as the crisis unfolded. He was later given a medal for his service by the Radio Corporation of America. Once Japan recovered and rebuilt, radio again became a priority. JOAK in Tokyo was operated by Masajiro Kotamura, who had invented some of the equipment the station used.[7] And when the station finally got on the air, it was an instant success. Among its unique features was that its chief announcer, Akiko Midorikawa, was a woman. This was highly unusual in an industry that tended to believe only men sounded authoritative over the airwaves. JOAK was soon followed by JOBK in Osaka and JOCK in Nagoya. But the Ministry of Communications made sure it held the power over radio. Regulations stated that "for the public benefit, the state may take control of the broadcasting facility," and independent stations were not encouraged. The national broadcasting service came to be known as NHK (Nippon Hoso Kyokai), and it was formally incorporated in late August 1926. But despite the popularity of radio in Japan, a 1932 report noted that "the number of listening sets per 1,000 persons [is] only 20, as compared to 122 in the Unites States and 115 in Great Britain."[8] As for what was on the air in those early years, a *New York Times* reporter listened in one day in September 1930 and was surprised to hear many elements similar to what was being broadcast on American stations: a cooking show, a business report, English-language lessons, play-by-play announcing of a local baseball tournament, weather, some traditional Japanese music, and a storyteller offering an adventure story from Japan's history. The government made sure there were programs with patriotic and educational themes, but a 1933 survey of the listeners found they preferred music and entertainment over educational programs. One big event for the Japanese listeners occurred in November 1934, when the baseball hero Babe Ruth, who, along with a number of Americans including Lou Gehrig and Connie Mack, had come to Japan to play some exhibition games, gave a radio talk. He discussed the progress Japanese teams had made and praised Japan for being so cordial to the American players.

In Korea, which was under Japanese control, the first station began to broadcast in February 1927 in Seoul; it used the call letters JODK (after the war, it was renamed HLKA). Korean radio in the late 1920s was operated in accordance with the wishes of the Japanese government, and press freedom was limited. However, the radio station did broadcast traditional Korean music, mostly performed by female artists called *gisaeng*. By 1929 performances from the Royal Music Institute were also broadcast, along with radio dramas. In the mid 1930s, some efforts were made to establish a national service, but these did not take hold fully until after the end of World War II in 1947, when the Korean Broadcasting Service

(KBS) was established. When Korea split into two countries, radio was often used by the respective leaders of each country to criticize the politics of the other.

Formosa, which would later be known as Taiwan, was also under Japanese control during its earliest radio experiments beginning in 1926. In the early 1930s, the Taipei Broadcasting Bureau was established; its role was to transmit news, educational programs, and pro-Japanese propaganda. What would become today's Taiwanese national broadcasting company (known as CBS) got its start under the Kuomintang (Nationalist Party) government in China, which put a station on the air in 1928 from Nanjing. Known as the Central Broadcasting Station, it moved to Taiwan in 1949 after the Communists established the People's Republic of China on the mainland. Taiwan's radio, just as the rest of its media, was controlled by a military dictatorship for the next several decades, and the number of stations was limited. Although some musical entertainment was broadcast, the emphasis was on cultural and educational programs,

THE EARLY RADIO YEARS IN OCEANIA

Unlike Hong Kong, where the British government seemed slow to allow radio to proceed, Australia, also under British control, was able to move forward in dramatic fashion. One of the first stations was 2SB in Sydney, owned by Amalgamated Wireless Australasia. The owners of 2SB had done experimental broadcasts as early as August 1919, and the station took to the air with official government approval in November of 1923, later changing its call letters to 2BL (Broadcasters Limited). In Melbourne, station 3LO was on the air in October 1924; not only did it have state of the art equipment, but it also offered performances by famous entertainers such as the internationally known soprano Dame Nellie Melba. By late 1925 Australia boasted seven high-power radio stations: in the United States, the typical station had 100 to 500 watts, but these Australian stations broadcast with 5,000 watts. As with many overseas stations, listeners supported the broadcasts by paying annual fees to own radio sets. The fees ranged from $5 to $10, which was a lot of money in the mid-1920s, but since radio was extremely popular, the public felt it was money well spent. As in the United States, stations broadcast both popular and classical music, educational shows, and programs for children, but sporting events were especially appreciated. The government's national service, the Australian Broadcasting Corporation, did not go on the air until July 1932.

As for New Zealand, radio was just as popular there as it was in Australia. Some early experimental broadcasts by amateur radio operators took place in 1919 and 1920. One of the best-known of the experimenters was D. G. "Toots" Mitchell, who founded one of the country's first stations, 4XD in Dunedin. It went on the air in 1922 (some sources say late 1921), operated by the Otago Radio Association. Putting forth its claim to being New Zealand's original radio station, it began using the slogan "We were here first." Another station that may have been the first to broadcast was 4XO, started by Professor Robert "Bobby" Jack at Otago University in Dunedin in November 1921. New Zealand's first broadcasting regulations were issued in 1923, at which time the country was divided up into four regions. One of the most influential of the professional stations was 4YA, also in Dunedin. It was owned by the British Electrical and Engineering Company, and in the spring of 1924, it was already using 1,000 watts. By early 1927 the Radio Broadcasting Company (RBC) of New Zealand had begun to establish stations in major cities across the country, including Auckland (1YA) and Christ Church (3YA). One of the most powerful stations in the country was Wellington's 2YA, which by 1930 was using 5,000 watts just as the high-power stations in Australia were doing. New Zealand radio fans especially enjoyed listening to distant broadcasts—sometimes reception was so good that they picked up stations in Chicago, Los Angeles, or New York, to the delight of the newspapers in those cities. While it may not seem like a news story in the current world of the Internet and satellites, in the 1920s radio signals provided listeners with the opportunity to hear what was happening in cities thousands of miles away. Owning a radio set in New Zealand cost about US$7.50, whether the owner was an amateur or a broadcast listener.

The popularity of early radio in Oceania could be seen in the number of stations. As of early 1930, Australia had twenty radio stations (including three in Adelaide, four in Melbourne, and seven in Sydney), and there were fourteen in New Zealand (including three in Auckland and five in Dunedin). This stood in sharp contrast to Hong Kong, which still had only one officially sanctioned station, or to Japan, which had only nine—one for each of the major cities.

A word should also be said about the importance of shortwave radio. Popular with hobbyists worldwide, the technology was developed by two American corporations: Westinghouse and General Electric. Shortwave listeners (SWLs) were able to hear stations in Asia and Oceania from the late 1920s on. Listening for distant stations was known as DXing. As might be expected, the first to take advantage of this technology was Australia, where Amalgamated Wireless installed VK3ME in Melbourne. Australia even had a station that broadcast from on board a ship. VK9MI was also unique for having a woman, Eileen M. Foley, in charge of the programming.

During the late 1920s and into the 1930s, the shortwave band became a sort of United Nations, where broadcasts took place in a number of languages. Many of the stations were operated by private citizens, but in countries such as China and Japan, there was government oversight. One important shortwave station in China was XGOY, set up by the Chinese government in Chungking in the 1930s. It called itself The Voice of China, and in its heyday, it broadcast in twenty languages.[9] The Japanese too, through NHK, began to send out hour-long programs that American SWLs picked up. But controlling the message soon became controversial. What had begun as an agent of local pride and entertainment changed from an entertaining hobby into something much more serious. As World War II loomed, shortwave stations began to send out propaganda broadcasts or jam stations that offered points of view with which they disagreed.

DEVELOPMENT AND GROWTH OF TELEVISION IN ASIA

In China, where the government had been slow to embrace radio, it was equally slow to embrace television. The first broadcasts did not occur till the late 1950s. One of the TV stations that went on the air during this time was Beijing Television, which began broadcasting in early May 1958. Its broadcast day was limited to approximately two to three hours of programming, four times a week. Another station was put on the air in Shanghai about a month later. As with Japan in its early days of television, not a lot of people had the equipment to watch the documentaries or enjoy the musical entertainment that the stations offered. One estimate was that no more than thirty TV sets existed in Beijing in 1958.[10] Throughout the 1950s and 1960s, the Chinese government remained more involved with radio, which by now was widely available, than with the newer technology of television, to which most people had no access. During the years of the Cultural Revolution, there was a lull in television development. It was not until the early 1970s that more television stations took to the air. By 1972 China had thirty-two stations in operation, and some programs were in color by 1973. But it was not until the early 1980s that the government seemed to embrace the importance of television; once that happened, the number of television stations increased dramatically, from 52 in 1983 to 422 by the end of 1988.[11]

In Hong Kong, which remained a British colony, the national broadcasting service got a new name in 1948 as Radio Hong Kong. In the mid 1950s, Hong Kong still did not have television, and the government seemed to be in no hurry to encourage or support its development. Although there were some TV programs during the 1960s, it was not until 1976 that the national service's name was again changed to reflect the increased production of TV shows: it became known as Radio Television Hong Kong (RTHK). RTHK is in operation currently and is still successful. Several commercial stations began in the 1960s as the media continued moving away from the British model and more toward the kinds of programming wanted by the Chinese residents of Hong Kong. Perhaps the most influential network was TVB (Television Broadcasts), which went on the air in mid-November 1967; by 1972 it was able to broadcast all its programs in color. Today, it remains a leading producer of Chinese-language programming and has an international reach: it provides an estimated 5,000 hours of Cantonese drama, comedy, kung fu, and action series, dubbed into over ten languages, to more than 20 million people in over thirty countries, including Taiwan and China.[12]

As for Taiwan, it, too, had to contend with a slow response from the government. Taiwan did not get its first television station till early 1962, when "the experimental National Education Television began broadcasting two hours of educational programming each day."[13] Not long after, Taiwan Television Enterprise (TTV) was founded. In 1969 TTV was joined by the China Television Company (CTV).

Although most history books credit inventors from the United States and Great Britain for television, in Japan people are justifiably proud of their own "father of television," Kenjiro Takayanagi, who performed successful experiments in the late 1920s; this was about the same time as the better-known Vladimir Zworykin and Charles Francis Jenkins in America and John Logie Baird in England began their work in this field. Some of the first Japanese television transmissions using Takayanagi's technology occurred in May 1937. The Toshiba company manufactured some of the early receivers. Unfortunately for Takayanagi, World War II intervened, and all television experiments were put on hold. After the war, it was Japan's national service, NHK, which finally put the first TV station on the air in February 1953. This was followed in late August by NTV (Nippon Television). But not many people were aware of either station. There were fewer than 1,000 receivers in the country, and TV was only available in Tokyo. Still, it was a start, and television gradually expanded its reach. By the summer of 1954, there were two stations in Tokyo and one each in Osaka and Nagoya, with more about to go on the air. Unlike some other countries in the region, Japan encouraged the growth of the industry and had a plan in place to mass produce television sets. By 1958 Tokyo's major department stores sold television sets in addition to transistor radios. There were several private television companies in operation during those postwar years, but NHK remained dominant. In theory, NHK was supposed to be independent; in reality, it was often the voice of the government. This affected which news stories were covered and which ones were not. It also affected how ethnic minorities such as Koreans were represented. Some modern media critics have observed that since the earliest years of Japanese TV, Japan's "official" television network has downplayed or entirely ignored stories that would cast the government in a bad light, such as Japan's oppression of Koreans; in this view, television has been used to promote the image of a benign and tolerant Japan.[14] Still, compared to some other countries in Asia, Japanese broadcasters had much more freedom.

In Korea, after liberation from Japan occurred in 1945, the country was then split into two separate entities: North Korea and South Korea. North Korea became a communist country, heavily influenced by the Soviet Union. The state-run broadcasting system, known as the

Korean Central Broadcasting Station, was set up in 1948. A state-run news service, Korean Central News Agency (KCNA) was also established that same year. Broadcasting was used mainly for education and propaganda purposes, with programs that praised the government's policies and stressed that the communist system of North Korea was superior to the system of South Korea. No criticism of the government or of its dictator, Kim Il-Sung, was permitted, and listening to any broadcasts from other countries was strictly forbidden. In fact, all radios were manufactured with fixed dials that could only receive the government stations.[15] It was not until the 1990s before North Koreans were able to hear stations from elsewhere, most notably Radio Free Asia, which, like Radio Free Europe, raised questions and tried to inform listeners about issues the government preferred to hide. But by all accounts, listening to such stations, while possible, could still result in punishment. As for television, as might be expected, North Korea was slow to develop it, and when TV finally was approved, Korean Central TV was just as rigidly controlled as was the government-run radio network. After Kim Il-Sung died, his son Kim Jong-il became the leader, and he maintained the same degree of control over the media that his father had. As of 2003, there were only thirty-eight television stations operating in North Korea, all spreading the government's point of view.

In South Korea the national service, KBS (Korean Broadcasting System), was established in late 1947. Another network, MBC (Munhwa Broadcasting Corporation), began radio broadcasts in 1961. Television broadcasting began in Seoul in mid-May 1956, when HLKZ-TV, operated by a Korean company affiliated with RCA, took to the air. As often happens with new ventures, this first station did not last long. In 1961 the government-run KBS began to offer television broadcasts in addition to continuing its radio broadcasts. MBC put some of its first television broadcasts on the air in 1969. But the fact that Korea had been split into two countries did not lead to freedom for the broadcast media in either of them. While today we think of South Korea as a free country, earlier it was run by a military dictatorship, led by President Park Chung-Hee, and broadcasting was seen as an effective way to disseminate government propaganda. It took many years before there was freedom for the broadcast media and the press. After President Park was assassinated in 1979, his immediate successor continued strict government oversight of media, including censorship of foreign news that was considered critical of the government.[16] This practice was not new in Asia: during the years before World War II, both China and Japan had tried to prevent Western journalists from reporting stories the governments believed to be too negative. Gradually, however, the public began expressing dissatisfaction with what was available on South Korean television, and policies began changing in the late 1980s.

DEVELOPMENT OF TELEVISION IN OCEANIA

Australia, as might be expected, has a far different television story from that of China or Japan. It, too, was affected by World War II, which slowed TV development worldwide. But by 1950 the government had decided there should be a national service similar to what had been created with radio, and the government also approved some commercial broadcasters. It took some years for the plan to be implemented, but in July 1956, test transmissions began in Sydney and Melbourne. Most sources say that station TCN9 in Sydney was the first to offer regular transmissions, beginning in mid-September that year. ABC, Australia's national service, put its first stations on the air in Sydney and Melbourne in November.[17] Not many people had televisions at that time, but the fact that the new stations were able to transmit portions of the Olympic games, which were held that year in Melbourne, increased public interest for the new medium. As happened in America, many successful radio programs began migrating to television, including quiz shows, musical variety shows, talent shows, and soap operas. The popularity of television led to the appearance of a new magazine, *татв-Radio Week*, later known as *TV Week*, which covered the stars and the programs. It began publishing in December 1957. By 1959 almost every major city in Australia had at least one television station, and a number of the performers and hosts were now considered local celebrities. Perhaps the first TV star in Australia was Graham Kennedy, a comedian who became the host of a popular variety show called *In Melbourne Tonight*; it was a role he maintained from 1957 until 1969. Unlike China or North Korea, where governments controlled what was seen and made sure broadcasts served propaganda needs, Australian programs were more often than not based on entertainment, with some news and sports as well. Even though there were three commercial networks, in addition to the ABC national service, in operation by 1965, full-color transmissions were not available till March 1975.

While New Zealand was far ahead of many other countries in radio experiments, it did not put the first TV station on the air until June 1960. There had been a few sporadic experiments in the 1950s, but the government had been slow to give TV the official go-ahead. Once that occurred, however, New Zealand's television industry began in Auckland, followed a few weeks later by a station in Wellington. A year later, in June 1961, a station was started in Christchurch, and another followed in Dunedin in July 1962. As of 1965, those were the only TV stations in the country. Similar to what happened in Australia, dramatic shows, talent shows, and quiz shows were the most popular. New Zealand also did well with cooking shows (Graham Kerr became a popular TV chef) and developed its own children's shows. Both Australia and New Zealand had some channels where advertising was permitted, and both imported shows from England. New Zealand was a market where there was also great interest in news, so when satellites came along, the ability to receive images from distant places made newsgathering much more timely. By 1971 New Zealanders were able to see news events the same day, rather than having to wait for a plane to bring footage from other countries. In 1974 New Zealand's TV stations began broadcasting some of their programs in color.

BROADCASTING MEETS THE MODERN WORLD

After World War II ended, a number of political and social changes occurred in Asia. The most notable was the communist takeover of China in 1949, after the civil war. Having lost that war, the Kuomintang (KMT) took up residence in Formosa (today Taiwan), which had been under Japanese control until the Axis powers had been defeated in World War II. Meanwhile, the victorious Communist Party established the People's Republic of China. In Korea, a civil war broke out in 1950 and continued till 1953; both North Korea and South Korea used their state-run radio stations to broadcast their versions of events, hoping to score propaganda points with listeners in the other country. The United States, too, was eager to broadcast to Korea during the conflict, and the Voice of America began offering expanded news and commentary. The broadcasts were heard in Seoul with no problems, but the U.S. government hoped the broadcasts would also reach areas where the communists were dominant. When the Korean War ended, North Korea became a totalitarian communist country, and South Korea, while also run by a dictator, tended to be pro-West and pro-United States.

Japan, which had been on the losing side in World War II, was occupied by the Allies until 1952. General Douglas MacArthur put all Japanese stations under American supervision during that time, forbidding content that was critical of the Allies and banning propaganda broadcasts. (Prior to losing the war, Japan had become well known for its sultry female broadcaster called Tokyo Rose, who aired anti-American propaganda to the U.S. troops via

Radio Tokyo.) By the time the occupation ended, Japan had begun to develop a fairly democratic broadcast medium compared to those of China and Formosa (Taiwan). Japan was quick to embrace modern technology, especially modern media. Sony manufactured one of the first transistor radios in 1955; as in America, the small portable radio became very popular with young people. Sony also manufactured a transistorized TV as early as 1960. Television became so popular in Japan that by 1982, a survey done by ACNielsen showed that the average Japanese person watched as much as eight hours of TV a day.[18]

In China during the 1950s and 1960s, the government continued to maintain strict control over all broadcasts. With the continuing emphasis on radio, the Communist Party used radio to promote "patriotic education" and to disseminate the teachings of Chairman Mao Zedong. The introduction of television did not change this substantially. Popular culture and entertainment programs were frowned upon. Traditional folk music or opera was acceptable, as were programs about art or literature. But much of the emphasis was on offering courses. In March 1960, Peking Teachers' University was among the first to broadcast college lectures on mathematics, physics, and chemistry.[19] Interest in television grew slowly. CCTV (China Central TV), China's national service, went on the air in 1958, serving only a limited area; by 1978 it was transmitting programs to more than twenty-six provinces and autonomous regions. News broadcasts were an important component of what was provided, and the general tone of the news was pro-Chinese government and anti-American. But after Chairman Mao's death in 1976, change began to occur. Beginning in the late 1970s, under the leadership of Deng Xiaopeng, the Chinese media started moving away from the model of broadcasting only education and propaganda, permitting more entertainment programming and encouraging more stations to broadcast. As of 2005, CCTV was operating 16 channels. There were a total of 350 channels across the country, with 60 of them in greater Beijing. The Communist Party still supervised what was on the air, especially when news was involved. However, it was no longer unusual to see music videos, soap operas, or sporting events. Chinese versions of HBO and MTV both became available, and commercials were an accepted part of life. Currently, Chinese television is still in transition as it moves farther away from a model that mainly emphasized educating viewers in communist doctrine. The government has become more accommodating toward entertainment programming, and stations have begun to offer more shows about business and about popular culture.

It was in Australia that the seeds of global media change were first sown, even though few people realized it at the time. In Canberra a new national newspaper, the *Australian*, began publication in mid-July 1964. The company that published the paper was the News Limited Group, headed by Rupert Murdoch. Murdoch had taken over his late father's newspaper in Melbourne, and he was busy expanding his newspaper holdings. By October 1969, in addition to other newspapers in Australia, he had purchased the *News of the World* and the *London Daily Sun*. He owned newspapers in New Zealand and Hong Kong as well, and by November 1976, he owned the *New York Post*. In fact, at that time he owned eighty-three newspapers and eleven magazines worldwide, and he was just getting started. In the United States, he became best known for creating the controversial *Fox News Channel* in October 1996, but internationally, he was becoming a major factor in both cable TV and satellite. In 1983 he started the satellite TV channel called Sky; by 1990, it became known as BSKyB after it merged with British Satellite Broadcasting. In 1993 Murdoch purchased a 64 percent share of a Hong Kong satellite broadcaster called Star TV, and in 1995, he acquired full control.[20] In the 1990s, thanks to the relaxation of worldwide media regulations, companies from one country were suddenly able to buy up properties in other countries. As a result, Rupert Murdoch became one of the most influential players in the rise of global media empires. Today his news corporation owns TV and radio networks, book publishing companies, movie studios, newspapers, and magazines. His personal political views continue to be expressed in the media he owns.

In addition to the growth of Murdoch's media holdings, media deregulation has enabled an American behemoth, Clear Channel Communications, to buy shares of stations in Australia and New Zealand. When bans on foreign ownership were eliminated in 1992 by Parliament's Broadcasting Services Act, Clear Channel was able to acquire a 50 percent share of the Australian Radio Network, which owns stations in cities throughout Australia. The arrival of Clear Channel has been controversial: some critics in those countries have accused Clear Channel of ignoring local culture and bringing in a lowest common denominator, cookie-cutter style of broadcasting. Despite what critics may have thought, though, Clear Channel has had a dramatic influence, contributing to the spread of American-style formats, such as classic rock, and influencing the way radio sounds throughout Oceania.

In addition to allowing media moguls such as Rupert Murdoch and giant conglomerates such as Clear Channel, which owns over 1,200 stations in the United States, to gain more power worldwide, the global revolution that started in the 1980s and 90s also can be seen in the various entertainment media. South Korea is now a major force in providing content to TV stations all over the world, and not just to the large Korean diaspora communities in American cities such as Los Angeles. Korean dramatic shows with subtitles can be seen in China, Hong Kong, Taiwan, the Philippines, and Singapore. *Hallyu*, or the Korean Wave, has become a factor all across Asia, spreading Korean hit songs and Korean culture. It has also been good for tourism: one Korean soap opera, *Jewel in the Palace*, has become so popular that Asian fans make trips to see the city where it was filmed.

And then there is music—while educational stations still preserve traditional programming such as Chinese Opera, the mass audience has become devoted to the hits. With a proliferation of hit music radio stations and video channels, Canto-pop, Mando-pop, and J-pop styles of music are heard everywhere. In a global world, these Cantonese, Mandarin, and Japanese music videos are sung in karaoke bars and played throughout Asia and beyond. Thus, the singers who perform in these genres now have fans in cities far beyond their home country. Thanks to MTV Asia, as well as to Korean music video channels such as m.net, popular artists have gained wider audiences. This has also been helped by the fact that most of the popular music video channels have Websites where young people can read about their favorite stars and download their songs. In Hong Kong, Canto-pop stars are so much a part of life that a series of postage stamps was issued to commemorate several performers who died tragically (among them, Wong Ka-Kui of the popular group Beyond, who died of injuries sustained in a fall from a stage during a performance, and the actress and singer Anita Mui, who died after a long battle with cancer). And although critics lament that Canto-, Mando- and J-pop are bland and formulaic, they have been around since the late 1970s and show no sign of going away. In fact, some of the founding fathers and mothers of the genre are now being heard on the Asian equivalent of "oldies" stations. And as in the United States, some of these early pop stars are now reuniting for nostalgia-oriented pop concerts.

Globalization has brought U.S. channels and programs to Asia (even *Desperate Housewives* was shown in China, although the Chinese audience had trouble identifying with the characters) and U.S. music formats to Australia and New Zealand. But in each country of Asia and Oceania, there are still a large number of local radio, TV, and music stars who have managed to maintain their popularity. The walls may have come down for consumer goods, so that cellular phones and video games from South Korea, Japan, and China are for sale all over the world, but not every country has freedom of the press (China and North Korea still do not) and of the broadcast media, and not every country is entirely comfortable with foreign ownership of the various media. Australian critics still worry that Clear Channel, as it is accused of doing in the United States, will stifle competition and further homogenize broadcasting, taking away even more of Australian media's uniqueness and localism.

Also, some media critics in Japan are concerned that global television has not necessarily improved society. One criticism from academics is that violent TV programs from the United States and elsewhere are creating a more violent generation of young people. This criticism is even being heard in countries that have embraced Western culture. In Japan, TV was once presented as a miracle, and American shows such as *Superman* were dubbed into Japanese for an adoring public.[21] Currently, however, while U.S. programs are still popular, there are also signs that the adoration has waned. "Dr. [Shizuo] Machizawa has identified a new youth symptom. He calls it *hikikomori*, a coined term for 'social withdrawal,' and has painted a portrait of the hikikomori youth which mirrors the ... 'couch-potato.'" While he is not accusing TV of creating delinquents, the group of delinquent boys he studied all exhibited similar behaviors: "Dr Machizawa says his defined youth avoids school, lolls in front of a television set, shuts himself (rather than herself) in his bedroom to play video games, talks online to any who will respond, and gorges on junk food."[22] In a similar way, Japanese health professionals are becoming increasingly concerned that even young people who are not delinquent in any way, and who do well in school, are becoming less physically fit. In a 2000 survey, health professionals found that more young people were eating junk food and watching hours of television instead of getting exercise.[23]

Whether the new global world of media is seen as positive or not, radio and television have dramatically impacted the way people live. These media have brought the biggest names in entertainment to rural areas of the world and have given people from all socioeconomic backgrounds equal access to newsmakers. Radio and TV have also helped create celebrities and spread new fads: with globalization, what may have been a local phenomenon can now be enjoyed worldwide. Although some media critics believe there is too much emphasis on consumerism, one result of globalization may be that people all over the world will come to know and respect each others' cultures a little more.

SOUTH AND SOUTHEAST ASIA

SHELTON A. GUNARATNE AND AMOS OWEN THOMAS

SOUTH ASIA

The second half of the twentieth century, and particularly its final years, witnessed an economic, technological, and cultural transformation of large parts of Asia in relation to radio and television broadcasting and reception, and this on a scale unprecedented for any communication media in this part of the world. The establishment of shortwave and satellite radio, and the arrival and consolidation of terrestrial, satellite, and digital television, together with the emergence of mass-mediated popular cultures that such phenomena entail, have changed the vary fabric of everyday life in many of the new nations of South and Southeast Asia. The extent, pervasiveness, and rapidity of the transformation have been particularly remarkable under the forces of globalization, which have swiftly ended older government monopolies on broadcasting in many places, and have also thrown state and private-sector enterprises into an unpredictable market "mix." Despite their obvious importance for the cultural survival and health of these nations, the cultural dimensions of the new broadcasting technologies have not yet begun to be studied with the necessary comprehensiveness.

Radio and television broadcasting have longer histories in some Southeast Asian countries than in some parts of South Asia. For a variety of geographical, historical, cultural, and political reasons, several nations in Southeast Asia—especially Malaysia, Singapore, Indonesia, and Thailand—have been at the forefront of innovation at the interface of society and contemporary technology. Since programs in these media are broadcast in dozens of disparate languages, and their audiences belong to different socioeconomic classes and to many different ethnicities, religions, and systems of social organization, the study of their content and their cultural impact still remains in its infancy. In order to arrive at a better comprehension of the mass-mediated and popular cultures that have emerged in this region in the course of the past 50 to 75 years, it is important to grasp the underlying transformations brought about by broadcasting and its economics, technology, and politics.

Given the relative sparseness of current literature on the content of the emergent media cultures in these complex, multilingual societies, this section focuses primarily on the recent history as well as on the economic and political conditions of broadcasting in five South Asian countries (Pakistan, India, Nepal, Bangladesh, and Sri Lanka), which can now be analyzed in the requisite detail for the first time. The section also explores the broad history, infrastructure, and political contexts of radio and television in six countries in Southeast Asia (Thailand, Vietnam, the Philippines, Malaysia, Singapore, and Indonesia).

Pakistan

Radio Broadcasting

The partition of 1947 compelled the emerging new nations of India and Pakistan to negotiate the latter's share of the assets of All India Radio, the broadcasting organization that earlier had operated in British India and the independent princely states on the subcontinent (see below). Pakistan inherited three low-power stations: two in what was then West Pakistan, with locations in Lahore and Peshawar, and one in East Pakistan (now Bangladesh), with a location in Dhaka. The following year the city of Karachi acquired a medium-wave radio station, which soon added two 50-kilowatt transmitters. Pakistan Broadcasting Service (later designated as Radio Pakistan) inaugurated five external services from Karachi in August 1949. Rawalpindi came on the air in 1950, Hyderabad in 1951, and Quetta in 1956. A receiving center at Peshawar and another station at Rawalpindi were established four years later. Ten years later, a training facility opened in Islamabad, and a station opened in Multan. Radio Pakistan World Service was inaugurated in April 1973 for Pakistanis overseas. Radio stations were also set up at Khairpur in 1974, and at Bahawalpur in 1975.

The Broadcasting Corporation Act converted Radio Pakistan into a statutory corporation in 1973. In 1977 the Pakistan Broadcasting Corporation at Islamabad moved its main unit to the new National Broadcasting House and opened stations in remote areas of Pakistan, such as Gilgit, Skardu, and Turbat. Stations established later at Dera Ismail Khan, Khuzdar, and Faisalabad further increased radio's reach.

Radio Pakistan opened a new broadcasting house in Khairpur in May 1986, as well as relay stations at Abbottabad and Sibi in 1989. Coverage extended to even remoter parts of the country with new stations at Chitral, Loralai, and Zhob in the 1990s. In 1997 the federal information minister computerized the Pakistan Broadcasting Corporation's news processing system and increased the availability of online news in text and audio form.

Although broadcasting has been a state monopoly from the outset, in 1995 the government of Prime Minister Benazir Bhutto allowed the introduction of private-sector FM broadcasting in Karachi, Lahore, and Islamabad. In October 1998 Radio Pakistan started its FM 101 network transmission, covering not only these three urban centers but also Faisalabad, Hyderabad, Peshawar, Sialkot, and Quetta; in 2005, it opened a new regular FM network covering Gawadar, Mianwali, Sargodha, Kohat, Bannu, and Mithi. Currently, Pakistan Broadcasting Corporation (also called Radio Pakistan) provides more than 300 hours of news and programs of general interest daily over its twenty-five radio stations in Punjab (seven), Northwest Frontier Province (four), Sindh (four), Baluchistan (six), Northern Area (two), and Azad Jammu and Kashmir (two). United Nations' data show that Pakistan has a radio density of 10.5 receivers for 100 inhabitants, which means there are approximately 17.5 million radio sets in the country.

The Home Service of Radio Pakistan broadcasts in twenty languages—including English, Urdu, Punjabi, Sindhi, Baluchi, Dari, and Pushto—to cover 75 percent of the land area and 95 percent of the population, which now stands at about 166 million. Information and education occupy almost half of its programming. The rest of its programming (the general programming) is made up of music (48 percent); religion (12.5 percent); news and current affairs (11 percent); rural and farm issues (10 percent); women, children, and labor (5 percent); youth (3 percent); sports (2.5 percent); special programs for the defense forces (2 percent); drama (2 percent); publicity campaigns (2 percent); and science, technology, and health (2 percent). An exclusive News and Current Affairs Channel broadcasts for seven hours daily from Islamabad over a network of eleven stations.

The World Service of Radio Pakistan strives to keep expatriate Pakistanis informed of the happenings in their mother country by providing ten hours of daily programming in Urdu and English. It operates five transmissions: one for Southeast Asia and two each for the Middle East and Europe. The separate External Service of Radio Pakistan broadcasts in fifteen languages: Arabic, English, Bangla, Chinese, Dari, Farsi, Gujarati, Hindi, Hazargi, Nepali, Russian, Sinhalese, Turkish, Turkic, and Tamil. This service is used as an instrument to project the country's policies from its own perspective to the world, especially to its neighbors.

FM100, the first 24-hour live commercial radio station in Pakistan, owned and operated by a private company, covers the three main urban population centers of the country—Karachi, Lahore, and Islamabad—and their surrounding areas. Its regular programs include Urdu pop music, Punjabi and Western music for younger listeners, the latest film-song hits aimed primarily at homemakers, and *ghazals* and folk songs for listeners of all ages. With stations in Sindh (Karachi and Hyderabad), Punjab (Islamabad, Sialkot, Lahore, and Faisalabad), Baluchistan (Quetta), and the Northwest Frontier Province (Peshawar), FM 100 competes with Radio Pakistan's FM 101 network and regular FM network (see above).

Other competing private-sector FM radio stations and networks include City FM 89 (Karachi, Lahore, Rawalpindi, Faisalabad, and Islamabad); Radio One FM 91 (Karachi); Radio Active FM 95 (Karachi); Power Radio FM 99 (Islamabad and Abbottabad); Mast FM 103 (Lahore); Radio Buraq FM 104 (Sialkot and Gujarat); Awaz Radio FM 105

(Gujarat and Gujranwala); Sachal Radio FM 105 (Hyderabad); Hum FM 106.2 (Karachi, Sukkur, Lahore, and Islamabad); and Apna Karachi FM 107 (Karachi).

Television

Television broadcasting in Pakistan began in November 1964 when a small pilot station (one of two, set up under an agreement with Nippon Electric Company of Japan) in Lahore conducted the first black-and-white television transmission. The experimental phase was completed in 1965, and control of the facilities went to Television Promoters, a private company that became a public limited company, the Pakistan Television Corporation, two years later. It established television centers in Karachi and Rawalpindi-Islamabad in 1967, and in Peshawar and Quetta in 1974. Color transmission began in December 1976, and in 1992 the corporation set up a second channel, PTV-2, for educational programming. In 1994 the corporation began beaming its programs via AsiaSat to thirty-eight countries. In 1998 it introduced its satellite channel, PTV World. It also began Prime TV to reach expatriate Pakistanis.

Shalimar Television Network, a combined public-private enterprise, established the country's second TV network in 1989. Now known as the ATV Network, it operates twenty stations. Shaheen Pay TV became the country's first subscriber television channel in 1996, but a legal challenge led to its early demise. In 2002 the government set up the Pakistan Electronic Media Regulatory Authority, which oversees the broadcasting industry. Although the available data are not sufficiently precise or current, a reasonable estimate suggests that in 2006, there may have been up to 20 million television sets in Pakistan, reaching a total viewership of roughly half the country's population (currently at about 166 million).

Pakistan Television Corporation today operates PTV 1 (the original TV channel), PTV National (a satellite channel providing regional programs in the various languages spoken in Pakistan), PTV World (a 24-hour global news channel), PTV Bolan (a regional satellite channel established in Quetta in 2005), and AJK TV (the Kashmiri channel, with programs highlighting the cause of Kashmir). The corporation takes special pride in its daily programs that broadcast translations, exegeses, and learned commentaries on Islamic scripture, the Qur'an.

Since 2000 a new open-media policy has eroded the near-monopolistic power of the Pakistan Television Corporation, and several private channels have emerged to compete with it. The ATV network (formerly Shalimar TV Network), which had its only transmitting station at Islamabad in 1990, now operates with twenty stations located at Islamabad, Karachi, Lahore, Faisalabad, Daska, Multan, Bahawalpur, Larkana, Hyderabad, Sukkur, Peshawar, Mangora, Qalat, Batkhail, Khuzdar, Thandyani, Sahiwal, Sibi, Quetta, and Tando Allahyar, covering more than 50 percent of the population. Its program mix includes entertainment (40 percent), information (37 percent), and education (23 percent).

Aaj TV (Today TV), a 24-hour entertainment channel started by the Business Recorder Group, provides four well-defined program features: news, current affairs, entertainment, and "infotainment." In collaboration with news sources from more than 100 countries, it provides a round-the-clock world news service. It is the only digital television service (with terrestrial transmission) in Pakistan, with bureaus in Karachi, Islamabad, and Lahore.

ARY Digital (formerly the Pakistan Channel), now operated from Dubai Media City in the United Arab Emirates and with studios in Pakistan and England, serves the Pakistani diaspora overseas with popular live English and Urdu programs. Its other services include QTV (religion), ARY Bangla, the City Channel, and the Musik.

Geo TV Network began programming in 2002 on the PAS 10 digital satellite. Owned by the Jang Group of newspapers, it is another Urdu language service operated from Dubai

Media City. It broadcasts interactive infotainment, daily serials (such as the popular *Jo Baat Ghar Main Hai* [The Issue in the House]), current events, political analyses (as in the hard-hitting *Follow up with Fahd*), and children's programs.

Another private satellite television operator is the Indus Media Group, which launched the Indus TV Network with its flagship channel Indus Vision. Its other channels are Indus Music, Indus News, and Indus Plus. In 2005 it launched Indus TV, which is targeted at audiences in Europe and North America.

Pakistan's regional television channels in the private sector include Apna TV, Punjab TV, and Ravi TV (all in Punjabi); Kashish TV, Sindh TV, and KTN (all in Sindhi, with KTN broadcasting nationally); and AVT Khyber (in Pashto). The foreign-owned TV channels broadcasting in the country are CNBC Pakistan, HBO Pakistan, Cartoon Network Pakistan, and 10 Sports Pakistan.

India

Radio Broadcasting

The Indian Broadcasting Company, a private enterprise, first sponsored radio broadcasting in British India in the cities of Bombay (now Mumbai) and Calcutta (now Kolkata) in 1927. Three years later, the colonial government took over the company's broadcasting and renamed it the Indian State Broadcasting Service, which became All India Radio in 1936. The same year, the British Broadcasting Corporation's Lionel Fielden arrived in India to streamline All India Radio's operations. At the time of partition and independence in 1947, India had eleven radio stations—six under the British colonial government and five in various princely states (Indian kingdoms not formally part of British India but nevertheless under British suzerainty on the subcontinent). After independence, radio became an important medium to promote the policies of the new Indian republic, which barred private enterprise in radio broadcasting until the turn of the twenty-first century.

All India Radio (AIR, also known as Akashwani in Hindi), India's main radio broadcasting network, is a division of Prasar Bharati (Broadcasting Corporation of India), created in 1997 as an autonomous body under the Ministry of Information and Broadcasting. The home services of AIR broadcast in 24 languages and 146 dialects, while its external services broadcast in 27 languages, including 10 foreign languages. AIR covers 99.4 percent of India's 1.1 billion people; United Nations figures show that in 2000, India had 12 radio receivers per 100 people, or over 130 million radio sets.

AIR operates a network of 215 broadcasting centers with 144 medium-wave, 54 short-wave, and 139 frequency-modulation transmitters, most of which are used to provide five regional services (in the north, the northeast, the east, the west, and the south) at distinct FM frequencies. Although AIR is a public service broadcaster, it also runs a popular nationwide commercial service, Vivid Bharati Seva (Multi-Indian Service), using separate medium-wave transmitters in eleven cities. Vivid Bharati offers a wide range of widely heard radio programs, including news, film and music programming, and comedy shows. Its typical programs include popular Hindi film songs (e.g., *Cibaca Geet Mala* [The Cibaca-sponsored Garland of Songs], skits (e.g., *Hawa-mahal* [The Wind Palace]), and jokes and humor (e.g., *Santojan ki Mehfil* [A Gathering of Good Folks]).

In addition, AIR provides the Yuva-Vani [The Voices of the Young] service, which encourages youth participation and experimentation with varied script ideas. Some Yuva-Vani shows, such as *The Roving Microphone*, *Mehfil* [Gathering], and *In the Groove,* have a rich history, having been on the air continuously for more than 30 years.

Radio and Television

AIR's monopoly of radio broadcasting came to an end in 2000 when the government decided to allow up to eleven new private FM channels in each major city. In 2001 expatriate steel magnate R. K. Mittal (based in the United Kingdom) set up India's first private FM radio station, Radio City, in Bangalore, with assistance from Australian Rupert Murdoch's STAR satellite broadcasting channel (see sidebar on the Zee Network). During this first phase of broadcasting liberalization, the license agreement banned private stations from broadcasting news and programs on public affairs. With the onset of the second phase of liberalization in 2006, the government was expected to lift this ban and allow private FM broadcasters to share the infrastructural facilities of the Prasar Bharati Corporation (the parent organization of AIR) in ninety-one cities on a license-fee basis. Under the new policy, 337 additional private FM radio channels will be available across the country.

Entertainment Network (India) Limited, India's first pure-play radio broadcasting company to go public, operates nine radio stations, one each in Mumbai, Delhi, Kolkata, Chennai, Bangalore, Indore, Ahmedabad, Pune, and Jaipur, under the name Radio Mirchi. This network is acknowledged to be the leader among the private FM radio broadcasters in terms of revenues and audience.

Television

Television was a state monopoly from its beginning in India. Television broadcasting began in 1959 as an educational experiment involving television clubs in New Delhi. Regular programming in this medium started in New Delhi in 1965. By 1975 only about a dozen cities—including New Delhi, Mumbai, Chennai, and Poona (now Pune)—were receiving television signals. In April 1976 the government separated the television unit from AIR and gave it the name Doordarshan, which retained its monopoly on television broadcasting in India for the next 16 years.

With the opening up of the market in 1992, TV18 emerged as India's premier private-sector business and consumer news broadcaster. It began to offer prime-time television content to most of the larger channels in India, including BBC, Star Plus, Sony Entertainment Television, Zee, MTV, and Discovery. Zee TV launched its round-the-clock news channel, Zee News, in 1995 with the motto *Sabse Pahle* (The Very First). Star News joined the 24-hour-news fray in 1998, signing a five-year contract with NDTV (New Delhi Television Company) to provide news content. In November 1999, TV18 and CNBC Asia joined to start CNBC India. TV Today, a company in the India Today Group (see the chapter on Periodicals), launched a popular 24-hour Hindi news channel named Aaj Tak [Until Today] in December 2000.

After the expiration of its contract with Star News, NDTV set up two 24-hour news channels, NDTV 24X7 (English) and NDTV India (Hindi). The Sahara India Parivar group also started a 24-hour national Hindi news channel, Sahara Samay, in March 2003, with Doordarshan News (the government's original channel) following suit in November 2003. The following year, the independent entrepreneurial and journalistic team of Rajat Sharma, Sohaib Ilyasi, and Tarun Tejpal set up India TV, a free-to-air Hindi news and current affairs channel. NDTV stepped into the high-quality business news segment with NDTV Profit, a 24-hour business channel, in January 2005. Meanwhile, CNBC India (TV18) set up Awaaz, a 24-hour consumer channel in Hindi. Another Hindi news channel, Channel 7 of Jagran TV, came into operation in March 2005.

As this summary suggests, the forces of globalization put a fairly drastic end to the monopoly on television broadcasting in India that Doordarshan, the state public-service

ZEE NETWORK: A CORPORATE SUCCESS STORY

The media conglomerate currently known as Zee Network (formerly Zee International) started in India in 1992 in the form of two sister companies: Zee TV (a satellite television channel) and Zee Telefilms (Zee TV's content supplier). Shortly afterward, Zee entered into a joint venture with the STAR group (Satellite Television Asia Region) to expand its broadcasting. In 1994 the Australian Rupert Murdoch's News Corporation acquired the satellite distribution business of STAR. The following year, Zee entered into a joint venture with News Corporation, launching the Zee News and Zee Cinema channels as well as Zee TV-Europe (based in the United Kingdom).

Zee and News Corporation then co-founded SitiCable Network, which enabled them to start Siti Channel, India's first cable television channel, in 1996. The same year Zee expanded its range by launching Zee TV-Africa; in 1997, it added the Zee Music channel; in the following year, it expanded into North America with Zee TV-USA. In 200, Zee ended its six-year joint venture by buying out News Corporation's 50 percent stakes in three companies: Asia Today (broadcasting), Programme Asia Trading (software), and SitiCable Network (cable distribution). With these three acquisitions as wholly owned subsidiaries, Zee became a fully integrated media company, with its own programming, broadcasting, and distribution in satellite, cable, and digital television.

Zee is unique because its content is produced entirely in Hindi and other South Asian languages (currently Bengali, Gujarati, Marathi, and Punjabi), and because, as founder and chief executive Subhash Chandra conceived of it at the start, this subscription service is aimed at a very specific audience: Indians, whether at home and abroad. By 2004 Zee had probably begun to reach roughly 20 million homes and over 100 million viewers in India alone, with as many as 225 million viewers in more than eighty countries spread across Asia, Africa, Europe, and North America.

Zee's television schedule for this enormous audience includes daytime serials (Bollywood-style counterparts of American soaps), children's shows, primetime comedy and drama, sports, miniseries, and specials as well as programs on current affairs, business, health, and religion—not to mention popular game shows and Bollywood and other South Asian movies. Zee already has more than 30,000 hours of television programming in its archives.

broadcaster, had held until the early 1990s. The breach occurred when a profusion of satellite-to-cable services clamored for the market after the nationwide impact of CNN's satellite broadcasts to India of the Gulf War in 1991. The liberalization of television broadcasting brought several international and Asia-regional services into the Indian market, which stimulated several existing large indigenous companies to expand into the multimedia broadcasting sector. According to Doordarshan, around the turn of the twenty-first century, 69 million homes in India had television sets, reaching approximately 362 million domestic viewers. At the end of 2004, the number of homes with television sets in India was estimated at 83 million, which, given communal viewing practices, corresponds to about 480 million domestic viewers.

Doordarshan, which continues to be India's dominant television broadcaster despite private-sector competition, is a division (like AIR) of the Prasar Bharati Corporation. In 2005 Doordarshan, with fifty-nine studio centers, operated twenty-seven television channels: five national channels, eleven regional-language satellite channels, eight *kendras* (centers) for the large Hindi-speaking region stretching from Rajasthan to Bihar, one international channel (Doordarshan India, which uses the PanAmSat 4 satellite to reach the Indian diaspora in some fifty countries), and two parliament channels (modeled on C-SPAN in the USA and covering proceedings in the two houses of the Indian Parliament). Except for the Hindi-region kendras, all Doordarshan channels now broadcast around the clock.

Doordarshan is the only terrestrial broadcaster in India, even though it cannot transmit all its channels in the terrestrial mode. In fact, the Prasar Bharati Corporation also operates Doordarshan Direct Plus, a free-to-air satellite direct-to-home platform, which carries nineteen Doordarshan channels, fourteen private-sector television channels (Sun TV, Star Utsav, MH1, Jain TV, Akash Bangla, Kairali, BBC World, ETC Punjabi, Smile TV, Aaj Tak, Headlines Today, TV 9, ETV Marathi, and Zee Music), as well as twelve audio channels. Two terrestrial channels broadcast nationwide: Doordarshan-1 National (focusing on news, entertainment, and education) and Doordarshan-2 News (focusing on news and current affairs).

Doordarshan follows a three-tier (national, regional, and local) program policy. At specific times, it beams regional programs on Doordarshan-1 National and also on the regional language satellite channels, catering to the interests of particular states, in the language(s) of those parts of the country. The local programs are area specific, cover local issues, and feature local people. Doordarshan's regional-language satellite channels televise infotainment programs in Assamese, Bengali, Gujarati, Malayalam, Marathi, Kannada, Telugu, Kashmiri, Oriya, and Tamil.

Although Doordarshan is a public service broadcaster, since 1976 it has accepted commercials to supplement its revenue earnings from license fees. With the advent of transnational commercial television in the early 1990s, Doordarshan had to adapt quickly in order to compete effectively with its private-sector counterparts. Among the early competitors were STAR Plus (launched in August 1991 by Richard Li), the first satellite channel to beam its signal to the subcontinent; Zee TV (started in October 1992 by Subhash Chandra), the first privately-owned Hindi channel; and subsequently Sony, followed by such domestic channels as Eenadu, Asianet, and Sun TV.

Moreover, Doordarshan was forced to compete with international channels such as the BBC and CNN in news and current events programs. In February 1995 Doordarshan began airing *News Tonight*, the national news program produced by Prannoy Roy's New Delhi TV (NDTV), the country's first private producer of national news. TV Today Network also aired *Aaj Tak*, a Hindi current affairs program, on the Doordarshan Metro channel.

Private providers such as ETV, Sun TV, and Asianet have emerged as strong leaders in regional TV broadcasting. The Zee Network currently has four regional-language channels, one each in Bengali, Gujarati, Marathi, and Punjabi. Star Network has introduced Star Vijay, a very popular entertainment channel, in Tamil. Moreover, the ETV Network, a part of the Ramoji Group, has established twelve dedicated regional channels, which target the speakers of eight different languages: Bengali, Gujarati, Hindi, Kannada, Marathi, Oriya, Telugu, and Urdu. ETV Network's broadcasting strategy is complex: Andhra Pradesh (the Telugu-speaking region), for example, can access all twelve channels, which include three news channels (ETV2, TV 9, and Teja News) as well as one song-based channel. Sahara India Pariwar offers five news channels as the bouquet of Sahara Samay: Sahara Samay NCR, Sahara Samay Mumbai, Sahara Samay Bihar & Jharkhand, Sahara Samay Madhya Pradesh & Chattisgarh, and Sahara Samay Uttar Pradesh & Uttaranchal. Finely tuned technological, programming, and marketing innovations of this kind appear to be the most successful means of catering to the size as well as the linguistic and cultural complexity of the open Indian television market.

> ## TELEVISION PROGRAMMING, IN A LIGHTER VEIN
>
> "Family dramas" and "romantic comedies" produced for Indian-language television, primarily in Hindi for several decades but now also in such languages as Bengali, Gujarati, Marathi, and Punjabi, often borrow their narrative formulas from Bollywood cinema. Viewers in the West are familiar with these paradigms and devices from American daytime soaps and their counterparts on Spanish-language television in Latin America. The following summaries of the frame stories of two prime-time shows broadcast weekly in half-hour episodes on Zee TV in 2006 capture the formulaic nature of such narratives in popular television programming in this decade.
>
> *Dulhan Banu Main Teri* [I'll Be Your Bride], a family drama from Zee TV (2006) showcases Vidya, a docile and illiterate girl from a small village in rural India, who finds her world utterly transformed when an arranged marriage makes her the bride of Aditya, the son of a rich modern *thakur* (estate owner). When she arrives at her new home, she encounters the deep hostility of her three sisters-in-law, especially Naina, who works in close cahoots with her own husband Aniket. Vidya's ailing father-in-law, a good man, unfortunately passes away shortly after Vidya's wedding; her mother-in-law, Gayatri, proves to be a weak matriarch, and Vidya's husband's sisters mistreat him—and her—at will. Helpless and diffident, Vidya nevertheless resolves to stand her ground and to change the ways of the household. But as she tries to reconcile Gayatri and Aditya (mother and son), to overcome hostility, and to be accepted as the legitimate *dulhan* (bride) in the family, she discovers that animosities run deep, and that things are not as they seem.
>
> *Jab Love Hua* [When Love "Happened"] is a romantic comedy on Zee TV (2006). It is the youthful, "fresh and hilarious love story" of Aanya (played by Priya Badlani) and Raghu (played by Sudeep Sahir). Aanya is a pretty, spirited, and thoroughly spoilt 18-year-old girl from a wealthy family, used to expensive clothes, cars, and holidays, who is surrounded by a host of similarly spoilt young men. She knows that she "has it all," and she "believes in the power of money and uses it to her advantage." But fate intervenes abruptly: a series of untoward events and an unwanted wish conspire to make her lose it all. Thrown suddenly into a new world, she encounters an unfamiliar kind of person in Raghu. "*Jab Love Hua* will make you laugh just when you are about to cry!"

Nepal

Radio Broadcasting

The government of Nepal owned and operated all broadcast media in the country until 1987. Broadcasting began in 1951 with the establishment of Radio Nepal, which operated a 250-watt transmitter. When Nepali was declared the medium of instruction in the nation's schools in 1965, Radio Nepal ceased its news broadcasts in Hindi and Newari. Today, however, news bulletins are delivered at various times in languages other than Nepali, including Newari and Hindi.

Five years after the 1991 communications task force headed by Narahari Acharya made its recommendations, the government granted a license to the Nepal Forum of Environmental Journalists to operate the first privately owned FM radio station, Radio Sagarmatha, in the Kathmandu Valley. It began regular broadcasting in March 1998. However, in 1995, the state-owned Radio Nepal gained a head start on FM radio when it established the first FM channel in Kathmandu. Since then, almost fifty private FM broadcasting services have emerged in Nepal, about one-third of them in Kathmandu. They include Kantipur FM (the first privately owned FM radio to go on air in Nepal), Image FM, Times FM, Hits FM, Nepal FM, HBC FM, Radio City, Star FM, Classic FM, Adhyatma Jyoti FM, and Bhaktapur FM. Additional FM channels are operated by British Forces Broadcasting Service, Kathmandu City Metropolitan Government, and Environmental Cycle Radio. FM stations outside Kathmandu started broadcasting in 2000, with Lumbini FM in Manigram leading the way.

Nepal has 3.9 radio receivers per 100 people, or roughly a total of 1 million radio sets. Radio Nepal broadcasts from thirteen transmitting stations: six medium-wave (at Kathmandu, Bardibas, Pokhara, Surkhet, Dipayal, and Dharan), six FM (at Burgunj, Hetauda, Bharatpur, Jomsom, Humla, and Illam), and one shortwave (at Khumaltar, with three transmitters). Radio Nepal's transmitters are thus able to reach all regions of the country. Its shortwave transmission is estimated to reach listeners throughout the kingdom, while its medium-wave transmission reaches 70 percent to 80 percent of the population (currently a little over 28 million).

Through its regional stations, Radio Nepal offers two hours of programs for listeners in different regions. It broadcasts national programs for 16 hours every day, using a variety of formats such as features, documentaries, documentary-dramas, dramas, talk shows, interviews, music shows, and live commentaries. It also offers educational programs on religion, literature, science and technology, agriculture, distance learning, women, health and sanitation, public health, and children and youth. Entertainment and commercials account for 58 percent of its total programming.

Television

The Nepalese government converted the Television Project, which it had initially set up to examine the feasibility of introducing the new medium, to Nepal Television Corporation (NTV) in 1985. NTV started broadcasting in the Kathmandu Valley in December of the same year. Its locally produced programs became so popular that it had to replace its low-power transmitter to extend its signals beyond the capital.

Satellite television entered Nepal in July 2001 when both NTV and the private-sector channel, Nepal Network (owned by cable operator Space Time Network), began transmitting their programs via the Intelsat and Thaicom satellites, respectively. Nepal 1 describes itself as "the first Nepali language satellite channel being beamed from India."[1] Kantipur TV network, an arm of the Kantipur Media Group and an affiliate channel of CNN, came into operation in July 2003. Pioneering private television channels in Nepal include Shangrila (still awaiting equipment for its operation), Image Metro, and the short-lived Young Nepal TV.

Television density in Nepal is 0.8 receivers per 100 people, the lowest in South Asia, which means about 250,000 television sets across the country. State-owned NTV remains the dominant broadcaster, covering about 42 percent of the country's population and 32 percent of the land area. It currently broadcasts 61 hours each week. News, current affairs, and related talk programs comprise about 30 percent of NTV content. It offers three 20-minute news bulletins a day, two of them in Nepali and one in English. Foreign programs make up 20 percent of the content.

Three private-sector television services are currently in operation: Kantipur TV, Image Metro TV, and Channel Nepal. Two other services, Shangrila TV and Avenues TV, have yet to start their broadcasts because of red tape and delays in acquiring equipment for satellite uplinking. Satellite channel Nepal 1 claims that it provides some of the most sought-after programs, such as Ramanand Sagar's *Ramayana* (a mammoth serial version of the ancient Sanskrit epic, produced in India in the 1980s, and now a "perennial" classic), dubbed in Nepali; news with a global Nepalese perspective (e.g., the role of the Gurkha Regiment as part of the international coalition forces serving in the Iraq war since 2003); career and health shows; and Nepali soap operas and Bollywood Hindi films.

Bangladesh

Radio Broadcasting

Radio transmission in what is now the nation of Bangladesh started in Dhaka on December 16, 1939, using a low-power transmitter. The first medium-wave and shortwave transmitters were installed in the city between 1959 and 1963 to improve communication between what were then East Pakistan and West Pakistan. Relaying stations were set up at that stage in Chittagong, Sylhet, Rangpur, Rajshahi, and Khulna.

The Dhaka radio station played a key role in the liberation war of 1971, when East Pakistan broke away from West Pakistan to become Bangladesh, and came to be known as the Shwadhin Bangla Betar Kendro [Independent Bengal Radio Station]. The war caused the destruction of most of the broadcasting facilities, particularly in Khulna. Soon after liberation, the new government created the Bangla Betar Radio [Radio Bangladesh], with eight regional stations. In 1975, thanks to an aid package of US$8 million from the Canadian International Development Agency, Bangladesh was able to open its first earth satellite radio station at Betbunia.

Bangladesh currently has fifteen AM, thirteen FM, and two shortwave radio broadcasting stations, with over 7 million radio sets in the country. Bangla Betar provides the national radio network with six regional services. Radio Bangladesh, the external service that broadcasts in English, Arabic, Bengali, Hindi, Nepalese, and Urdu, has its shortwave transmitters at Khabairpur and Shavar. Bangla Betar's FM radio stations now operate from Dhaka, Sylhet, Chittagong, Rajshahi, Rangpur, and Khulna.

Bangladesh has only one privately owned radio station, FM Metro Wave, but it does not carry political news. In 2002 the English- and Bengali-language services of Voice of America were allowed to retransmission in Dhaka on the state radio's FM frequencies. The BBC also transmits a Bengali service in the country.

Television

Television began in 1964 when Bangladesh was still part of Pakistan. Nippon Electric Company, as part owner of Pakistan's pilot television project, set up an experimental station in Dhaka. A satellite station in Chittagong and two relay stations in Khulna and Rajshahi were ready at the end of the decade; by 1970 these stations were broadcasting 35 hours of programming a week, mostly in Bengali. After the creation of Bangladesh in 1971, the government of President Mujibur Rahman nationalized the Bangladesh Television Corporation (BTV), with the government as the primary stockholder and Nippon Electric as a major stockholder. BTV's headquarters are now in the Rampura sector of Dhaka, signifying a significant expansion. It started color transmission in 1980 and introduced cable television in the early 1990s, which rapidly became very popular. About 1 million cable television homes had materialized by the end of the twentieth century, mostly in Dhaka and Chittagong, with about 2,000 cable operators, each serving 200–250 subscribers on average.

In the national elections of 1991 and 1996 in Bangladesh, the two main political parties—the Awami League and the Bangladesh Nationalist Party—called for a national, democratic broadcasting system free from government control. On September 9, 1996, the Awami League government then in power appointed a sixteen-member committee to recommend new measures and to authorize private-sector television and radio services. The committee submitted its report in 1997, and the government took the first step toward privatization in 1999 when it approved applications for seven privately owned satellite television stations. On July 12, 2001, Parliament granted autonomy to the state-run Bangladesh Television (BTV) and to Bangladesh Betar [Bangladesh Radio].

BTV is the state-owned but autonomous national television network. It has a potential coverage of about 93 percent of the country's population, which now stands at just over 147 million. BTV produces about 92 percent of the programming it broadcasts. Cultural and entertainment programs (35 percent) lead the program mix, followed by developmental and educational programs (30 percent), news (20 percent), and others programs (15 percent). The network was preparing for satellite transmission by the end of 2006, but the outcome remains uncertain due to the political turbulence in Bangladesh in late 2006 and early 2007, pending the resolution of problems surrounding the national elections scheduled for April 2007.

BTV's national channel uses its terrestrial network of fifteen stations (in Dhaka, Rangpur, Mymensingh, Noakhali, Satkhira, Sylhet, Khulna, Natore, Rangamal, Chittagong, Cox's Bazaar, Jenaidah, Thajurgaon, Brahmanpura, and Patunkhali) to cover the country, which by 2003 had an estimated 8.5 million sets. The BTV regional station in Chittagong broadcasts local programs in the evenings. BTV World, started in 2004, broadcasts programs to other countries in South and Southeast Asia, the Middle East, Europe, and North America.

Three private-sector television channels are now in operation: Channel i, ATN Bangla, and NTV. In 1999 the government gave permission to start seven private satellite television channels: Channel i, ATN Bangla, International Television (NTV), Inquilab Television (ITV), Universal Television (UTV), Jamuna Television (JTV), and Ekushey Television (ETV). However, only the first three went on the air; ITV, UTV and JTV failed to start broadcasting within 365 days of receiving permission, as required by the agreement, and ETV's contract was canceled by order of Bangladesh's Supreme Court.

Channel i, the first digital Bengali-language channel, has operated around the clock since its inception in October 1999. It transmits its signal via the PAS 10/4 satellite and provides a mixture of Bengali and English programs, including local news, Bengali drama, movies, and documentaries. ATN Bangla broadcasts various types of programs in Bengali, such as movies, drama, music, and documentaries, for viewers in Bangladesh as well in the state of West Bengal in India. NTV, operated by International Television Channel, is the only channel that uses a Bangladeshi satellite and transmits its programs without a satellite cable connection. It offers Bengali entertainment with serials, music, feature films, and children's features, as well as news, educational programs, and other specials during Bengali festivals (such the Durga Puja in the autumn).

Sri Lanka

Radio Broadcasting

On July 27, 1924, the broadcasting of the British governor's speech marked the first official demonstration of radio in Sri Lanka (then under colonial rule and known as Ceylon). The Government Broadcasting Station was established in December 1925. The year 1931 marked the first non-English broadcasts in Sinhala and Tamil. Sri Lanka began experimenting with shortwave broadcasting in 1934. The quality of transmissions improved after 1945 when

Great Britain turned over to Sri Lanka the powerful shortwave transmitters of its wartime South East Asia Command (SEAC).

After Sri Lanka gained its independence in 1948, the new national government formed the Department of Broadcasting, later known as Radio Ceylon, from the Government Broadcasting Station and Radio SEAC. An additional, commercial service was established in September 1950. That same year, stations began broadcasting simultaneously in Sinhala, Tamil, and English, the country's three languages. An educational service began in September 1951. Transmission began to improve four years later with the installation of a 10-kilowatt shortwave transmitter in Ekala, and in 1981, experimental stereo transmission began.

A special Farm Broadcasting Unit, created in 1967, began to air a daily rural service in 1969, featuring such popular programs as *Govi Jana Handa* [Voice of the Farmers] and the Young Farmers' Quiz Show. As with broadcasting in other former British colonies, broadcasting in Sri Lanka remained a government monopoly until the 1980s.

Today, Sri Lanka has 21.5 radio receivers per 100 people—the highest radio density in South Asia—which translates to about 4.3 million radios in a population of almost 20 million people. Although state-owned radio still dominates the country, a host of private commercial radio broadcasters provide stiff competition.

The island-wide domestic FM network of the Sri Lanka Broadcasting Corporation operates six regular program channels: Sinhala Swadeshiya Sevaya (Sinhala National Service); Tamil National Service; English Service; City FM (Sinhala); Velenda Sevaya (Sinhala Commercial Service); and Thendral (Tamil Commercial Service). The first three of these are public service channels; City FM targets young listeners, whereas the last two channels use an "adult contemporary" format while accommodating commercial content.

The corporation also operates a nationwide seventh channel, the Sports Service, which goes on the air only when major sports events, such as international cricket matches, take place. In addition it offers four regional services (in Rajarata, Ruhunu, Kandurata, and Thirayi), each of which broadcasts from its provincial studio center, as well as five community radio services (Pulathisi Ravaya, Uva Community Radio, Kothmale FM, and two Mahaweli services). Moreover, the corporation operates nine external services, transmitting on shortwave to South Asia, the Middle East, and Europe in Sinhala, English, Hindi, Tamil, Telugu, Kannada, and Malayalam. It also has a medium-wave transmitting facility for broadcasting mainly to the southern regions of India.

Seventeen private radio broadcasting services compete with the state-run services offered by the Sri Lanka Broadcasting Corporation. The Asia Broadcasting Corporation operates five services: Gold FM (English), Hiru FM (Sinhala), Sha (formerly Tharu) FM (Sinhala), Sooriyan FM (Tamil), and Sun FM (English). Maharaja Broadcasting Corporation offers four services: Shakthi FM (Tamil), Sirasa FM (Sinhala), y (formerly Classic) FM (Sinhala), and Yes FM (English). Telshan Networks provides four services: Elsira (Sinhala), Alsura (Sinhala), Lite 89.2, and TNL 1017 (English). Colombo Communications has three services: El FM (English), Raja FM (Sinhala), and Shree FM (Sinhala). Asset Radio Broadcasting operates a single service at present: Neth FM (Sinhala). Apart from these, under the ceasefire agreement with the government signed in 2002, the Liberation Tigers of Tamil Eelam (popularly known as the Tamil Tigers) operate the Voice of the Tigers service from Killinochchi in the north and from eastern Sri Lanka.

Television

Independent Television Network, a private terrestrial television channel started by Telshan, introduced television into Sri Lanka in 1979. The government, however, took over the company in 1981, citing concerns over its "commercial failure." The following year, the government used a gift from Japan to create the Sri Lanka Rupavahini Corporation to run the country's second TV channel, a nationwide network. The Independent Television Network, which also gets credit for being the first color television channel in South Asia, became a government company controlled by the Secretary of the Treasury, with its board of directors appointed by the government thereafter. In the mid-1990s, the government also took over Lakhanda [Sound of Lanka] Radio, an affiliate of Independent Television Network. The government permitted private commercial television channels in 1992 but placed them under the overall authority of the Sri Lanka Rupavahini Corporation. Under this arrangement, E. A. P. Edirisingha founded two television channels with the call name Extra Terrestrial Television—ETV 1 and ETV 2. In 1998 ETV 1 was renamed Swarnavahini [Golden Channel] with no ownership change, while ETV 2 became ETV (without the numeral), with its ownership subsequently taken over by Vanguard Lanka.

In 1993 Maharaja, a Sri Lankan business company, established the Maharaja TV (MTV) terrestrial network, which changed its call name to Sirasa TV in 1999, for consistency of name with its radio network, Sirasa FM. With this reconfiguration, Channel One MTV became Maharaja's English service, Sirasa its Sinhala service, and Shakthi its Tamil service. The newest Sinhala TV channel, Derana [My Land], started broadcasting in late 2005. Owned by Powerhouse, its initial programming was limited to the Western Province.

In 2003 Sri Lanka had an estimated 3.4 million TV sets and a TV audience of 13.6 million. Three state-owned television channels—Sri Lanka Rupavahini Corporation's national network, its Channel Eye, and the Independent Television Network—provide public service programming. Rupavahini's national network, the country's only 24-hour television channel, is notable for its popular teledramas. Independent Television Network covers 99 percent of the island, producing and broadcasting programs in all three languages of the country (Sinhala, English, and Tamil). Its programs and broadcasts are funded by television advertising and by government grants. Channel Eye also televises in all three languages.

Ten privately owned commercial TV channels complement the three state-run public service channels: ETV, Channel One MTV, ARTtv, and Dynavision (all only in English); Swarnavahini, Sirasa TV, Derana, and TV Lanka (all only in Sinhala); Shakthi TV (only in Tamil); and TNL (in both Sinhala and English).

Among the commercial services, ETV is considered the premier English channel in Sri Lanka, even though it broadcasts only within Colombo. It televises Channel News Asia, popular sitcoms and soaps from Nickelodeon, and content from MusicTV. Swarnavahini, a Sinhala news and entertainment channel, has gained popularity through its teledramas and news programs, such as *Live at 8* and the *8 O'clock News*. Another very popular show is *Sirasa Superstar*, a musical reality show offered by Maharaja's Sirasa TV.

SOUTHEAST ASIA

Thailand

Radio

Radio broadcasting began in Thailand in 1928, and although it was meant to help educate Thais about democracy after the end of the absolute monarchy, it degenerated into propaganda for the government. After World War II, various government agencies established radio stations, and broadcasting continued to proliferate. Yet all except about 30 of the more than 300 national and local stations in the 1980s belonged either to the Public Relations Department, the Ministry of Defense, or the Mass Communications Organization of Thailand.

Currently, there are over 500 radio stations, many of them regional affiliates of Radio Thailand; the majority of independent stations are FM services based in Bangkok. All stations other than those run by Radio Thailand and the Ministry of Education—including stations owned by other government ministries, by universities, and by the military—are incorporated as commercial entities. They operate under licenses from the government's Radio and Television Executive Committee, which also transmits their broadcast signals to over 100 million radio sets in the country. It is noteworthy that, during the periods of civil unrest in 1976 and 1992, the offices of Radio Thailand were burnt down twice, with an underground radio service beginning after the first instance, and state media reforms beginning after the second.

Television

Thailand was the first Southeast Asian country to have television broadcasts, which were launched in 1955 by the Thai Television Company, established with capital from the central government. It was then more a political instrument than a form of entertainment, targeting some 2,500 television sets marketed by the company. A second television channel (Channel 7) was started by the Thai Army as a commercial venture in 1958, but it, too, received government funding soon after. Several provincial channels were in operation by 1962. Color television was introduced in 1967 when the government began offering television franchises selectively to the private sector. Until the 1990s the government, including its armed forces, owned five of the six national channels as well as several regional channels, all of which served as instruments of state propaganda. Moreover, businessman Thaksin Shinawatra's successful bid for national power in the 2001 elections was attributed to his party's skillful manipulation of the media, which they influenced through their government as well as private-sector connections. Although UNESCO has recognized Thailand as a nation with freedom of the press, successive democratically elected governments in the 1990s have also overtly exercised media censorship, even taking certain television programs off the air because of their criticism or dissent. Freedom of the press in Thailand was further jeopardized after the military coup of October 2006.

By the first few years of the twenty-first century, Thailand had six free-to-air national television channels, three of them owned by the government (Channels 5, 9, and 11) and three by private-sector companies (Channels 3 and 7, and ITV). Entertainment comprised about 44 percent of their programming, while news and current affairs held a respectable 38 percent share, and documentaries came in at 16 percent. In the early 1990s, the government had licensed two companies to provide subscription television services: International Broadcasting Corporation (IBC), owned by the Shinawatra Group, and Thai Sky TV, owned by the Wattachak print media group. Catering primarily to up-market Bangkok, IBC launched four channels with imported programs (mostly from the United States), either dubbed or subtitled in Thai. Targeting provincial markets, Thai Sky TV launched three channels, all dubbed in Thai and subtitled in English. The company sourced news programming from Independent Television Network, the BBC, NBC, and Nippon Hoso Kyokai (NHK, Japan Broadcasting Corporation), and went to MTV, Virgin, MGM, and Paramount, among others, for programs for its entertainment channel. During the economic boom in the first half of the 1990s, the government also awarded new licenses for cable television services, including one to UTV Cable Network, a subsidiary of Telecom Holding Company. Affected by the economic troubles across Asia in the second half of the decade, UTV and IBC merged in 1998 to form UBC, which is now the sole cable service in the country, offering twenty-seven channels. In 1999 popular pressures for reform over price hikes, protests against the military's ownership of media, and demands for freer news culminated in the formation of two new regulatory bodies. These were to include representation from government as well as the civil society groups that spearheaded the reforms, but controversy has bedeviled their selection. Civil society reforms in Thailand remain suspended under the pro-monarchical military regime that came to power in October 2006.

Vietnam

Radio

The radio service Voice of Vietnam was established in 1945 in Hanoi following the declaration of independence by Ho Chi Minh, and it initially used old equipment introduced by the French colonials. As a result of civil conflicts over the next few years, the service had to broadcast from various parts of the northwest provinces until the formation of North Vietnam in 1954 allowed its consolidation in Hanoi. In South Vietnam, Radio Vietnam received sizeable American investments in infrastructure in the late 1950s, largely so that it could compete in the propaganda war against the radio broadcasts from North Vietnam, as well as against the clandestine broadcasts from the communist National Liberation Front underground in the south. In addition, South Vietnam had the U.S. Armed Forces in Vietnam Network, which also catered to other allied forces in the country during this period.

Since the unification of the north and the south during 1973–75 and the emergence of the new nation of Vietnam, the conditions for radio broadcasting have changed significantly. In the first decade of the twenty-first century, the public broadcaster Voice of Vietnam has been operating six different radio stations. VOV-1 is its primary news and current affairs service, which is also relayed by local medium-wave and FM stations. VOV-2 offers economic, social, cultural, and education programs; VOV-3 features entertainment, music, and news 24 hours a day on FM. VOV-4 provides programming in the minority languages of Vietnam, many of which it shares with neighboring countries. VOV-5 broadcasts in a wide range of languages—including Cantonese, Lao, Thai, Indonesian, Japanese, English, French, Russian, and Spanish—to listeners in the countries surrounding Vietnam; VOV-6 does the same for listeners around the world, with a reach as far as North and Central America, the Middle East, Africa, and Europe.

Television

In its early years, the South Vietnamese television channel THVN, inaugurated in 1966, was operated jointly with the U.S. Armed Forces in Vietnam Network. After surviving the collapse of the South Vietnamese government in 1975, it was incorporated into its Hanoi-based counterpart in the north to form a new national television service. North Vietnam had begun television broadcasting in 1970, with the support of East Germany and other socialist countries, but it had to evacuate to the countryside and remain experimental during the extended American bombing of Hanoi during this period. In 1976 the television service was formally separated from the radio service; only in 1987 was it named Vietnam Television and designated as the sole national broadcaster.

When Vietnam embarked on economic liberalization in the 1990s, it received considerable infrastructure aid from Thailand, such as satellite dishes for installation in offices, hotels, and embassies in Hanoi and Ho Chi Minh City. In 1994 Vietnam Television was the first foreign broadcaster to use Thaicom2, a satellite that had been expected to attract French broadcasters to the former colonies. However, under Communist Party control, Vietnam Television's satellite broadcasts primarily offered official information programming, thereby spawning a large video rental industry in the country as the alternative source of entertainment. Rather like Voice of Vietnam in radio broadcasting, Vietnam Television currently offers five free-to-air channels. VTV-1 concentrates on news and information, VTV-2 on education and science, and VTV-3 on entertainment, sports, and business news. As more recent additions to the stable, VTV-4 caters to overseas Vietnamese and is broadcast worldwide via three satellites, while VTV-5 targets the more than fifty ethnic minorities in the country with largely developmental programming.

Vietnam Television has also diversified recently into film production, subscription television service, Internet service, and print publication. Even though the government has prohibited access to satellite television other than through its VTV channels since 1996, Vietnam Television operates a limited microwave redistribution service. By 2000 it offered nine foreign channels through this service, including CNN, the French TV5, Discovery, OPT (French Polynesia), NBC, MTV, TNT, Cartoon Network, and Star Sports (besides its own VTV channels). By the middle of the present decade, Vietnam Television had two subscription services, by cable and direct-to-home, offering up to six local channels (with many programs featuring dubbed soap operas from other parts of Southeast and East Asia) and twenty-one international channels, but the subscription price has still been prohibitive for most citizens.

The Philippines

Radio

Owned by private American citizens living in the colony, radio service was inaugurated in Manila in 1922, barely two years after the first station was launched in the United States. The broadcast service was extended to the Philippine provinces within the next decade. Soon thereafter, even department stores had established radio stations to promote their products. Radio broadcasting in the Philippines took off after World War II and independence, with over 30 stations established within five years. By 1965, when Ferdinand Marcos came to power and declared martial law, there were about 350 stations across the country. Since advertising revenue was spread too thinly, many of these stations survived this period because of the sponsorship of political parties, In 1972 the Marcos regime shut down the nation's broadcast media, with the exception of the government radio and television station in Manila, the Voice of the Philippines, and the Radio Philippines Network. The last of these was privately owned by a crony of Marcos named Benedicto, who become a media oligarch soon after, taking control of two other radio and television networks and four telecommunications companies.

Despite the restoration of democracy in the "people's power" revolution of 1986, ownership of the media continued to be concentrated in the hands of the large conglomerates controlled by wealthy families, with the government owning only one radio and television network, PTV Channel 4. While there are now 40 government-owned radio stations, those in the private sector number over 500, about half of which are part of extensive regional and national networks of stations. Since private broadcast stations are licensed and regulated by various government bodies, they are unlike print media and tend to avoid political criticism, concentrating instead on entertainment. The few Philippine radio broadcasters who have investigated corruption in public office, organized crime, and the like have usually faced violent reprisals directed at property and person. Now on the air 24 hours a day and reaching the remotest parts of the country (in which more than 80 percent of all households own radio sets), radio remains a leading advertising medium, and economic or financial interests sometimes supercede editorial integrity.

Television

Television began in the Philippines on an experimental basis at its universities. It turned commercial with the establishment of Alto Broadcasting System in 1953, followed by Chronicle Broadcasting Network in 1957. Despite the lack of television sets, high production costs, and a limited advertising base, television continued to grow, with eighteen privately owned channels appearing by the mid-1960s. During the period of martial law that followed, Marcos's business crony Benedicto seized control of the Banahaw Broadcasting Corporation (with its two television stations) and the Inter-island Broadcasting Corporation (with its eight stations), adding them to the Radio Philippines Network (six stations) that he already owned. Marcos's cronies also took over the GMA network, a major broadcaster, on the grounds that its majority stock should be in the hands of local shareholders; the regime also closed down the ABS-CBN and ABC networks for being critical of the government.

In the first decade of the twenty-first century, Philippine television is dominated by six Manila-based national networks; in addition, the country has some 150 television stations, almost all of them private, including eleven religious and two educational stations. ABS-CBN made a dramatic comeback after the restoration of democracy in 1986; its Channel 2 now has over 60 percent of the audience share and about half of the advertising revenue nationally. Its success is attributed to its formula of sensational news and current affairs programming, which has been widely imitated by its competitors, in spite of the industry's self-regulation codes. GMA's Channel 7, second in the ratings, is noted for developing domestic programs in various genres, adapting successful foreign formats, and initiating broadcasts to Filipino expatriates abroad. ABC, now the third largest television network, also reopened after the revolution of 1986; roughly half of the programming on its Channel 5 is imported, and the other half is domestic. Two other private stations from the Marcos era, Channels 9 and 13, remain under government supervision 20 years later; their broadcasts are characterized by 80 percent and 50 percent foreign programming, respectively. These rival channels depend in part on their domestically produced soap operas and musical shows for their ratings; they are fueled in part by the real-life scandals surrounding their actors and artists. The government-owned but financially self-reliant National Broadcasting Network, which has undergone several name changes (even being called People's Television 4 at one stage), is mandated to provide citizens with a balanced programming mix of news, education, culture, and sports.

Although cable television service in the Philippines dates from the 1970s, the liberalization of laws governing ownership of cable networks, broadcast content, and satellite dish licensing after the "people's power" revolution of 1986 helps explain the current high viewership of transnational television. Many of the early satellite dishes were believed to be picking up signals from the Palapa, IntelSat, and AsiaSat satellites as well as from Japan's DBS satellites, some of them for unauthorized retransmission. The arrival of transnational television channels, such as CNN, Star TV, and ESPN, in the 1990s was a major impetus to the phenomenal growth of the cable industry in subsequent years. The cable operator Sky

Cable, set up by the ABS-CBN network, was soon offering over fifty-five transnational channels, including Star TV, Australia Television, MTV, TVBS (Taiwan), and CTN (the Christian Television Network), as well as French, Russian, and domestic programming. By 2000 there were nearly 1 million subscribers in the Philippines, served by more than 300 cable operators, most of which were small family businesses franchised by multisystem operators. Until the end of the twentieth century, there seemed to be a clear class division among Filipino audiences, between English-proficient middle-to-upper class viewers attracted to subscription television, and largely Tagalog-speaking lower-class viewers, confined to watching the free-to-air networks. In recent years, however, these class divisions have been increasingly blurred.

Malaysia

Radio

In 1921, Malaysia was one of the first British colonies to have a radio service, but it was launched at the initiative of radio enthusiasts. The colonial government, however, did not offer a temporary radio license until 1933; it did not award a license to the private British Malaya Broadcasting Company until 1935, which it was compelled to purchase on the eve of World War II. During the war, the company's facilities proved to be instrumental to the Japanese occupation forces, who used it for their propaganda broadcasts in local languages by local people. The British colonial government established Radio Malaya after 1945 to aid recovery and to deal with the communist insurgency. After independence in 1963, Radio Malaysia was established as a government department, which subsequently became Radio Television Malaysia

At present, Radio Television Malaysia has six radio channels, which broadcast 24 hours a day in Bahasa Melayu (Malay), English, Mandarin Chinese, and Tamil nationally, and also in several local languages for East Malaysia (Borneo). In addition, private radio broadcasters Suara Islam, Suara Malaysia, Redifusion Cable Network, and Time Highway cater primarily to West (Peninsular) Malaysia.

Television

Television in Malaysia began in 1963, soon after independence from Britain, and a second public channel was launched six years later. In keeping with the government's emphasis on national unity, almost three-quarters of the programming on Channel 1 is in the national language, Malay. Channel 2 is meant to cater to the nation's minority languages, and it has a 22 percent audience share. Together, both channels reach some 3 million Malaysian households, as well as most Singapore households by signal spillover. Channel 1's viewership has remained high among the Malay ethnic group; since the 1980s, Channel 2 has tried to cater to ethnic minorities with greater buying power by importing higher-quality foreign programs and adopting more provocative "Western" program formats.

In the early 1990s the Malaysian government decided to give up its monopoly on broadcasting; this was a major shift in policy and part of a wider commitment to privatization. However, it granted the license for a third television channel, TV3, to a consortium of Malaysian newspaper publishers, controlled financially by the political parties in the ruling coalition. The first commercial channel, TV3, was launched in 1994 and soon became the most popular in the country. Currently, it caters to largely urban Chinese viewers, who were neglected earlier for political reasons and usually had to turn to video rentals for their entertainment.

Other private-sector broadcasters have followed. Metrovision (TV4), a terrestrial service owned by a local consortium, was launched in 1995, with about 60 percent of its programming imported. It ceased transmission in 1999 but returned under new ownership as 8TV in 2004. NTV-7 started in 1998, targeting the upper middle class on the urban western coast of peninsular Malaysia. Channel 9 began in 2003, closed down in 2005, and resumed under new ownership as TV9 in 2006; most of its programs are now in Malay, but it also broadcasts some weekly programs in English, Mandarin, Tamil, Korean, and Japanese.

The first satellite subscription service, Mega TV, started operations in 1995, offering such transnational channels as CNN, Cartoon Network, Discovery, ESPN and HBO. Upon successfully launching its own domestic satellite, Measat-1, Malaysia licensed Astro All-Asia Networks to use the satellite for a twenty-two-channel direct-to-home subscription service. Astro expanded rapidly and drove Mega TV out of business in 2001. By 2006, using Measat-2, Astro was carrying fifty-six subscription and four pay-per-view television channels (plus seventeen radio channels). The latest subscription service, MiTV, is delivered over the World Wide Web and offers various packages, such as *Chitra*, which includes channels from Indonesia; *Spices*, which features popular channels from India; *Orient*, which has leading channels from Taiwan, Macau, and Hong Kong; and *International*, which includes Korean, Thai, Filipino, French and Japanese channels.

Singapore

Radio

Radio broadcasting began in Singapore as a private enterprise in 1936, but it was bought by the British colonial government in 1941 and reconstituted as the Malayan Broadcasting Corporation. During the Japanese occupation of Singapore, it operated as Syonan Hoso Kyoku, and when the British regained the city, it was renamed Radio Malaya. After Singapore's secession in 1965, the local branch of Radio Malaysia was placed under the city-state's new Ministry of Culture as Radio-Television Singapore. It was subsequently reorganized as the Singapore Broadcasting Corporation, and when it was semi-privatized, the radio division became the separate Radio Corporation of Singapore. Less well known is the fact that Rediffusion Vision Limited, the old British company (now defunct), which invented the world's first cable technology for radio and television in the 1930s and wired English towns such as Brighton and Hull before World War II, introduced cable radio into Singapore in 1949, carrying programming primarily in Chinese dialects. The city's old cable radio services went into rapid decline in the 1980s when government policies strongly encouraged the sole use of Mandarin.

New players entered the radio market in the 1990s, notably the Singapore Armed Forces Reservists Association (SAFRA) and the National Trades Union Congress (NTUC), the latter in conjunction with Singapore Press Holdings. But this was not a real opening up of the market because all these were government-controlled entities. At present, the state-controlled MediaCorp runs over a dozen radio stations, offering news, talk, music, and entertainment in English, Mandarin, Malay, and Tamil; Unionworks (NTUC) and SAFRA operate two stations each, one in English and the other in Mandarin. In addition, listeners have access to dozens of Malaysian and Indonesian radio channels, a few of which deliberately target the affluent Singapore market for advertisers, providing more liberal programming than that offered by their own government.

Television

Television broadcasts in black-and-white began in Singapore in 1963, ostensibly timed to distract citizens during a period of communal tensions. From the beginning, Radio-Television Singapore's Channel 5 broadcast in English and Malay, while its Channel 8 specialized in Chinese and Indian programs. In 1980 the organization was restructured as the Singapore Broadcasting Corporation, autonomous from the Ministry of Culture with regard to personnel, finances, and production. The autonomy ensured innovation, particularly in local drama, documentaries, talk shows, and current affairs programs, even though the content still remained quite guarded. Within a few years, the corporation launched Channel 12, which furthered the government's stated aim of creating a more cultured society by focusing on documentaries, drama, arts, educational programs, and art cinema.

In 1994, the government semi-privatized television. It formed Singapore International Media, under which the Television Corporation of Singapore came to own Channels 5 and 8, while Singapore Television Twelve (STV12) came to control Channel 12. STV12 then created two new channels: Prime 12, which took over all Indian programming from Channel 8, and Premiere 12, which continued the Channel 12 tradition of up-market programming. In 1999 STV12 replaced Prime 12 with Suria to cater to the Malay community, and it converted Premiere 12 into Central, which included children's, arts, and Tamil programs. In one more phase of reorganization, Singapore International Media metamorphosed into MediaCorp, and Television Corporation of Singapore became MediaCorp TV at the turn of the twenty-first century. At the same time, Singapore launched the satellite-based Channel News Asia, which offered regional and global news from an "Asian perspective." This service targeted transnational audiences stretching from the Middle East and South Asia to East Asia and to Australasia, but it also produced programming for Singapore's domestic channels.

Indonesia

Radio

The Dutch colonial government introduced radio-telegraphy communication into Indonesia in 1911, and then expanded its network to the major cities over the next 20 years, primarily for its military personnel and civilians. In 1933, about a dozen years after the transmission of the human voice over radio waves became commercially viable, an Indonesian sultan sponsored the first Javanese-language broadcasts from Surakarta, which became a model for others. Radio broadcasting from Jakarta was reorganized by the Japanese during World War II, and it was used subsequently by Indonesian nationalists to promote their anticolonial cause. Radio Republik Indonesia was set up as a government body soon after the declaration of independence in 1945, but it had to go underground until the Dutch conceded political control. By the early 1970s, the Indonesian government had 50 national and 100 regional stations, while there were over 300 other private and commercial broadcasters. At the end of the Suharto regime in the 1990s, there were 186 government-owned radio stations and 670 private ones, on which entertainment was the primary form of programming (46 percent), followed by news, information, and religion (30 percent).

There are currently over 1,100 licensed radio stations within Indonesia, and there are allegedly hundreds of others that operate without licenses. Radio Republik Indonesia itself runs over 50 stations, and provincial and local governments operate some 130 others. Voice of Indonesia, the overseas service, broadcasts in ten Asian and European languages. Since 2000 Radio Republik Indonesia has been a public-service broadcasting corporation instead of an entity directly owned and operated by the government. Also, private-sector broadcasting stations are no longer required to relay government news three times a day, to use Bahasa Indonesia, to pay a monthly tax, or to deal with complicated licensing procedures. As a result, there has been a burgeoning of community radio stations, many of them run by amateurs with low-power transmitters and licensed, at best, by local authorities. The policy of regional autonomy and the lack of a central regulator in the post-Suharto era have meant a saturation of the airwaves in Indonesia. Radio penetration now ranges from 70 percent to 90 percent in the major cities, with over 70 percent of the audience listening to music and entertainment programs, and less than 30 percent listening to news and information.

Television

Television broadcasting began in Indonesia in 1962 as a limited public service confined to the capital city of Jakarta; it was treated by the country's first president, Sukarno, as a means of personal communication with the masses. Under General Suharto's "New Order" regime, the public broadcaster Televisi Republik Indonesia was forced to collaborate with other government agencies to create development programming. In 1987 the Indonesian government revived domestic television by decreeing an encrypted commercial television service for the Jakarta area. In 1993 the Indonesian government allowed up to five commercial broadcasters access to its Palapa satellite for national transmission—but it restricted the language of broadcasts, regulated news retransmission, and censored programs.

The pioneering commercial station RCTI began broadcasting in 1987, targeting urban middle- and upper-class viewers. A second commercial station, SCTV, was licensed in 1990 and initially sought to reach a female audience. In 1991 a private-sector broadcaster, TPI, was mandated to provide an educational service, but the broadcaster was allowed to air some entertainment to generate advertising revenue. The fourth commercial channel, AnTeve, inaugurated in 1994, was noted early on for its "Western" programming. Soon after its launch in 1995, IVM challenged the dominance of RCTI by airing blockbuster Western movies. All five of these early commercial broadcasters had or still have ownership links with the Suharto family.

After Suharto's ouster, the interim government of President Habibie radically changed the broadcasting landscape by offering eight new commercial television licenses. Among the takers was Metro TV, approved in 1999 to run a CNN-like channel with an emphasis on news, current affairs, and documentaries. Another early entrant was Televisi Transformasi, which has challenged the older broadcasters, RCTI, SCTV, and IVM, by reaching the Indonesian upmarket with broad program offerings. A third new company, Global TV, features MTV videos, foreign sports, Nickelodeon cartoons, and other fare for young viewers. One outcome of this media liberalization has been a widespread increase in the number of news, current affairs, political forums, and talk-back programs. Another consequence has been greater freedom to broadcast Chinese programs and non-Muslim religious programs, to produce English-language business programs, and the like. Besides these national networks, there is now a plethora of city and provincial television stations, often run by local governments.

In recent years, RCTI has enhanced itself with more local productions, including serious news and current affairs programs. SCTV has become a leader in broadcasting Latin American *telenovelas*, Indonesian *sinetrons* (made-for-television movies), and Chinese kung fu films, thereby gaining loyal viewers among homemakers and younger adults in the middle class. TPI has abandoned its educational agenda and has repositioned itself as a "family" channel, with locally produced programs appealing to the lower socioeconomic segment. Although still lagging behind the other commercial stations, AnTeve has reinvented itself as a "youth-and-music" channel by offering much MTV programming and imported quiz and game shows, as well as their Indonesian clones.

The subscription service Indovision initially provided access to CNN, HBO, Discovery, ESPN, TNT, Cartoon Network, and StarTV, among others. When StarTV withdrew from Indonesia, its channels were replaced by other transnational channels, such as CNBC, BBC, Bloomberg, MTV, National Geographic, HBO, and Cinemax. Despite the Asian economic crisis of the late 1990s, which hit Indonesia particularly hard, the telecommunications carrier Indosat teamed up with SCTV to provide subscription channels via cable and microwave transmission ("wireless cable"). Other media companies have also joined the highly competitive cable television market since then, including Satelindo (teamed with RCTI), Indonusa TV (owned by RCTI), and Astro (from neighboring Malaysia). While satellite and cable television expand in the country, multichannel households in Indonesia are likely to be hemmed in by economic, linguistic, and cultural constraints, and might reach only 1 million by the end of the current decade.

RESOURCE GUIDE

PRINT SOURCES

East Asia and Oceania

Day, Mark. "Radio Wreckers? How U.S. Radio is Colonising Australia." *Australian* (2001, August 30, 2001): M01.

Fung, Anthony. "Think Globally, Act Locally: China's Rendezvous with MTV." *Global Media and Communication* 2.1 (April 2006): 71–88.

Greenwald, John. "Rupert's World: A Burst of Deals Puts Rupert Murdoch in the Forefront of Media Moguls Seeking Global Reach." *Time* 142.14 (1993, September 20).

Griffen-Foley, Bridget. "The Birth of a Hybrid: The Shaping of the Australian Radio Industry." *International Studies in Broadcast and Audio Media* 2.3 (Fall 2004): 153–169.

Hilliard, Robert L., and Michael C. Keith. *Global Broadcasting Systems.* Boston: Focal Press, 1996.

Howse, Hugh. "The Use of Radio in China." *China Quarterly* 2 (April/June 1960): 59–68.

Huang, Yu, and Xu Yu. "Broadcasting and Politics: Chinese Television in the Mao Era, 1958–1976." *Historical Journal of Film, Radio and TV* 17.4 (October 1997): 563-572

Langdale, John V. "East Asian Broadcasting Industries: Global, Regional, and National Perspectives." *Journal of Economic Geography* 73.3 (July 1997): 305-321.

Lo, Kwai-Cheung. "Look Who's Talking: The Politics of Orality in Transitional Hong Kong Mass Culture." *boundary 2* 25.3 (Autumn 1998): 151–168.

McCarroll, Thomas. "New Star over Asia: Media Baron Rupert Murdoch Buys Asia's Hottest TV Service." *Time* 142.6 (1993, August 9).

McKenzie, Robert. *Comparing Media from around the World.* New York: Pearson, 2006.

Quick, Amanda C., ed. *World Press Encyclopedia.* Vols. 1–2. Detroit: Gale, 2003

Robinson, Martin, Bender, Andrew, and Rob Whyte. *The Lonely Planet Guide to Korea.* Oakland, CA: Lonely Planet, 2004.

Shim, Doobo. "Hybridity and the Rise of Korean Popular Culture in Asia." *Media, Culture & Society* 28.1 (January 2006): 25–44.

Wei, Betty, and Elizabeth Li. *Culture Shock: A Survival Guide to Customs and Etiquette in Hong Kong.* Singapore: Marshall Cavendish, 2005.

Winfield, Betty Houchin, and Zengjun Peng. "Market or Party Controls: Chinese Media in Transition." *Gazette* 67.3 (Fall 2005): 255–270.

Zha, Jianying. *China Pop: How Soap Operas, Tabloids and Bestsellers Are Changing a Culture.* New York: New Press, 1995.

South and Southeast Asia

Agrawal, Binod C. *Television in South Asia: Cultural Scenario and Future Directions.* Lanham, MD: University Press of Americas, 2006.

Dudrah, Rajinder. "Zee TV: Diasporic Non-terrestrial Terrestrial Television in Europe." *South Asian Popular Culture* 3.1 (April 2005): 33–47.

Goonasekera, Anura, Lee Chun Wah, and S. Venkataraman, eds. *Asian Communication Handbook 2003.* Singapore: Asian Media Information and Communication Centre & Nanyang Technological University, 2003.

Gunaratne, Shelton A., ed. *Handbook of the Media in Asia.* New Delhi: Sage Publications, 2000.

Kumar, Shanti. "Inside the Home Theatre: The Hyper-real World of Television in India." *South Asian Popular Culture* 2.2 (October 2004): 127–144.

McDaniel, Drew O. (1994). *Broadcasting in the Malay World: Radio, Television, and Video in Brunei, Indonesia, Malaysia, and Singapore.* Norwood, NJ: Ablex Publishers.

Moran, Albert, and Michael Keane. *Television across Asia: Television Industries, Programme Formats and Globalization.* London & New York: RoutledgeCurzon, 2004.

Ostrowski, Ally. "The Framing of Religion: Nepal TV Explored." *South Asian Popular Culture* 4.1 (April 2006): 3–18.

Thomas, Amos Owen. *Imagi-Nations and Borderless Television: Media, Culture and Politics across Asia.* New Delhi: Sage Publications, 2005.

World Telecommunication Development Report: Access Indicators for the Information Society. Geneva: International Telecommunication Union, 2003.

WEBSITES

East Asia and Oceania

Australian. http://www.theaustralian.news.com.au/. Online edition of major Australian newspaper.

Australian Broadcasting Authority. Australian Government. http://www.aba.gov.au/. Official Website of Australia's regulator of radio, TV, and Internet.

CCTV. http://english.cctv.com/index.shtml. Website for the English-language 24-hour news channel of China Central Television, Mainland China's largest national TV network.

Korea Herald. http://www.koreaherald.co.kr/index.asp. Online edition of major Korean newspaper.

New Zealand Herald. http://www.nzherald.co.nz/. Online edition of major New Zealand newspaper.

NHK Online. NHK (Japan Broadcasting Corporation). http://www.nhk.or.jp/english/. Official Website of Radio Japan.

Radio New Zealand. http://www.radionz.co.nz/. Official Website of Radio New Zealand.

RTHK On Internet. Radio Television Hong Kong. http://www.rthk.org.hk/index_eng.htm. Official Website of Radio Television Hong Kong.

South China Morning Post. South China Morning Post Publishers. http://www.scmp.com/. Online edition of major China newspaper.

South and Southeast Asia

All India Radio. http://allindiaradio.org/. Site for India's national broadcasting service.

Asian Info. www.asiainfo.org. A listing of television stations by country, including links to individual Websites.

Asiawaves. www.asiawaves.net. Listings of television stations by country.

Bangladesh Betar. http://www.betar.org.bd/. Site for national radio network of Bangladesh.

Bangladesh Showbiz. http://www.bangladeshshowbiz.com/tv.htm. Site for information about popular television programming and television stars in Bangladesh.

BBC. http://www.bbc.co.uk. Official British Broadcasting Corporation Website.

Doordarshan. http://www.ddindia.gov.in/. Official Website of India's national broadcaster.

Pakistan Broadcasting Corporation. http://www.radio.gov.pk/index.asp. Official Website of the PBC.

Pakistan Television Corp. http://ptv.com.pk/webptv/index.asp. Official Website of Pakistan's television broadcasting company.

Nepal Television. http://www.explorenepal.com/ntv/. Official site of Nepal's television broadcasting company.

Press Reference. http://www.pressreference.com. Provides overviews of press, television, radio, and newspapers by country.

Rupavahini: The National Television. http://www.rupavahini.lk/. Official site of the Sri Lanka Rupavahini Corporation, the national television network.

Radio Nepal. http://www.radionepal.org/. Official site of Nepal's national broadcasting service.

Radio Station World. http://radiostationworld.com. Includes a list of radio and television stations by country, with links to individual Websites.

NOTES

East Asia and Oceania

1. Shim 2006 (in Resource Guide), p. 25.
2. See Chris Forrester, "Moving Pictures," *Television Asia* (May 1, 2005).
3. See Robert F. Gowen, "Teaching the Chinese Radio," radio broadcast March 1923, available at http://www-md1.csa.com.proxy.emerson.edu/ids70/p_search_form.php?field=au&query=hanada+tatsuro&log=literal&resolve_au&SID=q8munqp01ghju68n3edi1biac5, p. 384.
4. See *Radio News* (June 1923), p. 2161.
5. See George P. Jan, "Radio Propaganda in Chinese Villages," *Asian Survey* 7.5 (May 1967), p. 305.
6. See David Clayton, "The Consumption of Radio Broadcast Technologies in Hong Kong, c. 1930–1960," *Economic History Review* 57.4 (November 2004), p. 700.
7. See "Station JOAK of Japan," *Boston Herald* (April 11, 1926), p. 6.
8. See *Institute of Pacific Relations Report* (February 24, 1934), p. 1.
9. See Jerome S. Berg, *On the Shortwaves, 1923–1945* (Jefferson, NC: McFarland, 1999), pp. 89–90.
10. See Xiaoping Li, "The Chinese Television System and Television News," *China Quarterly* 126 (June 1991), p. 340.
11. Ibid., p. 341.
12. See Langdale (in Resource Guide), p. 310.
13. See *Taiwan Yearbook 2005*, http://www.gio.gov.tw/taiwan-website/5-gp/yearbook/p262.html.
14. See Tatsuro Hanada, "Cultural Diversity as Social Demand: The Korean Minority and Japanese Broadcasting," *Gazette* 65.4–5 (August 2003), pp. 393, 397.
15. See Andrei Lankov, "North Koreans Turned On but Tuned Out," *Asia Times Online* (June 28, 2006), http://www.atimes.com/>www.atimes.com.
16. See Young-han Kim, "The Broadcasting Audience Movement in Korea," *Media Culture & Society* 23.1 (January 2001): 94.
17. See *History of Australian Television*, http://televisionau.siv.net.au/fifties.htm.
18. Quoted in the *New York Times* (July 22, 1982), p. A1.
19. See Howse (in Resource Guide), p. 63.
20. See Langdale (in Resource Guide), p. 305.
21. See John Roderick, "TV Opens Windows Wide for Japan," *Hartford Courant* (August 2, 1959), p. 3G.
22. See R. Lamont-Brown, "Violence among Japanese Youth," *Contemporary Review* (August 2000).
23. See Ron Bailey, "Weight Loss Issues & Opportunities in Japan: Examining the Status of the Weight Loss Market in Japan," *Nutraceuticals World* (October 1, 2002).

South and Southeast Asia

1. Quoted on Nepal Television, http://www.explorenepal.com/ntv/. Accessed on October 12, 2006.

SPORTS AND RECREATION

EAST ASIA AND OCEANIA

JOUYEON YI-KOOK AND MONICA Z. LI

East Asia

People in most Asian countries enjoy their national/ethnic traditional sport activities as well as imported sport activities, such as football, baseball, and basketball. For example, in China, *wushu*, or martial arts, has been practiced for several thousand years in various types of set exercises, either with or without weapons, for physical training and self-defense. This traditional sport of China has won followers all over the world. In Japan and South Korea, traditional martial arts, such as judo or taekwondo, are still recommended for youth's physical well-being and mental discipline. Some of the traditional sports such as *ssireum* or sumo have become professionalized and have attracted as many people as other professional sports.

Western sports were introduced to the Asian countries in the nineteenth century. Since then, imported sports became as popular in Asia as they are in other parts of the world. They have further penetrated into Asian countries because of the development of technologies such as cable, satellite television, and the Internet, along with deregulation of broadcasting policies since the 1990s.[1] For example, watching the American basketball, baseball, and football leagues as well as the European Football Championship are common pastimes for many people in Asian countries. This has been encouraged in recent years by extensive television coverage and the success of Asian players—such as the Seattle Mariners' Ichiro Suzuki from Japan, the New York Mets' Chan Ho Park from Korea, and the Houston Rockets' Yao Ming from China—in American and European sport leagues.

The governments of Asian countries play a vital role in implementing national programs aiming to improve the fitness and health of the nation. Because of the support from the governments and the increasing concern about physical fitness and quality of life, people in Asian countries increasingly participate in recreation and sport activities in their leisure time. At the same time, Asian professional athletes have made remarkable achievements in competitive sports in recent years.

Sports and Recreation

China

With a long history of sport as an important part of its popular culture, China developed many traditional sport activities that are good for health as well as rich in artistic, recreational and educational values. Some sport activities, such as archery, horse riding, spear throwing, tree climbing, shuttlecock kicking, and *wushu* (martial arts), can be traced back several thousand years. Dragon boat racing, flying kites, and *yangge* dancing are traditional forms of recreation popular among both Han people and people of national minorities. The nature of China's traditional sport and recreation was often a product of philosophical directions, which stressed cooperation and harmony at the expense of competition.[2] For instance, two world-known forms of exercise for inner health that the Chinese have practiced for centuries—*taijiquan*, or *tai chi* (shadow boxing) and *qigong* (a system of deep breathing exercises)—stress the therapeutic nature of exercise, breathing, and mental state as opposed to the development of strength, musculature, and vigor. As a branch of Chinese martial arts with a history of hundreds of years, taijiquan grew out of the health maintenance exercises of ancient Taoism combined with the theories of *yin* and *yang*. It emphasizes body movement following mind movements, tempering toughness with gentleness, and graceful carriage. Qigong is a unique system of exercises aiming at controlling the mind and regulating the breath to keep fit, live long, overcome disease, and strengthen the physiological functions.

Modern sport was introduced into China at the end of the nineteenth century. Since then, sports, including basketball, gymnastics, volleyball, team handball, baseball, weightlifting, track and field, and soccer, gradually spread in the country. Since the founding of the People's Republic in 1949 and especially after the economic reforms initiated in 1978, sports activities in China have become rich in variety, and recreational sports have started to permeate all levels of society. As reported by the State Physical Education and Sports Commission of China (SPESC), popular sporting and recreational activities in China include formal sports (e.g., basketball, volleyball, soccer, badminton, table tennis, track and field, swimming, gymnastics, ice skating, weightlifting, and social dance), fitness and health-oriented activities (e.g., aerobic dancing, cycling, jogging, taijiquan, qigong, and wushu), play-oriented activities (e.g., tug-of-war, hopscotch, skipping, jumping rubber bands, and shuttlecock kicking), and ethnic minority-related activities (e.g., horse riding, dragon dancing, and dragon-boat racing).[3]

Aiming to improve the health and the overall physical condition of the general population, the State Council promulgated the National Program for Physical Fitness in 1995. This program encourages the Chinese public to engage in at least one sports activity every day, learn at least two health-building methods, and take a physical examination once a year. Starting in 2001, the State Physical Culture Administration has set aside the proceeds of the sports lottery[4] as pilot funds to build nationwide physical fitness centers in large and medium-sized cities throughout the country. Outdoor fitness centers, gymnasiums, and stadiums have been installed in urban communities in public parks, squares, schoolyards, and other convenient locations. Most of them are open to and widely used by the general public. With the flourishing of nationwide fitness activities, people's outlooks on life have also undergone great change. More and more people consider regular sports activities to be part of their daily lives. According to the survey released by the State Physical Culture Administration, 33.9 percent of the general population between seven and seventy exercises regularly, and 60.7 percent of the urban population go to sports clubs to engage in fitness activities.[5]

The government attaches great importance to physical education (PE) of youth, which it considers the foundation of national fitness. Children in China attend primary school from the ages of 6–12 years, during which time their PE focuses largely on basic athletics, games, and gymnastics. The PE curriculum for three years of junior and three years of senior middle school is mainly based on the areas of swimming, track and field, gymnastics, wushu, and ball sports (table tennis, basketball, soccer, and badminton). Schools have professional physical educators and exercise facilities, and students failing to reach the required physical standards are not allowed to go on to higher schools. Government regulations also determine that students of all subjects in higher education receive two hours of general sport per week during the first two years of the four-year undergraduate course. At the same time, sports schools are established at national and provincial level for children with high sporting potential. The government also stresses the construction of juvenile sports clubs. Using sports lottery proceeds, the State Physical Culture Administration had established some 3,000 juvenile sports clubs by the end of 2005.[6]

Beyond the government ministries, a variety of organizations are involved in organizing sport and fitness programs. Some of these organizations operate for specific groups of employees (e.g., railway workers), for specific groups of people (e.g., elderly), or for specific sports (e.g., the Badminton Association). In recent years, especially after the five-day work week was adopted in 1995, an increasing number of commercial sports clubs have opened in the major cities to meet the growing demand of people with greater income and more time for leisure. Clubs for some new sports, such as rock climbing, horse racing, bungee jumping, bowling, skateboard, woman's boxing, taekwondo and golf have become popular, especially among young urban populations. Wushu, taijiquan, qigong, and social dance remain common among many seniors. For instance, Yangge, a kind of folk dance accompanied by music with strongly accented rhythms, is a popular recreational activity among middle-aged and elderly women in many areas of north China.

Various entertaining and competitive sport activities are maintained and developed in the country's minority-inhabited areas. Examples of such activities are wrestling and horsemanship among Mongols, Uyghurs, and Kazakhs; yak racing among the Tibetans; "seesaw jumping" among ethnic Koreans; crossbow archery among the Miao; and dragon-boat racing among the Dai. These activities were rooted in the history of the ethnic groups, embedded in the local folk customs, and mostly performed in traditional festivals. For instance, in August of every year the Mongolians hold the Nadam Fair, a gala annual meeting in which ethnic sports programs including Mongolian-style wrestling and horse races are performed. A national sports meeting of minority ethnic groups is held once every four years to promote sport activities among ethnic populations.

Prior to the 1990s, competitive sport in China was government-funded. The training system of the competitive sports is based on juvenile amateur sports schools and basic-level clubs, with teams representing localities as the backbone, and the national team at the highest level. The situation began to change in 1994, when soccer became the first sport to take the professionalization road. Similar reforms have been carried out in basketball, volleyball, and table tennis. Some Chinese athletes have joined foreign professional sport leagues. For instance, basketball stars Wang Zhizhi and Yao Ming joined the American National Basketball Association (NBA), and soccer players Yang Chen and Sun Jihai play in European soccer leagues.

Since resuming its membership on the International Olympic Committee (IOC) in 1979, China has made remarkable achievements in the arena of competitive sports. By the end of 2004, Chinese athletes had won 1,800 world championships and broken 1,119 world records,[7] most notably in table tennis, women's volleyball, men's gymnastics, field and track, badminton, rhythmic gymnastics, diving, and weight lifting. Chinese athletes finished third in the medal count at the 2000 Sydney Olympics and second at the 2004 Athens Olympics. China's international sporting success owes much to its female athletes. Chinese women have made rapid progress in a range of international sport events including middle- and long-distance running, swimming, diving, weightlifting, chess, shooting, archery, wrestling,

BEIJING, HOST CITY OF THE 2008 OLYMPICS

On July 13, 2001, at the 112th IOC Session in Moscow, Beijing was elected the host city for the Games of the XXIX Olympiad in 2008, beating out Toronto, Paris, Istanbul, and Osaka. Prior to the session, five other cities, including Bangkok, Cairo, Havana, Kuala Lumpur, and Seville had submitted bids to the IOC but failed to make the shortlist in 2000. Beijing previously bid to host the 2000 Summer Olympics, but lost out to Sydney in 1993.

Beijing, also known as Peking, means "Northern Capital" and is situated toward the northeast corner of China at about 100 feet (30 meters) above sea level and about 110 miles (183 kilometers) from the sea. Beijing has served as China's capital city almost exclusively since the 1600s.

The 2008 Summer Olympics will be held in Beijing from August 8, 2008, to August 24, 2008, with the opening ceremony to take place at 8 PM on August 8, 2008. The number "8" is associated with prosperity in Chinese culture.

The official emblem of Beijing 2008, entitled "Chinese Seal, Dancing Beijing" combines the Chinese seal and the art of calligraphy with sporting features, transforming the elements into a human figure running forward and embracing triumph. The figure resembles the Chinese character *Jing*, which stands for the name of the host city and represents a particularly significant Chinese style.

rowing, badminton, gymnastics, volleyball, basketball softball, soccer, and table tennis.

In July 2001 China succeeded in its bid to bring the 2008 Olympic Games to its ancient capital Beijing. The Beijing government plans to invest US$2 billion on infrastructure construction to prepare and host the 2008 Olympic Games.[8] Established at the end of 2001, the Beijing Organizing Committee for the Games of the XXIX Olympiad (BOCOG) set the themes for the 2008 games as "Green Olympics," "High-tech Olympics" and "Humanistic Olympics," endeavoring to make the Beijing Olympic Games an occasion to spread modern Olympic ideas and display China's distinctive historical and cultural heritage.

Japan

In Japan, traditional sports, such as sumo and judo, and imported sports, including baseball, soccer, and volleyball, have been popular since the nineteenth century. Sumo is a competitive sport in which two wrestlers (*rikishi*) face each other in a circular area. Sumo has been used not only as a match of strength in combat but also for traditional Shinto rituals.[9] The history of sumo dates back to the early Edo period (1603–1867) as a form of sporting entertainment. Currently, professional sumo tournaments are run by the Japan Sumo Association, and the number of the association's members is approximately 700. Six-times-per-year regular tournaments once attracted many spectators; however, recently Sumo is losing its popularity with spectators in Japan. Judo (in English, "the way of pliancy") is a martial art, sport, and philosophy and was created by Dr. Jigoro Kano in 1882.[10] According to the International Federation of Associated Wrestlers Styles, judo is one of the four main forms of amateur competitive wrestling practiced globally today. It became an official Olympic sport at the Olympics Games of 1964 in Tokyo. There is an International Judo Federation and several different national organizations in the United States.

Japan has actively opened to the West and begun to modernize itself since the Meiji Restoration of 1867.[11] At that time modern sports were introduced one after another, usually in port towns such as Kobe and Yokohama. The first three decades of the twentieth century were the golden age of amateur baseball in Japan. Professional baseball appeared in 1936, and the expanded professional leagues began in 1950 with the Central and Pacific League, managed by the Nippon Professional Baseball organization. Since then, baseball became the most popular spectator sport in Japan. Currently, the Central League and the Pacific League each has six teams.[12] From March until October, each team in the Central League plays 146 games and the Pacific League 136 games. At the end of season, the league champions compete for the national championship in the Japan Series. Every team is owned by a major corporation that uses the team for promotional purposes. There are eleven baseball stadiums, and seven of them were built from 1988 through 1999.[13] During the 2003 seasons, professional baseball drew a total of 23.7 million in stadium attendance.[14]

European football, or soccer, is another popular sport in Japan, but it has not been popular for as long as baseball. Although the official name of the Japan Football Association (in Japanese, *Nippon Sakkaa Kyoukai*) uses the term "football," the term "soccer" is generally used among Japanese people. In 1921 the Japanese Football Association was created, and the Japan national football team won third place and achieved its first big success at the 1968 Mexico Olympic Games. In 2002 Japan co-hosted FIFA World Cup 2002 with Korea, and the Japan national team reached the round of sixteen.[15] The Japanese Professional Football League (J League) began in 1992 with ten teams, and it currently has eighteen J1, or top division, teams and twelve J2, or lower division, teams. The league seasons begin in March and end in December. In the 2004 season J1 games attracted an average of 18,965 spectators per game.[16]

In addition, K-1 events have strong potential in the Japanese professional sports industry. K-1 is a martial arts fighting sport that combines traditional martial arts such as karate, kung fu, taekwondo, and kickboxing (the "K") into a modern and electrifying spectator sport, to determine the single best stand-up fighter in the world (the "1"). K-1 was introduced in 1993 by Kazuyoshi Ishii, and it has become one of the world's fastest-growing sports.[17]

Successful professional players are very popular among the Japanese. Kazuhiro Kiyohara, born in 1967, is one of the best-known baseball players in Japan. Since 1986 he has played for the Seibu Lions (Tokorozawa), Yomiuri Giants (Tokyo), and Orix Buffaloes (Osaka/Kobe) with outstanding performances. Japanese athletes who play overseas are also very popular. In 2003 there were nine Japanese baseball players in the major leagues in the United States. Hideo Nomo, born in 1968, became the first Japanese player in the U.S. major leagues when he joined the Los Angeles Dodgers in 1995. He was followed by several other players, including Ichiro Suzuki of the Seattle Mariners, who was the American League's most valuable player in 2001. Hideki Matsui, nicknamed "Godzilla," won his third Central League Most Valuable Player Award and made his debut with the New York Yankees in March 2003. The latest Japanese baseball sensation is Daisuke Matsuzaka. Born in 1980, Matsuzaka made a name for himself pitching in the 2006 World Baseball Classic. After a frantic bidding war among American baseball powers, Matsuzaka—nicknamed "Dice-K," signed a 6 year $52 million contract with the Boston Red Sox in December 2006.

Sport fans of the professional athletes, teams, and even the national team are actively involved in the Japanese sports industry. In particular, it is worthwhile noting that Ultra-Nippon, a voluntary supporters association for the Japanese national soccer team, was created in 1992. It created its own homepage with which it shares information on football games and sells goods for fan activities.[18]

Japanese people enjoy participating in diverse sport activities in everyday life in addition to enjoying the spectator sports. For the promotion of sports for the public, the Ministry of Education, Culture, Sports, Science, and Technology (MEXT) laid out a "Basic Plan for the Promotion of Sports" in 1999, and the sports promotion lottery "Toto" was launched nationwide with the expectation of becoming a financial resource for sports.[19] According to the report of 2001 Survey on Time Use and Leisure Activities, Japanese people spent six hours and twenty-eight minutes per week on leisure activities.[20] The result of the 2004 National Sport-Life Survey, conducted by the Sasakawa Sports Foundation (SSF), revealed that 16.1 percent of the respondents were "active" sport participants who exercise moderately more than twice a week for over 30 minutes at a time to maintain and improve their health. The result of the same survey also showed that 19.2 percent of the respondents belonged to sport clubs or groups, whereas 55 percent of them had never joined. The same survey found that "taking a walk" and "walking" were the sport activities in which Japanese engaged most frequently (twice per week), and that Japanese men wanted to play golf and women wanted to swim in the next few years.[21]

Both schools and local communities offer sport programs to Japanese youth. According to the survey conducted by MEXT in 1998, more than half of the children (56.2 percent) were taking part in sporting activities through affiliation with sports clubs in the school, sport clubs in the community, or sport clubs run by commercial companies. The report of the Japanese Junior High School Physical Education Federation in 2000 showed that male students had a preference for baseball, basketball, table tennis, track and field, and soccer, whereas female students preferred volleyball, soft tennis (which differs from regular tennis in that it uses soft rubber balls, and is played primarily in Japan and Taiwan), basketball, track and field, and table tennis. However, the membership in sport clubs at school declined from 1.66 million in 1992 to 1.26 million in 1999. One of the greatest changes that occurred in the social environment surrounding youth was the increase in the amount of hours of staying home and playing video games, which corresponded to a decrease in the number of outdoor activities. Thus, Japan became more concerned about youth sport to improve physical fitness as well as to develop their emotional and social well-being. In addition to sport for youth, Japan has developed diverse sport programs for older adults, since Japan is an aging society. The various sport programs and opportunities for the elderly include gateball games (Japanese croquet), new sport programs (e.g., ground golf, lawn bowls, and flying disks), and walking events at the national and local levels. According to the 2000 SSF National Sport-Life Survey, about 60 percent of the respondents aged 60–69 and about 50 percent of the respondents aged over 70 had participated in sport and physical activities more than once in the last 12 months. Main activities included walking, light exercises, and calisthenics.[22]

Most sport and exercise programs in Japan are being offered at the following four settings: schools, workplaces, private sport clubs, and community sport clubs. MEXT has surveyed the current number of the public facilities. According to the investigation in 2002 made by MEXT, the number of public sport facilities was 47,321: prefecture facilities, 677; municipal facilities, 33,159; association facilities, 269; and corporation-related facilities, 13, 216.[23] It can be said that the sport facility per person in Japan is not inferior to those of any country, and, in particular, public support at the local community level is well developed in Japan.

South Korea

Since the twentieth century three main sports sectors have been present in Korea: Korean traditional sports, such as taekwondo (also known by its older name, *taekkyon*) and ssireum (Korean style wrestling); organized sports from Europe, such as badminton, tennis, and football; and organized sports from the United States, such as basketball and baseball.[24] Taekwondo is a Korean traditional martial art sport, and its inception dates back to the first century BCE. The ancient Korean people performed a unique exercise for physical training during religious ceremonies, and the exercise is the origin of taekwondo.[25] The Korean Taekwondo Association, founded in 1961, modernized rules to guide the practice of taekwondo. Taekwondo became an official entry in the 2000 Sydney Olympic Games. In 2004 the number of registered training centers for taekwondo was over 7,000 in Korea, and

80–90 percent of the trainees were children.[26] Ssireum is a form of Korean traditional wrestling, established as a military art in ancient times. The professional ssireum leagues began in 1983. The number of professional ssireum teams has decreased to two in 2004 from fifteen in 1991,[27] but ssireum is still one of the most popular sports in Korea.

The development of modern sports in Korea has been significantly influenced by Western culture. In the early twentieth century, when Japan began to occupy Korea, Koreans believed that the acceptance of Western culture could help to modernize their nation, and that building up physical strength and public morale through sport could help to fight against the danger of losing the nation.[28] As a result, British and American sports were widespread in the Korean education system. In particular, Western missionaries were significantly involved in the development of modern physical education in Korea.[29] The Korean YMCA (Young Men's Christian Organization) was officially created in 1903, and it built an indoor gymnasium for the first time in Korea. In 1962 the Korean legislative body enacted a law for the encouragement of people's general participation in sports. However, elite-oriented training programs dominated until the 1980s, and the governmental support for the elite athletes' training peaked in the mid-1980s because of the 1986 Asian Games and 1988 Seoul Olympic Games. Sports programs for the public had not been seriously considered until the late 1990s in Korea.[30]

As the Korean gross national product increased dramatically in the 1980s, professional sport leagues began to be launched. A professional baseball league started in 1982, and professional ssireum and soccer leagues started in 1983. As of April 2005, there were thirteen professional soccer teams, eight professional baseball teams, ten men's basketball teams, six women's basketball teams, two ssireum teams, and six men's and five women's volleyball teams.[31] The Korea Professional Golfers' Association, established in 1968, had 3,704 members in 2005, and the Korea Ladies Professional Golf Association, created in 1978, had 761 members in 2005.[32] Soccer, baseball, and men's basketball are the most popular spectator sports among Koreans. As Korea went to the semifinals in the 2002 FIFA World Cup Korea/Japan, the professional soccer series became more popular than ever. Likewise, after Korea got into the semifinals in the 2006 World Baseball Classic, more Korean people became interested in the baseball games. In 2004 the professional baseball games attracted about 2.3 million visitors, soccer games 2.4 million onlookers, and men's basketball games 1.1 million spectators.[33] The Korean professional baseball teams, however, do not own their own stadiums, nor do other professional teams in Korea.[34] Preparing the 2002 World Cup, the Korean government constructed ten world-class football stadiums. Korea had 156 public football fields and twenty-one public baseball stadiums as of 2002.[35] In 2004 the number of golf courses was 262, and the gross area of the golf courses accounted for 0.2 percent of the entire country's land, which was five times more than the gross area of the golf courses in Japan.[36] In this sense, it can be said that golf is also popular in Korea, although the number of people who play golf is not really known. Golf became more popular as it came to be considered a symbol of higher social status.[37] Gambling on sport activities, such as horseracing and cycle racing, has become more popular in Korea. According to Korea Racing Association (horseracing), the total amount bet in 2000 was approximately $48 billion, an increase from $20 billion in 1995.[38] During the same period, the total amount bet on cycle racing rose from $ 0.8 billion in 1995 to about $12.5 billion in 2000.[39]

Professional athletes are very popular among Koreans, especially those who became successful in the overseas professional leagues. Cha Bum-Kun, born in 1951, was selected as "Asia's best player of the century" by the International Federation of Football History and Statistics.[40] He began his soccer career in 1971, and from 1978 until 1989 he played in Germany. Since returning to Korea, he has worked as a coach for a professional team and has run "Cha Bum-Kun's football school for children." Park Ji-Sung, who became famous during the 2002

World Cup Games, is currently one of the most popular soccer players. He plays for Manchester United in the English Premier division. Chan-Ho Park is one of the most popular baseball players. Since 1994 he has played for Major League Baseball as a pitcher in the United States. Lee Seung-Yup is another baseball player; he has been very successful as a hitter for Yomiuri Giants in Japan since 2003. Currently, more than thirty Koreans play on the LPGA tour in the United States. The best-known Korean golfer is Se Ri Pak, who became a professional in 1996 and joined the LPGA tour full-time in 1998. Since then, Pak has won more than twenty events on the tour, including four majors; hence, she became qualified for the World Golf Hall of Fame, although she cannot be inducted until she has been a tour member for ten years. Another well-known golf player is Sung Mi Wie (Michelle Wie). She is a Korean-American professional golfer born in Hawaii. Wie began playing golf at the age of four. In October 2005, less than a week before her sixteenth birthday, Wie became professional. Recently Koreans began to watch world-class professional leagues on TV, which helped them become more interested in internationally known Korean professional players than before.

Sport fans and clubs are also actively engaged in the development of spectator sports in Korea. Of particular note is the "Red-devil," a voluntary association supporting the Korean national soccer team. It organized for massive cheering in the stadiums and organized millions into street demonstrations of support at the 2002 FIFA World Cup Games; it amazed the world because all this cheering was never tainted with any violence or other trouble.[41]

Korean people on average spent 24 minutes per day for sport and outdoor recreation activities.[42] According to the 2004 Sport White Paper, each Korean household, on average, spent $200 per year purchasing sport equipment and sport services, which accounted for 0.9 percent of the total expenditure. A recent study on Koreans' sporting life reported that approximately 40 percent of the respondents were "active" sports participants who exercise moderately more than twice a week for over 30 minutes at a time to maintain and improve their health, and 14 percent of the respondents had joined an amateur sport association, such as a community football team.[43] The same study also found that popular sports activities included running, jogging, and hiking mountains, and that Koreans wanted to participate in swimming, hiking, and golf in the next few years. Playing and broadcasting cyber games, which is called the "e-sports industry," has become popular among young Koreans.[44] A 500-seat stadium exclusively for e-sport games was built in 2005. Korean youth, however, did not participate in sport activities as much as they wanted. According to a survey conducted by the National Council of Sports for All in 1998, most students of elementary, middle, and high schools could not participate in sports activities because of the lack of time and of appropriate facilities. In fact, the survey conducted by the Korean national statistical office in 2004 revealed that only 10 percent of the respondents between 15 and 19 years old participated in sports during weekend and holidays, whereas 61 percent of them participated in computer-related activities.[45] In general, turning to the twenty-first century, Koreans have become more concerned about "well-being" and their physical body image; as a result, the number of fitness centers has increased. In the future, the pattern of participation in sport and outdoor recreation activities among Koreans will change dramatically considering the fact that the five-day work week just began in 2005.

OCEANIA

Australia and New Zealand

With sport and recreation being an integral part of its popular culture, Australia is recognized internationally as a nation with a strong interest in sport. The interest has its roots in the nation's geographical location in the Southern Hemisphere. Blessed with year-round temperate, subtropical sunshine, and thousands of kilometers of coastline, the overall climatic conditions in Australia are favorable for all kinds of sports, especially open-air pursuits such as swimming, tennis, and surfing. In addition, Australians enjoy a 40-hour work week, which gives everyone ample time to participate in sport. A significant proportion of the Australian public (approximately 39 percent) is active in sport at one level or another.[46] The ten most popular physical activities undertaken by Australians aged 15 and over include walking, aerobics/fitness, swimming, cycling, tennis, golf, running, bushwalking, soccer, and netball.[47]

Among the population who participate in sports on a regular basis, many Australians choose to register at sport and recreation clubs or organizations to play organized sport. The ten sport organizations with the largest numbers of registered members include golf, basketball, Australian football, netball, soccer, bowls, cricket, tennis, rugby league, and rugby union.[48] Informal recreational sport is also popular in the country. Many Australians use municipal facilities such as tennis courts, outdoor fields, swimming pools, and golf courses, or commercial facilities such as squash courts, skating rinks, and bowling alleys, to develop their skills in a sport before becoming a club member and taking part in regular competition. Coaches are available at many of these venues to teach the basic skills. Australian youth are also active in sports. According to the Australian Bureau of Statistics, in 2003 an estimated 1.6 million (62 percent) children aged 5–14 years participated in sport organized by school, club, or association, with the most popular sport for children being swimming, followed by outdoor soccer.[49]

Australians also enjoy watching sporting events, on television and in person. One of the most popular spectator sports is Australia Rules Football. The pinnacle of the sporting year for the Australian Rules Teams is the Grand Final, which matches the two best teams in a playoff. In New South Wales and Queensland, rugby league is a popular sport. Every year there is a major tournament called the State of Origin, which matches the best New South Wales players against a similar Queensland team. Cricket is also popular, with the Australian national team having a lot of success in recent years. Since the late 1870s, Australian cricketers have been known for their resolute style of play. The tradition has been carried out by current cricketers, who are officially world champions and generally described one of the best teams in the world.

Australians have always loved sport and excelled at it. Having joined the International Olympic Committee as a founding member in 1894, Australia is one of the only two countries that have competed in every Olympics since 1896, and one of the only five that have hosted more than one Olympics. Australia finished fourth in the medal count at the 2000 Sydney games and the 2004 Athens Olympics. Many people believe that the climate and the healthy lifestyle generally enjoyed by the Australian population provide the perfect breeding ground for its elite athletes. Australia has produced a long list of champions who have distinguished themselves in the international arena at tennis, cricket, swimming, rowing, motor car racing, cycling, golf, boxing, surfing, yachting, and equestrian events. Olympic swim champion Ian Thorpe, world women's surfing champion Layne Beachley, and the former world number one professional tennis player Lleyton Hewitt are just a few examples. Women have contributed significantly to the rich sport history of Australia. From the pool of more than 3.5 million women and girls participating in sport and physical activity[50] have come the country's world or Olympic champions in a range of sports, such as Dawn Fraser in swimming, Karrie Webb and Jan Stephenson in golf, and Michelle Timms in basketball. Australia also has a reputation as a leader in the field of sport for disabled people. Paralympic athletes of Australia ranked fifth in the world, with a total of 100 medals.[51]

Sports and Recreation

Australian government at all levels plays an important role in the development of Australian sport and recreation. For 2004–05, the Australian government provided approximately $170 million in sports funding. As a priority, the Australian Olympic Committee has allocated $17 million to prepare its elite athletes for the 2008 Beijing Olympics.[52]

Various programs aimed at stimulating higher levels of mass physical fitness are initiated by the government. For instance, the "Active Australia" program was established by the sports commission in 1996 to provide quality sport and recreation facilities to encourage more active participation of Australians in sport, community recreation, fitness, outdoor recreation, and other physical activities. Funded by the Australian government, the Australian Institute of Sport (AIS) leads the development of Australia's elite athletes with sports facilities and support services of the highest standards. The Australian Sports Commission also has programs in place to promote sport for people with disability. For instance, in partnership with the Australian Paralympic Committee, Project CONNECT provides national sporting organizations with comprehensive support to include people with disability, from grassroots to the elite level.

Self-described as a "great little sporting nation,"[53] New Zealand is a country of low population density and spectacular scenery. With an abundance of open space accessible to everyone, sport is an important activity for many New Zealanders. In the early 2000s, 68 percent of New Zealand adults and children over five spent at least 2.5 hours a week in physical activity. Self-directed physical activities such as walking and jogging are popular: 72 percent of New Zealanders walked for exercise and enjoyment during the year 2000.[54] There is also an extensive range of organized sports throughout the country. Some are dependent on the season, and others are available throughout the year. Considered the national game of New Zealand, rugby is the most popular winter sport. It is played by New Zealanders of all ages and both sexes. The New Zealand All Blacks rugby team has won the World Cup once and been a finalist twice. Rugby players such as Colin Meads and Jonah Lomu remain national heroes. The most popular sport among women in terms of participation and public interest is netball. This team sport has been encouraged by extensive television coverage and the success of the national Silver Ferns team, who were world champions in 2003. Soccer is also popular in New Zealand. Almost all schools have soccer teams for both boys and girls. New Zealand hosted the FIFA under-17 years World Championships in 2000. Other popular organized summer sports in New Zealand include cricket and lawn bowls.

New Zealanders have a love of their landscape and the outdoors. The many beaches, rivers, and lakes around New Zealand allow a great number and variety of water sports to be played. The beach has been a favorite place of relaxation and physical activity for New Zealanders. Beach recreation, in the form of swimming, boogie boarding, beach cricket, surfing, diving, and windsurfing, are popular countrywide. Lakes, rivers, and hot pools are also sites for swimming and water sports such as waterskiing, kayaking, yachting, and fishing. With the fantastic scenery, New Zealand has been called a golf lover's paradise. There are almost 400 golf courses in the country (the highest number per capita in the world).[55] Golf is a popular participation sport for both men and women in the country. In the wild areas close to cities, bush-walking, tramping, and hiking in the forests and mountains become favorite recreation and leisure activities. Skiing and snowboarding also attract people into the mountains in the winter months when there is enough snow.

In the arena of competitive sports, New Zealand's elite sportsmen and women have had gold medal success in events such as rowing, windsurfing (boardsailing), canoeing, equestrianism, and yachting. At the 2004 Olympics, New Zealand athletes won gold and silver medals in rowing, cycling, triathlon, and canoeing. The country's most successful female Olympian is windsurfer is Barbara Kendall, who has won three world championships. Yachting attracted passionate national interest with the success of New Zealand boats in the America's Cup in 1995 and 2000. Maori and Pacific Islanders are strongly represented among the elite athletes. There are many sport activities in which Maori have gained international recognition, including golf (Phil Tataurangi, Michael Campbell, and Bradley Iles), surfing (Daniel Kereopa), and basketball.

Founded by the government and through the New Zealand Lottery Grants Board, Sport and Recreation New Zealand (SPARC) is the country's leading agency in promoting participation in sport and physical recreation. Push Play is one of the nationwide SPARC campaigns to encourage more New Zealanders to be more active physically. SPARC is also committed to providing facilities and services to nurture and develop the talents of the country's elite athletes. As a government initiative managed by the New Zealand Academy of Sport, the Prime Minister's Athlete Scholarship program aims to assist talented and elite athletes achieve educational goals while pursuing excellence in sport. More than 580 athletes across fifty-one sports were awarded scholarships for 2006.[56]

RESOURCE GUIDE

PRINT SOURCES

Adair, D., and Vamplew, W. *Sport in Australian History.* Melbourne: Oxford University Press, 1997.

Andrews, David L., and Steve J. Jackson, eds. *Sport Stars: The Cultural Politics of Sporting Celebrity.* London: Routledge, 2001.

Baker, J., et al. "Sport Administration in the People's Republic of China." *Journal of Sport Management,* 7 (1993): 71–77.

Birchall, Jonathan. *Ultra Nippon: How Japan Reinvented Football.* London: Headline Book Publishing, 2000.

Bloomfield, J. *Australia's Sporting Success: The Inside Story.* Sydney: University of New South Wales Press, 2003.

Brownell, Susan. *Training the Body for the People's Republic of China.* London: University of Chicago Press, 1995.

Carr, K. G. "Making Way: War, Philosophy, and Sport in Japanese Judo." *Journal of Sport History* 20.2 (1993): 167–188.

Cashman, R. *Australian Sport through Time: The History of Sport in Australia.* Sydney: Random House, 1997.

Collins, C., ed. *Sport in New Zealand Society.* Palmerston North: Dunmore Press, 2000.

Gordon, H. *Australia and the Olympic Games.* Brisbane: University of Queensland Press, 1994.

Guttmann, Allen, and Lee Thompson. *Japanese Sports: A History.* Hawaii: University of Hawaii Press, 2001.

Ha, Nam-Gil. "East Meets West and West Meets East: Celebrating the International Journal of the History of Sport." *International Journal of the History of Sport* 20.4 (2003): 136–138.

Han, Sang-Jin. Confucian Tradition and the Young Generation in Korea: The effect of Post-Traditional Global Testing. Paper prepared for presentation at the International Symposium for the Dialogue among Youth in East Asia Project held at Yingjie Exchange Center of Peking University, January 14, 2004.

Hong, F. "Commercialism and Sport in China: Present Situation and Future Expectations." *Journal of Sport Management* 11 (1997): 343–354.

Howard, G., Q. Ma, and Z. Wu, eds. *Sports in China.* Champaign, IL: Human Kinetics, 1990.

Kim, B., O. Cho, and Y. Jung. "The Research about Taekwondo Trainees' Satisfaction of Training Program and Instructors According to Socio-Demographic Characteristics." *Korean Journal of Sport Management* 10.3 (2005): 71–80.

Kim, Moon Kyum. *Sociology of Leisure—Korean Leisure and Culture.* Seoul: Hanwool, 1993.

Korean Overseas Culture and Information Service. *A Guide to Korean Cultural Heritage.* Seoul: Author, 2004.

Maguire, J., and N. Masayoshi, eds. *Japan, Sport and Society—Sport in the Global Society.* London: Rutledge, 2006.

Mangan, J., and J. Nauright. *Sport in Australasian Society: Past and Present.* (Cass Series, Sport in the Global Society, 18). London: Frank Cass Publishers, 2000.

Ministry of Culture and Tourism. *Statistics of Sport for All in Korea.* Seoul: Author, 2003.

Morris, A. D. *Marrow of the Nation: A History of Sport and Physical Culture in Republican China.* Berkeley, CA: University of California Press, 2004.

Ok, Gwang "The Political Significance of Sport: An Asian Case Study—Sport, Japanese Colonial Policy and Korean National Resistance, 1910–1945." *The International Journal of the History of Sport* 22.4 (2005): 649–670.

Riordan, J., and R. Jones, eds. *Sport and Physical Education in China.* New York: International Society for Competitive Physical Education and Sport, 1999.

Sports Bureau in the Ministry of Culture and Tourism. *A Sport White Paper.* Seoul: Ministry of Culture and Tourism, 2004.

West, D. "Legal Rules and Social Norms in Japan's Secret World of Sumo." *Journal of Legal Studies* 26.1 (1977): 165–201.

POPULAR SPORT MAGAZINES

Australian Golf Digest. Federal Publishing Company, Sydney, 1970. http://www.australiangolfdigest.com.au/.

Baseball. Sports Media., Ltd., Seoul, 2005. www.ebaseball.co.kr. Korea's leading baseball magazine.

Best Eleven. Best Eleven, Ltd., Seoul, 1970. http://www.besteleven.co.kr/. Korea's leading soccer magazine.

Inside Sport. Horwitz Publications, Sydney, 1991. http://www.insidesport.com.au/is/index. Australia's premier sports magazine.

Monthly Golf. Monthly Golf, Seoul, 1970. www.imgolf.co.kr. Korea's leading golf magazine.

New Zealand Fishing News. Fairfax Media, Auckland, 1978. http://www.fishnz.co.nz.

New Zealand Rugby World. Image Center Publishing, Auckland, 1997. http://www.nzrugbyworld.com/index.aspx.

Slugger. Nippon Sports Kikaku Publishing, 1998. http://www.sluggernet.com/. Japan's monthly baseball magazine.

Sportiva. Shueisah, 2001. http://sports.nifty.com/sportiva/index.jsp. Japan's leading monthly sports magazine.

Sports Business. Monthly Sports Business, Seoul, 1998. http://www.sportbusiness.co.kr/. Korea's leading sports business magazine.

Sports Graphic Number. Bungeishunju Ltd., 1980. http://number.goo.ne.jp/. Japan's leading weekly sports magazine.

Wilderness. Lifestyle Publishing Ltd, Auckland, 1991. http://www.wildernessmag.com/. New Zealand's magazine of the outdoors.

World Soccer Graphic. Fullcast Sports Co., 1993. http://www.wsg.ne.jp/. Japan's monthly football magazine.

Xin Ti Yu [New Sports]. Zhong Guo Ti Yu Bao Ye Zong She [China Sports Newspaper Society], Beijing, 1950. China's leading sport magazine.

WEBSITES

Australian Bureau of Statistics—National Centre for Culture and Recreation Statistics. http://www.abs.gov.au/websitedbs/c311215.nsf/20564c23f3183fdaca25672100813ef1/8086c7185b84f467ca256b260020f899!OpenDocument.

China Interactive Sports. http://www.sports.cn/.

China Sports on Web. http://www.sportschina.com/.
Culture and Recreation Portal (CRP). http://www.cultureandrecreation.gov.au/. Australia's online services and information in the fields of culture and recreation.
Foreign Press Center Japan. "Facts and Figures of Japan." http://www.fpcj.jp/e/mres/publication/ff/index.html.
Japan: A Web Guide. http://www.fpcj.jp/e/mres/publication/jp/index.html.
Japanese Statistic Bureau. http://www.stat.go.jp/english/data/shakai/2001/kodo/yoyakuk.htm.
Korea National Statistics Office. Outline of the 2001 Survey on Time Use and Leisure Activities. http://kosis.nso.go.kr:7001/ups/chapter.jsp?pubcode=KP&pub=3&ch_id=11&full=F. Report on the time use survey.
The Official Website of the Beijing 2008 Olympic Games. http://en.beijing2008.com/.
The Official Web Portal of the Central People's Government of the People's Republic of China. http://english.gov.cn/.
Sasakawa Sports Foundation. http://nippon.zaidan.info/seikabutsu/2004/00220/contents/0001.htm. SSF's National Sport-Life Survey Executive Summary.

VIDEOS/FILMS

New Beijing, Great Olympics (promotion video). Dir. Zhang, Y. M. China. 2006. http://en.beijing2008.com/97/70/article212007097.shtml. Features Chinese people's enthusiasm for staging the 2008 Beijing Olympic Games.
The Olympic Gold Medalists of China (documentary). China Central Television (CCTV). Features stories of eighty-seven Chinese Olympic Champions since 1984.

ORGANIZATIONS AND MUSEUMS

All China Sports Federation (ACSF). http://www.sport.org.cn/.
Australian Institute of Sport (AIS). http://www.ais.org.au.
Australian Sport Commission (ASC). http://www.ausport.gov.au/.
The Baseball Hall of Fame and Museum (Japan). 1-3-61, Koraku, Bunkyo-ku, Tokyo 112-0004. Tel: +81-03-3811-3600. http://english.baseball-museum.or.jp/index.html. The first baseball museum in Japan, opened in 1959.
China General Administration of Sport. Tel: +86(10) 87182998, 87182280. http://www.sport.gov.cn/.
China Sport Museum. Anding Men Wai, Anding Road, #3A, Beijing, China. Tel: +86 (10) 64912167. http://www.chinamuseums.com/China%20_sports.htm.
The Chinese Olympic Committee. http://en.olympic.cn/.
Korea Institute of Sports Science (KISS). 223-19, Gongneung 2-Dong, Nowon-Gu, Seoul, 139-242. Tel: +82-2-970-9500. http://www.sports.re.kr/. A research institute conducting studies related to the improvement of national health and the development of Korean sports.
Ministry of Culture & Tourism of Republic Korea. 82-1, Sejongno, Jongno-gu, Seoul, 110-703, Korea. Tel: 82-2-3704-9114. http://www.mct.go.kr/english/index.jsp.
Ministry of Education, Culture, Sports, Science and Technology (Japan). Japan 2-5-1 Marunouchi Chiyoda-ku, Tokyo 100-8959. Tel: 81-(0)3-5253-4111. http://www.mext.go.jp/english/index.htm.
National Council of Sport for All (Korea). The Olympic Tennis Field, 2nd Floor, 88, Bangeui-Dong, Songpa-Gu, Seoul, 138-050. http://www.sportal.or.kr/vm/unite/main/main.html. A government organization founded in 1991 with primary focus on the promotion of sports for the public.
National Sport Information Centre, Australian Sports Commission. Leverrier Crescent Bruce ACT 2617 Australia, PO Box 176 Belconnen ACT 2616 Australia. Tel: +61 2 6214 1369. www.ausport.gov.au/nsic. A comprehensive directory of Australian sports libraries, museums, and halls of fame.
New Zealand Institute of Sport. http://www.nzis.co.nz/.
New Zealand Recreation Association. http://www.nzrecreation.org.nz/.

SPORTS AND RECREATION

New Zealand Rugby Museum. 87 Cuba Street, PO Box 36, Palmerston North. Tel: +64 (6) 358 6947. http://www.rugbymuseum.co.nz/. New Zealand's biggest collection of rugby memorabilia and records.

New Zealand Sports Hall of Fame. Railway Station, Anzac Avenue, PO Box 643, Dunedin. Tel: +64 (3) 477 7775. http://www.nzhalloffame.co.nz/.

Sasakawa Sports Foundation (SSF). 1-15-16 Toranomon, Minato-ku, Tokyo, Japan. Tel: +81-3-3580-5854. http://www.ssf.or.jp/index_english.html. A nonprofit organization founded in 1991 under the auspices of the Ministry of Education with primary focus on the promotion of "Sports for All."

Sport and Recreation New Zealand (SPARC). http://www.sparc.org.nz/.

NOTES

1. Hans Westerbeek and Aaron Smith. *Sport Business in the Global Marketplace*. Hampshire, NY: Palgrave Macmillan, 2003.
2. See M. Speak, "Recreation and Sport in Ancient China," in Riordan and Jones (in Resource Guide).
3. See S. Reekie, "Mass Fitness," in Riordan and Jones (in Resource Guide).
4. See http://www.china.org.cn/english/features/China2004/107178.htm (accessed March 11, 2007).
5. See http://english.gov.cn/2006-02/08/content_182552.htm (accessed April 10, 2006).
6. See http://english.gov.cn/2006-02/08/content_182562.htm (accessed April 10, 2006).
7. See http://english.gov.cn/2006-02/08/content_182573.htm (accessed April 10, 2006).
8. See http://english.gov.cn/2006-02/08/content_182581.htm (accessed April 10, 2006).
9. See Mark D. West (in Resource Guide).
10. See Kevin Gray Carr (in Resource Guide).
11. See Maguire and Nakayam (in Resource Guide).
12. See the section of culture and sports in Japan: A Web Guide (in Resource Guide).
13. See Japanese Baseball Parks, Domes and Stadiums, http://baseballguru.com/jalbright/stadiums.htm (accessed April 8, 2006).
14. See the section of culture and sports in *Japan: A Web Guide* (in Resource Guide).
15. See the homepage of Japanese Football Association, http://www.jfa.or.jp/e/index.html (accessed April 5, 2006).
16. See the section of culture and sports in *Japan: A Web Guide* (in Resource Guide).
17. See the official Website of K-1, http://www.so-net.ne.jp/feg/k-1gp/index.htm. (accessed March 23, 2006).
18. See Jonathan Birchall (in Resource Guide).
19. See Sasakawa Sports Foundation, Sport for All in Japan, http://nippon.zaidan.info/seikabutsu/2001/00132/mokuji.htm (accessed March 31, 2006).
20. See Statistics Bureau, Outline of the 2001 Survey on Time Use and Leisure Activities. http://www.stat.go.jp/english/data/shakai/2001/kodo/yoyakuk.htm (accessed March 30, 2006).
21. Ibid.
22. Ibid.
23. See Ministry of Education, Culture, Sports, Science and Technology, "Physical education and sports," http://www.mext.go.jp/english/statist/index16.htm (accessed March 15, 2007).
24. See Nam-Gil Ha (in Resource Guide).
25. See Korean Overseas Culture and Information Service (in Resource Guide).
26. See Kim, Cho, and Jung (in Resource Guide).
27. See Sports Bureau in the Ministry of Culture and Tourism (in Resource Guide).
28. See Gwang Ok (in Resource Guide).
29. See Horace Horton Underwood, *Modern Education in Korea*, New York: International Press, 1926.
30. Ibid.
31. See Sports Bureau in the Ministry of Culture and Tourism (in Resource Guide).

32. Ibid.
33. Ibid.
34. Ibid.
35. Ibid.
36. See article on golf courses in *The Hankyoreh* 21 (March 23, 2006).
37. Ibid.
38. See the homepage of Korea Racing Association, http://www.kra.co.kr/ (accessed April 23, 2006).
39. See the homepage of Cycle Racing Association, http://www.cyclerace.or.kr/ (accessed April 23, 2006).
40. See the official Asian Player of the Century Thread, http://www.bigsoccer.com/forum/showthread.php?t=10880 (accessed April 13, 2006).
41. See Sang-Jin Han (in Resource Guide).
42. See Korea National Statistics Office, 2004, Report on the Time Use Survey, http://kosis.nso.go.kr:7001/ups/chapter.jsp?pubcode=KP&pub=3&ch_id=11&full=F (accessed April 20, 2006).
43. See Ministry of Culture and Tourism (in Resource Guide).
44. See Yun-Sook Sung, "Online Games and Cyber Delinquency among Adolescents," *The Journal of the Korean Home Management* 22.2 (2004): 37–57.
45. See Ministry of Culture and Tourism (in Resource Guide).
46. See J. Bloomfield (in Resource Guide).
47. See the Website of the Australian Government Department of Foreign Affairs and Trade, http://www.dfat.gov.au/aib/sport.html (accessed April 10, 2006).
48. See J. Bloomfield (in Resource Guide).
49. See the Website of Australian Bureau of Statistics (in Resource Guide).
50. See S. Phillips, *History of Women in Sport in Australia*, http://www.ausport.gov.au/fulltext/2001/ascpub/women_history.asp (accessed April 10, 2006).
51. See the Website of the Australian Government Department of Foreign Affairs and Trade, http://www.dfat.gov.au/aib/sport.html (accessed April 10, 2006).
52. Ibid.
53. See S. Jackson and D. Andrews, D. (1996). "Excavating the (Trans) National Basketball Association: Locating the Global/Local Nexus of America's World and the World's America." *Australian Journal of American Studies*, 15 (1996): 57–64.
54. See Te Ara, http://www.teara.govt.nz/NewZealandInBrief/SportsAndLeisure/4/en (accessed April 10, 2006).
55. Ibid.
56. See SPARC Website, http://www.sparc.org.nz/elite-sport/prime-ministers-athlete-scholarships (accessed April 10, 2006).

LITERATURE

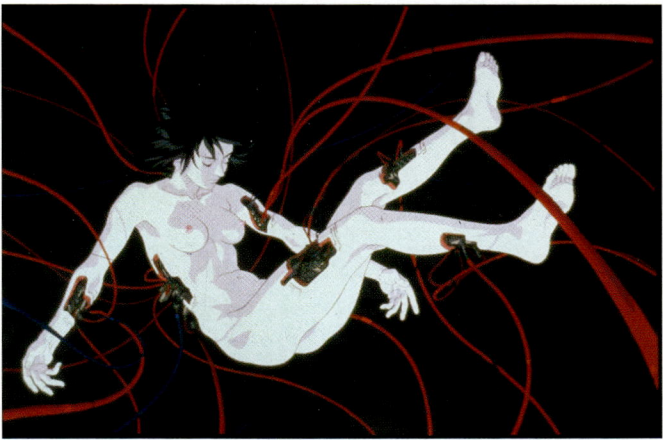

LITERATURE: A scene from the film version of the popular manga story, *Ghost in the Shell* (1995). Directed by Mamoru Oshii. © Manga Entertainment/Photofest.

LITERATURE: Portrait of Pramoedya Ananta Toer, Indonesia's most famous literary man, at his home in Bogor, Indonesia, July 27, 2001. Pramoedya, rumored to be nominated for a Nobel prize for literature for years, is the author of such classics as the *Buru Quartet*. © AP Photo/John Stanmeyer/VII.

LITERATURE: Indian-born British novelist Salman Rushdie presents his book, *The Moor's Last Sigh*, December 1995 in Sydney, Australia. Rushdie, who had lived in hiding since February 1989 when Iran promoted a fatwa (death threat) against him for blasphemy against the Islamic religion, was finally able to live in the open when the fatwa was officially removed by Iran in 1998. © AP Photo/Russell McPhedran.

LOVE, SEX, AND MARRIAGE

LOVE, SEX, AND MARRIAGE: A farmer rides past a billboard which promotes China's one-child policy, on the outskirts of a village near Dongying, in Shandong province. The sign urges people to "improve the quality of the population" and "control the population increase." Though the one-child policy is strictly enforced in the cities, in rural areas many people ignore the rules, or willingly pay fines in order to have more children. © AP Photo/Greg Baker.

MUSIC

MUSIC: Cui Jian, known as the "Father of China's Rock-and-Roll," performs during his solo concert at Hongshan Stadium in Wuhan, capital city of central China's Hubei Province, June 3, 2005. © AP Photo Xinhua, Zhou Guoqiang.

MUSIC: Many ensemble traditions, such as the Javanese *gamelan* in Indonesia, the Thai *pi phat*, the Burmese *pat waing*, and the Vietnamese *vong co*, have been celebrated internationally for their musical subtlety and stately refinement. Here a young boy in an ensemble in Thailand sits inside and plays a circular gong instrument called a *khawng wong lek*. Courtesy of Shutterstock.

PERIODICALS

PERIODICALS: A passerby stops to read a copy of a newspaper reporting the Pakistani-made missile Ghauri II in Islamabad, April 12, 1999. Foreign Minister Sartaj Aziz had said that Pakistan was mulling over the response to India's test firing of its newest nuclear-capable Agni II missile. © AP Photo/B.K. Bangash.

PERIODICALS: A newspaper vendor sits during a protest rally in front of the Jamia mosque in New Delhi, India, March 7, 2003. Indian Muslims shouted anti-American slogans, waved portraits of Saddam Hussein and cheered Islamic unity as they assembled after the Friday prayers. © AP Photo/Aijaz Rahi.

RADIO AND TELEVISION

RADIO AND TELEVISION: The Tokyo Tower at Tokyo, Japan. Television as well as radio stations broadcast from the tower, which opened in 1958. It is one of the world's highest steel-supported towers. Courtesy of Shutterstock.

RADIO AND TELEVISION: News readers of the Jaya TV channel read the news at their studio in Madras, on August 31, 1999. Jaya TV, a private 24-hour satellite channel in Tamil, went on the air on August 22, 1999. The channel has four news bulletins, including one in English. The channel was started by the All India Dravida Munnetra Kazhagam party leader Jayalalitha Jayaram to counter her arch rival and the state chief minister M. Karunanidhi's Sun Channel. © AP Photo/Desikan Krishnan.

SPORTS AND RECREATION

SPORTS AND RECREATION: A girl in Taiwan enthusiastically performs Chinese martial art. Courtesy of Shutterstock.

SPORTS AND RECREATION: A rugby scrum between the New Zealand and Australian teams, played in Auckland. Courtesy of Shutterstock.

SPORTS AND RECREATION: Grand champion Asashoryu defeats Kotooshu, foreground, to stay in sole possession of the lead in the Nagoya Grand Sumo tournament on July 20, 2006 in Nagoya, central Japan. © AP Photo/Kydo News.

THEATER AND PERFORMANCE

THEATER AND PERFORMANCE: Cambodian dancers perform traditional dance as part of the third Angkor International Ramayana Festival in Siem Reap, the northern province of Cambodia, November 29, 1997. Troupes from India, Laos, Vietnam and Cambodia participated in the festival through which the organizer of the four-day event hopes to carry a message to the world's tourists to come back to the country. © AP Photo/Ou Neakiry.

THEATER AND PERFORMANCE: Artists from Nagpur, Maharashtra state, perform during a dance drama *Sita Swayambar*, which is based on the Hindu holy book *Ramayana* fusing the Indian classical dances Kuchhipudi, Kathak, and Bharatnatyam in a cultural presentation program. © Sanjeev Gupta/epa/Corbis.

TRANSPORTATION AND TRAVEL

TRANSPORTATION AND TRAVEL: Fireworks at Petronas Twin Towers, Kuala Lumpur, Malaysia. The Petronas Towers were the world's tallest buildings until Taipei 101 in Taiwan was completed in 2003. Courtesy of Shutterstock.

TRANSPORTATION AND TRAVEL: Bayon Temple at Angkor Thom, Angkor, Cambodia. Courtesy of Shutterstock.

THEATER AND PERFORMANCE

EAST ASIA AND OCEANIA

GARY XU

OVERVIEW

Theater has existed in East Asia and Oceania for as long as there have been civilizations in these parts of the world. For each region—China, Japan, the Korean Peninsula, Australia, New Zealand, and the South Pacific islands—the origins and exact dates of the earliest theater vary. Debates and controversies abound. One thing is certain, however: no matter the region, theater consists of two components, that of oral and physical performance, and that of written drama with its considerable literary value. Theater as literature—read and appreciated by a select few—was all developed much later in these regions than theater as oral and physical performance in which all people can participate. Both components are integral parts of each region's cultural identity.

To qualify as theater, at least one of these four elements is required in the Chinese tradition: *chang* (to sing), *nian* (to converse in a rhythmic and poetic way), *zuo* (to strike a pose, to express ideas in body movement), and *da* (to fight, to perform martial arts). Because of a long history in China of elaborating on and perfecting these elements, and through cultural influence, in Japan and in Korea, some consider any performance with one of the four elements to be the equivalent of theater. Others argue that each one of these performances—be it aria, cross-talk, mime, or acrobatics—deserves its own independent status and should not be discussed under the general rubric of theater.

For this chapter that surveys East Asian and Oceanian theater, it is unnecessary and unproductive to engage in debate on what theater is or on how widely the study of theater should range. For the sake of clarity, however, I do want to draw attention to referentiality as a crucial criterion for determining whether a performance qualifies as theater in East Asia and in Oceania. By referentiality, I mean that a theatrical performance clearly demarcates the boundary between performance and reality by referring to its own fictitiousness and by making sure the audience understands that the performance is fictitious. Because all theatrical performances are live actions, certain devices must be utilized in order that the performance not be confused with reality. A clearly marked stage, for instance, is one of those devices. A high-pitched artificial singing voice is another. In ancient civilizations such as China's or Japan's, in which the worlds of fantasy and reality were often mixed in people's minds, referentiality was important for theater to be enjoyed without feelings of confusion or fear of threat from the spiritual. The most important referentiality device in early East Asian and aboriginal Oceanian theater is the mask and, by extension, the painting of the face.

People often trace the origin of the theatrical mask to ancient shaman rituals. Not all shaman rituals belong to the realm of theater, however. Shamans want people to believe that the spiritual has possessed the medium behind the mask, whereas theater uses the mask to express an idea, to represent certain types of character, to indicate morals, and to externalize emotions. Reality is condensed, abstracted, and represented—but *not imitated*—through the mask as a referentiality device.

Inherent referentiality not only differentiates theater from other forms of performance—such as shaman rituals, dance, and martial arts display—it also marks the most crucial difference between East Asian theater and Western theater. To elucidate this point, I'd like to use the example here of one of the earliest complete Chinese plays, *Daimian* [The Mask]. Popular in the Tang Dynasty (618–907), *Daimian* is about a brave and handsome prince. This prince's face is so fair that he cannot intimidate his enemies. He is thus forced to wear an ugly wooden mask for every battle. Once he is ambushed outside his home city. The troops on the city wall do not recognize the prince because of the mask. They let him in and shoot arrows to fend off the enemy only after the prince takes off his mask and identifies himself. The play is built on the dramatic tension between the masked identity and the true identity, between what the mask represents and the reality behind the mask. Without the mutual reference, the play could not have become one of the archetypes of Chinese theater.

Traditional East Asian and South Pacific island theaters are mostly *expressionistic* because of their inherent referentiality. This is different from the *mimetic* theater dominant in the Western classical traditions. For the latter, a play should imitate reality and should create a stage setting and a story resembling as much reality as possible. For the former, a play must be clearly separated from reality and should express aesthetic, ethical, and emotional ideals that do not have to strictly correspond to reality. Reality is mirrored in Western theater, but is distilled and transcended in East Asian theater. Hence, on a Chinese stage, a mere stick can be a horse whip, a rowing oar, or a staff as a weapon, depending on the context. The stage setting is thus minimalist and abstract; an actor could raise the stick to signify a long journey on horseback, a boat ride, or a breathtaking fight.

The expressionistic and minimalist theater is characteristic of traditional theaters in East Asia and in South Pacific islands. In modern China, Japan, Korea, Australia, and New Zealand, Western influences are visible on theater stages as much as they are in people's daily lives. Shakespearean theater is as popular in China as it is in Europe. Most of the Shakespearean plays have been translated and are regularly staged in China. The earliest translated play was *Hamlet*, masterfully rendered into Chinese by the playwright Tian Han in 1921. On a typically mimetic stage that resembles Victorian England, actors and actresses wear wigs and English clothing and express in Chinese the feelings of Romeo and Juliet.

The modern cultural trafficking is not, however, unidirectional. While Western mimetic theater has become increasingly popular in East Asia and Oceania, the expressionistic Chinese and Japanese theater has also cast tremendous impact on Western modernist and postmodernist theater. Bertolt Brecht (1898–1956) and Antonin Artaud (1895–1948) are two prominent examples of integrating East Asian theater and aesthetics into their respective challenges to conventional Western theater. Brecht's most famous notion of theater theory, *verfremdungseffekt* (distancing effect or alienation effect), is precisely his way to stress what he understood as oriental theater's inherent referentiality. Whether the requirement of speaking in an unnaturally high-pitched voice or the effort to engage the audience in a clearly theatrical setting, Brecht's theater theory is based on conscious reflection on the difference between theatrical representation and reality.

As for Antonin Artaud, the rebellious French playwright who claimed that Western theater was "dead," he found his inspiration in the Pacific islands' theaters, especially the Balinese theater. He described passionately how the Balinese theater displayed a panoply of pure and superior theatrical conventions: gestures, angular and abruptly abandoned attitudes, syncopated modulations formed at the back of the throat, musical phrases that break off short, flights of elytra, rustlings of branches, sounds of hollow drums, robot squeakings, dances of animated manikins, and so on. "In the Oriental theater of metaphysical tendencies," Artaud explains, "this whole complex of gestures, signs, postures, and sonorities which constitute the language of stage performance, this language which develops all its physical and poetic effects on every level of consciousness and in all the senses, necessarily induces thought to adopt profound attitudes which could be called *metaphysics-in-action*."[1] This is the "theater of cruelty," a term Artaud uses to refer specifically to the theatricality of the "extreme action" that is "pushed beyond all limits."[2] In his own words, the "cruelty" is "a matter of neither sadism nor bloodshed"—from "the point of view of the mind, cruelty signifies rigor, implacable intention and decision, irreversible and absolute determination."[3]

Brecht grasped East Asian theater's inherent referentiality, whereas Artaud became fascinated with the pure action of the Oceanians' theater. These traits—the expressionism and the theatrical action unbound by language—speak volumes about the heterogeneity of East Asian and Oceanian theaters as well as about the strong presence of these theaters in modern Western theater. East Asia and Oceania may have been completely reshaped by Western value systems and Western popular cultures in the modern age, but their own local cultures, including their theaters, continue to contribute—in whatever form—to the richness of human lives around the globe.

CHINA

Theater is called *xiju* in Chinese. This is a combination of the two words *xi* and *ju*, each representing a distinctive subgenre most important in the history of Chinese theater. *Xi* is *nan-xi*, the theater of the literati from the South; whereas *ju* is *zai-ju*, Northern performances that encompass acrobatics, martial arts, singing, and slapstick. The differentiation has to do with the fact that China proper was divided into separate Northern and Southern regimes more often than not during China's long history. Each regime has developed distinctive cultural features.

Zai-ju became a mature form of public performance during the Northern Song Dynasty (960–1127). Song's capital, Kaifeng, with its population of more than one million, demanded a variety of entertainment forms. The most popular entertainment place was the theater, called *goulan* or *wasi*, which was complete with a stage, an audience section, and a backstage. Many poems, paintings, and essays from the Northern Song describe with great admiration the busy scene of the theater.

Nan-xi experienced many years of development along China's southeast coastal area, especially around the city of Wenzhou, before it became a national form of theater and literature in the Southern Song Dynasty (1127–1279). The Song rulers were driven to the south of the Yangtze River by the Tartars. There was no essential difference between nan-xi and zai-ju because the former would not have been possible without the zai-ju talents that migrated to the South. The element that stands out for nan-xi is the refinement of its plays for not only public performance but also for literary appreciation. Many plays, previously transferred orally from teachers to disciples, were written down and revised to perfection by the literati. The scholars mixed stage direction with beautiful poems, lyrics, and narratives that strengthen the characterization; they even managed to have some of the plays printed and circulated. Before nan-xi's coming to the fore, all evidence of Chinese theater's development was through indirect sources—travelogues, fiction, historical records, and so on. There was no play extant in the written form. Nan-xi gave Chinese theater the first batch of actual plays that are still staged and also included in China's literary legacy.

The earliest extant nan-xi play is *Zhang Xie Zhuangyuan* [Zhang Xie, No. 1 in Civil Service Examinations], dated at around the early twelfth century. The four most famous nan-xi plays are *Baiyue ting* [The Peony for Moon Worshipping], *Jingchai ji* [The Story of the Thorn Hairpin], *Baitu ji* [The Story of a White Bunny], *Shagou ji* [The Aftermath of a Dog's Death]. These plays were repeatedly performed and further revised during the golden years of Chinese drama—the Yuan Dynasty (1206–1370), when the aesthetics and conventions of Chinese theater became stabilized.

During the Yuan Dynasty, which was ruled by the Mongols, Chinese civil service examinations were abolished. Chinese literati, who normally would devote their entire energy to studies of Confucian classics in preparation for the examinations, lost their means for upward mobility and had to find ways to make a living. Many chose to write plays and lead theatrical troupes. The most famous Yuan playwright is Guan Hanqing (1240–1310), widely considered the best in the entire history of Chinese theater. Guan wrote such plays as *Dou'e yuan* [The injustices to Lady Dou'e], the best-known tragedy in China. The most crucial contribution by Guan and his contemporaries to theater lies in their combination of zai-ju and nan-xi, in their effort to popularize theater for people from all walks of life, and in their formulation of the following generic features of Chinese theater:

1. Role categorization. Theatrical characters are divided into several categories based on their roles in the play and their attributes. These categories include the *sheng* (the male lead; young and handsome), *dan* (the female lead; young and beautiful), *jing* (the supporting character; middle-aged and respectful), *mo* (aged character), and *chou* (clown). Some of the categories have different names during the Yuan or in localized drama forms. Each role has a variety of face paintings corresponding to their character: red represents loyalty, black represents anger, white represents treachery, and so on.
2. Mixture of song lyric, prose, and prosody.
3. Multiple acts. A play can be staged in its entirety or in separate acts. Because of this arrangement, theatrical appreciation goes beyond the tight plot or the final climax, and nuances and different interpretations are more important to the Chinese audience than theatrical intrigues.
4. Lyricism and expressionism. Realism was never a concern for Guan Hanqing or his colleagues. Reality, as mentioned in the overview, was condensed, intensified, distilled, and transcended in Guan's plays.

The lyricism was carried to its extreme in the two most important plays of Chinese theater: *Xixiang ji* [Romance of the West Chamber] and *Mudan ting* [The Peony Pavilion], of the late Yuan and the late Ming (the early seventeenth century), respectively.

Romance of the West Chamber was written by Wang Shifu, who took over a popular story and created several of the most unforgettable characters in Chinese culture. One of the characters goes by the name *Hongniang* [The Red Lady], a maid who serves as go-between to help her mistress and a talented scholar consummate their love in marriage despite tremendous obstacles. "Hongniang" has since become synonymous with the go-betweens and dating services of modern times. One of the dating services, for instance, uses the Website www.chinahongniang.cn. The play's most important contribution is its creation of the scholar-beauty motif, which has become ubiquitous in Chinese theater. Emphasizing chance encounters and love at first sight, the scholar-beauty motif defies social hierarchy and arranged marriage; its celebration of genuine love is highly lyrical and its expressions of human emotions intense.

The Peony Pavilion was created by Tang Xianzu (1550–1616), who has been dubbed "China's Shakespeare." This dubbing has to do with the coincidence that both Tang and Shakespeare died in the same year; it also tries to establish that Tang was the first Chinese playwright with a wide range of works and with such Shakespearean theatrical originality and linguistic ingenuity that all of Chinese culture has to some extent been impacted by him. *The Peony Pavilion* was both the ultimate text of *qing*—human love and passion—and an encyclopedia of Chinese society during the late Ming. It has been regularly performed and adapted to other forms of arts. The most recent and spectacular production of *The Peony Pavilion* was staged at New York's Lincoln Center during the summer of 1998. Directed by Chen Shizheng, this postmodern 25-hour-long reproduction of *The Peony Pavilion* restages vividly Tang's time; it also accentuates Tang's central theme: "Qing can make one live and die."

Besides the long line of theater as China's literary treasure—from nan-xi to *The Peony Pavilion*—theater has also become fully embedded in China's popular culture as oral and physical performance. Every major region in China has its own version of operatic theater performance; every village has theater at the center of its festivities and market gatherings. Puppet theater is another important branch of Chinese theater. None claimed superiority over the others until Peking (Beijing) Opera became the national theater during China's last dynasty—the Qing. In 1790, four theatrical troupes from the South were summoned to Beijing to entertain the Qing emperor and his consorts. The imperial clan liked the singing and dancing so much that they kept the troupes in Beijing. This was the beginning of Peking Opera, which, because of Beijing's increasing importance as China's capital in the early modern and modern periods, became the most popular form of Chinese theater. Nowadays, with other local forms of theater becoming increasingly unpopular because of their slow pace and classical lyricism, Peking Opera continues to enjoy government endorsement as part of China's cultural heritage and to reinvent itself in modern and postmodern ways.

The twentieth century saw profound Western influence on Chinese theater. Shakespeare was significant; as were Eastern European playwrights such as Henrik Ibsen (1828–1906), widely revered as the father of modern drama. Ibsen's *A Doll's House* was staged in China numerous times. A new Westernized theater genre developed in modern China under the name *huaju*—spoken drama. That the words are only spoken not only sets this genre apart from traditional Chinese operas, but also speaks volumes about the ideological transformation that shaped modern China. At the center of the clashes of words and melodramatic battles between good and evil are notions of class struggle and antitraditionalism.

Cao Yu's (1910–96) *Leiyu* [The Thunderstorm] (1933) is one of the modern classics. In a well-off family in Shanghai, deeply hidden are the secrets of an illegitimate son, of incest, of murder and violence, and of generation gaps intensified by class struggle and the clash between tradition and modernity. All the tensions come to a climactic end on a stormy night in the most quintessential melodramatic fashion.

Western-educated Chinese intellectuals like Cao Yu used theater to expose the evils of traditional Chinese society, whereas the communists realized the potential of theater as a powerful tool for mass mobilization. In the 1930s, one of the most effective plays for

Theater and Performance

> ### FIRST CHINESE WINNER OF NOBLE LITERATURE PRIZE
>
> As if to acknowledge the dynamic and diverse theater scene in contemporary China, the Nobel Prize Committee awarded the 2000 Nobel Prize for Literature to the Chinese playwright and novelist Gao Xingjian (b. 1940). Gao is known for his avant-garde plays *Absolute Signal* (1982), *Bus Station* (1983), *Wilderness Man* (1985), and *The Other Shore* (1986). Inspired by Western modernist playwrights including Brecht, Gao combines the theater's inherent referentiality with scenes of Chinese society in post-Mao transition. Gao was forced into exile after the 1989 Tiananmen Incident and currently resides in France. His plays are regularly staged around the world and in multiple languages, including Chinese, English, French, Spanish, German, and Swedish.

mass mobilization was *Fangxia nide bianzi* [Put Down Your Whip], a one-act mini play always performed live on city streets. The male lead would repeatedly whip a young girl in public. Standers-by, without knowing they were watching a play, would often intervene and snatch the whip away. The scene would end with the actors leading the audience in a slogan shouting out against feudalism and the Japanese invasion. The inherent referentiality of traditional Chinese theater had given way to a deliberate blurring of reality and drama for maximum didactic effect.

The make-believe technique was further reinforced in the so-called revolutionary model plays of the Cultural Revolution (1966–76). The entire country was in practically a cultural vacuum. Traditional theater was denounced as feudalistic poison, and the only productions allowed were those with explicit communist didacticism and overt melodramatic motifs. The situation ended only after traditional culture was given its proper position in Chinese society at the end of the Cultural Revolution when not only the traditional but also the avant-garde theater again became prevalent.

JAPAN

The earliest theater in Japan was based on both Japan's local traditions in ritualism and the theatrical performance imported from China. Around 612, a Buddhist monk brought to Japan a set of theater instruments and plays from south China. The performances regularly held afterward were limited to those presented within Buddhist temples and were meant to spread Buddhist teachings. Gradually, three major forms of theater came into shape, increasingly secularized and embedded in Japan's popular culture.

The first form is Noh. It became a mature theater genre during the Kamakura period (1185–1333) when Japan's cultural and political center shifted from Kyoto to Edo (present-day Tokyo). The rise of the samurai warrior class demanded a form of entertainment that could both carry on the aristocratic refinement of the previous Hei'an period and relate to the booming urban life. When Noh was originally created, it thus catered exclusively to the samurai's tastes and needs. Commoners had no access to Noh performances.

Noh is most representative of minimalist and expressionist theater. The stage is always simple, with minimal decoration—no more than several pine trees in the background, serving as the only constant element in a world of impermanence. There are no props and no facial expression—characters all wear masks. There are only three roles—*shite* (the "doer," who sings and initiates action), *waki* (sideman), and *tsure* (companion). The music, too, is simple and pure, consisting only of several flutes and drums.

Characteristic of Noh are slow, elaborate, carefully measured foot and hand movements; a mixture of simple dialog, poems, singing, and dancing; males performing all female roles; and a ghostly aura. The key criterion for judging the quality of a Noh play or performance is known as *yugen*—deep in meaning and most plain in appearance. Having originated in Zen Buddhism, yugen expresses things that are beyond and transcendent of what their appearance might suggest. Thematically, under this principle, one must see through the appearance of the characters and realize that their suffering as ghosts is the result of their attachment to illusory worldly possessions and desires. Stylistically, the action and words do not stop at the moment they are supposed to stop—they carry over and pierce through. In short, yugen generates the power of suggestion.

The greatest Noh master in Japanese history is Zeami Motokiyo (1364–1443), who has been credited with about fifty Noh plays, all of which are considered Japan's national cultural treasure. One of Motokiyo's plays, *Atsumori*, is representative of the conventions and aesthetics of the Noh theater. In this play, an old warrior-turned-monk—the waki—comes to a beach to pray for Atsumori, a handsome young aristocrat he killed in a last battle that practically ended the aristocracy-dominated Hei'an period. The monk runs into a flute-playing lad—the tsure, who turns out to be Atsumori's ghost. The ghost lingers at this place because he is unable to cut his attachment from the past glory of his clan. After some conversation, the ghost shows his real face—in the role of the shite—and dances a spectacular dance accompanied by the sound of the flute. Together, the monk and Atsumori pray for eternal salvation and rebirth in the Western Paradise. Sharing the same story as the segment on Atsumori in the great Japanese novels *The Tale of Genji* and *The Tale of the Heike*, the play is part of Japan's cultural memory.

The second major form of Japanese theater is Kabuki, which has been widely performed since the seventeenth century. Kabuki can be seen as almost the reverse of everything Noh is known for. It is for the newly arisen townspeople and is free of the aristocratic tendency in Noh. Kabuki takes off the Noh mask, showing the real faces of the actors; allows female performers; and is burlesquely full of eroticism, everyday subjects, and the expression of people from all walks of life.

The third major form of Japanese theater is Jooruri, the puppet theater, which is similar to Kabuki in themes and target audiences.

The most famous Kabuki and Jooruri playwright is Chikamatsu Monzaemon (1653–1725), widely known in modern times as "Japan's Shakespeare." The very term—similar to calling Tang Xianzu "China's Shakespeare"—is absurd, fraught with unnecessary envy of Western culture under the influence of modernity. As Donald Keene points out: "Western readers who hope that Chikamatsu will prove a second Shakespeare are bound to be disappointed: there never lived a second Shakespeare. Chikamatsu's plays offer instead a vivid picture of a unique age in Japan, and have a special importance among the dramas of the world in that they constitute the first mature tragedies written about the common man."[4]

Indeed, Chikamatsu's plays, be they Kabuki or Jooruri, typically depict townspeople's lives—their financial worries, their travel adventures, and their romances with ladies of pleasure, which often conclude in elopement or double suicide. Chikamatsu also wrote about the samurai, but not those who enjoyed social privileges; instead, he wrote about the samurai with no master, those who struggled in poverty and yet were required to carry out vendettas to avenge their master's death. He also wrote about Japanese history, asserting an identity independent of China. These plays, such as *The Love Suicides at Sonezaki*, *The Battles of Coxinga*, *The Uprooted Pine*, and *The Love Suicides at Amijima*, contain as much theatrical spectacle as the hustles and bustles of early modern Japanese society.

THEATER AND PERFORMANCE

KOREA

As in China and in Japan, the mask was crucial also to early Korean theater until the nineteenth century. Called *Talchum*, mask theater showcases multiple characters wearing masks. The plays are mostly about exposing the true identities behind the masks, but—similar to the Chinese play *Daimian*—they also generate their theatrical, often satirical, effect from the difference between reality and illusion made possible by the mask.

Another important theater form in Korea is *Pansori*, a storytelling form wildly popular in both traditional and contemporary Korean society. Featuring a storyteller and a drummer/backup vocalist onstage, this form is more theater than strict storytelling. The storyteller impersonates different characters in the story and creates dramatic tension by using different voices. One of the most prevalent *Pansori* performances is the story of Chun'hyang. The daughter of a courtesan, she goes through numerous obstacles, including physical torture, before she consummates in marriage her love for the son of a government official. A recent film version of the story, titled *The Legend of Chun'hyang*, captures well both the story of this legendary girl and the theatricality of the Pansori performance. The film juxtaposes a real public performance of the story of Chun'hyang with the realistically produced scenes of Chun'hyang's love stories. We see how the storyteller's voices change and how engaged the audience is; when the actual story unfolds on the silver screen, the storyteller's voice becomes voiceover, explaining the characters' actions and venting anger at social injustice.

AUSTRALIA AND NEW ZEALAND

European settlers brought Western traditions of theater to Australia in the 1780s, and to New Zealand in the early nineteenth century. Almost all popular forms of European theater found their way to Australia and New Zealand while these two countries also developed their own troupes and built their own public theaters. In 1973, Australia's landmark Sydney Opera House opened and has since accommodated countless world-class performances by traveling European and local troupes.

SOUTH AND SOUTHEAST ASIA

BETH OSNES

INTRODUCTION

When we look at the great diversity of dramatic art, theatrical practice, and staged performance across South and Southeast Asia, three accomplishments stand out in particular. First and perhaps most striking is the antiquity of India's classical theater and epic literature, which together have shaped not only the subcontinent's later arts, but also pervasively influenced the verbal and performance arts of Thailand, Cambodia, Malaysia, and Indonesia (from Java to Bali). The ancient Indian traditions include comprehensive works of dramatic

VARIETIES OF HINDUISM

Hinduism is organized around the worship of three main gods: Brahma, Vishnu, and Shiva. Among them, Vishnu and Shiva constitute the primary pair. Hindus who choose to worship Vishnu are called Vaishnavas, and their beliefs and practices constitute the branch of the religion known as Vaishnavism. Hindus who devote themselves to Shiva are called Shaivas or Shaivites, and their beliefs and practices represent the branch identified as Shaivism. Historically and today, the great majority of practicing Hindus are Vaishnavas; Shaivas make up a minority. As a result of this demographic imbalance, many characteristics attributed to Hinduism as a whole are actually features of Vaishnavism, and are not necessarily shared by Shaivism.

One crucial divide between Vaishnavism and Shaivism is that Lord Shiva has one fixed form, whereas Lord Vishnu does not. Vishnu has avatars, concrete incarnations in which he periodically descends to earth in order to intervene in human affairs—specifically, to destroy a source of evil whose presence has begun to dangerously affect the moral-ethical balance of the world. A standard "short list" attributes ten avatars to Vishnu (longer lists ascribe twenty-five or more avatars to him). In Vaishnava mythology, each of these avatars has a particular life history, or biography, on earth, and performs distinctive miracles that help destroy a given source or form of evil.

Among the ten main avatars of Vishnu, the two most popular are Rama and Krishna, both anthropomorphic (i.e., human-like) incarnations of divinity. Vishnu is said to have descended to earth as Rama at the historical time when Ravana, the demon-king of the island country of Lanka, had become so demonic and powerful that all the other gods in the Hindu pantheon were powerless to control or stop him. The goal of Vishnu's Rama incarnation on earth thus was to destroy Ravana and restore peace, justice, prosperity, and happiness among human beings. The Sanskrit epic the *Ramayana* (composed between the sixth and second centuries BCE and attributed to the sage poet Valmiki) tells the complete story of Rama's life on earth as Vishnu's incarnation (and as heir to the throne of Ayodhya), destined to battle and defeat the evil Ravana.

At a different (later) time in history, Vishnu descends in his avatar as Krishna in order to rid the world of another set of evils, one of which is an internecine war between two branches of a royal family in Kurukshetra, a town north of modern Delhi. The two branches are the Kauravas (consisting of 100 brothers) and the Pandavas (five brothers). Being cousins, they are potentially equal claimants to the throne of Kurukshetra. The Kauravas, led by eldest brother Duryodhana, use intrigue and foul play to try to eliminate the Pandavas. The Pandavas are led by their eldest, Yudhishtira, and include Arjuna, the middle sibling. Because Duryodhana and his brothers are inclined toward evil and because the Kauravas are collectively very powerful, their contest for the throne with the far fewer Pandavas is unequal. Without outside intervention, the Kauravas are virtually certain to destroy the Pandavas, and in the process devastate much of the surrounding country.

In this context, Vishnu comes to earth as Krishna, partly to help the good Pandavas wage a successful war (mostly of resistance and response) against their evil and more numerous cousins and reclaim their rightful portion of a kingdom that ought to be proportionally divided between the two branches of the family. The other Sanskrit epic, the *Mahabharata* (fourth century BCE to the fourth century CE), tells the entire story of the conflict between the Kauravas and the Pandavas, as well as the related narrative of Krishna, Vishnu's warrior-god avatar. Thus, the two famous ancient Indian epics are poems related specifically to the Vaishnava branch of the Hindu religious and literary tradition, with the *Ramayana* devoted to Lord Rama and the *Mahabharata* devoted to Lord Krishna.

theory, theatrical discipline, and rhetoric and poetics. Examples are Bharata's *Natyashastra* (second century CE); the *Ramayana* (sixth through second century BCE), an epic poem in 24,000 verses ascribed to the sage Valmiki; and the *Mahabharata* (fourth century BCE to fourth century CE), the world's longest poem in 100,000 verses, of which the *Bhagavad Gita* is a small part. While Bharata's text (or other dramaturgical works like it) has often served directly and indirectly as a code book of aesthetic principles and as a manual of stagecraft, the two Sanskrit epics have provided many of the stories, episodes, characters, or contexts for actual plays in several theatrical forms. The appearance of the story of Rama, for example, in numerous guises from northern India to Bali over a period of centuries is one of the most remarkable facts of the history of popular theater around the world.

Asia's second achievement in the dramatic arts is a unique repertoire of parallel and interlinked puppet theaters found in India and Sri Lanka; in Myanmar, Thailand, Cambodia, and Vietnam; and also in Malaysia and Indonesia. The puppets of this long-standing tradition range from small hand puppets to large cutouts and life-size marionette puppets; and the performance modes range from staged puppet shows to shadow plays and water puppetry, with an amazing variety of representations, accessories, settings, and cultural codes in play. The crafts of puppet-making, the arts of manipulating elaborate arrays of puppets, and the poetics of narration and musical accompaniment are singular to this region of the globe.

The third collective accomplishment of South and Southeast Asian theater traditions is the distinctive evolution of modern urban theater and performance in unprecedented local, national, and regional environments. Although modern urban theater, based on original literary drama, has not spread uniformly across Asia, it has invented distinctive forms for itself in specific settings, especially in India and Indonesia. Urban theater in cities such as Mumbai (Bombay), Kolkata (Calcutta), Delhi, Chennai (Madras), Bangalore, Pune, and Chandigarh, as well as in Jakarta, Singapore, Kuala Lumpur, Bangkok, and Manila, brings world drama and contemporary plays to thousands of viewers every week, most often in high-quality amateur performances, but sometimes also in commercial and professional productions. Even when not as widespread as folk and traditional forms and stage practices, cosmopolitan urban theater significantly alters Asian audiences' understanding of the world, their cultures, and themselves.

Against this backdrop and with the help of particular examples, the following discussion surveys two main types of theater and performance in South and Southeast Asia: contemporary urban theater in India, Singapore, and Indonesia; and popular performance practices in older indigenous, folk, and traditional forms in India and Indonesia, as well as in Sri Lanka, Myanmar, Thailand, Cambodia, Vietnam, the Philippines, and Malaysia.

Modern Urban Theater

India

The first Western-style playhouse in India (and also in Asia) with a proscenium stage was the Bombay Theatre, built around 1776. Between 1776 and 1835, it staged only English plays for white colonial audiences (with wealthy Indians starting to attend performances in the early 1820s). The first Indian plays in "modern" form were staged in the languages of Marathi, Gujarati, Hindi, Hindustani, and Urdu for Indian audiences between 1843 and 1871. This early theater was a mixture of modes: Indian-language plays based on ancient Indian literary and religious texts, and Indian and Persian historical accounts; Indian-language translations and adaptations of classical Sanskrit drama; Indian-language versions of English plays, including some Shakespeare; and original new plays written by Indians in indigenous languages. Some of the early initiatives came from amateur groups, but in 1853 Parsi entrepreneurs began to organize commercial theater companies that performed at new proscenium playhouses in Bombay, and also on tours in Maharashtra and northern India. Commercial "Parsi theater"—an enterprise that brought together Zoroastrian, Hindu, Muslim, and Christian theater personnel to collaborate on numerous new Gujarati, Hindi, and Urdu plays—dominated the urban Indian stage until the late 1920s, when the emergent Indian film industry rapidly displaced drama as the most popular form of public entertainment.

After about 1930, modern urban theater in India became chiefly an "amateur" endeavor, with private groups and noncommercial theater organizations (such as the Indian People's Theater Association, active from 1943 through the late 1950s) providing fresh momentum. Since independence in 1947, modern urban theater in India has reinvented itself in the age of mass media as a nationwide amateur and commercial enterprise. It now has vibrant performance traditions in the Marathi, Bengali, Gujarati, Hindi, Urdu, Punjabi, Manipuri, Kannada, Malayalam, Telugu, Tamil, and English languages, with primary centers of activity in Mumbai, Kolkata, and Delhi. There is also significant theatrical activity in modern forms in the smaller cities of Bangalore, Bhopal, Chandigarh, Imphal, Chennai, Pune, and Trivandrum, as well as in Ahmedabad, Baroda, Gwalior, Hyderabad, Jaipur, Lucknow, Mysore, Nagpur, and Patna.

Much of modern urban Indian theater revolves around the work of major directors and the groups or companies they run. Principal theater directors of the post-1947 period, all of whom have worked in multiple languages, and the languages in which they directed include Ebrahim Alkazi (English, Hindi, Hindustani); Satyadev Dubey (Hindi, Urdu, Marathi, Gujarati, English); B. V. Karanth (Kannada, Hindi, Sanskrit, other languages); and Habib Tanvir (Hindi, Chattisgarhi, Urdu, English). Among the major directors are some who have worked in two languages, such as Utpal Dutt (Bengali, English), Shyamanand Jalan (Hindi, Bengali), Alyque Padamsee (English, Hindi), and K. N. Panikkar (Malayalam, Sanskrit); and some who limit their work to a single language, such as Mahesh Dattani (English), Arvind Deshpande (Marathi), Shombhu Mitra (Bengali), Rajinder Nath (Hindi), Jabbar Patel (Marathi), Badal Sircar (Bengali), K. V. Subanna (Kannada), and Ratan Thiyam (Manipuri). Their numbers also include several important women directors, among whom are Vijaya Mehta (Marathi, Hindi, Sanskrit), Neelam Mansingh Chowdhry (Punjabi, Hindi), and Usha Ganguli (Bengali, Hindi).

Among the most prominent theater groups or companies of the past 30 years are Satyadev Dubey's Theater Unit, Alyque Padamsee's Theater Group, and Vijaya Mehta's Rangayan in Bombay; Badal Sircar's Satabdi, Shyamanand Jalan's Padatik, and Usha Ganguli's Rangakarmee in Kolkata; and Habib Tanvir's Naya Theater and Rajindernath's Abhiyan in New Delhi. Other groups of the first importance in this period include K. V. Subanna's Ninasam in Heggodu, Karnataka; K. N. Panikkar's Sopanam in Trivandrum; Jabbar Patel's Theatre Academy in Pune; Ratan Thiyam's Chorus Repertory Theatre in Imphal; Neelam Mansingh Chowdhry's The Company in Chandigarh; and Mahesh Dattani's Playpen in Bangalore. Each of these groups has produced major work on the Indian stage, and has received national as well as international recognition. Their productions—of the best new plays in the Indian languages and in English, of a broad range of world drama in English and Indian-language translations, and of Indian theater classics—constitute a significant portion of modern urban theatrical performance in the country today.

The vitality of contemporary urban Indian theater groups and the directors associated with them has directly sustained theater-going audiences in the principal cities, often against great financial odds, and especially against stiff competition from India's enormous film and mass-media entertainment industries. The groups' vitality has contributed greatly to the growth and success of modern Indian drama as a literary art, providing stage outlets for new and original work by playwrights in a number of indigenous languages and in English. Among the major post-independence dramatists who have flourished in this environment are Vijay Tendulkar, G. P. Deshpande, Mahesh Elkunchwar, and Satish Alekar (Marathi); Badal Sircar and Utpal Dutt (Bengali); Mohan Rakesh, Dharamvir Bharati, and Habib Tanvir (Hindi); Chandrashekahr Kambar and Girish Karnad (Kannada); K. N. Panikkar (Malayalam); Ratan Thiyam (Manipuri); and Mahesh Dattani (English).

Since the early 1950s, this modern urban theater has accomplished an unparalleled transformation of India's dramatic and performance traditions. Within the broad confines of the proscenium stage, it has exposed educated Indian audiences to some of the most innovative and provocative recent writing in their indigenous languages. It has energized its viewers into dealing with urgent social problems, political issues, and historical conundrums, whether concerning the general situation of women, the conflict between religious belief and secular modernity, human trafficking, the collapse of the traditional order, or the integration of the caste system's former "untouchables" (now identified as the Dalits) into the rest of contemporary society. The modern urban theater has also focused public debate on such contentious problems as domestic violence, alcoholism and abuse, gender and sexuality, AIDS, the harvesting of human organs, religious fundamentalism and terrorism, and fascist politics. Formally and technically, this urban theater has been immensely innovative. It constantly explores varieties of realism and anti-realism, folk performance styles and method acting, elaborate stage machinery and minimalist theater, traditional Indian musical theater and contemporary Euro-American forms of the musical, rigorous translation and free adaptation, and dramatic texts and workshop productions. Its repertoire has been persistently global for several decades: Aeschylus and Shakespeare, Bertolt Brecht and Dario Fo, Henrik Ibsen and Wole Soyinka appear side-by-side with Kalidasa and Bhasa, Vijay Tendulkar and Girish Karnad, and Mahasweta Devi and Manjula Padmanabhan. Among the Asian nations, the urban theater of India in various modern forms and styles remains the most vital on the aggregate, occupying a unique position in world theater today.

Singapore

Singapore was a part of Malaysia until 1963, and its earliest modern urban theater was an English-language amateur theater performed and watched by its British colonial residents (mostly administrators, businessmen, and armed services personnel). Since independence, Singapore has defined itself as a predominantly Chinese immigrant city, with significant minorities of Malays and immigrant Indians. It launched its Cultural Centre as a state-sponsored institution in 1965, a multiracial organization designed to nurture the city's arts, including drama and theater. Professional theater companies were formed subsequently, with Theatreworks, for example, being established in 1985. These initiatives have created an admixture of Western and indigenous theater forms. Since the 1970s, local dramatists have succeeded in reaching the stage; the early box-office success of Robert Yeo's *Are You There, Singapore?* at the Cultural Centre set the trend. Most amateur and experimental theater groups now perform plays in "Singlish," Singapore's distinctive brand of English (parallel to "Hinglish" in India's so-called Bollywood movies and in its broadcasting media). Beijing Opera is also popular, and is called Chinese *Wayang* [the Malay word for performance] when staged in Singapore. Moreover, the city has a Malay theater, which is performed at distinctive playhouses such as Sriwana, led for many years by Kalim Hamidy. Singapore has also witnessed some unusual cross-cultural and "cross-over" theater. Kuo Pao Kun, for instance, a dramatist and director trained in Australia, started his illustrious career in Mandarin drama, before switching to English. Over more than 40 years, his successes have included *The Coffin Is Too Big for the Hole* (1985), as well as *Mama Looking for Her Cat* (1988), performed with a mixed-race cast. Overall, however, theater based on the works of indigenous authors still lags behind the performance of canonical Anglo-American drama.

Indonesia

Among the Southeast Asian nations, Indonesia has the most active and successful modern urban theater, most often associated with the larger-than-life career and achievements of W. S. Rendra (b. 1935). Rendra was trained in the dramatic arts and in theater in New York in the mid-1960s, and returned to Jakarta to found his *Bengkel Teater* [theater workshop] in 1967, the first such initiative in the country. During the next 11 years (until imprisoned as a political dissident by the Suharto regime in 1979), Rendra's workshop techniques and other innovations utterly changed contemporary theatrical practice as well as audience expectations in urban Indonesia. During this period, the most important site for Rendra's experiments and productions was the Taman Ismail Marzuki, Jakarta's arts center, founded in 1968 by Ali Sadikin, then the anti-communist and anti-Suharto governor of Jakarta, in collaboration with a group of artists who broadly shared his views. It was at this time that Rendra wrote, directed, and staged some of his most trenchant protest plays, attacking the government's corruption, its repression of dissent, and its systematic depredation of Indonesia's natural environment.

Rendra's principal achievements as a theater craftsman had emerged by this phase of his career. He is famous for what is frequently called "the Rendra method," in which he takes a well-known play from the Euro-American dramatic canon and adapts it so freely into Bahasa Indonesia that, when the process is complete, there is little or no remaining resemblance between the original and its "rendition"—even though the latter cannot be created without beginning with the former. This is a workshop practice that is virtually universal in modern theater, but in Rendra's hands it has yielded remarkable adaptations and new texts in Bahasa Indonesia, transforming the imaginative landscape of the language and its cultural heritage. He is also famous for his mini-*kata* plays, which constitute a "theater of minimal text" in which theatrical signification is achieved through multiple means—from the actor's body to stage setting—even while minimizing the role of explicit expression and narrative structure in language.

The issues and positions that Rendra has highlighted through his method of adapting Western plays, use of minimal text, and experiments in stagecraft have since become characteristic of modern urban theater in Indonesia. Its popular concerns include the quest for social justice; restoration and preservation of the environment (especially in the presence of multinational "world factories" in Indonesia); protection of women against violence and abuse; rethinking Indonesian precolonial and colonial history in the light of postcolonial experience; critical recognition of the troubling continuity between Dutch colonial rule in the past and self-government in the present; and freedom from corruption in public office and from the repression of political dissent.

INDIGENOUS THEATER

Distinguished from modern urban theater as a whole, the forms of indigenous theater in South and Southeast Asia fall into four main categories: (1) forms developed in or derived from classical literary drama, such as the plays of Kalidasa or Bhasa in Sanskrit; (2) forms of religious ritual enactment, often linked to festivals and particular occasions and contexts of worship; (3) forms evolved in post-classic times, of nonliterary and nonreligious origin, often related to contexts of popular entertainment; and (4) forms of folk origin, with no clear precursors in canonical literature or religion, with connections to folktales and folksongs in oral culture. The first three of these categories can be grouped together under the label of "traditional forms," whereas the fourth category consists of "folk forms." The following survey of indigenous forms in nine countries highlights only a few prominent examples. Left out are many other interesting traditions that deserve attention in more detailed studies of the region.

India

Some of the most popular traditional forms of theater in India are connected to Hinduism. The *Ram Lila*, the most famous of the religious theatrical forms, is a sacred pageant play based on the story of the *Ramayana*, and is performed annually at the end of the Hindu solar calendar that culminates in the festival of Dasehra (September or October), foreshadowing the new year festival of Diwali (October or November). The *Ram Lila* is traditionally performed by, in, and for particular Hindu communities. Whether in villages, small towns, or city neighborhoods, each community plans and produces its own pageant play, raising money for the production and providing props, costumes, amateur stagehands, musicians, directors, and actors. The pageant is usually performed in multiple sessions, extending from several days to a month, with one or more episodes (of several hours' duration) staged each evening to reenact the story of Rama, Sita, and Ravana in either synoptic form or in entirety. The performances usually take place in an open-air setting, with a stage or playing area set up temporarily for the occasion, and with the audience seated on the ground before it. In recent decades, wealthier communities have turned to more elaborate outdoor arrangements featuring tents and chairs, or to indoor community halls with facilities for the comfort of large audiences. Some communities have also sponsored trained performance troupes or touring companies to stage their pageants. In the Banaras-Allahabad region (known as "the Hindu heartland" of central northern India), the annual *Ram Lila* has been a much more elaborate sacred pageant, with extended Vaishnava rituals incorporated into the performance cycle each year, and with actors and production staff trained in more specialized pageantcraft.

Each September and October, the *Ram Lila* is performed at tens of thousands of small and large public locations all over India, involving millions of participants nationwide in its production and performance, and drawing a total audience in the range of 200 to 300 million spectators. It is a continual multi-day public event, with carnivalesque elements in the theatrical experience (although as a sacred pageant it imposes considerable restraint on audience behavior). The enactment onstage of the Rama story emphasizes multiple emotions, almost as a collective catharsis of the ups and downs of everyday life: anger at the injustice of court intrigue in Ayodhya that deprives Rama of his rightful throne; grief over the banishment of Rama, Sita, and Lakshmana to their 14-year forest exile; fear and horror in response to Ravana's abduction of Sita to his island fortress in Lanka; laughter at the clever antics of Hanuman, the monkey god who helps Rama and Lakshmana locate Sita; and

THE STORY OF THE *RAMAYANA*

The "original" *Ramayana*, attributed to an ancient sage poet named Valmiki, was composed in epic Sanskrit between the sixth and second centuries BCE, with continual revisions and refinements by several generations of anonymous authors. This canonical text is 24,000 couplets long, and is divided into seven books. It tells the full story of Rama as an avatar or incarnation of Lord Vishnu, and the main narrative runs as follows.

Dasharatha, the king of Ayodhya (now a holy city in central northern India), has three wives who among them give birth to four sons. Rama, the eldest prince, is presumed the heir apparent; he wins a suitors' contest for the hand of Sita, the foundling daughter of Janaka, ruler of a neighboring republic. In Dasharatha's last days, however, a palace intrigue deprives Rama of the throne and banishes him from Ayodhya for 14 years. Rama's wife Sita and his favorite half-brother Lakshmana insist on accompanying him into exile, and the three young people travel southward until they reach the Dandaka forest (on the Deccan Plateau, in central India), where they build a simple hut for themselves and settle down for the long duration of the exile.

One day, however, Ravana, the powerful demon king of Lanka (an island kingdom in the far south), chances upon Sita in the forest. Immediately attracted to her, he devises an elaborate subterfuge to abduct her and carries her off to his fortified palace. Rama and Lakshmana, distraught beyond grief, search high and low for Sita. Finally, with the help of a clan of intelligent monkeys led by Sugriva and Hanuman, they locate her on Ravana's palace grounds. Rama and Lakshmana then lead their army of monkeys across the straits to Lanka, wage war with Ravana and his brothers, and finally defeat the demon king and his army. They find Sita apparently unharmed; she proves she has remained chaste by walking through a fire (a test of purity and purification). Happily reunited, Rama, Lakshmana, and Sita return to Ayodhya with the prescribed period of exile at an end. The people of the city celebrate the return of their favorite prince, and Rama ascends its throne as the rightful king.

In this core form, the *Ramayana* portrays an ideal prince and king, an ideally faithful wife, and a true brother; it also represents the ultimate triumph of good over evil, justice over injustice, temperance over lust, and love over adversity. The numerous subsidiary characters and incidents woven into the fabric of the main narrative populate the many smaller tales that grow out of this epic. Over the past two millennia, some 300 different versions of the Rama story have appeared in about three dozen languages across South and Southeast Asia (the Thai epic *Ramkien* being one of them). Among them, they encompass every possible variation on the canonical Sanskrit version.

reaffirmation in Rama's victory over Ravana at the end of the main story. The style of the local community performances is usually playful and improvisational, with physical comedy, stunts, and stage machinery (especially for Hanuman's flying) that greatly entertain children and younger audiences. The *Ram Lila* culminates in the festival of Dasehra, on the tenth day after the new moon in late September (with Divali occurring on the night of the following new moon). Conducted, for safety, on the outskirts of town or in a large open field some distance from the performance area, the Dasehra festival involves the spectacular public ritual of burning large wooden effigies of Ravana and his brothers to mark the cyclic victory of good over evil following the autumn harvest, which coincides with the end of the Hindu solar calendar.

Other traditional theatrical forms based on Hindu religious practices include the *Ras Lila*, which is performed widely among Vaishnava communities across northern India, but not on the same scale as the *Ram Lila*. The *Ras Lila* is a community reenactment and celebration of Lord Krishna's life as a young cowherd in the Vrindavan region (near Mathura, north of Agra), particularly of his representation as an erotic god. Another religious theatrical form is the *Yakshagana*, a sacred folk opera that appeared about 500 years ago in the Kannada-speaking Karnataka region of southern India, with related developments in the Andhra and Tamil regions. Popularized in the postcolonial period, *Yakshagana* brings together stylized heroic action; acrobatics; song (in classical Carnatic ragas); music; and elaborate costumes, masks, makeup, and the symbolism of color to enact stories about the gods of Hindu mythology or celebrate the various avatars of Vishnu (including Rama and Krishna). In recent decades, *Yakshagana*-style music, movement, costumes, and masks have been used prominently in some experimental urban Indian theater.

Of the indigenous theater forms based on ancient literature, the most famous in modern times is *Kutiyattam*, unique to a small community of ritually trained caste performers in the southern Indian state of Kerala who reenact select episodes from select Sanskrit plays by Bhasa and lesser classical authors in highly stylized versions in sacred temple auditoriums. Among the relatively secular folk/popular theater forms, the most famous are *Nautanki* (developed in Hindi-speaking northern India), *Tamasha* (Marathi, Maharashtra), and *Jatra* (Bengali, the Bengal region). *Nautanki* is a secular entertainment, narrative in structure and operatic in style, with variable content: it retells episodes from the epics or from history and popular legend, or it depicts contemporary events. *Tamasha*, in contrast, focuses on a combination of the comic and the erotic. It tells a basic story with romantic, heroic, and comedic elements but is structured as explicitly bawdy song-and-dance entertainment featuring several male actors, jesters, and women performers onstage accompanied by instrumental music and choral singing. *Jatra*, in further contrast, is a more flexible folk form used by traveling troupes in the Bengal region, which offers plays specially composed for rural audiences on domestic issues, contemporary problems, or historical events; the plays are performed in makeshift open-air settings, featuring improvised dialog and an emphasis on song. These three forms are among dozens of less well-known but locally popular indigenous theatrical forms that have flourished over the past half-millennium or so all over the subcontinent.

Sri Lanka

Among the island nation's indigenous traditions, *Kolam* is a folk form of masked theater from the southern region that may have evolved from ancient fertility ceremonies. In Sinhala, *kolam* means "comic disguise," so humorous comedy is a primary function. Performances usually occur in an outdoor clearing, and continue from sundown to sunup. In the opening dances and incantations, the musicians chant verses providing the background of each character in the story while the actor playing that role performs an individual dance, wearing a mask. In the more dramatic parts that follow, the performers discard their masks so they can deliver the dialog more easily.

Sri Lanka is a Buddhist-majority nation that includes old Muslim, Hindu, and Christian minorities. Among several specifically Christian theatrical forms, *Pasku* is a Passion play that depicts Christ's suffering before his crucifixion. It is performed during Holy Week (preceding Easter), and originated in northern Sri Lanka in the late nineteenth century. The action is portrayed either by actors, or by means of life-size statues manipulated from behind a six-foot wall. A narrator describes the action; painted scenery 20 feet tall serves as the backdrop; and sacred music, sometimes played on a church organ, accompanies the performance.

A form of folk theater called *Nadagama* evolved as a secular form of Pasku, and became very popular in the nineteenth century. Subsequently, the Nadagama form heavily influenced *Rukada*, a marionette theater performed only in southwestern Sri Lanka, most of whose puppeteers are former Nadagama performers. The puppets are between three and four feet tall, and are manipulated by strings by puppeteers located out of sight above the puppets' stage. The stage itself is divided into three distinct sections, all with scenic drops behind them and a curtain in front to conceal scene changes. The music is provided by an orchestra consisting of harmonium, violin, and pair of complementary tabla drums.

Myanmar

Because of its location, Myanmar (formerly Burma) has borrowed culturally from China to the north, Thailand to the east, and India to the west. However, Burmese theater remains very much its own tradition, centered around a joyful marionette theater and dominated by clown characters. The marionette theater form known as *Yokthe Pwe* originated in the fourteenth century. Customarily performed at temple festivals, it initially offered simple animal plays to amuse children. Subsequently, the theater produced complete puppet plays of greater depth and magnitude, in the likeness of *Zat Gyi*, Burmese court drama, and enacted from the *Jataka* the stories of the former births of Gautama Buddha. Yokthe Pwe puppets are carved from wood, and appear to wear masks like those of Thai *Khon* dancers. Because the puppets have up to sixty strings, the technique for moving them is extremely complicated. The lively movements and dancing of these puppets is often imitated in stylized form in Burmese dance.

The *Anyein Pwe* is a more modern form of theater that combines dance, music, opera, and comedy skits based on everyday life. Troupes traditionally traveled to different locations to entertain at events such as weddings, pagoda festivals, ear-piercing ceremonies, and funerals. The most famous contemporary practitioners of the Anyein Pwe form are the Moustache Brothers of Mandalay, who were persecuted by Myanmar's military regime in the late 1990s. At an Independence Day performance in 1996 at the compound of Nobel Peace Prize Laureate and dissident Aung San Suu Kyi, eldest brother U Pa Pa Lay satirized government corruption under the current dictatorship. In retaliation, he and his cousin U Lu Zaw were sentenced to seven years' hard labor, with metal bars chained between their legs. Their release was won only in 2001, following massive international pressure.

Thailand

The oldest known indigenous Thai theater form is the dance drama *Lakon Jatri*, from the southern region of the mainland, in which only male actors perform song, pantomime, and dialog. It enacts stories from the Buddhist *Jataka*, often over a span of several nights. Traditional performances had three male performers: one portrayed all the male parts; the second, all the female parts; and the third, all the animal and clown parts (usually wearing a mask to play the jester). Indian classical dance has influenced the movement style in Lakon Jatri. One unusual movement characteristic of this form is a backbend, in which the dancer's head appears between his legs—a remnant of the style of Thai dancing before courtly refinement. A flute, drums, and cymbals provide musical accompaniment. In recent times,

Theater and Performance

Lakon Jatri performances have become more like modern variety shows, with women often performing the female roles.

Puppet theater and shadow play are highly evolved forms, enjoying a rich history in Thailand that goes back to the fifteenth century. One of the world's most spectacular forms of shadow theater is the *Nang Yai* (probably derived from the Cambodian *Nang Sbek* form in the fifteenth century), which uses large, flat, carved shadow figures that range up to five feet tall. An entire scene is intricately carved into the large rawhide shadow figures, usually featuring one or two characters with some surroundings. Each of these square figures with rounded corners is secured to two poles that hold them up, and is painted with heavy paint so as to cast a dark shadow. Two narrators seated to the side of the screen narrate the show and perform the dialog.

Up to twelve performers hold the shadow figures and move in stylized ways, in front of and behind a large muslin screen that is backlit by flames, making them appear alternately in shadow and silhouette. The performers move in a style befitting the character depicted in the shadow figure they hold. In nearly every other form of shadow puppet theater in Asia, the puppeteers keep any part of themselves from appearing to the audience; but in Nang Yai the human performers intentionally make themselves visible. They move so evocatively, while manipulating the shadow figures and communicating the action, that human performer and puppet become one in the flow of the narrative. The stories enacted in this form are drawn from the *Ramakien*, the Thai version of the Indian *Ramayana*. The accompanying traditional orchestra is called *Pin Peat*, and consists of an oboe, a set of tuned bronze bowls, a xylophone, drums, and cymbals.

Cambodia

Cambodia's best-known puppet shadow theater form is the *Nang Sbek* (very similar to its Thai derivation, the Nang Yai), which uses huge cutout shadow figures. Six to eight performers manipulate these figures, holding them high over their heads while moving stylistically behind and in front of a huge shadow screen that measures 30 feet wide and 15 feet high. The source of light for casting shadows is a large fire behind the screen. Two narrators sit to the side, performing dialog and chanting verses. The shadow figures are intricately carved from rawhide, painted, and attached to two supporting bamboo rods that serve as handles. These figures measure as much as six feet high and five feet wide, and may portray either an entire scene with several characters and background, or a single important character, such as Rama or Sita. The performers take on the movement attributes of the character or scene they carry, so that puppeteer and puppet blend into one dancing image. When behind the screen, they appear in shadow; when in front, they are in silhouette. The scenes on the carved shadow figures resemble the relief sculptures on the Khmer temples at Angkor Wat; the enacted stories are drawn from the *Ramayana*; and the accompanying music is provided by a *Pin Peat* orchestra with oboe, bronze bowls, xylophone, and drums.

Another form of shadow puppet theater, *Nang Sbek Touch* (also called *Ayang* or *Nang Kaloun*) literally means "theater of small hides." Here a single puppet master, seated cross-legged behind a muslin screen, manipulates the shadow puppets, narrates the story, and delivers all the dialog, while also leading the Pin Peat orchestra seated behind him. The shadows are cast by an oil lamp that hangs in front of the puppet master. The performance technique is similar to that of the Thai *Nang Talung* and the Malaysian *Wayang Siam*. The puppets are modeled on figures in the bas-relief sculptures at the Angkor Wat temple complex. Carved intricately from rawhide, the puppets are then painted and for support are sewn onto a slit wooden rod, the end of which extends from the bottom for use as a handle. The stories narrated in the Nang Sbek Touch form are also drawn from the *Ramayana*, and music is provided by a Pin Peat orchestra.

The *Lakon Bassak*, literally "Theater of the Bassak," is a popular dance-drama from the early twentieth century, created by Cambodians living in southern Vietnam near the Bassak River. This form, influenced by the Chinese Beijing Opera, by classical Cambodian dance, and by Vietnamese performance styles, was developed to appeal to lower- and middle-class audiences. It includes songs and movement accompanied by Vietnamese-style strings and cymbals as well as a Cambodian Pin Peat orchestra. The Lakon Bassak is performed by many professional troupes in Phnom Penh, Battambang, and other towns.

Vietnam

Vietnam is unique for a highly developed form of water puppetry known as *Mua Roi Nuoc*, which has existed since at least the twelfth century. The performance area for this theater is a pond where a stage house is constructed to hide the puppeteers from view. The puppets are two to three feet in height, and are mounted to long poles held underwater, out of sight. The stories enacted in this form are either popular Vietnamese tales or well-known Chinese stories. The puppet clown Chu Teu adds humor, liveliness, and energy to the performances. The Mua Roi Nuoc form is practiced by groups formed by village puppet societies, and is also taught at Vietnam's National Film and Theatre Academy.

The Philippines

One of the few indigenous theater forms in the Philippines is the *Fagfagto*, a symbolic enactment of war and defense. This form is practiced by the men of the aboriginal Bontac tribe, who live in the mountains of central Luzon, an area almost completely inaccessible to outsiders—its very isolation explains why the form survived into modern times. The ritualized Fagfagto performances dramatize the rivalry between different tribes, and the skill of the Bontacs in protecting their cultivated land. The daylong play, which represents two groups at war with each other, is performed in the early summer to celebrate the successful planting of crops.

A popular Christian form of theater is the *Cenaculo*, an annual realistic reenactment of the Passion of Christ during Holy Week (which precedes Easter). It probably dates to the sixteenth or seventeenth centuries, and evolved from the Spanish *Auto Sacramentale* during the early decades of the Spanish-Mexican colonization of the Philippines. In this sacred theater practiced in rural villages, amateur actors perform the Last Supper, the Crucifixion, and the Resurrection. The performer who portrays Christ actually drags a cross through the streets. When the cross is erected, the actor is symbolically placed on it. The role of Christ, as well as other important roles, are handed down from generation to generation in particular families. In any given instance, the whole village becomes the stage for the Cenaculo performance, so that actors and audience move from location to appropriate location for the enactment of different scenes.

Malaysia

One of the most prominent theater forms on the Malaysian peninsula is the *Wayang Kulit* shadow puppet theater, which varies in style and name in different parts of the country. The *Wayang Siam* variation, very similar to the Thai *Nang Talung*, is popular along the eastern coast. The *Wayang Melayu* (or *Wayang Jawa*) variation, an aristocratic form in the style of the Javanese Wayang Kulit, is predominant in the north. In all such variations, a single puppet master (*dalang*) manipulates intricately carved rawhide puppets between a hanging light and a muslin screen upon which the shadows are cast. The audience sits on the other side, witnessing the drama of the ancient Hindu epics (the *Ramayana* and the *Mahabharata*) brought to life in the play of the shadows.

The shadow puppets in this form are usually one to two feet tall, and are supported by either a carved buffalo horn rod or a bamboo rod sewn vertically along the body of the puppet. The rod is longer than the puppet, and its extra length serves as a handle for the puppeteer. The rod on the puppet may also be thrust into a banana log set along the base of the screen, to hold the puppet up to view when it is not being manipulated. Most of the puppets have only one articulated arm, which can be moved by means of a thin rod attached to its end.

One of the distinctive characters in this theater is a local clown god of supernatural origin; in the Wayang Siam form he is known as Pak Dogol, whereas in the Wayang Melayu form he is called Semar. His story, of strong local interest, is interwoven into stories drawn mainly from the *Ramayana*. Music is provided by an orchestra (*gamelan*) consisting of drums, gongs, cymbals, and a melodic reed instrument (which accompanies most traditional performances on the peninsula). Wayang performances take place in a raised hut, which has a shadow screen stretched across the side facing the audience, with the dalang and the gamelan located inside the structure. Traditionally, a performance begins at sundown and continues until sunrise, with no breaks for the performers.

Most dalangs also serve as *bomoh*s—spiritual healers—and supplement their income from puppeteering with income from healing. Notable puppet masters in the Kelantan area include Dalang Abdullah Abrahim (or Baju Merah, which translates to "red shirt," his signature performance attire), Dalang Husain Kualessaurt, and Dalang Hamzah Awang Hamat.

Indonesia

The best documented theater forms exist on the islands of Java and Bali. The powerful influence of Indian culture and dance styles and of the Hindu epics on the arts of Java and Bali cannot be overestimated. When some of the populations of Southeast Asia converted to Islam (between roughly 1300 and 1750), the people of western Java, already Hindu as a result of earlier Indian migration and influence (during the fifth through seventh centuries), avoided conversion by fleeing to Bali. Isolated on that island for centuries, they practiced a form of Hinduism that has evolved into a form found nowhere else in the world. The rest of the Javanese people converted to Islam, but Hindu mythology and literature still largely define their national character, especially as it is expressed in their theater.

One of the oldest forms of performance storytelling in Java is *Wayang Beber*, which dates to the fourth or fifth century. The storytelling is done by a narrator who with one hand unrolls a scroll wrapped around a pole, while winding onto a second pole with the other hand the other end of the scroll. The story-pictures on the scroll follow the narrator's dramatization. This tradition of using visual aids in telling the stories of the *Ramayana* and the *Mahabharata* was greatly elaborated in the Wayang Kulit theatrical form. Wayang Kulit combines intricately designed rawhide puppets that cast shadows on a screen with hypnotic music from a *gamelan* (traditional orchestra) and dramatized narration by a *dalang* (puppet master), using tales from the *Ramayana* or the *Mahabharata*. This form likely originated in Java around the tenth century, although some claim it was brought from India or China, both of which have ancient shadow puppet traditions. Many rituals are integral to a Wayang

Kulit performance, designed to gain the favor of the gods and to protect against evil spirits, both gods and spirits being brought into the material world in the puppets' shadows.

Puppets used in this theatrical form are intricately carved from rawhide, beautifully painted with gold and other colors, and secured to thin split rods of carved water buffalo horn. Their articulated arms have thin horn rods attached at the fingers for manipulation by the dalang. So evolved is the artistry of these figures that they stand as works of fine art in themselves. Moved behind the shadow screen, the fluttering puppets cast shadows as intricate as an insect's wing and as beautiful as the finest carvings. The design of the characters portrayed by the puppets is highly stylized. The more refined characters have long faces, pronounced angular noses, and long thin arms; whereas the rougher characters have bulbous eyes, blunt noses, and upturned arrogant heads. With the predominance of Islam in Indonesia after the middle of the last millennium, the puppets were made to look less realistic in deference to the Qur'anic injunction against creating images of humans (because Allah is believed to be the only creator).

Wayang Kulit performances take place outdoors, from sundown to the early morning hours. It often takes several consecutive nights to complete a single episode. The dalang manipulates all the puppets, delivers all the dialog and narrative, and leads the gamelan with the help of a wooden clapper placed under the knee or on the side of the puppet chest. He can hit the clapper with hand, knee, or foot. Sitting cross-legged behind a wide muslin screen with a hanging light, the dalang passes the puppets in front of the light to cast their shadows on the screen. He does not use a script, but improvises the narrative and the dialog, based on his thorough knowledge of the epic stories. A dalang must have great range of voice and oral style to represent the diversity of characters, and must also possess quick wit and timing for the comic scenes with the clown god Semar (a local element integrated into the tales of the *Ramayana* and the *Mahabharata*). The gamelan provides a variety of background music and musical interludes, with songs and the instrumental accompaniment of gongs, drums, cymbals, and sometimes a melodic reed instrument.

Recent innovations and changes in the Wayang Kulit include the use of an electric light instead of an oil lamp to cast the shadows. Electronic amplification systems are also now in common use to serve large audiences. Popular puppet masters broadcast their dramatic narrations on the radio, and "superstar" dalangs command high fees and attract large crowds to their performances. Narto Sabdho (1925–85) was an innovative dalang who achieved great fame as an artist and contributed significantly to the contemporary evolution of the form.

A number of specialized forms of shadow puppet theater have evolved from the Wayang Kulit tradition. Their performance conventions are the same, but they tell other stories. *Wayang Djawa*, for instance, dramatizes the *Panji* tales, as well as stories about Prince Diponegoro, famous for rebelling against Dutch colonizers in the nineteenth century. *Wayang Madya* performs stories about the East Javanese kings. Some forms of shadow puppet theater have evolved into political propaganda, indicating how central this form is to the Javanese national character: *Wayang Suluh* was used to support the Indonesian revolution against the Dutch in 1945–49, whereas *Wayang Pantja* Sila was used subsequently to promote Indonesian nationalism and patriotism. The *Wayang Klitik* form deviates from the Wayang Kulit tradition by replacing the carved rawhide puppets with flat wooden puppets. *Wayang Golek*, which emerged in Sunda, western Java, about 150 years ago, uses three-dimensional puppets in full view, not casting shadows from behind a screen. The apparent reason for this variation is that the Sundanese people wanted to watch puppet theater during the day, and preferred the realism of three-dimensional wooden puppets in broad daylight.

In addition, Wayang Kulit has given rise to *Wayang Wong* (also known as *Wayang Orang*), a form of theater performed by humans in which actors mimic the stylized movements of the shadow puppets. Wayang Wong began in the eighteenth century under the patronage of the Javanese courts of Yogyakarta and Surakarta, and weeklong performances in this mode were quite common until the 1940s. The elaborate Wayang Wong form has given rise to *Sendratari*, a dance-drama in condensed format developed specially for tourists in the 1960s and 1970s. The latter has no narration or dialog; all its dramatic content is pantomimed and draws on short, easy-to-follow episodes from the *Ramayana*.

In spite of the enormous fecundity of Javanese theatrical traditions, Bali offers even more fertile ground for artistic expression. A relatively small island in the Indonesian archipelago, Bali is home to some of the most exquisite performance forms known to the world, especially in dance and dance-drama (see the chapter on Dance). Highly refined styles are executed with dignity and confidence by ordinary villagers in honor of the Hindu gods. There is no "star system" and no personal gain for the performers, who practice their art as pure worship. Bali's most important theatrical form is also the Wayang Kulit shadow puppet theater, a performance that is a treat at any celebration or festival (which are surprisingly frequent). The Balinese form differs from the Javanese in that the puppets are more full-bodied and realistic, and the performance style is likewise more robust and lively. Bali is probably the only place where an oil lamp is still used to cast the shadows, with the flame on the wick fluttering to create shadow images that seem restlessly alive on their own. Dalang Wija (b. 1952) is one of today's leading Balinese puppeteers, a maker of exquisite puppets and a master at performing the clown scenes. Because he speaks English fluently, he has performed his Wayang Kulit all over the world—including New York City, where in 1992 he designed and crafted ant puppets out of rawhide for Lee Breuer's production of *The Warrior Ant: The MahabharaANTa*.

RESOURCE GUIDE

PRINT SOURCES

East Asia and Oceania

Brandon, James R., ed. *The Cambridge Guide to Asian Theatre.* Cambridge: Cambridge University Press, 1997.

Brazell, Karen. *Traditional Japanese Theater.* New York: Columbia University Press, 1999.

Cavaye, Ronald, and Paul Griffith and Akihiko Senda. *A Guide to the Japanese Stage: From Traditional to Cutting Edge.* Tokyo: Kodansha International, 2005.

Chen, Xiaomei. *Acting the Right Part: Political Theater and Popular Drama in Contemporary China.* Honolulu: University of Hawaii Press, 2002.

Chikamatsu. *Four Major Plays of Chikamatsu.* Translated by Donald Keene. New York: Columbia University Press, 1961.

Crump, James Irving. *Chinese Theater in the Days of Kublai Khan.* Ann Arbor: University of Michigan Asian Center, 1990.

Fei, Faye Chunfang, ed. *Chinese Theories of Theater and Performance from Confucius to the Present.* Ann Arbor: University of Michigan Press, 2002.

Gao, Xingjian. *The Other Shore: Plays by Gao Xingjian.* Translated by Gilbert C. F. Fong. Hong Kong: The Chinese University Press, 1999.

Keen, Donald. *Noh and Bunraku.* New York: Columbia University Press, 1990.

Lovrick, Peter, and Wang-Ngai Siu. *Chinese Opera: Images and Stories.* Seattle: University of Washington Press, 1997.

Ma, Qian. *Women in Traditional Chinese Theater: The Heroine's Play.* Lanham, MD: University Press of America, 2005.

MacKerrras, Colin, ed. *Chinese Theater: From Its Origins to the Present Day.* Honolulu: University of Hawaii Press, 1989.
Ortolani, Benito. *The Japanese Theater.* Princeton: Princeton University Press, 1995.
———, and Samuel Leiter, eds. *Japanese Theater in the World.* New York: Japan Foundation, 1997.
Quah, Sy Ren. *Gao Xingjian and Transcultural Chinese Theater.* Honolulu: University of Hawaii Press, 2004.
Sieber, Patricia. *Theaters of Desire: Authors, Readers, and the Reproduction of Early Chinese Song-Drama, 1300–2000.* New York: Palgrave Macmillan, 2003.
Sponsler, Claire, and Xiaomei Chen, eds. *East of West: Cross-cultural Performance and the Staging of Difference.* New York: Palgrave Macmillan, 2000.
Tam, Kwok-kan. *Ibsen in China, 1908–1997.* Hong Kong: The Chinese University Press, 2001.
Tyler, Royall, ed. *Japanese Noh Dramas.* Translated by Royall Tyler. New York: Penguin Books, 1992.

South and Southeast Asia

Awasthi, Suresh. "Shadow Plays of India and Their Affinities with the Shadow Plays of Southeast Asia." Pp. 112–119 in Mohammed Taib Osman (ed.), *Traditional Drama and Music of Southeast Asia.* Kuala Lumpur: Dewan Bahasa Dan Pustaka Kementerian Pelajaran Malaysia, 1974.
Birch, David. "The Life and Times of Singapore English Drama: Loosening the Chains, 1958–63." *Performing Arts* 3, 1 (1986):28–32.
Brandon, James. *On Thrones of Gold.* Cambridge, MA: Harvard University Press, 1970.
———. *Theatre in Southeast Asia.* Cambridge, MA: Harvard University Press, 1974.
———. *The Cambridge Guide to Asian Theatre.* New York: Cambridge University Press, 1993.
Dharwadker, Aparna Bhargava. *Theatres of Independence: Drama, Theory, and Urban Performance in India since 1947.* Iowa City: University of Iowa Press, 2005; New Delhi: Oxford University Press, 2006.
Eiseman, Fred. *Bali Sekala & Niskala: Essays on Religion, Ritual, and Art.* Berkeley, CA: Periplus Editions, 1989.
Gunawardana, A. J. *Theatre in Sri Lanka.* Colombo: Department of Cultural Affairs, Sri Lanka, 1976.
Keeler, Ward. *Javanese Shadow Plays, Javanese Selves.* Princeton, NJ: Princeton University Press, 1987.
Osnes, Beth. *A Survey of Shadow Play in the Malaysian Traditional Shadow Puppet Theatre.* Ann Arbor, MI: Proquest, 1992.
Pich Tum Kravel. *Sbek Thom: Khmer Shadow Theatre.* Ithaca, NY: Cornell University Southeast Asia Program, 1995.
Ratnam, Perala, ed. *Laos and Its Culture.* New Delhi: Tulsi, 1982.
Singer, Noel. *Burmese Puppets.* New York: Oxford University Press, 1992.
———. *Burmese Dance and Theatre.* New York: Oxford University Press, 1995.
Sweeney, P. L. *The Ramayana and the Malay Shadow-Play.* Kuala Lumpur: National University of Malaysia Press, 1972.
Tilakasiri, J. *Puppetry in Ceylon.* Colombo: Department of Cultural Affairs, 1961.
Tran Van Khe. *Traditional Theatre in Vietnam.* Edited by James Brandon. Paris: UNESCO, 1971.
Yeo, Robert. "Towards an English Language Singaporean Theatre." *Southeast Asian Review of English* 4 (1982, July): 59–73.

WEBSITES

East Asia and Oceania

Australian Theater. www.cultureandrecreation.gov.au/articles/theatre. Accessed March 26, 2007. Australian government's official site for Australian theater; contains detailed timeline of Australian theater history.
History of World Theater. "Chinese" and "Japanese." Accessed March 26, 2007. www.theatrehistory.com/asian/chinese.html *and* www.theatrehistory.com/asian/japanese.html. Contains useful information on Chinese and Japanese theaters.

Modern Chinese Drama. Accessed March 26, 2007. Web.cecs.pdx.edu/~fli/bajin/work/drama.htm. A concise introduction to modern Chinese huaju.

VIDEOS/FILMS

East Asia and Oceania

Chunhyang (South Korea, 2000). Directed by Im Kwon Taek.
Farewell My Concubine (China, 1993). Directed by Chen Kaige. A film about the lives of two Peking Opera actors through China's twentieth-century history.
The King of Masks (China, 2000). Directed by Wu Tian-ming. A film on a master of Sichuan local opera's mask play.
The Peony Pavilion (USA, 2002). Directed by Chen Shizheng. A DVD version of the Lincoln Center 1998 staging of the classical Chinese play.
The Puppet Master (Taiwan, 2001). Directed by Hou Hsiao-hsien. A docudrama on a contemporary Taiwanese puppet theater master.

NOTES

East Asia and Oceania

1. Antonin Artaud, *The Theater and Its Double*, translated by Mary Caroline Richards (New York: Grove Press, 1958), p. 44.
2. Ibid., p. 85.
3. Ibid., p. 101.
4. Keene 1961 (in Resource Guide), p. 1.

TRANSPORTATION AND TRAVEL

EAST ASIA AND OCEANIA

BOB LEE, ERWEI DONG, AND AIHUA ZHANG

East Asia and Oceania is one of the fastest-growing regions in the transportation and travel industry. Its rapid economic development has made the region a most favorable spot for travelers and tourists from all over the world. Experts have predicted that East Asia and Oceania will remain a dominant high-traffic area in the next decade.

The United States and Europe are the major sources of the tourism for this region. China's Great Wall, Australia's wild kangaroo population, Japan's Mt. Fuji, and Korea's traditional Folk Village remain as the most popular attractions in the area. China alone registered more than 1.3 million American travelers in 2005. In return, the United States and Europe are the most favorite destinations for the travelers from East Asia and Oceania.

East Asia and Oceania has been recognized as the world's biggest regional supplier of travelers. The outbound growth rate and travel potential in this area have far surpassed those in Europe or America.[1] Traveling from East Asia and Oceania to other parts of the world has grown 8 percent a year. The Japanese and Australians are well-known interregional tourists, who love to visit long-haul destinations. In recent years, the emerging new economic powers of China, Taiwan, and Korea have been producing most of the region's international travelers.

In particular, China has become one of the strongest generating markets in the leisure travel industry. The Chinese have already begun to travel extensively within their own country, with about 1.2 billion travelers moving around the country in 2005; regional and global trips will be their next steps. Approximately 31 million Chinese visited other countries in 2005.[2] It has been forecast by the World Travel and Tourism Council that overseas tourists from China will surge to 100 million in ten years.

With the number of regional and interregional travelers steadily increasing, there is a growing concern for the efficient movement of people and for an effective transportation infrastructure in this region. Japan, South Korea, China, and Taiwan have constructed high speed railways in their countries. Australia has also planned to build a high speed railway connecting Sydney with Canberra. Moreover, since they share similar geographical attributes, are

East Asia

China

As a newborn economic power in the world, China is generating numerous middle-class and leisure travelers. Although it relies heavily on land transportation, China faces a severe challenge to its transportation infrastructure. Air transport has been recognized as an alternative travel mode to help ease the pressure on ground transportation and allow for the establishment of a new, more efficient mass transit system for the nation. In the past few years, China's civil aviation has become a fast-growing sector in the travel industry. By the end of 2005, China had 489 airports (142 civil airports) and 1,245 civil aircrafts. Additionally, forty-two new airports were under construction as of 2006. Chinese airlines carried a record of 138 million passengers in 2005.[4] As a result, the country has been ranked as the largest aviation market outside the United States. The air traffic in China is expected to continue growing at a rate of 7.6 percent a year. Thanks to the open door policy initiated by the government in 1978 that invited many foreign airline companies to participate in China's aviation market, more than thirty foreign airline companies have set up their offices in China and have been providing international air transport services. Those companies include major international air carriers such as United Airlines, Northwest Airlines, British Airways, and KLM.

In spite of increased air travel activities, highways and railways remain the dominating choices among China's public transportation services. In combination, railway and highway transports account for 98 percent of the total passenger traffic each year. The length of the railway lines had been extended to 75,000 kilometers by the end of 2005. The total length of highways has reached 1.87 million kilometers.[5] The highway network has connected 99.8 percent of the villages in the nation. More recently, expressway construction has been a main focus of Chinese ground transportation development. By 2005 the length of expressways had totaled 35,000 kilometers, which has lifted China into second place in the world behind the United States, whose system is 88,000 kilometers long.[6] To ensure effectiveness and efficiency in transportation and travel services, the Chinese government has recently raised the speed limit for its expressways to the maximum speed of 120 kilometers per hour.

The well-established highway network promotes the ownership of civilian vehicles. There were about 30 million civilian vehicles on the roads in 2006.[7] However, given the population of 1.3 billion, the average vehicle ownership remains relatively low—only twenty-four vehicles per thousand people. Thus, there is still great growth potential for the Chinese automobile market.

Contrary to the rapid development in air and land transports, the waterway operation in China has declined. Although China owns 110,000 kilometers of navigable waterways, less than 1 percent of all passengers were transported via water traffic during 2004.[8] However, marine shipping activities have shown an enormous increase. A number of harbor cities in the northeast China, such as Dalian, Qingdao, and Tianjin, have joined in the competition to become the port of call and the port of embarkation for international cruise lines.

The development of transportation services and relevant infrastructure is inseparable from the growth of travel and tourism. By establishing the policy that requires three mandatory week-long holidays (the week of May 1, the week of October 1, and the week of Spring Festival holidays) in 2000, the Chinese government encouraged its citizens to enjoy leisure travel. There were millions of tourists on the roads during the so-called May 1 Golden Week. It was reported that 120 million people traveled during the week of May 1 in 2005.[9] Domestic travelers spent 40 billion yuan (US$5 billion) during the period. Consequently, travel and tourism have an enormous impact on the nation's economic growth. The travel industry, including direct and indirect expenditure, contributes approximately US$218 billion to the gross domestic product (GDP), equivalent to about 12 percent of the total GDP. The money citizens spend on travel activities was estimated to be about 11 percent of total personal consumption. Collectively, personal expenditure for Chinese travel and tourism is US$72 billion a year.[10]

> **AVIATION ON DISPLAY**
>
> Synchronized with the fast growth of air transport services, China's National Aviation Museum, founded in 1989 in Beijing, has significantly expanded its collection of aviation treasures, including aircraft, aviation bombs and cameras, and ground-to-air missiles. Today, there are more than 200 airplanes stored and displayed in the museum.

Unlike during the twentieth century, in which the prevalent travel mode in China was the bicycle, an ordinary citizen of this century has a variety of travel means available to choose from for a leisure trip. For instance, a luxury motor coach may serve a visitor viewing a local rural scenic area, a railway train may carry a traveler to Beijing or Shanghai for sightseeing or shopping, or an aircraft may carry a visitor over the Tibetan Plateau for a challenging adventure. Of these numerous tourist attractions, sightseeing in a variety of cities and visiting cultural relics, such as on a tour of one of the five famous mountains (including the Eastern Tai, the Western Hua, the Southern and the Northern Hengs, and the Center Song Mountains), are some of the favorite leisure trips for the Chinese.

Even though various travel modes are available in China, the most accessible and affordable means for the general public to visit a long-haul destination is still by train. Growth of air travel and motor-coach services has diffused some of the market share for long-distance travel, but the railway traffic service still accounted for more than 80 percent of the country's medium and long-distance transportation in 2004.

In 2005 domestic travel registered a record 1.2 billion tourists, while inbound international arrivals climbed to 109 million in the same year. Four countries had over a million visitors coming to China in 2004: Japan (3.33 million), South Korea (2.84 million), Russia (1.79 million) and the United States (1.30 million). Outbound Chinese tourists surged to 30 million as of 2006.[11] Currently, more than sixty countries have been granted Approved Destination Status (ADS) by China's officials, allowing Chinese citizens to travel to those countries in tour groups. According to a recent report, the most favorite international destinations for Chinese travelers were Japan, Russia, South Korea, Thailand, and United States.[12]

Hong Kong, China

Hong Kong, as a Special Administrative Region (SAR) under the sovereignty of China, has a high degree of autonomy. Partially situated on the South China Sea, Hong Kong's territory includes the Kowloon Peninsula and an additional 254 outlying islands. Distinctive geographical characteristics afford Hong Kong a 733-kilometer coastline and a wealthy marine shipping business. Hong Kong has about 1,000 ships, more than half of them owned by foreign companies. Air transportation also plays an important part in Hong Kong's transportation service. There are three paved airports in the area. The northern part of the SAR connects to an extension of the Zhu Jiang Delta from Mainland China—a 34-kilometer railroad built to connect the harbor with Guang Dong province of China. Hong Kong has 1,865 kilometers of highways, but it also has the one of the highest vehicle densities in the world. There are more than 500,000 automobiles in use on Hong Kong's 1,042 square kilometers of land.[13]

Each year, Hong Kong, owing to its rich cultural heritage, fashion merchandising, luxury hotels, gourmet food, and numerous business opportunities, brings in about US$20 billion in international tourism receipts. In addition to the city amenities, 28-year-old Ocean Park, the newly developed Disneyland, and an ecotourism site, Tin Shui Wai, also attract thousands of domestic and international tourists. Hong Kong is the largest tourism market for Chinese, followed by visitors from Taiwan, Japan, the United States and the United Kingdom. Hong Kong is famous for its hospitality, and it also ranked as the ninth largest source of overseas tourist expenditure in the world in 2002. The residents spent US$12.9 billion outside Hong Kong last year. The top-ranked tourist destinations for Hong Kong residents are China, Japan, and the United States.[14]

Macau, China

Macau is another Special Administrative Region under China's sovereignty. For years, Macau has been the only place in China where gambling is legally permitted. The gaming industry has provided Macau with an exceptional economy, with which the travel industry is heavily involved. In 2004, the total gaming revenue was US$5.3 billion, surpassing that of Las Vegas, Nevada. Macau's prosperous gaming economy attracted Las Vegas's Sands Corporation, which invested US$6 billion in the development of a game center, Cotai Strip. The new center contains 10,000 rooms, combining business, entertainment, recreation, and gambling into one holistic facility.[15] Most inbound tourists to Macau are from mainland China, Hong Kong, Taiwan, Japan, and the United States. In 2004 a total 16 million arrivals were registered. The personal travel-tourism expenditure per person by residents has been estimated at US$601 million, about 17 percent of the total personal consumption a year.[16]

Transportation infrastructure is being built to improve travelers' accessibility to Macau. The Hong Kong-Zhuhai-Macau Bridge, with a span of 29 kilometers, is under construction at a cost of US$3 billion. There is only one airport in Macau, handling 5 percent of the visitors a year. Most visitors came in either by sea or land. Roadways have also been extended to cover 345 kilometers in Macau's 28-square-kilometer area.

Taiwan

Taiwan consists of many islands; it is situated in the southeastern waters of China, and its area totals 35,980 square kilometers. As a result of its unique geographical location, Taiwan can only be accessed by air or water, and air carriers play a dominant role in international transportation. About 99 percent of visitors arrive in Taiwan by air. There are a total of forty-two (including two international) airports in Taiwan. Domestic travel is easy and convenient because of a well-developed railway system and highway network: 2,497 kilometers of railroads and 37,299 kilometers of roadways have been laid on the island, including 1,789 kilometers of expressways.[17] Because of the crowding issue (23 million residents live on the island), the motorcycle is a very popular mode of transportation among local residents.

According to 2004 statistics, there were 12.8 million motorcycles registered in Taiwan. The mass transit in Taiwan is primarily bus service: nearly 59 percent of intercity passengers traveled by bus in 2004.[18] However, to make traveling easier and faster around the island, a high speed mass transit rail system is now underway. It will link the island's major cities and carry 300,000 commuters daily.

Taiwan's travel industry is constantly growing. In 2004 the Taiwanese government launched the campaign "Taiwan: touch your heart" to promote leisure travel on the island. International visitors to Taiwan numbered about 1.9 million, and they spent US$4.3 million there in the same year.[19] The two biggest contributors of international tourists in Taiwan are Japan and Hong Kong. However, Mainland China can be a most important source in the future if governments on both sides (Mainland and Taiwan) ease restrictions and allow their residents to freely visit each other. The major outbound tourism destination for Taiwanese is Hong Kong. For many, however, their final destination is Mainland China. They use this longer route because of restrictions on direct transportation between the two locations. Japan, South Korea and the United States are also among the top favorite outbound destinations for travelers from Taiwan.

One popular domestic travel activity among island residents is spa tourism. There are a number of natural thermal springs spread out over the island. Taiwan is situated in a volcano band with rich, natural seismic activities. More than 110 kinds of minerals have been found on the island. It is believed that hot spring water with rich minerals may heal many diseases and illnesses. In addition, Nan-Kuen-Shen and Ma-Do temples, Sun Moon Lake, and Targo Gorge are also very popular tourist attractions.

Mongolia

Mongolia is a country with the rich history of a nomadic lifestyle. In the thirteenth century, legendary Genghis Khan used his cavalry to conquer a huge territory across Asia and Europe. Even now, the horse is still a popular means of transportation for civilians traveling between villages. However, the main access gateway to Mongolia today is not riding on horseback but flying to its international airport, Buyant Ukhaa, located 18 kilometers to the southwest of its capital, Ulaanbaatar. Mongolia has forty-eight airports in total, but only one serves international travelers. The railway is another way to enter Mongolia. The length of railway track is 1,810 kilometers, and a major route stretches 1,118 kilometers, connecting Moscow and Beijing. Highway construction is underdeveloped. Of the 49,250 kilometers of roadways, only 1,724 kilometers are paved.[20]

Travel and tourism development centers on its traditional culture and unexplored nature scenic attributes. Wide, untouched landscapes; historical and cultural relics; and a traditional nomadic way of life, including raising livestock and sleeping in the *gers* in the country, attract thousands of international visitors. There were more than 300,000 international arrivals in 2004, and 98 percent of them were leisure travelers. International travelers brought in US$181 million in tourism receipts in 2004.[21]

Domestic travel has focused on visits to sites connected with the historical heritage of Genghis Khan, and on travel linked to two major public holidays: Naadam and Tsagaan. Naadam is a traditional festival celebration to display and compete in three prevailing games: horse racing, wrestling, and archery. Tsagaan is the Mongolian Lunar New Year. An optimistic statistical report on outbound tourism shows that 626,000 Mongolians traveled abroad in 2004. The top-ranked travel destinations for the Mongolians are China, Russia, Korea, Japan, and the United States.[22]

> **HISTORY MEETS INNOVATION IN JAPAN**
>
> The Modern Transportation Museum in Japan opened in 1962. Its exhibitions not only reflect cultural and historical aspects of railway but also unveil the newest trends of the innovative transportation industry.

Japan

Japan is an island country. Situated by the west Pacific Rim, it consists of four large islands (Hokkaido, Honshu, Shikoku, and Kyushu) and about 1,000 other smaller adjacent islands. Early on, Japan recognized the importance of developing an effective air transport service for this nation surrounded by the sea. Since the 1970s, Japan's civil aviation has grown steadily in terms of passenger and cargo volume. In 2005 Japan had 173 airports and handled about 100 million passengers a year.[23]

Even though air transportation in Japan plays an important role in its travel industry, this is the country that invented the first high speed train (also known as the bullet train) in 1964. Shinkansen is a well-known high speed train line that allows a bullet train to run at 300 kilometers per hour. However, using Shinkansen can be very expensive; currently, for example, it costs more than US$150 for a one-way ticket from Tokyo to Hakata, a city about 1,000 kilometers away. Alternatively, regular rail travel is easy and convenient in Japan. By 2005 a total of 27,400 kilometers (17,000 miles) of railways had been laid over various islands throughout the country.[24] As a result, trains are the most favorite mass transit in Japan. The Japanese usually prefer to take the train to commute to work or school, or to travel on holidays, because of its availability. A foreigner may also take advantage of the convenience of railway travel by purchasing the Japan Rail Pass overseas. Just like the Euro Pass, its price is cheaper if the pass is purchased overseas rather than in Japan. Currently, a seven-day pass costs approximately US$250. When it comes to Japan's high-tech railway system, the Modern Transportation Museum, founded in 1962, comes into the spotlight—it is a site that preserves the history of technological advancement in transportation and features future developments in land, water, and air technology.

As for ground transportation, Japan also has a well-developed highway network. A total of 1,177,278 kilometers of roadways had been constructed by 2005, including eighty-nine expressways that totaled 8,730 kilometers in length.[25] According to the Japan Automobile Service Promotion Association's statistics for 2006, Japan had approximately 67 million cars. The speed limit for cars is usually 80 kilometers (50 miles) or 100 kilometers (62 miles) per hour on the expressways. Unlike the United States, all highways in Japan are toll roads, with maximum tolls up to US$350 for a long trip. Traffic moves on the left. Streets and roads are generally congested with cars, trucks, buses, motorbikes, and bicycles. Public transportation services are provided in major cities and include buses, subways, and trains. In addition, taxi services are also available in all cities.

A well-developed transportation infrastructure and associated services are essential provisions for growth in travel and tourism. Japan has many tourism spots that vary from historical, cultural, or natural sites to most modernized cities. For example, Japanese citizens often enjoy visiting the futuristic Tokyo, the beautiful Mount Fuji, and the traditional Kyoto. However, the most favorite tourist spots in Japan are the natural hot springs (*onsen* in Japanese). There are quite a few spa sites across the nation. According to the Japan Association of Travel Agents, the total travel expenses for the Japanese in 2002 amounted to US$208 billion, including US$184 billion for domestic travel expenditures and US$24 billion for the international visitations. A report from the Statistics Bureau of Japan indicated that the average travel expense of each household in 2003 was approximately US $1,000.[26]

Japan is known as one of the leading international tourist countries in the world, and its people love traveling around their own country as well. In the past few years, Japan has become the number one tourist-generating country in East Asia and the Pacific region. In 2005 more than 17 million Japanese tourists traveled outside of Japan. The United States, China, South Korea, and Hong Kong are the top travel destinations for the Japanese. In 2003 America alone hosted 5 million Japanese visitors.[27]

Democratic Republic of Korea (North Korea)

Because of its political differences with most Western countries, North Korea is one of the world's most isolated states. Its travel and transportation development reflects such detachment. An inadequate transportation infrastructure, insufficient travel-related information, and underdeveloped services have produced great challenges for this nation in its efforts to attract foreign tourists and foreign currency. Independent travel to the country is not permitted unless the tour is guided under control of the government.

North Korea has seventy-nine airports, but only a few have civil aviation routes.[28] Flights to North Korea are mainly via China. China Air and Koryo Air (the North Korean airline) provide three trips a week. It usually takes about two hours to fly from Beijing to Pyongyang, the capital of North Korea. However, most long-distance travelers often rely on the railway because of frequent snowfalls in the late fall and winter and extensive rainfall in the summer, both of which often make it extremely difficult to drive or fly around the country. A railway system has been well developed, with a total length of 5,200 kilometers.

By 2004 highways have been extended to 31,200 kilometers.[29] Bus service is provided in and between most cities. Very few people own cars in North Korea. A foreigner is not allowed to drive in the country, and even North Korean citizens are not encouraged to travel freely around the country without official permission. However, North Korea possesses numerous exquisite national parks and untouched natural scenic sites, largely because the whole country has been completely unexploited by commercial tourist activities. A number of well-preserved nature resources may offer North Korea great potential in developing nature-oriented tourism.

Republic of Korea (South Korea)

South Korea lies in the southern portion of the Korean Peninsula, sharing a border with North Korea by land and separating itself from Japan by sea.

South Korean transportation development was fueled by its rapid economic growth. Just as other newly industrialized nations, South Korea has encountered serious urban traffic problems, including road congestion, parking difficulties, and high numbers of traffic accidents. Thanks to the 1988 Seoul Summer Olympics, roads were constructed and greatly improved. By 2005 South Korea has paved 74,641 kilometers of highways and had built twenty-three expressways, with a total length of 2,778 kilometers. The road system plays a dominant role and handles 90 percent of the nation's transportation.[30] In general, the speed limit on the expressways is 110 kilometers per hour. In 2005, according to the Ministry of Construction and Transport of Korea, approximately 15 million cars were registered.[31]

South Korea's railway system, however, is more efficient than is the system of automobile transport. By 2005 railway lines had been expanded to 3,472 kilometers. Riding on the trains is a favorite mass transit option in the South Korea.[32] Trains are clean, safe, comfortable, punctual, and inexpensive. In addition, a high speed railway was built in 2004. Currently the

Korea Train Express (KTX), which used French TGV technology, runs between Seoul and Busan, with a maximum speed of 300 kilometers per hour.

Unlike in Japan, in South Korea the central and local governments run the train network. The Korea Railroad Corporation is the only national railroad company; it provides train services across Korea. For intracity transport, only the metropolitan cities of Seoul (the capital of Korea), Busan (the second largest city in Korea), and the other two cities have subway services, which are run by local municipal governments. Just as in Japan, the Korea Railroad Cooperation offers train passes (KR Pass) for foreigners. Similar to the EURAIL Pass and JR Pass, the KR Pass can be purchased in overseas Korea Railways ticket offices before visiting South Korea. The price is much cheaper than the JR Pass: currently, costs vary from approximately $61 for a three-day pass to approximately $166 for a ten-day pass.

South Korea has 109 airports.[33] Even though the major cities are linked by airlines, most Koreans would rather use land travel because the country is small in size, and the distance is short to fly. However, international travelers usually come to South Korea by air. Air travel accounts for 92 percent foreign visitors.[34] The capital, Seoul, has an international airport: Incheon International Airport, which began to serve international travelers in 2001, replacing the old Gimpo International Airport, which now operates only domestic flights. The airport serves as a hub for international flights and cargo transportation in East Asia.

South Korea has 5,000 years of civilized history, and there are many remarkable cultural relics in cities such as Gyeongiu, as well as a number of natural scenic locations, including the mountain range of Baekdudaegan, the caves of Danyan, and the rural scenery of Samcheok. According to the Korea Tourism Organization's statistics for 2006, the total tourism expenditures in 2004 were US$9.5 billion and international arrivals to South Korea were recorded at 5.2 million.[35] On the other hand, Korean people also love to travel to other countries. In 2005 nearly 10 million Koreans traveled outside Korea. China was the most favorite destination, hosting about 2.7 million Korean visitors a year, followed by Japan, the United States, and Thailand.[36]

OCEANIA

Australia

Australia is the only nation occupying an entire continent and its outlying islands. Owing to its vast area, Australians rely on aviation so heavily that approximately 80 percent of long-distance trips by public transport are made by air. By 2005, 450 airports were in use, constituting a comprehensive airline network connecting all parts of the country.[37]

Australia has a well-maintained roadway network totaling 811,601 kilometers of roadways, nearly 40 percent of which are paved. According to 2005 data issued by the Australian Bureau of Statistics, 10.9 million passenger vehicles and 72,620 buses were registered there.[38] The Greyhound Pioneer provides an excellent national coach service among major cities. Coaches are one of the cheapest ways to travel around Australia, as well as one of most comfortable, since most have adjustable seats, air conditioning, on-board bathrooms, and television/video shows. For a short-distance trip with a relaxed schedule, travel by car is much preferred. In Australia traffic drives on the left, and road signs are international. The maximum speed limit in cities and towns is 60 kilometers an hour, but in some suburban areas the speed is limited to 50 kilometers an hour. On country roads and highways, the maximum speed is usually 110 kilometers an hour.

Based on statistics from 2004, Australia has a 54,624-kilometer railway system, with 3,859 kilometers electrified.[39] Prior to federation, each state has its own rail network, and as a consequence, the gauge varies from one state to another. To unify the differences, a program to standardize railroad gauges throughout Australia is in progress. In contrast to countries where the most popular way to travel for long distances is by train, few people in Australia take long journeys by train because it is usually the slowest mode of overland transportation and remains relatively expensive.

In terms of water transportation, Australia has more than 8,000 kilometers of waterways, mainly used by small, shallow-draft craft.[40] Large numbers of ships are used for merchant purposes. Adelaide, Brisbane, Cairns, Darwin, Fremantal, Hobart, Launceston, Mackay, Melbourne and Sydney are famous ports and harbors for waterway shipping businesses. Coastal and transoceanic shipping plays a vital role in Australia's economic development.

As a significant international tourism destination, Australia has a well-developed tourism industry, boasting abundant tourist resources. These resources reflect a perfect combination of natural environment and multicultural heritage, creating diversified tourist attractions, notably Canberra, Sydney, Red Centre, Darwin, Kakadu National Park, Tennant Creek Back, Uluru-Kata Tjuta National Park, the Great Barrier Reef, Adelaide, and Tasmania. Additionally, an extensive coastline surrounds Australia, and lakes dot its immense land, both of which provide an unparallel advantage for boat touring and various types of aquatic entertainment and sports such as diving and surfing. Each year Australia attracts countless tourists from all over the world. In 2005 the number of visitors reached 5.5 million, an increase of 5.4 percent relative to 2004.[41] The major source countries for international arrivals are New Zealand, the United Kingdom, Japan, the United States, China, Singapore, and Korea. For outbound tourism, the major destinations for Australian residents include New Zealand, the United States, the United Kingdom, Fiji, and such East Asian countries as China, Thailand, Hong Kong, and Singapore.

In terms of travel expenditures, according to a publication issued by Tourism Research Australia in 2006, domestic day and overnight visitors in 2005 spent US$51.7 billion in Australia, while international visitors contributed US$12.7 billion.[42]

The World Travel and Tourism Council (WTTC) estimated that Australia's travel and tourism would grow 2.8 percent in 2007 and by another 3.8 percent per annum in the next ten years. It is evident that Australian tourism is one of the most valuable sectors of the economy, and its great potential will continue to be tapped.

New Zealand

New Zealand is one of the most aviation-oriented nations in the world because of its remote geographic location. The overwhelming majority of visitors arrive by air. The three busiest airports for international flights are Auckland, Wellington, and Christchurch. Even though New Zealand itself is compact and easy to get around in, air travel is still a good choice, especially for scenic views over the mountains and volcanoes. At the present, 117 airports are in service, which weave a thorough network that covers the whole country.[43]

The total length of highways in New Zealand is over 92,000 kilometers, most of which are not engineered to meet international highway standards.[44] In many respects, its highways are simply the major roads between significant places, open not only to vehicles but also to cyclists, pedestrians, and even farm animals. New Zealand's bus lines extend widely. Service on the main routes is frequent but can be expensive and slow. A desirable alternative is to use shuttle buses operated by small companies, which are not only cheaper and friendlier but also more flexible in scheduling service. Car driving is still a generally welcome transport mode because it gives more convenience and freedom. According to 2005 motor vehicle

Transportation and Travel

registration statistics, 235,666 cars were registered.[45] New Zealand is also well known as a cyclist-friendly country with good road conditions, little traffic, and clean air. Many people like to ride bicycles for traveling and relaxation. Just as in Australia, driving in New Zealand is on the left. In urban areas, the speed limit is 50 kilometers per hour unless there are signs indicating otherwise. The speed limit on the main highways and motorways is 100 kilometers per hour for cars, but only 90 kilometers per hour for buses and trucks and 80 kilometers per hour for vehicles towing trailers.

The rail network in New Zealand has around 3,898 kilometers of available track, with about 506 kilometers electrified.[46] Most freight operations are carried out by the Toll Company, formerly Tranz Rail, owned by a private consortium. Main passenger train routes are few, although train travel is reasonably fast, comfortable, and sometimes cheaper than bus travel along the same routes.

New Zealand is a port country, and most of its exports and imports are carried by sea. In terms of passenger shipping, New Zealand statistics indicate that 28,166 passengers arrived and departed by cruise ship in 2004.[47] In addition, an inter-island ferry operates between Wellington and Picton to transport both freight and passengers.

As far as leisure travel is concerned, New Zealand is blessed with a diversity of natural landscapes: from volcanic and thermal activity to beautiful bays, and from serene lakes to picturesque cliffs. Wellington and Auckland are the most popular attractions. The former is of historic significance, and the latter is rich in maritime history. Such spots add to New Zealand's charm, attracting overseas tourists, whose numbers are steadily increasing. According to the Tourism Research Council, in 2005 New Zealand hosted a total of 2.2 million international visitors, up about 2 percent from 2004.[48] The total visitor expenditure for the 2005 period was NZ6.5 billion (about US$4.1 billion). Countries such as Australia, the United Kingdom, the United States, China, Japan, and Germany have large shares of the international arrivals in New Zealand. In regard to its overseas travel, New Zealand had a record of 1.86 million travelers in 2005.[49] The main destinations for New Zealand residents are Australia, Fiji, the United States, the United Kingdom, and China. Travel and tourism has boosted New Zealand's economy and will continue to make it sustainable.

Fiji, Papua New Guinea, and Other Pacific Island Countries

There are a number of small island countries scattered across the west-central parts of the Pacific Ocean. Because of their geographical isolation, travelers often describe a visit to this region as "a world away from others." A subtropical climate, white sand beaches, waving palm trees, and romantic amenities possessed by these island countries offer exotic traveling experiences. Sharing similarities of natural resources and native culture traditions, most of the countries chose to develop tourism as their economic vehicle for foreign exchange. In 2006 travel and tourism were expected to generate about US$977 million of Fiji's economic activities, offer Papua New Guinea 194,000 jobs, and contribute a 13 percent increase in the gross domestic product of the Oceania region.[50] Most international arrivals are from Australia, the United States, New Zealand, Japan, and now China.

Distance and isolation are major constraints for access to these Pacific islands. Railways are rarely used in these countries except for Fiji, which has a population of 905,949 and 18,270 square kilometers of land. Instead, air travel is the more popular travel option in the region.

Most island countries have at least one airport; some counties such as Fiji and French Polynesia operate as many as thirty and fifty airports, respectively. Roadway construction is well developed throughout these islands. Fiji, with 3,440 kilometers of roadway, leads in highway construction in the region. Bus, motor coach, and taxi are frequently used and favorite modes of transportation for visitors and local residents.

SOUTH AND SOUTHEAST ASIA

DAVID ATHERTON AND VINAY DHARWADKER

INTRODUCTION

Transportation and travel in South and Southeast Asia have been influenced for a long time by the topography and environmental features of these regions. As in other parts of the world, they have also been determined by economic and technological factors, especially in relation to modes of transportation, their invention and development, their costs and cost-effectiveness, and their accessibility, efficiency, and utility. Equally importantly, travel and transportation in these regions have been constrained by the infrastructures built and maintained for them, and by the availability of the services, supplies, and technical know-how needed to support them. The success of the travel and transportation industries in a particular nation also depends vitally on the socioeconomic class affiliations of their consumers, the overall economic organization of that society, and the general political conditions under which they have to operate, including conditions of law, order, and public safety.

The natural environment in South Asia is immensely varied. Nepal, Bhutan, and parts of northern Pakistan and India, for example, are ruggedly mountainous. In contrast, the vast Indo-Gangetic plain as well as the Deccan Plateau region are relatively flat and easy to traverse, except in densely forested areas. Portions of western India and eastern Pakistan are desert or semi-arid wilderness, whereas much of the deltaic land that constitutes Bangladesh is waterlogged for several months of the year. Traditionally, travel in different areas on the subcontinental mainland was on foot; on the backs of trained animals (horses, elephants, camels); in palanquins carried by two or more men; in carts or carriages drawn by such animals as bulls, oxen, horses, camels, mules, and donkeys; and on boats, rafts, or barges that plied rivers, canals, or seas.

In premodern Southeast Asia, where heavily forested and often mountainous interiors presented formidable barriers to the construction of roads, river travel proved a vital form of transportation, augmented in some terrains and cities by networks of canals. Sea travel along coasts and between islands was also crucial in peninsular Southeast Asia, as well as in parts of the mainland that border the sea. Overland travel was accomplished by foot or with the aid of animals; the domesticated elephant, which could cover large distances and navigate narrow forest tracks effectively, proved particularly important in this region as a whole.

Transportation and Travel

Modern, technologically sophisticated modes of transportation arrived in South and Southeast Asia mainly with European traders, missionaries, and colonizers, starting at the turn of the sixteenth century. The first modern modes of transportation were ships and boats built in Europe or constructed in Asia in the European style, with steamboats and steamships—as well as large new ports with mechanical equipment to move goods—appearing in the nineteenth century. Transportation by rail was introduced starting in the 1860s, and railway lines, stations, and service yards were constructed all over the Indian subcontinent during the next several decades. This was also the period when railway lines were built in Vietnam and Cambodia (then part of French Indochina), the island of Java in Dutch Batavia (now part of Indonesia), British Burma (now Myanmar), the American Philippines, and Siam (which was not colonized by European powers and is now known as Thailand).

In many parts of Asia, modern paved roads were first built under colonial initiatives in the twentieth century, even as cars (and later, buses and trucks) began to be imported from Europe and the United States in significant numbers. Air travel was initially established in the 1920s, catering to the needs of colonial governments, especially their armed forces. By the 1930s air transportation for civilian passengers and commercial goods had become more common. Air travel remained rather rudimentary in various parts of Asia until the 1950s, and it expanded both domestically and internationally only in the following decade.

In order to grasp the complexities of travel and transportation in present-day South and Southeast Asia, it is important to keep this basic history in mind, and to recognize the remarkable geographical and economic diversity of the region. The conditions and modes of transportation vary significantly between the highly developed and prosperous city-state of Singapore, for example, and the vast, rugged island of Sumatra in Indonesia, just across the Straits of Melaka; or between India, where large numbers of people can afford air travel, and neighboring Bhutan and Nepal, where very few people can. Air and sea transport are vital in the Maldives, the Philippines, and Indonesia, each with its hundreds or thousands of islands, as well as in an island nation like Sri Lanka. In contrast, inland river travel remains crucial in mountainous, landlocked Laos, Vietnam, and Bangladesh.

Conditions and modes of transportation can vary significantly within a single country as well. In Thailand, the capital city of Bangkok has approximately 9 million residents and an extensive bus, metro, and elevated train system to accommodate them; Chiang Mai, the next largest city in the country, has only several hundred thousand residents and lacks even a formal bus system. Similarly, transportation is significantly different between the mountainous highlands of central Vietnam and the riverine network of the Mekong Delta in the country's south. Brunei, which lies on the island of Borneo, has one of the highest ratios of per capita automobile ownership in the world, while roads remain largely undeveloped in the rest of the island. Income also makes a large difference, determining whether people will fly, take a train, or travel by bus—or private automobile, for that matter—in a variety of countries. The relatively low cost of scooters and motorcycles has made them very popular in much of South and Southeast Asia; in many countries, it is not uncommon to see a family of four zipping around together on a single scooter or on a 150cc motorbike.

While South and Southeast Asia on aggregate now welcome tens of millions of international tourists every year, domestic travel within individual countries involves much more than travel for travel's sake. Domestic and regional tourism has been on the rise under globalization, with the emerging middle classes being able to afford short package tours to neighboring countries. For many South and Southeast Asians, however, "tourism" remains a local or domestic affair. A family or group of friends may borrow a car or minivan and drive to a nearby waterfall for a picnic, or take a daytrip to a local city or site of historical or cultural interest.

Moreover, much of the travel in these regions has nothing to do with "tourism" at all. In Myanmar, for example, domestic package tours of the country are designed to facilitate pilgrimages to holy sites—a phenomenon with parallels or equivalents in most of the nations of South and Southeast Asia. For many people, the first experience of long-distance travel may be a school trip for an educational purpose. At holiday times, it is common for people working in the cities to return to their hometowns, while people from the countryside may go to visit their friends or relatives in the cities. Many Southeast Asians perform long-distance travel solely for the purpose of business, whether as a company salaryman boarding an international flight in Singapore or as a petty trader loading a minivan with goods in Cambodia.

INTERNATIONAL TOURISM

Under the forces of economic and political globalization, South and Southeast Asia have witnessed a massive growth in international tourism since about 1990. This growth has had a measurable impact on various national economies in these regions, whether of Nepal and India, or of Singapore and Thailand. For popular destinations in such countries, a massive influx of foreign travelers has meant an increase in employment in the local transportation and hospitality industries, demands for more and better services, improvements in local infrastructures, and especially the inflow of foreign currencies and transnational capital as well as cross-cultural interaction and transformations of local culture.

According to the Association of Southeast Asian Nations (ASEAN), the total number of foreign tourists per year in Brunei, Cambodia, Indonesia, Laos, Malaysia, Myanmar, the Philippines, Singapore, Thailand, and Vietnam taken together, for example, more than doubled in the last decade of the twentieth century, rising from just over 20 million in 1991 to more than 42 million in 2001. The increase in international tourist traffic has been phenomenal for the region as a whole, but the proportions of the number of travelers from different parts

---

GROWTH OF INTERNATIONAL TOURISM IN SOUTHEAST ASIA, 1991–2001

A. Total number of international tourist arrivals in ASEAN countries

1991: 20.2 million
1996: 30.9 million
2001: 42.2 million

B. Approximate proportions of international tourist arrivals in ASEAN countries by selective area of origin in the period 1991–2001

Tourists from within ASEAN: 38–42 percent
Tourists from parts of Asia outside ASEAN: 27–33 percent
Tourists from Europe: 12–15 percent
Tourists from North America: 4–6 percent
Tourists from Australia/Oceania: 3–4 percent

C. Total number of foreign tourists in ASEAN countries in 2001 by country of origin

From within ASEAN:
   From Singapore: 9.2 million
   From Malaysia: 3.1 million
   From Indonesia: 2.4 million
   From Thailand: 1.8 million
   From the Philippines: 0.7 million

From the rest of Asia:
   From Japan: 3.5 million
   From China: 2.4 million
   From Taiwan: 1.9 million
   From South Korea: 1.5 million
   From Hong Kong: 1.2 million
   From India: 0.8 million

From Europe, North America, and Australasia:
   From the United States: 1.9 million
   From Australia: 1.7 million
   From the United Kingdom: 1.6 million
   From Germany: 0.9 million

(*Source*: ASEAN, http://www.aseansec.org, accessed October 14, 2006.)

of the world have remained roughly constant. Thus, throughout the period from 1991 to 2001, roughly two-fifths of all of the international tourist traffic originated within the ASEAN countries themselves; one-third came from other parts of Asia; and the remainder (about one-fourth of the total) came predominantly from Europe, North America, and Australasia.

If this trend continues as expected in the present decade, then roughly three-fourths of all international tourists in the ASEAN nations will still be from Asia itself, and no more than one-fourth will be from outside Asia. Within the ASEAN group, the five most prosperous nations—Singapore, Malaysia, Indonesia, Thailand, and the Philippines—provide the bulk of international tourist traffic within the region. From the rest of Asia, the majority of international tourists come from the wealthiest parts of East Asia: Japan, China and Hong Kong, Taiwan, and South Korea. Among non-Asian tourists, the great majority originate in the United States, the United Kingdom, Germany, and Australia. The number of international tourists visiting Southeast Asia from Central and South America, Africa, northern and eastern Europe, the Mediterranean region and the Middle East, and Central Asia remains negligible.

POPULAR TOURIST ACTIVITIES AND DESTINATIONS

Since about 1990, economic globalization has not only "opened up" Asia's nations to foreign investment and foreign workers and visitors, but it has also "liberalized" political systems domestically and increased economic and social mobility for Asian countries' own populations. This has meant a new consolidation of middle class cultures in Asian societies, with modern, "Westernized" lifestyles especially predominating in urban areas. In addition to changes in family structures, everyday life at home and in communities, work environments, and patterns of education, such transformations have also brought with them significant surpluses of income, with a focus on entertainment, cultural pursuits, and travel. The growth of international tourism across Asia since the 1990s has therefore mirrored a corresponding rise in domestic tourism in the more prosperous countries. To a great extent, the travel and hospitality industries in many parts of South and Southeast Asia today cater as much to big-city middle- and upper-class domestic consumers as to international tourists, since both groups now have comparable purchasing power.

Among the types of destinations and activities that are most popular among such domestic as well as international tourists are resorts and spas in "exotic" locations, which offer unusual landscapes, beautiful natural and man-made settings, high-quality accommodations, personalized services, and multiple forms of entertainment, physical exercise, and health-enhancing activities—often as a contrast to repetitive, sedentary, or high-pressure urban and professional lifestyles. Such resorts attract couples, families, and groups of families and/or friends; they also attract business and professional groups on sightseeing tours and office or company retreats, as well as special interest groups on package tours (such as groups interested in a spiritual or health-and-well-being retreat). They often offer special facilities and activities for children and families (such as theme parks and water parks); health spas with au courant therapies; and activities ranging from golfing and walking tours to yoga and meditation. General and family vacation resorts of this type are especially popular in India, the Philippines, and Malaysia, among other countries.

A second, very popular choice is an expensive and glamorous "party" destination, which often appeals to younger, wealthier, and celebrity travelers interested in music, dancing, and socializing, often accompanied by the consumption of alcohol and recreational drugs. Party destinations often go through cycles of high and low popularity over time, depending on current trends: over the past 15 years, Goa (western India), Kathmandu (Nepal), and Koh Samui (Thailand) have been among the hottest spots around the world for film stars, media personalities, politicians, and other public figures, as well as for the general public.

A third major type of popular destination has included sites that offer unusual opportunities for outdoor sports and recreation in "extreme" forms. Nepal, for example, promotes Himalayan mountaineering, glacier treks, high-altitude biking, motorcycle tours, motor rallies, rock climbing, cave exploration, paragliding, canyon-swinging, and rafting and boating through rapids. The Maldives offer diving safaris, scuba diving, and snorkeling in the Indian Ocean, as well as surfing and submarine dives. Thailand advertises white-water rafting, mountain biking, rock climbing, wake boarding, wind surfing, and jet skiing, whereas Malaysia promotes diving as well as the thrills of high-speed car racing at the Sepang International Circuit (a leg of the Formula One Grand Prix).

A fourth type of activity and destination seeks out ecotourists interested in natural environments and their preservation, as well as in less intrusive and less strenuous activities. India offers a wide variety of ecologically conservative destinations and activities at national wildlife parks and bird sanctuaries (such as the Siriska Bird Sanctuary and the Jim Corbett National Park in north India); the Maldives have popularized whale and dolphin watching in the Indian Ocean; the Philippines promotes its wildlife parks; and Thailand has developed special locations for bird watching and butterfly watching. Each of these activities and destinations attracts tens of thousands, if not hundreds of thousands, of domestic and international tourists to specific parts of South and Southeast Asia every year.

HISTORIC SITES

Most parts of Asia have long and distinguished histories of human civilization, with numerous centers of political, cultural, and religious importance dating back centuries, if not millennia. Places of great historical and cultural interest are among the most attractive destinations for domestic as well as international tourists in South and Southeast Asia, outweighing most other categories in the industry.

In South Asia, Pakistan's rich background includes the archaeological sites of Mohenjodaro and the Indus Valley civilization (third millennium BCE.); the Indo-Greek settlement of Gandhara (a legacy of the army of Alexander the Great); the great monuments of the Mughal empire, especially the Shalimar Garden, the Badshahi Mosque, and the Fort at Lahore (seventeenth century); and the Grand Trunk Road, from Lahore in Pakistan to Delhi in India, originally built by the Mughal emperor Shah Jahan (who also built the Taj Mahal at Agra in the mid-seventeenth century). In addition to its historic capital, Kathmandu, Nepal has the ancient cities of Patan, Bhaktapur, Lumbini, and Janakpur, variously associated with illustrious moments in the histories of Hinduism and Buddhism. Among these, UNESCO has designated specific locations at Kathmandu, Patan, and Bhaktapur as World Heritage sites.

Bangladesh offers a plethora of Muslim mosques, Hindu temples, Buddhist monasteries, and Christian churches, dating from the eleventh to the twentieth centuries. It also attracts visitors to the Rajshahi provincial area, one of the oldest and most distinguished centers of silk production in the world. Among the country's most unusual sites are several associated with poets, writers, and modern public figures: the National Poet's Grave, dedicated to Kazi Nazrul Islam; two family estates associated with Rabindranath Tagore, who won the 1913 Nobel Prize for Literature; Sagordari, Jessore District, the birthplace of Michael Madhusudan Dutt, a major nineteenth-century English and Bengali writer; and the famous ashram or retreat in Noakhali District, built and used by Mahatma Gandhi.

TRANSPORTATION AND TRAVEL

> ## INDIA'S POPULAR HISTORICAL SITES
>
> Among the countries of South and Southeast Asia, India has the largest number and greatest variety of sites from different historical periods that have survived into modern times. Among them are
>
> Lothal (Gujarat): prehistoric port city, part of Indus-Harappan civilization, flourished about 2000 BCE–1500 BCE.
> Kurukshetra (Haryana) and Indraprastha (Delhi): cities associated with events narrated in the Sanskrit epic, the *Mahabharata*, flourished about 500 BCE.
> Ayodhya: capital of ancient republic of Kosala; associated with story of the Sanskrit epic, the *Ramayana*, flourished about 500 BCE or earlier.
> Bodh-Gaya, Nalanda (both Bihar), and Sarnath (Uttar Pradesh): places associated with Siddhartha Gautama, the Buddha, and early history of Buddhism (sixth–second century BCE).
> Ajanta and Ellora (Maharashtra): locations of Buddhist rock-caves with paintings (fifth–eighth century CE).
>
> Delhi:
> > Sultanate period (1206–1526): Qutub Minar complex, Tughlaqabad, Hauz Khas complex, Feroze Shah Kotla, Lodi Gardens.
> > Mughal period (1526–1858): Red Fort, Jama Masjid, Chandni Chowk.
> > British period (1808–1947): Rashtrapati Bhavan and Secretariat complex, New Delhi.
>
> Chittor (Rajasthan): Ancient mountain fort with palaces, flourished thirteenth century.
> Goa: Portuguese colony, 1510–1961.
> Agra and Fatehpur Sikri: Mughal capitals, late sixteenth through the mid-seventeenth centuries; Agra Fort, Taj Mahal, Fatehpur Sikri fort and palace complex.
> Surat (Gujarat): major Indian port since at least twelfth century; primary Mughal port; first English factory in India, built in 1619.
> Calcutta (now Kolkata): founded as British colonial city; Fort William, built 1690; capital of British India, 1757–1911.
> Madras (now Chennai): founded as British colonial city; Fort St. George, built 1639.
> Bombay (now Mumbai): founded by Portuguese; acquired by British in 1660; premier colonial city.
> Jaipur and Udaipur (Rajasthan): capitals of important Hindu kingdoms (seventeenth–twentieth centuries).
> Mysore and Shrirangapattana (Karnataka): capitals of early modern kingdom in south India; latter associated with Tipu Sultan (late eighteenth century).
> Pune: capital and cultural center of Maratha kingdom (seventeenth–eighteenth centuries.
> Lucknow: late Mughal city, provincial capital (eighteenth century); British Residency (nineteenth–twentieth centuries); major site of Indian Rebellion of 1857.
> Hyderabad: capital of largest Muslim principality in south India (eighteenth–twentieth centuries).

Sri Lanka, likewise, has a range of notable Buddhist, Hindu, Muslim, and Christian sites of great antiquity and public interest. Six World Heritage sites (as designated by UNESCO) particularly attract domestic as well as international tourist traffic. These include the ruins of the ancient sacred city of Anuradhapura (fifth century BCE), and the cave temples at the Dambulla Vihara (first century BCE), which is said to stand at the geometrical center of

Sri Lanka. Among them also are the Sigiriya Rock Fortress (fifth century CE), the medieval capital of Polonnaruwa (tenth century), and the royal city of Kandy (fifteenth century). The most recent site is that of the Dutch fortifications at Galle (seventeenth century), which now memorialize the first European colony on the island.

In Southeast Asia, Thailand has preserved a rich political and cultural legacy. Relics of the Khmer kingdom survive at Phimai, Phanom Rung, Muang Tham, Muang Singh, and Lop Buri. The monuments of the Dvaravati kingdom stand around Nakhon Pathom and include a massive, bell-shaped shrine, considered the tallest Buddhist structure in the world at a height of nearly 400 feet. Visitors are also fascinated by the ruins of the Sukhothai kingdom, and especially of the Ayuthaya kingdom (1350–1767), considered the greatest in Thai history. Each of these four sites is now preserved in the form of a tourist-friendly "historical park."

In Cambodia the greatest draw is the magnificent, sprawling Angkor Wat temple complex, built by Khmer kings between 802 and 1220. The main set of structures was constructed during the reign of Suryavaman II in the early twelfth century: it is dedicated to the Hindu god Vishnu and is a comprehensive symbolic representation of Hindu cosmology. More than 100 temples survive at Angkor Wat, a reminder of one of the greatest architectural, engineering, and imaginative feats ever accomplished. (For information on Vishnu and related Hindu mythology, see the chapter on Theater and Performance.)

Other major historical sites in the region include the gilded pagoda at Yangon, as well as the cities of Mandalay and Bagan in Myanmar; the imperial cities of My Son, Hoi An, and Hue in Vietnam; the Vigan Heritage Village (sixteenth century), the best-preserved Spanish colonial town in Asia, together with various baroque churches (mid-sixteenth to early eighteenth centuries) as well as the five remarkable Ifugao Rice Terraces, preserved as World Heritage sites, all in the Philippines; the historical city of Malacca in Malaysia, founded by a Hindu king and ruled successively by the Portuguese, the Dutch, and the English; and the relics of the famous kingdom of Aceh in Indonesia. All these places attract thousands or tens of thousands of visitors every year, including numerous groups on international sightseeing tours and groups of school and college students on educational tours.

RELIGIOUS PILGRIMAGES

Every year, tens of millions of people in South and Southeast Asia travel to specific destinations of religious significance, most often in small and large groups on popular pilgrimages and to attend religious festivals. Devout Muslims in Pakistan, India, Bangladesh, Malaysia, and Indonesia, for example, undertake the annual hajj or pilgrimage to the Kaaba in Mecca, Saudi Arabia, in very large numbers. Government agencies and private tour operators in these and other countries routinely organize transportation for millions of people to and from Mecca, providing domestic chartered bus, train, boat, and/or air travel and the full array of hospitality and support services. International pilgrimages by the tens of thousands of Shia Muslims to their holy sites—such as Karbala and Najaf in Iraq—are also organized along the same lines. Within South Asia, smaller-scale Muslim pilgrimages also take thousands of devotees every year to the shrines of Sufi saints, in cities such as Ajmer (Rajasthan) and New Delhi.

Among orthodox Hindus, pilgrimages are common to a large number of holy sites all over India. Among popular Hindu destinations are Banaras, Allahabad, Mathura, and Vrindavan (all in Uttar Pradesh); Puri (Orissa); and Haridwar, Rishikesh, Joshimath, Kedarnath, Badrinath, Gangotri, Jamnotri, Amarnath, and Vaishnodevi (all near or in the

Himalayan mountain range). Each of these destinations has major, often ancient Hindu temples; the journeys to many of them, especially those located at high altitudes, are long and arduous. In south India, millions of Hindus converge annually on the major temple towns of Tirupati, Mahabalipuram, Kanchipuram, and Rameshwaram, among other destinations. In rural India, shorter pilgrimages on a smaller scale are more popular: in the Maharashtra countryside, for example, farmers routinely trek on foot to Pandharpur, associated with the folk god Vitthala.

For orthodox Hindus, the Kumbha Mela, held four times in every 12-year cycle, is the most important pilgrimage festival, celebrated as a huge "riverside fair" with mass bathing in a river's holy waters. The four locations, by rotation, are Haridwar, on the River Ganges; Ujjain, on the River Shipra; Nasik, on the River Godavari; and Allahabad, at the confluence of the Rivers Ganges and Yamuna. The ritual river bath cleanses body and soul, preparing the individual for "liberation" from the effects of karma and the circle of death and rebirth. Each Kumbha Mela attracts millions of people; the Allahabad festival, held once in 12 years, attracts tens of millions of Hindus. The Kumbha Mela has a history of nearly 2,000 years; the earliest historical description of the Allahabad festival was recorded by Hsuan-tsang, the famous Chinese Buddhist traveler, who attended it in the company of King Harshavardhana in the seventh century.

For Sikhs in India, important destinations included their temples (*gurudwaras*) in Amritsar, Anandpur Sahib, Delhi, and elsewhere. Among Buddhists, destinations in India range from Bodh-Gaya and Sarnath to Dharamsala; in Sri Lanka, they include the temple of the Buddha's tooth relic at Dalada Maligawa in Kandy (fourth century), the Kelaniya temple near Colombo, with its famous image of the reclining Buddha (said to be 2,563 years old in 2006), and the Dambulla cave temples (first century BCE).

TRANSPORTATION INFRASTRUCTURE

The various nations of South and Southeast Asia today accomplish the movement of large numbers of people and large quantities of goods over long distances on a routine basis. Nevertheless, the infrastructure for travel and transportation in these regions is multifarious and uneven, and it does not always meet international expectations. A brief survey of different types of infrastructure in select Southeast Asian countries can indicate the complexities involved in the transportation and tourism industries in this part of the world.[1]

Thailand

Transportation in Thailand is extremely varied, with long-distance travel relying on road, rail, river, canal, sea, and air. The country has an elaborate road system of some 33,000 miles, almost all of which is paved. Bus is the most common form of intercity public transportation, and various classes of bus connect all parts of the kingdom, from cramped local buses to luxurious, air-conditioned "VIP" buses. The state rail network covers more than 2,500 miles, but it is a narrow-gauge system, so travel can be rather slow. Thailand has the same length of navigable waterways, with the Chao Phraya River serving as the primary artery, on which the capital, Bangkok, is an important international shipping port. Boat and ferry travel is also common along the coastline and between the mainland and various islands.

Thailand's cities are linked by air routes, and the deregulation of the airline industry in 2000 created a number of competitive private airlines, which offer low fares and make domestic air travel an increasingly popular option. Bangkok remains an important hub for international aviation, and the new Suvarnabhumi International Airport, featuring the world's largest terminal building, opened early in 2007 (though it was beset with problems relating to its construction and quality past its launch-date).

In 2001 Thailand had nearly 2.3 million registered passenger cars, and 15.2 million motorcycles and scooters. In addition to these types of private vehicles, Bangkok has a complicated system of public bus lines, which share the road with metered sedan taxis, noisy motorized three-wheelers known as *tuk-tuk*s, and motorcycle taxis. Since 1999, the city has been served by the elevated Bangkok Mass Transit System (popularly known as the Skytrain), and since 2004 it has also had a Mass Rapid Transit system, a network of underground metro trains. In addition, river taxis carry passengers along the Chao Phraya River and Bangkok's canals. Common forms of public transportation in smaller Thai cities and towns include pedicabs (*samlor*s) and pickup trucks converted to carry passengers along semiregular lines (*songthaew*).

Cambodia

Largely because of the policies of the Khmer Rouge regime and wartime conditions over decades, the transportation infrastructure of Cambodia remains severely underdeveloped. While various modes of transportation are available throughout the country—road, rail, water, and air—travel is often hard and dangerous for several reasons. Although Cambodia has some 7,600 miles of roads, only about 1,250 miles are paved, and even these are often in poor repair. Many roads become impassable in the rainy season (July–November), and on less-traveled roads, mines left over from Cambodia's many years of civil war remain a threat. Buses and converted pickup trucks carry travelers throughout the country, but banditry constitutes a real danger. The rail system, with two main lines covering about 400 miles, is also in disrepair and equally unsafe. The country's 1,500 miles of navigable waterways lie primarily along the Mekong River, the Tonle Sap River, and the large Tonle Sap Lake, with boats carrying freight and passengers. Cambodia has two international airports, at Phnom Penh and Siem Riap, home to the ancient temple complex of Angkor Wat. Several airlines provide domestic service to major towns in the country.

In 2002 Cambodia had 209,128 registered passenger cars and 586,278 motorcycles and scooters. Public transportation in the cities usually consists of motorcycle taxis and pedicabs. Pedicabs are known as "cyclos" here; the driver sits behind the passenger(s) and propels the vehicle using bicycle pedals. The country also has homemade bicycle-type contraptions that can be pedaled using the hands rather than the feet—a sad testament to the continued effects of wartime landmines, which have created a large number of leg amputees.

The Philippines

As an archipelago of 7,107 islands, the Philippines relies heavily on sea and air transportation, as well as on road and rail. Boats and ferries are important means of transportation along coasts and between islands, as also on about 2,000 miles of inland waterways. Air provides another important means of inter-island transportation. In 1999 the Philippines had 92 national airports and 103 private airports, together with 4 main international airports. Inland, road transport is the most common mode, with a road network of roughly 125,000 miles, of which some 12,000 miles are paved and nearly 19,000 miles are highways. Several classes of bus provide the most common form of long-distance passenger transport, and a rail network of about 550 miles offers inland transportation, primarily on the island of Luzon.

TRANSPORTATION AND TRAVEL

Several modes of transportation compete for city and short-distance travel. "Jeepneys," jeeps converted to hold a large number of passengers, are common and are similar to converted pickup trucks in other parts of Southeast Asia. Motorized three-wheeled vehicles, called "tricycles" here, are also popular, as are nonmotorized pedicabs. In 2004 the Philippines had over 1.8 million registered motorcycles, scooters, and tricycles, as well as some 2.6 million passenger cars, SUVs, and utility vehicles, all told. The capital features the Manila Light Rail System, the oldest metro system in Southeast Asia, which was recently augmented with the Manila Metro Rail Transit System. In some of the more touristy areas, horse-drawn carriages (*calesas*) remain in use.

Malaysia

Malaysia has one of the best-developed transportation infrastructures in Southeast Asia, with road, rail, sea, river, and air all used effectively. The road network covers more than 40,000 miles, about three-fourths of which are paved; but the network is more extensive and better developed in peninsular Malaysia than in the states of Sabah and Sarawak on the island of Borneo. Bus travel between towns and cities tends to be efficient and affordable. A rail network runs the length of peninsular Malaysia, stretching for a total of nearly 1,200 miles from Singapore to the border with Thailand. The capital, Kuala Lumpur, opened a new, state-of-the-art international airport in 1998; five airports also provide regional service within Southeast Asia; and a number of domestic airports link different parts of the country. Water remains an important means of transportation: ferries connect islands to the peninsula, and boats provide transportation along coasts. Of Malaysia's 4,500 miles of waterways, nearly 2,500 miles are on Borneo, where, in the states of Sabah and Sarawak, rivers provide vital access to the interior.

Local transportation in Malaysia is equally varied. In 2002 the country had just over 5 million registered passenger cars and nearly 6 million motorcycles and scooters. Taxis are available in large cities, while in smaller towns, pedicabs known as "trishaws" are common. Some cities feature public bus routes; Kuala Lumpur features a comprehensive city bus network as well as an elevated light rail system.

Singapore

Singapore's transportation system is unique in Southeast Asia, mainly because of its characteristics as a compact city-state and its considerable wealth. Although only about 270 square miles in area, Singapore has nearly 2,000 miles of roads, almost all paved and in good repair, including some 90 miles of expressways. When completed in 2008, the new 7.5-mile Kallang-Paya Lebar Expressway will directly link the city's south and northeast; about 5.6 miles of it will be underground, making it the longest road tunnel in Southeast Asia. In 2004 Singapore had 417,103 registered passenger cars and 136,122 motorcycles and scooters. It has tried various means to control congestion at peak travel hours on heavily used roads, and since 1998 has employed a system known as Electronic Road Pricing, in which a toll is electronically collected from vehicles on select expressways.

Although taxis are available everywhere, Singapore also has a very comprehensive and efficient public bus system. The Mass Rapid Transit system provides another highly efficient mode of transportation: operational since 1987, this metro rail system covers over 50 miles, with two main lines and fifty-one stations, and a new circle line around the island scheduled for completion in 2010. Since 1998 this network has been augmented by an elevated Light Rapid Transit system that connects it to outlying housing estates. In addition, some 16 miles of regular railway line, owned and operated by Malayan Railways, connect Singapore to the Malaysian railway system.

As an island at the center of the Melaka Strait—one of the most vital sea corridors in Southeast Asia—Singapore plays a decisive role in the maritime transportation of passengers as well as goods. The city is linked to peninsular Southeast Asia as well as to the islands of Indonesia (particularly nearby Sumatra) via ferries and express boats. It is also one of the world's busiest commercial ports, with 133,185 shipping vessels docking there in 2004. At the same time, Singapore serves as a crucial aviation hub for Southeast Asia as a whole. Changi International Airport is one of the world's most state-of-the-art and busiest airports; when its third terminal is completed in 2008, it will have the capacity to handle 64 million passengers annually.

Indonesia

Transportation in Indonesia is extremely varied, owing to the diversity of terrain, development, and population density in this archipelago of 17,508 islands. For long-distance transportation, sea and air travel are very important. Indonesia's national shipping company, P. T. Pelayaran Nasional Indonesia, operates a fleet of passenger ships across the archipelago, serving a large number of island ports approximately biweekly. Ferries also make shorter journeys from island to island. Indonesia has almost 13,500 miles of navigable waterways, making river travel into island interiors another viable means of transportation in the country.

In 2002 Indonesia had some 215,000 miles of roads, of which just under half were paved, with road quality and density varying greatly across various islands. Extensive road travel is possible on the more-developed islands, such as Java, Sumatra, Sulawesi, Kalimantan, Bali, and Madura, where buses are the most popular mode of public transportation. But in areas such as the mountainous, jungle-clad island of Papua, light aircraft, boats, and foot travel are more convenient and common. Indonesia also has over 4,000 miles of rail line, nearly all of it on Java, with limited services on Sumatra and Madura. The passenger trains can be slow and do not always run on time, but they offer more comfort than do the frequently overcrowded buses. In addition, air transport plays a major role: in 2004 Indonesia had 7 international airports and 179 commercial airports serviced by twenty-four domestic airlines.

As in much of the rest of Southeast Asia, motorcycles and scooters comprise a major form of private transportation. In 2000 Indonesia had more than 13.5 million registered motorcycles and scooters, and just over 3 million cars. Some cities offer public bus networks; in most cities, public transportation is dominated by pedicab taxis known as *becak*s and minivans known as *bemo*s. The bemos ply the streets constantly, picking up as many passengers as possible along regular or semiregular routes. Some cities also feature *bajaj*, a form of motorized three-wheeled rickshaw taxi. Although the government announced the construction of a Mass Rapid Transit metro rail system in Jakarta in 1995, the plans have yet to come to fruition.

RESOURCE GUIDE

PRINT SOURCES

East Asia and Oceania

Bender, Andrew, and Martin Robinson. *Korea*, 6th edition. Victoria, AU: Lonely Planet Publications, 2004.
Collins, Darrian, and Kathryn Galliano. *Travel Expenditure by Domestic and International Visitors in Australia's Regions*. Canberra, AU: Tourism Research Australia, 2005.

Department of Transport and Regional Services, Australia. *Australian Transport Statistics, June, 2005.* http://www.btre.gov.au/statistics/statsindex.aspx (June 11, 2006).

Economist Intelligence Unit. *Industry Forecast: Asia and Australasia, June 2005.* http://www.store.eiu.com (June 8, 2006).

Harrison, David. *Pacific Island Tourism.* New York: Cognizant Communication, 2003.

Kim, Samuel Seongseop, Yingzhi Guo, and Jerome Agrusa. "Preference and Positioning Analyses of Overseas Destinations by Mainland Chinese Outbound Pleasure Tourists." *Journal of Travel Research* 44 (2005): 212–220.

Lan, Lawrence, Ming-Te Wang, and April Kuo. "Development and Deployment of Public Transport Policy and Planning in Taiwan." *Transportation* 33 (2006): 153–170.

Ministry of Roads, Transport, and Tourism of Mongolia. *The Yearbook of Tourism Statistics, 2005.* http://www.mongoliatourism.gov.mn/Statistc_year_book.pdf (June 16, 2006).

Pearce, Douglas, and David Simmons. "New Zealand: Tourism—the Challenges of Growth." Pp. 197–219 in Frank Go and Carson Jenkins (eds.), *Tourism and Economic Development in Asia and Australasia.* London: Pinter, 1997.

Rowthorn, Chris, Andrew Bender, John Ashburne, Sara Benson, David Atkinson, and Craig McLachlan. *Japan,* 9th edition. Victoria, AU: Lonely Planet Publications, 2005.

World Travel & Tourism Council. *China, China Hong Kong SAR and China Macau SAR April 2006.* http://www.wttc.org (June 5, 2006).

Zhang, Hanqin Qui, Ray Pine, and Terry Lam. *Tourism and Hotel Development in China.* New York: Haworth Hospitality Press, 2005.

South and Southeast Asia

Bhardwaj, Surinder Mohan. *Hindu Places of Pilgrimage in India: A Study in Cultural Geography.* Berkeley: University of California Press, 1973.

The Europa World Year Book 2005. Vols. 1–2. London/New York: Routledge, 2005.

South Asian Popular Culture. Journal. London/New York: Routledge, 2003–.

Wolpert, Stanley. *A New History of India,* 4th edition. New York: Oxford University Press, 1993.

WEBSITES

East Asia and Oceania

Asia Source: A Resource of the Asia Society. Asia Society. http://www.asiasource.org.

japan-guide.com. http://www.japan-guide.com. A Website featuring information on traveling and living in Japan.

Japan Rail Pass. http://www.japanrailpass.net. The online guide to buying Japanese rail passes.

Korail of Korea. Korea Railroad Corporation. http://www.korail.go.kr/2005/eng/index.html. The online guide to buying Korea rail passes.

Ministry of Tourism. http://www.trcnz.govt.nz. Home page of the New Zealand Ministry of Tourism.

National Bureau of Statistics of China. http://www.stats.gov.cn/english.

National Statistics: Republic of China (Taiwan). Directorate General of Budget. http://eng.stat.gov.tw/.

PATA: Pacific Asia Travel Association. Lonely Planet Travel Guides. http://north-korea.travelwithpata.com.

Tour2Korea. http://english.tour2korea.com. The official Korea Tourism Organization's travel guide.

South and Southeast Asia

Association of Southeast Asian Nations. http://www.aseansec.org.

British Broadcasting Corporation. http://www.bbc.co.uk. The BBC homepage offers "Country Profiles," with useful overviews of each country discussed in this chapter; each Country Profile includes a section of tourism, with links to important sources of official information.

Consular Information Sheets. U.S. Department of State. http://travel.state.gov/travel/cis_pa_tw/cis/cis_1765.html#c.

Ministry of Culture and Tourism, Republic of Indonesia. http://www.budpar.go.id.
Philippine Tourism Authority. http://www.philtourism.gov.ph.
Singapore Tourism Board. http://www.stb.com.sg.
Tourism Authority of Thailand. http://www.tat.or.th.
Tourism Malaysia. http://www.tourism.gov.my.
Vietnam National Administration of Tourism. http://www.vietnamtourism.com.
World Factbook. U.S. Central Intelligence Agency. https://www.cia.gov/cia/publications/factbook/index.html.

ORGANIZATIONS

East Asia and Oceania

China National Tourist Office, New York. Phone: 1-888-760-8218. http://www.cnto.org/aboutcnto.asp. An overseas office of the China National Tourism Administration (CNTA) whose headquarter is in Beijing. CNTA has fifteen overseas tourist offices around the world including two in the United States: New York and Los Angeles.

Japan National Tourism Organization, Tokyo, Japan. Phone: +81(3)32013331. http://www.jnto.go.jp/eng. Responsible for organizing a broad range of activities to promote travel to Japan.

South and Southeast Asia

Pacific Asia Travel Association, Bangkok, Thailand. Phone: 66-2-658-2000. http://www.pata.org. Founded in 1951, the association is a leader in developing Asia Pacific's travel and tourism industry.

NOTES

East Asia and Oceania

1. See Omar Nawaz, "Asia Outbound Tourism Take off," *World Tourism Organization*, http://www.unwto.org/newsroom/Releases/2006/june/asianoutbound.html (accessed March 11, 2007).
2. See Aiping Ma, "China's Outbound Tourism in its Primary Stage," *China Daily*, http://www.chinadaily.com.cn (accessed June 5, 2006).
3. See Jing Fu, "Spending on Airports to Soar in 5 Years," *China Daily*, http://www.chinadaily.com.cn/china/2006-05/09/content_584844.htm (accessed June 5, 2006).
4. Ibid.
5. "Overview of Transportation," *Annual Statistics*, National Bureau of Statistics of China (in Resource Guide).
6. See "The 2006 Report of Investigations and Investments on Highway Transport," China Reported Net, http://www.ccmnet.com (accessed June 9, 2006).
7. "Overview of Transportation," *Annual Statistics*, National Bureau of Statistics of China (in Resource Guide).
8. Ibid.
9. See "Millions Travel on 1st Day of Golden Week Holidays," Xinhua News Agency, http://www.china.org.cn/english/Life/167426.htm (accessed June 9, 2006).
10. "The 2005 Travel & Tourism Economic Research in China," World Travel & Tourism Council (in Resource Guide).
11. Ibid.
12. Ibid.

13. "Overview of Transportation," *Annual Statistics,* National Bureau of Statistics of China (in Resource Guide).
14. "The 2005 Travel & Tourism Economic Research in Hong Kong," World Travel & Tourism Council (in Resource Guide).
15. See Michael Brush, "Las Vegas Bets Gig on Macau," *MSN Money,* http://moneycentral.msn.com/content/P143804.asp (accessed June 8, 2006).
16. "The 2005 Travel & Tourism Economic Research in Macau," World Travel & Tourism Council (in Resource Guide).
17. Lan, Lawrence, Ming-Te Wang, and April Kuo 2006 (in Resource Guide).
18. Ibid.
19. "Chinese Taipei," *WTTC 2006 Tourism Satellite Accounts: Country Reports,* World Travel & Tourism Council, (in Resource Guide).
20. "Tourism Sector Overview," *The Yearbook of Mongolian Tourism Statistics,* Ministry of Roads, Transport, and Tourism of Mongolia 2005 (in Resource Guide).
21. Ibid., p. 11.
22. Ibid., p. 49.
23. Ibid.
24. "Japan," Asia Society (in Resource Guide), http://www.asiasource.org/profiles/ap_mp_02_eastasia.cfm.
25. Ibid.
26. See "Survey on Time Use and Leisure Activities," Statistics Bureau of Japan, http://www.stat.go.jp/english/data (accessed June 12, 2006).
27. See "Tourism Statistics," Japan Tourism Marketing Company, http://www.tourism.jp/english/statistics (accessed June 12, 2006).
28. See "Korea, North, Transportation 2006," Countries Profiles, Information Technology Associates, http://www.theodora.com/wfbcurrent/korea_north/index.html (accessed June 11, 2006).
29. Ibid.
30. See "Transportation," Korean Overseas Information Services, http://www.korea.net/korea/kor_loca.asp?code=F0301 (accessed June 11, 2006).
31. Ibid.
32. Ibid.
33. See "Airport," Korea Civil Aviation Development Association, http://www.airtransport.or.kr/english/airports.html (accessed June 13, 2006).
34. See "Airport Introduction," Korea Airports Cooperation, http://www.gimhaeairport.co.kr/eng/info/information.jsp (accessed June 13, 2006).
35. See "Korea, Monthly Statistics Tourism," Korea Tourism Organization, http://www.etourkorea.com/jsp/eng/about/research/research01_02_01.jsp (accessed June 13, 2006).
36. Ibid.
37. See "Australia Transportation 2006," Countries Profiles, Information Technology Associates, http://www.theodora.com/wfbcurrent/australia/index.html (accessed June 18, 2006).
38. See "Motor Vehicle Census, Australia," Australian Bureau of Statistics, http://www.abs.gov.au (accessed June 15, 2006).
39. See "Australia Transportation 2006," Countries Profiles, Information Technology Associates, http://www.theodora.com/wfbcurrent/australia/index.html (accessed June 18, 2006).
40. Ibid.
41. See "Visitor Arrivals Data," Tourism Australia, June 17, 2005, http://www.tourismaustralia.com.
42. Darrian Collins and Kathryn Galliano 2005 (in Resource Guide), p. 2616.
43. See "New Zealand Transportation 2006," Countries Profiles, Information Technology Associates, http://www.theodora.com/wfbcurrent/new_zealand/index.html (accessed June 17, 2006).
44. Ibid.
45. See "Motor Vehicle Registration 2005," Land Transport New Zealand, http://www.ltsa.govt.nz/statistics/motor-vehicle-registration/2005/index.html (accessed June 17, 2006).

46. See "New Zealand Transportation 2006," Countries Profiles, Information Technology Associates, http://www.theodora.com/wfbcurrent/new_zealand/index.html (accessed June 17, 2006).
47. See "Cruise Passengers 2004," Statistics New Zealand, http://www.stats.govt.nz/default.htm (accessed June 17, 2006).
48. See "International Visitor Arrivals 2005," Tourism Research Council, http://www.tourismresearch.govt.nz/Datasets/International+Visitor+Arrivals/Data+and+Analysis (accessed June 17, 2006).
49. See "Asmal New Zealand Report," Asmal Travel Reports, http://www.asmal.com/nzlqtl.htm (accessed June 18, 2006).
50. "Fiji," *WTTC 2006 Tourism Satellite Accounts: Country Reports*; "Papua New Guinea," *WTTC 2006 Tourism Satellite Accounts: Country Reports*, World Travel & Tourism Council (in Resource Guide).

South and Southeast Asia

1. The information about various modes of transportation in countries summarized in the rest of this section is consolidated mainly from the *Europa World Year Book 2005* and the *World Factbook* Website, listed in the Resource Guide. Distances have been converted to miles and rounded off as appropriate to the context of the section; figures for vehicle registration, population, land area, and so forth have also been rounded off as required by context.

GENERAL BIBLIOGRAPHY

EAST ASIA AND OCEANIA

Ang, Ien, Sharon Chalmers, Lisa Law, and Mandy Thomas, eds. *Alter/Asians: Asian-Australian Identities in Art, Media and Popular Culture.* London: Pluto Press, 2000.

Australian Government Culture and Recreation Portal. Directory of Australian Cultural Organisations and Resources. http://www.cultureandrecreation.gov.au/.

Bennett, Tony, and David Carter, eds. *Culture in Australia: Policies, Publics and Programs.* Cambridge: Cambridge University Press, 2001.

Brown, Ju, and John Brown. *China, Japan, Korea Culture and Customs.* North Charleston, SC: BookSurge Publishing, 2006.

Burrows, Toby, and Grant Stone, eds. *Comics in Australia and New Zealand: The Collections, the Collectors, the Creators.* Binghamton, NY: Haworth Press, 1994.

Bush, Laurence. *Asian Horror Encyclopedia: Asian Horror Culture in Literature, Manga, and Folklore.* Writers Club Press, 2001.

Chen, Zishan. *Food and Chinese Culture: Essays on Popular Cuisines.* San Francisco: Long River Press, 2006.

Ciecko, Anne T. *Contemporary Asian Cinema: Popular Culture in a Global Frame.* Oxford, UK: Berg Publishers, 2006.

Clancy, Laurie. *Culture and Customs of Australia.* Westport, CT: Greenwood Press, 2004.

Craig, Timothy J., ed. *Japan Pop!: Inside the World of Japanese Popular Culture.* Armonk, NY: M. E. Sharpe, 2000.

Craig, Timothy J., and Richard King. eds. *Global Goes Local: Popular Culture in Asia.* Honolulu: University of Hawaii Press, 2002.

Craven, Ian, ed. *Australian Popular Culture.* Cambridge: Cambridge University Press, 1994.

Eng, Robert Y. East and Southeast Asia: An Annotated Directory of Internet Resources. http://newton.uor.edu/Departments&Programs/AsianStudiesDept/general-pop.html

Erni, John N., and Siew Keng Chua, eds. *Asian Media Studies: Politics of Subjectivities.* London: Blackwell, 2004.

Iwabuchi, Koichi, Stephen Muecke, and Mandy Thomas, eds. *Rogue Flows: Trans-Asian Cultural Traffic.* Hong Kong: Hong Kong University Press, 2004.

JVC Video Anthology of World Music and Dance [30 VHS Tapes]. Dir. Katsumori Ichikawa, Kunihiko Nakagawa, Yuji Ichihashi, Tomoaki Fujii. Rounder Records [distributor], 1990. Note: vol. 1–2, Korea; vol. 3–4, China; vol. 5, China/Mongolia; vol. 29, Micronesia/Melanesia/Australia; vol. 30, Polynesia/New Zealand.

Lau, Jenny Kwok Wah, ed. *Multiple Modernities: Cinemas and Popular Media in Transcultural East Asia.* Philadelphia: Temple University Press, 2003.

GENERAL BIBLIOGRAPHY

Lent, John A., ed. *Asian Popular Culture.* Boulder, CO: Westview Press, 1996.
Ma, Eric Kit-wai. *Culture, Politics and Television in Hong Kong.* New York: Routledge, 1999.
Martinez, Dolores, ed. *The Worlds of Japanese Popular Culture: Gender, Shifting Boundaries and Global Cultures.* Cambridge: Cambridge University Press, 1998.
Robertson, Jennifer. *Takarazuka: Sexual Politics and Popular Culture in Modern Japan.* Berkeley: University of California Press, 1998.
Schilling, Mark. *The Encyclopedia of Japanese Pop Culture.* New York: Weatherhill, 1997.
Treat, John W. *Contemporary Japan and Popular Culture.* New York: RoutledgeCurzon, 1996.
Turner, Graeme. *Making It National: Nationalism and Australian Popular Culture.* Sydney: Allen & Unwin.
Vamplew, Wray, and Brian Stoddart, eds. *Sport in Australia: A Social History.* Cambridge: Cambridge University Press, 1995.
Wu, Dingbo, and Patrick Murphy, eds. *Handbook of Chinese Popular Culture.* Westport, CT: Greenwood Press, 1994.

SOUTH AND SOUTHEAST ASIA

Acharya, K. T. *A Historical Dictionary of Indian Food.* New Delhi: Oxford University Press, 1998.
Agrawal, Binod C. *Television in South Asia: Cultural Scenario and Future Directions.* Lanham, MD: University Press of Americas, 2006.
Barendregt, Bart, and Wim van Zanten. "Popular Music in Indonesia since 1998, in Particular Fusion, Indie and Islamic Music on Video Compact Discs and the Internet." *Yearbook for Traditional Music* 34 (2002): 67–113.
Biddle, Arthur W., gen. ed. *Contemporary Literature of Asia.* Upper Saddle River, NJ: Prentice Hall, 1996. Contains introductions to and selections of contemporary short stories and poems from Pakistan, India, Nepal, Sri Lanka, Vietnam, the Philippines, Malaysia, and Indonesia.
Bowers, Faubion. *Dance in India.* New York: Columbia University Press, 1953.
Brandon, James. *The Cambridge Guide to Asian Theatre.* New York: Cambridge University Press, 1993.
Cheah, Pheng. "Chinese Cosmopolitanism in Two Senses and Postcolonial National Memory." Pp. 133–169 in *Cosmopolitan Geographies: New Locations in Literature and Culture,* ed. Vinay Dharwadker. New York: Routledge, 2001.
Ciecko, Anne Tereska. *Contemporary Asian Cinemas.* New York: Berg, 2006.
Comrie, Bernard, ed. *The World's Major Languages.* New York: Oxford University Press, 1990.
Coomaraswamy, A. K. *The Dance of Shiva: Fourteen Indian Essays.* Rev. edition. New York: Noonday Press, 1962.
Coronel, Sheila S., ed. *Access to Information in Southeast Asia and Beyond.* Uppsala: Dag Hammarskjold Centre, 2003.
Craven, Roy C. *Indian Art: A Concise History.* New York: Thames and Hudson, 1985, 1991.
Das Gupta, Ashin. *The World of the Indian Ocean Merchant, 1500–1800: Collected Essays.* Ed. Uma Das Gupta. New Delhi: Oxford University Press, 2001.
Dharwadker, Aparna Bhargava. *Theatres of Independence: Drama, Theory, and Urban Performance in India since 1947.* Iowa City: University of Iowa Press, 2005; New Delhi: Oxford University Press, 2006.
Dharwadker, Vinay, ed. and trans. *Kabir: The Weaver's Songs.* New Delhi: Penguin Classics, 2004.
———, gen. ed. *The Collected Essays of A. K. Ramanujan.* New Delhi: Oxford University Press, 1999. Excellent essays on Indian and South Asian literatures and folklore.
———. "Print Culture and Literary Markets in Colonial India." Pp. 108–133 in *Language Machines: Technologies of Literary and Cultural Production,* ed. Jeffrey Masten, Peter Stallybrass, and Nancy J. Vickers. New York: Routledge, 1997.
———, and A. K. Ramanujan, eds. *The Oxford Anthology of Modern Indian Poetry.* Delhi: Oxford University Press, 1994.
Dissanayake, Wimal. *Melodrama and Asian Cinema.* Cambridge: Cambridge University Press, 1993.

GENERAL BIBLIOGRAPHY

———. *Colonialism and Nationalism in Asian Cinema*. Bloomington: Indiana University Press, 1994.
The Europa World year Book 2005, Vols. 1–2. London and New York: Routledge, 2005.
Flood, Gavin. *An Introduction to Hinduism*. Cambridge: Cambridge University Press, 1996.
Gahlaut, Kanika. "Designs on the World." *India Today*, II.38 (16–22 September 2003): 30–39.
Ganti, Tejaswini. *Bollywood*. Routledge Film Guidebooks. New York: Routledge, 2004.
Goonasekera, Anura, Lee Chun Wah, and S. Venkataraman, eds. *Asian Communication Handbook 2003*. Singapore: Asian Media Information and Communication Centre and Nanyang Technological University, 2003.
Gunaratne, Shelton A., ed.. *Handbook of the Media in Asia*. New Delhi: Sage Publications, 2000.
Katz, Solomon H., and William Woys Weaver, eds. *Encyclopedia of Food and Culture*. Scribner, 2002.
Lapidus, Ira M. *A History of Islamic Societies*. Cambridge: Cambridge University Press, 1988.
Lockard, Craig. *Dance of Life: Popular Music and Politics in Southeast Asia*. Honolulu: University of Hawaii Press, 1998.
Lopez, Donald S., Jr., ed. *Religions of India in Practice*. Princeton, NJ: Princeton University Press, 1995.
———, ed. *Buddhism in Practice*. Princeton, NJ: Princeton University Press, 1995.
Massey, Reginald. *India's Dances: Their History, Technique, and Repertoire*. New Delhi: Abhinav Prakashan, 2004.
McDaniel, Drew O. *Broadcasting in the Malay World: Radio, Television, and Video in Brunei, Indonesia, Malaysia, and Singapore*. Norwood, NJ: Ablex Publishers, 1994.
McLeod, W. H. *Sikhs and Sikhism*. New Delhi: Oxford University Press, 1999.
Moran, Albert, and Michael Keane. *Television across Asia: Television Industries, Programme Formats and Globalization*. London and New York: RoutledgeCurzon, 2004.
Natarajan, Nalini, ed. *Handbook of Twentieth Century Literatures of India*. Westport, CT: Greenwood, 1996.
Neuman, Daniel M. *The Life of Music in North India: The Organization of an Artistic Tradition*. Chicago: University of Chicago Press, 1990.
Osnes, Beth, dir. *Cambodia: The People and the Performing Arts*. [Video] University of Colorado Theatre Department, 2003.
Parks, Lisa, and Shanti Kumar, ed. *Planet TV: A Global Television Reader*. New York: New York University Press, 2003.
Pollock, Sheldon. *The Language of the Gods in the World of Men: Sanskrit, Culture, and Power in Premodern India*. Berkeley: University of California Press, 2006.
———, ed. *Literary Cultures in History: Reconstructions from South Asia*. Berkeley: University of California Press, 2003.
Rajadhyaksha, Asish, ed. *Encyclopedia of Indian Cinema*. 2nd rev. ed. London: British Film Institute, 1999.
Rawson, Philip S. *The Art of Southeast Asia: Cambodia, Vietnam, Thailand, Laos, Burma, Java, Bali*. New York: Thames and Hudson, 1990.
Romano, Angela Rose, and Michael Bromley, ed. *Journalism and Democracy in Asia*. London: RoutledgeCurzon, 2005.
Rowland, Benjamin. *The Art and Architecture of India: Buddhist, Hindu, Jain*. New York: Penguin, 1977.
Salmons, Lynn Garry. http://www.thesalmons.org/lynn. Accessed December 19, 2006. Provides links to text and pictures relating to all UNESCO World Heritage sites in South and Southeast Asia.
Sanga, Jaina, ed. *South Asian Literature in English: An Encyclopedia*. Westport, CT: Greenwood, 2004.
Singer, Noel. *Burmese Dance and Theatre*. New York: Oxford University Press, 1995.
Sivaramamurti, Calambur. *The Art of India*. New York: Abrams, 1977.
South Asian Popular Culture. Journal published by Routledge, 2003–.
Tan, Sooi Beng. "The Performing Arts in Malaysia: State and Society." *Asian Music* 21.1 (1989/1990): 137–171.
Thomas, Amos Owen. *Imagi-Nations and Borderless Television: Media, Culture and Politics across Asia*. New Delhi: Sage Publications, 2005.
Wolpert, Stanley. *A New History of India*. 4th edition. New York: Oxford University Press, 1993.

ABOUT THE EDITORS AND CONTRIBUTORS

THE VOLUME EDITORS

GARY XU has a Ph.D. from Columbia University and is currently associate professor of Chinese literature, comparative literature, and cinema studies at the University of Illinois, Urbana-Champaign. His teaching and research focus on modern China: its literature, cinema, and popular culture in general. He is the author of *Sinascape: Contemporary Chinese Cinema* (2007) and editor of *The Cross-Cultural Zizek Reader* (2006).

VINAY DHARWADKER is currently a professor in the department of languages and cultures of Asia at the University of Wisconsin-Madison, where he has also served as the Director of the Center for South Asia (2002–04) and as the faculty coordinator of the Mellon Workshop on Cosmopolitan Cultures, Cosmopolitan Histories (2005–07). A poet, painter, translator, scholar, and teacher, Dharwadker is the principal editor of *The Oxford Anthology of Modern Indian Poetry* (1994) and the general editor of *The Collected Essays of A. K. Ramanujan* (1999). His recent publications include *Cosmopolitan Geographies: New Locations in Literature and Culture* (2001) and *Kabir: The Weaver's Songs* (2003, 2005). Among his forthcoming works are *The Columbia Book of South Asian Poetry* and *Mirza Ghalib: Selected Poetry and Prose*.

THE GENERAL EDITOR

GARY HOPPENSTAND is professor of American studies at Michigan State University and the author of numerous books and articles in the field of popular culture studies. He is the former president of the national Popular Culture Association and the current editor-in-chief of *The Journal of Popular Culture*.

THE CONTRIBUTORS

DAVID ATHERTON is a Ph.D. candidate in the department of East Asian languages and cultures at Columbia University. He has traveled extensively throughout South, Southeast, and East Asia and has published his travel writing in the *Let's Go* travel guide series and the *Los Angeles Times*.

About the Editors and Contributors

VALERIE H. BARSKE is working on her Ph.D. in East Asian studies from the University of Illinois, Urbana-Champaign. She has been involved in the study of various forms of dancing for most of her professional life. Through the support of a Fulbright-Hays Grant, Barske has completed her field research and is writing her dissertation, entitled "Embodying History, Dancing Politics: Performing Peace, Gender, and Ethnicity in Okinawa, Japan." She has also served as a dance researcher for a team project on Lahu hill tribe dances in Northern Thailand. Currently, Barske is teaching courses in women's studies as an associate lecturer at the University of Wisconsin, Stevens Point.

LÉJARIE BATTIESTE received a B.A. in East Asian studies with a focus on Japanese in 1995 from the University of California at Los Angeles. She has also worked in Japan for three years as an English teacher and currently resides in the Los Angeles area, where she is a freelance journalist and researcher specializing in Japanese culture.

KATARZYNA J. CWIERTKA works at the Center for Japanese and Korean Studies, Leiden University, The Netherlands.

ERIC DALLE is a Ph.D. student in the department of comparative and world literature at the University of Illinois, Urbana-Champaign. His research interests include modern Chinese and French literature, as well as cinema studies.

WIMAL DISSANAYAKE is a professor at the Academy for Creative Media in the University of Hawaii. Dissanayake is the author and editor of over thirty books, including *Melodrama and Asian Cinema*; *New Chinese Cinema*; and *Narratives of Agency*.

ERWEI DONG is a lecturer in the department of recreation and leisure studies, SUNY Cortland, New York. He has a master's in physical and health education from Tokyo Gakugei University, Japan, and a Ph.D. in leisure studies from Pennsylvania State University. His research interests focus on cross-cultural leisure research and tourism research.

SHELTON A. GUNARATNE is professor of mass communications at Minnesota State University, Moorhead. A specialist in international communication, he has applied Eastern philosophy to communication theory building in his most recent work: *The Dao of the Press: A Humanocentric Theory* (2005) and *Public Sphere and Communicative Rationality: Interrogating Habermas's Eurocentrism* (2006).

DONNA L. HALPER, adjunct professor of journalism at Emerson College, Boston, is a media historian who has spent more than 30 years as a broadcaster and freelance journalist. She is the author of three books and is currently working on a fourth. Her expertise is in women and minorities in media history.

YIJU HUANG is currently a Ph.D. candidate at the University of Illinois, Urbana-Champaign. She is in the department of East Asian languages and cultures, where she also completed her M.A. in 2006. Her interests include philosophy, architecture, modern Chinese cinema, and literature.

SHUYONG JIANG is assistant professor of library administration at University of Illinois, Urbana-Champaign. She has written articles on Chinese literary theories and knowledge classifications in prestigious journals, and she has edited two volumes in *Zhongguo gudai wenyi lilun zhuantiziliao congkan* [A Source Book, Chinese Traditional Literary Theories].

BOB LEE is assistant professor of recreation and tourism at Bowling Green State University. His research interest focuses on recreation and tourism services for older adults. He has written extensively on outdoor recreation promotion, tourism marketing, and applications of information communication technology in park, recreation, and tourism administrations.

About the Editors and Contributors

MONICA Z. LI is currently a doctoral candidate at the department of recreation, sport and tourism at the University of Illinois, Urbana-Champaign. Her primary research interests lie in leisure and travel experiences of transmigrant populations in North America. She seeks to explore how leisure and travel experiences are influenced by the transnational status of the population, and how, through leisure and travel, the transnational linkages are manifested, fostered, or enforced. Other areas of her research include recreation and physical activity participation and park use of minority populations, leisure constraints, cross-cultural aspects of leisure, and travel information search behavior and its marketing implications. Prior to her education in the United States, she worked as a travel counselor and a corporate travel supervisor for six years at one of the leading Chinese travel companies: China International Travel Service (CITS) Group in Beijing.

JING LUO is professor of French/Chinese and second language learning at Bloomsburg University of Pennsylvania. He received his B.A. and M.A. from Peking University and Ph.D. from Pennsylvania State University. He is editor of *China Today: An Encyclopedia of the People's Republic* (Greenwood Press, 2005).

BETH OSNES teaches theater at the University of Colorado in Boulder. She was a Fulbright Scholar in Malaysia, where she conducted field research on the shadow puppet theater. She is author of *Acting: An International Encyclopedia* (2001) and numerous articles on the Asian performing arts and on activism and women in performance.

JAINA SANGA is a scholar of Indian and South Asian literature in English and has taught most recently at Southern Methodist University. She is the author of *Salman Rushdie's Postcolonial Metaphors* (2001), and the editor of *South Asian Novelists in English* (2003) and *South Asian Literature in English: An Encyclopedia* (2004). She is also a fiction writer and currently lives in Dallas, where she is devoting herself full-time to completing her first novel.

E. K. TAN is assistant professor of comparative literature at SUNY Stony Brook. His areas of interest include diaspora studies, psychoanalysis, and film theory. He is presently working on a book manuscript on Southeast Asian Chinese diaspora writers and filmmakers.

ALOKE THAKORE is a media consultant, journalist, and teacher currently based in Kolkata, India. His research interests are in media ethics, law, and sociology. His dissertation at the University of Wisconsin-Madison was on media coverage of ethnic violence, which he plans to turn into a book.

AMOS OWEN THOMAS is associate professor of international business and marketing at the Maastricht School of Management in the Netherlands. He has taught previously in Australia, Papua New Guinea, and Singapore. He is the author of *Imagi-Nations and Borderless Television: Media, Culture and Politics across Asia* (2005) and *Transnational Media and Contoured Markets: Redefining Asian Television and Advertising* (2006).

JEREMY WALLACH is an assistant professor in the department of popular culture, Bowling Green State University. His research interests include music and technology, globalization, postcolonialism, and the musics of Southeast Asia. He is author of the forthcoming book *Modern Noise, Fluid Genres: Popular Music in Indonesia, 1997–2001*.

HUI XIAO is a Ph.D. candidate in the department of East Asian languages and cultures at the University of Illinois, Urbana-Champaign. Her areas of interest are modern Chinese literature, film studies, and gender studies. Her articles have appeared in journals such as *Asian Cinema*, *Frontiers (Tianya)*, *China Media Research*, and *Concentric*, and in collections such as *Globalization and Chineseness: Postcolonial Readings of Contemporary Culture* and *From Camera Lens to Critical*

About the Editors and Contributors

Lens: A Collection of Best Essays on Film Adaptation. Currently she is working on her dissertation project, an investigation of the intersections of gender, family, and class through an examination of divorce narratives in post-Mao literature and culture.

JOUYEON YI-KOOK earned her bachelor's and master's degrees, both in sociology, from Yonsei University of Korea. She worked at the Korea Cultural Administration Research Institute and the Korea Cultural Policy Research Institute before studying toward her master's degree in community arts management at the University of Illinois, Springfield. She is now a doctoral candidate in recreation, sport, and tourism at the University of Illinois, Urbana-Champaign. She is also working as a researcher at the Tourism and Recreation Research Laboratory in the Research Institute for Agriculture and Life Sciences at Seoul National University, Korea.

AIHUA ZHANG is an English lecturer of the School of Foreign Languages in Shandong University, China. Her research interests include East Asian culture and history.

SHERI ZHANG is a professor at the University of Ottawa. Her research areas are international education, second language acquisition, and cultural studies. Her recent publications include the book *Understanding Modern China through Its Language and Culture*. She was honored as the Canadian representative at the European Educational Research Association.

INDEX

Note: Chinese, Japanese, and Koreans commonly use the family name first followed by the given (first) name. If Americans followed this style, Bill Smith would be commonly called Smith Bill. In this index, cited individuals are listed under family names followed by given (first) names. For example, the Chinese architect Wu Liangyong is indexed under W as "Wu Liangyong" because the family name is Wu.

Abbas, Khwaja Ahmad, 177
Aboriginal peoples
    artistic traditions of, 21
    dance performances of traditional, 38
    influence on Australian popular music, 209, 210
    preservation of dance forms of, 32
    and settling of Australia, 151, 156
    Tjapukai Aboriginal Cultural Park, 38
    toys and games of, 156
AC/DC, 209
Ahmad, Shahnon, 177, 179
Ainu people
    dance and preservation of culture of, 36
    traditional clothing among, 65
Anand, Mulk Raj, 176, 178
Ankor Wat, 353
Architecture and urban planning
    in Australia, 8, 9–10
        Australia Square, 9
        Bank of China tower (Hong Kong), 5
        baseball stadiums (Japan), 6
        Bligh Lobb Sports Architects, 10
        Burnett, B. C. G., 9
        Cathedral of the Blessed Sacrament (Melbourne), 9
    in China, 2–5
    of churches (Australia), 9
    colonial legacies and, 1, 23
    Conder, Josiah, 6
    conservation of traditional Chinese, 5
    Continental Bank Building (Beijing), 3
    Le Corbusier (Charles-Edouard Jeanneret), 6
    courtyard houses (*siheyuan*), 3
    courtyards, and Qing Dynasty, 3
    early business districts and modern cities, 9
    emulating Western styles, 3
    European influence on, in Australia and New Zealand, 8
    Fragrant Hill Hotel, 5
    fusion of art and architecture, 28
    German expressionism and, 6
    Golden Grove Street Housing (Australia), 10
    Grand People's Study House, 7
    Gulf Station (Yura Valley, Australia), 9
    Hussey, Henry H., 3
    imported European traditions, 3, 4–5, 6, 7, 8
    influence of Japanese, 6
    international influences on, 1–2
    the International Style and, 2
    in Japan, 5–6
    Japanese influences on Korean, 7
    Juer Hutong project (Beijing), 5
    Kim Il-Sung Stadium, 7
    Lu Xun, 15
    Meiji-era, 6
    modernization and, 2–3
    Myongdon Cathedral, 7

Index

Architecture and urban planning (*continued*)
  Nara Imperial Museum (Japan), 6
  neoclassical styles, 1
  in New Zealand, 8
  in North Korea, 7
  the Olympic Games and, 5
  Pak Kil-yong, 7
  Pak Tong-jin, 7
  Pei, I. M., 4–5
  Peking Union Medical College, 3
  Philip Cox Richardson Taylor & Partners, 10
  prefabricated homes, 9
  Pyongyang redevelopment, 7
  Rose House (Sydney), 9
  in rural Australia, 9
  Ryugyong Hotel, 7
  and sculpture in South and Southeast Asia, 22–23
  Seidler, Harry, 9
  Seoul City Hall, 7
  Seoul Railroad Station, 7
  Shanghai's foreign quarter, 2
  sliding doors and walls in Japanese, 6
  in South Korea, 7–8
  Soviet Exhibition Hall, 3
  Soviet influences on, 2, 3, 7
  Soviet model for standardized housing, 3–4
  Sydney Opera House (Australia), 9–10
  Taipei 101, 5
  Tange, Kenzo, 6
  technological advances and, 1
  Telstra Stadium (Australia), 10
  temple, 3, 5
  theme parks (South Korea), 7–8
  tiled roofs, 3
  Toksugung Palace, 7
  traditional Japanese, 5–6
  traditional styles, 3
  urbanization and, 1
  Utzon, Joern, 9–10
  Victorian Arts Center (Australia), 9
  Western influences on Japanese, 6
  Western influences on Korean, 7
  world's tallest buildings, 4, 5
  Wright, Frank Lloyd, 6
  World Cup Stadium (South Korea), 8
  Wu Liangyong, 5
  in Xi'an, 5
  Xi'an city walls and moat, 2
  Yulara Tourist Village (Australia), 10
Armstrong, Gillian, 104

Art
  Aboriginal artistic traditions, 21
  abstract painting in China, 16
  in Australia, 21–22
  avant-garde style in Chinese, 16
  avant-garde movement in Japan, 18–19
  Bhattacharya, Bikash, 26
  Broota, Rameshwar, 26
  Buddhist influences on, 23
  Caur, Arpana, 27
  Chandra, Shruti Gupta, 27
  changing responses to abstract style, 17
  communism and (North Korea), 20
  the Communist Revolution (China) and, 15
  Confucian ethnics and Chinese, 14
  Daoism and, 14
  Den Xiaoping, art and reforms of, 16
  depiction of male genitalia in, 21
  diversity in modern Chinese, 16
  Dongfang Huazhan (Eastern painting exhibition), 17
  end of Cold War and, 17
  Fahey, Jacqueline, 22
  "Faith + the City" exhibition, 27
  folk-art forms in modern Chinese, 15–16
  fusion of architecture and, 28
  galleries, 24
  globalization and, 24
  government control of (North Korea), 20
  The Great Wave, 18
  Gujral, Satish, 26
  Gu Wenda, 17
  Heidelberg School (Australia), 22
  Hindu influences on, 23
  Hokusai, Katsushika, 18
  Hussain, M. F., 25–26
  indigenous modifications of Western concepts in, 25
  Islamic control of, in South and Southeast Asia, 23
  in Japan, 17–19
  Japanese influences on, 17
  Khakhar, Bhupen, 26
  Komu, Riyas, 27
  in Korea, 19–20
  Kumar, Ram, 27
  Liu Kuo-Sung, 17
  manga, 19
  Mao collectibles, 16
  Maoism and, 15
  Maori crafts, 21
  Mao Zedong [Tse-tung] and Chinese art, 15

markets for, 24–25
after Meji Restoration (Japan), 18
Mehta, Tyeb, 26
Menon, Anjolie, 27
Minjung Cultural Movement, 20
modern art in, 23–25
modern Western styles and, 23–24
monumental sculpture in China, 16
Monument of the People's Heroes (Tiananmen Square), 16
Morimura Yasumasa, 19
Munakata Shiko, 18
museums, 24
Neo Dada movement, 18
neolithic traditions in Oceania, 20
in New Zealand, 21–22
Nihonga masters, 17
in North Korea, 20
in Oceania, 20, 21
Okada, Kenzo, 18
The Old Foolish Man Removing Mountains, 15
Padamsee, Akbar, 26
Patel, Gieve, 27
Patwardhan, Sudhir, 26–27
Playing with Gods, 19
postmodernist, 25
Progressive Artists Group, 26
as propaganda, 15–16, 20
Raza, S. H., 26
rural influence on classical Chinese, 13–14
Sabavala, Jehangir, 26
Santosh, G. R., 27
schools for, 24
sculpture in China after the Liberation, 16
Sheikh, Ghulam Mohammed, 27
Shepard, Carole, 22
Sikandar, Shahzia, 25
in South and Southeast Asia, 22–28
in South Korea, 20
Souza, F. N., 26
spirituality and, 21
Stone Age (Neolithic) traditions, 20, 21
"Telah Terbit [Out Now]" exhibition, 27
tourism and, 28
traditional arts today, 26–27
tribal traditions and carvings, 21
Western influences on, 23–24
Western influences on Japanese, 18
Western influences on modern Chinese, 16
women and, 27
Women's Art Movement (New Zealand), 22
woodblock, in Japan, 18
wood carvings, 21
wood-cut movement in Chinese, 15
writers and, 27
Xin Chao (*New Wave*) movement, 16
Xu Beihong, 14–15
Zhu Yongin, 16
Artaud, Antonin, and, 315
Association of South-East Asian Nations (ASEAN), xxi-xxii
The Atlantics, 209
Australia
    Aboriginal artistic traditions in, 21
    Aboriginal games and toys in, 156
    Anglophone literary traditions, 168
    architecture in, 8, 9–10
    art in, 21–22
    birth-rates, 198
    British influence on food in, 135–136
    children's literature traditions in, 168–170
    Chinatowns in, 137
    climate, 8
    dance in, 37–39
    demographics, 8
    education in, 198
    ethnic diversity in modern, 137
    European migration to, 198
    fashion and appearance in, 67–69
    film in, 103–104
    food in, 135–137
    geography, 21
    Hollywood dominance and local film production in, 103
    international recognition for music from, 209–210
    literature in, 168–170
    marriage and sexual relationships in, 198–200
    music in, 208–210
    Olympic Games, 305
    the Olympic Games and television, 267
    periodicals in, 228, 237–238
    radio in, 264
    spending on clothing in, 68
    sports in, 304–306
    television in, 267–268
    theater in, 320
    tourism in, 344–345
    toys and games market in, 155–156

INDEX

Australia (*continued*)
    toys, games, and pastimes in, 155–156
    transportation in, 344–345

Baku, Ishii, 32, 35
Bali
    classical dance in, 45–46, 49–50
    indigenous theater in, 334
    recently created dance forms in, 53
Bangladesh
    broadcasting in, 281–282
    films in, 113–114
    founding of, 113
    historic sites in, 351
    import restrictions on foreign films, 113
    languages in, 245–246
    the partition and literature of, 173–175
    the partition and periodicals in, 246
    periodicals in, 245–246
    tourism and, 351
    war of independence and broadcasting, 281
    war of independence and literature, 174–175
Barba, Eugenio, 50
The Bee Gees, 209
Berliner, Emil, 214
Bernal, Ishmael, 118–119
Bhattacharya, Bikash, 26
Billy Thorpe & the Aztecs, 209
BoA, 208
Bond, Ruskin, 180
Brecht, Bertolt, 314–315
Brocka, Lino, 118
Broota, Rameshwar, 26
Brunei, 216–217
The Bund (Shanghai), 2
Burj Tower (Dubai), 4
Burma. *See* Myanmar
Burnett, B. C. G., 9

Cambodia
    Ankor Wat, 353
    classical dance in, 48–49
    folk dance in, 51–52
    historic sites in, 353
    indigenous theater in, 330–331
    landmines and roads in, 355
    languages in, 249
    National Khmer Classical Ballet Troupe, 49
    periodicals in, 249
    under Pol Pot, 249
    tourism and, 353
    transportation infrastructure in, 355
Campion, Jane, 104–105
Cao Yu, 317
Carey, Peter, 168
Caro, Niki, 104
Caur, Arpana, 27
Ceylon. *See* Sri Lanka
Cha, Louis (Jinyong, Zha Lianyong), 164
Chandra, Shruti Gupta, 27
Chandra, Subhash, and broadcasting, 277
Chan, Jackie, 95
Chan, Peter, 96
Chatterjee, Saratchandra, 177
Chauncey, Nan, 169
Chen Kaige, 93
Cheung, Leslie, 205
Chikamatsu Monzaemon, 319
Children's literature. *See* Literature, for children
China (including People's Republic of China). *See also* China, Republic of
    agriculture in, 13–14
    architecture in, 2–5
    art in, 13–17
    autonomous regions in, 14
    canonical novels of, 163
    censorship, 232
    changing broadcast programming in, 269
    "China Magazine Square" project, 231
    climate of, 2
    coffee consumption in, 128
    communism and dance in, 33–34
    communism, marriage, and sexual relationships in, 191
    Communist Party publications (Chinese), 231
    the Communist Revolution and art in, 15
    Confucian ethics, 14
    the Cultural Revolution and film production in, 93
    the Cultural Revolution and TV in, 265
    dance in, 33–34
    Den Xiaoping, reforms of, 16
    disposable income and fashions, 61
    emergence as fashion center, 60–61
    ethnic diversity of, 14, 33
    fashion industry in, 59–62
    film in, 93–94
    food in, 128–130
    foreign origins of communications in, 260
    freedom of the press, 232
    general and family magazines, in China, 231
    geography of, 13

INDEX

government control of the press, 231–232
the Great Cultural Revolution, 16
the Great Leap Famine (1959–1961), 129
Great Wall Hotel (Beijing), 4
leisure travel industry in, 337
literature in, 162–164
Mao collectibles, 16
Mao Zedong and broadcasting, 269
marriage and sexual relationships in, 190–192
modern games linked to ancient, 151
music in, 203–204
National Aviation Museum (Beijing), 339
New Cultural Movement (China), 14
Olympic Games (2008) in, 300
one-child policy, 190
open door policy and outside music influences, 203
"patriotic education" and broadcasting, 269
the Peking [Beijing] Opera, 163, 164
periodicals in, 230–232
political reforms in, 16
preference for male children, 190
Qing Dynasty architecture, 3
radio in, 260–261, 265
the *Readers* magazine, 231
regional Chinese cuisines, 128
revolutionary operas, 164
rural art movement, 15–16
sports in, 297–300
Sun Yat-sen, 14
tai chi, 298
Taoism and sports in, 298
television in, 265–266
textile exports, 60–61
theater in, 315–318
tourism and, 337, 338–339
toys, games, and pastimes in, 151–153
urbanization and fashions in, 61
Western influences, 14
Wu Shaoyun, 15
Yangtze River as dividing line for culture in, 13
China, Republic of (Taiwan)
art in, 17
dance and, 33–34
end of Cold War and art in, 17
film in, 96–99
food in, 130
influence on mainland Chinese music, 203
Japanese "educational" dance in, 33
Japanese occupation of, 17, 33, 96
the Kuomintang and radio in, 264
Kuomintang (KMT) takeover of Taiwan and films, 96
marriage and sexual relationships in, 192–193
Minzu Wudao [national/ethnic dance] Propagation Movement, 32, 34
Nationalist Kuomintang (KMT) Party retreat to Taiwan, 17
post-martial law period and film production in, 97
radio in, 264
Sino-Japanese War (1937) and film in, 96
television in, 266
tourism and, 341
transportation in, 340–341
women and dance in, 33
Chow, Stephen, 96
Clavell, James, 168
Clothing
Asian fashion designers, 75–76
Asian influences on Western designers of, 75
body wrap garments, 79
changing economies and, 70
Chinese exports of, 59–60, 66, 68
colors and sari wear, 80
custom tailoring and, 74–75
the dhoti, 79
economic liberalization and, 74
exports to Western markets, 75–77
first stitched garments, 79
Gandhi, Mahatma, and the dhoti, 79
ghaghra-choli ensembles, 82
globalization and production of, 75
governmental controls on, 73–74, 82–84
Gypsy (Roma) clothing origins, 82
haute couture market, 76
hybrid styles and, 72–73
import restrictions and, 74
for Indian diaspora communities, 76–77
indigenous, 79–85
indigenous in Thailand, 84
Islam and sari styles, 80
jeans and T-shirts, 73
jodhpurs, origin of, 82
the *kurta*, 80
the longyi, 82–84
market for ready made, 76
mass-produced, 60
in Myanmar, 82–84
New Zealand exports of, 69
the *paijama*, 80

375

Index

Clothing (*continued*)
    ready-made garment market, 74–75
    religious restrictions on, 73–74
    retail outlets for, 74–75
    the sari, 79–80
    the sari-blouse, 80
    sarongs, 82
    South Korean markets and, 66
    sportswear, 73
    stitched garments of Asian origin, 80, 82
    synthetic fabrics and, 73
    the tehband, 79
    in Thailand, 84
    in Vietnam, 84–85
    Western adaptations of Asian, 80, 82
    Western influences on, 72–74
Comics
    the *animé* film style and, 164
    in Japan, 165
    manga, 19, 164–166
    manhwa, 167–168
    in South Korea, 167–168
Computers. *See* Electronic media (including radio, television, and computers)
Conder, Josiah, 6
Le Corbusier (Charles-Edouard Jeanneret), 6
Cosmetics
    the *bindi*, 83
    in China, 62–63
    Chinese spending on, 62
    indigenous, 83
    in Japan, 64, 65
    the *kumkum*, 83
    mehndi, 83
    the *meinu jingji* (beauty economy) in China, 63
    shampoo and its origins, 81
    in South Korea, 67
Council on Tall Buildings and Urban Habitat, 4
Crowded House, 211
Cui Jian, 204

Daguio, Amador, 181
Dalits ("untouchables"), 175, 324
Dance
    Aboriginal, 32, 38
    ancient religions and Myanmar, 51
    the *ankoku butō* [dance of darkness] movement, 35
    Aotearoa Traditional Maori Performing Arts Festival, 39
    the *Ardja* form, 49
    in Australia, 37–39
    avant garde, 35
    Baku, Ishii, 32, 35
    in Bali, 45–46, 53
    ballet companies, 32
    ballet influences on Burmese, 47
    ballet in New Zealand, 39
    Bangara Dance Theatre, 38
    Barba, Eugenio, 50
    the *Baris* (war dance, Java), 52
    the *Barong* (Bali), 45–46
    the *Bedoyo* (Java), 45
    Bhangra folk dances (India), 50
    Bharata natyam style, 44, 45
    Bollywood films and, 41, 42–43
    Buddhist influences on Vietnamese, 52
    buyo-geki dance-dramas, 34–35
    in Cambodia, 48–49, 51–52
    Chamo [Alphabet] System of Dance Notation, 37
    Chennai Dance and Music Festival, 47
    in China, 33–34
    Chinese influences on Korean, 36
    Chinese influences on Vietnamese, 52
    Chinese minorities and, 33
    Chosun Dance Education Institute, 37
    Christian missionaries and, 31
    classical, 43–50
    colonialism and, 31
    communism and, in mainland China, 33–34
    contemporary, 41–43
    courtship (Cambodia), 51–52
    cultural and religious heritages and, 31
    Cultural Revolution (People's Republic of China) and, 34
    Dance, Dance, Dance Revolution, 32
    dance clubs, 42
    dance-dramas, 46–50
    dance-drama styles (China), 33, 34
    dance-drama styles (Thailand), 48
    dance festivals in India, 44, 47
    dance halls, social (Shanghai), 34
    development of uniquely Australian, 38
    Disco *Bhangra*, 42, 50–51
    Elephanta Music and Dance Festival, 44
    erotic dancing, 42
    ethnic Han folk-dances, 33
    ethnic minorities and Indian folk, 51
    exotic dancers, 42
    films and, in Australia, 38
    first Chinese ballet (Beijing), 32
    first Chinese ballet (Taiwan), 32
    folk, 50–53
    folk dances and political movements

INDEX

(Korea), 37
gamelan orchestras and, 45, 50
governmental control efforts, 41
Hindi cinema and, 42–43, 45
Hindu influences on, 45
hip hop, influence of, 32, 35, 40
historical forms, 43
Hong Sin-cha, 37
incorporation with other art forms, 31
in India, 43–45, 46–47
Indian epics and dance, 46
Indian folk dances, 50–51
indigenous classical forms, 43
in Indonesia, 45–46, 49–50, 52–53
in Japan, 34–36
Japanese occupation of Taiwan and, 33
in Java, 45, 49
kabuki, 34–35
Kathak, 43
Kathakali style, 46–47
the *Kebyar* (Bali), 53
the *Ketjak* (Bali), 53
Khajuraho Dance Festival, 44
the *Khon* form, 48
Konark Music and Dance Festival, 44
in Korea, 36–37
Kuchipudi style, 46
and kungfu, 32
kungqu dance-drama, 33, 34
the *Lakon Kbach Boran* form, 49
the *Lakon Nai*, 48
Legong form (Bali), 49–50
lion dances, 34
the *Ludruk Bendang*, 52
in Malaysia, 52
Mamallapuram Dance Festival, 47
Manipuri style, 46
Manora style (Malaysia), 52
Manora style (Thailand), 48
Maori, 32, 39, 40
Maori dance troupes, 39
Maori influences on New Zealand, 40
Mehndi, Daler, 42, 50
the middle class and, 41
Minzu Wudao [national/ethnic dance] Propagation Movement, 32
modern, in Korea, 36–37
Modhera Dance Festival, 44
Mua Chay Cay (plow dance; Vietnam), 52
Mua Luc Cung (dance of six offerings; Vietnam), 52
Mua Phy Thuy (sorcerer's dance; Vietnam), 52
music video industry and, 41
in Myanmar, 47–48, 51
nationalist movements and, 32
National Khmer Classical Ballet Troupe, 49
Natyanjali Festival (Chidambaram), 47
in New Zealand, 39–40
in North Korea, 37
Odissi form of, 44
in Okinawa, 35, 36
The Other Festival, 47
Pattadackal Dance Festival, 47
The Peony Pavilion and, 34
politics and, 36
ragas and, 43
recent dance crazes in Japan, 36
The Red Detachment of Women, 34
Reddy, Raja and Radha, 46
retro movement, 35
rugby matches and, 39
Seoul International Dance Festival, 37
Seung-hee, Choi, 36–37
shin buyō movement, 35
shinmuyong [new dance] movement (Korea), 36
Shi-zheng, Chen, 34
Shizuki, Fujikage (Fujima Shizue), 35
in South and Southeast Asia, 40–43
in South Korea, 37
stag dance (*Trott*) in Cambodia, 51
street-dance and street-dance competitions, 32
Swapnasundari, 46
Taj Mahotsav, 44
Tatsumi, Hijikata, 32
Te Matatini National Festival, 39
in Thailand, 48
Tjapukai Aboriginal Cultural Park, 38
tourism and Aboriginal, 38
tourism and contemporary, 42
tourism and Indonesian, 50
transnational dance trends, 32
urban professionals and, 41
in Vietnam, 52
the *Wayang Topeng* form, 49
Western popular music and, 41
The White-Haired Girl, 34
women in Japanese, 35
World Wide Web and Australian, 38–39
World Wide Web and spread of dance crazes, 32–33
yangge song-dances, 34
Zat Pwe form, 47–48
Daratista, Inul, 218

377

INDEX

Den Xiaoping
    and Chinese fashions, 62
    reforms of, 16
De Silva, Sugathapala, 185
Devi, Mahasweta, 177, 179
Djarot, Eros, 121
Drama
    De Silva, Sugathapala, 185
    in Hindi, 184
    in India, 184–185
    in Indonesia, 185
    in Kannada, 184
    in Marathi, 184
    Rendra, W.S., 185
    in Sinhala, 185
    in Sri Lanka, 185
    Tanvir, Habib, 184
    Tendulkar, Vijay, 184
Dravidian peoples, influence of foods of, 144
Duangjan, Pompuang, 216
Dusty, Slim, 210

East Asia
    dance in, 31
    overview of food in, 127–128
    overview of literature in, 161–162
    overview of theater in, 313–315
East Timor, emergence of, xxii
Edison, Thomas Alva, 214
Electronic media (including radio, television, and computers). *For computer games, see also* Toys, games, and pastimes
    AIR (All India Radio), 275–276
    all news channels, 276
    amateur ("Ham") radio, 261, 262
    AM radio, 259
    annual fees (tax) for receivers, 264
    Asian resistance to broadcasting, 260
    audiences for Malaysian, 289–290
    in Australia, 269
    in Bangladesh, 281–282
    the BBC and broadcasting in India, 275
    BBC influence on early Asian broadcasting, 262
    Beijing Television, 265
    Bollywood cinema and TV programming, 279
    Bollywood style daytime serials, 277
    the British Forces Broadcasting Service and Nepalese, 280
    broadcasting equipment illegal in China, 261
    broadcasting liberalization in India, 276, 277
    broadcasting liberalization in Pakistan, 274
    cable radio, 290
    cable television, 277, 285–286, 287, 288, 293
    censorship and, 262, 285–286
    Chandra, Subhash, 277
    in China, 265–266, 269
    Chinese communist Party and broadcasting, 261
    colonial control and radio in Malaysia, 289
    colonial control and radio in Singapore, 290
    commercial radio, 273
    computer and video games in Japan, 153
    computer and video games in New Zealand, 157
    conglomerates, media, 270
    control of, in post-World War II Japan, 268–269
    the Cultural Revolution and TV, 265
    digital television, 282
    Doordarshan, 276–278
    the Dutch and early broadcasting in Indonesia, 291
    DXing, 265
    early Asian radio broadcasting, 260
    economic liberalization and, in Vietnam, 287
    education and early broadcasting, 262
    for expatriate audiences, 273
    Extra Terrestrial Television, 284
    fixed dial radio receivers, 267
    foreign ownership concerns, 270–271
    freedom of the press and, 285
    gisaeng performers and radio, 263
    globalization and broadcasting, 276–277
    globalization and program distribution, 270
    government control of broadcasting, 260, 261, 263, 265, 266, 267, 269, 276, 283, 285, 287, 288, 289, 290, 292
    government shutdown of, 287
    Gowen, Robert F., 261
    Hong Kong and radio broadcasting, 261–263
    Hong Kong and television, 266
    the Hong Kong Telegraph and first radio station in Hong Kong, 262
    in India, 275–279
    in Indonesia, 291–293
    influence of *Dae Jang Geum* TV drama

INDEX

on fashion, 67
the Internet and broadcasting in Malaysia, 290
the Internet and music, 211
the Internet and periodical publishing, 230
Internet games, in China, 153
Internet games, in Japan, 153
jamming, 265
Japan and Bangladeshi, 281
Japanese occupation and, 289
JOAK radio, 263
JODK radio, 263
juvenile development and, 271
liberalization of programming control in Indonesia, 292
the Korean Wave, popularity of, 270
in Malaysia, 289–290
Mao Zedong [Tse-tung] and broadcasting, 261, 269
Marcos, Ferdinand, and Philippine broadcasting, 287, 288
mass media and play in New Zealand, 157
media deregulation and ownership of, 270
Mitchell, D. G.; "Toots," 264
MTV influences, 259, 270
Murdoch, Rupert, and broadcast ownership, 269–270
in Nepal, 279–281
news dispatches and telegraph service, 261
in New Zealand, 264
NHK national broadcasting service (Japan), 263
in North Korea, 266–267
in Oceania, 265
for overseas audiences, 272, 291
pay TV, 274
in Pakistan, 272–275
in the Philippines, 287–289
politics and, 287, 288
"pop" cultures and, 259–260
"pop" music and, 270
portable radios, 269
private FM stations, 276, 281, 283, 285
private ownership versus state monopolies, 273
private sector Indian TV, 278
private sector Indonesian, 292
private sector Nepalese, 280–281
private sector Pakistani, 273–274

private sector Sri Lankan, 284
privatization of, 282, 285, 289, 291
propaganda and, 265, 267, 268, 269, 284, 286
The Radio Atlas of the World, 259
radio, early Asian interest in, 259
"radio golf," 259
Radio Hong Kong, 262
radio in Australia, 264
radio in Bangladesh, 281
radio in China, 260–261
radio in India, 275–276
radio in Indonesia, 291–292
radio in Japan, 263
radio in Korea, 263–264
radio in Malaysia, 289
radio in Nepal, 279–281
radio in New Zealand, 264–265
radio in the Philippines, 287–288
radio in Singapore, 290
radio in Sri Lanka, 282–283
radio in Taiwan, 264
radio in Thailand, 284–285
radio in Vietnam, 286
Radio Pakistan, 272–274
Robertson, Charles H., 261
role of broadcasting in 1920s, 262
rural services, 283
satellite television, 269, 274, 278, 280, 282, 285, 287, 290, 291
in Singapore, 290–291
in Shanghai, 261
Shanghai and early Asian broadcasting, 260
Shen Bao newspaper and radio broadcasting in China, 260–261
shortwave radio, 259, 265, 282–283
in South Asia, 271–272
in South Korea, 267
Sports Service in Sri Lanka, 283
in Sri Lanka, 282–284
state ownership of media, 280, 282
subscription services, 287, 290, 293
Takayanagi, Kenjiro, 266
television and manga in Japan, 165
television in Australia, 267–268
television in Bangladesh, 281–282
television in India, 276–279
television in Indonesia, 292–293
television in Japan, 266
television in Malaysia, 289–290
television in Nepal, 280–281
television in New Zealand, 268

Index

Electronic media (*continued*)
- television in North Korea, 267
- television in Pakistan, 274–275
- television in the Philippines, 288–289
- television in Singapore, 291
- television in Sri Lanka, 283–284
- television in Taiwan, 266
- television in Thailand, 285–286
- television in Vietnam, 286–287
- television violence concerns, 271
- Tokyo Rose, 268–269
- transistors and, 269
- transnational television, 288–289, 293
- unlicensed, 292
- U.S. military and broadcasting in Vietnam, 286
- in Vietnam, 286–287
- Voice of the Tigers service, 283
- war and broadcasting in Bangladesh, 281
- Western influences on, 259, 263
- as Western technology, 259
- women and broadcasting, 262
- the Zee Network, 277, 278

Embroidery, 78

Fahey, Jacqueline, 22
Faiman, Peter, 103
Fashion and appearance. *See also* Clothing; Cosmetics; Obesity; Textiles
- Asian fashion designers and world markets, 75–76
- in Australia, 67–69
- "Australian Fashion Week" magazine, 68
- beauty pageants and, 71–72
- body art, 83
- body image and, in China, 61
- body image in Oceania, 68
- body images and, 70–72
- body piercing, 83
- Bollywood films and, 71, 72
- brand names and, 66–67
- Buddhism and, 74
- burkas and, 73
- casual wear in Japan, 65
- Changan (now Xian) as fashion center, 59
- changing economies and, 70
- in China, 59–63
- in China after death of Mao, 62
- Chinese exports and Japanese, 63
- class differences and, 70–71
- cosmetics use in China, 61, 62, 63
- cultures and, 85
- designers in China, 62, 63
- for diaspora communities, 76–77
- disposable income and, in China, 61
- diversified fashion scene in Australia and New Zealand, 67
- early fashion influences, 60
- among ethnic minorities in Japan, 65
- export market for, 60–61
- foreign influences and, 65, 66
- Fraser Crowe brand and, 69
- globalization and changing styles, 60
- governmental controls and, 73–74
- grooming of head and facial hair, 81
- *hanboks*, 66, 67
- hat and caps, 81
- haute couture market, 76
- "Hello Kitty" products, 64
- hybrid standards of judgment and, 71
- indigenous garments, 79–80, 82
- indigenous versus international aesthetic norms and, 70–71
- influence of *Dae Jang Geum* TV drama on, 67
- influence of films on, 61–62
- international beauty pageants, 63
- international exchanges and, 70
- Islam (Sharia) law and, 73
- in Japan, 60, 63–65
- Japanese influence on Korean, 66
- Japanese spending on, 64
- jewelry, 83
- the kimono, 63
- the Korean Wave, 66, 67
- magazines about, in China, 62
- male standards and, 72
- Mao-style suits, 62
- Mao Zedong [Tse-tung] and, 62
- the *meinu jingji* (beauty economy) in China, 63
- minorities in China and fashions, 63
- Miss Universe pageant, 71–72
- Miss World beauty pageant, 72
- mixed post-colonial cultures and, 72–73
- "Modern Girl" image in China, 61
- "Modern Girl" image in Japan, 64
- "Modern Girl" image in South Korea, 66
- in New Zealand, 67–69
- in North Korea, 65
- obesity and, 61, 66, 68
- during premodern period, 59
- poverty and, 70
- the *qipao* (*cheung sam*), 61–62
- religion and, 73–74
- in Shanghai during 1930s, 61

INDEX

Sikhs and grooming, 81
the Silk Road and, 59–60
in South Korea, 66–67
stratification of market for, in China, 63
synthetic fabrics and, 73
tattoos, 83
textiles and, 77–79
totalitarian political regimes and, 74
tourism and, 68–69
turbans, 81
the "veil" and, 73
Western fashion trends, 60, 72–74
Western influences on, 62, 64–65
Westernization of Japanese dress, 64–65
as a Western phenomenon, 59
Fiji, and tourism, 346
Film(s)
adaptations of "scar literature" in China, 93
and adapting to the post–World War II world, 91
Alam Ara, 106
animation (*animé*) and popular Japanese, 100, 164
Armstrong, Gillian, 104
art cinema in Sri Lanka, 116
in Australia, 103–104
avant-garde Korean, 103
in Bangladesh, 113–114
based on popular literature, 177
Bayan Ko, 118
Bernal, Ishmael, 118–119
blockbuster potential of Korean, 102
Boat People, 95
Bollywood cinema style, 111–112
Bollywood films and fashions, 71, 72
Bollywood influence, 114
Bollywood, origin of term, 111
Brocka, Lino, 118
The Brotherhood of War, 102
Campion, Jane, 104–105
Caro, Niki, 104
censorship and Pakistani, 113
censorship of Bangladeshi, 113
censorship of South Korean, 101
Chan, Jackie, 95
Chan, Peter, 96
Chen Kaige, 93
in China, 93–94
Chinese influences on Indonesian, 120
Chinese opera genre, 94
Chow, Stephen, 96
Chungking Express, 96
Chunhyang, 102
A City of Sadness, 97
civil war and films in Sri Lanka, 116
comedy, 95, 96
communism and, 93
Crocodile Dundee, 103
Crouching Tiger, Hidden Dragon, 95, 98
culture and, 91, 108
Devadas, 106, 108
"Dhakai cinema," 113
distinctive Indian popular, 106, 108
Dixit, Madhuri, and hybrid fashions, 71
Djarot, Eros, 121
Dragon Gate Inn, 94–95
Dutch colonial rule and film in Indonesia, 120
early filming in India, 106
early films in Malaysia, 119
early films in Thailand, 117
early films in the Philippines, 118
Faiman, Peter, 103
family dynasties in Indian, 111
Farewell My Concubine, 93
first feature film made in South India, 106
first sound film in India, 106
foreign film institutes and, 95
gangster genre (Japanese), 101
Ghatak, Ritwik, 108, 110
Gibson, Mel, 104
globalization and Bangladeshi, 114
globalization and Thai, 117
global transactions and production of, 92
Godzilla series, 100
as government propaganda, 92, 93, 102
Hafsham, Othman, 119–120
Hindi, 108
history of, in Indonesia, 120–121
Hogan, Paul, 103
Hollywood musicals and Indian, 110
Hollywood remakes of Japanese, 99, 100
Hollywood remakes of Korean, 101
Hollywood standards and, 92
Hollywood success of Ang Lee, 98
Honda, Ishiro, 100
in Hong Kong, 92, 94–96
in Hong Kong after turnover, 95–96
Hou Hsiao-hsien, 97–98
horror films (Japanese), 100
Hui, Ann, 95
hybrid standards of appearance and, 71
Im Kwon-taek, 102
in India, 106–112, 115

381

Index

Film(s) (*continued*)
- Indian "classics" (1950–1975), 107
- Indian cultural heritage and film, 110
- Indian "greats" (1976–2006), 109
- Indian influences on Pakistani, 112, 113
- Indian influences on Sri Lankan, 116
- Indian market for, 115
- in Indonesia, 120–121
- influence of "Hello Kitty" cartoons, 64
- influence of Indian on American and European, 110
- influence of *The Piano* on fashions, 68
- influence on fashions, 61–62
- influences on Philippine, 118
- international co-productions, 113
- international film festivals and, 92
- international response to Bangladeshi, 114
- Ismail, Usmar, 120
- Jackson, Peter, 104, 105
- in Japan, 99–101
- Japanese New Wave, 100
- Jaywant-Samarth-Behl-Mukherjee-Devgan clan and, 111
- joint productions, 92
- *Kadavunu Poronduva*, 114
- Kang Je-gyu, 102
- Kapoor family and Indian, 111
- Kapoor, Raj, 108
- Karya, Teguh, 121
- *Katar Singh*, 112
- Khan, Aamir, 72
- in Korea, 101–103
- kung fu genre, 94
- Kurosawa, Akira, 99
- Lai, Stan, 97
- *Lakhon Mein Ek*, 112
- Lee, Ang, 95, 98–99
- Lee, Bruce, 94–95
- *Long March Silwangi*, 120
- *The Lord of the Rings* and tourism in New Zealand, 68
- *The Lord of the Rings* trilogy, 104, 105
- *Lost in Translation* and changing Japanese fashions, 65
- Luhrmann, Baz, 104
- Lumière brothers and, 106
- *Mad Max* series, 104
- in Malaysia, 119–120
- *Mandala*, 102
- manga comics and film, 100, 165
- market for, in Indonesia, 120
- martial arts and, 94–95
- *Maula Jat*, 112
- media censorship and underground production of, 94
- melodrama genre, 96–97, 114
- Middle Cinema (India), 110
- Miller, George, 104
- Minh, Dang Nhat, 118
- Miyazaki, Hayao, 100
- Mizoguchi, Kenji, 99–100
- modernization and Indian, 110
- *In the Mood for Love* and fashions, 61
- the Mukherjee family and Indian, 111
- multilingual tradition in Indian, 106
- *Moulin Rouge*, 104
- in Mumbai (Bombay), 106
- musical theater heritage in India and, 110
- music for Hindi, 221–222
- music videos and Indian, 110
- mythological film genre, 106
- national cinemas, 92
- and nation building, 92
- nativist films, 97
- new genres for, 92
- new genres in Pakistani, 112–113
- New (Filipina) Cinema, 119
- New Indian Cinema, 110
- New Korean Cinema, 102
- in New Zealand, 104–105
- Noorjahan, 112
- ocker comedy genre, 103
- overview of film industry in South and Southeast Asia, 105
- Ozu, Yasujiro, 100
- in Pakistan, 112–113
- Park Chan-wook, 102
- Parsi theater companies and Indian, 110
- Pasha, Anwar Kamal, 112
- *Pather Panchali*, 108
- *Penarek Becak*, 119
- Peries, Lester James, 114, 115–116
- Phalke, Dhundiraj Govind, 106
- in the Philippines, 118–119
- *The Piano*, 104
- *Picnic at Hanging Rock*, 103
- popular and art films in Sri Lanka, 114–117
- as propaganda in Vietnam, 118
- Rahi, Sultan, 112
- *Raise the Red Lantern*, 94
- *Raja Harishcandra*, 106
- Ramlee, P., 119
- *Rashomon*, 99
- Ray, Satyajit, 108
- rebirth of Korean under Lee Seung-man, 101

Rekhava, 115
Ringu, 100
sci-fi/action thriller genre, 104
Seven Samurai, 99
Shanghai and early production of, 93
Shaolin Soccer, 96
the Shaw Brothers and Hong Kong, 94
Shiri, 102
Sholay, 110
silent films (Korean), 101
Soldadu Unnahe, 116
in South Korea, 101–103
Spirited Away, 100
in Sri Lanka, 114–117
studio system in Hong Kong, 95
sword-fighting genre, 94
Taiwanese New Cinema, 97, 98
in Taiwan (Republic of China), 96–99
television and, in South Korea, 102
in Thailand, 117
Throne of Blood, 99
Tjoet Nja dhien, 121
the triad action genre, 95
Tsai Ming-liang, 98
Tsui Hark, 95
underground productions of, in China, 94
urbanization and Indian, 108
in Vietnam, 117–118
The Wedding Bouquet, 98
Weir, Peter, 103–104
Western professionalism and development of, 91–92
The Whale Rider, 104
The Whale Rider and dance, 40
Wong Kar-wai, 96
Woo, John, 95
Zhang Yimou, 93–94
Zhang Ziyi, 98

Food and foodways
    afternoon tea custom, 137
    alcoholic beverages and, 129, 133, 135
    American fast food chains, 127, 129, 131, 134, 137, 145–146
    American influences on Australian and New Zealand, 137
    American influences on South Korean, 134
    Asian identity issues and, 128
    in Australia, 135–137
    in Bangkok, 139–140
    barbequed meat (in South Korea), 133
    beer, 133, 135
    Beijing cuisine, 128
    British influence on, in Australia and New Zealand, 135–136
    buffalo milk products, 144
    canned green tea, 133
    carbonated beverages, 133
    caste restrictions and, 145
    changing diets in Japan, 64
    in China, 128–130
    Chinese influences on other national cuisines, 127
    Chinese Restaurant Syndrome, 130
    coconut in Thai cuisine, 143
    coffee-drinking in Asia, 128
    Colombo (Sri Lanka) cuisine, 139
    cooking methods, North Indian cuisine, 141, 142
    cooking methods, Thai cuisine, 143
    curry, 141
    dairy products, 144
    diet modifications during Ramadan, 145
    dining out, 131, 138–141
    of Dravidian peoples, 144
    economic development and diets, 135
    economic influences on food, 127–128, 133
    ethnicity and, 144–145
    flatbreads, 141
    Fujian cuisine, 128
    Gangzhou cuisine, 128
    ghee (clarified butter), 141
    globalization and, 145–146
    the Great Leap Famine (China, 1959–1961), 129
    herbal tea trends, 129
    Hindu dietary laws and, 145
    Hindu niche hotels, 145
    holiday foods in Korea, 134
    in Hong Kong, 129
    influence of Thai cuisine on other cuisines, 144
    Islam and, 145
    among the Jains, 145
    in Jakarta, 140
    in Japan, 131–133
    Japanese influences on Taiwanese cuisine, 130
    kaiseki cuisine (Japan), 132
    in Karachi, 138
    kimch'i (pickled vegetables), 133
    Korean resistance to dietary globalization, 135
    Korean royal cuisine, 134

INDEX

Food and foodways (*continued*)
    Korean-style barbeque in Japan, 131
    in Kuala Lumpur, 140
    in Lahore, 138
    makkōli, 135
    meat consumption in South Korea, 133
    meats in North Indian cuisine, 141–142
    the media and Japanese, 132
    monosodium glutamate (MSG) usage, 130
    in New Delhi, 139
    and New Year's celebrations (Japan), 133
    in New Zealand, 135–137
    noodles, 134, 136
    in Northeast Asia region, 127
    North Indian cuisine, 141–142
    Northwest Frontier (India) cuisine, 139
    Nyonya cuisine, 140
    obento, 131
    obesity and diets in South Korea, 66
    and obesity in China, 61
    in Pakistan, 138
    penal colony diets and Australian, 136
    pho, 143
    porich'a (scorched-rice tea), 135
    prohibition on pork consumption, 145
    religion and, 145–146
    religious rituals and Japanese, 132–133
    in Republic of China (Taiwan), 130
    rice, 131, 144
    rural versus urban, 129
    sake, 133
    seasonings in North Indian cuisine, 141
    seasonings in South Korea, 133
    seasonings in Thai cuisine, 143
    sheep grazing and Australian, 136–137
    Sichuan cuisine, 128
    side dishes, 131, 134
    in Singapore, 140
    snacks, 135
    soju, 135
    in South Korea, 128, 133–135
    soybean paste, 131, 133
    soybeans, 144
    soy sauce, 131, 133
    Starbucks and coffee consumption, 128
    stir-fries, 131
    street food, 140–141
    the Taejanggum TV series and, 134
    the tea ceremony (Japan), 132
    tea consumption in Korea, 135
    Thai cuisine, 142–144
    urban eating patterns, 138–141
    vegetables and vegetarian dishes in North Indian cuisine, 142
    vegetarianism, 145
    Vietnamese restaurants abroad, 143
    Wagamama dining, 136
    Western influences on Japanese, 131
    wheat, 144
    Zen influences on Japanese, 132
    Zhejiang cuisine, 128
Football (European). *See also* Sports
    Australian Rules, 305
    Cha Bum-Kun, 303
    in Japan, 301
    in New Zealand, 306
    replacing cuju in China, 152
    in South Korea, 303–304
Formosa. *See* China, Republic of
Fox, Mem, 169–170
French Polynesia and tourism, 346–347

Games. *See* Toys, games, and pastimes
Gandhi, Mahatma, and the dhoti, 79
Gao Xingjian, 318
Garment industry. *See* Clothing
Ghalib (Mirza Asadullah Khan), 174
Gibson, Mel, 104
Gordon, Gaelyn, 171
Gowen, Robert F., 261
The Gramaphone Company, 214
Guan Hanqing, 316
Gujral, Satish, 26
Gu Wenda, 17

Hafsham, Othman, 119–120
Harris, Rolf, 209
Hibari, Misora, 205
Hicky, James Augustus, 239
Hinduism, overview of, 321
Hogan, Paul, 103
Hokusai, Katsushika, 18
Honda, Ishiro, 100
Hong Kong
    film genres from, 94
    film industry in, 92, 94–96
    food in, 129
    Hollywood remakes of films from, 96
    the Hong Kong-Zhuhai-Macau Bridge, 340
    kung fu films, 94
    marriage and sexual relationships in, 192–193
    periodicals in, 232–233
    radio in, 261–263

INDEX

    the Shaw Brothers and film in, 94
    Sino-Japanese War and periodicals in, 232
    television in, 266
    tourism and, 339–340
    transportation and, 340
    triad-action genre films, 95
    turnover to China and films in, 95–96
    turnover to China and food in, 129
Hong Sin-cha, 37
Hou Hsiao-hsien, 97
Hsu Chen-ya, 164
Hui, Ann, 95
Hussain, M. F., 25–26, 71
Hussey, Henry H., 3
Hyder, Qurratulain, 176

Im Kwon-taek, 102
India
    Bollywood films and contemporary dance in, 41
    broadcasting in, 275–279
    the caste system in literature, 175
    Chandra, Subhash, and broadcasting, 277
    classical dance-drama in, 46–47
    classical dance in, 43–45
    "classic" films of (1950–1975), 107
    Dalits ("untouchables"), 175
    dance festivals in, 44, 47
    diversity of periodicals in, 243–244
    ethnic minorities and folk dance in, 51
    family dynasties in film industry in, 111
    film industry in, 106–112
    folk dance in, 50–51
    "great" films of (1976–2006), 109
    Hinduism and theater in, 326–328
    historic sites in, 352
    indigenous theater in, 326–328
    languages and periodicals in, 243
    leading role of fashion industry in, 76
    modern urban theater in, 322–324
    multilingualism in, xxv–xxvi
    the partition and literature, 173–175, 181
    periodicals in, 241, 243–245
    popular historic sites in, 352
    radio in, 275–276
    television in, 276–279
    theater in, 322–324, 326–328
    themes in literature of, 173–175
    tourism and, 351, 352
Indigenous Australians. *See* Aboriginal peoples
Indonesia
    Bali, 45
    broadcasting in, 291–293
    classical dance in, 45–46, 49–50
    Dutch colonial rule and broadcasting in, 291
    Dutch colonial rule and film in, 120
    Dutch East Indian Company and, 252
    efforts to unify, 120
    ethnic diversity of, 120
    film in, 120–121
    folk dance in, 52–53
    freedom of the press and "Guided Democracy" in, 252
    Hindu influences on theater in, 332
    indigenous theater in, 332–334
    Japanese occupation and film in, 120
    Java, 45, 52, 332–334
    languages in, 251
    music in, 217–218
    periodicals in, 251–252
    radio in, 291–293
    Suharto regime and broadcasting in, 292
    Suharto regime and Pramoedya Ananta Toer, 179
    television in, 292–293
    theater in, 325–326
    transportation infrastructure in, 357
Inoue, Yosui, 206
Iran, first stitched garments from, 79
Ismail, Usmar, 120

Jackson, Peter, 104, 105
Japan
    American influence on toys and games in, 153
    ancient settlement of, 17
    animé film style, 164
    architecture in, 5–6
    art in, 17–19
    birth rate declines and demographics, 193
    and China, 17–18, 153
    climate of, 5
    comics in, 164–166
    dance in, 34–36
    demographics, 17
    fashion designers in, 64
    "father of television," 266
    film and manga in, 165
    film in, 99–101
    first film studios in, 99
    first magazine in, 228
    food in, 131–133
    influence of Chinese culture in, 17–18, 153
    influence on Korean dance, 36

385

INDEX

Japan (*continued*)
- judo, 300
- *kabuki* dances, 34–35
- karaoke origin in, 207
- literature in, 164–166
- manga, 19, 164–166
- marriage and sexual relationships in, 193–196
- Meji Restoration and art in, 18
- the Modern Transportation Museum, 342
- music in, 205–207
- periodicals in, 228, 234–236
- recent dance crazes in, 36
- the Samurai, 18
- sports in, 300–302
- sumo wrestling, 300
- television in, 266
- textile design and manufacture after World War II, 76
- theater in, 318–319
- tourism and, 342–343
- toys, games, and pastimes in, 153–154
- transportation in, 342
- Westernization in, 18
- woodblock art heritage, 18
- World War II period and dance in, 35
- World War II period and film in, 99
- World War II period and literature in, 165
- Zen influences on theater in, 319

Java. *See also* Indonesia
- ancient language (Kawi) of, 49
- *Bahasa* language and dance-opera, 49
- dance in, 45, 49
- folk dance in, 52
- indigenous theater in, 332–334

Jinyong (Zha Lianyong, Louis Cha), 164
Joaquin, Nick, 178, 179, 181

Kang Je-gyu, 102
Kapoor, Raj, 108
Karnad, Girish, 177
Karya, Teguh, 121
Khakhar, Bhupen, 26
Khan, Aamir, 72
Komu, Riyas, 27
Korea. *See also* North Korea; South Korea
- architecture in, 6–8
- art in, 19–20
- Chinese cultural influences in, 19, 36
- climate in, 6–7
- dance in, 36–37
- film in, 101
- first newspaper in, 228
- history of, 19
- Japanese occupation and film in, 101
- Japanese occupation and literature in, 167
- Japanese occupation and periodicals in, 236
- Japanese occupation of, 7, 36
- Korean War, 19
- Korean War and architecture in, 7
- Korean War and dance in, 37
- literature in, 166–168
- marriage and sexual relationships in, 197–198
- outside influences on toys and games in, 154
- periodicals in, 228, 236–237
- radio in, 263–264
- silent films in, 101
- theater in, 320
- toys, games, and pastimes in, 154–155
- Western architecture in, 7

Kumar, Ram, 27
Kurosawa, Akira, 99

Laila, Runa, 221
Lai, Stan, 97
Laos
- communism in, 248
- languages in, 248
- periodicals in, 248

Lee, Ang, 95, 98–99
Lim, Shirley Geok-lin, 184
Literature. *See also* Drama; Poetry
- *Aag ka Darya* (*River of Fire*), 176
- Abbas, Khwaja Ahmad, 177
- adaptations of canonical novels in China, 163
- Ahmad, Shahnon, 177, 179, 181
- Anand, Mulk Raj, 176, 178
- Anglophone traditions, 162, 168
- *Anil's Ghost*, 175
- *The Asian Saga*, 168
- in Australia, 168–170
- in Bengali, 176, 180
- *Bhookh* (*Hunger*), 176
- blogs and, 162
- Bond, Ruskin, 180
- *Buru Quartet*, 173, 179
- business genre, 167
- Carey, Peter, 168
- the caste system in, 175
- celebrating indigenous cultures, 175

changing audiences for manga, 165
Chatterjee, Saratchandra, 177
Chauncey, Nan, 169
for children, 163, 168–170, 171
for children, first Australian, 169
in China, 162–164
Chinese influences on Korean and Japanese, 161
chuanqi dramas, 163
Clavell, James, 168
comics, 164–166, 167–168
common themes in, 173–175
Daguio, Amador, 181
decolonialization theme, 173–174
detective fiction, 170
Devi, Mahasweta, 177, 179
Dragon Ball, 166
Dream of Red Mansions, 163
early Australian, for children, 169
familial narratives, 173
family and home as metaphors, 173
"feminist" writers, 175, 181
film adaptations of popular, 177
Fox, Mem, 169–170
genres within manga, 165–166
Ghalib (Mirza Asadullah Khan), 174
Ghost in the Shell, 166
global marketing and, 162, 167
Gordon, Gaelyn, 171
Harry Potter series, 162
in Hindi, 175–176, 180
historical fiction in New Zealand, 171
Hsu Chen-ya, 164
hybrid literary traditions, 162
Hyder, Qurratulain, 176
idealistic realism, 175–176
Indian-English literature, 176–177
Indian women writers, 176
indigenous languages and, 172
international influence of manga, 165–166
the Internet and changing ideas of, 161
Jade Pear Spirit, 164
in Japan, 164–166
Jinyong (Zha Lianyong, Louis Cha), 164
Joaquin, Nick, 178, 179, 181
Journey to the West, 161, 163
kamishibqi (picture card shows), 165
Karnad, Girish, 177
King Rat, 168
in Korea, 166–168
kunqu operatic style and, 163
literary traditions and popular consciousness, 161

Littleton, Edith, 170
Mahy, Margaret, 171
"The Management of Grief," 173
for Maori children, 171
Maori depicted in, 171
in Malaysia, 181
manga, 164–166, 235
manhwa, 167–168
Mann, Philip, 171
Marsh, Ngaio, 170
the martial arts genre, 164
Masters of Rome, 168
the May Fourth Movement, 164
McCullough, Colleen, 168
Midnight's Children, 178
Morrissey, Di, 168
A Mother's Offering to Her Children, 169
Mukherjee, Bharati, 173
multilingualism and, 172–173
Muzi Mei, 162
mystery genre, 170
Nagar, Amritlal, 176
Nai Kahani (new short story) movement, 180
Narayan, R. K., 176, 178
national identity and struggle theme in, 173
in Nepal, 180
in New Zealand, 170–171
the novel form, 175–176, 178
Ondaatje, Michael, 175
overview of, in South and Southeast Asia, 173
in Pakistan, 181
Peel, Colin, 170
Peony Pavilion, 163
picture books, 171
pornographic manga, 165
Premchand, Munshi (Dhanpat Rai Shrivastava), 174, 175–176
the publishing industry and, in Korea, 167
Ramanujan, A. K., 173
Rao, Raja, 176, 178
"reformist" writers, 175
robots in Japanese manga, 165
romance novels, 164, 170
The Romance of the Three Kingdoms, 161, 163
Rowling, J. K., 162
Rushdie, Salman, 178
Sailor Moon, 166
"School of Mandarin Ducks and Butterflies," 164

Index

Literature (*continued*)
    science fiction genre, 171
    self-help genre, 167
    Sexual Diary of a Young Chinese Woman on the Internet (blog), 162
    Shirow, Masamune, 166
    Shogun, 168
    short stories, 180
    "Small-Scale Reflections of a Great House," 173
    in South Korea, 167–168
    Summers, Essie, 170
    Tagore, Rabindranath (Gurudev), 174, 180
    Takeuchi, Naoko, 166
    Tang Xianzu, 163
    Tendulkar, Vijay, 177
    themes in, 173–175
    Thiep, Nguyen Huy, 182
    Thomas, Paul, 171
    The Thorn Birds, 168
    thriller novels, 170
    Toer, Pramoedya Ananta, 173, 178, 179
    Toriyama, Akira, 166
    traditional dramas and contemporary literature in China, 163
    Turner, Ethel, 169
    "untouchables" (Dalits) and, 175
    Upadhyay, Samrat, 180
    in Urdu, 175–176
    Verma, Nirmal, 176
    in Vietnam, 181–182
    White, Patrick, 168
Littleton, Edith, 170
Liu Kuo-Sung, 17
Lomu, Jonah, 306
Luhrmann, Baz, 104
Lu Xun, 15

Macau, tourism and, 340
Malaysia
    broadcasting in, 289–290
    folk dance in, 52
    immigration and culture in, 216
    indigenous theater in, 331–332
    languages in, 250
    literature in, 181
    music in, 216–217
    periodicals in, 242, 250–251
    radio in, 289
    television in, 289–290
    transportation infrastructure in, 356
Manchu Dynasty (China). *See* China, Qing Dynasty

Mann, Philip, 171
Maori people
    artistic traditions, 21
    crafts, 21
    dance and rugby matches, 39
    dance forms preservation, 32
    dance troupes, 39
    popularity of dance of, 40
    and popular music in New Zealand, 210–211
    and settling of New Zealand, 151
    Te Matatini National Festival, 39
    toys and games among, 157
Mao Zedong [Tse-tung]
    and broadcasting, 261
    and Chinese art, 15
    collectibles related to, 16
    and fashions, 62
Marcos, Ferdinand, and Philippine broadcasting, 287, 288
Marriage and sexual relationships
    abortions, 190, 196, 198, 199, 200
    abortions, sex selective, 192
    arranged marriages, 190, 191–192
    in Australia, 198–200
    bigamy, 193
    birth rate decline, 193
    Buddhism and, 194
    changing attitudes toward sexual relationships, 191
    child bearing incentives, 200
    childcare and leave policies in Japan, 193–194
    child custody (Japan), 195
    in China, 190–192
    Christianity and, 198–199
    cohabitation, 199
    collectivism and, 200
    communism and, in China, 191
    concubines, 192
    Confucian traditions and, 189, 190, 194, 197, 198
    consumerism and, 192
    the Cultural Revolution (in China) and, 190
    dating, 191
    divorce, 191, 193, 194–195, 197, 199
    educational pressures and, 193, 196, 197
    entertainment visas, 196
    European traditions and, 189
    extramarital relationships, 191
    family planning, 190, 196
    homosexuality, 191, 195, 198, 199

Index

in Hong Kong, 192–193
intermarriage, 199–200
in Japan, 193–196
in Korea, 197–198
late marriage, 190, 193, 194, 199
manga, 195
marriage laws, in China
matchmaking, 192
Mizuko Jizo figures, 196
in New Zealand, 198–200
one-child policy in China, 190
oyaji girls, 195–196
polygamy, 192
pornography, 193, 195
pornography, manga, 195
preference for male children in China, 190
premarital sex, 190, 191
prenatal sex determination, 192
prostitution, 196
in Republic of China, 192–193
same-sex unions, 199
the sex trade, 196
the sexual revolution (1970s), and, 189
the Shinto faith and, 194
single parents and single-parent families, 199, 200
"single" persons and, 197
in South Korea, 197–198
Taoism and, 194
teen pregnancy, 199
traditional culture and, 193, 194, 197–198
virginity issues, 190
visitation rights (Japan), 195
Western influences on, 191, 192–193, 194, 197, 200
Western influences on Asian, 189
young professional women and, in Japan, 195–196
Marsh, Ngaio, 170
Matsutoya, Yumi, 206
McCullough, Colleen, 168
Meads, Colin, 306
Mehndi, Daler, 42, 50
Mehta, Tyeb, 26
Menon, Anjolie, 27
Midnight Oil, 210
Miller, George, 104
Minh, Dang Nhat, 118
Mitchell, D. G.; "Toots," 264
Miyazaki, Hayao, 100
Mizoguchi, Kenji, 99–100
Mongolia
tourism and, 341
traditional nomadic lifestyles and, 341
transportation in, 341
Monosodium glutamate (MSG) usage and health, 130
Morimura Yasumasa, 19
Morrissey, Di, 168
Mui, Anita, 205
Mukherjee, Bharati, 173
Munakata Shiko, 18
Murdoch, Rupert, and broadcast ownership, 269–270
Music
Aboriginal performers and, 209, 210
AC/DC, 209
American domination of popular styles of, 212
American popular styles in Asia, 205–206
the Atlantics, 209
in Australia, 208–210
Bahasa language, 217
The Bee Gees, 209
Berliner, Emil, 214
bhangra, 221
Billy Thorpe & the Aztecs, 209
BoA, 208
in Brunei, 216–217
cai luong style, 215
in Cambodia, 215–216
Cantopop style, 204, 205
Carnatic classical, 213, 219–220
Chennai Dance and Music Festival, 47
Cheung, Leslie, 205
in China, 203–204
colonialism and, 212
Crowded House, 211
Cui Jian, 204
dangdut genre, 217–218
Daratista, Inul, 218
diaspora people and, 215
Duangjan, Pompuang, 216
Dusty, Slim, 210
early twentieth century Japanese, 205
early twentieth century popular, in Korea, 207
Edison, Thomas Alva, 214
Elephanta Music and Dance Festival, 44
for films, 213
folk traditions and, 221
foreign recordings of, 215–216
gamelan orchestras and dance, 45, 52
gangtai, 203
genres in Indonesian, 217–218
the *ghazal* poetry form and, 220–221

389

Index

Music (*continued*)
    ghazal vocalists, 221
    Gisaeng singers, 207
    government control of, 215
    The Gramaphone Company, 214
    hallyu ("Korean Wave"), 208
    the harmonium and, 213
    Harris, Rolf, 209
    Hibari, Misora, 205
    Hindi film, 221–222
    Hinduism and, 213
    Hindustani classical, 213, 219–220
    hip-hop, in New Zealand, 211
    hybrid nature of, 213
    illegal downloads of, 206
    in India, 213, 214
    indigenous ensemble traditions, 212
    in Indonesia, 217–218
    influence of Taiwanese on mainland Chinese, 203, 204
    Inoue, Yosui, 206
    instruments, Indian classical, 220
    Islam and, 213, 217, 218
    in Japan, 205–207
    Japanese domination of Korean (1930s), 207
    karaoke, 207
    the Khmer Rouge and music in Cambodia, 215
    Konark Music and Dance Festival, 44
    in Korea, 207–208
    the Korean War and, 207
    the "Korean Wave" (*hallyu*), 208
    K-pop, 208, 209
    Krakatau genre, 219
    kunqu operatic style, 163
    Laila, Runa, 221
    in Laos, 215–216
    Listen to My Heart album, 208
    liuxing style, 203
    Luktoong style, 216
    in Malaysia, 216–217
    and Malaysian indigenous theater, 332
    Mandopop style, 204
    Maori performers and, 210–211
    Matsutoya, Yumi, 206
    media promotion of local talent (Australia), 209
    merging of Aboriginal and contemporary, 209, 210
    Midnight Oil, 210
    MTV and popular, 212–213
    Mui, Anita, 205
    music industry in South Korea, 208
    music piracy, 204
    Mustapha, Sabah Habas (Colin Bass), 219
    in Myanmar, 215
    nasyid genre, 217
    Newton-John, Olivia, 209
    in New Zealand, 210–211
    nostalgia for the pre-Communist era, 216
    Nusrat Fateh Ali Khan, 221
    O'Keefe, Johnny "The Wild One," 208–209
    Orang asli ("original people") and Malay music, 217
    The Other Festival, 47
    overseas markets for Australian, 209–210
    the Peking [Beijing] Opera, 163, 164
    in the Philippines, 218
    Poi E, 40
    politics and, 216
    post-World War II Japanese, 205–206
    post-World War II Korean, 207
    Prime, Dalvanius, 40
    as propaganda, 215
    punk, 210
    the *raga*, 213
    Raihan, 217
    RAIN, 209
    regional genres in Malaysia, 217
    revolutionary operas, 164, 203
    rock, Australian, 208–209
    rock, Chinese, 204
    Rock N Roll on the New Long March album, 204
    rock, popularity of, 218
    Saijo, Hideki, 206
    Saing orchestras and *Zat Pwe* dance dramas, 48
    Sakamoto, Kyu, 205
    Sakon style, 216
    Shankar, Ravi, 220
    Siddi Goma, 221
    in Singapore, 216–217
    "slow rock" genre, 217
    SMAP, 206
    smuggled, 204
    sound recording, history of, 214
    in South and Southeast Asia, overview and history, 212–213
    in South Asia, 218–219
    in South Korea, 207–208
    Sufi folk, 221
    Taj Mahotsav, 44
    the *tala*, 213

INDEX

talent agencies and pop idols, 206, 207–208
Teng, Teresa, 203
in Thailand, 216
Tiananmen Square demonstration and, 204
Tie Me Kangaroo Down, Sport, 209
Urban Pasifika style, 211
in Urdu, 220–221
Vedic chants, ritual, 213
in Vietnam, 215–216
violins and, 213
Waltzing Matilda, 210
Western influences on, 205, 207–208, 212, 217, 218
White Snake, 163
World-beat fusion groups, 219
xibeifeng (northwest wind) style, 204
yaogun (rock), 204
the Yellow Magic Orchestra, 206
Yindi, Yothu, 210
Mustapha, Sabah Habas (Colin Bass), 219
Muzi Mei, 162
Myanmar
    classical dance in, 47–48
    dictatorship and culture in, 215
    folk dance in, 51
    indigenous theater in, 329
    languages in, 247
    music in, 215
    periodicals in, 247

Nagar, Amritlal, 176
Narayan, R. K., 176, 178
Nepal
    broadcasting in, 279–281
    languages in, 245
    Maoist insurgency and periodicals in, 245
    periodicals in, 242, 245
Newton-John, Olivia, 209
New Zealand
    architecture in, 8
    art in, 21–22
    birth-rates, 198
    British influence on food in, 135–136
    climate, 8
    dance in, 39–40
    demographics, 8
    education in, 198
    European influence on architecture in, 8
    European migration to, 198
    fashion and appearance in, 67–69
    first radio stations in, 264
    food in, 135–137
    Fraser Crowe fashions, 69
    geography, 21
    international sporting success, 306
    the Maori and traditional games, 157
    Maori arts and crafts, 21
    Maori dance, 39, 40
    Maori musicians, popular, 210–211
    marriage and sexual relationships in, 198–200
    music in, 210–211
    periodicals in, 238
    radio in, 264–265
    settling of, 151, 156–157
    sports in, 306–307
    television in, 268
    theater in, 320
    toys, games, and pastimes in, 156–157
Noorjahan, 112
North Korea. *See also* Korea
    architecture in, 7
    art in, 20
    communism and art in, 20
    communism and broadcasting in, 266–267
    dance in, 37
    fashion in, 65
    isolation of, 343
    lack of artistic freedom in, 20
    periodicals in, 236
    redesign of Pyongyang, 7
    television in, 266–267
    tourism and, 343
    transportation in, 343
Nusrat Fateh Ali Khan, 221

Obesity
    in Australia, 68
    in China, 61
    in Japan, 64
    in New Zealand, 68
    in South Korea, 66
Oceania
    art in, 20, 21
    dance heritage in, 31
    overview of literature in, 161–162
    overview of theater in, 313–315
    radio in, 265
    settling of, 151
    Stone Age (Neolithic) traditions in art, 20, 21
Okada, Kenzo, 18
O'Keefe, Johnny "The Wild One," 208–209

INDEX

Okinawa, dance in, 35, 36. *See also* Japan
Olympic Games
    and architecture in South Korea, 8
    in Australia, 305
    in Beijing (2008), 300
    and competitive sports, 299
    and South Korean road systems, 343
Ondaatje, Michael, 175
Orang asli ("original people") and Malay music, 217
Ozu, Yasujiro, 100

Padamsee, Akbar, 26
Pakistan
    broadcasting in, 272–275
    films in, 112–113
    historic sites in, 351
    languages in, 242
    the partition and literature of, 173–175, 181
    the partition and periodicals in, 242–243
    periodicals in, 242–243
    television in, 274–275
    themes in literature of, 173–175
    tourism and, 351
Pak Kil-yong, 7
Pak Tong-jin, 7
Papua New Guinea and tourism, 346
Park Chan-wook, 102
Pasha, Anwar Kamal, 112
Patel, Gieve, 27
Patwardhan, Sudhir, 26–27
Peel, Colin, 170
Pei, I. M., 4–5
Peries, Lester James, 114, 115–116
Periodicals
    adaptations of manga (comics), 236
    advertising and, 230, 233, 240–241, 244
    the Asian financial crisis and, 247
    audience relationships and, 229
    in Australia, 228, 237–238
    "Australian Fashion Week," 68
    Australia Women's Weekly, 237–238
    in Bangladesh, 245–246
    in Bengali, 246
    brand-making for publishing houses, 235
    the *Bulletin*, 238
    in Cambodia, 249
    censorship of, 232, 236, 240, 246
    in China, 230–232
    "China Magazine Square" project, 231
    Christian missionaries and, 228, 239
    colonial rule and, 239–240
    comics, 235–236, 250
    Communist Party publications, 231
    dailies, 243
    "digital press" development, 237
    diversity of Indian periodicals, 244
    the doi moi policy and Vietnamese, 249
    earliest publication in Indonesia, 252
    early newspapers and news sheets, 227–228
    economic liberalization and, 241, 244
    e-journals, 230
    English-language, 244, 250
    fashion magazines, 62, 233
    fiction magazines (Chinese), 229
    first Australian newspaper, 228
    first English manga, 236
    first magazine in Thailand, 248
    first newsletter in the Philippines, 250
    first newspaper in Malaysia, 250
    first newspaper in the Philippines, 250
    first newspaper in Thailand, 248
    first newspaper on Indian subcontinent, 239
    first newspapers in Myanmar, 247
    first New Zealand newspaper, 238
    first Sri Lankan newspaper, 246
    freedom of the press, 232, 233–234, 236–237, 240–241, 241–242, 243, 245, 246, 247, 249, 252
    general and family magazines (Chinese), 231
    global markets and, 230
    government attitudes toward, 236–237
    government control of, 231–232, 233–234, 241, 245, 246, 248, 249, 250–251, 252
    government support and, 241
    Gujarati language, 244
    Hicky, James Augustus, 239, 243
    the *Hindustan Times*, 244
    in Hong Kong, 232–233
    in India, 239–240, 241, 243–245
    indigenous languages and, 240
    in Indonesia, 251–252
    "intermediate novels," 229, 235
    international distribution and, 230
    international titles, 233, 237, 252
    the Internet and, 230
    in Japan, 228, 234–236
    in Korea, 228, 236
    languages and, in India, 243
    in Laos, 248–249
    literary magazines, 235

INDEX

and literature, 229
major Japanese, 234
"Komics," 250
in Malaysia, 242, 250–251
manga, 235–236, 250
monthly, 233, 234
movie magazines, 250
multicity newspapers, 244
multinational, 232–233
in Myanmar, 247
nationalist movements and, 239–240
in Nepal, 242, 245
The New Light of Myanmar newspaper, 247
in New Zealand, 238
niche audiences and, 229–230, 252
non-news publications in Singapore, 251
ownership and politics and, 242, 246, 250, 251
in Pakistan, 242–243
the "Papers Past" project, 238
paper supplies and control of, 241, 244, 246
in the Philippines, 250
political, 245
political parties and, 252
popular culture and, 230, 235
"popular," defined, 227
popularizing writers, 229
in post-colonial era, 240
post–World War II period and, 229
press freedom and 1988 Olympics in South Korea, 236
proletarian media idea in Japan, 235
the *Readers* magazine, 231
relationship between newspapers and magazines in Japan, 234–235
in Republic of China (Taiwan), 233–234
self-regulation of, 234
in Singapore, 242, 251
Sino-Japanese War and publishing of, 232
in South Korea, 236–237
South Korean attitudes toward magazines, 237
spin-offs of manga, 236
in Sri Lanka, 246–247
the *Storytelling Club*, 231
subcultures and trends and, 230
subscriptions and, 241
in Thailand, 247–248
the *Times of India*, 244
types of, in South and Southeast Asia, 242
in Urdu, 243

as venue for political and opinioned voices, 228
in Vietnam, 249
war and, 229
weekly periodicals, 228–229
women's magazines, 234, 237–238
Persia, first stitched garments and, 79
Petrona Twin Towers, 4
Phalke, Dhundiraj Govind, 106
The Philippines
   broadcasting in, 287–289
   colonial languages in, 172
   early broadcasting in, 287
   "Faith + the City" exhibition, 27
   film in, 118–119
   foreign influences on music in, 218
   government control and broadcasting in, 287–288
   indigenous theater in, 331
   languages in, 250
   music in, 218
   periodicals in, 250
   radio in, 287–288
   television in, 288–289
   transportation infrastructure in, 355–356
Poetry
   anthologies of Asian, 182
   in Bengali, 182–183
   in English but by Asians, 183–184
   the *ghazal* form and music, 220–221
   in Hindi, 183
   Indian-English, 183
   Lim, Shirley Geok-lin, 184
   in Marathi, 183
   popular response to, 182
   in Punjabi, 183
   Tagore, Rabindranath, 182
   in Telugu, 183
   Thumbo, Edwin, 184
   in Vietnam, 182
Premchand, Munshi (Dhanpat Rai Shrivastava), 174, 176
Prime, Dalvanius, 40

Quotations of Chairman Mao, 16

Radio. *See* Electronic media (including radio, television, and computers)
Rahi, Sultan, 112
Raihan, 217
RAIN, 209
Ramanujan, A. K., 173
The *Ramayana*, 327

INDEX

Ramlee, P., 119
Rao, Raja, 176, 178
Ray, Satyajit, 108
Raza, S. H., 26
Reddy, Raja and Radha, 46
Rendra, W. S., 185, 325
Robertson, Charles H., 261
Rushdie, Salman, 178

Sabavala, Jehangir, 26
Saijo, Hideki, 206
Sakamoto, Kyu, 205
Santosh, G. R., 27
Sculpture
    and architecture in South and Southeast Asia, 22–23
    Chinese monumental, 16
Sears Tower, 4
Seidler, Harry, 9
Seung-hee, Choi, 36–37
Shanghai
    early radio broadcasting in, 260
    film production and, 93
    radio broadcasting in, 261
    social dance halls in, 34
Shankar, Ravi, 220
The Shaw Brothers and films in Hong Kong, 94
Sheikh, Ghulam Mohammed, 27
Shepard, Carole, 22
Shi-zheng, Chen, 34
Shizuki, Fujikage (Fujima Shizue), 35
Siddi Goma, 221
Sikandar, Shahzia, 25
Singapore
    broadcasting in, 290–291
    immigration and culture in, 216
    languages in, 251
    music in, 216–217
    periodicals in, 251
    radio in, 290
    "Telah Terbit [Out Now]" exhibition, 27
    television in, 291
    theater in, 324–325
    transportation infrastructure in, 356–357
SMAP, 206
Soccer. *See* Football (European)
South and Southeast Asia
    antiquity and cultures in, xxiv
    art and tourism in, 28
    art in, 22–28
    authoritarian regimes in, xxvii
    Buddhism in, xxiv
    Buddhist influences in, 23
    capitalism and economies in, 69
    Chinese influence in, xxiv
    Christianity and, xxiv–xxv
    colonialism and, 23
    contemporary dance in, 41–43
    convergence in fashions, xxvi
    cultural elements in, xxvi
    cultural interconnects in, xxiv
    cultural patterns, xxiv–xxvi
    decolonialization in, xxvi
    democracy and national economies of, 69
    development of film industry in, 105
    economic globalization and, xxix
    European powers and, xxvi
    fusion of art and architecture in, 28
    fusions of cultural heritages, xxvi
    globalization and, xxviii–xxix
    globalization and economies in, 69
    globalization and rural life in, xxix
    Hindu influences in, 23
    Indian influences on art in, 22–23
    international war or large-scale internal civil conflict in, xxvii
    the Internet and music in, 211
    Islamic control of art and architecture in, 23
    multiethnic character of, xxv
    multilingualism in, xxv
    national film industries in, 105
    overview of dance in, 40–41
    overview of foods in, 137–138
    overview of literature in 172–173
    overview of popular music in, 211–213
    overview of periodicals in, 239–242
    overview of theater in, 320, 322
    overview of transportation and tourism in, 347–348
    political changes and popular cultures in, xxviii
    popular themes in literature of, 173–175
    religion and culture in, xxix–xxx
    religious diversity in, xxix
    shared classical Hindu-Sanskrit past, xxiv
    socialist or communist regimes in, xxvii
    traditional modes of travel in, 347
    Western influence on cultures in, xxx, 23–24
    World Heritage Sites and tourism in, 28
South Asia
    defined, xxi–xxii
    music in, 218–219
    nations, cities, languages, and religions in, xxii

INDEX

South Asian Association for Regional Cooperation (SAARC), xxi
South Korea. *See also* Korea
    architecture in, 7–8
    art in, 20
    broadcasting in, 267
    censorship of films in, 101
    dance in, 37
    development in Seoul, 7–8
    economic growth and transportation in, 343
    electronic games market in, 155
    fashion in, 65–67
    film in, 101–103
    Kwangju Massacre and art in, 20
    literature in, 167–168
    marriage and sexual relationships in, 197–198
    Minjung Cultural Movement, 20
    periodicals in, 236–237
    recent growth of film industry in, 101
    sports in, 302–304
    toys, games, and pastimes in, 154–155
Souza, F. N., 26
Spinning and weaving
    British influence on technology of, 77
    dyes and, 78
    history of, 77–78
    synthetic fibers and, 78
Sports. *See also individual sports*
    aging populations and, 302
    in Australia, 304–306
    Australian Rules Football, 305
    baseball, 300–301
    baseball stadiums (Japan), 6
    Beijing Olympic Games (2008), 300
    Bligh Lobb Sports Architects, 10
    in China, 297–300
    commercial sports clubs, 299
    competitive, 299, 305, 306–307
    cricket, 305
    economic advancement and, 299
    for the disabled, 305
    fans and fan organizations, 301, 304
    female athletes and, 299, 305
    golf, 304, 306
    government promotion of, 301, 306, 307
    in Japan, 300–302
    judo, 300
    Kim Il-Sung Stadium, 7
    K-1 martial arts events, 301
    Lomu, Jonah, 306
    lotteries and, 298, 301
    martial arts, 297, 301
    Meads, Colin, 306
    minority ethnic groups in China and, 299
    netball, 306
    in New Zealand, 306–307
    Olympic Games, 299, 300
    Olympic Games and architecture, 8, 10
    overview of East Asian, 297
    Park Ji-Sung, 303–304
    physical education programs and, 298, 302
    professional baseball in Japan, 300–301
    professionalization of, 297, 299
    professional sports, 301, 303
    the Red Devils (fan organization), 304
    rugby, 305, 306
    in South Korea, 302–304
    ssireum wrestling, 303
    statistical data on, 301–302, 304
    sumo wrestling, 300
    Taekwondo, 302–303
    tai chi and, 298
    Taoism and, 298
    television coverage and, 297
    traditional, 297, 298
    video games and, 302
    walking, 302, 306
    water sports, 306
    Western, 297, 298
    Western missionaries and, 303
    Wie, Michelle (Sung Mi Wie), 304
    World Cup Stadium (South Korea), 8
Sri Lanka
    broadcasting in, 282–284
    civil war and literature in, 175
    civil war and periodicals in, 247
    film in, 114–117
    historic sites in, 352–353
    indigenous theater in, 328–329
    languages in, 246
    periodicals in, 246–247
    radio in, 282–283
    Tamil-speaking minority in, 247
    television in, 283–284
    tourism and, 352–353
Summers, Essie, 170
Sun Yat-sen, 14
Swapnasundari, 46

Tagore, Rabindranath (Gurudev), 174, 182
Taipei 101, 4, 5
Taiwan. *See* China, Republic of (Taiwan)
Takayanagi, Kenjiro, 266

Index

Takeuchi, Naoko, 166
Tamil people
    and civil war in Sri Lanka, 175
    Voice of the Tigers broadcast service, 283
Tang Xianzu, 163, 317
Tatsumi, Hijikata, 32
Television. *See* Electronic media (including radio, television, and computers)
Tendulkar, Vijay, 177, 184
Teng, Teresa, 203
Textiles. *See also* Clothing; Fashion and appearance; Weaving and spinning
    batik methods of dying, 78
    cashmere, 78
    Changan (modern Xian), China and, 59
    Chinese exports and, 60
    Chinese exports of silk during Tang Dynasty, 59–60
    cotton, 77
    dyes and dying, 78
    embroidery and, 78
    export markets, 60–61
    in Japan after World War II, 76
    New Zealand exports, 69
    and saris, 80
    silk, 77
    the Silk Road and, 59
Thailand
    broadcasting in, 284–286
    classical dance in, 48
    dance-dramas, 48
    food in, 142–144
    historic sites in, 353
    indigenous clothing in, 84
    indigenous theater in, 329–330
    languages in, 248
    the monarchy and freedom of the press, 248
    music in, 216
    periodicals in, 247–248
    popular foods in, 143–144
    radio in, 284–285
    television in, 285–286
    tourism and, 353
    transportation infrastructure in, 354–355
Theater. *See also* Drama; Literature
    "amateur," in India, 323
    Anyein Pwe form, 329
    Artaud, Antonin, and, 315
    Atsumori, 319
    in Australia, 320
    in Bali, 334
    the Beijing (Peking) Opera, 163, 317
    Brecht, Bertolt, and, 314-315

Cao Yu, 317
Chikamatsu Monzaemon, 319
in China, 315–318
Christian influences on indigenous, 328, 331
chuanqi style of drama, 163
commercial, in India, 323
communism and Chinese, 317–318
the Cultural Centre (Singapore) and, 324
dalangs (puppet masters), 332, 333
Dalits ("untouchables") and, 324
the Dasehra festival, 327–328
defined, 313
dramatic writing, 184–185
expressionism and, 314
face painting and, 314
Fagfagto form, 331
Gao Xingjian, 318
Guan Hanqing, 316
Hindu influences on, 326–328, 332
Hindu texts and, 322
in India, 184–185, 322–324, 326–328
indigenous theater, 326–334
in Indonesia, 185, 325, 332–334
in Japan, 318–319
in Java, 332–334
Kabuki, 319
Kolam form, 328
in Korea, 320
kunqu operatic style, 163
Kutiyattam, 328
Lakon Bassak dance-dramas, 331
Lakon Jatri form, 329
Leiyu (*The Thunderstorm*), 317
in Malaysia, 331–332
masks, 318, 320
masks, origins of, 314
minimalist, 314, 318
modern urban theater, 322–326
modern urban theater versus indigenous, 326
Mongol rule and Chinese, 316
music and indigenous Malaysian, 332
in Myanmar, 329
Nadagama form, 329
Nang Sbek form, 330
Nang Sbek Touch form, 330–331
Nan-xi, 315–316
in New Zealand, 320
Noh, 318–319
overview of, in East Asia and Oceania, 313–315
Pansori form of, 320

INDEX

passion plays, 328–329
Peony Pavilion, 163, 317
puppet, 319, 322, 329, 330, 331–332, 332–334, 333
puppetry, water, 331
the *Ramakien* and, 330
the *Ramayana* and, 327, 330
Ram Lila, 326–328
Ras Lila, 328
referentiality and, 313–315
Rendra, W. S., 185, 325
Romance of the West Chamber (*Xixiang ji*), 316–317
shadow theater, 330, 330–331, 331–332
shaman rituals and, 314
in Singapore, 324–325
social change and modern Indian, 324
in Sri Lanka, 328–329
stages and, 314
Talchum mask form of, 320
Tang Xianzu, 317
in Thailand, 329–330
traditional Chinese requirements for, 313, 316
traditional dramas (China), 163
the "untouchables" (Dalits) and, 324
water puppetry, 331
Wayang Beber form, 332
Wayang Kulit form, 332–333
Wayang Wong form, 333–334
Western influences on Asian, 314–315, 317
Western versus Asian, 314–315
women playwrights, 184
the *Yakshagana* folk opera, 328
Zai-ju, 315
Zeami Motokiyo, 319
Zen influences on Japanese, 319
Thiep, Nguyen Huy, 182
Thomas, Paul, 171
Thumbo, Edwin, 184
Tibet, influence on folk dance in India, 51
Toer, Pramoedya Ananta, 173, 178, 179
Tokyo Rose, 268–269
Toriyama, Akira, 166
Tourism
Aboriginal dance and, 38
Ankor Wat and, 353
the arts and, 28
Australia and, 344–345
in Bangladesh, 351
Buddhist holy sites, 354
Cambodia and, 353
in China, 337, 338–339

Chinese nationals going abroad, 339
and dance in Indonesia, 50
and dance in South and Southeast Asia, 42
domestic travel and, 348–349
economic development and, 348
eco-tourism, 340, 351
"exotic" locations and, 350
and "extreme" sports, 351
and Fiji, 346
French Polynesia and, 346–347
the gaming industry and Macau, 340
globalization and, 348, 350
Himalayan holy sites, 354
Hindu holy sites, 353–354
historic sites and, 351–353
in Hong Kong, 339–340
India and, 352
international cruise lines and China, 338
Japan and, 342–343
The Lord of the Rings films and, in New Zealand, 68
in Macau, 340
in Mongolia, 341
Muslim holy sites, 353
National Aviation Museum (Beijing), 339
New Zealand and, 345–346
in North Korea, 343
overview of leisure travel industry, 337–338
overview of international, 349–350
in Pakistan, 351
and Papua New guinea, 346
"party" destinations and, 350–351
religious pilgrimages and, 349, 353–354
in Republic of China (Taiwan), 340–341
Sikh holy sites, 354
and South Korea, 343–344
spa tourism, 341, 342
in Sri Lanka, 352–353
statistics for international, 349
Thailand and, 353
Tjapukai Aboriginal Cultural Park and, 38
traditional nomadic lifestyles and, 341
travel restrictions in North Korea, 343
within Asia, 350
World Heritage Sites and, 28, 352, 353
Toys, games, and pastimes. *See also* Electronic media (including radio, television, and computers)
adaptation of pinball (pachinko), 154
animal strength games, 151–152
arcade games, 153, 154

397

INDEX

Toys, games, and pastimes (*continued*)
    board games, 155
    Chajon Nori, 155
    in China, 151–153
    Chinese chess (*xiangqi*), 152
    computer and video games, 153, 156, 157
    cricket fighting, 151–153
    cuju, 152
    electronic games market (South Korea), 155
    European games, 156, 157
    folk toys (Chinese), 152–153
    folk toys (Japanese), 154
    gambling games, 152, 154
    games of strength, 151, 154, 155, 157
    girls' games, 155
    Go (*weiqi, Igo*), 152, 153
    hagoita, 154
    Hwatu (flower card game), 155
    indigenous Australian, 156
    indigenous Korean, 154
    intelligence games, 152
    Internet games, 153
    jianzi, 152
    jumping jack, 157
    lawn bowling, 156, 157
    lawn games, traditional European, 156
    kee'an, 156
    Kolap, 156
    in Korea, 154–155
    knucklebones, 157
    Lantern Riddles, 152
    Mahjong, 152
    Maori and games in New Zealand, 157
    mass media and play in New Zealand, 157
    munhanganingin, 156
    online Mahjong and Igo, 153
    origami, 153
    pachinko, 154
    poker, 152
    riddle games, 152
    skipping rope, 152
    self-made toys among Aboriginal peoples, 156
    sports and games regarded as the same in China, 152
    sports games, 154
    table games, 156
    Tarnambai, 156
    video games and sports, 302
    Western cultures and Japanese folk toys, 154
    Yut-nori, 155

Transportation. *See also* Tourism
    air travel, 338, 339–340, 341, 342, 343, 344, 345, 354–355, 355, 356, 357
    in Australia, 344–345
    the bullet train, 342
    bus and motor coach services, 339, 340, 341, 343, 344, 345, 355, 356, 357
    in Cambodia, 355
    in China, 338–339
    globalization and transportation, 248
    in Hong Kong, 339–340
    the Hong Kong-Zhuhai-Macau Bridge, 340
    by horse, 341
    in Indonesia, 357
    international cruise lines, 338
    in Japan, 342
    landmines and roads (Cambodia), 355
    in Macau, 340
    in Malaysia, 356
    marine shipping, 338, 339, 354, 357
    modernization of, in South and Southeast Asia, 348
    the Modern Transportation Museum (Japan), 342
    in Mongolia, 341
    motorcycles, 340–341
    in New Zealand, 345–346
    in North Korea, 343
    Olympic Games and, in South Korea, 343
    in the Philippines, 355–356
    public transportation in Cambodia, 355
    rail systems, 338, 339, 340, 341, 342, 343–344, 344–345, 346, 356, 357
    in Republic of China (Taiwan), 340–341
    river taxis, 355
    road systems, 338, 339, 340, 342, 343, 344, 345, 348, 355, 356, 357
    in Singapore, 356–357
    in South Korea, 343–344
    in Thailand, 354–355
    toll roads, 342, 356
    waterways, 338, 345, 346, 354, 355, 356, 357
Travel. *See* Tourism; Transportation
Tsai Ming-liang, 98
Tsui Hark, 95
Turner, Ethel, 169

Upadhyay, Samrat, 180
Urban planning. *See* Architecture and urban planning
Utzon, Joern, 9–10

Verma, Nirmal, 176
Vietnam
    broadcasting in, 286–287
    film in, 117–118
    indigenous dress in, 84–85
    indigenous theater in, 331
    languages in, 249
    periodicals in, 249
    short story literature in, 181–182
    patriotism and war themes in films of, 117–118
    television in, 286–287
    U.S. military and broadcasting in, 286

Weaving and spinning, new technologies and fashion trends, 60
Weir, Peter, 103–104
White, Patrick, 168
Wie, Michelle (Sung Mi Wie), 304
Women
    beauty pageants and, 71–72
    and broadcasting, 262
    burkas and, 73
    changing fashion styles in Japan, 64–65
    changing gender relationships and fashions, 65
    changing roles of, in Japan, 193
    changing roles of, in Korea, 197–198
    clothing restrictions and, 73–74
    combination of Asian and Western qualities in fashions for, 71
    Japanese efforts to protect rights of, 193
    the "Modern Girl" image, 61, 64
    participation in sports, 299, 305
    status and treatment of, in literature, 175
    the "veil" and, 73
    writers, in India, 176
    young professional, 195–196
Wong Kar-wai, 96
Woo, John, 95
Wright, Frank Lloyd, 6
Wu Liangyong, 5
Wu Shaoyun, 15

Xu Beihong, 14–15

the Yellow Magic Orchestra, 206
Yindi, Yothu, 210

Zeami Motokiyo, 319
Zha Liangyong (Jinyong, Louis Cha), 164
Zhang Yimou, 93–94
Zhang Ziyi, 98
Zhu Yongin, 16